A HISTORY OF RUSSIA

A HISTORY OF

RUSSIA

SIXTH REVISED EDITION

BY GEORGE VERNADSKY

NEW HAVEN, YALE UNIVERSITY PRESS

First published, May 1929.
Issued as a Yale Paperbound, June 1961.
Sixth revised edition, March 1969.

Library of Congress catalog card number: 61–11405
ISBN: 0–300–00247–5 (paper)

Printed in the United States of America by
BookCrafters, Inc., Chelsea, Michigan.

30   29   28   27   26   25   24   23   22   21   20

AUTHOR'S NOTE

THE FIFTH EDITION of this book appeared in 1961. Much has happened since then in Russia and the rest of the world.

In the present edition the course of events and the main trends of life in contemporary Russia have been related and analyzed. The Bibliography has been expanded in order to list a number of important books published after 1960. The Appendix contains brief statistical data on the Soviet Union for 1966.

G. V.

New Haven, Connecticut
July 1, 1968

CONTENTS

GENEALOGICAL TABLES

MAPS

INTRODUCTION

1. *The Russian people and their expansion*

RUSSIAN history is sometimes thought to be unduly long and complicated. It isn't. It is no longer than the history of most modern nations, and the complications are more apparent than real. It is true that geographically Russia covers a vast and varied territory which may be unfamiliar to many readers. It is also true that within that country live many peoples whose origins are likely to be obscure to most Americans and whose names nearly always have an outlandish sound to non-Russian ears. But these are at most surface difficulties: a good look at a map, the repetition aloud of a few names, and a brief consideration of the broad framework of Russian history will do much to remove them. The first two suggestions are left to the reader; it is the business of this introduction to provide the third—a brief and general survey of the material of Russian history.

Today the Union of Soviet Socialist Republics is the largest country in the world. Nearly three times the size of the United States, it includes within its boundaries roughly one-sixth of the land surface of the earth, an area of about 8,700,000 square miles spread over the vast expanse of two continents from the North Pacific to the Gulf of Finland. Its population was estimated in 1966 to be more than 234,000,000, and though representatives of over a hundred nationalities contributed to this total, around 182,000,000, or three-fourths are Eastern Slavs (Russians, Ukrainians, and Belorussians). The great number of the Russian people and the tremendous area they occupy are among the factors that have made Russia a major force in the world today.

Russia's becoming a leading actor on the world stage is a comparatively recent development. A thousand years ago the Russian people numbered but a few million and occupied only a fraction of the land now within the borders of the Soviet Union. Their history since then has been a varied one; since 1550 it has showed one consistent and striking characteristic: steady growth in numbers and in territory.

And the Russians are not merely prolific. They are a gifted people whose contributions to world culture in literature, music, the fine arts, the theater, and ballet have long been appreciated by all who have more than passing acquaintance with the history of the arts. By 1800 western civilization had struck deep roots in Russia, and by 1850 Russian science had become a living part of the general body of world science. In the late 19th and 20th centuries Russia has gone through a process of rapid industrialization. In view of the peculiar form of government established after 1917, and the tension in the 1940's and 50's between that government and the western powers, Russia's technological progress has evoked varied feelings in the western world, ranging from admiration to incredulity and fear. One thing is certain in any case: Russia's scientific and technological advance is not a by-product of her internal politics but an expression of a basic urge of the human mind, a current in the general evolution of mankind.

2. *The Russians basically a Slavic people*

It is wise, perhaps, to begin the story of Russia with a word about her people. The Russians are basically Slavs, a part of the greater Slavonic family belonging to the Indo-European group of peoples. The family includes, among others, the Czechs, Poles, Serbs, and Bulgarians. Their language, like all Slavonic languages, has many characteristics in common with Lithuanian, German, Greek, Iranian, and other Aryan tongues.

This great Slavonic family to which the Russians belong can be divided roughly into three parts: a western section which includes the Czechs and the Poles; a southern segment made up of a group of Balkan Slavs; and a large eastern section, of which the Russians form the backbone. Like all modern peoples, the Russians have acquired through the centuries a certain admixture of alien blood. During the course of the 8th and 9th centuries A.D. they fell under the control of Norsemen who swept down upon them from Scandinavia; but these Norse invaders—Varangians, as they were then called—were few in number and rapidly absorbed by the Slavs. Both before and after the Norse invasion the eastern Slavs mixed freely with peoples of the Ural-Altaic family—the Mongols, Turks, and Finns. Though there is of course no way of estimating the extent of the Ural-Altaic admixture, it is clear that it was not enough to change the racial characteristics of the Slavs appreciably.

So the Russians remain essentially a Slavonic people. In time certain cultural and language differences grew up among the Eastern Slavs which resulted in their division into three major branches: the Great Russians (now usually called just Russians) who today comprise about 65 per cent of the total; the Ukrainians (or Little Russians, as they were once called), something more than 25 per cent; and the balance, less than 10 per cent, of White Russians (Belorussians). The beginnings of this subdivision have been traced as far back as the 12th century; its persistence has been due in large part to political events. From the 14th to the 18th centuries the Russians were divided between two states, the eastern, or Tsardom of Moscow, and the western, under the domination of the Poles and Lithuanians. Though parts of Little and White Russia were annexed to the Tsardom of Moscow about the mid-17th century, other parts were added only at the end of the 18th century at the time of the partition of Poland. Thus it was not until the 19th century that the three branches were reunited in a single state. Naturally enough, the Polish influence to which the Ukrainians and Belorussians had been subjected for several centuries was reflected in both their culture and their language.

3. *The three branches of the Russian people*

In the Middle Ages people of all branches of the Eastern Slavs were known as Russians (Rus'). Originally, language differences among them were of no importance. As time went on, however, the differences became more marked. In discussing these variations it is important to distinguish between the literary or written languages and the spoken languages or folk dialects of the people. In Russia as elsewhere dialects are not confined by national or provincial boundaries. Within each of the three Russian groups the popular speech varies considerably from section to section—so much so, indeed, that it is impossible to speak of any one dialect as the language of Great Russia or of Ukraine or White Russia. Since the branches of the Russian people are not separated by impenetrable partitions, their languages tend to merge by gradual stages and are differentiated largely on the basis of usage and custom.

The literary languages, however, are separated by a more distinct line of demarcation. Up to the 19th century the literary language of the Russian Empire was based primarily on old church Slavonic and the Moscow dialect of the Great Russians. It included, however, many elements of Ukrainian origin which had been absorbed during the late 17th and early 18th centuries when the Ukrainians played an important role in church and state. Because of these additions and modifications it became to a considerable degree an all-Russian tongue rather than merely the language of the Great Russians.

Nevertheless, in the 19th century movements were instituted by both Ukrainian and Belorussian intellectuals to emancipate their respective languages by stressing their differences from Russian. New terms were frequently invented or borrowed from foreign languages for the sole purpose, apparently, of providing forms distinct from the Russian; this was especially true of scientific terms and technical modes of expression. However, both languages seem to have enlisted popular support and today have been adopted officially by the Ukrainian and Belorussian Socialist Soviet Republics.

4. *Geographic limits of Russian expansion. Eurasia as its natural area*

During the 18th and 19th centuries German and Russian geographers devised a purely arbitrary division of Russia into two parts, so-called European Russia and Asiatic Russia. This conception is not only historically unjustified and unreal but also geographically misleading. According to this theory, the Ural Mts. were to be considered the eastern limit of European Russia, but a moment's consideration will show that the Urals are in no sense a natural boundary and cannot even be made to look like one. No amount of rationalization can alter the plain fact that geographically Euro-

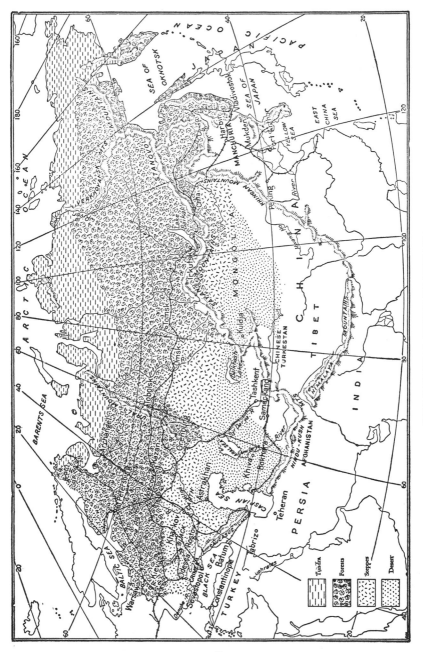

THE NATURAL ZONES OF EURASIA

pean and Asiatic Russia are one, that on both sides of the Urals there stretch the same zones of tundra, forest, and steppe that have played such an important role in the development of the Russian people. Far from separating the country, the Urals by their topographical and geological peculiarities have actually bound the eastern and western parts of Russia together into the only real unity possible, Eurasian Russia.

The Russia that we are to consider is this single geographical unit, Eurasia, and it is worth understanding that term in order to clear up misconceptions which have grown up around it. As I shall use it, Eurasia refers not to a vague sociohistorical combination of Europe and Asia but to a specific geographical area of the great central continental land mass. It is made up of a series of large, interlocking plains—the White Sea–Caucasian, the western Siberian, and the Turkistan. This great area is in turn divided into several long latitudinal strips which are distinguished from each other largely by variations in vegetation and soil. Since much of Russian history hinges on the relationship of these bands, it is well to get them clearly in mind at the very beginning. The first, stretching along the whole shore of the Arctic Ocean, is the tundra, a bleak, unforested, and untillable land. Immediately below it lies a zone of deep forests, its southern boundary extending from the southern Carpathians approximately along the line of Kiev-Kazan-Tiumen to the Altai Mts. and from there along the northern edge of the Mongolian steppes and deserts. South of the forests lie the steppes, vast plains spreading over the black earth belt. The fourth and southernmost strip is the desert zone of the Aral-Caspian and Mongolian area which, like the northern tundra, is broad in the east and grows narrower and finally disappears altogether in the west.

All the vast expanses of this Eurasian area have been occupied by the Russians in the course of a long historical process. When first the Russian people came upon the stage of history, in the period between the 3rd and 9th centuries, they occupied only the western corner of Eurasia north of the Black Sea. From this small corner they spread eastward against the sun until by 1650 Russian settlers had reached the Pacific and two centuries later had touched Tien Shan in central Asia. Both in this great eastward expansion and in the remarkable persistence with which they meanwhile held their western frontier along the Carpathian Mts. against the attacks of their neighbors, the Russian people have demonstrated much fortitude and determination.

The fundamental urge which directed the Russian people eastward lies deep in history and is not easily summarized in a paragraph. It was not "imperialism," nor was it the consequence of the petty political ambitions of Russian statesmen. It was in the last analysis, perhaps, simply the inevitable logic of geography which lies at the basis of all history.

5. *Ethnological limits of Russian expansion. The nomadic tribes of Eurasia*

All civilizations are to some extent the product of geographical factors, but history provides no clearer example of the profound influence of geography upon a culture than in the historical development of the Russian people. Eurasia is, as we have seen, divided into four distinct zones, and in the central two of these—the forests in the north and the steppes spreading southward below them—there developed the two dominant culture patterns upon which Russian civilization is based. Today there is little to differentiate these bands, which through the centuries have been wielded into a single broad agricultural area, but in ancient times the forests and the steppes were sharply divided. Rugged, difficult, and sometimes almost impenetrable, the forest area was inhabited originally by a hunting people widely dispersed and organized into small, independent states. The steppes, on the other hand, were vast open areas over which herdsmen wandered with comparative ease and where, in time, they were able to establish huge states based upon their nomadic way of life.

The part played in history by nomadic cultures deserves some special mention. Too often the cultural level of nomads is thought to have been invariably low, and their part in the development of modern society is frequently represented as a purely negative one. Such generalizations are, of course, misleading. The cultural level of nomads, like that of any other group, has no constant and absolute limits. It has varied with peoples and times and places. The Mongol tribes, to take a convenient example, clearly made considerable progress in political and social forms and organization during the 12th and 13th centuries. History is filled with cases of two or more groups of nomads living side by side, in different stages of cultural development. So it is well to remember that in the cultural sense "nomadic" is not a qualitative measure but a descriptive term, used only to indicate a *type* of civilization and not its relative state of development.

The role of the nomadic peoples in the cultural history of Eurasia—and, indeed, of the whole ancient world—was of great significance. There were, in those days, three principal centers of agricultural civilization in the world: one in the Far East, in China; another farther west in the central Asian area called Khorezm; and a third in the Mediterranean basin in the southwest.

Beside and between these areas of settled populations lay the steppes, the realm of the nomads. This vast region, which along its southern border blended imperceptibly into the desert, served the nomads as the sea served maritime peoples. Near at hand it was a fertile and hospitable source of livelihood, and beyond the horizon a shifting, dangerous highway over which hardy traders fared on peaceful missions and bands of warriors rode on swift, stabbing raids for plunder. But whether they came in peace or war, the nomads maintained through the centuries the cultural links between the scattered outposts of settled civilization. The horses, cattle, hides, and wool which were the products of the herdsmen's flocks were essential to the economy of their far-flung neighbors, and in return for them the nomadic traders received the grain and other agricultural produce that they needed. In addition to these primary items of commerce, wealthy herdsmen and tribal chieftains often dealt in artistic wares, precious cloth, gold and silver vessels, jewelry and ornaments of all sorts. At times large workshops were developed within the tribal organizations, and craftsmen were engaged in the manufacture of weapons, utensils, harness, and richly ornamented gear. By trade and by plunder tribes were able occasionally to accumulate great riches in their tents; but whatever their economic condition they roamed the length and breadth of the steppes and in their trains traveled cultural elements of all the civilizations which they touched.

Beyond the normal and constant contacts developed within this pattern, the steppes were from time to time swept by great waves of migrations. Before the beginning of our era the central region lying between the Black Sea, the Caucasus, and Khorezm was occupied by the Scythians, while the eastern connecting link between Khorezm and China was held by the Huns. In the 4th and 5th centuries the Huns, surging west, attempted to seize control of the whole area of the steppes and to become the main intermediary between east and west. Centuries later the Mongols aspired to the same position, and under Genghis Khan and his descendants in the 13th century were able to found an empire which stretched from the Pacific Ocean to the Balkans. Each of these invasions brought new cultural patterns and each, when it retreated years or centuries later, left its imprint indelibly on the land that was to become Russia.

6. *The economic development of Eurasia*

In the border zone between the area of the forests of northern Russia and that of the cattle- and horse-breeding economy of the southern steppes, agriculture was practiced from time immemorial. The natural conditions, such as soil and climate, make it possible to raise crops in both steppe and forest zone, although in the extreme north of the forest zone the severe climate makes agriculture unprofitable. The entire steppe zone with its rich *chernoziom* ("black earth") is tillable, and the only major technical problem that confronts the farmer is the need of irrigation in border regions between the steppe and arid desert zones. It was solely for political reasons that in the early periods of Russian history most of the steppe was closed to agriculture and used instead by the nomads as grazing grounds for their horses and cattle. Farmers were tolerated in only a few sections of the steppe and had to be satisfied with the narrow belt between the steppes and the forests, the so-called "forest-steppe zone" which, in fact, was also well suited for agriculture, or with transforming sections of the forest for agriculture as best as they could. The first step was to cut trees and burn the underbrush. The first two or three years' yield on such burned-out patches was high, since wood ashes make good fertilizer. After three or four years, however, the yield of a given patch fell off and the farmers turned to new patches. When eventually he returned to the first patch, he was likely to find it covered with young growth which must be burned anew. The task of clearing and maintaining such lands entailed hard work by a good number of laborers and was beyond the powers of a single peasant family. Thus the practice of primitive agriculture in the forest zone presupposed the existence of cooperative peasant guilds.

With the utilization of the forest zone, agriculture steadily expanded northward. Whenever the pressure of the nomads eased in the south, the farmer tried to establish himself in the steppes, more often than not to be expelled again later on. It was only after the emancipation of the Russians from Mongol domination that a steady Russian advance to the south and southeast became possible. After that the agricultural wedge between forests and steppes. expanded in both directions, so that by 1800 a considerable part of both zones could or had been adapted for agriculture. Historically speaking, this expansion of Russian agriculture constituted the basis of the economic unification of Eurasia. In this sense the Russian peasant may be called the main hero of Russian history. His role was symbolized in the folk epos in the figure of the giant plowman, Mikula Selianinovich (Nicholas the Villager's Son).

Even after the plowman had become dominant all over Russia, a marked difference persisted between the economy of the original forest area and the steppes. While wheat became the staple crop in the south, rye and flax were preferred in the north. In the 19th century beet cultivation expanded rapidly in the south owing to the progress in sugar refining. Among other economically important crops cotton, which was raised from ancient times in Turkistan, an area not annexed to Russia till 1864–76, is today being planted in south Russia as well. Many forests remained intact in the northern area, especially the extreme north; and while hunting lost its former importance with the decrease or extermination of the more valuable fur-bearing animals, other kinds of forest industries, like timber, tar, and potash, were continually developed. Cattle and horse breeding, on the other hand, continued to play an important role in the south alongside agriculture. Fishing industries flourished in both north and south, the variations between each region depending on the distribution of various kinds of fish. Sturgeon caviar is perhaps the best known fishery product of the south.

In the early period of their history the Russians were not sufficiently acquainted with mining techniques to make proper use of the deep iron deposits in what is today the Ukraine. Besides, they were soon excluded from that region by the nomads. On the other hand, there were vast areas at their disposal in both west and north Russia containing plenty of near-surface iron ore, chiefly in swamps and on lake shores. On the sites of many early Russian settlements dating from the 9th century on, evidence of the extraction and smelting of iron has been found. In some regions of north Russia the swamp iron deposits were exploited by neighboring peasants as late as the 19th century. With the formation of a strong centralized state—the Tsardom of Moscow—in the 16th century and the building up of a strong army and artillery, the old iron deposits proved inadequate and new methods were sought for using the deep mineral deposits. At first with the help of foreign technicians, and later, from Peter the Great on, by acquainting Russians with western technology, the nation was able to develop the rich deposits of the Ural area and then, after the conquest of the south, those of the Donets Basin and of Ukraine. On the whole the Russian expansion, together with the mastering of western techniques, resulted in the course of the 18th and 19th centuries in providing the peoples of what is now the Soviet Union with a vast territory well stocked with mineral ores and natural resources of various kinds. The steady development of Russian industries from the time of Peter the Great, and especially the rapid industrial growth from the 1880's on, became a factor of tremendous importance in the modernization of the country and the changing of her economy.

In order to understand the role of trade in Russian history we must consider both Russia's international position and the difference between various regions within the country. The two main reasons for the growth of domestic trade in Russia as in other countries may be seen in the contrast between the cities and rural districts and in the diversity of natural resources in the various regions. The city dwellers were dependent for agricultural produce on the farmers; the latter needed tools and other goods manufactured by the city artisans. As regards regional diversity, the fundamental contrast between north and south—forest zone and steppe zone—was of paramount importance in Russian history. Even if agriculture expanded in the north, not enough grain could be produced there for the cities. The difference between the grain-producing provinces of the black earth belt and the bread-consuming provinces of the north runs through the whole of Russian history and is valid even in our times. The early development of trade in iron and salt was also the result of divergencies in Russian economic geography.

The expansion of Russia's foreign trade was facilitated by the country's favorable position between East and West. From time immemorial the Eurasian nomads had maintained commercial routes between the Far and Middle East on one hand and the Azov and Black Sea region on the other. The early Greek and the later Italian colonies in the Crimea provided a convenient link between the Eurasian and the Mediterranean trade. A connection between the Khoresmian and Black Sea trade on one hand and that of the Baltic Sea on the other could be, and was, established through Russia. The rich profits of that commerce lured the Norsemen to Russia in the 8th and 9th centuries. In the Mongol period the city of Novgorod in north Russia served as a link between the Baltic and the oriental commerce. In the 16th century the English explored the possibilities of establishing trade with Persia through Russia. The city of Nizhni Novgorod (now called Gorky) on the upper Volga, with its big annual fair, served in the 19th century as the main clearing place for Russia's eastern trade. Trade with the West was greatly facilitated by the conquest of the northern shores of the Black Sea in the late 18th century, after which the newly founded city of Odessa became the chief outlet for the export of south Russian wheat.

Commerce requries good roads for proper functioning. Here we touch a sore spot in Russian life and economy. Enormous distances, severe climatic conditions, and scarcity of stone account for the fact that ballasted roads appeared in Russia only shortly before railroads. Before the era of railroads, it was easier to travel in northern Russia in winter, by sleigh or sledge, than in summer on a road deformed by ruts and holes. For at least a month in spring and another in autumn, land travel was almost impossible in northern Russia and in Ukraine. In winter the rivers in most of Russia are frozen, yet in spite of the comparatively short season of open water Russian internal and transit commerce depended mainly on rivers up to the era of railroads. Russia possesses a network of riverways which, in recent times, has been considerably improved by building of huge dams and canals. The

main rivers, discharging into different peripheral seas, all start
in the same central region northwest of Moscow. This is true of
the Dnieper, Western Dvina, Neva, Northern Dvina, and Volga.
It is easy to travel and to ship goods from the upper reaches of
one of these main rivers to another through tributaries and por-
tages. The fact that in the Ural region the upper reaches of the
Kama River and its tributaries come close to the tributaries of
the great rivers of western Siberia, the Ob and Irtysh, proved an
important factor in facilitating the colonization of Siberia. Russia's
rivers have thus played a significant role in her history with respect
to commerce and colonization, as well as to strategic considerations. And control of the rivers was also essential in getting access
to the seas and oceans into which various streams discharged.
Essentially a continental power, Russia needs outlets through the
neighboring seas both for international trade and cultural intercourse with the western world. Through the Black Sea medieval
Russia established early connections with Byzantium and obtained
Christianity from Constantinople. Through the Baltic Sea Novgorod made contact with the German Hansa in the late Middle
Ages. In the mid-16th century, when Russia was cut off from both
the Baltic and the Black Sea, the English found a new maritime
route to Russia through the Arctic Ocean and the White Sea.
Peter the Great in the early 18th century restored Russia's position on the Baltic shores, and his newly built capital of St. Petersburg has served since then as the main channel for the Europeanization of Russia.

7. Cultural development of the Russian people.
The role of Byzantium

The roots of Russian civilization go deep into the ancient Indo-
European background common to all European nations. In both
their basic spiritual notions, from the pre-Christian era, and the
rudiments of their material culture, the ancient Slavs did not differ
much from such other Indo-European peoples outside of the
Mediterranean area as the Germans and the Balts (Lithuanians).
In the Mediterranean, however, the Greeks and later the Romans,
starting from the same Indo-European bases, developed a brilliant
civilization much earlier than their northern kin. The Slavs in the
Scythian and Sarmation epochs profited much by their intercourse

with another branch of the Indo-European family, the Iranians, then firmly established in the south Russian steppes. Slavic mythology is permeated with Iranian themes; there are many Iranian motifs in old Russian folklore, and there is much similarity between the Iranian and Turkish epos on the one hand and some of the *byliny* (heroic songs) of old Russia on the other. The art of ancient Russia too was greatly influenced by the Iranian civilization. Many designs in medieval and even modern Russian folk art derive from Iranian patterns of the Scythian and Sarmatian periods. Ancient Russian civilization is thus a combination of original Slavic and related Iranian elements.

In the course of the 9th and the 10th centuries a new element appeared which proved to be of tremendous importance for the whole subsequent course of Russian intellectual and cultural history. This was Christianity in its Byzantine form. By 1000 A.D. Russia was officially converted to the new faith. At that time Constantinople was one of the cultural capitals of the world, and the differences between the Roman and the Greek churches did not as yet amount to a formal break between the two. Thus Russia's acceptance of Christianity from Byzantium did not, at first, separate her from the West but was rather a move uniting her with the Christian world at large. All the principal elements of Byzantine civilization entered Russia with the teachings of the church, and though the transplanted culture reached the Russian people only after many modifications it did lay the basis for a closer relation between Europe and Eurasia. This unifying influence was, however, of comparatively short duration, for Russian adherence to Greek Orthodoxy at the time of the breach between the Roman and Byzantine churches in the middle of the 11th century tended to separate Russia from the western peoples. Later on the separation was further widened by the constant military pressure exerted against Russia's borders by her western neighbors—the Poles, Germans, and Swedes. This new cleavage between East and West persisted until the end of the 17th century, when the necessity of acquiring the technical skills which the Europeans had developed led to another attempt at cultural rapprochement. But by this time the breach had so widened that the government had to apply coercion to accelerate the process of adaptation to western ways. The upper classes led the way in absorbing western civilization, while the bulk of the nation followed slowly behind. The circumstances of this final meeting of Russia with the West were, perhaps, the primary sources of the dualism and crises in the religious and national psychology of the people which were evident throughout the 18th, 19th, and 20th centuries.

8. *The periods of Russian history*

History is a continuing process which does not pause at regular intervals for the convenience of the student, and any divisions we set up must, of course, be purely schematic and arbitrary. Nevertheless, history can be studied only in segments, and the necessary division into periods can have positive value if it is not merely mechanical but significant events of the historical process. The preceding sections have been intended to indicate in broadest outline the objective and subjective events upon which the divisions of the present history will be based. A recapitulation of those events with reference to their relative positions in the development of the Russian people may provide for the reader a historical perspective which will be useful in the chapters to follow.

The fundamental basis for the divisions adopted here is the shifting relationship between the forest and the steppe zones, a relationship which will be considered largely from the standpoint of its sociological implications and effects. On the eve of Russian history, efforts had already begun to unify these two areas so that both might benefit through the exchange of their natural wealth. These first elemental attempts, begun long before the appearance of Russia as an independent historical entity, were made by the inhabitants of both forests and steppes, and after the emergence of the Russian people were carried on first by the Khazars and later by the Varangian princes. The final attempt at unification during this period was directed by Prince Sviatoslav, who strove to unite under his power the Dnieper, lower Volga, and lower Danube. The period closed with the crumbling of Sviatoslav's empire after his death in 972, a time which was important also as marking the gradual approach of the Russians to Christianity.

The next two and a half centuries—or, more exactly, 972–1237 —were characterized by a protracted struggle between the forest and the steppe. In the course of this the Russians all but lost their access to the Black Sea; the southern steppes were occupied by Turkish tribes—first by the Pecheniegs and then by the Cumans. The Russians were able to keep the intermediate forest-steppe zone, but the bulk of their resources was now in the forest zone. While the periodical Turkish raids on the border regions were harassing enough and caused great damage and heavy losses, the Turks were not, in this period, strong enough seriously to endanger the existence of the Russian nation. In the 12th century a kind of balance of forces was established, and in the early 13th century the relations between Russians and Cumans became more friendly. On the whole, the pressure of the steppe nomads did not prevent the Russians from developing their free political institutions or promoting their civilization. In fact this period—called Kievan since Kiev was at that time both the political and ecclesiastical capital of Russia—saw the blossoming of Russo-Byzantine culture. Close contacts were maintained by the Russians with both Byzantium and the nations of the West, and even the ecclesiastical breach between Constantinople and Rome did not, at first, seriously affect the intercourse between the Russians and their western neighbors—the Hungarians, Czechs, Poles, and Germans.

The third great period of Russian history (1237–1452) began with the Mongol invasion, which at last brought to an end the long conflict between forest and steppe. The victory of the invading nomads was a decisive one for the steppes and resulted in the unification of the several Russian states under the domination of the Golden Horde. Mongol rule over western Russia lasted about a century and was then replaced by the domination of Poland and Lithuania. Eastern Russia, which remained under Mongol control for another century, gradually became centered around Moscow. While the Russians accumulated strength and resources, the Golden Horde began to disintegrate and in the middle of the 15th century broke into several smaller khanates. The rulers of Moscow were shrewd enough to profit by new circumstances and to assert their virtual independence from the khan. With the founding of a vassal Tatar princedom in Kasimov in 1452, Moscow had signaled its assumption of the role of successor to the Golden Horde.

The internal peace which the Mongols were able to enforce during the greater part of two centuries allowed the Russians gradu-

ally to recover from the terrible shock of the invasion and to start
building a strong state of their own under the tutelage of the khans.
Because of the wholesale destruction of most Russian cities at the
time of the invasion, it took several decades for Russian crafts
and industries to gather new strength. Agriculture, however, continued to expand throughout the period, and international trade
was under the special protection of the khans. The strict obedience
required by the khan of all the Russian princes, and the severe
regime of taxation and military conscription introduced by the
Mongols, resulted in changing the traditional system of government
and administration. The free political institutions of the Kievan
period failed to survive the trial, except in Novgorod which enjoyed autonomy under the Mongols. When events made resistance
to the Mongols possible and national leadership was assumed by
the grand duke of Moscow, he used for his own and his nation's
benefit the system of administration and taxation built up by
the khans. In the matters of religion the Russian church had been
greatly strengthened when the Mongol khan chose to give it his
patronage, and the gradual weakening of the Byzantine Empire
further freed the Russians from administrative dependence on
Constantinople. The position of the Russian church was enhanced
still more when at the time of the Florentine union of 1439 it remained independent while the Byzantine church submitted temporarily to the authority of the pope. With the collapse of the
Byzantine Empire and the capture of Constantinople by the Ottoman Turks in 1453, Russia became in the eyes of her people the
leading state in Orthodox Christendom.

The fourth period was characterized by the great Russian expansion southeast and the consequent reassertion of the power of
the forest zone over the nomadic culture of the steppes. The two
and a half centuries following 1452 witnessed the conquest of
Kazan and Astrakhan and the colonization of Siberia, as well as
the reoccupation after many centuries of the mouth of the Don.
The capture of Azov by Peter the Great in 1696 brought this era
to a close. Russia's hard struggle against the Mongols and the
Turks as well as against the Poles and the Swedes required the
strenuous efforts of the whole nation. Individual and political
freedom had to be sacrificed for the sake of national survival. As
a result, people of every social class were compelled to perform

services for the state in one form or another. The peasants were subjected to serfdom. The church, on the whole, cooperated with the tsars in their policies. The chief events in the religious field were the division of the Russian church into two metropolitan districts—Moscow and western Russia—and the establishment of the patriarchate in Moscow; the defense of Orthodoxy against the pressure of Roman Catholicism from the West; and the schism of the Old Ritualists.

The fifth period, extending from 1696 to the revolution of 1917, saw the gradual expansion of the Russian Empire to the natural boundaries of Eurasia. In this age the final unification of forest and steppe was achieved, the two great zones being welded into a single economic unit. Agriculture reached a dominant position throughout all Eurasia, and as the area of cultivation spread across the continent industries sprang up to exploit the rich natural resources discovered and developed in the land. The cultural history of the time was marked by resurgent conflicts and fermentation, and the spiritual life of the day was stirred by a severe crisis in the religious consciousness of the people when the church, in its administrative branches, became subject to the authority of the state.

The present era of Russian history began, of course, with the revolution of 1917.

CHAPTER 1

THE ORIGINS OF THE RUSSIAN STATE

1. *Western Eurasia as the cradle of the Russian state*

THE Russian state came into existence in the western corner of the area we have called Eurasia, where, at least by the 3d century, the territory lying between the Baltic Sea, the Don River, the Black Sea, and the lower Danube had been settled in part by east Slavic tribes. In the course of the 8th and 9th centuries these tribes were united under the Norsemen who had penetrated to the mainland by way of the Baltic, and it is this event which is commonly taken as the date of the founding of the Russian state. In fact, however, political life in the territories occupied by the eastern Slavs had originated much earlier in southern Russia, in the social and political forms centering around the trade between the wooded regions and the pasture lands of western Eurasia, the Black Sea, and the East.

2. *The foundations of political life in western Eurasia. The nomadic empires. Scythians and Sarmatians*

The first inhabitants of the south Russian steppes of whom we have definite knowledge were the Scythians, a tribe belonging linguistically to the Iranian peoples but in its mode of life closely similar to the Turko-Mongols. In fact, it is probable that even at this time there had been a mixture of racial groups and that among the Scythians there was at least a sprinkling of Turks and Mongols.

These Scythians—whose favorite occupation seems to have been war and whose closest companion was the horse—appeared in southern Russia sometime during the 7th century B.C. On the Eurasian steppes they found themselves neighbors of the Turks who inhabited Altai and Mongolia, and together these two groups maintained the connecting links between China and Greece. The northern shore of the Black Sea was occupied at that time by Greek colonies—Olbia at the mouth of the Bug, Chersonesus close to the present city of Sevastopol, Panticapaeum on the site of the city of Kerch, and many others—and the Scythians conducted a lively trade with these outposts of Greek civilization. Greek artisans and craftsmen made household articles for the Scythian kings and for the wealthier classes, and many examples of Greco-Scythian art, some of which are now in the Hermitage Museum in Leningrad, have been found by excavators in southern Russia.

Greek authors have left us interesting information about the life and customs of the Scythians. Herodotus, the 5th-century B.C. Greek historian, in a description of Scythia tells us that it extended from the mouth of the Ister (the Danube) up the rivers Borysthenes (the Dnieper) and Tanais (the Don) far to the north and east of the Black Sea. From the data available on the Scythians and particularly from the information on the volume of their trade with the Greeks to the south and the Turks, Mongols, and Chinese to the east, it seems probable that they succeeded at times in uniting under their power not only the steppes but also part of the wooded north; and indeed there exists archaeological proof that trading settlements were founded along the boundary of this forest area.

3. *The Alans and the Antes*

At the beginning of the 4th century B.C. another Iranian people, the Sarmatians, began to press upon the Scythians, and by the end of the 2d century B.C. they had occupied the shores of the Black Sea.

Among the Sarmatians the most powerful tribe was the Alans who, until the coming of the Huns, were considered the best horsemen of the steppes. They are described in contemporary accounts as tall, handsome, and blond. For centuries they were famous as highly skilled armorers and jewelers, and many of their favorite weapons, the long spear and long iron sword, have been uncovered in the barrows of the north Caucasus and southern Russia. They developed a peculiar artistic style of their own, a variation of the Scythian "animal style" in which the lavish use of enamel and precious stones for incrustation was characteristic. The famous treasure of Novocherkassk which was discovered in 1864 is thought to represent a part of the riches of an Alanic queen who lived, presumably, during the 1st century A.D.

Though the Alans were originally typical nomads, in time some of their clans settled down and, as they mixed with the native agricultural population, gradually came to dominate several of the east Slavic tribes. Many of the early Slavic princes bore Alanic names, and the old name of the strongest of the east Slavic tribes —the Antes—is itself of Iranian origin. The Caucasian Alans were called As or Os—a name which their descendants, the Ossetians, still bear. Their "outer" clans were known as Antes. A leading Alanic clan was called Rukhs, "the Radiant," and it is from this name that Ros or Rus (hence Russia, Russians) presumably derives.

These Rus (in the variation Rhos) are mentioned in a Syriac chronicle of the middle of the 6th century; at about the same time the Goth historian Jordanes, who wrote in Latin, mentioned the Antes in connection with events of the 4th century when they had already developed an organized state. Archaeological and linguistic evidence leads us to believe that the Antes—who must have existed in southern Russia as a Slavic tribe under the domination of Alanic chieftains since the 3d century A.D.—early reached a comparatively high degree of civilization. They were engaged in both agriculture and cattle breeding; they had orchards and vegetable gardens; they developed handicrafts such as weaving and ceramics; they forged iron tools and weapons. At times the smaller clans and family communes bound themselves together in larger tribal unions and associations; and there can be no doubt that they held well-defined ideas about social order and organization. It is interesting to remember in this connection that the words for "justice" (*pravda*) and "law" (*zakon*) are among the oldest in the Slavic vocabulary.

From time immemorial the Slavs had been an artistic people who were known for their particular fondness for music and singing. Their religion was a conglomerate system of beliefs drawn from a variety of sources, originally involving the worship of clan ancestors and natural forces such as lightning, and including rivers and trees which were considered the abodes of nymphs and spirits. Subsequently a more elaborate system developed under the influence of Iranian religious beliefs on the one hand and of Norse mythology on the other. While the Slavic Perun, god of thunder and lightning, resembles the Teutonic Thor, other deities of the early Russian pantheon are more akin to the Iranian gods and genii. Throughout the Sarmatian period the worship of the Great Goddess of the Scythians was continued, and her image imprinted itself firmly in Russian folk art, becoming, for instance, a prominent motif in early embroideries. The "Mother Earth" of Russian folklore is another interesting example of the persistence of the memory, in another form, of this same Iranian age.

According to the 6th-century Byzantine historian, Procopius of Caesarea, the Antes lived originally in a political democracy in which all public affairs were discussed in clan or tribal assemblies. From other sources, however, it is known that some of the Antic princes were endowed with considerable personal authority, and apparently an aristocratic class gradually came into being as the chieftains enriched themselves with war booty and prisoners. A rich hoard of gold and jewelry which is thought to have been part of the treasury of one of these princes was found at Pereshchepino in Poltava province and is now in the Hermitage Museum. Various less spectacular ornaments which apparently belonged to ordinary members of the tribe—plaques and rings of bronze, silver, and gold—have been found and serve as additional evidence of a highly developed artistic sense and skill among the people.

4. The Goths and the Huns

In the 3d century A.D. the Sarmatians who dominated the southern Russian steppes were displaced by German tribes of Goths who descended from the north along the Dnieper and the Don rivers. Having conquered this western corner of the Eurasian steppes, the Goths soon acquired both the nomadic customs and the material culture of the people they had displaced. They themselves became in time mounted warriors and about the middle of the 4th century organized a strong military power under the leadership of Ermenrich. For a time, as they succeeded in subduing one after another of the east Slavic tribes and forcing the peasants to work for them, it seemed that they were about to achieve a permanent subjugation of the Slav by the Teuton.

However, toward the end of the 4th century a new invasion from the east in turn destroyed the power of the Goths. This time the invaders were the Huns, a Turkish tribe led by a militaristic aristocracy similar to that of the Mongols who overran Russia much later during the 13th century.

The Hunnic khan first made vassals of the Alans and then turned against the Goths, whom he easily defeated. Shamed by this defeat, Ermenrich, the Goth king, committed suicide, and the tribe began a retreat westward in the direction of the lower Danube. However, in the Bug area which lay between them and their refuge there lived a tribe of the Antes, and the refusal of this group to allow the Goths passage resulted in a bloody conflict. The Goths crushed one of the Antic armies and Ermenrich's successsor ordered their king, Boz, all of his sons, and some seventy boyars crucified. By this time, however, the Hunnic khan had given permission to the Alans under his rule to come to the rescue of their kin, the Antes, and the Goths were again defeated and driven farther west. Even then they did not completely escape Hunnic suzerainty, for the Huns eventually followed them westward and in the reign of Attila brought most of central Europe under their control.

During the last years of his life the center of Attila's power lay in Pannonia, the western outpost of the Eurasian steppes, now known as Hungary. Strategically situated for marauding expeditions against the Mediterranean coast, Rome, and Byzantium, Pannonia was long the favorite goal of nomadic invasions and it was finally occupied by the Magyars at the end of the 9th century. Though the empire of Attila at one time extended over an enormous area from east to west, following his death it rapidly fell apart and made way for the formation of new political organizations; the remnants of the Huns eventually retired to the Azov area where they came to be known as the Bulgars.

5. The Lithuanians and the Finns

While the nomadic Iranian and Turkish tribes were displacing each other on the southern Russian steppes, the forests on both sides of the Ural Mts. were being occupied by the Finno-Ugrian tribes. The Finns constituted the northern or Ural branch of the Finno-Ugrian peoples, whose southern group was made up of Magyars, a group culturally related to the Turks. The northern Finnish tribes lived submerged in the forest regions and were consequently a hunting and fishing people; fish was their chief food, and furs served them both as clothing and as the major article of trade with their neighbors. Since their contact with each other was limited to a tenuous one along the rivers and waterways, they did not succeed in establishing a strong military power, and when the wave of Slavonic colonization started northward they were unable to resist its pressure. As the Slavs advanced into their territory, the Finns either retreated or were gradually absorbed by the ever-increasing number of invaders.

In northwestern Russia, in the basins of the Western Dvina and Nieman rivers, there lived a group of Baltic or Lithuanian tribes who belonged linguistically to the Indo-Europeans. The country they occupied was chiefly forest land not unlike that of the Finns, but even in this early period parts of it had been cleared and numbers of the people were engaged in agriculture. These early Lithuanians appear to have lived not in the village communities common to the time but on isolated farms just as their descendants did much later in the 16th and 17th centuries. The basic social unit was the family whose head wielded absolute authority over its members and the household servants they held. In the event of external danger several of these family clans would unite in common defense, and it was from these unions that the larger Lithuanian tribes were eventually constituted. In time they became a warlike people, and the barrows of that region have yielded many examples of iron halberds, spears, and swords as well as bits, stirrups, and various other horse trappings.

6. *Byzantium, the Antes, and the Avars*

During the time of the Hunnic predominance the Antes had occupied the region around the Donets and the Bug rivers and had also made settlements and enclaves in the area of the lower Don, the Crimea, and even as far as the north Caucasus. Advancing toward the southwest in the period following the dismemberment of the Hunnic Empire, certain groups of the Antes swept over Bessarabia and in the course of the 6th century joined with other Slavic tribes in devastating raids on the Byzantine possessions south of the Danube.

In a maneuver typical of their diplomacy, the Byzantine em-

perors endeavored to check the Anto-Slavic menace by both diplomatic and military measures. Seeds of discord were assiduously
sown to induce strife among various ethnic and social groups, and
at times the stratagem worked so well that Antes and Sclaveni
(Slavs) forgot the common enemy, Byzantium, and fell upon one
another instead. On the whole, however, Byzantium was forced to
rely chiefly upon its armed forces, part of whom, it is interesting
to note, were hired "barbarians" of the same racial stock as the
enemy. Many of these mercenaries held high administrative and
army positions, and it was to one of them—Chilbudius, a general
of Antic ancestry—that Emperor Justinian I entrusted the defense
of the Danubian fortified line. Though Chilbudius fought loyally
and valiantly against the Anto-Slavs, dealing them severe blows in
a campaign north of the Danube, he was eventually killed in battle (534). However, some years later a rumor spread among the
Antes that Chilbudius had not been slain but had secretly deserted
to his kin with whom he lived in hiding. In due time a man who
called himself Chilbudius was indeed produced and acclaimed by
the whole tribe as their leader, but this first of a long line of pretenders in Russian history failed miserably. Lured to Constantinople under the pretext of negotiations, he was treacherously arrested on the way and so disappeared from the stage of history. In
spite of this episode, however, the Antes later allied themselves
with the empire for a short time.

About 560 the political equilibrium of the Pontic steppes was
again upset by two more nomadic tribes driving westward. The
leading group was a tribe of Avars, that appeared in the east hotly
pursued by a tribe of Turks who had originally inhabited the
Altaic region. When the Antes in Bessarabia valiantly resisted their
attempts to break through, the Avars offered to negotiate for passage. This offer, however, proved to be merely a ruse, for in the
midst of negotiations the Antic envoy was killed and the Avars
suddenly renewed the attack in the hope of catching the Antes
unawares. Though the Antes were not completely annihilated at
the first shock as the Avars had hoped, they were so badly disorganized that the attackers were finally able to cut their way
through their lines into Pannonia (568) and to subjugate a substantial part of the Pannonian and Balkan Slavs.

While these attacks and counterattacks in southern Russia were in progress, however, the Slavs as a whole maintained a steady pressure against the Byzantine possessions to the south of the Danube and in the course of the 7th century were eventually able to occupy most of the Balkan Peninsula to the Aegean and the Adriatic.

7. *The Turks and the Khazars*

The Altaic Turks who had driven the Avars across southern Russia now established themselves on the steppes between the lower Volga and the Don and in the north Caucasus. Out of the mixture of Turks, conquered Hunno-Bulgar tribes, and Caucasian aborigines there grew a new people, the Khazars, who by 650 had established a stable state. Those Bulgar tribes who were unwilling to submit to Khazar rule were forced to emigrate, and spread north and west from the new state. One Bulgar horde settled along the middle course of the Volga and in the Kama basin, while another, driving westward into the lower Danube region, defeated the Byzantines and gradually extended their control over the whole eastern Balkan Peninsula. Though they conquered the Antic and Sclavenian tribes who held this region, they themselves fell under the influence of Slavic culture and in time even adopted the language as their own. Thus, while the name Bulgar originally applied specifically to this ruling horde of conquerors, it later came to mean that heterogeneous Slavic people who emerged from this mixed background—the modern Bulgarians.

At about the same time another "barbaric" horde, the Ugrians or Magyars, was pushed north from the Caucasus. They first settled the territory along the Donets River and, while they themselves recognized the suzerainty of the Khazars, they in turn compelled the Antes who had long lived in that region to submit to their rule. Later the Magyars moved on to the Bug and from there, at the end of the 9th century, migrated to Pannonia, which became their permanent home under the name of Hungary.

Meanwhile the Alans and Slavs of the lower Don and Azov area —the old As and Rus tribes—also became Khazar subjects. In a sense they were really allies, for they were allowed a considerable degree of autonomy. In times of danger they were obligated to send auxiliary troops to the assistance of the Khazars, but these troops retained their identity and fought under their own officers.

The whole Alano-Slavic brigade was led by a commander known as *As-tarkhan*, "the chieftain of the Alans"; it was presumably from this title that the city of Astrakhan derived its name.

During this period Khazar power reached its height in a state extending from the Caspian Sea and the lower Volga to the Dnieper and the Black Sea. Authority was legally divided between two chieftains, the kagan (the great khan) and the *beg*. While the kagan held formal authority in matters pertaining to the state and to religion, the *beg* exercised the real power since he was the recognized head of the army.

Though some of the Khazars had by this time developed considerable agricultural skill—they were engaged in cattle breeding, cultivation of the land, and fishing enterprises—their principle interest lay in trade. The great trade route of the north lay along the upper reaches of the Volga, through Bulgar territory to the Caspian, and on across the Caucasus into the Near and Middle East which at that time (700 A.D.) was under Arab rule. Along this route the Khazars developed a thriving commerce between the Far East and the Black Sea on one hand and between the Arabian south and Slavonic north on the other.

One of the results of these commercial contacts with such widely divergent peoples was the variety of religious influences to which the Khazars were subjected. Though the Arabs offered them Islam and the Greeks Christianity, the Khazar kagan, possibly for political reasons, was reluctant to accept either, fearing that a foreign faith might well be followed by foreign domination. He solved the dilemma eventually by choosing a neutral faith, Judaism, which carried with it no political threat.

From the middle of the 7th century on the Khazars and their allies the Alans had waged a series of protracted and inconclusive wars against the Arabs to the south. They had repeatedly gathered the strength to drive a wedge into Transcaucasia, only to be driven out by the Arabs. In 737, however, the Arabs were able to administer a crushing defeat to the Khazars and, sweeping on through the north Caucasus, penetrated as far north as the Don. Some 20,000 Slavs were taken prisoner in the campaign and transported to Syria. The political results of this invasion were far reaching, for both Alans and Slavs—the As and the Rus allies and vassals—lost faith in the ability of the Khazars to protect them and began a search for new allies whom they eventually found in the invading Norsemen.

8. *The Norsemen and the first Russian Kaganate*

The Norsemen—or Vikings, as they are sometimes called—had long before this established a reputation as intrepid mariners, and pirates, traders and explorers. As early as the 6th and 7th centuries the Swedes in particular had explored the eastern shores of the Baltic and eventually, ranging up the Dvina waterway, reached the Russian "Mesopotamia," the region of the upper Volga and Oka rivers. By 700 they had established themselves around Iaroslavl, Rostov, and Suzdal and were sharing the control of the native Finnish tribes with Slavic settlers from Novgorod and Smolensk. The record of this colonization is confirmed by archaeological discoveries of numerous objects such as iron clasps and swords which are unmistakably Scandinavian in origin.

Around 750 the Swedes penetrated into south Russia, where they mixed with the Rus and even assumed their name.* Originally an Iranian tribe, like the Antes, the Rus like them were gradually Slavicized. The earliest Rus activity in this period that we know of is the story of the attack on the Crimean city of Sugdaea (Surozh) as recorded in the list of miracles of St. Stephan of Surozh (appended to his "Life"). According to this source the attack took place "a few years" after the saint's death (he died in 786). From the Crimea the Rus crossed the Strait of Kerch and penetrated into the Taman Peninsula. At first they recognized the authority of the Khazar kagan. However, profiting by the weakening of Khazar power after another Arabian attack, about the year 825 the Swedish-Russian commander defied the authority of the Khazars and proclaimed himself independent. Assuming the title of Russian kagan, he established his headquarters, presumably, at Tmutorokan in the Taman Peninsula.

* The origin of the name Rus (Rus' as the name of the country and the people collectively) constitutes a highly controversial problem. An influential school of philologists and historians either disregards the evidence of the early existence of the name Ros in the south or denies its connection with the name Rus'. In the opinion of this group, Rus' derives from *Ruotsi*, the Finns' name for the Swedes. Hence, they argue, the name Rus' must have been imported to south Russia from the north.

This first Russian Kaganate captured from the Khazars and the Volga Bulgars part of the international trade in which they had been engaged and, in carrying it on, fulfilled the same sociological and economic functions. The chief article of trade appears to have been precious furs from the forests of northern Russia. The area lying along the southern shore of Lake Ilmen and centering in a town which still bears the name Old Rus (Staraia Russa) became an important northern trading outpost for the Russian Kaganate. A steady flow of merchandise was sent down the Donets-Don waterways and a lively export trade instituted not only with Byzantium but also with the Orient where the records of the postmaster general of the Caliphate indicate that during the 9th century Russian merchants were regular visitors to such cities as Bagdad.

The political emancipation of the Russians and their economic competition were regarded by the Khazars as nearly equal threats. As a defense against both, the Khazar kagan appealed to the Byzantine emperor to send architects and engineers to erect a chain of forts along the course of the lower Don and Donets rivers. The emperor was pleased to grant the request and by 835 the Byzantines had built on the Don near the present town of Tsymlianskaia a strong fortress called Sarkel (the name, in Ugric, means "White House") which is mentioned in early Russian chronicles. Protected by these fortifications, the Khazars were now in a position not only to control the Russian routes to the east but to sever the connections between the Taman Rus and northern Russia. Using this advantage skillfully, within a few years of the building of Sarkel the Khazars had conquered the Slavs of the Oka region and established their Magyar vassals in control of the Kiev area.

Finding himself thus virtually encircled, and having experienced the results of the negotiations which his enemies the Khazars had carried through with the Byzantine emperor, the Russian kagan decided in 838 to send his own envoys to Constantinople. The emperor, however, was cold to his proposition, and not only declined to conclude a treaty with the Russians but delayed the envoys and prevented them from returning to their homes. Using as a pretext the troublesome political situation which had by that time developed around the lower Danube, he urged the envoys to return by a more roundabout way and at last advised them to travel with an embassy of his own which he was just then dispatching to the Frankish emperor, Louis. According to the so-called Bertinian Annals, the envoys arrived in Ingelheim, Franconia, with the Byzantine embassy on January 17, 839. Even then their difculties had not ended, for when they proved to be Swedes by birth rather than Russians Emperor Louis became suspicious of them and ordered them arrested pending investigation. How long they were held is not known, but it does appear that at last they were allowed to return to Russia.

It is hardly surprising that the Byzantine emperor's treatment of the Russian envoys aroused the resentment of the kagan, who must immediately have set about devising a suitable retaliation. There are indications that about 840 the Russians raided Amastris, a Byzantine city on the southern shore of the Black Sea, and twenty years later Constantinople itself came under Russian attack. This last raid, however, seems to have been made in cooperation with another Russian group which had in the meantime risen in the north; and we must now turn our attention to the origins of the second branch.

9. The formation of the Kievan state

The aggressive Khazar policy which, as we have seen, resulted in the severance of commercial relations between the Taman Russians and the producing areas to the north affected not only the Russian Kaganate but also Staraia Russa and the whole region around Lake Ilmen. It soon became obvious that sending a strong expeditionary force from the north to reopen the trade routes was the only solution to the serious economic crisis which had rapidly developed throughout the area. That plan, however, could not be carried out immediately for there were not, apparently, enough Norse troops available in north Russia to attempt such a serious undertaking. That shortage of troops seems to have been the reason for "calling the Varangians from over the sea," which for centuries has been considered the "beginning of Russian history"—according to tradition in 862, but actually about 856.

The call was answered by Riurik (in the Frankish Annals, Roric), the famous Norse adventurer and pirate who, as vassal of Emperor Lothaire, was then the ruler of southern Jutland and Friesland. Though he soon restored order to north Russia and established himself firmly in Ladoga and later in Novgorod, he displayed no interest in extending his dominions southward as the Russians had hoped. His chief concern continued to be developments in western Europe and on several occasions he was forced to hasten west to secure his holdings in Friesland. While Riurik himself did nothing to relieve the Swedish-Russian merchants of Staraia Russia, he raised no objections to their organizing an expedition on their own account. This they did, and about 858 a band of their warriors succeeded in reaching Kiev and establishing themselves there under an agreement with the Magyars. From Kiev they were able to rejoin forces with the Taman Russians and with them to make the attack of June 860 on Constantinople which has been mentioned.

However, even this union of the two Russian groups did not provide sufficient military strength to attain their objectives and they were finally forced to retire. But the campaign had one important indirect result: the Byzantine Patriarch Photius seized the opportunity to send missionaries after the retreating Russians. Several years later a considerable part of the Russians were baptized and in 867 they accepted a bishop whose see was probably at Tmutorokan on the Taman Peninsula.

When Riurik died, about 873, his successor Oleg, who was a Norwegian by birth, shifted his attention to the south. Some five years later he entered Kiev at the head of a strong force and, after killing the leaders of the Swedish Rus who had been in control there, set himself up as an independent ruler. Thus a new state, so-called Kievan Russia, came into being.

The Kievan state, military and trading in character, was based economically on control of the Dnieper waterway instead of the Azov area. It continued as the intermediary between the wooded north, the southern steppes, and Byzantium, and the Russians tried also to keep open the old trade route to the caliphate. Twice during the first half of the 10th century they staged military campaigns in the Caucasus and along the southwestern shores of the Caspian Sea—campaigns which had an additional and secondary commercial aspect in the loot they yielded.

The trading character of the new state was exemplified in more orthodox fashion by the relations with Byzantium, which were, on the whole, of a more organized character. Every spring expeditions of Varangian and Slavonic traders set out down the Dnieper from Kiev in crude longboats hewn from the trunks of trees. They carried furs, wax, honey, and slaves and in Constantinople received in exchange fine wines, jewelry, and rich fabrics. The military protection necessary for such a valuable cargo was provided by the prince and his retinue, or *druzhina,* and consequently the prince participated in the undertaking as one of the largest shareholders and chief beneficiaries.

In spite of their commercial connections with Constantinople, the Russians several times during the first half of the 10th century launched military campaigns against the Byzantine Empire. While several of these raids were instituted purely for plunder, others were intended to protect the rights of the Russian traders and to defend their freedom to trade in Byzantium. Throughout this period the Russians seem to have worked assiduously to develop trade alliances in the south, and in 911 and again in 944 were able to conclude treaties with the Greeks.

However Byzantium, which had first attracted Russian warriors and traders by its riches and by the brilliance of the court and the capital, affected them in a more general way as well. Soon those Russians engaged in the southern trade began to fall under the influence of Byzantium's spiritual culture and by the middle of the century quite a number had been converted to Christianity. That these conversions created a delicate diplomatic situation is indicated by the treaty of 944, which specifically provided that a part of the Russian traders were to perform their rites according to Christian customs while the rest continued in the old pagan manner. Later, however, Princess Olga herself was converted and received by the court in 957, where, according to the Ceremonial Book of Emperor Constantine Porphyrogenitus, which contains a detailed description of her reception in the great Byzantine palace in Constantinople, she was recognized as head of the Russians but was not accorded the highest honors.

10. *The expansion of the Kievan state: Prince Sviatoslav*

The real expansion of the Kievan state began with the reign of Olga's son, Sviatoslav, a man of dynamic strength and resourcefulness and certainly one of the most energetic characters in early Russian history. Though he took over the reins of government during the lifetime of his mother, he had little interest in the internal administration of the country, which he left almost completely in Olga's hands. He preferred to spend most of his reign, which lasted from 964 to 972, campaigning far from the capital.

Sviatoslav seems to have gloried in the hard life of the military campaigner. In the words of the old chronicler, he was as brave and quick as a panther. His armies moved without baggage trains, and Sviatoslav himself shared the hardships of his men: he ate no boiled meat, but cooked horseflesh or game over the coals of the campfire; he carried no tent but slept in the open on a saddle cloth with a saddle for a pillow. When he attacked, he scorned stealth and sent messengers ahead announcing, "I come against you."

Sviatoslav's first campaigns were against the Khazars. After he had conquered one of their vassal Slavonic tribes along the Oka River, he attacked the Khazars themselves and by 965 had despoiled their empire and captured their chief towns, Sarkel on the Don and Itil on the Volga. In contrast to the marauding expeditions which the Russians had conducted during the early part of the century primarily to obtain plunder, Sviatoslav's campaigns were essentially political in character. Having overthrown the Khazar Empire, he intended to entrench himself on the lower Volga and erect a new empire on the ruins of the old, and had he been content to remain there it seems likely that he would have become the natural successor to the Khazars.

However, Sviatoslav was a restless character, and when the Byzantine emperor called on him for aid against the Bulgars on the Danube, he left Itil—stationing a small force there, perhaps to guard the newly conquered territory. His campaign against the Bulgars in 967 proved highly successful, and when he had occupied the town of Pereyaslavets on the Danube he was at last satisfied to entrench himself and give up dreams of further conquests. "I desire to live in this place on the Danube," he said. "Here is the center of my lands. Here are to be had all good things: gold, cloth, wines, and fruits of the Greeks, silver and horses of the Czechs and Hungarians, and furs, wax, honey, and slaves from Russia."

Indeed, with the conquest of the Bulgars Sviatoslav had carried to completion a political plan of broad vision. He had become the successor of the nomadic emperors and so occupied a unique and strategic position.

At that time he controlled an empire of tremendous proportions, greater than that of the Avars or Khazars, for it included within its sweep the mouths of both the Volga and the Danube. In size it could be compared only to the Hunnic Empire of the 4th and 5th centuries; but to the south Russian steppes which the Huns had ruled Sviatoslav had added the vast expanses of the forest states of Kiev and Novgorod.

After the conquest of the Khazars, and the occupation of Tmutorokan Sviatoslav must have assumed the title of kagan to follow in the tradition of the first Russian Kaganate. We know that his successors bore the title and there is a record of Metropolitan Bishop Hilarion ascribing it in the middle of the 11th century to Vladimir the Saint and Iaroslav the Wise.

The empire of Sviatoslav first began to crumble in the east. Following the decline and later dissolution of Khazar power, a new force appeared in the south of Russia, another Turkish tribe called the Pecheniegs. Taking advantage of the absence of Sviatoslav with the main Russian armies, they besieged Kiev and forced him to return hastily from the Danube to save his mother and the citizens of the beleagured city. He relieved Kiev, but after the death of Olga in 969 did not remain long in the capital, preferring to establish his sons as rulers of the principal towns while he himself returned to the Danube. But by now the whole eastern frontier of the empire was aflame with revolt. In addition, the Greeks could never reconcile themselves to the fact that by enlisting Sviatoslav's aid against the Bulgarians they had merely replaced one enemy by another, the Russians. Finally, Emperor John Tsimiskes, one of Byzantium's most skillful military leaders, personally led a campaign against Sviatoslav, defeated him, and besieged him in a fortress. In 971 Sviatoslav was forced to accept peace terms which required him to leave Bulgaria; and the following year, while the dispirited Russian armies were returning to Kiev, they were surprised and defeated by the Pecheniegs. In the battle Sviatoslav was killed and—so the old story goes—a Pechenieg prince had a drinking cup made of his skull.

CHAPTER 2

KIEVAN RUSSIA

1. *The area occupied by the Russian people*

BY the year 1000 the Russian people occupied almost all the great area from the Finnish Gulf and Lake Ladoga in the north to the lower Danube, and the Black, Azov, and Caspian seas in the south. From east to west their territory stretched from the Don River to the boundaries of present-day Hungary. But between then and 1200 the area did not remain unaltered. The nomadic peoples of the steppes wedged themselves in between the southern seas and the territories of the Russians. The southern steppe zone was gradually lost and communication cut off with the southern seas. Bitter struggles characterized the whole period. The Russian princes at times attempted to fight Turkish tribes with the help of Turkish allies and offered their Turkish auxiliaries lands in Russia to settle on. The Russians also attempted to fortify themselves against the steppe by the construction of trenches and forts, as the tsars would do again in the 16th to 18th centuries. But in spite of all their efforts they were forced to retreat to the north.

About 1200 the southern frontier of the Russian people followed a line from Moldavia to the lower course of the Oka and northeast to Viatka. The losses of territory in the south may be illustrated by the case of Tmutorokan. In the 11th century Tmutorokan, a town near the straits of Kerch, was a strong Russian center. In the 12th-century chronicles it is no longer mentioned. The Russians remained strongly entrenched, however, in the southwestern corner of Eurasia, the Carpathian Mts., and Moldavia, in spite of the ferocious attacks of the Pecheniegs and the Cumans. Russian settlements existed on the lower Danube as late as the 14th century.

North of the Carpathians the Russians were subjected to the pressure of Hungarians and Poles, but in most cases successfully resisted them. Farther north the Russian land, up to the 13th century, was relatively peaceful. The old lines still ran from the Nieman to Lake Peipus and along the river Narova to the Gulf of Finland. In the 11th century the town of Iuriev (now Tartu) was founded west of Lake Peipus. North and northeast the Russians moved forward and occupied new territories reaching the White Sea, the Arctic Ocean, and the northern section of the Ural Mts. Similarly Russian colonists in the east moved during the 13th century to the lower course of the Oka and the middle Volga.

2. The conversion of Russia to Christianity. Prince Vladimir the Saint

The death of Sviatoslav was followed by the collapse of his ambitious plan to unite forests and steppes and control the trade of both Black and Caspian seas. The Russian princes were forced to concentrate most of their attention upon the internal organization of their states and defense of the forest-steppe belt against the invaders from the steppes. The nomadic tribesmen who, like the Khazars, in earlier times had united forests and steppes under one rule now became again dangerous enemies. One wave succeeded another; after the Pecheniegs appeared the Cumans. For a long time neither forest nor steppe succeeded in getting the upper hand. The forces of the Kievan state and the nomadic tribes in the south of Russia were approximately equal, and their struggle was long and indecisive.

After the death of Sviatoslav his sons fell into dispute. Vladimir was victorious in 978.

As we have seen above, part of the Russian people were converted to Christianity in the 9th and 10th centuries. The pagan religious ideology was broken down. There was a need for a new faith. The ancient Russian chronicles contain an account of Vladimir's christening after a long period of indecision. According to the chronicler, in 986 Vladimir was visited by religious missions of different faiths and churches: Mohammedans from the Bulgars of the Volga, Roman Catholics from Germany, Khazars professing Judaism, and a Greek philosopher of the Orthodox faith. This picture was not a mere rhetorical figure but an exact reflection of the facts. These different religions were professed partly by neighbors and partly even by inhabitants of the Kievan state.

The acceptance of one or another of these faiths must necessarily have determined the future cultural and political development of Russia. The acceptance of Islam would have drawn Russia into the circle of Near Eastern culture. Accepting Roman Christianity from the Germans would have made Russia a country of Latin or European culture. The acceptance of either Judaism or Orthodox Christianity ensured to Russia cultural independence of both East and West.

Political arguments could be mustered for both Judaism and Orthodoxy. On the one hand, there were the arguments that had converted the khan of the Khazars to Judaism, playing upon the desire to secure political and religious independence from the strongest churches and states of the eastern Mediterranean. On the other hand, in favor of Orthodoxy, there were arguments of a different nature—the advantages of a cultural union with Byzantium, which already had close trade relations with Russia. Political calculation aside, the question of faith also had to be considered with regard to spiritual needs, because of the inadequacy of the old paganism.

According to the chronicler, after listening to the representatives of the various religious missions, Vladimir seemed to be favorably impressed by the Greek philosopher. But before making a final decision he dispatched emissaries to the neighboring countries to observe "by whom and how God was worshiped." The emissaries who attended a service in Saint Sophia in Constantinople related that they did not know whether they were on earth or in heaven. Their accounts finally determined Vladimir to accept baptism into the Orthodox Church (988). This most important event of his reign led to the institution of Christianity as the official religion not only of the princely house but of the whole Russian people. The earlier baptism of the Princess Olga had not had this result. When Olga had entreated Sviatoslav to accept Christianity, he is said to have replied, "How can I alone change my faith? The druzhina would laugh at me."

Prior to the official conversion of Russia to Christianity, political complications with Byzantium occurred. Vladimir undertook a campaign against the Greek town of Chersonesus, which surrendered after a long siege. The Byzantine emperor agreed to give Vladimir the princess Anne in marriage. Upon his return from the Chersonesus campaign, Vladimir organized a general christening of his subjects (about 990 A.D.). The people of Novgorod were also christened, but by force, since their paganism was more strongly entrenched. Christian churches were built upon the former places of pagan worship. The legal position of the church was fixed by an order of Vladimir's regarding the collection of a tithe for the benefit of the church of Our Lady in Kiev, about 996, and the statute regarding church courts in 1010.*

3. Prince Iaroslav the Wise and his policy

Upon the death of Vladimir the Saint strife broke out among his sons as it had among Sviatoslav's. His eldest son, Sviatopolk, seized the throne, and to protect himself against his brothers had recourse to murder. At his orders Boris and Gleb, later venerated by the Russian church as saints, were put to death. But Sviatopolk did not succeed in getting rid of his most dangerous rival, his brother Iaroslav, the prince of Novgorod. A protracted struggle began between the two. Iaroslav received support from his subjects and from the Varangians, whose forces were augmented by mercenaries brought from across the sea. Sviatopolk concluded an alliance with his father-in-law, the Polish king, Boleslav the Brave. While Iaroslav remained true to Orthodoxy, Sviatopolk counted on support from Roman Catholicism. The struggle between the brothers took on far wider significance than a family disagreement. The victory of Sviatopolk would have subjected Russia to Polish and Catholic influence.

After a long period of indecisive struggle Iaroslav finally defeated his brother in 1019. Sviatopolk perished during his retreat. Following this victory and the subjection of Kiev, Iaroslav entered into conflict with his remaining brother, Mstislav. The latter was an interesting figure in the history of ancient Russia. He had attempted on a smaller scale to re-create the empire of his grandfather, Sviatoslav, starting not from the north but from the south. He ruled over the eastern corner of the Black Sea coast from the city of Tmutorokan and attempted to extend his power northward.

* Long after his death, Vladimir was canonized by the Russian church.

In this respect his policy followed the tradition of the Khazar khans of adding the forest regions of the Dnieper to their empire of the steppes. The two-year war between the brothers resulted in the victory of Mstislav. Iaroslav was forced to agree to a division of the Russian state along the line of the Dnieper. Several years later Mstislav died, and in 1036 Iaroslav became head of both parts of the Russian lands. The same year Iaroslav routed the Pecheniegs who had advanced again on Kiev but who never after attacked the town.

The internal policy of Iaroslav was of great significance. During his reign the first laws were drawn up, a collection known as the Russian Law. Iaroslav first granted these to his Novgorod subjects as a reward for their aid in his struggle against Sviatopolk. Later, the law was also promulgated in Kiev. The laws of Iaroslav attempted to limit the prevailing custom of blood vengeance for murder by empowering only certain relatives to avenge a murder; in their absence the murderer was fined by the treasury of the prince. The Russian Law was based on old Slavonic customs, and later expanded and modernized. Jurists acquainted with Byzantine law took part in its formulation.

Furthermore, in 1037, Iaroslav made an agreement with the Byzantine authorities about the status of the Russian church, whose relations with Constantinople had not been well defined under Vladimir. The church was now organized as a diocese of the patriarchate of Constantinople, with the metropolitan of Kiev at its head. The metropolitan was to be ordained by the patriarch but the bishops were to be appointed upon the recommendation of the prince of Kiev. There were ten bishoprics in the time of Iaroslav. Later the number increased slightly. All the metropolitans of Russia in the Kievan period were Greeks, except for Hilarion in the 11th century and Clement in the 12th. Some of the bishops were Greeks but the majority were Russians.

Imitating the Byzantine emperors, Iaroslav wanted to make Kiev an imperial city like Constantinople. He embellished it with handsome buildings, some of which, like the church of St. Sophia, were constructed by Greek masters. Both a library and a divinity school were connected with St. Sophia. Iaroslav also organized schools for the children of the druzhina. During his own life or that of his immediate successor, the World History of the Greek chron-

icler, George Hamartolos, and the collection of laws regulating ecclesiastical matters (*nomokanon*) were translated into Slavonic.

In Iaroslav's reign there appeared a remarkable leader in the
Russian church, Hilarion, the first metropolitan of Russian origin
(1051). He was fully educated in Greek ecclesiastical matters,
and his profound wisdom and oratorical power are evidenced by
one of his surviving sermons in which he spoke of the significance
of Russian conversion to Christianity. Hilarion, even before he
became metropolitan, was known for his deeply religious life. In
his earlier days he had dug himself a cave in a hill near Kiev,
for spiritual meditation. He may therefore be regarded as the
founder of the Kiev Monastery of the Caves, which flourished under the sons of Iaroslav and became a leading institution in Russian religious life of the Kievan period.

4. *Russia divided into several principalities.*
Internal and external struggle

After Iaroslav's death in 1054 Russia was divided into principalities ruled by his sons. As the royal house increased with each generation, these principalities were broken up into more pieces. But
the subdivision was not permanent. The princes frequently moved
from one town to another. The eldest of the family always tried to
occupy the throne of Kiev, which was regarded as the highest. At
the death of each Kiev prince, a general shifting of princes took
place. The power was vested in the whole royal clan and was continually being reallocated within the family.

As might be expected, the distribution of power was frequently
complicated by the personal ambitions of individual princes. Of
considerable moment, too, were the desires of the population of
the large towns. The popular council or *veche* often refused to accept a new prince and called in another. However, with one exception the prince was always selected from the dynasty of Vladimir.

Principally in view of this custom, Russian history from 1050
to 1250 is full of civil strife between princes. To strengthen their
power some of these princes frequently allied themselves with
foreigners—Hungarians, Poles, or Cumans. In the decades around
1100 efforts were made to form an alliance among the princes. A
family council was called on several occasions. The idea of a general alliance of princes was supported by one of the best men of

the time, a grandson of Iaroslav, Vladimir Monomakh, prince of Kiev. His death in 1125 brought to an end the efforts to form an alliance. Russia began to fall apart. In place of a single cultural and national center in Kiev, in the middle of the 12th century a number of local centers came into existence: the Galician principality in the west; Novgorod in the north; the Vladimir-Suzdal principality in the northeast; and Kiev in the south. The importance of Kiev was shaken in 1169 when it was captured from Vladimir by the armies of Prince Andrew Bogolubsky. The city also suffered indirectly—through the cutting off of its trade—from the sacking of Constantinople by the Crusaders in 1204. A Latin empire was founded in Constantinople and lasted until 1261 when the Greeks overthrew it; but the Greek Empire never regained its former strength. Until these events the Greeks had played an important part in the political life of the Russians. Byzantium sent to Kiev metropolitans who then headed the Russian church and constantly attempted to secure alliances of Russian princes by marriage with Byzantine princesses or aristocrats. The mother of Vladimir Monomakh was a Greek princess.

Byzantium attempted to employ the Russian princes in its own politics. Thus in the 12th century, during a war with Hungary, Byzantium sought to form an alliance with the Galician princes for the purpose of attacking Hungary from the northeast, and with the Suzdalian princes to contain Kiev. Later, when the Galician princes allied themselves with Hungary, Byzantium sought an alliance with the Kievan princes, setting them up against the Galicians.

The Russian princes waged a continual struggle against the Cumans, nomadic tribesmen in the steppe zone who made frequent raids upon the Russian principalities, devastating them and enslaving the inhabitants. The princes from time to time undertook campaigns against the tribesmen, but although occasionally defeated the mounted nomads invariably saved themselves by flight. The nomadic enemy could not be completely subdued; and sometimes the Russian campaigns in the steppes ended in catastrophe. The Cumans would trap the Russian armies and surround them on all sides. One of these unfortunate incidents in 1185 is the subject of an old Russian epic poem, "Lay of Igor's Campaign."

In the 13th century the pressure of the Cumans weakened, and separate alliances between Russian princes and Cuman khans increased in frequency. At this time new enemies arose, Germans, Swedes, and Lithuanians in the northwest, and in the southeast the Mongols.

The Germans appeared at the mouth of the Western Dvina in the middle of the 12th century, their first contacts with the natives being peaceful. Most of them were traders and missionaries. In 1200 Bishop Albert founded the town of Riga at the mouth of the Dvina. The inhabitants of the region, Lithuanians and Letts, were converted, though with difficulty, to Christianity. Then warriors came in support of the missionaries. An order of knights similar to those who fought against the Moslems in the Holy land was organized: the Sword-bearers, whose distinguishing mark was a white cape with a red cross and a sword on the shoulder. The Sword-bearers were subject to the orders of the *magister* and not to the Livonian bishop. They extended their power rapidly eastward from Riga in the direction of Pskov and Polotsk. The region southwest of the Livonian Order of Sword-bearers, between the Nieman and the Vistula, was occupied by the Teutonic Order of Knights, those of the black cape and white cross. The Teutonic Order first came into existence to fight the Moslems, but the hopelessness of the struggle in the Holy Land led the order to move around 1230 to the Baltic Sea at the invitation of a Polish prince who asked them to protect him against the attacks of a Lithuanian tribe of Prussians. The knights conquered the Prussians and created a new German state, which was later to be known as Prussia.

Tribes of Letts and Lithuanians united to struggle against the German knights. For the most part they were unsuccessful, and the result was a movement of Letts and Lithuanians eastward into the Russian lands. Thus arose the threat of Lithuanian pressure in the northern principalities.

Meanwhile civil strife among the Russian princes continued. A leading part was played in the early 13th century by Prince Mstislav the Daring, a gallant fighter but unsuccessful in his policies. Mstislav took part in the wars between Smolensk and Kiev, Novgorod and Suzdal. He was allied with the Cumans and defended the Galician principality against the Hungarians, but nowhere did he achieve permanent political conquests. The glory of fighting was all he desired; everything else was unimportant. In character he resembled many of the western knights of his time, being perhaps most akin to Richard the Lion-Hearted.

While the Russian princes feuded, a new danger appeared in the east. A wave of nomadic peoples was advancing westward with unprecedented force. This wave was to flood Russia, submerging the princes and their quarrels.

In 1223 the Mongols, or Tatars as they were known in Russia, appeared in the southeast. Fleeing before them, the Cumans sought the aid of the Russian princes. "Today they have taken our land; tomorrow they will take yours," Khan Kotian, father-in-law of Mstislav the Daring, told the princes. Mstislav undertook to organize an alliance of Russian princes against the Tatars. The emissaries sent by the Mongols to the Russian princes were killed; and it was decided at a conference called in Kiev not to await the enemy but to go out and meet him in the midst of the steppes. The meeting took place by the Kalka River near the Sea of Azov. The Russian troops fought bravely but without cooperation among themselves or with the Cumans. The Mongol armies were led by the experienced generals Jebe and Subudey. They had defeated the Cumans and part of the Russian troops before the warriors of Kiev could enter the struggle. The prince of Kiev then shut himself up in an armed camp on the shore of the Kalka and for three days resisted the enemy. Finally he accepted a truce, but the Mongols did not abide by the convention and killed their enemies. The prince of Kiev was crushed to death under planks.

The Mongols now turned back. For fourteen years Russia heard nothing of them. The chronicler wrote of those "evil Tatars": "Only God knows whence they came and whither they went."

5. *Economic development*

In spite of all their political and military troubles the Russians were able, during the Kievan period, to promote their crafts, commerce, and agriculture and to build up remarkable political institutions based on political and individual freedom. Cultural progress, mainly on the basis of Byzantine patterns, was impressive too in many respects.

Even without most of the southern steppes, Russia in this period was rich in natural resources. Agriculture flourished in the northern sections of the steppes and in the forest-steppe zone. The original system of using the rich black earth in the steppe zone was to let the land, after the first harvests, lie fallow a number of years, although for no set and regular period. In the steppes the virgin soil was so rich that after being plowed once it secured good harvests for a number of seasons, even without new tilling. Such lavishness in the use of land was possible only so long as people were scarce. In the more thickly settled areas the supply of new land soon ran out and private ownership was established, which resulted in the appearance of the two-field, and later three-field, crop rotation system. Plowing was done with horses or oxen. In north Russia originally a light wooden plow (*sokha*) was used which could be pulled by one horse. Later on it was made more effective by the addition of iron plowshares. People of every social class could own land. The average farm was small, but large landed estates came into being as well as horse and cattle ranches owned by the princes and boyars. In addition to agriculture and cattle raising, hunting, fishing, and bee keeping played important roles in the national economy.

The art of metallurgy attained a comparatively high level. Foundries and smithies and their workers are mentioned in a number of sources. The building industry too was well developed. In northern Russia houses were made of wood, which was plentiful. Novgorod master builders and carpenters were considered particularly skillful. The art of masonry was transplanted to Russia from Byzantium in the course of the 10th and 11th centuries. In the late 12th century the city of Vladimir in Suzdalia became the most important center of the Russian stone and brick-building crafts. The art of weaving had been known to the Slavs for ages past. Both hemp and flax yarn served for fabrics. In Kievan Russia, with the growth of population and the development of handicrafts and commerce, the demand for textile products increased rapidly. The increase in wealth among the upper classes resulted in a certain refinement of life and taste for luxury. Finer linen was now to be procured. The new demands were partly satisfied by imported goods but must also have led to improvement in the methods of domestic handicraft. Woolen fabrics and cloth were also produced in Kievan Russia, being used chiefly for winter garments. In north Russia fur coats were a necessity during the long and severe winters, which stimulated both the hunting of fur-

bearing animals and the craft of furriery. Among other branches
of Russian artisanship of this period, pottery and tanning may be
mentioned.

The diversity of the country's natural resources and of the goods
produced, on the one hand, and the rise of a wealthy upper class
on the other were conducive to the development of commerce. And
indeed, trade—both foreign and domestic—played a role of paramount importance in Russian economic life of this period. The
Dnieper riverway was then the principal artery of Russian commerce. It served as the main route from the Baltic to the Black
Sea, "from the Varangians to the Greeks" as the saying went. Constantinople was its main southern outlet. The rise of both Novgorod and Kiev was due to the pivotal position of these two cities
on the great riverways. An overland road branched off from Kiev
westward to Bohemia and Germany. As for oriental trade, part
of it was carried by caravans from the Caspian and Azov areas
to Kiev through the Cuman steppes. The neutrality of the merchants was recognized by both Cumans and Russians. The Volga
River was another important artery for oriental commerce, the city
of Bulgar on the Volga below its confluence with the Kama being
the main meeting place of Russian and oriental merchants. Among
the main items of Russian export furs, honey, and wax may be
mentioned. Linen and woolen cloth were also exported to the
orient, and in certain periods silver and silverware were sent to
the West. From Byzantium Russia imported wines, silk fabrics,
jewelry, and glassware. The oriental trade brought her spices,
precious stones, silks, and weapons of Damask steel. Imports
from the West included woolen cloth of a finer quality than that
produced domestically.

An indication of the importance of the domestic commerce was
the significant role of the market place in the life of each Russian
city of this period. It was associated with political life and administration as well as with trade, and all sorts of official an-
nouncements were made there. Goods of every kind were bought
and sold in the market place and once a week it was turned into
a local fair. Novgorodian merchants played an important role in
both domestic and foreign trade, and Smolensk, Kiev, and some
other Russian cities also had powerful merchant corporations. In
the revised Russian Law (1164) considerable attention was paid

to commercial regulations. Another important document of this kind was the commercial treaty between Smolensk and a number of the German cities signed in 1229.

6. *Political organization*

The political organization of the Russian principalities in the pre-Mongol period was a combination of monarchical, aristocratic, and democratic government. The monarchical element was the prince, who however in ancient Russia was not an autocratic ruler. His chief function was military. His primary duty was to defend the town from enemies outside. Another of his functions was judicial. He appointed local judges to try cases among his subjects. In major cases the prince himself functioned as chief justice.

The aristocratic element was represented by the council, composed of the high officers of the princely druzhina and other grandees commonly known as the boyars, a term of Bulgar origin. The prince's councilors met daily at his palace, and a plenary session was convoked whenever necessary, to discuss the most important governmental matters and to introduce new legislation. It should be borne in mind that the boyars were entirely free in their service to the prince. A boyar could always retire from the court or enter the service of another prince. Since the boyars owned landed estates in their own right, they would not forfeit their land rights by so doing. Sometimes it happened that a boyar who owned lands in one principality served the prince of another. On the whole, however, the growth of the landed estates tended to make the boyars more settled and to identify their interests with some particular principality.

The democratic element of government was to be found in the city assembly known as the veche. This was not a representative body, but consisted of all the adult males in the population. Unanimity was necessary for any decision. In practice this requirement occasionally led to armed encounters between the opposing groups in the veche, after which the defeated side would acquiesce in the decision of the victors. The veche of the capital of the principality had authority over the smaller towns.

These three elements of power appeared in all Russian principalities of the Kievan period, but their relative importance differed from place to place. The veche was especially powerful in the large

trading city of northern Russia—Novgorod. In fact, Novgorod
should be called a city-state rather than a principality. In 1136
the office of the prince of Novgorod became elective, and sovereignty rested with the city—Lord Novgorod the Great as it was
called. To prevent any ambitious prince from becoming firmly entrenched in the Novgorodian land the city assembly passed a law
that deprived the prince and his non-Novgorodian retainers of the
right to own landed estates within the boundaries of the Novgorodian state. Every newly elected prince had to sign a special
contract with the city of Novgorod. According to the usual terms
of such contracts the prince had to pledge himself not to interfere with the elections of the city officials by the veche and not
to dismiss any city official without a veche decision or a court
trial. Furthermore, the assembly retained supreme judicial authority. The two major city officials were the mayor (*posadnik*)
and the commander of the city militia (*tysiatsky*). Any former
posadnik was considered a notable and continued to have a part
in directing Novgorodian affairs through the boyar council which
was known in Novgorod as "the Lords." Legally, that council was
not an upper chamber but a committee of the veche for preliminary
discussion of matters to be submitted to the general assembly.
Actually, "the Lords" were able, on many occasions, to direct
policy, and the existence of such a council guaranteed a degree of
continuity in that policy. Thus the constitution of the Novgorodian
city-state may be said to have been a democracy limited to a
certain extent by the interests of the upper classes.

Spiritually, life in Novgorod centered around the cathedral—
St. Sophia. The archbishop of Novgorod enjoyed considerable
political influence and acted as moderator when conflict occurred
between the veche and the prince or between opposing parties
within the veche.

Internally, the Novgorodian commonwealth consisted of five
autonomous communes, one in each of the five wards into which
the city was divided. Each ward elected its own mayor.

Novgorod, however, was not merely a city; it was the metropolis
of a state, commanding a vast territory stretching from the Gulf of
Finland to the northern Urals and from Lake Ilmen to the White
Sea and the Arctic Ocean. This was a territory rich in natural
resources, with the exception of grain, and able to provide the

metropolitan merchants with varied items for export. It may be added that elements of the city-state which were to develop fully in Novgorod were potentially inherent in the constitution of all the main Russian cities of this period, even if in some of the principalities they were eclipsed by the growth of divergent political factors.

The aristocratic element was particularly strong in southwestern Russia, in the principalities of Galicia and Volynia. The council of boyars dominated the political life of these principalities. It is possible that one of the contributing causes of the aristocratic domination in western Russia was the influence of western feudalism coming through Poland and Hungary. The prince was forced to submit to the boyars or to fight them. One of the energetic princes of southwestern Russia, Roman of Galicia, said of the boyars, "honey cannot be eaten without crushing the bees," referring to the custom of keeping bees in hollow tree trunks, which necessitated killing the bees to obtain the honey. In this case it proved not so easy to crush the bees. Seven years after Roman's death the boyar Vladislav was proclaimed prince of Galicia—the only known case in the Kievan period of a princely title in one of the Russian lands being held by a man not a member of the house of Riurik (1212). His reign did not last long, however, for the Poles and Hungarians interfered in Galician affairs. Boyar-prince Vladislav was deported to Hungary and imprisoned there. A Hungarian prince next assumed the title of king of Galicia, but before long the old dynasty was back in saddle. Occasional conflicts between the prince and the boyars occurred in other parts of Russia as well, but on the whole they cooperated closely within each principality, since it was to each side's interest to do so.

The monarchical element was particularly developed in Suzdalia, in northeastern Russia, where the dominating personality of Prince Andrew Bogoliubsky had much to do with the increase of princely power. His arrogance was resented by many of his servitors and he was killed in 1175. Later his brother Vsevolod, nicknamed "the Big Nest" because of the size of his family, succeeded, by using subtler methods than Andrew, in raising the prince's prestige to a higher level than in any other part of Russia. The Suzdalian monarchy was, however, a constitutional one, and not absolute, since both the boyar council and the city assembly continued to function. Most of the Suzdalian princes were great builders of new cities, churches, and palaces, able managers of their estates, and active colonizers. Through its various branches the house of Suzdalia controlled a huge area in the region of the upper Volga and the Oka rivers. In the north, the Suzdalian princes extended their possessions to Beloozero (southeast of Lake Onega) and to the upper reaches of the Northern Dvina, wedging into the Novgorodian dominions. The capital of the senior branch of the Suzdalian princes was Vladimir-in-Suzdalia. Rostov and Iaroslavl were among the important cities; later on, in the Mongol period, Moscow, Tver, and Nizhni Novgorod became prominent. Historically speaking, Suzdalia was the nucleus of the future Tsardom of Moscow.

7. Society

Russian political institutions of the Kievan period were based upon a free society. There were no impenetrable barriers between various groups of freemen, no hereditary castes or classes, and it was easy to pass from one group or occupation to another. It is, then, only with reservations that one can speak of the existence of social classes in Russia at that time. The boyars and other owners of large landed estates, together with the richest merchants in the cities, may be called Russia's upper class of the period. The middle class in the cities consisted of the merchants of average means and of master artisans; in the rural districts of the owners of medium and small-size estates. The lower classes were represented by the poorer artisans and unskilled labor in the cities; in the rural districts by agricultural laborers and the peasants settled on the state lands, the so-called *smerdy*. This, however, is not the whole picture, since in addition to freemen there were also the half-free and slaves in Kievan Russia; the two latter groups constituted but a small fraction of the total population.

The boyars as a group were of heterogeneous origin. The backbone consisted of the descendants of the old clan aristocracy of the Antes. Some of the boyars, especially in Novgorod, came from the merchant families. With the rise of princely power in Kiev the prince's retinue became an important factor in the formation of the boyar class. The druzhina was a melting pot in itself, since it included, besides the Norsemen and the Slavs, knights and adventurers of other nationalities, such as Ossetians (As), Circassians

(Kasogians), Magyars (Ugrians), and Turks, who were eager to win glory and to grow rich under the banner of the Kievan prince. In the heroic songs of old Russia—the byliny of the so-called Kievan cycle—the knights of the druzhina are represented as alert defenders of the Russian people against the inroads of the steppe nomads. By contrast, in the Novgorodian byliny the hero is more often a wealthy merchant than a professional warrior, and the adventures of the maritime trading expeditions replace those of steppe warfare. The wealthiest overseas importers and exporters in Novgorod formed an exclusive corporation known as the St. John's Guild. Lesser merchants established guilds and joint stock companies of their own. Artisans of each trade usually settled together in the same street, forming their own associations or "street" guilds. In other cases, artisans joined professional co-operative groups of the type which later became known as an artel.

In the rural districts the traditional Slavic "greater family" commune (*zadruga*) was gradually replaced by smaller families and individual ownership of land. Even when several former members of the zadruga, or just several neighbors, owned land co-operatively, each cultivated his plot individually. In addition to such farmers, there was the group of peasants settled on state lands, known as the smerdy. These, while freemen, were under the special protection and special jurisdiction of the prince. They had to pay the state tax (called "tribute") to which neither the townspeople nor the middle-class farmers were subjected. When a smerd left no sons the land reverted to the prince.

With the growth of the church, a new social group came into being, the so-called "church people." Not only the clergy and their families belonged to this group but also assistants in the charitable institutions of various kind supported by the church, as well as freedmen. All of the church people were under the jurisdiction of the special church courts. In this period as well as later, the Russian clergy was divided into two groups: the "black clergy" (i.e. monks) and the "white clergy" (priests and deacons). Following the Byzantine pattern, it has been an established custom in the Russian church that only monks are ordained bishops; and, contrary to the practice of the Roman Church, Russian priests are usually chosen from among married men.

Let us now turn to the slaves. The coexistence of this group with a society of free citizens is a feature in the social and economic set-up of Kievan Russia reminiscent of ancient Greece. Slavery in Kievan Russia was of two kinds: temporary and permanent. The latter was known as "full slavery" and was hereditary. The main source of temporary slavery was war captivity. At the close of a war captives were released for a ransom. If unable to pay the ransom, the captive remained at the disposal of his captor, his work being credited toward the payment of the ransom. If and when the full amount was made up the captive was released. Full slaves were considered chattels of the owner and could be bought and sold. Some of them were employed in the master's household, others in the fields. Some of the trusted household slaves succeeded in becoming prosperous and were eventually able to buy their freedom. On the other hand, if a freeman lost his property owing to inroads of the steppe nomads or for any other reasons, and found himself in a desperate position, he could sell himself into slavery, by this action excluding himself, of course, from the ranks of citizens. He had, however, an alternative course: to borrow money and to work for his creditor and to pay debt and interest. This made him "half-free," an indentured laborer temporarily bound to his creditor. If he succeeded in fulfilling his obligation, his citizen's rights were restored; if he broke the contract and attempted to flee from his lord he became the latter's slave.

8. *Cultural development*

After Russia's conversion to Christianity the church became the main vehicle of Byzantine civilization in Russia, playing a leading part not only in the field of religion but in literature, fine arts, and music as well. Paganism was stamped out in the cities without much opposition. In the rural districts, however, pagan notions persisted in the popular beliefs, and even pagan rites were long practiced. Significantly enough, almost all the monasteries and convents founded in the Kievan period were located in or near the cities. The most renowned of these was the Monastery of the Caves at Kiev, an important Russian spiritual center of the period. According to Abbot Theodosius of this monastery (who later was canonized) the foundations of monasticism were prayer, humility, work, and charity. Following those rules himself the abbot wore shabby clothes and did not shun any manual work. Perhaps the most important result of the introduction of Christianity in old Russia was the new sense of moral responsibility it brought for one's own deeds, and even thoughts; the idea of a future life and the Last Judgment strengthened this. At first only a few could appreciate the symbolism of church ritual; but there were many elements in the service that appealed to a greater or lesser degree to the majority of the congregation, such as the reading of the Old and New Testaments, hymn singing, and prayers. Icon paintings and murals representing biblical scenes were meant to illustrate the contents of the readings. Further explanation was supplied in sermons.

It must be borne in mind that the church services were performed not in Latin or Greek but in Church Slavonic. The Slavic language was introduced into the service, and the Gospel translated from the Greek, by the Byzantine missionaries S.S. Cyril and Methodius who were born in Macedonia and became known as the Apostles of the Slavs. They came to Moravia in 863. Their work was continued by their disciples in Bulgaria. In the early Middle Ages the difference between single Slavic languages was less marked than in modern times, and Church Slavonic, while based on Macedonian, Moravian, and Bulgarian dialects, was easily understood by the Russians. In fact, it became the foundation of the Russian literary language. While a number of Slavic books were brought to Russia from Moravia and Bulgaria, the translation of others was undertaken in Kiev. In that way, by the late 11th century Russian readers had at their disposal a comparatively well-stocked library of manuscript books, mainly on religious subjects. Moreover, an intellectual élite had formed by that time, some of whose members learned Greek.

Gradually a native literature emerged in Russia based on the Byzantine and Bulgarian patterns. Sermons of the leading Russian bishops and the lives of the first Russian saints were part of this literature. The life of St. Theodosius was written in the late 11th century by Nestor, a learned monk of the Monastery of the Caves. He is also usually considered the chief contributor to the first History of Russia, the so-called *Povest' vremennykh let* (Annals), although there is no definite proof for it. Completed in 1116, the *Povest'* was based on earlier records of events compiled by Kievan and Novgorodian monks. It contains valuable information on the history of the Russian tribe and the formation of the Kievan state. The editors used some documents of the princely archives, such as the Russo-Byzantine treaties of the 10th century, as well as a number of historical tales and legends. The cultural unity of the Slavs and the importance of their conversion to Christianity were emphasized. In the Byzantine tradition, this first History of Russia is permeated with religious ideas; historical events are interpreted in the light of the struggle between Christianity and the evil forces in the human soul.

Russian art of the Kievan period also was closely connected with the church. Instrumental music was not used in the Greek Orthodox Church but singing (apparently always in unison) played a very important role in the service. At first Greek singers and conductors were engaged to perform and to train Russian choirs, but before long the Russians mastered the art.

Religious painting, following the Byzantine style, took two major forms: frescoes on the walls of the churches and icons. These were executed at first by Greek masters and only later by Russians. Some icons were imported from Constantinople. Icons were a characteristic expression of the customs of the Orthodox Church. They might represent Jesus Christ, Our Lady, the saints, or scenes from the lives of any of these. The icon, however, is not a portrait but an object of veneration. This usage was recognized after the defeat of the iconoclastic party in Byzantium in the middle of the 9th century. The Orthodox believer places his icon in a prominent place in his home, in Russia usually in a corner. A wick is lighted before it and prayers are said facing the icon. It is in fact a symbol or a reminder of the spiritual world to the believer, and its purpose is to raise corresponding emotions in the soul. For this reason the ancient Russian icons had a much more powerful psychological influence than ordinary painting. The old icon painters approached their task with religious feeling, in this too differing from lay artists.

Mosaics were also used in ancient Russia. The remains of some fine examples exist in St. Sophia in Kiev.

Sculpture had only a subordinate place in Byzantine art, and in Russia especially the church frowned on it, identifying it with the pagan art of classical antiquity. While icons became highly popular, there were no statues of saints in Russian churches. What sculpture there was in old Russia—the bas-reliefs—was mostly used for decorative purposes. The best known examples are the bas-reliefs of the Suzdalian churches of around 1200, some of them in stucco, others executed in stone.

The sumptuous stone cathedrals built in Kiev, Novgorod, and a number of other Russian cities in the late 10th and 11th centuries were all created by Byzantine or Byzantine-trained masters. Some of the latter came not from Constantinople, however, but from the Byzantine provinces or the Caucasus. The Suzdalian churches of the 12th and early 13th centuries, most of which were built by Russian masters, were smaller than St. Sophia in Kiev but artistically no less remarkable. The type is characterized by strikingly harmonious composition and graciousness of lines and decoration. The Suzdalian style has been called by an American art historian, K. J. Conant, "authentically classic" and "worthy of the hellenistic spirit." It has some features in common with both the Romanesque and the Transcaucasian (Armenian and Georgian) types of architecture.

The applied arts, such as cloisonné enamel, filigree, and niello, also reached a high level in the Kievan period. Both church and princes patronized them. While the church needed them to embellish crosses, vessels, and the bindings of copies of the Gospels that were used in the service, the princes and boyars—or their womenfolk—craved jewelry and ornaments. Kiev was an important center of this production.

Thus by no means all the manifestations of Byzantine or Byzantine-inspired art in Russia were church art; and princes built palaces as well as churches. Nor was all lay art in Russia of that period Byzantine. Folk art of various kinds, such as embroidery and wood carving, kept alive the themes and designs of pre-Byzantine times.

The same is true of folk music and folklore. Russian folk song has its own melodic, harmonic, and rhythmic peculiarities. Various cultural elements must have contributed to its growth. While some Russian songs followed the traditions of ancient Greek music, others were composed in the pentatonic scale in which the shortest step is the whole tone. This scale was also used in Celtic folk song, among the Scotch, the Irish, and in Brittany, as well as in the East, in the folk music of the Turkish tribes of the Volga basin, in central Asia, Siam, Burma, and Indochina. Most Russian folk songs are polyphonic. The song is begun by the leader who carries the main theme, while the other singers modulate and embellish it to create a contrapuntal effect. Among the knights of the princely courts heroic ballads were popular. These differed from the folk epos by having a more individualistic and dramatic style. The only one to be preserved in full in a 16th-century copy is the famous "Lay of Igor's Campaign." It described poetically the unsuccessful campaign against the Cumans undertaken by one of the lesser Chernigov princes in 1185. The author must have been a member of the druzhina of Prince Igor and participated in the campaign.

CHAPTER 3

RUSSIA IN THE MONGOL PERIOD

1. *Territorial distribution of the Russians*

THE Mongols' raid of 1223 was but a reconnoitering expedition. Fourteen years later they again appeared on Russian soil and this time conquered all of Russia. They controlled West Russia for about a century, East Russia for about two centuries. As the Mongols withdrew from West Russia, the Poles and Lithuanians moved in; by the time East Russia emancipated herself from the Mongols Polish rule in Galicia was firmly established, while Belorussia and most of Ukraine had become parts of the Lithuanian state. Political division was gradually accentuated by religious and cultural differences between East and West Russia, that is between the Great Russians on the one hand and the Ukrainians and Belorussians on the other. In addition to the political changes it caused, the Mongol invasion affected the territorial distribution of the Russian people in many respects. The destruction of several major Russian cities during the invasion lowered the ratio of the urban population to the total. The Russian lands on the fringe of the steppes, like the Kiev and the Pereiaslav provinces, were thoroughly devastated, and a good part of their population moved to the neighboring regions north, northwest, and northeast. The southern steppes became once more grazing grounds for the nomads' horses and cattle. In East Russia, people from the border regions most exposed to the Mongol raids moved north to the better protected parts of the country—to the Moscow and Tver regions as well as to Kostroma province beyond the Volga. This movement had important political repercussions as it became one of the factors in the growth of Moscow. On the other hand, quite a number of Russians settled in the capital of the Golden Horde, Saray, on the lower Volga. Merchants

and artisans constituted the core of this settlement. A bishopric
of the Russian church was established there for their spiritual
needs. Russian merchants also visited the city of Urgenj in central Asia, the Caucasus, and the Crimea. There were a number of
Russian trading cities in Moldavia too. The Russian element in the
regions of the lower Dnieper and the Bug River was temporarily
strengthened by the advance of the Lithuanian-Russian army south
to the Black Sea in the second half of the 14th century.

A continual drain on Russian manpower caused by conscription
of recruits to the Mongol army and of artisans for the khan's industrial shops was another characteristic of the Mongol period.
Punitive expeditions sent by the khan at every attempt at rebellion
added to the plight of the Russians: many thousands were seized
and enslaved. The Russian conscripts were used to strengthen the
armies not only of the khans of the Golden Horde but of the great
khan of China as well. In the 14th century a Russian guard division
was formed in Peking and received lands for settlement in the
neighboring province. Russian captives and slaves were exported
from the Golden Horde to both China and Egypt. In China a number of these also received lands for settlement. In Egypt some of
them were impressed into the Sultan's guard troops.

2. *The Mongol invasion*

Historically speaking, the Mongol invasion was the last great
drive of the Eurasian nomads to the west. It continued the traditions of the Scythians, the Sarmatians, the Huns, the Avars, and
the Khazars. Before the invention of firearms cavalry reigned
supreme in steppe warfare; and the Mongol army, which was
based on cavalry, was the best organized and best trained of all
the nomadic armies of the past. Booty and the use of the great
commercial routes between the Pacific and the Mediterranean were
the immediate objectives of the Mongol war lords. No less important was their conscious striving for control of the world. Their
aim was to establish a world empire under which international
peace, the *pax mongolica,* would be achieved. A commendable
feature of Mongol imperial policies was the principle of religious
toleration. Thus, lofty ideas intermingled with savage greed and
physical brutality, and the whole edifice was built on the ruthless
efficiency of the imperial army and administration.

Unification of the Mongol tribes was achieved in the late 12th century by Temuchin, a clan leader of unusual power of will and vision born in 1167. Having suffered much from the rivalries of other Mongol chieftains as well as the intrigues of agents of the kingdom of North China, Temuchin, supported by a group of farsighted knights who were devoted to him, attempted to end the chaos of permanent tribal warfare by superimposing imperial institutions on the primitive feudal society of the Mongols. The goal was achieved by stages. First the nearest clans had to recognize Temuchin's authority and to elect him their khan. Then other Mongol tribes were brought to submission, and in 1206 the assembly of the whole Mongol nation (*kuriltay*) gathered at the source of the Orkhon River in Mongolia to proclaim Temuchin great khan of the nation, giving him the new name Chingis (usually spelt Genghis in English) which denotes "limitless strength." On that occasion the organization of the imperial army and administration took definite shape and the first draft of the new imperial law (*Yasa*) was approved. The Mongol army as finally organized by Chingis-Khan was based on the decimal principle, with units consisting of ten, one hundred, one thousand, and ten thousand soldiers respectively. The imperial guards, who were always on duty even in peacetime, were selected from the best fighters of each larger unit. It was through these guards that the emperor controlled the army and the nation. Over all his troops Chingis-Khan wielded an iron discipline.

As soon as the empire was constituted, it started expanding. The first stage of that expansion was the conquest of the kingdom of North China. Peking surrendered to the Mongols in 1215. In addition to its military significance, the conquest of North China was important in that it placed vast material and human resources at the Mongols' disposal. A number of high officials of the kingdom of North China agreed to enter the Mongol service and helped the Mongols to establish an efficient administration. The best known among them was Ye-liu Chu-tsai, statesman, astrologer, poet, and scholar. While the military organization of the Mongol Empire must be credited to Chingis-Khan, the administrative mechanism was the work of Ye-liu Chu-tsai and other foreign experts among the khan's assistants. From the military point of view, by conquering North China the Mongols acquired the services of thousands

of Chinese army engineers and technicians who greatly helped the
Mongols in their sieges of fortified cities during their subsequent
campaigns.

The next stage of Mongol expansion was the campaign against
the powerful Khorezmian Empire in central Asia and Persia. War
was made inevitable when the Khorezm-shah ordered the execution of the Mongol envoys who accompanied a trade caravan, in
1218. Within two years most of the Khorezmian Empire was in
the hands of the Mongols. The shah fled south and died on an
island in the Caspian Sea. Two divisions of choice Mongol troops
commanded by the prominent generals Jebe and Subudey were
sent to capture the fleeing ruler. Unable to locate him, they asked
for, and received, instructions to reconnoiter the "western lands."
They went first to northern Persia and Transcausia, then turned
north and appeared in the south Russian steppes in 1223. It was
their force which defeated the Russians and Cumans at the Kalka
River. The expedition having served its purpose, the Mongols
turned back east.

Chingis-Khan died in 1227. Two years later, the kuriltay elected
one of his sons, Ugedey, great khan. Ye-liu Chu-tsai continued to
advise the new emperor. In Ugedey's reign the Mongol imperial
institutions took final shape. The newly built city of Karakorum
in Mongolia became the capital of the empire. In 1235 a new session of the kuriltay met there to discuss plans for further expansion. It was decided to continue and complete the conquest of
both China and Persia and to start the conquest of the western
lands. That last decision put Russia on the danger list. At the head
of the Russian expedition Ugedey placed his nephew Batu, whose
father Juchi, Chingis-Khan's eldest son, had died the same year
as Chingis-Khan. Batu was accompanied by princes of all branches
of the Chingisids. The veteran of the 1223 campaign, Subudey, was
appointed his chief adviser. The army under Batu's command
was about 120,000 strong, including the newly recruited central
Asian Turks.

Batu's first move was to subdue the prosperous kingdom of the
Volga Bulgars. This task accomplished, he crossed the Volga
River in December 1237 and entered the land of Riazan. The
Russians were caught unawares since they had not expected the
power of the Volga Bulgars to disintegrate so fast. The lessons

of the Kalka defeat, fourteen years before, had obviously not been learned by the Russians. There was even less unity among them than before, and the Mongols were able to conquer one principality after another. First they demanded tribute from Riazan. Refused it, they stormed and destroyed the city. From Riazan they went to Moscow—at that time a minor principality—and burned the town. They then turned against the rich and prosperous city of Vladimir, the capital of Suzdalia. At the news of their approach Grand Duke George II went north beyond the Volga to gather more troops, leaving his family and a suitable garrison behind the city's strong walls. The city fell after six days of desperate resistance. The survivors were slain and the city destroyed. The Mongols then hastened north and attacked George's army from several quarters, killing the grand duke in battle and defeating his troops. After that they marched toward Novgorod but stopped sixty-five miles short of their goal. It was March by that time and they feared approaching spring and the thawing which would make the roads impassable. So they turned south to the Cuman steppes where their army was given a long period of rest. In the course of the next year Mongol authority was firmly established in the lower Don area as well as in the north Caucasus. About 40,000 Cumans migrated to Hungary rather than recognize Batu's authority.

In 1240 the Mongol drive was resumed, and both Chernigov and Kiev were captured and destroyed. By that time the western nations were well aware of the Mongol threat. Both Poland and Hungary sent urgent messages for help to the pope, the German emperor, and the king of France. There was no unity, however, among the European nations, and the open feud between pope and emperor made the situation even worse. The Swedes and the Teutonic Knights considered the moment appropriate for an attack on Russia. In July 1240, about the time Mongols were besieging Chernigov, the Swedes appeared at the mouth of the Neva River threatening Novgorod. They were defeated and repulsed by young Prince Alexander, George II's nephew, who became known as Nevsky ("of the Neva") after this victory. The Livonian Knights (affiliated with the Teutonic Order) directed their efforts against Pskov but scored no decisive success. Meanwhile the Mongols, proceeding west from Kiev, entered Poland and Hungary in the spring of 1241. In spite of the assistance of the Teutonic Knights the Poles suffered a severe defeat. Hungary too was at the mercy of the invaders, and her king, fleeing south, sought refuge on an island in the Adriatic. The Mongols overran the Dalmatian littoral down to Dubrovnik (Ragusa) and Cattaro; another Mongol detachment appeared at Klosterneuburg near Vienna and still no help reached Hungary from the west. In the Baltic area the Teutonic and Livonian Knights resumed their drive against Pskov and Novgorod. Pskov was taken in 1241 and in March of 1242 the knights set forth to conquer Novgorod. They were met by Alexander Nevsky on the frozen surface of Lake Peipus and routed in the so-called "battle on the ice" (April 5, 1242).

At that time the situation in Hungary changed drastically. Batu received the news that Great Khan Ugedey had died in Mongolia on December 11, 1241. Batu and other Mongol princes around him decided to go back to take part in the electoral campaign for the nomination of the new great khan. Batu himself had good chances for nomination and did not want to let them slip. Thus Mongol politics prevailed over Mongol strategy, and Batu ordered the withdrawal of his whole army from Hungary, through Bulgaria and Moldavia, back to the south Russian steppes, completing a circle.

Batu's great campaign had resulted in the conquest of an enormous territory. He had brought under his sway not only the south Russian steppes and the north Russian forests but also the region of the lower Danube. While Hungary remained a Mongol province for only one year, Bulgaria and Moldavia became parts of the Mongol Empire for a century.

At approximately the same time, the eastern Mongol armies completed the conquest of North China and Korea, and the southern army advanced in Persia and Transcaucasia. The Mongol Empire now included the whole Eurasian subcontinent from the Pacific Ocean to the Balkans.

3. The first century of Mongol rule

Batu's hopes for leadership in the Mongol Empire were frustrated since the majority of the Mongol princes and clan leaders proved ready to support the candidacy of Ugedey's son Guyuk. Because of the lack of agreement between the two parties the pre-electoral campaign lasted four years. Guyuk was formally elected and solemnly enthroned in 1246. Batu had to be satisfied with the position he already enjoyed—that of head of the strongest of the regional khanates. He established his capital in the newly built city of Saray on the lower Volga, north of Astrakhan. His authority was recognized both in those regions he inherited from his father Juchi (Kazakhstan, Khorezm, and western Siberia) and in those he conquered himself (the Volga basin, the north Caucasus, the Cuman steppes, and Russia). That vast territory was known as Juchi's Ulus (regional state). The western part of Juchi's Ulus (west of the Iaik River), which Batu's sons inherited from him in due course, eventually became known as the Golden Horde, the connotation being that of imperial power and wealth. While this name first appears in 16th-century sources, we shall use it for the earlier period as well for convenience sake.

Endowed with lands rich in natural resources of various kinds, the Golden Horde profited much by controlling the western section of the great overland commercial route stretching from China to the Black Sea. From Khorezm the western extension of that route led to Saray, to Azov (Tana), and then to the Crimean ports. The Italian merchants who established a number of "factories" (trade agencies) in the Crimea shipped the goods they received from the Orient to the Mediterranean countries and the West. A brisk west-east trade also developed over the northern route: by the Baltic Sea and Novgorod and then down the Volga to Saray. The development of trade and industry in the Golden Horde resulted in the growth and prosperity of its main cities. While the bulk of the Mongols and Turks remained nomads, large groups of their subjects were settled peoples engaged in agriculture and various handicrafts. It should be mentioned that the Mongols, while occupying the most important posts in the army and administration, constituted but a fraction of the total population. In the southern part of the Golden Horde, as well as in the basin of the middle and lower Volga, the Turks predominated, and in the north and west the Slavs. Most of these Turks were known in Russia as Tatars (such as the Kazan Tatars and the Crimean Tatars). Even the Mongols themselves were called Tatars in the Russian chronicles. We will use the term Mongols for the earlier period of Mongol rule, down to the disintegration of the Mongol Empire, and Tatars for the later periods.

With all his wealth and power, the khan of the Golden Horde was not an independent ruler but a vassal of the great khan. The first four great khans resided in Mongolia. The fifth, Kubilay (1260–94), whose wisdom and power the Venetian merchant traveler Marco Polo described with so much enthusiasm, moved his capital to Peking, China, and embraced Buddhism. All China recognized him as its emperor. His dynasty became known as the Yuan. In spite of the distance from China to Russia, the great khans interfered with Russian affairs on many occasions. In the first period of Mongol rule taxes were established and recruits conscripted in Russia by orders of the great khan countersigned by the khan of the Golden Horde, and a quota of both the money collected and the soldiers drafted went to the great khan. In the reign of Guyuk a number of Russian princes were summoned to Mongolia to receive the patents on their thrones. Later on, a journey to Saray was considered sufficient; but the khan of the Golden Horde who then issued patents to the Russian princes himself had to be confirmed in office by the great khan at the beginning of the latter's reign. At times misunderstandings arose between the great khan and the regional khans. During Kubilay's reign as well as in that of his successor some of the central Asian regional khans attempted to defy the authority of the great khan, which led to many troubles. Later on, however, the great khan's prestige was restored. Clashes occurred among regional khans as well. The feud between the khans of the Golden Horde and those of Iran lasted, with some intermissions, for about a century, in spite of the fact that the rulers of both houses continued to consider themselves vassals of the great khans. All this shows that the governmental mechanism of the Mongol Empire was not perfect. Yet it worked reasonably well until the very downfall of the Yuan dynasty in China. The last emperor of that dynasty was overthrown by a national revolution of the Chinese; and a native Chinese dynasty, the Ming, was established in Peking in 1368. Thus ended the Mongol Empire. Some of the regional khanates continued much longer, now as independent states.

The first twenty-five years of Mongol rule in Russia proved the hardest for the Russians. Dazed by their misfortunes, they were at first uncertain what course of action to take. All the Russian princes were required to acknowledge themselves vassals of the khan, and none was allowed to occupy his throne without the khan's patent, which he could not get without appearing personally before the khan. The journeys "to the Horde"—to the khan's camp—were both dangerous and humiliating. Nevertheless, first the East Russian princes and then the West Russian traveled to get their patents. After thus gaining time some of them started secret preparations for rebellion. Others who entertained no hope for immediate emancipation from Mongol rule, especially while the pressure of the Teutonic Knights from the west lasted, recommended loyalty to the khan as the only sensible course of action. Outstanding among the princes of the former group was Daniel of Galicia; among the latter, Alexander Nevsky. Daniel decided to turn to the West for assistance and asked the pope to urge a crusade of the Roman Catholic rulers against the Mongols. The pope first of all demanded that the Russian clergy recognize his authority. Receiving this assurance from Daniel, he sent the latter a royal crown (1253). While Daniel was at first much encouraged by this token of western sympathy, he kept asking for auxiliary troops to support his kingdom and was naturally disappointed when none were forthcoming. The pope on the other hand was dissatisfied with the delay in recognition of his authority by the Russian clergy. Finally Daniel ventured to oppose the Mongols singlehanded. He had some success at first, but before long more Mongol troops were sent to Galicia by the new khan Berke which Daniel had no means to oppose. He fled to Poland and then to Hungary, and both Galicia and Volynia were devastated by the Mongols (1260). Daniel had no alternative but to accept the inevitable and acknowledge himself the khan's vassal once more. He died, thoroughly disillusioned, in 1264.

Alexander Nevsky received the patent for the throne of Kiev from Great Khan Guyuk; he did not go to that devastated city, however, but remained in Novgorod. Several years later Batu's son granted him the grand ducal throne of Vladimir. Being convinced that Russia could not oppose both Germans and Mongols at once, Alexander adopted the firm political course of accepting the khan's suzerainty; he never deviated from this and his successors followed this policy for about a century. Not only was Alexander personally a loyal vassal of the khan but he insisted that his subjects abstain from hostilities against the Mongols. In his opinion any uprising would be suicidal under the circumstances.

Alexander's policy was put to a bitter test in 1257 when a general census of population was ordered by the khan. Hosts of Mongol officials were sent to Russia to fix taxation districts and to supervise the drafting of recruits into the Mongol army. While the people of Suzdalia at first grudgingly let the officials proceed with the census, the citizens of Novgorod objected violently and started a revolt, which Alexander suppressed by force. Simultaneously, however, he succeeded in persuading the Mongols to promise to withdraw their officials from Novgorod after the census was completed. Collection of taxes in the future was left to the authority of the Novgorod officials.

In 1262 an uprising against the Mongols took place in the Suzdalian cities as a protest against the hardships imposed on the population by the system of farming out taxes to Moslem merchants. The tax farmers were allowed to seize the delinquent taxpayers and make them work for the interest on the unpaid amount of taxes, or even sell them into slavery. Unable either to prevent or to suppress the revolt, Alexander hurried to Berke's camp "to implore the khan," as the chronicler puts it, "to pardon the people." Alexander spent several months in the Horde and succeeded in his mission: Berke agreed not to send any punitive expedition to Suzdalia. The rebellious cities, however, had to pay the damages. This was Alexander's last service to the Russian people. He fell ill during his stay in the Horde and died on his way back (1263).

Berke died three years later. His successor Mangu-Temir abrogated the farming of taxes in Russia and sent regular tax collectors there instead. He also issued a charter granting the Russian church and the church people exemption from both taxes and conscription. These two measures were welcomed as a relaxation of the previous intolerable regime. Furthermore, Mangu-Temir guaranteed the constitutional autonomy of Novgorod and its rights to free trade. This action gave new impetus to Baltic commerce. To promote Black Sea commerce Mangu-Temir granted the Genoese special privileges for their trade in Crimean ports.

His policy made Mongol rule more acceptable to the Russians, and most of the Russian princes were quite loyal to the tsar (as the Russians called the khan) during his reign. After his death the authority of the next three khans was challenged by a relative of his, Prince Nogay, who became virtual coruler in the western section of the Golden Horde. Some of the Russian princes, including those of Moscow and of Tver, pledged their loyalty to Nogay instead of to the khan of Saray. Clashes started between them and the princes loyal to Saray. Each group looked for protection to its respective suzerain. The result was a brief and undecisive but devastating civil war in which Mongols of both camps participated. The net profit for those Russian princes who were Nogay's vassals was that they were commissioned by the khan to collect taxes for him in their principalities; the Mongol tax collectors were withdrawn from these principalities. No less important psychologically was the new feeling among the Russians that the Mongol rule was not as solid as it had been and that liberation would be feasible in the not too distant future.

These hopes proved premature, however. The unity of government in the Golden Horde was restored by Khan Tokhta in 1300. Both he and his successor Uzbeg (1313–41) were able rulers, and under them the Golden Horde reached the height of its power and prosperity. In this period Islam became the official faith of the Horde. The original religion of the Mongols had been a mixture of Sky worship and Shamanism. After the expansion of the empire, the Mongol rulers were gradually influenced by the old established religions of the peoples they conquered. Thus in China they accepted Buddhism. In south Russia they wavered for some time between Christianity and Islam. One of Batu's sons was a Christian; Batu's brother Berke became a Moslem. Berke's successors were again Sky worshippers. Uzbeg, on the other hand, not only was personally converted to Islam but gave it the full support of the state.

Conversion to Islam greatly enhanced Uzbeg's prestige in the Near East; the Moslem merchants of central Asia were particularly pleased. Uzbeg moved his capital from Old Saray, founded by Batu, to New Saray (founded by Berke) which was situated on the eastern bank of the Volga not far from present-day Stalingrad. New Saray now became the main commercial center of the Golden

Horde, while at the mouth of the Volga Astrakhan rose in competition to decaying Old Saray. In his policy toward Russia Uzbeg tried to keep a balance of power among the Russian princes, allowing no one of them to become too strong. The activities of each were closely supervised by the khan's commissioners. This course was continued by Uzbeg's son Janibeg (1342–57). As a result, in addition to the Grand Duchy of Vladimir three other grand duchies were created in East Russia, those of Tver, of Nizhni Novgorod, and of Riazan. Each of the grand dukes was commissioned to collect taxes for the khan within his grand duchy. This policy proved only partly successful, since eventually the authority of the grand duke of Vladimir became closely associated with the strongest of the local principalities, that of Moscow, which as a result became much stronger than the other three. The steady rise of Moscow and the competition between Moscow and Tver were the most significant factors in Russian politics of this period. The growth of Moscow was due to its central location in Russian "Mesopotamia"—that region of the upper Volga and Oka rivers; to the influx of population from the cities and regions more exposed to the Mongol raids; to the skillful policies of the Moscow princes; and to the support of the church. After the devastation of Kiev in 1240, and because of the pro-Catholic policies of Daniel of Galicia, the metropolitans of the Russian church preferred to stay in East Russia; and in 1326 Moscow became the metropolitan's see in fact if not yet in name.

While the Mongols seemed to be firmly in the saddle in East Russia, their authority in West Russia was challenged by the rising power of Poland and Lithuania. Under the pressure of the Teutonic Knights the Lithuanians moved eastward and entered some of the Russian lands. By 1250 they controlled the Novgorodok region in the basin of the upper Nieman River. Association with the Russians proved useful to the Lithuanians in many respects, especially in reorganizing their army and administration. Gradually, more West Russian lands recognized the authority of the grand dukes of Lithuania, whose rule the Russians preferred to the Mongols'. Thus a Lithuanian-Russian state came into existence, taking definite shape in the reign of Grand Duke Gedymin (1316–41). Combining the resources and manpower of Lithuania and Belorussia, this able ruler made his grand duchy a major power in eastern Europe. His attempt to establish his suzerainty over Smolensk worried Uzbeg, who sent his East Russian vassals to protect the city against the Lithuanians. Checked in that direction, Gedymin decided to cooperate with the Mongols against the Poles in Galicia and Volynia. Galicia, weakened by the Mongol raids of 1240, 1260, and 1287, had little if any chance of fending off the increasing pressure of Poland, Hungary, and Lithuania. Moreover, there was a perennial conflict between the Galician prince and boyars. In 1340 the last prince died, apparently poisoned by the boyars. King Casimir the Great of Poland, immediately went to Galich. The city, however, refused to surrender to the Poles and offered the throne to Gedymin's son Lubart. Since the latter had pledged allegiance to Khan Uzbeg, a detachment of Mongol troops was sent to assist him against the Poles. Casimir was obliged to retreat, though he did not give up his claims. Nine years later he launched another campaign against Galicia and Volynia. Lubart again asked the Mongols for help, and the Poles were ousted from Volynia but kept Galicia.

4. *The Mongol system of administration*

Both in China and in Persia the Mongols overthrew the ruling dynasties and assumed direct control. By contrast, in most of Russia they left the princes of the House of Riurik in power as their vassals. This difference in policy may be explained by the fact that they found no centralized state in Russia and none of the local Russian princes seemed dangerous to the khan, especially since most of them proved ready to recognize his authority. Besides, while the Mongols found the south Russian steppes suited to their ways of life and habits, they had no desire to settle in the forest area of the north; they were interested only in exploiting its manpower and financial resources. The exploitation of the Russian regions closest to the steppes, such as the Pereiaslav and Kievan lands, as well as Podolia, presented no difficulty. The Mongols ousted the princes from these regions and put the area under Mongol governors. In other parts of Russia the princes continued to rule under the khan's suzerainty but with their authority drastically curbed.

The tsar—as the Russians used to call the khan—was not only their political suzerain; he also had supreme power in judicial,

military, and financial matters. All Russian princes were subject
to the Supreme Court of the Golden Horde and a number of them
were tried and executed for real or alleged crimes. All litigation
between Russians and Mongols was tried by Mongol courts. In
addition all Russian soldiers drafted into the Mongol armies were
subject to Mongol military law. However, the khan left the trial
of litigation among the Russians themselves to the authority of
their princes. In fact in the first period of Mongol rule that was
almost the only field of public affairs in which Russian princes
could exercise their authority.

For the purpose of conscripting recruits and collecting taxes the
Mongols took three censuses of the population of Russia, in 1245,
1257, and 1274. The Mongol administrative system was closely
connected with the army and like it was based on the decimal
principle. The quota of soldiers to be drafted from each district
determined the size of the district. Each district able to raise ten
soldiers was counted as a unit of ten, and so on, up to the ten-
thousand unit (the myriad or *t'ma*). Consequently Russia was
divided into "tens," "hundreds," "thousands," and "t'my" (the
plural of t'ma). The Mongols conscripted in Russia one recruit
out of every ten males, which means that the ratio of soldiers was
10 per cent of the male population or about 5 per cent of the total
population. Therefore the population of a hundred was approximately 2,000; of a t'ma 200,000.

Each district was a unit of taxation as well as of conscription.
The total tribute to be collected in rural Russia was tabulated according to the number of t'my. Thus the grand duchy of Vladimir
was counted as 15 t'my; the grand duchy of Nizhni Novgorod
paid for 5 t'my. In all East and West Russia over 43 t'my were
established. From that it may be assumed that the population of
all the t'my districts was around 8,600,000. Adding that of the
large cities and of certain regions not included in the t'my network,
we may arrive at about 10,000,000 for the total population of
Russia in this period. As most of the Russians were then occupied
in agriculture, the tribute took the form of a land tax paid from
each agricultural unit ("plow"). The merchants in the cities at
first had to pay a capital levy; later on this was replaced by a
tax on the turnover of goods and was collected as customs duties.
In order to ensure the system's working smoothly Mongol gar-

risons were stationed at strategic points. In case of any serious disturbance, punitive expeditions were sent by the khan to break the resistance. In this way Russian taxpayers were taught strict obedience to the law, so that when the Mongol officials and troops were withdrawn and the Russian princes themselves were commissioned by the khan to collect taxes, they had no difficulty in performing their duties. On the contrary, they found the system very expedient and even profitable: in some areas more money was collected than was due to the khan and the prince was able to pocket the surplus.

5. *The decline of Mongol power and the resurgence of Russia*

A few years after Janibeg's death a protracted political crisis started in the Golden Horde. At its basis lay the growth of the apanages (or land grants) of the Juchid princes and the rise of the feudal power of the Mongol and Turkish aristocracy, which sapped the unity and strength of the state. Dissensions started among Janibeg's sons, and a series of palace revolutions occurred which served as an incentive to the khans of the eastern part of Juchi's Ulus to intervene in the affairs of the Golden Horde. As by that time the Yuan empire in China had been first paralyzed by the revolution and then overthrown altogether, the regional khanates were left entirely to themselves with no higher authority able to mediate their disputes. It was only around 1370 that order was restored in that part of the Golden Horde west of the Volga River by a high officer of the Mongol army, Mamay, who, not being a Juchid, was not entitled to occupy the throne and had to rule through a puppet khan. Another khan, not subject to Mamay's authority, ruled in Saray. The turn of events was extremely favorable to the Russians and Lithuanians in spite of their being handicapped by lack of unity. The first to profit by the situation was Grand Duke Olgerd of Lithuania, son of Gedymin. In 1362 he occupied Kiev and the next year led his combined Lithuanian-Russian army south to the Black Sea; his victory over the Mongols at the mouth of the Bug River made him master of a large part of Ukraine. Had Olgerd cooperated with young Grand Duke Dmitri of Moscow (1362–89), they might have freed all Russia from the Mongols then and there. Instead, Olgerd supported Tver against Moscow and twice attempted to storm the Kremlin, but failed both times. In 1375 the grand duke of Tver had to recognize Dmitri's suzerainty.

Dmitri now felt himself strong enough to assume a more independent attitude toward the Mongols and stopped paying the tribute regularly to the khan, sending only token payments from time to time. Disturbed by this change in attitude of his main Russian vassal, Mamay started gathering forces for a punitive expedition against Moscow. At that juncture, however, Mamay's authority was challenged by a new pretender to the throne, the khan of the eastern part of Juchi's Ulus, Tokhtamysh. Behind Tokhtamysh loomed an even more powerful figure, Tamerlane, the ruler of Samarkand, who already entertained ambitious plans to follow Chingis-Khan's path and found a world empire. Like Mamay, Tamerlane was handicapped by not being a Chingisid; he too had to rule through puppet khans, but he succeeded much better than Mamay. It was Tamerlane who helped Tokhtamysh to seize power in the eastern part of Juchi's Ulus. That done, Tokhtamysh was ready to establish his authority over the Golden Horde as well. Faced with the dilemma of whom to oppose first—Dmitri or Tokhtamysh—Mamay decided to re-establish his authority in Russia and then, with Russia's resources at his disposal, turn against Tokhtamysh. In the summer of 1380 Mamay led against Moscow an army reinforced with Genoese infantry as well as with Ossetian and Circassian auxiliary troops. The total strength of his field army must have been not less than 30,000. To assure success, Mamay concluded an alliance with the new grand duke of Lithuania, Iagailo, son of Olgerd (who had died in 1377). It was agreed that the Mongol and the Lithuanian armies would converge in the upper Don basin by September 1.

Against the combined forces of Mamay and Iagailo Dmitri hastily mobilized the troops of the Grand Duchy of Vladimir which, it will be recalled, was counted as 15 t'my and thus, according to the Mongol system of recruiting in Russia, could produce 150,000 soldiers. Of these, hardly more than a third could be actually mobilized on short notice, and part of those mobilized had to be used to garrison Moscow and some of the other cities. Tver, which was bound by the treaty of 1375 to help, refused to send any troops. The Nizhni Novgorod troops were used locally to prevent the

Mongols from attempting to envelop the army of the Grand Duchy of Vladimir from the east. All said, Dmitri's field army must have been about equal to Mamay's in size but had a smaller proportion of cavalry. In spite of this disadvantage the Muscovites displayed a grim determination and were greatly encouraged by the blessing sent to the troops by the venerated Abbot Sergius of the Trinity Monastery. The Russians had to act fast to prevent the merging of the Mongol and Lithuanian armies. When the Russians crossed the upper Don River, Iagailo's forces were only about twenty-five miles away from the Mongol camp. Mamay however had no alternative but to accept the Russian challenge. The battle was fought on the Kulikovo Pole (Snipes' Field). The losses were tremendous on both sides, but the Russians won the day. Mamay and the remnants of his army fled south in complete disorder. Iagailo ordered retreat back to Lithuania as soon as he received news of the defeat. There was great rejoicing in Russia but also great sorrow because of the heavy casualties. Everyone understood, however, the historical importance of the victory on the Don. The spell of Mongol invincibility was broken. Grand Duke Dmitri became known as Donskoy ("of the Don").

The blow the Russians had administered to the Mongols, while heavy, was not mortal. Mamay immediately started preparations for a new campaign against Moscow. But instead he had to fight Tokhtamysh' rapidly advancing forces. Mamay's army was defeated and he fled to the Crimea where the Genoese killed him. Tokhtamysh now became undisputed master of all of Juchi's Ulus. He at once assumed the task in which Mamay had failed, of reestablishing Mongol authority over Russia. Exhausted by the effort of 1380, Russia was not prepared for another war. The Russian princes sent their greetings to the new tsar but were reluctant to resume their old obligations, trying to gain time. Tokhtamysh did not underestimate Russia's strength by any means and understood well that his only chance lay in secrecy and speed. When news of his advance was received in Moscow in the fall of 1382, Grand Duke Dmitri had no field troops at his disposal and went north to mobilize a new army. But he left a strong garrison in Moscow equipped with cannon—the first mention in the chronicles of the use of firearms by the Russians. Failing in his attempt to storm the city walls, Tokhtamysh offered a truce to the Russians, then violated it and seized the city by ruse. Moscow was looted and burned and all its defenders either slain or made captive. After all the region around Moscow had been laid waste Tokhtamysh led his booty-laden caravan back to Saray. Thus, at one stroke, everything gained by the Russians since 1362 had been wiped out and the Mongols seemed to be firmly in the saddle once more. All the Russian princes including Grand Duke Dmitri had to apply for the khan's patent, and regular payment of the tribute had to be resumed without delay.

It was fortunate for Russia that the revival of the might of the Golden Horde under Tokhtamysh proved ephemeral. A third power intervened in the politics of western Eurasia—Tamerlane's growing world empire. The conflict between Tamerlane and Tokhtamysh lasted about eight years. Tokhtamysh was finally defeated in 1395. In the course of this war Tamerlane's forces destroyed all the major cities of the Golden Horde including Saray, thus sapping both the Horde's trade and industry. From this blow the khanate was never able fully to recover. After having administered the coup de grâce to Tokhtamysh Tamerlane undertook a campaign against Moscow. This time Russia was well prepared and Dmitri's son Basil I (1389–1425) deployed his strong army along the line of the Oka River ready for any eventuality. There was no battle, however. Tamerlane stopped in the southern section of the principality of Riazan, then turned back and returned to Samarkand. While he could have hoped to defeat the Russians, he realized that the victory would be costly; besides, the center of his empire lay too far east and the control of the Russian forests presented no attraction to him. The Russians ascribed Tamerlane's unexpected retreat to the miraculous intercession of Holy Virgin.

The net result of these events was that the Russians could resume their plans for liberation. Tribute payment again became irregular, and Moscow became virtually a semiautonomous state. The Golden Horde now seemed to the Muscovites a less dangerous adversary than the Grand Duchy of Lithuania. In 1385 a treaty of union was signed between Lithuania and Poland. Grand Duke Iagailo of Lithuania married the queen of Poland and was himself elected king of Poland. The Roman Catholic Church was recognized as the state church of Lithuania, and the Lithuanian nobility received all the rights and privileges of the Polish nobility.

Grand Duchy of Vladimir ·····

Grand Duchy of Lithuania ////

0   100   200   300
Miles

WHITE SEA

Solovki Monastery

KARELIANS

N O V G O R O D   D O M I N I O N S

N. Dvina

Ustiug

FINLAND

Valaam Monastery

L. Onega

L. Ladoga

Neva R.

Oreshek

Beloozero

Vologda

BALTIC SEA

Kolyvan (Revel)

ESTONIA

Rugodiv

Iuriev

L. Peipus

Novgorod

Volkhov

Msta

Sit

Kostroma

LIVONIA

Riga

Pskov

Volga

Tver

Rostov

Suzdal

Gorodet

PRUSSIA

ZHMUD

W. Duina

Polotsk

MOSCOW

Vladimir

Nizhni Novgorod

Niemen

Troki

Vilna

Vitebsk

Smolensk

Murom

Gorodets (Kasimov)

Grodno

Novgorodok

Serpukhov

Kolomna

Liubutsk

Odoev

Riazan

POLAND

Warsaw

W. Bug

Drogichin

Brest

Starodub

Briansk

Novosil

Elets

Lublin

Kholm

Gorodlo

Vladimir

Lutsk

Turov

Chernigov

Novgorod in Severia

Rylsk

Putivl

Kursk

Don

Kopor

Volga

Kraków

Sokal

Lvov

Kremenets

Kiev

Pereiaslav

Psiol

Sanok

Galich

Kamenets

Vinnitsa

Cherkasy

Dnieper

Vorskla

Donets

Saray

Braslav

Bug

Dniester

HUNGARY

TRANSYLVANIA

MOLDAVIA

Iasi

Prut

BESSARABIA

Tana (Azov)

WALLACHIA

CRIMEA

SEA of AZOV

BULGARIA

Kaffa

Soldaia

BLACK   SEA

Terek

Dadakov

CAUCASIAN

MTS.

Tbilisi

Constantinople

R.B.B.

RUSSIA AROUND 1396

The combination of forces greatly helped Poland and Lithuania in their struggle against the Teutonic Knights. The treaty of 1385 was meant not only as a personal union but as an incorporation of the Grand Duchy of Lithuania into the Kingdom of Poland. Actually, however, Lithuania retained her identity as a state, and in 1393 Iagailo's cousin Vitovt was recognized as grand duke of Lithuania under Iagailo's nominal suzerainty. Before long Vitovt became the most powerful ruler in eastern Europe. He entertained ambitious plans for pushing the Tatars out of the Dnieper steppes as well as extending his sway over all the Russian principalities. In 1395 he conquered Smolensk and started making preparations for an offensive against Novgorod. Three years later an unexpected turn in Tatar politics gave him a pretext for intervening in the affairs of the Golden Horde. After Tamerlane's withdrawal from Russia, Tokhtamysh made an attempt to regain his control over the Golden Horde but he was ousted by the khan left there in power by Tamerlane. Actual authority in the Horde belonged at this time to Amir Edigey, whose position was similar to Mamay's. Tokhtamysh then fled to Lithuania and asked Vitovt for protection. A treaty was signed between these two leaders by which Vitovt was to help Tokhtamysh regain the throne of the Golden Horde and Tokhtamysh ceded Vitovt his suzerainty rights over Russia. In 1399 Vitovt led his great army, well equipped with cannon, to the steppes beyond the Dnieper River. Besides the Lithuanian and West Russian troops, Vitovt had under his command auxiliary forces sent to him by the Poles and the Teutonic Knights, as well as Tokhtamysh' Tatars. Edigey met them at the banks of the Vorskla River (not far from the spot where Peter the Great was to defeat the Swedes three centuries later). The day ended in a complete victory for Edigey. Vitovt and Tokhtamysh fled back to Lithuania.

It took Vitovt several years to restore his prestige and rebuild his army. In 1410 he joined Iagailo in the latter's campaign against the Teutonic Knights. The combined Polish, Lithuanian, and West Russian armies completely defeated the knights at Tannenberg in East Prussia. The Teutonic Order was never able fully to recover from this blow and in 1464 recognized the suzerainty of the king of Poland. In 1425 Grand Duke Basil I of Moscow died leaving his ten-year-old son Basil II as his successor. The boy's

mother—Vitovt's daughter Sophia—immediately asked her father
to protect her son against the rival princes of the Grand Duchy
of Vladimir. Protection was given but meanwhile Vitovt resumed
his attempts to extend his authority over all Russia. The grand
dukes of Riazan and of Tver acknowledged themselves his vassals.

6. *The end of Mongol rule*

Vitovt died in 1430 an octogenarian. After his death troubles
started both in Lithuania and in Muscovy. It was not until 1445
that the authority of young Grand Duke Casimir, son of Iagailo,
was recognized by most of the dissenting groups in Lithuania. Soon
after, he was elected king of Poland (as Casimir IV), while remaining grand duke of Lithuania. On that occasion he issued a
charter which became the cornerstone of constitutional government
of the grand duchy (1447).

In Muscovy, meanwhile, a lengthy conflict developed between
Basil II and his uncle, and after the latter's death between his sons
and Basil. The interprincely struggle was aggravated by the intervention of the Tatars. By that time the Golden Horde had broken
into several groups. One of them, led by Khan Ulug-Mahmed,
moved close to the Russian border in the region of the Oka River.
The khan asked Basil to cede him a city in this area, promising
in return to protect the border from the other Tatar hordes. Basil
refused, and war started between the two rulers. Both sides had
only small forces. When a detachment of Tatar troops 3,500
strong under the command of the khan's sons approached Suzdal,
Basil attacked it with but 1,500 troops and was taken prisoner.
Thus a casual encounter unexpectedly assumed great historical
importance (1445).

The Tatars, who did not expect such a decisive success, at first
did not know what to do with their prisoner. Ulug-Mahmed's horde
was not strong enough to dominate Russia directly. The khan's
plan was to establish himself in Kazan beyond the Volga and exploit Russia as a source of income. So he made Basil promise a
huge ransom and then set him free. To supervise the collection of
the ransom as well as of the regular tribute, Ulug-Mahmed sent
some of his sons and other Tatar princes to Russia with strong
detachments of troops. Basil assigned the Tatars suitable quarters

in various Russian cities. The Russians were stunned. The days of Batu and Berke seemed to have returned and the Tatars to be ruling Russia again through Basil as their stooge. Basil's cousin and long-time opponent, Dmitri Shemiaka, organized a conspiracy and was proclaimed grand duke; Basil was arrested and blinded by his order. Before long, however, Basil's supporters rallied to his aid. The core of this group was the lower gentry centered around Basil's court. Several impoverished princes of the House of Riurik who had entered Basil's service also remained loyal to him; the church prelates also were against Shemiaka; and last but not least, two Tatar tsarevichi, Ulug-Mahmed's sons, brought their troops to help Basil. He was put back on the throne a year after his over-throw. Shemiaka retreated beyond the Volga where he tried to continue resistance. Defeated several times, he fled to Novgorod and was poisoned there by a Muscovite agent.

The civil war was over. Its net result was a considerable strength-ening of the authority of the grand duke of Moscow. The apanages of the rebel princes—as well as of some of the loyal ones—were an-nexed to the grand duchy. The Grand Duchy of Nizhni Novgorod which had been annexed to Moscow by Basil I at the time of weak-ening of Tokhtamysh' power, and whose independence Shemiaka had promised to restore, again became part of Muscovy. The autonomy even of Novgorod the Great was somewhat curtailed by Basil II after a victory of the Muscovite troops over the Nov-gorodians in 1456. As for Russo-Tatar relations, the turn of events favored Moscow. Khan Ulug-Mahmed was killed by his eldest son Mahmudek, who became khan of Kazan. Mahmudek's brothers and a number of Tatar grandees refused to recognize his authority; some of them went over to another Tatar khan who established his camp in the middle Dnieper region; others entered the service of the grand duke of Moscow, among them Ulug-Mahmed's son, Tsarevich Kasim. Thus, instead of controlling Russia some of the Tatars now became servitors of the Moscow grand duke. Ac-tually, this amounted to the end of Mongol rule over Russia. To prevent misunderstandings between "loyal" Tatars and the Rus-sians, Basil II made an agreement that these Tatars would evacu-ate the cities in central Russia which they had occupied in 1445 and receive lands for settlement at the southern borders of Muscovy instead. As a part of this plan, a vassal Tatar Khanate was created

around 1452 in the region of the middle Oka River under the
rule of Tsarevich Kasim. Its capital became known as Kasimov
and the khanate as the Tsardom of Kasimov.

The creation of this vassal Tatar state under Moscow's suzerainty greatly enhanced the prestige of the grand duke of Moscow
in the Tatar world, which already lacked unity. The Golden Horde
now controlled only the lower Volga region; in the middle Volga,
the new Khanate of Kazan came into being (1445); one more independent khanate was established in 1449 in the Crimea by
Khan Haji-Geray, founder of the Geray dynasty which ruled
the Crimea until the late 18th century. The division among the
Tatars greatly undermined their power and made Russia's position
relatively stronger. Different Tatar groups continued raiding Russian borders from time to time and in some cases even reached the
outskirts of Moscow, but they no longer constituted a mortal danger. Moscow continued paying token tribute now to one khan
and now to another, but became virtually independent. It was left
to Basil II's son Ivan III to make a formal declaration of independence, which he did in 1480.

7. The Mongol impact on Russia

Mongol rule could not but affect the whole political and economic
structure of Russia deeply and left many indelible traces in Russian life which were noticeable for a long time after the emancipation. The devastation caused by the Mongol invasion of 1237–41
amounted in itself to a national catastrophe. The protracted drain
on Russia's manpower and financial resources which followed
prevented any quick recovery of the nation. The destruction of the
major Russian cities during the invasion was a serious blow to
the urban civilization which had flourished in the preceding period.
The periodic conscription of skilled artisans for the khan's service
completely disorganized Russian industrial production. A number of Russian industries, including such arts as enamel, filigree,
and niello work, as well as stone cutting, ceased to exist. There
was no sign of industrial revival until about 1350. But while city
crafts declined, agriculture continued to expand and became the
main foundation of the Russian economy. It was in the Mongol
period that Russia became a predominantly agrarian country.

Politically, the decline of the cities meant the weakening of the authority of the city assembly or veche. Besides, the Mongols deliberately attempted to curb the veche since they considered the townspeople responsible for whatever opposition to their power was left in Russia. The princes in most cases were themselves suspicious of the veche and therefore ready to follow the khan's instructions in regard to city politics. The city militia was disbanded. As a result of all this, the veche ceased to function in Muscovy except for brief sporadic revivals at times of crisis as, for example, during Tokhtamysh' invasion. Thus the democratic element in the old Russian system of government was shattered except in Novgorod and Pskov. The boyar council which represented the aristocratic element of government in Kievan Russia continued to assist the prince but failed to acquire any constitutional rights. While the prince was completely subordinated to the khan, the khan's patent now protected him against political claims of either the townspeople or the boyars. To be sure, the boyars were still considered free to move from one prince to another while retaining their patrimonial landed estates. With the growth of Moscow, however, the grand duke looked askance on those boyars who left his service, especially in time of war or of interprincely conflicts. In the reign of Dmitri Donskoy and after there were several cases of confiscation of the estates belonging to a boyar whom the grand duke considered a traitor, and in at least one case the boyar was executed.

The very nature of princely authority underwent a change. In the first century of Mongol rule that authority was drastically curbed by the khan. The prince was allowed to keep a retinue, but it was the Mongols who supervised the drafting of soldiers into their army. The prince retained his judicial authority in trials among his subjects, which he exercised either personally or through his lieutenants. Beyond this he had almost no administrative duties and had to be satisfied with the narrow sphere of managing his estates. Thus, his manorial rights and duties assumed greater importance, and his court became the core of his state. The heads of administrative departments in the management of his estates became his most influential councillors. The prince's servitors— the lower gentry centering around his court—were the main prop of his authority, as a social group. When the khan commissioned his Russian vassals to collect taxes for him, the competence of

the grand duke became wider. It widened even more when, in
the time of Dmitri Donskoy, the grand duke became a virtually
autonomous ruler. In that period the grand duke was able to use
for his own benefit the administrative and military machine built
up in Russia by the Mongols. He thus emerged from the Mongol
period a much stronger ruler than his predecessors had been in
the Kievan age.

What was of considerable importance was that the people were
trained by the Mongols to take orders, to pay taxes, and to supply
soldiers without delay. They continued to perform the same duties
for their own grand duke, who became their leader in the national
struggle against the Mongols. This change in attitude gradually
resulted in a new concept of state and society. The old free political
institutions were replaced by the authority of the grand duke.
The free society was gradually transformed into a network of social
classes bound to state service. The new order took definite shape
in the post-Mongol period but its beginnings are to be found in
the changes introduced into Russia by the Mongols or as a result
of their rule.

8. *The church and religion; literature and the arts*

The first shock of the Mongol invasion was as painful to the
church as to the other aspects of Russian life and culture. Many
outstanding clergymen perished in the destroyed cities; many
cathedrals, monasteries, and churches were burned or looted; hosts
of parishioners were killed or enslaved. Kiev, the metropolis of
the old Russian church, was so devastated that for many years it
was not fit to serve as the center of church administration. Not
until the issuance of Mangu-Temir's immunity charter to the
Russian clergy did the church find itself on firm ground once more
and able gradually to reorganize; as years went by, it became even
stronger in some respects than before. Indeed, ruled by Greek
metropolitans or by Russian metropolitans ordained in Constantinople, and protected by the khan's charter, the church in Russia
was in this period less dependent on princely power than in any
other period of Russian history.

Among the tasks the church faced in the Mongol period, the
first was that of giving spiritual advice and moral support to an
embittered and exasperated people—from princes to commoners.

Connected with it was a more general mission, completing the Christianization of the Russian people. It will be recalled that in the Kievan period Christianity became firmly established among the upper classes and the townspeople but did not penetrate deeply into the rural districts. It was in the Mongol period that the rural population too was Christianized. This was achieved both by the strenuous effort of the clergy and by the growth of religious feeling among the people themselves. The number of churches and monasteries grew steadily in both cities and rural districts. A characteristic feature of the new monastic movement was the initiative shown by individuals, young men of ardent religious spirit who took monastic orders in order to go to "the wilderness"—deep into the woods—to work hard in primitive conditions as well as to pray and meditate. The disasters of the Mongol invasion and of the interprincely strife as well as the harsh conditions of life in general were conducive to the development of this mentality. When what started as a hermitage grew into a large and wealthy monastery surrounded by prosperous peasant villages, the original hermits, or monks of similar spirit, would find the new atmosphere stifling, and would leave the monastery they had created to establish another hermitage deeper in the woods or farther north. Thus each monastery served as a nursery for several more. A venerated leader and pioneer of this movement was St. Sergius of Radonezh, founder of the Trinity Monastery about forty miles northeast of Moscow. His saintly personality was a source of inspiration to many who never met him.

As a branch of the Byzantine church, the Russian church was deeply affected by the grave political and religious crisis which developed in the Near East between 1350 and 1450. In 1355 the Ottoman Turks crossed the Dardanelles and entrenched themselves in Gallipoli. From there they rapidly extended their authority over the Balkan Peninsula, enveloping the remnants of the Byzantine Empire. By 1400 both Bulgaria and Serbia had been conquered by the Turks. The Byzantine emperor in Constantinople found himself in a desperate situation. His only hope was for assistance from the West. The pope was ready to preach a crusade against the Turks only on condition that the Greek church would recognize his authority. An ecumenical council was convoked in Italy, to which the Byzantines were invited, to discuss the possibility of union of the Roman and Greek churches. A declaration of such a union was approved by the council in Florence in 1439 with only one dissenting vote among the prelates of the Greek church. However, in Constantinople a considerable group of the clergy and the majority of the people refused to accept the union. Dissents and confusion were the result of mixing religion with international politics. On the political side, the crusade organized by the pope failed miserably (1444). Nine years later Constantinople was stormed by the Turks. The Byzantine Empire was overthrown and the Cathedral of St. Sophia turned into a mosque. The Turks, however, did not destroy the Greek church as an institution and permitted a new patriarch to be elected. The church union was now repudiated and the Greeks returned to Orthodoxy.

The Russian church was represented at the council of Florence by its metropolitan, Isidor, a Greek or Hellenized Slav, who had been ordained by the patriarch of Constantinople in 1437. It was with grave misgivings that the Russian authorities allowed him to proceed to Italy. At the council, Isidor proved a strong supporter of the union and was made cardinal. He came back to Moscow in 1441 and read the declaration of union at a solemn mass in Moscow's main cathedral. This caused a commotion among the Moscow clergy, who refused to accept the union. Grand Duke Basil II ordered Isidor's temporary arrest. Later on, Isidor went to Rome and was sent as the pope's legate to Constantinople where he was taken prisoner by the Turks in 1453. Having got rid of Isidor, the Russians were at a loss what to do next. They had no intention of breaking with their mother church in Constantinople but at the same time they now considered that church schismatic. They waited vainly for several years for the restoration of Orthodoxy in Byzantium. Finally Basil II convoked a council of Russian bishops to elect a new metropolitan. Bishop Iona, a wise old prelate, thus became the first head of an autonomous Russian church (1448). This act was not meant, however, as a definite separation from Constantinople. It was considered an emergency measure, and it was explained that when Orthodoxy was restored in Byzantium the patriarch's blessings would again be sought for future candidates to the see of Moscow. Orthodoxy was restored in Constantinople in 1453 but under political conditions which made it psychologically difficult for the Russians to subordinate their church to the patriarch once more since that patriarch's see was in the camp of infidels. Thus the Russian church became self-governing through the course of events and not as a result of any deliberate opposition to the patriarch.

Even more than in the Kievan period, the church remained in the Mongol age a leading factor in the growth of literature and arts. The spirit of the church found expression in the bishops' sermons and in the lives of saints, as well as in the biographies of such princes as Alexander Nevsky—who, it was felt, deserved to be canonized—which were written in the style of the lives of saints. The underlying idea of these works was that the Mongol yoke was God's visitation for the sins of the Russian people, and only true Christianity could lead the Russians out of their plight. As in the Kievan period, the clergy of the Mongol era played an important role in the compilation of the Russian chronicles. The work all but stopped after the Mongol invasion but was resumed and expanded in the 14th and 15th centuries. An indication of the leading role of the clergy in literature may also be found in the fact that the most famous heroic poem of the period, the "Zadonshchina" ("Deeds beyond the Don"), in which the battle of Kulikovo Pole was glorified, was written by a priest. From the literary point of view it is an imitation of the 12th-century "Lay of Igor's Campaign," which as we know was created by a member of the princely druzhina. In addition to "Zadonshchina," other stories of Kulikovo Pole were composed in this period and some of them were recorded in the chronicles. In the domain of folklore, the byliny of the Kievan age were revised by the popular reciters to fit the new situation, and the name of the new enemy, the Tatars, was substituted for the Cumans. Simultaneously new byliny and historical legends were created dealing with the Mongol phase of Russia's struggle against the steppe nomads. Batu's destruction of Kiev and Nogay's raids on Russia served as topics for contemporaneous Russian folklore.

An important aspect of the religious revival in Russia in the Mongol age was the church art. Architecture fell into a state of decay everywhere but in Novgorod, because of the utter disorganization of the Suzdalian building crafts by the Mongol conscription of skilled craftsmen. In contrast religious painting in the form of both frescoes and icons entered a period of blossoming, both in Novgorod and Muscovy. An important role in this artistic renaissance was played by the great Greek painter Theophanes, who spent the last thirty years of his life and artistic career in Russia. Both his personality and his masterpieces were admired by the Russians, and the painters profited greatly by studying his technique of free brush stroke. They did not attempt, however, to copy his individualistic and dramatic style. The greatest Russian painter of this period was Andrew Rublev, who spent his youth in the Trinity Monastery and later on painted his famed icon, "The Old Testament Trinity," for that monastery. The charm of Rublev's creations is in the serene quietness of composition and the symphony of delicate colors. There is a certain similarity between his works and those of his contemporary, the Italian painter Fra Angelico.

CHAPTER 4

THE TSARDOM OF MOSCOW IN THE 16TH CENTURY

1. *Russian expansion in the 16th century*

RUSSIA'S emancipation from the Mongol yoke was an important landmark in her struggle with the steppes. That struggle, however, was far from over. While politically independent, Russia continued to be exposed to perennial Tatar raids. The fluid situation in the steppes required constant vigilance and strenuous military effort on the part of the Muscovite government. The only solution seemed to be controlling the steppes —by either diplomatic or military means. By 1550 Russia was strong enough to start a counterattack against the steppes, and Tsar Ivan IV succeeded in conquering the khanates of Kazan and Astrakhan, thus establishing his rule over the whole course of the Volga River. Simultaneously with state expansion, an elemental colonization movement was going on among the people. Having been excluded for centuries from the fertile lands in the south and southeast, the Russians now took advantage of the changing situation and started moving to "the wild prairie," as the saying went. The government protected them by building, from the late 16th century on, several fortified lines to prevent the Tatars from destroying the new settlements. With the progress of colonization, the existing lines were extended and new lines added. While the Tatars proved able, on many occasions, to pierce these lines, on the whole they served their purpose. In the northeast, fur-bearing animals instead of agricultural lands constituted the main attraction to the Russians. At least as early as the 1300's trappers and hunters crossed the northern section of the Ural Mts. into the lower Ob basin close to the Arctic; in the late 1500's the Russians entered Siberia from the Perm region in the middle Ural area. There is also some evidence indicating that late in that century a group of Novgorodians, fleeing from Ivan IV's terror, took ship and eventually reached Alaska via the Arctic Ocean. In the extreme northwest of European Russia, Russian fishermen continued to explore the Arctic coast and a number of Russian monks preached Christianity to the Lapps. A Russian monastery was founded on Petsamo Bay, close to the Norwegian frontier, in 1533.

A number of Russians and Ukrainians settled in the river valleys of the steppe zone far beyond the fortified lines. These pioneers had to rely on their own resources for survival and organized themselves in so many military communes. They became known as Cossacks. More will be said of them later in this chapter.

2. *The growth of Muscovy and the fall of Novgorod*

The process of liberation of East Russia from Mongol control was long and tortuous. As we know, it was accompanied by important changes in government and administration. Muscovy became the leading Russian state, and the authority of its grand duke was immensely strengthened. The new face of Muscovy as well as its international stature was suddenly revealed to the world in the reign of Ivan III (1462–1505). A farsighted and cautious ruler, conscious of the high dignity of his position, Ivan III subjected Novgorod and Tver to his authority and laid claim to West Russia as his patrimony, as a descendant of Vladimir the Saint. In domestic policies he bound both the Russian princes and boyars firmly to his service. He was the first of the Muscovite rulers to introduce on a large scale the system of military fiefs (*pomestie*) which was to be fully developed by his grandson Ivan IV. He established diplomatic relations with a wide circle of both western and oriental rulers. His marriage to a Byzantine princess heightened his prestige in the West as well as in the East. The Italian artists and technicians he engaged embellished the Kremlin with sumptuous churches, towers, and palaces, and modernized the Russian artillery. In short, Moscow, which had been until then an obscure and remote provincial town of whose existence few Westerners were aware, now became widely known as the capital of a young empire, even if that empire was considered half barbarian.

Ivan's Byzantine marriage was arranged by the pope, who hoped through it to achieve a double objective: to bring Russia into the fold of the Roman Catholic Church and to engage Moscow's assistance against the Ottoman Turks. Neither goal was realized, and it was Ivan who obtained most benefit from the transaction. His bride, Sophia Paleologus (his second wife), was a niece of the last Byzantine emperor. Though she had been brought up in Rome in the ideas of church union and was accompanied to Russia by the pope's legate, she agreed to accept Greek Orthodoxy as soon as she arrived in Moscow (1472). The Greeks and Italians who accompanied her to Moscow brought with them the traditions of Byzantine splendor coupled with some of the artistic notions of the Renaissance. With her arrival, the ritual at the Moscow court grew much more elaborate. The Byzantine double-headed eagle made its appearance on the state seal of Moscow.

THE FIRST MUSCOVITE DYNASTY
(*House of Riurik*)

Alexander Nevsky
(Descendant of Vladimir the Saint)

Daniel (1283–1304)

George (1304–25)   Ivan I (1325–41)

Simeon (1341–53)   Ivan II (1353–59)

Dmitri Donskoy (1359–89)

Basil I (1389–1425)

Basil II (1425–62)

Ivan III (1462–1505)

Basil III (1505–33)

Ivan IV (1533–84)

Theodore I (1584–98)

A year before his marriage to Sophia, Ivan III made the opening move in his attempt to subjugate Novgorod. Since the early 13th century Novgorod had traditionally chosen each new grand

duke of Vladimir as her prince; each prince had to sign a covenant
pledging himself not to violate the Novgorodian constitution. Furthermore, the autonomy of Novgorod was guaranteed by the
Mongol khan, and later on was indirectly strengthened by the
rivalry between Tver and Moscow. Now the khan lost his authority and Tver was so weakened that she could no longer limit
the ambitions of the Moscow rulers. Novgorod seemed to have no
alternative but to turn to Casimir, king of Poland and grand duke
of Lithuania, for protection. The Novgorodian boyars, headed by
an energetic woman politician, Martha Boretsky, widow of a former
mayor of Novgorod, all favored an agreement with Lithuania. The
sympathies of the commoners, however, were mostly with Moscow. Moreover, Casimir represented a Roman Catholic power,
which made him suspect to many Novgorodians. Nevertheless,
the advice of the boyars prevailed, and the Novgorod veche concluded a treaty with Casimir. The king guaranteed the Novgorodian constitution and freedom of religion, and promised protection against Moscow. As might be expected, Ivan III refused
to tolerate Lithuania's intervention in what he considered purely
Russian affairs and sent his army against Novgorod. Defeated in
a decisive battle and receiving none of the assistance which had
been promised from Lithuania, the Novgorodians had to sue for
peace (1471). By the provisions of the peace treaty, they had to
pay a substantial fine and agree to the grand duke's having increased judicial authority; otherwise, Novgorod's former liberties
were confirmed by Ivan. The Novgorodians also had to promise
not to enter into any alliance with Lithuania.

The treaty of 1471 proved but a temporary truce. Relations between boyars and commoners in Novgorod were strained, and riots
started in 1475. Many of the commoners appealed to Ivan. He
came in person to Novgorod for the trial of the offenders; several
boyars were accused and imprisoned. When Ivan returned to Moscow, a number of Novgorodians visited him there to submit complaints. On one such occasion two Novgorod officials addressed
him as their "sovereign." Ivan was quick to grasp the opportunity
and announce that he was willing to assume full sovereignty over
Novgorod. The citizens protested that the officials in question were
not entitled to change the form of address and that Novgorod was
satisfied with the agreement of 1471. In spite of this, Ivan once

more sent troops against Novgorod. Casimir, as before, gave no help; and the city, being no match for Moscow, had to surrender unconditionally. The constitution was abrogated, the veche dissolved, and its symbol—the liberty bell—was shipped to Moscow (1478). Martha Boretsky was arrested and sent to a nunnery in Nizhni Novgorod.

This, however, is not the end of the story. Two years later a conspiracy was uncovered in Novgorod against Moscow and in favor of Lithuania. Ivan III personally led a punitive expedition. This time he took drastic measures to secure obedience once and for all. One hundred and fifty boyars were executed and their property confiscated. Eight thousand prominent families were deported and received landholdings in various districts of Muscovy; on their former lands in Novgorod an equal number of Muscovites were settled. In 1487 fifty of the richest Novgorod merchants with their families were deported to Vladimir. Within the next two years around 10,000 middle-class burghers were moved from Novgorod to Muscovy, chiefly to Nizhni Novgorod. Furthermore, by 1500 most of the church lands in Novgorod had been confiscated and assigned as landholdings to Muscovite army officers.

This was the end of Novgorod the Great. The top layer of Novgorodian society had been skimmed off and most of the middle class similarly dispersed. The commoners were left an amorphous mass, without leaders or political rights. Ivan's Novgorodian policies had, however, an even wider significance, affecting as they did the nature of the Moscow regime itself. Neither the Novgorodians deported to Muscovy nor the Muscovites settled in Novgorod received lands in their own right; the landholdings were conditional, recompense for past or future services to the grand duke. Control of these holdings greatly increased the duke's authority and strengthened his position with respect to the boyar class in Muscovy as well.

It should be mentioned in this connection that the status of the boyars and the composition of the boyar class underwent a drastic change in this period. With the annexation to Moscow of most of the regional principalities (the last, Riazan, was annexed in the reign of Ivan III's son), the princes had either to enter the service of the grand duke of Moscow or emigrate to Lithuania. Most of them stayed in Muscovy and formed the top layer of boyars. The disappearance of independent principalities affected the position of the nontitled boyars as well. The old principle of freedom of boyar service now lost its meaning since there was only one prince in East Russia whom they could serve. Thus, both East Russian princes and boyars were now permanently bound to Moscow. The term "boyar" acquired a new connotation—that of member of the boyar council (Duma) of the first rank. The boyars also filled the highest positions in the Muscovite army and administration. To prevent personal conflicts and confusion, an elaborate system of coordination of genealogical seniority of the boyar families with the rank of service of each was established, based on precedent. Thus the Moscow grand duke (later the tsar) was bound by tradition in the choice of his councilors and high officials. As the historian, Basil Kliuchevsky, put it, "the autocratic tsar had to rule through an aristocratic administration." This eventually led to a serious political conflict which reached its climax in the middle of the 16th century.

In his relations with the Tatar world Ivan III took full advantage of the dissensions among Tatar hordes. His vassal, the khan of Kasimov, was closely related to the khans of both Kazan and the Crimea, and was always ready to help Ivan's emissaries at the courts of other Moslem rulers as well. Hence Moscow was well informed of the situation in the Near and Middle East. Moscow's agents even appeared in Herat, Afghanistan. Ivan's main objective was a diplomatic and strategic encirclement of the Golden Horde. For this purpose he concluded an alliance with the khan of the Crimea, Mengli-Geray, who became a vassal of the Ottoman sultan in 1475. Friendship with the Crimean Horde proved beneficial to Russia economically as well as politically, since a lively trade developed between Moscow and the Crimean ports. In addition, Ivan established friendly relations with the khan of Tiumen, Siberia, as well as with the Nogay Horde, whose home was the steppes in the basin of the Iaik River. To counter these moves Ahmad, khan of the Golden Horde, concluded an agreement with Casimir of Poland and Lithuania. Ahmad then demanded that Ivan formally recognize his suzerainty. Around 1479 his envoy appeared in Moscow offering Ivan the khan's patent to the throne. The offer was flatly rejected. Ahmad had no alternative but to attempt to restore his authority by force. He led his army to the Ugra

River, which was then the boundary between Muscovy and Lithuania. Casimir's army was to join him there. Ivan concentrated his troops on the Muscovite side of the Ugra. Tatar and Muscovite armies faced each other for a long time without either side initiating action. Ivan tried to gain time. Ahmad waited vainly for Casimir. Meanwhile Ivan's ally Mengli-Geray raided the Ukrainian provinces of the Grand Duchy of Lithuania, thus diverting Casimir's attention. Ivan also sent Mengli-Geray's brother, who had entered his service with his Tatars, as well as a detachment of Muscovite cavalry to raid Ahmad's camp near Saray where the khan's wives resided. News of this raid compelled the khan to order immediate retreat. Simultaneously the Russian army hastily retreated to Moscow. This event had been traditionally considered the "end of the Mongol yoke" (1480).

The next year the Golden Horde was raided by Ivan's friend, the khan of Tiumen, supported by the Nogays. Ahmad was killed in his tent. His sons continued to rule the remnants of his horde for about a decade. Finally, the Golden Horde was destroyed by Mengli-Geray. It was replaced by the Khanate of Astrakhan which, however, was weak and represented no threat to Moscow. Following Ahmad's death Ivan III turned his attention to the affairs of the Khanate of Kazan, where dissension had arisen between two sons of the former khan. One of them was a friend of Mengli-Geray and through him became a friend of Ivan. When he was ousted from Kazan by the rival party, he appealed to Ivan for protection. A Russian army was sent to Kazan and put Ivan's candidate on the throne (1487).

In the west, Ivan III's relations with Casimir of Poland and Lithuania were strained, as might be expected. Following Casimir's death (1492), one of his sons was elected king of Poland and another, Alexander, grand duke of Lithuania. In an attempt to gain Moscow's friendship, Alexander married Ivan's daughter, Helen. It was stipulated that they were not to try to convert her to Roman Catholicism and she would have a Greek Orthodox chapel at court. She indeed remained Greek Orthodox, but complained of constant pressure by her husband and his officials to get her to renounce her faith, which caused considerable friction. Alexander, on his part, complained that Ivan had accepted into his service a number of Chernigov princes who were Alexander's subjects, with

their lands. An indecisive war between Moscow and Lithuania
which lasted from 1500 to 1503 grew out of the mutual offenses.
As in his dealings with the Golden Horde, Ivan attempted a diplomatic and strategic encirclement of Poland. He entertained lively
relations with Moldavia, Hungary, and the German Empire. In
1489 the German emperor Frederick III, bidding for Ivan's friendship, offered him a royal crown. To his amazement Ivan refused
to accept it. His answer to the emperor's envoy was characteristic:
"By the grace of God we and our forefathers have been sovereigns
of our land from aboriginal times; we have been invested with
power by God and do not need investiture by anyone else."

3. West Russia

In contrast to Muscovy, the authority of the grand duke of Lithuania decreased as years went by, and an aristocratic form of constitutional government developed there. The grand duchy of "Lithuania and Russia" (as it was officially known) was not a centralized state but a federation based on extensive autonomy of the
lands and principalities which constituted it. Its core was Lithuania
proper, divided for administrative purposes into two provinces,
Vilno and Troki. The autonomy of the Russian lands subject to the
authority of the grand duke—Polotsk, Vitebsk, Smolensk, Volynia, Kiev, Chernigov,—was guaranteed by special charters. Both
in the grand duchy as a whole and in each of its component parts
the nobility enjoyed a privileged position. District assemblies of
gentry were established after the Polish pattern; and in the late
15th century a national Diet (*Seim*) was organized in which the
gentry (*szlachta*) of all the provinces were represented. The
magnates formed a special body known as the Council of Lords,
which advised the grand duke on all important matters of foreign
and domestic policy, especially those pertaining to taxation and
the organization of the army. It should be borne in mind that the
magnates were more powerful in Lithuania than in Poland and
that no "szlachta democracy" of the Polish type ever developed in
Lithuania.

The princes and magnates enjoyed full ownership and seigniorial
rights on their estates. Each had a large retinue and in time of war
mobilized cavalry contingents from the population of his land;
these units constituted a good proportion of the Lithuanian army.

The gentry had to appear personally and to bring their retainers when called to serve in a campaign. If they failed to appear, their estates were subject to confiscation. Thus their rights on their estates were not as secure as those of the lords and the princes. Some of the gentry received landholdings from the grand duke, out of crown lands. Such grants were usually made to each holder for the term of his natural life; after his death the estate reverted to the crown. In other cases grants were for "two lives" (the holder's and his son's) or for "three lives" (the holder's, his son's, and his grandson's). Landholdings of this type were similar to the military fiefs in Muscovy, but the system never assumed the significance in Lithuania that it had in Muscovy.

The political climate in the grand duchy was definitely unfavorable to city democracy, and the importance of the veche in the West Russian cities rapidly declined. The introduction of the German municipal law in West Russian cities administered a final blow to the remnants of the old Kievan type of democracy. The corporate councils and guilds of the German law eliminated the popular assembly altogether. As regards the rural population, most of the farmers gradually lost their rights to land and became tenants on either crown lands or the estates of the magnates and gentry. In 1447 the peasants settled on private estates were forbidden to move to the crown lands. This amounted to serfdom. As to the slaves, their position remained the same as in the Kievan period.

All said, changes in social organization were as profound in West Russia as in Muscovy, although of a somewhat different nature. Under Polish influence, the Kievan type of free society was transformed in West Russia into a ladder of "estates of the realm" of the western type. The social and political constitution of the Grand Duchy of Lithuania was well reflected in the Lithuanian Statute (Code of Laws) of 1529, a remarkable juridical document of West Russian law (written in Russian, i.e. in this case Old Belorussian).

While in the days of Vitovt the Grand Duchy of Lithuania had been stronger than the Grand Duchy of Moscow, the balance of power shifted later in favor of Moscow, and in the 16th century it became more and more difficult for the Lithuanians and West Russians to contain the Muscovite pressure. In 1514 the Muscovites took Smolensk and kept it. Ivan IV's attack on Livonia in

1558 (of which more will be said later in this chapter) precipitated
a serious crisis in Muscovite-Lithuanian relations. Unable to withstand the pressure of the Muscovite armies, the Livonian Knights
put themselves under the protection of King Sigismund August of
Poland in his capacity as grand duke of Lithuania (he occupied
both thrones). As a result, war broke out between Lithuania and
Moscow, and in 1563 the Muscovites seized Polotsk. Closer cooperation between Lithuania and Poland seemed imperative to
strengthen both these states in their struggle against Muscovy. So
the Poles proposed to transform the personal union between the
two states (through the person of their common ruler) into a real
state union. The reaction to this in Lithuania was mixed. The
Lithuanian grandees, in spite of being thoroughly Polonized by
that time, cherished their influential and privileged position in the
grand duchy and would agree only to a loose federation. A section
of the Ukrainian gentry, however, favored a close union since
the gentry enjoyed much more power in Poland than in Lithuania.
In December 1568 a joint session of the Polish and Lithuanian
diets was convoked in Lublin to discuss the form of union. To
crush the Lithuanian opposition, Sigismund August by his own
authority transferred the Ukrainian provinces of Volynia, Kiev,
and Podolia from Lithuania to Poland. This action broke the resistance of the opposition, and at the end of June 1569 the Lithuanian Council of Lords reluctantly announced acceptance of the
union. The lords wept on this occasion, and it is said that some
of the Poles wept too from sympathy with their Lithuanian colleagues. In any case, the Poles won the day. By the treaty of
union Poland and Lithuania were merged into a single commonwealth under a ruler to be elected at a joint session of the lords
and szlachta of the two peoples. The Lithuanian Diet as a separate
institution was abolished. All treaties with foreign powers were
to be concluded in the name of the commonwealth. Even after that,
however, the Grand Duchy of Lithuania kept its own army and
financial administration and its own code of laws. A revision of the
Lithuanian Statute was published in 1588.

4. *The Cossacks*

The combination of the three basic elements of government—
the monarchic, aristocratic, and democratic—which constituted the

foundation of Russian political life in the Kievan age was broken up in the Mongol and post-Mongol periods. As we have seen, the monarchic element became dominant in Muscovy and the aristocratic in the Grand Duchy of Lithuania. The city assembly was stamped out in both these states. However, the old democratic traditions were not dead and were now revived in a new form in the Cossack communities of the south and southeast.

The Cossacks as a peculiar type of social group appeared in the 15th century at the time of the disintegration of the Golden Horde. The origin of the name Cossack is disputed and it would be out of place to discuss it here.* Suffice it to say that in the Tatar language of the period *kazak* meant "free man," "free adventurer," and hence "frontiersman." A number of Cossack groups, some of them Tatar, others Russian, were formed on the fringes of Muscovy and Lithuania, on the one hand, and of the Tatar succession states, on the other. The Russian Cossacks are first mentioned in the chronicles for the year 1444. That particular group was organized in the southern part of the principality of Riazan. Both the Muscovite and the Lithuanian governments understood the usefulness of such frontiersmen in assisting the regular armies to protect the border regions. At the end of the 15th and in the early 16th centuries several Cossack detachments entered the service of either the grand duke of Moscow or the grand duke of Lithuania. They were given weapons and supplies and while subordinate to the commander of the nearest regular army division were allowed a measure of self-government. It was not, however, these "service Cossacks" but the free Cossacks settled beyond the borders of either Muscovy or Lithuania who succeeded in fully developing the new social type of military democracy. Their ranks were swelled by all those who found regimentation and heavy taxation in the mother country not to their liking. The Lublin union of 1569, with its transfer of the Ukrainian provinces from Lithuania to Poland and the ensuing intensification of serfdom, greatly contributed to the growth of the Ukrainian Cossacks. The influx of newcomers to the East Russian Cossack communities increased after the issuance of the first ukase limiting freedom of movement of the peasants in Muscovy (1581).

* See G. Vernadsky, *The Mongols and Russia* (Yale University Press), pp. 291–292.

By 1600 there were in existence four major communes of free Cossacks or Cossack armies as they were known. One was the Ukrainian or Zaporozhie Cossacks, whose main stronghold was an island of the Dnieper below the cataracts (the word *zaporozhie* means "beyond the cataracts"). The other three were Great Russian, all of them situated in river valleys, in the basins of the lower Don, the Iaik, and the Terek (in the eastern part of the north Caucasus) respectively. There were two main reasons for the Cossacks preferring to settle in river valleys, one economic and the other strategic. In the first place, they depended mainly on fisheries for subsistence. They practiced no agriculture at that early stage of their history, and in addition to fishing and hunting lived on war booty or by robbing commercial caravans from time to time. Second, they were more or less protected from Tatar raids on a river island or fortified river bank—and the Tatar cavalry usually avoided river valleys in their campaigns and followed the watersheds.

The Zaporozhie Cossacks were a fraternity of bachelors; no one could bring a woman to their stronghold save under penalty of death. The other Cossacks were allowed to marry and to raise families. In other respects the Cossack hosts were organized on similar principles. All Cossacks had equal rights and a voice in the general assembly, which was known at Zaporozhie as the council and among the Don Cossacks as the circle. The assembly elected all officers, including the head of the host, whom the Ukrainian Cossacks called the hetman and the East Russian Cossacks the ataman. In wartime the hetman or ataman had absolute power. In peace he was merely president of the assembly which discussed and settled all important affairs. The assembly also functioned as supreme court. In the earlier period of Cossack history membership in the host was open to anyone who was ready to pledge loyalty to the Greek Orthodox Church and promise to obey the Cossack laws.

The first definite mention of the Don Cossacks is for 1549. In this year a Nogay prince lodged a complaint against the Cossacks with Ivan IV for looting a Tatar merchant caravan. This episode shows that in spite of the Cossacks' independence their neighbors the Turks and Tatars for practical reasons considered them the tsar's subjects. Moscow, on her part, had no objection to using Cossack aid frequently in expanding southward and eastward. At the same time conflicts between the Muscovite government and the Cossacks were not rare, especially because the Cossacks flatly refused to return any fugitive subject to the tsar, making it one of their principles that "there is no extradition from the Don." Because the Polish government encountered the same difficulties in its relations with the Zaporozhie Cossacks, King Stephen Batory proposed, around 1576, to transform the community of free Cossacks into a militia subordinated to the Polish authorities, promising the "registered Cossacks" good pay and plenty of supplies. The militia was created, but the free Cossacks refused to disband or to destroy their stronghold at Zaporozhie. In 1594 Emperor Rudolf II's envoy appeared with an offer of alliance with the German Empire against the Turks, which is indicative of the high military reputation acquired by that time by the Zaporozhie Cossacks.

5. *The tsardom*

With Russia's emancipation from the Mongols and the growth of the power of the grand duke of Moscow, his title ceased to satisfy the Muscovites. In old Russian an independent ruler of the highest degree of authority was called "tsar," a title first applied by the Russians to the Byzantine emperor and then to the Mongol khan.*

The ruler of Moscow could claim the title of tsar on two grounds. In the first place, he had formally announced his independence of his former suzerain, the Mongol tsar. Second, the Byzantine Empire had been destroyed by the Turks, and the Greek Orthodox world thus left without a tsar. And yet, according to the Byzantine theory of "symphony" of church and state, Christian society needed two heads, tsar and patriarch. Thus, it was argued, the grand duke of Moscow, as the only independent Greek Orthodox ruler, had not only the right but the duty to assume the title of tsar so as not to leave Orthodox society without a protector. Both Ivan III and his son used the title occasionally. His grandson, Ivan IV the Dread (usually called "the Terrible" in English), was

* "Tsar" is usually considered a contraction of "caesar." However, the old Slavic form of the latter is not "tsar" but "kesar." Besides, in the Byzantine Empire the title "caesar" was applied to a secondary rank of office. The Byzantine emperor was called in Greek *basileus autocrator*. This the Russians translated as "tsar and autocrat."

officially crowned tsar in 1547. Fourteen years later the patriarch of Constantinople recognized Ivan's title and sent him his blessing.

Ivan IV's reign lasted half a century (1533–84) and was full of momentous events. The tsar had a complex personality. Endowed with many intellectual gifts and a ruler of broad vision, he was at the same time impetuous, cruel, and neurotic, and suffered from a persecution complex which grew especially strong in the last twenty years of his life. His nature was essentially artistic; aestheticism prevailed in him over moral sense. He was attracted by the dramatic and, one may say, theatrical effects of political conflicts and actions. Whatever the occasion—whether coronation or mass execution of political opponents—it was staged as a pageant, gay or grim depending on circumstances. When he created the oprichnina, his dreaded political police, its headquarters assumed all the aspects of a monastery, with himself as abbot.

Various psychopathic traits in Ivan's character were the result of the unfortunate circumstances of his childhood. When his father died, Ivan (b.1530) was an infant of three. His mother assumed the regency, which she shared with the boyar duma. There was continual friction between her and the boyars, as well as among the latter, because of the rivalry of two powerful princely boyar families. In 1538 Ivan's mother died, presumably poisoned by her rivals. The boyar council was left to rule the country, but the factional strife continued unabated. At every new turn of political fortune, the leaders of the defeated faction were imprisoned or exiled. The atmosphere in the palace was far from healthy for the boy Ivan, and he often had reason to fear for his life. He was also repeatedly offended by the arrogant behavior of the leading boyars, a gross contrast to their outward servility to him on state occasions, such as receptions for foreign ambassadors, when he had to sit on the throne in gorgeous robes. Ivan soon noticed that boyars in positions of power freely took from the palace whatever jewelry or other art objects they liked without troubling to ask his permission. The only man whom he could trust and whom he esteemed in those years was the head of the Russian church, Metropolitan Makari. Under the metropolitan's guidance Ivan read a number of theological and historical books that were available in Slavic. It was also Makari who inspired him with ideas of the high dignity and responsibilities of the Christian ruler.

The boyar rule came to an end in 1546. That year Ivan became sixteen and, apparently acting on Makari's advice, announced to the boyars his decision to marry and to assume the title of tsar. Both the marriage and the coronation took place the next year. Ivan's bride, Anastasia Romanov, belonged to an old boyar family, though not a princely one. According to contemporary evidence, she was beautiful, intelligent, and virtuous, and had a sound and soothing influence on her husband. No less important for Ivan was the formation around him of an informal council of able advisers, men of high integrity, who actually directed state affairs in the early part of his reign. Prominent among them were a priest, Sylvester; a palace official, Alexis Adashev; and Prince Andrew Kurbsky.

Guided by the council, Ivan undertook a series of important reforms in the Muscovite government and administration. A new institution was created, the zemsky sobor (assembly of the land) which first met in 1550. It consisted of two houses which, however, met jointly whenever the sobor was in full session. The upper house consisted of the boyar duma, the council of bishops, and the highest officials of the realm. In the lower house sat the representatives of the gentry and the merchants. Politically, this house was meant to counterbalance the exclusive influence of the boyars on state affairs. With the sanction of the sobor Ivan changed the whole system of local administration (1555). Up until then the Tsar had appointed a governor of each district to collect taxes and combat crime; instead of salary the governor was entitled to receive food and other supplies from the population of the district according to established quotas which he often exceeded. This was the so-called "feeding" system which had grown to be quite a burden to the people. Now the governors were revoked and the people received the right—and the duty—of electing their own officers to collect taxes and apprehend and try criminals. The sobor also approved a new code of laws, called the Tsar's Code. (1550) Furthermore, the system of military fiefs was greatly expanded. One thousand army officers received pomestie, or fiefs, around Moscow and formed a battalion of guard troops; strict norms for grants of fiefs to the provincial gentry were announced at the same time. The pomestie reform was completed at another session of the zemsky sobor in 1566. The grants were not issued in full ownership and were personal and conditional, not hereditary—for services rendered by the recipient as army officer. A nucleus of a standing infantry army was also formed, the so-called *streltsy* (musketeers; literally, "shooters"). Five thousand of these were stationed in Moscow and 7,000 in various border towns. In the first half of the 17th century their total strength was increased to 25,000 and in the second half to 50,000.

The reorganized army was immediately put to the test in a campaign against the Khanate of Kazan. As a matter of fact, following the death of Ivan III relations between Muscovy and the Tatar world had become strained. The friendship established by Ivan with the Crimean khans came to an end and the khans shifted their support to Lithuania. In Kazan the anti-Russian party came to power. During the regency of the boyar duma in Ivan IV's childhood, both the Crimean and Kazan Tatars frequently raided Muscovy. Ivan IV and his advisers decided to deal with the Tatar khanates one by one, starting with Kazan. In 1551 the Muscovites built a fortress at Sviazhsk on the Volga about twenty miles above Kazan. This served as a base for the big Russian offensive against Kazan the next year. The Muscovite army was well supplied with artillery and powder for mining the city's walls. A Danish technician was put in charge of the mines. On October 2, 1552, Kazan was stormed by the Russians, and the khan was taken prisoner. Soon the whole Khanate of Kazan was in Russian hands. Russian garrisons were stationed at several strategic points. The establishment of Russian rule was made easier by the heterogeneous composition of the population of the khanate. The Tatars constituted the ruling class. It did not matter much to the various Finnish and Turkish or half-Turkish tribes whom they had to pay taxes to—the khan or the tsar. With the approval of Metropolitan Makari a policy of religious tolerance was announced. Christian churches were built in the newly conquered land for the Russian officials and settlers, but there was no forcible conversion of the Moslems. After consolidating their control of the basin of the middle Volga, the Russians were ready to conquer the lower Volga basin as well. The Khanate of Astrakhan was weak, and besides there was a pro-Russian party at the khan's court. So the Russians had little difficulty in annexing Astrakhan, in 1556.

It so happened that the year after the Russian conquest of Kazan English mariners, in search of an Arctic route to India, discovered instead the northern maritime route to Russia via the White Sea. English merchants were quick to grasp the importance of this discovery, and a joint-stock company, the Russia Company, was formed to trade with Muscovy. With the conquest of Astrakhan the English became interested in using the Volga River way for transit trade with central Asia, and through it with China and Persia. In 1558 an agent of the Russia Company, Anthony Jenkinson, went down the Volga and through the Caspian Sea to Khiva and Bukhara. But he found the central Asian trade less profitable than he had thought, owing to chaotic political conditions prevailing in Turkistan and lack of commercial relations between central Asia and China at that time.

6. *The Livonian war and the oprichnina*

In the opinion of both Adashev and Prince Kurbsky the conquest of Kazan and Astrakhan should have been followed up with an attempt to subordinate the Khanate of the Crimea to Moscow in order to end the Tatar menace once and for all. By that time, however, their relations with the tsar had become strained. As the years went by, Ivan resented more and more the tutelage of his advisers. He wanted to rule by himself and grew suspicious of the political designs of his old friends. When Tsaritsa Anastasia died in 1560 he believed the malignant and absurd rumor that she had been poisoned by order of his councilors. With her death, there was nobody left to check his fits of rage. Under the circumstances, Ivan's disagreement with his old advisers on matters of foreign policy resulted in a complete break with them and in his assuming personal control of state affairs. He decided to win Russia access to the Baltic instead of to the Black Sea.

This decision was not a mere personal whim. Russia needed an outlet to the West both for trade and to promote cultural relations. The English monopolized the roundabout northern route they had established. Since the time of Ivan III Russia had employed many western experts and technicians, and she needed more. But her western neighbors—the Livonian Knights, Poland,

and Sweden—used every pretext for not letting foreign specialists into Muscovy, hoping to prevent her using western techniques for her aggrandizement. A kind of "iron curtain" was thus built against Russia along her western frontier. Hence many Russian statesmen and merchants sympathized with Ivan's Baltic policies. As opening move in his struggle for the Baltic provinces Ivan demanded that the Livonian Knights pay him tribute. They agreed in principle but failed to make the first payment on time. In 1558 the tsar's armies invaded Livonia, producing an international crisis. As has been mentioned, the Livonian Knights put themselves under the protection of Lithuania. Courland became a vassal state of Poland, and Estonia gave herself up to Sweden. The Island of Oesel recognized the authority of Denmark. Muscovy now had to face war with several powerful states. Ivan IV accepted the challenge and tried to detach Denmark from his other three adversaries. The Danish duke, Magnus, who ruled Oesel agreed to pledge vassal allegiance to Ivan and married the latter's niece. Ivan proposed to extend Magnus' authority to Livonia and Estonia in order to create a buffer state in the Baltic area under his own protection. The plan fell through with Russia's final defeat in the war.

While the first years of the Livonian war on the whole went well for Russia, the Muscovite troops had defeats as well as victories. Every defeat Ivan would attribute to the treason of the boyar commanders. Several of them were imprisoned or executed. In 1564 one of the ablest Muscovite generals, Ivan's former adviser Prince Kurbsky, lost a battle to the Lithuanians. Not willing meekly to await his disgrace, he went over to the Lithuanian side and was warmly received by King Sigismund August, who granted landed estates to the fugitive and gave him an important position in the Lithuanian army. From his point of view, Kurbsky merely took advantage of the traditional Russian principle of freedom of boyar service. In Ivan's view Kurbsky was a traitor. A curious exchange of letters took place between the two, each defending his position and heaping abuses on the other.

Kurbsky's defection produced an extremely painful impression on Ivan and all but threw him off mental balance. His suspicions now knew no limits. He decided finally to break the opposition of the boyars and to take extraordinary measures both for his personal protection and to increase his control of the army and administration. In December 1564, Ivan secretly left Moscow and established his headquarters in Alexandrov, a small town about forty-five miles east of the capital. From there he sent a message to the people of Moscow announcing that he was abdicating because of the treachery of the boyars. As he must have expected, the dumbfounded Muscovites sent a delegation asking him not to abandon the throne. He agreed on condition that he be given dictatorial powers to punish the traitors and be allowed to establish a separate court as a new center of administration, unrestricted by any traditional institutions. This was the beginning of the oprichnina. The meaning of the term is precisely "a separate (or private) household (or court)." Ivan's new court was actually organized along the lines of a monastery; prayer alternated with wild orgies, and the oprichniki (members of the oprichnina) wore black garments and were called "brethren." No boyar was admitted to the oprichnina unless he was ready to break from his class politically and give a special pledge of allegiance. It was the lower gentry whom Ivan considered loyal to him and on whose support he relied. Besides the gentry, some commoners and a number of Baltic German prisoners of war and other German adventurers were allowed to join the oprichnina guards. Their total number reached six thousand. All of them received confiscated boyar estates as fiefs. More and more towns and districts were assigned for the upkeep of the oprichnina regime, so that at the time of the fullest expansion of the oprichnina Muscovy was divided into two almost equal parts. While the central region and the north were placed under the oprichnina regime, the border provinces in the west and south continued to be administered in the traditional way and became known as "the Land" (*zemshchina*). The boyars' patrimonial estates in the oprichnina area were confiscated and their former owners, if they were not executed, received fiefs in the Land. Confiscations were carried out in a disorderly manner with much brutality and looting. They served Ivan's purpose, however, since they ruined a good part of the boyar class. Many boyars and their servitors were executed as traitors under the tsar's personal supervision. In 1570 the whole city of Novgorod was proscribed and sacked by the oprichniki. As the horrors of the oprichnina affected mostly the boyars at first, the commoners did not protest against it. In 1566 three hundred boyars asked to be received in audience and admonished the tsar to stop the persecutions. They were imprisoned and tortured. Two years later the head of the Russian church, Metropolitan Philip (ordained in 1567), openly denounced the oprichnina in his sermons. He was arrested, deported to a provincial monastery, and there quietly strangled by the head oprichnik. Another open opponent of the oprichnina was a self-styled prophet ("Christ's fool," as such men were known in Muscovy), Nicholas Salos of Pskov. Following the raid on Novgorod the tsar led his oprichniki to Pskov. In the midst of the sack of this city Nicholas publicly reprimanded the tsar with such vehemence that Ivan called off the expedition and went back to Alexandrov. As a result, Pskov suffered much less than Novgorod.

The oprichniki ran riot for almost seven years until it became obvious to Ivan that the terror was undermining the whole Muscovite state and becoming dangerous to his own government. In 1572 the oprichniki corps was disbanded, although most of its members continued to serve in the army and at the tsar's court. The administrative division between the court (as the oprichnina area now became known) and the zemshchina was not abolished, but on the whole things assumed a more orderly tenor. The boyar estates which had been confiscated earlier were now returned to those of their owners who had survived the terror.

Meanwhile, the Livonian war was not yet over. That and the terror all but exhausted the strength of the people. When the new Polish king Stephen Batory (elected in 1576) led his well-trained army against Russia in 1579, the only resistance he met was from Pskov, whose garrison refused to surrender and which the Poles were unable to storm. Hard pressed by both Poles and Swedes, Ivan IV appealed to the pope to mediate. The pope's ambassador, the Jesuit Antonio Possevino, succeeded in persuading King Stephen to agree to a ten-year armistice. Ivan had to give up Livonia but kept all his former possessions along the Lithuanian border. The armistice with Sweden signed the next year was less favorable to Russia, since Ivan was compelled to cede Ingria, including the mouth of the Neva River, which cut Russia off completely from the Gulf of Finland.

Checked and thrown back in the west, the Russians at that very time started a new expansion in the east. The initiative in this case was taken not by the Muscovite government but by the Stroganov family. In the course of the 16th century the Stroganovs, rich merchants and industrialists of Novgorodian extraction, had established a prosperous business in the Perm area. Interested in the furs and other resources of western Siberia, they sent across the Urals a detachment of Cossacks who had entered their service. This detachment, under the command of Ataman Ermak, was 540 strong, and reinforced by 300 soldiers recruited among the tenants of the Stroganov domains. That small force which started its campaign in 1581 was equipped with firearms, which gave it a definite advantage over its adversaries. Within two years Ermak conquered the Tatar khanate of western Siberia and sent a deputation to Tsar Ivan IV asking him to take the newly conquered lands under his protection. The deputation was graciously received by the tsar. By that time however, Ermak's military position had been weakened owing to a vigorous attempt of the Tatars to regain power, and Ermak himself perished in an ambush in August 1584. Meanwhile Ivan IV had died. Not willing to let the opportunity of controlling western Siberia slip out of its hands, the Muscovite government sent several hundred more troops which completed the conquest. In 1585 the first Russian fortress in Siberia was built at Tiumen, which became the main base for further expansion.

The Livonian war ended none too soon for Russia; she was in the midst of a profound crisis, social, economic, and political. Both the city crafts and agriculture in the central regions were suffering from a labor shortage because of the continued conscription of soldiers. Many peasants had been affected by the oprichnina lootings and fled south; while the conquest of Kazan, which opened rich virgin lands in the middle Volga basin to agricultural colonization, contributed to the exodus from the central region. This was disastrous because the whole pomestie system was based, economically, on the produce of the tenant farmers of the pomestie estates. The patrimonial estates of the boyars were in a better position since most of the boyars owned slaves and could use their labor in addition to that of the peasants. Until this time the peasants had been free to move from one estate to another, or to migrate at the end of the agricultural year, which was set at St. George's Day, November 26. Now the holders of the military fiefs complained that they were ruined by the fluidity of agricultural labor. The tsar saw no way out except to restrict the peasants' freedom. As a preliminary measure the government reserved for itself the right to proclaim certain years "prohibited." No peasant was allowed to move in those years. The first "prohibited year" was 1581.

Ivan's family affairs added to the general confusion and jeopardized the very existence of his dynasty. Anastasia had borne him two sons: Ivan, who seemed to be normal and intelligent, and Theodore, a saintly and sickly simpleton. After Anastasia's death Ivan took six more wives in succession, disregarding canon law. By his seventh wife, Maria Nagoy, whom he married in 1580, he had one more son, Dmitri, in 1582. The same year he decided to marry once more (although Maria was still living and still his wife) and to combine diplomacy with matrimony in order to raise his prestige in Europe. He sent his envoys to England to look for a suitable fiancée among the relatives of Queen Elizabeth. Reluctant to lose the benefits of the Russian trade, the queen did not want to offend Ivan by a plain refusal. Hence the Russian envoy was told that Elizabeth's niece, Mary Hastings, was eligible but that she was ill at the moment. The negotiations continued but nothing came of them. Meanwhile Ivan IV in a fit of anger accidentally killed his eldest son Ivan (1582). Thus when Ivan IV died, in 1584, the weak Theodore became his successor and proved the last tsar of the dynasty.

7. Political and religious thought

The period 1450–1600 was one of religious and intellectual ferment in Russia. The liberation of the Muscovite state from the Tatars and separation of the church from Byzantium, the fall of Novgorod, the establishment of the tsardom, the conflict between tsar and boyars, and the intensified contacts with the West all called for a reappraisal of traditions and adjustment to the new circumstances. New ideas clashed with old, and under their impact some of the old intellectual currents took an unexpected turn.

Two different attitudes toward the role of the church in society crystallized among Russian religious leaders in the late 15th century. One may be called idealistic and mystical, the other practical and social. The former group continued the traditions of Russian monasticism of the second half of the 14th century and was strengthened by a new influx of Byzantine mysticism. An outstanding representative of this group was the monk Nil Sorsky, who established his hermitage in north Russia beyond the Volga, near Beloozero. According to the Trans-Volga hermits, as he and his followers were known, the vehicle of religion was prayer and meditation; salvation could be achieved only through the regeneration of inner spiritual forces. The Trans-Volga hermits disapproved of the church and monasteries acquiring lands and wealth. They asked no protection of the state and wanted the church completely free of interference by the state. In contrast their opponents the Josephites (named after their leader Joseph, abbot of the Monastery of Volokolamsk) emphasized the importance of the social services the church performed, which, they argued, required wealth as well as the protection of the state; the Josephites in turn were ready to give the state their full blessing.

Before long a new movement came upon the scene, the so-called heresy of the Judaizers. It started in Novgorod and was stimulated by the visit, in 1471, of a learned Jew of Kiev, Zechariah by name, a student of both philosophy and astronomy. Impressed with his learning, a number of Novgorodians, including two priests, became interested in Judaism as well as in astronomy and astrology. In 1478 Ivan III met the two Judaizing priests, liked them, and invited them to Moscow. They made many new converts there among both clergy and state officials. Not all the Judaizers accepted Judaism in full. Most of them used the Judaic literature to criticize various Christian dogmas as well as certain features of the organization and practices of the Russian church. Among other things they objected to the use of icons and questioned the right of the church to own landed estates. On the whole the Judaizers were permeated with a rationalistic and reforming spirit.

It was the Josephites who first became alarmed at the spread of the Judaizing movement and called for strong measures to suppress it. They cited the activities of the Spanish Inquisition as the best method to employ. The Trans-Volga hermits, on the contrary, argued that the only Christian way to combat heresy was persuasion. For a number of years Ivan III hesitated to take action against the Judaizers. From a practical point of view he favored the negative attitude of both the Trans-Volga hermits and the Judaizers to the church estates. Around 1500, as we know, Ivan confiscated church lands in the Novgorod area, and he planned to follow a similar policy in Muscovy. However, at the meeting of an ecclesiastical council in 1503 the Josephites proved to be in the majority. Reluctantly Ivan had to abandon his plans; the Josephites, in return, promised the church's full support to autocracy. The next year another session of the church council met, with the Josephites in full control. This council condemned the ringleaders of the Judaizers to be burned at the stake. Within a few years the heresy was stamped out. From that time on the Josephites were in full control of the Russian church administration. The influence of the Trans-Volga hermits gradually declined in spite of the fact that a number of boyars were in sympathy with their teachings.

Both the Muscovite government and the church prelates— whether Josephites or not—considered lack of scholarship among the Russian clergy one cause of the spread of heresies. Cooperation with either Roman Catholic or Greek scholars in translating more religious works seemed desirable. It was but natural that Greeks were preferred. In 1516 an outstanding Greek humanistic scholar, Michael Triboles, better known by his monastic name of Maxim, was invited to Moscow, where he was to remain the rest of his life since he was never allowed to leave Russia. He translated a number of Byzantine theological works into Slavic and corrected some of the church books previously translated. He also recommended the return of the Muscovite church to the fold of the patriarchate of Constantinople, which was much resented by the Josephites. On the other hand, Maxim the Greek made friends among the followers of the Trans-Volga hermits, who greatly admired his learning and personality.

The victory of the Josephites called for a new definition of the role of the ruler and church of Moscow in the Christian world. Hence the idea of the Third Rome. It arose as an adaptation of the Byzantine doctrine of the symphony of church and state to the new international situation. Byzantine writers argued that in the early Middle Ages the center of the Christian state had shifted from Rome to Constantinople, the Second Rome. Now, with the overthrow of the Byzantine Empire by the Turks, Moscow, in the opinion of some Russian writers, became the Third Rome in both a political and religious sense. And, it was added, this was the last

Rome—there would be no other. The coronation of Ivan IV as tsar in 1547 was in line with this doctrine To complete the organization of the Third Rome, the metropolitan of Moscow had to assume the title of patriarch. That was done in 1589 in the reign of Theodore I. Bishop Job became Russia's first patriarch.

The doctrine of the Third Rome has often been interpreted as Moscow's aggressive claim to political as well as religious world leadership. Originally the doctrine had no such meaning. Those who first formulated it believed the end of the world was approaching and the Last Judgment. They were merely trying to keep Orthodox Christianity alive as a last refuge to the end. Their followers were less pessimistic and hoped for a Christian millennium; but they too were concerned only with the fate of Orthodox Christianity and preached no crusade against the outside world. Their aim was first of all to clean their own house and improve the organization of the Russian church. A church council was convoked in 1551, known as the Stoglav (the Hundred Chapters) since its proceedings were divided into a hundred sections. That council decided to stamp out various abuses in church administration and to improve learning. It recommended using only corrected copies of church books. To prevent further mistakes in copying, Metropolitan Makari established a printing office in Moscow in 1553. The printing of Slavic books had been started in Poland in 1491, in Bohemia in 1515, and in Lithuania in 1525. Now Moscow followed suit. The first Russian master printer, Ivan Fedorov, worked in Moscow until 1565 when he left for West Russia and continued his activities there. Printing in Moscow became a state monopoly.

The religious polemics and new ideas on church and state found expression in an abundant literature of pamphlets, epistles, and treatises. The political conflict of the reign of Ivan IV was accompanied by a similar development of political literature. Among the outstanding specimens of it are the writings of Ivan Peresvetov who belonged to a gentry family of the region of Briansk. In his youth he served in the Polish and Hungarian armies, traveled in Moldavia, and grew well acquainted with the Turkish regime. In a sense he became a Turkophile. In 1538 he came to Moscow and entered government service. When Ivan IV was crowned, Peresvetov wrote several pamphlets and allegorical tales in which he advised the tsar to reduce the power of the boyars and establish a strong government based on a well organized and well paid army and administration. In this program he was partly influenced by the pattern of the Turkish administration, which he idealized. Peresvetov may be considered a mouthpiece of the lower Russian gentry, expressing their readiness to become the mainstay of the tsar's power.

Another important body of political writings of the period is the polemical correspondence between Ivan IV and Prince Kurbsky. The former, naturally, defended autocracy; the latter argued for a constitutional government of an aristocratic type. While Ivan IV's private letters to various persons show his ability to write in a lively and informal style, his political writings are rather unwieldy, overburdened with long quotations from various theological and historical works. Kurbsky's works are better organized and on the whole more readable. Their exchange of opinion is characteristic of the intellectual ferment in Russia of this period; the mere fact that Ivan wished to convince his opponents of the rightness of his position and not merely crush them is significant.

8. *Fine arts*

The late Mongol and the early post-Mongol period may be called the age of the Renaissance in Russian arts. The blossoming of Russian painting around 1500 was a reflection of the earlier revival of Byzantine art—the so-called Renaissance of the Paleologi. In architecture a revival of Suzdalian forms took place late in the 15th century under Italian architects, and through them the Italian Renaissance had a direct influence on Muscovite architecture.

The greatest of the Italian artists engaged by Ivan III was Aristotle Fieravanti * of Bologna, who was equally skillful as architect and engineer. He came to Moscow in 1475 and was entrusted with building Moscow's main church, the Cathedral of the Assumption in the Kremlin. Definite instructions were given that the new cathedral was to be in the Suzdalian style, like the 12th-century Cathedral of the Assumption in Vladimir. Fieravanti studied the architectural forms of the cathedral in Vladimir as well

* Often spelt Fioravanti.

as of the other churches in Suzdalia and found them congenial to his taste. The wonderful cathedral he built in the Kremlin—much larger in size than the Suzdalian churches—was not a mere replica of any of them but a re-creation of their spirit. Fieravanti also had a share in planning the rebuilding of the Kremlin's walls and towers. Another cathedral was built in the Kremlin by the architect Aloisio Novi of Milan, and a palace (the Hall of the Facets) by Pietro Antonio Solari and Marco Ruffo. The building of the third Kremlin cathedral was entrusted to Pskovian architects. Thus within a period of about thirty years the inimitable architectural ensemble of the Kremlin was created.

After 1530 an entirely new architectural style became popular in Muscovy which represented a complete break with Byzantine tradition. A characteristic feature of the churches built in it was the tower-like shape of the main body of the church, capped by a pyramidal or in certain cases a cone-shaped roof. These became known as "tent" churches, which is what the roof suggests. The first outstanding example of this style is the church in the village of Kolomenskoe, about twelve miles from Moscow, which was completed in 1532 and attributed to Aloisio Novi. If Aloisio was indeed the architect he must have received as precise instructions as Fieravanti in 1475 on what style to follow. In the opinion of many art historians the style was an adaptation in stone of the wooden buildings of north Russia. The point is a disputed one, and there is another possible answer—the influence of central Asian forms, and through them of Indian forms, on Muscovite architecture. In any case the Muscovite style of the 16th century is certainly remarkable. Of a peculiar style is the Cathedral of the Intercession of Our Lady (better known as the Church of Basil the Blessed) built in the Red Square in Moscow in 1555–60 to commemorate the conquest of Kazan. The builders were two Russian architects, Barma and Postnik, the latter a Pskovian. The cathedral is a weird ensemble of domes crowned with onion-shaped cupolas, the central tower, which rises much higher than the others, being close to the tent form. The decoration is exuberant; and the first impression the church makes on the modern sightseer is of the fantasy of Russian fairy tales with touches of the Italian Renaissance added.

The Novgorod school of icon painting reached its full flowering in the last twenty years of Novgorod's independence. The Novgorodian style, at its best, is characterized by rhythmic lines and bright yet delicate colors. After Moscow annexed Novgorod a number of Novgorodian painters moved to Moscow and reinforced the cadres of artists there. The greatest Russian painter of this period was Dionysius, a Muscovite best known for his wall paintings at St. Therapont Monastery southeast of Beloozero (1500). His art was influenced by the school of Andrew Rublev but he was a creative artist in his own right. His wall paintings are distinguished by delicate drawing and subtle coloring. His predilection in design was for lean elongated figures and faces. His two sons and other pupils carried on his traditions but none of them was his equal.

CHAPTER 5

THE TSARDOM OF MOSCOW IN THE 17TH CENTURY

1. *The Time of Trouble*

AFTER the death of Ivan IV the administration of Moscow assumed a more orderly character. The leading figure in the government was now the boyar Boris Godunov, the new tsar's brother-in-law. In Theodore I's name Boris actually ruled Russia. He was a statesman of great ability, and it seemed at first that Muscovy would be able to return to normalcy under his guidance. However, the inner contradictions in the political and social regime, as well as the economic crisis, could not be solved at once. The boyar class, which had been shattered by the oprichnina, now rallied to defend its old privileges. The boyars resented Boris' rule and envied his high position. As a matter of fact, Boris followed the main line of Ivan IV's policy, promoting the interests of the gentry and merchants against those of the boyars. This compelled him also to follow Ivan's plan of restricting the freedom of the peasants, which caused growing discontent among them.

MOSCOW TSARS AND PRETENDERS
OF THE TIME OF TROUBLE

1598–1605	Boris Godunov
1605	Theodore II (son of Boris)
1605–06	Pseudo-Dmitri I
1606–10	Basil IV (Shuisky)
1607–10	Pseudo-Dmitri II (rival tsar)
1610–13	Vladislav of Poland (tsar elect)

Meanwhile, the situation in the tsar's family added to a general feeling of instability. By their father's will Theodore's half brother, the boy Dmitri, received Uglich, a small town on the upper Volga, in appanage. For several years he lived there quietly with his mother and her relatives of the Nagoy family under the supervision of a government commissioner. Then one day in 1591 he was found dead in the courtyard with his throat slashed. The Nagoys accused the commissioner of the crime, and the excited townspeople of Uglich killed the commissioner and his clerks. A commission of inquiry was then sent from Moscow headed by a prominent boyar, Prince Basil Shuisky. The commission reported that Dmitri, who was an epileptic, had killed himself accidentally in a fit while playing with a knife. The Nagoys were accused of taking law into their own hands by inciting the people of Uglich against the commissioner. Dmitri's mother, Tsaritsa Maria, was put in a nunnery, and a number of other members of the Nagoy family were deported to distant towns. There the matter seemed to have ended. Soon after Dmitri's death Tsaritsa Irene (Theodore's wife) gave birth to a daughter; the child died, however, three years later, leaving the tsar without heirs. Since Theodore himself was in poor health, a dynastic crisis was obviously approaching.

Theodore died in 1598, bequeathing the realm to his wife. Irene, however, refused to accept the throne and entered a nunnery. A zemsky sobor was then convoked to elect a new tsar. Boris, as the actual ruler during Theodore's reign, was a logical candidate, but several other names were mentioned, among them that of the boyar Theodore Romanov, second cousin of the deceased tsar. A favorite of Moscow society and a man of pleasing personality, Romanov enjoyed considerable popularity among both boyars and townspeople. Patriarch Job, however, favored Boris, and his opinion prevailed. Boris was elected tsar.

Boris' personality and tragic fate have made his name widely known. A man of sound judgment, a ruler of good intentions, a model husband and father, Boris at first glance does not resemble the villain legend has made him. At the reception in the palace after his coronation he touched the pearl-studded collar of his royal shirt and promised to share all his riches with the people. He meant, indeed, to improve the lot of his subjects. Understanding the superiority of western education and technique, he was friendly toward foreigners and was the first of the Moscow rulers to send Russian youths abroad for training. He gave both his son and his daughter a good education and arranged the latter's betrothal to a Danish prince. But, as if fate itself was against him, none of his plans succeeded: his subjects were famine-stricken; his daughter's bridegroom fell ill and died; none of the young Russians he sent abroad ever returned. And his memory became subject to slander and hatred. He was accused of a series of crimes: of poisoning Tsar Ivan IV as well as his own brother-in-law, Tsar Theodore, and his daughter's Danish bridegroom—and, above all, of murdering Tsarevich Dmitri. The historian Nicholas Karamzin rejected as slander all the accusations except the last. Karamzin's point of view has prevailed in subsequent historical studies, with but few dissenting voices. In his play, *Boris Godunov,* the poet Alexander Pushkin, following Karamzin, represented Boris as having that one crime on his conscience and suffering to expiate it. This is also the approach the composer Musorgsky took in his opera. And yet, there is no positive proof that Tsarevich Dmitri did not commit suicide. The case remains a mystery.

Whatever the truth may be, when Boris ascended the throne his position was not secure, in spite of the sanction of the sobor. He lacked the prestige of the hereditary dynasty, and the boyars now claimed a greater role in the government which Boris was not prepared to grant them. An elemental misfortune added to the new tsar's and the nation's troubles. Beginning with the summer of 1601 the crops failed three years in succession. To provide employment for more people the tsar initiated a vast program of public works and building in Moscow, which, however, could not support all those in need. Mortality was high and brigandage spread.

Against this background of confusion and discontent, the boyars grew more insistent in their claims. Boris struck back by accusing several leading boyars of conspiracy and treason. Theodore Romanov was made a monk against his will, taking monastic orders under the name of Philaret. By that action he was considered automatically divorced from his wife who entered a nunnery under the name of Martha. Other members of the Romanov family were deported to distant towns in the north (1601). A number of boyars now decided to incite the nation against the tsar by playing on the people's traditional reverence for the old dynasty. Rumors were circulated that the official report on the circumstances of Tsarevich

Dmitri's death had been false; that Boris' agents had been ordered
to kill Dmitri but had killed the wrong boy; and that the real
Dmitri succeeded in escaping and was now about to reappear to
take revenge. Incidentally, this was the first occasion on which it
was alleged that Boris was responsible for Dmitri's death ten
years earlier. The boyars did not merely agitate. They had a definite plan of action: to produce a pretender. While there is no
direct evidence, from some hints in the sources as well as from
subsequent events it seems likely that a suitable boy must have
been secretly trained by boyar agents to assume the role of Dmitri.
His origin is not known.*

In 1603 the news reached Moscow that Tsarevich Dmitri had
appeared at the court of a West Russian prince and later been
given refuge at the castle of a Polish lord, George Mniszek, in
Sambor, Galicia. Whoever the Sambor Dmitri may have been, it
is clear from his actions and behavior that he was firmly convinced
of his royal origin and in that sense was not an impostor. At this
juncture the boyar intrigue assumed international significance.
King Sigismund III of Poland and the Jesuits decided to make
the pretender a pretext for intervening in Russian affairs and attempting to convert the Russian people to Roman Catholicism.
Dmitri himself agreed to become a member of the Roman church
(his conversion being kept secret) and was promised the hand of
the beautiful Marina Mniszek, his host's daughter.

While the Polish government gave Dmitri no direct military
support, it allowed him to recruit volunteers for a campaign against
Moscow; a number of Muscovite fugitives, Ukrainians, and Poles
answered his call. In the autumn of 1604 Dmitri led his motley
troops to Novgorod-in-Severia but was defeated and had to retreat hastily to the border town of Putivl. His cause was saved
by the service Cossacks and petty squires of this frontier region
who had grievances of their own against Moscow. A detachment of
Don Cossacks also joined them. Together they dashed north
toward Orel and seized the fortress of Kromy; there they were
stopped and besieged by Muscovite troops. The situation, while
serious for the Moscow government, was not hopeless by any

* After the appearance of the pretender the Moscow government announced
that he was a former novice of a Moscow monastery, Gregory Otrepiev. This
identification is hardly credible.

means, since Boris was still firmly in saddle. It was only after Boris' death, in April 1605, that Dmitri's fifth column in Moscow got their chance to seize power in his name. In June Dmitri entered the city in triumph. A month later he was crowned tsar; in November he was betrothed to Marina by proxy. Marina with her father and his retinue of two thousand Polish noblemen and servants entered Moscow on May 2, 1606, in solemn procession. Dmitri and Marina were married six days later, and banquets and festivities continued for several days. Entranced with all this splendor and happiness, Dmitri lost his sense of reality an did not suspect that he was sitting on top of a volcano. The arrogant behavior of the Poles irritated the Muscovites, and the boyars had no difficulty in inciting the populace against them. On May 17 riots started in the city and the boyar conspirators, profiting by the general confusion, penetrated into the palace. Dmitri was killed, Marina sent back to Poland. Thus ended the pretender's brief career. A disorderly crowd gathered in the Red Square and shouted for the leader of the boyar conspiracy, Prince Basil Shuisky. He graciously accepted the throne.

The boyars had never intended to let the pretender actually rule Russia unless he agreed to be their puppet. Dmitri had refused to be anybody's tool and assumed the throne in all seriousness; besides, he proved an intelligent man of considerable ability. So the boyars had conspired against him almost on the first day of his reign. Now they seemed to be victorious. But they soon discovered that it was easier to conjure a ghost than to get rid of one. Popular discontent ran high, and the peasants and slaves rose in many localities against the boyars. While the peasant army was defeated and the ringleaders of the insurrection executed, the movement was not crushed. Before long the news spread that Dmitri was alive. The old pattern was repeated. It was announced that the man Shuisky's agents had killed in the palace in Moscow was not Dmitri, that the latter had miraculously escaped and reappeared. The new pretender seems to have been the son of a Ukrainian priest and a man of vulgar and dissolute character. Nobody, however, cared about his personality. The name Dmitri became a symbol of discontent around which all those who resented the boyar rule rallied.

Even some of the boyars, for example Prince Dmitri Trubetskoy, joined the second pretender, having lost faith in Tsar Basil's ability to restore the order. The false Dmitri's prestige was also heightened by Tsaritsa Marina's recognition of him as her husband. Having once tasted the splendor of tsardom, Marina did not want to let a chance of regaining it slip by. The second pretender was soon heading a large army composed of Polish adventurers, Zaporozhie Cossacks, Kasimov Tatars, Don Cossacks, and Muscovite service Cossacks. The latter two groups represented the Russian element in the coalition and had a definite political plan—to reorganize the Muscovite state along Cossack democratic lines. Most of the others were chiefly interested in plunder and booty. In 1608 the second Dmitri defeated Basil's army and established his camp in the village of Tushino close to Moscow. A protracted stalemate followed, neither side being strong enough to overcome the other. Agents of both tsars were sent all over Russia demanding the submission of the people in the name of Dmitri or Basil, depending on whom they represented. Armed Polish, Ukrainian, and Russian bands roamed at will, looting boyar estates as well as towns and churches. The Poles and Ukrainians besieged the large and prosperous Trinity Monastery northeast of Moscow but were unable to take it. Russia seemed to be rapidly disintegrating and people were in confusion and despair.

Tsar Basil decided to ask Sweden for help. Sweden was at war with Poland, and the Swedes agreed to send Basil auxiliary troops only on condition that he sign a permanent alliance with Sweden against Poland, besides ceding Karelia to Sweden. The conditions were accepted, and with the help of the Swedes Basil's generals were able to undertake an offensive against Tushino. At the news of the approach of the Swedes Dmitri lost courage and fled to Kaluga. The civil war was not over, however, and now a new element entered the picture. King Sigismund of Poland could not tolerate Moscow's alliance with Sweden and declared war on Moscow. In June 1610 Basil's army was defeated by the Poles. Soon afterward the angry Muscovites deposed Basil. After that two alternatives were open to them: to negotiate with the Poles or to recognize Dmitri. The latter raced to Moscow, trying to get there before the Poles. The conservative groups of Russians, led by the boyars, preferred to negotiate with the Poles, and in August 1610 an agreement was reached recognizing Sigismund's son Vladislav as tsar of Russia provided he was converted to Greek Orthodoxy. He was to rule with the assistance of the boyar duma and the zemsky sobor. The people of Moscow were ordered to swear allegiance to Vladislav, and a grand embassy was sent to Poland to conclude the formal treaty. Among many notables in the embassy was Philaret Romanov (ordained bishop in 1606). As a measure of protection against Dmitri's troops the boyars asked the Polish commander to place a Polish garrison in the Kremlin, which he readily hastened to do.

The agreement with the Poles was looked upon with much suspicion by both the Russian clergy and the lower classes. Among the latter Dmitri was still popular. His days, however, were numbered. In December of that year Dmitri killed his associate, the Tatar khan of Kasimov, suspecting him of treason. A friend of the khan then killed Dmitri. Few among those who were close to Dmitri lamented him. Tsaritsa Marina at once found a new protector in the person of the Don Cossack ataman Ivan Zarutsky. Presumably in this case her motive was love, as well as politics.

With Dmitri's removal from the stage Vladislav appeared to have a good chance of establishing himself firmly in power. But when the specter disappeared Sigismund changed his mind and instead of sending his son to Moscow offered himself for the Russian throne. This changed the whole picture. The Muscovite embassy insisted on the conditions of the preliminary agreement being honored. When they refused to budge from this position, their leading members, including Bishop Philaret, were arrested by Sigismund's order. Russia had now to face the threat of subjection to a foreign ruler and one of different religious denomination at that. This the nation was not ready to tolerate. The response to Sigismund's action was a desperate effort of the Russians to put their house in order by themselves.

The first calls for national unity were issued by Russian church leaders—Patriarch Hermogen (ordained in 1606), and abbot Dionysius of the Trinity Monastery. Each of them wrote letters to various Russian political groups, to cities and rural communes, and to the people at large, urging them to organize an army and to oust the Poles from Moscow. When the Poles discovered Hermo-

gen's activities they put him in prison (where he died of malnutrition in February 1612), but his work was done. In the summer
of 1611 the new Russian army appeared before Moscow. It consisted of three groups: the service Cossacks, the Don Cossacks,
and the gentry militia. In June an agreement had been reached
between these parties vesting supreme authority, Cossack fashion,
in the army's general council. The executive power was given
to the "triumvirs"—Prince Dmitri Trubetskoy, representing the
service Cossacks; Ivan Zarutsky, ataman of the Don Cossacks;
and Procopius Liapunov, leader of the gentry militia. Before long,
however, dissension arose between the Don Cossacks and the
gentry, and Liapunov was killed by the Cossacks. The gentry militia then disbanded, and the Cossacks remained alone to face the
Poles. Marina, who took an active part in politics beside Zarutsky,
now succeeded in persuading the Don Cossacks to proclaim her
one-year-old son Ivan the tsar-designate of Russia. The Cossacks
had no proper equipment and were not strong enough to storm the
Kremlin, so they made preparations for a long siege. Their chance
of success, however, was slim since King Sigismund was known to
be about to send a new Polish army to relieve the Polish garrison
at Moscow.

Losing faith in the Cossacks, the gentry and the towns now resolved to take matters into their own hands. The prime mover in
this was a Nizhni Novgorod merchant, Kuzma Minin, an able
financier and a man of indomitable energy. While he took on himself the business management of the drive, a boyar, Prince Dmitri
Pozharsky, assumed command of the troops. In the spring of 1612
the new army was concentrated at Iaroslavl on the upper Volga
and a session of the zemsky sobor was convoked there. News
reached Iaroslavl in July that the Polish relief army was on its
way to Moscow. Pozharsky too hastened to the city. As his army
approached, the Don Cossacks retreated south. The service Cossacks held their ground but showed no desire to join forces with
Pozharsky. The latter, in his turn, was suspicious of the Cossacks.
However, at the last moment, when the Poles attacked Pozharsky's
camp in force, the Cossacks rushed to his assistance. The Polish
relief army was turned back (October 22). The Polish garrison in
the Kremlin, their food and other supplies exhausted, had no
alternative but to surrender. Moscow was back in Russian hands.

2. *The Romanov dynasty*

In January 1613 a solemn session of the zemsky sobor was convoked in Moscow to elect a new tsar; representatives of all groups except the serfs and slaves were present. After careful consideration of the possible candidates, young Michael Romanov, son of Bishop Philaret, was nominated. His candidacy proved especially popular among the townspeople and the service Cossacks. A two-week period was set for presenting objections to Michael. None were submitted, and on February 21, 1613, he was unanimously elected tsar. Michael was sixteen at the time, a youth amiable but passive. His father was still imprisoned in Poland, and the decision whether Michael should accept the throne or not had to be made by his mother, the nun Martha, with whom Michael was living in Kostroma province. She agreed to let her son rule on condition that the zemsky sobor remain permanently in session to assist the young tsar in his difficult task. Thus the Romanov dynasty was established, which was destined to rule Russia for three centuries.

The task of restoring order in Russia was no light one. The nation was poverty-stricken, its resources all but exhausted, its economy in decay. Armed bands still roamed the country; the Poles held Smolensk and might be expected to start a new offensive against Moscow at any moment; the Swedes had taken Novgorod and were besieging Pskov; the English contemplated seizing the White Sea region; Zarutsky with Marina at his side had established himself in Astrakhan and was busily trying to build up a federation of the Cossack armies against Moscow. It was only through the concerted effort of the whole nation, guided by the zemsky sobor, that the most urgent problems of the day were solved one by one. The damage was too vast to be repaired at once. The new government needed money, and quantities of it. Old taxes had to be restored and a number of new taxes imposed to enable the administration to function.

As regards foreign affairs, the Cossack danger was eliminated first. Zarutsky and Marina were ousted from Astrakhan in 1614 and their army defeated. They fled to the Iaik River but got no support from the Iaik Cossack Army when the Muscovite troops arrived on their heels. Seized by the streltsy, Zarutsky and Marina as well as Marina's son, Tsarevich Ivan, were brought to Moscow. The two Ivans—Zarutsky and the tsarevich—were executed; Marina, defiant to the end, died in prison. The upshot of these events was that the Don Cossacks proved willing to recognize the protectorate of the tsar over their host (1614).

In 1617 peace was made with Sweden. The Swedes agreed to return Novgorod but kept Ingria and Karelia, so that Russia remained cut off from the Baltic. The next year a fourteen-and-a-half year armistice was concluded with Poland. Vladislav did not give up his claims to the throne of Moscow (his father had withdrawn his own claims by that time); the Poles were to keep Smolensk. An exchange of prisoners was stipulated, the Poles specifically agreeing to free Bishop Philaret.

Soon after Philaret's return he was installed in the patriarchal see which had been purposely left vacant after the death of Patriarch Hermogen. Philaret was given the title of great sovereign, which had so far been applied only to the tsar. This was a reflection not only of the family tie between the patriarch and the tsar but also of Philaret's notion of the dignity of his office. With Philaret's return everybody felt that Russia had at last found her master. Philaret, now over sixty, was an ambitious and irritable man, with a strong will and marked ability as a statesman. The tsar regarded him with filial awe, and the courtiers feared him. While Philaret did not hesitate to take the initiative in both church and state affairs, he cooperated closely with the zemsky sobor. In cultural matters he was very conservative and suspicious of the West and western ways. He was openly hostile to Roman Catholicism, as might be expected after his own and Russia's painful experiences in the Time of Trouble. Protestants were less frowned upon.

A number of foreign merchants and experts of various kinds settled in Moscow in this period, and this foreign colony was to grow steadily. In 1652 all the foreigners were ordered to move from the city to a nearby area which became known as the German Suburb (all north Europeans were called Germans in Russia then). This soon became a prosperous town, a corner of Europe within Muscovy, with a life of its own. While several Lutheran and Calvinist churches were built there, no Roman Catholic churches were allowed, although there were Roman Catholics among the inhabitants of the Suburb. In the reign of Tsar Michael a prominent foreign merchant and industrialist residing in Russia was the Dutchman Andrew Vinius, who established Russia's first modern iron works at Tula in 1632. That same year King Sigismund of Poland died, the term of the Polish armistice expired, and a new war started between Russia and Poland, whose end Patriarch Philaret would not live to see. The Russians tried to recover Smolensk but failed. In 1634 a peace was signed which forced Moscow to pay 20,000 rubles as indemnity and renounce her claims to Smolensk. For his part, the new Polish king Vladislav renounced his claim to the Muscovite throne and recognized Michael as tsar. The Russians rightly attributed their failure in the war to their backwardness in training and technique. More western technicians and army officers were now engaged and the Tula iron works enlarged.

Michael died in 1645 and his son Alexis was proclaimed tsar, coming to the throne, like his father, at sixteen. Alexis had a lively mind and pleasant personality. An adept at falconry and, toward the end of his life, an admirer of the theater, he was sympathetic to western culture although he took no drastic steps to impose it on the nation. During the first years of his reign he interfered little in state affairs, handing the reins of government to his tutor, the boyar Boris Morozov, who became his brother-in-law by marrying a sister of Alexis' wife. Morozov became highly unpopular because of the tax on salt he introduced in 1646 as well as for his harsh methods of administration and his nepotism. An uprising took place in Moscow in 1648. To placate the populace, Tsar Alexis was obliged to dismiss Morozov, and two of the latter's assistants were executed. A new session of the zemsky sobor was called to consider the grievances of the people and to prepare a new code of laws to rectify them. The code was approved by the sobor in 1649, and two thousand copies were printed—an innovation, since previous codes had been in manuscript. The new code guaranteed more even distribution of taxes to the town communities and satisfied the gentry by removing all restrictions on the right of estate owners to reclaim runaway serfs, which amounted to the final establishment of serfdom. On the whole it may be said that the new code of laws was meant to satisfy the demands, and to protect the interests, of the gentry and merchants rather than of the boyar aristocracy and the peasants. This was in line with the policy initiated by Ivan

IV and continued by the zemsky sobor under Michael. Irrespective of its social tendencies, the new code was an important document of jurisprudence and served as a basis for Russian legislation for many years.

3. The Cossacks and Siberia

A significant feature of Russian history of this period was the expansion to the east. While economic recovery in Muscovy itself was slow and the nation was still threatened by its western neighbors, the Russians quietly built themselves a new empire in Siberia. Simultaneously, the Cossack armies of the Don, the Terek, and the Iaik continued to grow, and while they were at that time independent or in any case autonomous, they served the purpose of Russian colonization in the east just the same. In fact, there was a direct connection between the Cossack and the Siberian expansion, since the service Cossacks played a large role in the Russian advance in Siberia, and from time to time detachments of free Cossacks joined them, lured by tales of the fabulous riches of the new country.

In 1614 Tsar Michael presented the Don Cossacks with a new banner, symbol of his protectorate over them. But the Cossacks did not become direct subjects of the tsar or have to take any oath of allegiance. The Don Army remained a separate state and the Muscovite government dealt with it through its Department of Foreign Affairs (called then the Department of the Embassies). On many occasions Moscow tried to restrain the Don Cossacks from raids on the Crimea and the Turkish possessions, fearful lest they involve the tsar in a war with Turkey for which Moscow was not prepared. Since the Cossacks paid no attention to the tsar's admonitions, Patriarch Philaret, in 1629, threatened them with excommunication. The next year the tsar sent an envoy to the Don to demand obedience. The envoy was executed by order of the Cossack Circle. Moscow broke off diplomatic relations, but no further measures were taken since the government's attention was diverted by the Polish war of 1632–34. In 1637 the Cossacks seized the Turkish fortress of Azov, which barred their entrance to the Sea of Azov. Cossack flotillas of light boats then raided the shores of the Azov and even of the Black Sea. A Turkish army was sent to retake the fortress, but the Cossacks repulsed this attack (1641) and asked Tsar Michael to take possession of Azov and send Muscovite troops to hold it. The zemsky sobor, however, advised against accepting Azov, arguing that Moscow was not in a position to start a war against Turkey; state finances had already been overstrained by the Polish war. The Cossacks reluctantly abandoned Azov.

In Siberia the west Siberian khanate was the only large-scale organized state. After its conquest, there was no further barrier to Russian expansion, for the various native tribes of heterogeneous extraction were not in a position to prevent the advance of the newcomers. The Tatars had been the only ruling clan in the west Siberian khanate; they collected tribute from the Finnish and Turkish tribes subordinate to them. Those tribes now had to pay approximately the same amount of tribute to the Russians. Siberia's main attraction for the Russians was the furs. Small bands of adventurers—trappers, Cossacks, fur traders—moved quickly east along the network of Siberian rivers and their tributaries. In addition to the produce of their own enterprises they collected furs from the native tribes. As soon as an area was explored the Moscow government sent its own agents and troops, and built forts at strategic points.

The main objective of Moscow's Siberian policies at that time was to exploit the fur resources. Private merchants had to pay a tax in kind to the government on the furs they exported from Siberia. And tribute in furs was regularly collected from the natives. Since the proceeds of the tribute were of great value to the tsar's government, it assumed a policy of enlightened self-interest by trying to protect the natives against injury by Russian merchants and traders as well as against abuses by the local agents of administration. Actually, of course, it was difficult for the central government to control its local agents, and the natives were often subjected to illegal exploitation.

The Russian drive eastward across the continent of Asia was in many ways like the westward drive of the Anglo-Saxons across the American continent. The two movements started about the same time: Ermak's Siberian venture took place almost simultaneously with the first settlement on Roanoke Island; and Jamestown in Virginia was founded in 1607, three years after the building of Tomsk, in western Siberia. Iakutsk in eastern Siberia was founded in 1632, six years before New Haven, Connecticut. Russian expansion in Siberia had, however, a much more rapid tempo than the American progress to the Pacific. By 1648 the Cossack Semen Dezhnev had already reached the strait dividing Asia and America which later received the name of Bering. On the other hand, the numerical growth of the white population was more substantial in America. In 1662 there were about 70,000 Russians in Siberia and in 1783 about 1,000,000. The corresponding figures for the white population of what is now the United States are 200,000 (1690) and 3,200,000 (1789). The sparsity of the Russian colonization in Siberia may be explained by the fact that in the early phase there was no rapid influx of agriculturists. There was so much virgin land closer to central Russia in the middle Volga and the upper Don regions that the peasant had no incentive to travel farther east. To ensure the raising of crops in Western Siberia the government had to attract new settlers by subsidies and special privileges, such as exemption from taxes for several years. Another method was forcible colonization; political offenders and criminals were sent to Siberia to till land and do other kinds of work.

Around 1640 the Russians penetrated into the Amur River valley, and small parties descended the Amur to the Sea of Okhotsk. By 1650 they had occupied a good part of the Amur River basin. This was bound to lead to international complications. It was the first time in their progress through Siberia since the conquest of the khanate of western Siberia that the Russians had come into contact with a large and well organized state. The native population of the Amur basin were Manchu subjects and paid tribute to the Manchu emperor (this was the period of the extension of the Manchu dynasty's control over China). A series of clashes took place between the Russian Cossacks and the Manchu troops, but it was not until the 1680's that Chinese troops appeared in force in the upper Amur valley. Further Russian expansion in this direction was thus checked.

4. The Ukrainian revolution and the union of Ukraine and Muscovy

While relations between Moscow and the Don Cossacks were not always friendly, Poland had her own troubles with the Zaporozhie

Cossacks. In her case, however, the situation was much more serious since Zaporozhie was but one facet of the Ukrainian problem. It will be recalled that at the time of the Lublin union between Poland and Lithuania (1569) Ukraine was incorporated into Poland. Large estates of the Polish magnates were then established there, and serfdom was tightened, much to the dissatisfaction of the Ukrainian peasants. Economic exploitation was aggravated by religious pressure. In 1596 the union of the west Russian church with Rome was announced at a convention in Brest-Litovsk. Actually, the majority of the delegates were against it, being loyal to the traditional Greek Orthodox denomination. But most of the bishops recognized the authority of the pope, and the Polish government confirmed the validity of the Uniate Church; in fact, it attempted to dissolve the Greek Orthodox Church in Belorussia and Ukraine altogether. Church buildings were handed over to the Uniate clergy. Books and pamphlets published by Greek Orthodox scholars against the church union were confiscated. It should be added that by this time most of the west Russian princes who until the middle of the 16th century had been staunch defenders of Greek Orthodoxy had been converted to Roman Catholicism. It was the Zaporozhie Cossacks who now assumed the role of protectors of the Greek Orthodox faith in Ukraine. In 1620 an Orthodox church convention gathered in Kiev in which the Cossacks took an active part. Patriarch Theophanes of Jerusalem ordained several new bishops, and the west Russian Orthodox hierarchy was thus restored. The Polish government reluctantly had to recognize the existence of the Greek Orthodox Church in Ukraine, even if it granted it but limited rights.

While church matters were thus temporarily settled, the gulf between the Polish lords and Ukrainian peasants remained open. The latter were unwilling to accept serfdom, and a number of uprisings occurred in which the Zaporozhie Cossacks took a leading part. Until 1648 all of these uprisings were crushed by the Poles. That year the movement assumed the proportions of a national revolution.

A dynamic leader appeared in the person of Bogdan Khmelnitsky, whose family belonged to the Ukrainian gentry. Offended by a Polish squire and finding no protection in the Polish courts, Bogdan went to Zaporozhie and eventually was elected hetman.

He was a shrewd politician, an able diplomat, and a well educated man. To ensure military success he made an agreement with the Crimean khan against the Poles. After the choice Polish troops had twice been defeated by the combined forces of the Cossacks and the Crimean Tatars, the peasants rose against their landlords all over Ukraine. Ghastly atrocities were committed by each side against the other. The plight of the Jews, whom the peasants considered financial agents of the Polish regime, was especially tragic. In 1649 a peace treaty was signed. Poland recognized the Cossacks as an autonomous army, though not to be over 40,000 strong. Polish troops were not allowed to enter the Ukraine, but the Polish lords were to keep their estates. Serfdom was not abolished. These terms were not acceptable to the peasants, many of whom accused the Cossacks of betraying their interests. Thousands of peasants migrated to the boundaries of the Muscovite state and were settled on the banks of the Donets River.

On their part, the Poles considered the conditions of the peace humiliating. War broke out again. This time the Cossacks were betrayed by the Tatars and suffered a severe defeat. Bogdan now asked Tsar Alexis to intervene and to take the Ukrainian Cossack Army under his protection. The Muscovite leaders were at first reluctant to take this action since they understood that it would mean a new war between Moscow and Poland. The zemsky sobor debated the question for two years (1651–53). Finally the Ukraine was taken under the tsar's protection. On January 18, 1654, the general Cossack council which gathered in Pereiaslav unanimously voted to recognize the tsar's suzerainty over the army. Two months later the Cossack envoys came to Moscow to negotiate a detailed treaty of union. Its main provisions were that the Cossack Army was to consist of 60,000 men; all the rights and privileges given by the Polish kings to the Cossacks, the Ukrainian gentry, and the towns were confirmed; and the hetman was given authority to treat with foreign powers except Poland and Turkey, the Tsar's special authorization being required for any negotiation with these two. While the legal nature of the treaty is open to different interpretations, it amounted in any case to the end of Polish landlordism and to far-reaching autonomy of Ukraine under the tsar's protection.

As was expected, war broke out between Muscovy and Ukraine

on the one hand and Poland on the other. During its first years things went in favor of the Russians and Ukrainians. The Cossacks freed all Ukraine from the Poles; the Russians conquered most of Belorussia. Alexis now assumed the title of "tsar of all the Great, the Little, and the White Russias." However, after the death of Bogdan Khmelnitsky (1657) dissension arose between the Muscovites and the highest officers of the Cossack Host, many of whom were of gentry origin and favored the Polish constitution. Hetman Ivan Vygovsky went over to the Polish side. At that point the Swedes in their turn attacked Poland, and war started between Muscovy and Sweden over the division of the spoils, neither side achieving a decisive victory. The Poles knew how to take advantage of the dissension among their enemies and regained much of the ground they had lost. After thirteen years of conflict which exhausted both sides an armistice was signed in 1667. Moscow gave up White Russia but kept Smolensk. The Ukraine was divided in two, the Right Bank (west of the Dnieper) being returned to Poland and the Left Bank (east of the Dnieper) remaining united with Moscow. Poland ceded the city of Kiev (on the Right Bank) to Moscow for two years, and in 1686 agreed to cede it permanently to Russia.

5. *The religious crisis*

In connection with Ukrainian affairs a serious religious crisis developed in Muscovy. It had been latent for many years and now came into the open and reached a climax.

It will be recalled that by 1550 the Muscovite church had consolidated itself in both ideology and organization and seemed to have become the foundation of "Holy Russia." However, the horrors of the oprichnina and even more the catastrophe of the Time of Trouble, which brought Russia to the brink of ruin, shattered the nation's self-confidence. While order was gradually restored economically, confusion persisted in spiritual matters. Increased contact with foreigners raised Russian interest in western religious thought. Few Russians at that time showed any inclination toward Roman Catholicism but many were influenced by Protestantism. The Russians were forbidden by their government to leave the Greek Orthodox Church, and cases of open conversion to Protestantism were rare, but there are indications in the sources that a number of government officials as well as merchants were in secret sympathy with Protestant doctrine.

The overwhelming majority of the people still clung to their traditional church. However, while they considered Greek Orthodoxy the foundation of Russia's spiritual life, many church leaders admitted the necessity of certain reforms within the church as well as of a new definition of the relations between church and state. On the latter point, it was felt by some prelates that Russia's misfortunes were partly caused by the passivity of the church during periods of political crises. It was argued that the church must offer stronger guidance to the nation. Patriarch Philaret's assumption of the title of great sovereign was intended as such a move; but the next two patriarchs abandoned the claim. As regards reforms, it was felt that the work of correcting and editing the church ritual and prayer books started by Maxim the Greek should be continued. Abbot Dionysius of the Trinity Monastery, an admirer of Maxim's writings, was entrusted with the task. He was handicapped, however, by his assistants' lack of scholarship; few Muscovite clergymen of that time knew Greek and Latin. It became clear to Dionysius that the advice of Greek and Ukrainian scholars was needed. But many conservative Muscovites were reluctant to recognize the superiority of either Ukrainians or Greeks. In fact, Dionysius' position amounted to admission of the failure of the Third Rome idea; Moscow was found wanting. Time was required to overcome the opposition of the conservatives, and until the middle of the century the reform developed slowly; then, all at once, it assumed a revolutionary tempo under the new patriarch, Nikon, a prelate of dynamic and impetuous personality and dictatorial inclinations, who was filled with a sense of the dignity of his office and the historical importance of his task.

Nikon was born in 1605 of a peasant family in the district of Nizhni Novgorod. He started his ecclesiastical career as a village priest, but after the death of his children he persuaded his wife to take the veil while he became a monk. In 1648 he was ordained metropolitan of Novgorod. When four years later the patriarchal throne became vacant it was offered to Nikon. He agreed to accept only on condition that the tsar and the bishops promise "to obey him in everything as their shepherd and father." In accordance with Byzantine doctrine as expressed by Patriarch Photius in the 9th century, Nikon believed that patriarch and tsar were to rule Orthodox society jointly, and that the patriarch, "the living image of Christ," was more important than the tsar. Like Patriarch Philaret, Nikon was granted the title of great sovereign. A Grecophile and partisan of reform, Nikon brooked no delay in correcting the text of the church books and in changing the Russian church ritual wherever it was found to differ from the Greek and Ukrainian. He was in constant consultation with the eastern patriarchs and brought a number of Greek and Ukrainian scholars to Moscow to assist him. The council of Russian bishops approved Nikon's actions in spite of the fact that some of its members doubted their wisdom. One bishop protested openly and was promptly exiled. Within four years (1653–56) the Russian prayer books and liturgy had been altered in many ways.

While the essence of Nikon's reform was religious, there was a political motive behind it too. The reform coincided with the Ukrainian crisis. It was believed in Moscow that the adjustment of the Russian liturgy to the Ukrainian would make it easier for Ukrainians at large to accept the tsar's protectorate and for the Kievan clergy in particular to shift their allegiance from the patriarch of Constantinople to that of Moscow.

Most of the changes introduced by Nikon dealt with the religious ritual. The most noticeable change in everyday religious symbols was the new way of making the sign of the cross. Nikon ordered believers to join three fingers, to symbolize the Trinity, instead of two fingers after the ancient custom in Russia (to symbolize the dual nature of Christ). Changes in the text of the prayer books concerned not only ritual but the wording of the dogma as well. Through old copyists' mistakes a word had been added in the Creed, as read in the churches before Nikon, to the characterization of the Holy Ghost: "vivifying" had become "true and vivifying." This was now eliminated. To the modern reader such matters may seem small and unimportant, but to the Orthodox believer of the old days church ritual was the symbol and vehicle of religious emotion. The feeling of the faithful was associated with every detail of the church service, and every word in the prayer book had its traditional meaning. Besides, the alterations were made by Nikon in a sudden and peremptory manner, and it is not surprising that many believers proved ready to defend their right to worship in their own way against the orders of both the church and lay authorities. Moreover, some of Nikon's opponents pointed out, and rightly, that the work of his editors and correctors was at times hasty and superficial, and that on certain occasions it was not the old verified Greek manuscripts which served as the basis for correction but recent editions of the Greek service books printed in Italy, which themselves were not devoid of mistakes.

At first the Russians seemed stunned by the innovations, and few churchmen raised their voices against them. Before long, however, the anti-Nikonian movement gained momentum. Harsh measures of suppression only added fuel to the fire. Priests, monks, aristocratic ladies, merchants, peasants were aroused, and many proved ready to become martyrs for the cause. Outstanding among the leaders of the Old Ritualists, as the anti-Nikonians eventually became known, was the archpriest Avvakum, a man of vast energy and great spiritual powers, intransigent and defiant, for whom life outside the true church had no meaning. In 1653 Avvakum was arrested and exiled to Siberia. Many other members of the opposition movement were subjected to various punishments. On the surface, Nikon seemed to be winning. But now his relations with Tsar Alexis became strained. As time went by, the tsar, in spite of all his respect for the patriarch, had grown weary of the latter's tutelage. The boyars, who resented the rise of a plebeian to the highest position in the state, in their turn objected to Nikon's interference in state affairs. Nikon considered the new independent attitude of the tsar a breach of the original conditions stipulated by him and accepted by the tsar and boyars at the time of his election to the patriarchal see. Consequently, on July 20, 1658, Nikon laid down the patriarchal insignia and left for the monastery which he had built for himself about forty miles west of Moscow known as New Jerusalem. While he ceased to perform the duties of a patriarch, he did not resign from the office. A protracted crisis in church administration followed, and the tsar temporarily took actual control over church administration with the assistance of the senior bishops.

This break with the patriarch did not affect the tsar's basic attitude toward the church reform. Nikon was out, but the church remained Nikonian. However, as Alexis was of a milder disposition than Nikon, he rescinded some of the latter's punitive orders against the leaders of the Old Ritualists. In 1664 Avvakum was allowed to return to Moscow. Embittered by his exile and elated by the fall of the patriarch, Avvakum refused to make any concessions to the official church, and no reconciliation between the two church groups followed. Meanwhile a Great Church Council was convoked in Moscow in 1666, in which the eastern patriarchs participated. Two of them—those of Alexandria and of Antioch—attended in person; the other two—those of Constantinople and of Jerusalem—sent their legates. The council had two main tasks on its agenda: to try Nikon for abandoning the patriarchal see, and to make a decision on the church reform. By unanimous vote Nikon was demoted to a monk of the lowest grade and ordered deported to a remote monastery in northern Russia. With patriarchal see thus made vacant a new patriarch was ordained. It was not until 1681 that Nikon was set free and allowed to return to New Jerusalem; he died on the way. While the council sentenced Nikon, it upheld his church reform. More than that, it anathematized the Old Ritualists and by this action made the schism final.

On the basis of the decisions of the Great Council, both church and lay authorities in Russia initiated a harsh policy of repression against the Old Ritualists. Several of their leaders were sentenced to death. Avvakum was burned at the stake in 1681. When the monks of the Solovki Monastery on the White Sea island of that name refused to accept the new ritual, troops were sent against them. It was only after an eight-year siege that the government's soldiers succeeded in breaking the monks' resistance (1668–76). Great numbers of Old Ritualists now began to think that the end of the world was approaching and the Antichrist about to appear. Exasperated by persecutions, some of them became hysterical and preferred dying to waiting passively for the end. Hundreds would confine themselves, together with their spiritual leaders, in wooden barns and set fire to the building. It is estimated that over 20,000 perished through such self-immolation. By 1700 the wave of suicidal hysteria had subsided and after that only a few cases of it were recorded.

6. *Peasants, Cossacks, and Streltsy*

The basic causes of the schism with the Old Ritualists were doctrinal and psychological. However, when the break became final, the Old Believers found themselves in sharp opposition to the Moscow government, and hence their movement attracted the sympathies of all who were dissatisfied with the Moscow regime for their own reasons. Generally speaking, the period 1650–1700 saw the growth of social and political discontent in Russia. In 1662 there were riots over the government's monetary policy and the resulting inflation. Eight years later the Don Cossacks led a peasant uprising which all but shook the foundations of the Muscovite state. In 1682 the streltsy mutinied in Moscow.

The confirmation of serfdom in the Code of Laws of 1649 was bitterly resented by the peasants affected by it. More and more peasants abandoned their homes, and in some cases their families, and escaped south to "the wild prairie." A number went to the Don area. The influx of newcomers created a serious problem for the Don Cossack Army and resulted in a social cleavage between "old" and "new" Cossacks. The former, also known as the "house-owning Cossacks" had priority on the best fishing grounds. Most of these grew prosperous, accumulating wealth not only from fishing but also from war booty of earlier expeditions. Now they became well settled and wanted to enjoy things as they were. The "new Cossacks," or the "Naked" (i.e. poor), found themselves in a precarious position. Many of them had been farmers and wanted to continue farming, but no tilling was allowed by the Army Circle because the "old Cossacks" were afraid that the transformation of the Don area into agricultural country would open the way to landlordism and serfdom. The "Naked" seemed to have no means of improving their condition except war or raiding. In 1667 a band of them under the vigorous leadership of Stephen Razin, whom they had elected their ataman, undertook a successful maritime expedition across the Caspian Sea against Persia and returned with loads of valuable booty. As a result, Razin became a popular leader among all the Cossacks, new and old. Encouraged by his success he now conceived a daring plan of war against Moscow. He rightly expected that the peasant tenants on the estates of the boyars and gentry would give him all the support they could. Razin's strategy was based on seizing the Volga waterway as pivot for his operations, which started in May 1670. Taken unawares, the Moscow government had at first no army strong enough to stop the invaders. The Cossacks were able to overcome the garrisons of the cities along the Volga one by one, starting with Tsaritsyn. Before long, Astrakhan, Saratov, and Samara were in their possession. They executed the commanding officers of each garrison, as well as all the boyars and rich merchants they could lay their hands on. The captured streltsy and other rank-and-file soldiers were invited to join the rebel army. The municipal government in the conquered cities was then reorganized in accordance with Cossack principles; in each town the general assembly of the citizens was put in charge, all municipal officers were to be elected by the assembly. The same pattern was followed in the administration of the rural districts the Cossacks seized. Before long the peasants rose against their landlords on the west side of the middle Volga; the Turkish and Finnish tribes both west and east of the Volga joined the movement too. His army swelled by irregulars, Razin seemed ready to march on Moscow itself. But by September 1670 the Moscow government succeeded in putting a well equipped army in the field, a good part of it trained by foreign officers. In October, after bitter fighting, the tsar's army broke the resistance of Razin's motley troops. Razin fled to the Don and the remnants of his army dispersed. Punitive expeditions gradually restored the tsar's authority everywhere by harsh measures. If Razin counted on obtaining a refuge in the Don area, he miscalculated. The "house-owning" Cossacks refused him support and, contrary to the basic principle of the Don constitution, seized him and handed him over to the Muscovite authorities. He was executed in the Red Square in June 1671. His popularity did not die with him, however, and he became a favorite figure in peasant and Cossack song and folklore. To guard against any repetition of his exploit in future the Moscow government now decided to curb the liberties of the Don. All the Don Cossacks had to take an oath of allegiance to the tsar and thus became his subjects. The internal autonomy of the Don Army was not abrogated, however.

The sharp social cleavage which reached its climax in the Razin rebellion, together with the schism in the Russian church, undermined the constitutional foundations of the Moscow government. Owing to the lack of cooperation between various social and religious groups, the tsar's administration became more authoritarian than in the first half of the 17th century. The zemsky sobor now seemed superfluous to the Muscovite leaders. In fact, it had held no full session since 1654. Whenever necessary, special committees of experts were convoked instead. The boyar duma continued to function, but the principle of genealogical seniority and precedent in appointments of higher army and administrative officers was abolished in 1682, which freed the tsar from restrictions in selecting his assistants.

Unfortunately for Muscovy, just about this time troubles occurred in the Romanov family which for a while lowered the prestige of the dynasty. Tsar Alexis married twice; his first wife was Maria Miloslavsky, the second Natalie Naryshkin. Following his second marriage the court became divided into two factions, one centered around the Miloslavskys and the other around the Naryshkins. When Alexis died in 1676, he was succeeded by his eldest son by the first marriage, the fourteen-year-old Theodore. Theodore was a well intentioned youth and received a good education, but illness prevented him from taking any active part in the government. When he died childless, in April 1682, the strife between the two court parties came into the open. Next in line by seniority was Theodore's brother Ivan, a sickly and apathetic youth of fifteen, incapable of ruling. In contrast, their half-brother Peter (Natalie Naryshkin's son) was a healthy, vigorous, and intelligent boy of ten. It was obvious to many high officials that in the interest of the dynasty as well as of Russia preference should be given to Peter. The patriarch too favored Peter and urged his selection before a huge crowd of notables and commoners who gathered in the Red Square. Peter was proclaimed tsar.

Ivan did not mind being passed over, but his elder sister Sophia, then twenty-five, was not willing to accept the decision. She was an ambitious and energetic young woman who now became the leader of the Miloslavsky party and decided to use the streltsy as her tool. In Theodore's reign the discipline of the streltsy corps had become extremely lax. They were allowed in peacetime to engage in trade and crafts since their pay was not enough to live on. Now they complained of not receiving regularly such pay as was due them, since their commanding officers cheated them and kept part of the pay roll money for themselves; besides, the officers compelled the streltsy to work for them. The administration satisfied some of these claims, which made the streltsy even bolder. In addition, quite a number of them sympathized with the Old Ritualists and opposed the government on that ground. In short, in April 1682 the streltsy were on the verge of mutiny, and it was not difficult for Sophia and her partisans to incite them to action. Rumors were circulated that the Naryshkins had killed Tsarevich Ivan, and the streltsy rushed to the palace. They were baffled at first when they saw the live Ivan standing timidly beside Peter, but they ran wild just the same and killed several boyars of the Naryshkin party. Next they demanded that Ivan be proclaimed tsar together with Peter and that Tsarevna Sophia be recognized as regent. Thus the coup d'état was completed. Sophia soon realized that her government was actually at the mercy of the streltsy. They now demanded that the Old Ritualists be allowed to submit their case to the government. A discussion between the leaders of the two church groups was held in the Hall of Facets in the Kremlin, in the presence of the two tsars, the regent, and the highest church and state authorities. No decision was taken, but the Old Ritualists boasted that their arguments prevailed. Presently Sophia received information that the streltsy were preparing to seize power openly. She withdrew with the two tsars to a suburban estate and summoned the gentry militia as well as several army regiments. The streltsy took fright, and order was restored (September 1682).

During Sophia's regency, which lasted seven years, her closest associate was Prince Basil Golitsyn, an enlightened aristocrat and an admirer of western civilization. He contemplated far-reaching reforms, said to include abolition of serfdom. But his foreign policy interfered with internal stability. He was in favor of a close understanding with Poland, and in 1686 a permanent peace was signed with that country; by its provisions Moscow agreed to join the coalition of Christian powers against Turkey, in which Poland played an important role. As her share in the coalition Moscow undertook to attack the Khanate of the Crimea. In 1687 Golitsyn personally led the Muscovite army, supported by the Ukrainians under their hetman, to the Crimean isthmus but failed to defeat the Tatars. The second campaign, two years later, had no better results. Simultaneously with the failure in the south, Moscow's foreign policy met a check in the Far East. In 1689 a treaty was concluded in Nerchinsk between Muscovy and China by which the

Russians abandoned their claims on the Amur River Valley. Russia thus lost direct access to the Sea of Okhotsk.

7. First steps of Peter the Great

The failures in foreign policy hurt the prestige of Tsarevna Sophia's government. Meanwhile, Sophia realized that Peter, the younger of the tsars, in whose name she ruled, was nearing his majority. She knew, as did all her courtiers, that Peter was endowed with extraordinary energy, intellectual curiosity, and a lively temperament. It was clear that as soon as he came of age he would seize power for himself.

During Sophia's rule Peter lived in a village near Moscow. He grew up outside the influence of the palace, and left to his own resources he made the acquaintance of a number of Dutch technicians from the German Suburb of Moscow. From them he learned all they were able to tell him about shipbuilding and shipping, which greatly interested him. Peter also studied arithmetic and geometry. He organized among his playmates two youth regiments and gave them regular training.

This period of Peter's life was brought to an end by the news that agents of Tsarevna Sophia were preparing an attempt against his life. He was only seventeen years old at this time but he succeeded in carrying out a coup d'état with the help of the Naryshkin party. Tsarevna Sophia was arrested and shut up in a convent in 1689; Prince Golitsyn was deported to a remote town in northern Russia.

The young Tsar Peter began to occupy himself on a larger scale with military and naval matters. He did some sailing in the White Sea near Archangel. The direction of government affairs fell to Peter's mother and her group of supporters, among whom the patriarch played an important role. The Polish alliance continued to be the cornerstone of Russian policy, and in 1695 war with Turkey was resumed. This gave Peter the opportunity to apply his military and technical knowledge. Anxious to avoid the military errors of Sophia's administration, he chose for his point of assault the Turkish fortress of Azov at the mouth of the Don. Prominent in the army Peter led into the field were the two guard regiments formed from the play detachments of his boyhood. In Voronezh Peter rapidly constructed ships to descend the Don. The first attack upon Azov was unsuccessful, but the next year, 1696, Peter captured the fortress. The seizure of Azov he regarded as a successful test of his new army and his new military methods.

Now Peter took the reins into his own hands and carried out a policy of close political and cultural contact with Europe.

8. *Economic development*

The economic development of Russia was painfully affected by the crisis of the late 16th century and even more so by the devastations of the Time of Trouble. The wounds were not healed until about 1630; then a new upward trend became noticeable in most branches of economic life. Both domestic and foreign trade expanded rapidly, connecting areas of production with markets. Russia's national economy was able gradually to overcome local isolation and to assume an organic unity.

Rye in central Russia and flax in the Novgorod area continued to be the two main staple agricultural products. Cattle breeding made considerable progress, supplying the market with butter, lard, and hides. Small peasant farms prevailed in the north, and large landed estates operated with serf and slave labor in central Russia. Among the various kinds of industries, the extraction of potash, tar, and pitch in the wooded regions was important. Small-scale peasant shops competed with larger establishments. Peasant women wove linen cloth and burlap in their homes, and the men in some localities manufactured nails and various metal and other articles. This type of home or cottage industry became known in Russia as *kustarnaia* industry; the term is said to derive from the German *Kunst*, "art," "artifice." Side by side with the cottage industries and crafts there grew larger industrial concerns, each operating numbers of smaller shops. The largest enterprise of this sort belonged to the Stroganovs. In the remote area in which they operated, they were able to survive the Time of Trouble, and they now expanded their activities. They owned salt and ironworks, and manufactured potash and tar, employing 10,000 free workers and 5,000 serfs in their shops. They also traded in furs, fish, and grain.

Not only the middle-class industrialists but the tsar and many of the boyars also developed crafts and industries on their estates. After 1630 Dutch industrialists were invited by the government to build ironworks to supply the armament industries. These were

modern in type (for that time) and introduced new techniques and
large-scale production. Tula in central Russia and the Olonets
region in the north were the two main centers of iron production
until around 1680, when the attention of both the government and
private metallurgists shifted to the Ural area. Foreign businessmen
also built a glass factory and a paper mill near Moscow, as well as
velvet and silk factories.

Foreigners played an important role too in Russian commerce.
Russia's foreign trade with western countries was almost entirely
in the hands of foreign merchants. The maritime trade via the
White Sea was at first monopolized by the English; later on the
Dutch succeeded in breaking the monopoly and took an active
part. The city of Archangel, founded in 1584, became its main outlet. The growth of the northern maritime trade is best indicated by
comparing the number of foreign commercial vessels which visited
Archangel: 21 in 1600, 154 in 1708. Through Archangel Russia
exported grain, furs, flax, hemp, tar, potash, linen and sailcloth,
and leather. Among the goods imported from the West were metal-
ware, weapons, cloth, wines, tobacco, drugs and medicaments.

Not satisfied with practically monopolizing Russia's foreign
trade with the West, western merchants, contrary to the original
agreements, took an active part in Russian domestic trade, the
Dutch being especially interested in the grain trade. The Russian
merchants resented the intrusion of foreigners and on many occasions demanded that foreign merchants be allowed to reside in
Archangel only, or, failing that, be forbidden to conduct retail trade.
Their complaints were long disregarded by the government. It was
only in 1650 that the privileges of the English merchants were canceled, for both economic and political reasons; Tsar Alexis was out-
raged by Charles I's execution the previous year. The English were
ordered to confine their operations to Arkhangelsk; but the order
was not strictly observed. In 1667 the tsar issued a new commercial
ordinance forbidding foreigners to engage in retail trade. The Russian merchants had won an important point of their program, an
indication of their growing strength. As a matter of fact, in spite
of their complaints some Russian merchants did not fare too badly
even before 1667. There were a number of "millionaires" besides
the Stroganovs among the merchants and industrialists, some of
whom controlled a considerable share of the Volga River trade.

The city of Moscow became the main center of trade and handicrafts. Its population about 1650 was around 200,000. An observation of the Austrian envoy Baron Augustin von Mayerberg, who visited Moscow in 1661–62, indicates its prosperity: "There is in Moscow such an abundance of the things necessary for life, comfort, and luxury, available at reasonable prices, that it should not be envious of any other country in the world."

9. State and society

The basic feature of the organization of Muscovite society was its adaptation to the needs of the state. All social classes had to perform service to the state of one kind or another. Ironically enough, the slaves were the only group free from governmental regimentation. The principle of universal obligatory service of all freemen to the state was established in the Mongol and early post-Mongol period; it was reinforced by the urgent need to restore order after the chaos and devastation of the Time of Trouble. Service to the state took two main forms: serving as officers in the army or officials in the court and administration, and supplying labor and paying direct taxes. Thus a distinction arose between the men of "service" and the men of "burden." The "service" (in that sense) became a characteristic of the nobleman, the "burden" that of a commoner.

The top layer of the men of service was the boyars, who occupied all the highest positions in the tsar's administration. Below them were the gentry of the Moscow region and then the provincial gentry. Lower still were the petty officers of the frontier guards on the fringe of the steppe and the service Cossacks. Eventually a number of these were promoted and entered the gentry class; the bulk became free farmers. The boyar class which had been shattered by the oprichnina and discredited by its lack of statesmanship during the Time of Trouble only partly regained its former prestige under the first Romanovs. Many old princely families became extinct, and the ranks of the boyars were refilled by newcomers from the gentry of the Moscow region. On the whole, the middle gentry now became the mainstay of the tsar's power. Because of this their rights to landholdings (pomestie) gradually increased, as it became customary for the tsar to confirm the son's rights to his father's fief. By the end of the 17th century there was little difference left between the rights of the boyars to their patrimonial estates and those of the gentry to their fiefs.

The townspeople were organized into closed communes, from whose jurisdiction the wholesale merchants and rich industrialists were, however, excluded. These constituted a group by themselves, and since they were used by the tsar as the agents of his financial administration their personal status came close to that of the men of service. With this exception, the townspeople were permanently bound each to his commune. According to the Code of Laws of 1649 any member who left the commune without the government's permission was to be punished by banishment to Siberia. This measure was passed to ensure equal distribution of taxes and other liabilities among the townspeople.

The peasants were divided into two approximately equal sections. Those who lived on state lands remained personally free but like the townspeople were bound to their communes and liable to direct taxes and compulsory work whenever necessary, such as improving roads, building bridges, and so on. The other category now became serfs attached to the landlords' estates. They still were recognized as persons in the juridical sense, not as slaves; they could sue in court and own property. But as time went by they found themselves more and more helpless before their masters' increasing authority. As for the slaves on the boyar estates, a new group of conditional slaves (the so-called *kabala* slaves) was added in the Muscovite period to the old category of full slaves. These were indentured workers whose work was counted as meeting the interest on the money they had borrowed from their masters. The kabala slave was not in a position ever to repay the principal and had to serve until his own or his master's death. If the master died first, the kabala slave was set free.

At the top of the sociopolitical pyramid stood "the tsar and autocrat of all Russia." His authority, although tremendous, was not absolute. In religious matters it was limited by that of the church and, as we know, the patriarchs at times interfered even with state affairs. In administrative matters the tsar had to rule with the concurrence of the boyar duma. It will also be recalled that until the mid-17th century the tsar was assisted by the zemsky sobor, which often made the actual decision. Current affairs were handled by the administrative departments (*prikazy*). The board of each prikaz included one or more boyars. Decisions must be unanimous. There was much overlapping among departments, as they had been created at various times, according to no general plan but rather casually, because of an accumulation of matters or the tsar's special interest in some particular branch of administration at a given time. Some of the departments had authority over all Russia, others over only a region. In the late 17th century there were over forty permanent departments. The institutions of local self-government continued to function but, except in north Russia, its agents after 1650 were subordinated to the provincial governors appointed by the tsars.

Beginning with the Mongol period the basic direct tax was that on tilled land, assessed according to the cadastre. In the late 17th century it was decided to collect this tax from each household, irrespective of the amount of land tilled. This was done as an incentive to farmers to increase production. Two other important sources of state revenue were customs duties and the liquor monopoly. The total annual revenue as of 1680 was around 1,500,000 rubles, the equivalent of approximately 26,000,000 gold rubles as of 1913.

10. Cultural development

Two basic trends are clear in Russia of the 17th century: the decline of the role of the church in the national culture, and the increase of western influence. These new developments were present in latent form at the beginning of the century but became apparent only in the second half. They affected many aspects of Russian life, such as religion, the arts, music, and education.

The religious crisis has already been discussed. As regards architecture, the "tent" style, with variations, remained the preferred form until the middle of the century, when Patriarch Nikon came strongly out against it on the ground that it did not follow the patterns of Byzantine architecture. The result (which Nikon could not foresee) was an increase of western forms in Russian architecture, and particularly of the baroque style. The latter became especially popular in Ukraine, but many of its characteristics appeared in Muscovite architecture as well. In icon painting, a new school patronized by the Stroganovs became prominent between 1580 and 1630. The icons painted by the masters of this school

are mostly small, and even the larger ones are done in the manner
of miniatures. Black, deep brown, and red are their characteristic
colors. The outstanding Russian painter of the second half of the
17th century was Simeon Ushakov, who frankly used the western
techniques of painting. His creations are no longer "icons" (in the
essence of their style) but pictures on religious themes.

The years 1500 to 1650 saw the flowering of the old Russian
church singing. The Russian chant originally introduced by the
Greeks came in the post-Mongol period to differ from the Byzantine patterns in many ways, because of its close relations with Russian folk song. Elements of polyphony also entered church singing
in the 16th century; and in the Ukrainian church polyphonic singing influenced by western patterns prevailed in the 17th century.
After Nikon's reform the so-called Kievan chant was introduced
in Muscovy as well, and simultaneously line notation replaced the
old system of "hook" notation—though the Old Ritualists accepted neither the new melodies nor the new notation. The principles of Kievan polyphony were used by Russian composers of the
late 17th century for secular songs as well. This was the beginning of modern Russian vocal lyrics.

As before, no instrumental music was allowed in the church
services, but with the 1660's the upper classes of Moscow society
became acquainted with secular instrumental music, the musicians
being imported from abroad. Both instrumental music and singing
were used in the theater. Until then there had been no theater in
Muscovy in the western sense of the word. Religious pageants, such
as the representation of Christ's entrance into Jerusalem, in which
both the tsar and the patriarch participated, answered the Russians' craving for dramatics. Puppet shows (*Petrushka*) on the
city streets in festival time were popular among commoners. In
Ukraine, religious theater developed at the divinity schools. A
prominent Ukrainian scholar, Simeon Polotsky, who settled in
Moscow (he was Tsar Theodore's tutor), wrote several religious
plays which may be considered the first samples of Russian dramatic literature. Simultaneously, the tsar and some of the boyars
became interested in the western theater, and occasional spectacles
were staged in the tsar's palace and in the boyar houses. In 1672
a theater was built in the tsar's suburban residence, where several
plays translated from the German were produced by a pastor from

the German Suburb, Johann Gottfried Gregory. Most of them were on biblical or classical themes—*Esther* and *Judith,* and the ballet *Orpheus.*

The tragic events of the Time of Trouble served as a basis for numerous historical treatises and tales in most of which the misfortunes of the Russian people were explained as God's punishment for the sins of both the rulers and the people. Tsar Boris Godunov, and of course the two false Dmitris, were represented as the main villains, the former on the assumption (never proved) that it was his agent who killed the true Dmitri. In the next period the historical novel became popular. To this type belong the story of the seizure of Azov by the Don Cossacks and the semifantastic story of the young merchant Savva Grudtsyn who allegedly took part in the campaign against the Poles in 1632. Of a quite different sort is the novel *Frol Skobeev* written at the end of the century. It is a realistic and even cynical story of a successful rascal, in a sense a forerunner of 19th-century realistic satire. A unique monument of 17th-century Russian literature is the autobiography of the leader of the Old Ritualists, the archpriest Avvakum. It is a human document of great psychological and historical significance in which Avvakum's fiery personality and religious fervor found vigorous expression. Not less remarkable is his language, a racy colloquial Russian, which he used in a period when Church Slavonic was considered the only proper vehicle for cultivated literature.

Elementary schools were the only ones that existed in Muscovy until the late 17th century. Small groups of children were taught by local deacons and sextons, in some cases by lay teachers. Emphasis was put on reading and writing, but some arithmetic also was required. The main purpose of these schools was to train future deacons and priests, as well as government clerks. In Ukraine the situation was different. The Orthodox clergy there had to face the constant pressure of Roman Catholicism and so were forced by circumstances to hold to the same intellectual level as the Roman Catholics and to build up similar educational equipment. The elementary schools were better organized in Ukraine than in Muscovy; and in 1631 a divinity college of a higher type (later called an academy in Russian) was created in Kiev and became the main center of learning for Ukraine. With the calling of many Ukrainian scholars to Moscow in the second half of the century, Kievan scholarship became a leading factor in modernizing Muscovite culture as well. To break the monopoly of the Ukrainians, the patriarch invited to Moscow two Greek scholars, the Likhuda brothers, who opened a divinity school in Moscow in 1687 similar to the Kievan college but with more emphasis on the Greek language. Later this school became known as the Slavo-Greek-Latin Academy.

While there were at that time no schools for science and technology, either in Moscow or in Ukraine, the knowledge of Latin acquired by the students of both the Kiev and Moscow academies opened the gates to western learning to many Russians and Ukrainians. Instruction in languages, both western and oriental, was also offered by the Department of the Embassies for its employees, some of whom had to study geography and political history as well. Incidentally the Russian exploration of Siberia constituted an important contribution to geographical science at large. Russian painters and architects of the second half of the 17th century acquired considerable familiarity with western techniques. And many Russian assistants of the foreign engineers in metallurgical and other plants learned enough to take over part of the work formerly done by only foreigners.

To sum up, a thin layer of westernized cultural élite had formed in Russia by the end of the 17th century which could serve both as a connecting link between Russia and the West and as a center for the spread of new ideas in Russia itself. What was needed was a signal on the part of the government to disregard old traditions and prejudices and to go ahead with westernization. That signal was given by Peter the Great.

THE ROMANOV DYNASTY
Part I

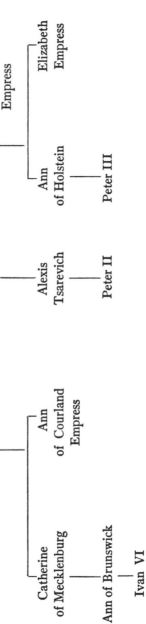

CHAPTER 6

THE RUSSIAN EMPIRE IN THE
18TH CENTURY

1. *Aspects of the imperial period*

THE reign of Peter the Great opened a new period in Russian history. Russia became a westernized state and a member of the European community of nations. The administration and the judiciary, the army, and the various social classes were reorganized along western lines. Industry and trade developed rapidly, and great improvements in technical training and science took place.

The Russian people in the course of the 18th and 19th centuries reached the natural geographic limits of their expansion: the Baltic and Black seas in the west, the Pacific Ocean in the east, and the Pamir Plateau in the south. With the exception of the inhabitants of the southwest regions—Galicia, Bukovina, and Carpatho-Russia—all branches of the Russian people were united during these centuries in a single state.

But the great achievements of the imperial period were accompanied by profound internal conflicts. The chief crisis was one in the national psychology. The Europeanization of Russia brought with it new political, religious, and social ideas, which were absorbed by the governing and upper classes of society before they reached the masses of the people. Consequently a split occurred between the top and the bottom of society, between the "intellectuals" and the "people." The chief psychological basis of the old Russian state, the Orthodox Church, was shaken in the course of the 17th century, and gradually lost its influence from 1700 until the revolution of 1917, when it had to face a threat of disintegration. Political and social problems also became acute. The political emergency was brought about by the abolition of the zemsky

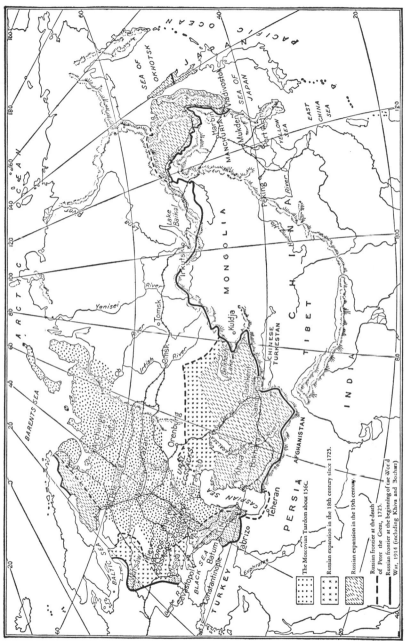

THE GROWTH OF THE RUSSIAN EMPIRE TO 1914

149

sobors, which deprived the people of political power, and the abrogation of local self-government in 1708.

The government keenly felt its lack of contact with the people following Peter's reforms. It soon became clear that the majority did not sympathize with the program of Europeanization. To carry out its reforms the government was consequently forced to act harshly, as, in fact, Peter the Great did. Later the concept of absolutism became habitual and traditional. Meanwhile western political thought influenced the Europeanized circles of Russian society, which absorbed ideas of political progress and eventually became ready to fight absolutism. Thus Peter's reforms set in motion political forces which the government later was not capable of controlling.

The political crisis was complicated by social instability. The barriers between classes became sharper as time went on, and the point was finally reached where only autocratic government was capable of mediating between the various groups in society.

2. *The personality of Peter the Great*

The character of Peter the Great reached its full development following the Azov campaigns in 1695–96. His chief traits were enormous physical energy and endurance combined with intellectual activity and determination. Peter had no respect for tradition and authority. His mind was as constantly in search of knowledge as his hands were of work. He could not be inactive for a moment. Not content with theoretical knowledge, he wanted to try everything himself. He worked as a carpenter on the docks when he was building the new Russian navy, and pulled teeth when he wanted to learn medicine. And with all this, Peter was of an imperious nature that brooked no contradiction. He demanded that everyone submit without question to his will, and he was capable of great cruelty.

His primary concern was the good, not exactly of the Russian people, but rather of the Russian state. His famous order before the Battle of Poltava illustrates this principle: "Do not think of Peter; all that matters is that Russia shall survive." He made exacting demands both on himself and on others, and stopped at nothing in pursuing the interest of the state as he conceived it. Having acquired great respect for European science and tech-

nology, Peter expected the same of all his subordinates. He succeeded in doing great things: he created a first-class army, a navy,
the best state chancellery that Moscow had ever had, and a learned
Academy of Sciences. He also attended to details, demanding that
all his subjects dress in European clothes and shave off their beards.
In this he succeeded only as far as the military officers, civil servants, and nobles were concerned. He personally supervised the
execution of his orders, making no distinction between large matters and small, and threatened severe punishment for nonfulfill-
ment.

In carrying out his reforms Peter came into conflict with national conservatism. For this reason both his admirers and his enemies regarded him as a man alien to the Russian spirit. But with
all his apparent opposition to Russian tradition and habits, Peter
was a true Russian, of that dynamic variation of the national type
to which the merchant Kuzma Minin, the patriarch Nikon, and the
Cossack Stephen Razin belonged.

3. His foreign policy

The capture of Azov was the first test of the new "regular" army.
Peter realized that Russia was capable of fighting Turkey and
securing a foothold on the coast of the Black Sea. He wanted to
continue the war with Turkey on a large scale and for this purpose
considered it essential to enter into alliances with European states.
Thus arose the idea of the Extraordinary Russian Embassy which
was to tour the chief courts of Europe. The embassy left Moscow
in the spring of 1697. The personnel included Peter, who traveled
incognito under the name of Peter Mikhailov. The route taken was
first to Riga, at the time a Swedish town, then to Courland, the
Electorate of Brandenburg (Prussia), Holland, England, and back
through Holland to Vienna. From Vienna Peter was to have continued to Venice, but news arrived from Moscow that the streltsy
had revolted, and Peter hurriedly returned to his capital in the
summer of 1698.

The embassy was not successful in accomplishing what had been
planned by Russian diplomacy, namely, the creation of an all-
European alliance against the Turks. The moment was ill chosen.
Europe was occupied by the struggle between the Hapsburgs and
the Bourbons. The only state directly interested in the struggle

against the Turks was Venice, and that state Peter failed to visit. But the embassy did have important consequences. It brought a number of talented Russians into direct contact with Europe and particularly influenced Tsar Peter. He had a chance to satisfy his thirst for learning European technique. In Holland and England he studied shipbuilding—in Holland working as a carpenter in the shipyard. The embassy made decided advances toward the cultural Europeanization of Russia.

It also had diplomatic consequences. It drew Peter's attention away from the Turks to other matters. He observed that in a number of Baltic states, among them Brandenburg (Prussia), Poland, and Denmark, there was growing the idea of a war with Sweden which then controlled the greater part of the coast of the Baltic Sea. Peter decided to take advantage of this situation and to participate in the struggle. So it turned out that Peter went to Europe with the idea of fighting the Turks and returned with the idea of fighting the Swedes.

On his return to Moscow in August 1698 Peter first investigated the uprising of the streltsy, which had been suppressed in his absence. He personally supervised the execution of the ringleaders of the rebellion; and the streltsy corps was disbanded. Then he began to prepare for war with Sweden. Treaties were signed with the Polish king, Augustus II, and King Christian of Denmark, but Peter refused to begin a new war before making peace with the Turks. In the summer of 1700 a Russian plenipotentiary concluded a treaty of peace with Turkey in Constantinople, by which Azov was ceded to Russia. Immediately upon receiving news of this treaty Peter moved an army to the Swedish town of Narva in the Gulf of Finland. This was Moscow's customary opening move in all its wars with Sweden.

The war began very unfavorably for Peter and his allies. The young king Charles XII vanquished Denmark at one stroke and then turned against Russia. The Russian army was defeated at Narva. Charles, thinking that he had finished with the Russians, then turned against Augustus. This drew him away from Russia, and in Peter's words, "He got stuck in Poland." This circumstance was Peter's salvation. The defeat at Narva instead of breaking his military ambition gave it a powerful stimulus. He began rapidly to reorganize the Russian army along new lines. He dispatched auxiliary forces to Poland and Lithuania to aid Augustus, but his attention was chiefly directed to the Baltic coast.

In the course of 1701–04 Peter conquered Ingria. In May 1703 he founded the new city of St. Petersburg. Its construction in the swamps of the Gulf of Finland, the conscription of recruits for the army, together with the supply and transportation of foodstuffs for it all demanded great sacrifices of the population. Peter continually needed more money and more men. Popular discontent found expression in a series of revolts. In 1705 an uprising took place in Astrakhan against the boyars and "the Germans" or foreigners. At the same time another occurred among the Bashkirs, which was not suppressed until 1709. In 1707 the Don Cossacks rose when Peter sent a detachment of troops to the Don to recapture escaped robbers and runaway serfs. The poorer Cossacks under the leadership of Kondrat Bulavin overpowered the house-owning Cossacks, and the uprising took on a threatening aspect. Peter was forced to send large forces to the Don. Bulavin was caught in Cherkassk, where he committed suicide in 1708. His accomplices took refuge in the Kuban region. All these uprisings were suppressed with great difficulty. At one time it looked as if all southeast Russia would revolt. The situation was saved by the Kalmyks, whose khan sent a force of over 20,000 men to aid in restoring order.

Simultaneously the Swedish danger grew. Charles drove Augustus from Poland, pursued him to the boundaries of Saxony, and compelled him to conclude a separate peace in 1707. Poland elected a new king, Stanislav Leszczynski, under the pressure of Charles whom he supported. At the end of 1707 the Swedes moved against Russia. Early in 1708 Charles took the town of Grodno, and the Russian army barely escaped a crushing defeat. From Grodno Charles moved on Mogilev; Peter expected a further advance against Smolensk and Moscow, and Moscow was hurriedly fortified. But Charles unexpectedly turned south to the Ukraine without awaiting the arrival from Latvia of an auxiliary corps that accompanied large quantities of military supplies and provisions. He relied solely upon the assistance of Hetman Ivan Mazepa, who, planning to abandon Peter, had opened negotiations with Stanislav Leszczynski as early as 1705. Charles planned to supplement his military attack upon Russia by an organized political uprising of the Ukrainians against the Russian Government. In this respect Austria-Hungary and Germany during the first World War followed his example. But he overestimated the strength of Mazepa, who joined him with an insignificant force of Cossacks. The majority of the rank-and-file Cossacks remained loyal to Russia. A new hetman was elected under the supervision of the Russians, and Ukrainian autonomy was severely curbed. By not waiting at Mogilev, Charles had committed a great mistake. In September 1708 Peter defeated the Swedish auxiliary force near the village Lesnaia and captured the whole supply train.

The climax came in 1709. Peter considered it necessary to save Poltava from Charles and Mazepa, for this city was the key to the route to Voronezh, the chief base of Peter's southern fleet, containing large reserve stores of grain. The battle of Poltava was decided principally by the superiority of Peter's artillery. The Swedish army was completely defeated. Several days afterward the remnants surrendered to Peter's chief assistant, Gen. Alexander Menshikov, who overtook them at the crossing of the Dnieper. Only Charles and Mazepa succeeded in crossing the Dnieper with a small following and escaped to Turkey. The victory of Poltava had great consequences. Stanislav Leszczynski was forced to leave Poland, and Augustus, regaining the throne, declared war upon Sweden.

Charles did not hasten to return to Sweden but attempted to use his presence in Turkey to draw that country into war with Russia. His intrigues met with success, and toward the end of 1710 Turkey declared war upon Russia. Peter decided to take the offensive. A European alliance against Turkey proving impossible, he tried to utilize for his purpose the sympathies of the Orthodox subjects of the Sultan—the Slavs, Rumanians, and Greeks. He received promises of assistance from the princes of Moldavia and Wallachia, and moved toward the Danube with an army not more than about 40,000 men. His troops soon began to suffer from lack of provisions, which had been promised by the prince of Wallachia but which never came. Having reached the river Pruth, Peter found himself surrounded by a great Turkish army of 200,000 men. He considered it a stroke of luck that the Turkish vizier agreed to negotiate a peace, though he had to cede back to the Turks the hard-won town of Azov.

The Pruth campaign undermined the military prestige Peter

had acquired by the victory at Poltava, and this lengthened the Swedish war. Peter, however, continued it with great energy. In 1714 the Russian fleet was victorious over the Swedish fleet at Gangut. Peter also captured the Aaland Islands, and from them was able to threaten Stockholm. This was the turning point. In 1717–18 peace parleys began between Peter and Charles, who meanwhile had returned to Sweden from Turkey.

Negotiations were interrupted by Charles' death, and the war continued another three years. In the end Sweden was forced to conclude peace. By the Treaty of Nystadt of August 30, 1721, she ceded Ingria, Estonia, and Latvia to Russia. St. Petersburg—the proverbial "window to Europe"—was formally secured, and Russia gained easy access to the shores of the Baltic Sea. The struggle of centuries, it seemed, had at last given her a favorable position. By the Treaty of Brest-Litovsk of March 3, 1918, Russia was to lose all Peter's Baltic acquisitions with the exception of Ingria.

The Senate presented Peter with the titles father of his country, emperor, and great (*pater patriae, imperator, maximus*). The Byzantine idea of the tsar was exchanged for the Roman idea of the emperor. Peter hastened to make Russia's position in the Baltic Sea secure by a series of diplomatic marriages. One of his nieces, Ann, was married to the duke of Courland, and another, Catherine, to the duke of Mecklenburg. Peter also arranged for the marriage of his daughter Ann to the duke of Holstein. These Baltic connections of the Russian imperial house later gave the nation considerable anxiety and frequently exercised an unfortunate influence upon Russian policies.

4. *His domestic reforms and the opposition to them*

The great tension caused by unceasing war resulted in continual disorders, first in Moscow, as in the uprising of the streltsy in 1698, and later in the provinces, led by Bulavin, Mazepa, and others. All these rebellions Peter successfully suppressed, thanks to the new organization of the army and of the state. Peter had combined the new European techniques with some principles of the old Muscovite organization of the army. The secret of the discipline of his army lay in the Guards regiments, composed entirely of nobles.

The system of administration was also reformed in accordance with European principles. Russia was divided into governmental provinces in 1708. The Senate was placed at the head of the administration in 1711. Later, to direct the separate functions of the central government, departments ("colleges") were formed which were supervised by councils and not by individual ministers.

In 1716 the Army Statutes, based on Swedish and German models, were published. The harsh rules of military procedure were applied to criminal and civil offenses in general. Prior to these reforms, the new direction of policy was symbolized by the transfer of the capital from Moscow to St. Petersburg. The "regulated" state created by Peter was based even more than the Muscovite monarchy had been upon strict subjection of all persons and classes to its interests. Peter looked upon himself as its first servant. The nobility were called upon to give unlimited military service, the merchant and manufacturing classes to give economic assistance, the peasants to supply recruits for the army and workmen and horses for the construction of new towns and factories. Peter regarded both the serfs and the peasants on state lands as state servitors. Those belonging to the nobility merely paid smaller state taxes, since they had already had the task of sustaining their masters.

The increasing burden of services to the state created extensive dissatisfaction among the people. This reaction was perhaps even more dangerous to Peter than open uprisings. High and low were seething with discontent. The top circles of the Moscow aristocracy —the boyars—were especially disturbed at Peter's disregard for seniority and reward only of individual capacity. This attitude of Peter's was later formulated in the Table of Ranks published in 1722. The lowest officer's rank, that of lieutenant, conferred hereditary nobility on the holder. The nobility of service replaced the nobility of birth. Naturally the old aristocracy were displeased with Peter's reforms.

The church also was disaffected, for Peter lowered its position. He was not an atheist, but his faith was not the traditional Russian faith. Strongly influenced by Lutheranism, he believed that the Russian church should be reorganized after European models, on the central European principle that the ruler's religion is the state religion—*"Cujus regio, ejus religio."*

Under the influence of Lutheranism, and wanting to prevent any possibility of another Nikon appearing, Peter came to the conclusion that an independent church was harmful and that it should be subordinated to the civil power. Upon the death of Patriarch Adrian in 1700 Peter refused to allow the election of a new patriarch. The patriarchal throne remained vacant and then was abolished.

In reorganizing the higher branches of administration during the second half of his reign, Peter introduced a clerical "college" to govern the Russian church. This body was later renamed the Holy Synod. Thus, the highest organ of church government became a bureaucratic agency subject to the emperor. The number of the clergy was limited, and Peter passed several laws to curb monasticism. An "all-comic and all-drunken council" was created, in grotesque parody of the church rituals, to amuse Peter. Its principal characters were "Prince Pope" and "Prince Patriarch."

The opposition of the church, aristocracy, and peasants was not well enough organized to lead to a general uprising against Peter. But it did find a leader very close to the emperor, in the Tsarevich Alexis, Peter's son by his first marriage. Peter soon separated from his wife and began living with a Latvian prisoner, Skavronskaia, whom he later married and who took the name of Catherine. Ann and Elizabeth were the children of this second marriage. The political rivalry led to a family tragedy. After a quarrel with his father Alexis fled abroad. Fearing that some foreign power would use Alexis as a means to disturb the internal situation in Russia, Peter sent agents who succeeded by fraudulent promises in persuading Alexis to return to Russia. There he was arrested, tried, and sentenced to death in 1718. He died, from nervous shock and the effects of torture, several hours before the time set for the execution. A number of his followers were tortured and executed. After this the opposition subsided.

5. *Political struggle after Peter's death*

Peter died in 1725, having made no arrangements for the succession of the throne. At the insistence of the Guards regiments, the widow Catherine was named Peter's successor, but power passed in fact to the Supreme Privy Council, comprised of the leading personages in Peter's new nobility, Gen. Alexander Menshikov, Count Peter Tolstoy, Baron Andrew Osterman, and others. Only one member of the council, Prince Golitsyn, belonged to the old aristocracy. The Supreme Privy Council continued to control governmental affairs even after Catherine's death in 1727, but very soon the political situation changed. The new emperor, Peter II, Alexis' son, was only twelve years old. The old opposition to Peter's reforms raised its head. The church and boyar parties reappeared in the political arena. The imperial court moved to Moscow. The membership of the Supreme Privy Council was completely changed by the intrigues of the reactionary group which succeeded in driving out its members one by one. The new members of the council were of the old aristocratic party. Soon, with the exception of Osterman, all were of the Golitsyn or Dolgoruky families. When the young emperor died of smallpox before his coronation in 1730, the council acted as regent. It decided to invite to the throne one of Peter's Baltic nieces, Ann of Courland.

Before she was vested with imperial power Ann was called upon to sign certain "conditions," which transferred the actual power from the empress to the Supreme Privy Council. The Russian Empire would thus become an oligarchy. News of the "conditions" in favor of the council aroused the Guards officers who had assembled in Moscow in great numbers for Peter II's coronation. The city became the scene of unusual political activity; meetings were called; plans were made to create a chamber of nobles to assist the Supreme Privy Council. It soon became clear that the majority of the Guards officers were opposed to the oligarchical privileges of the council. They were greatly concerned with limiting military service, and desired to end the service of nobles as privates in the Guards regiments. Under Peter the nobles had been compelled to serve in the army without time limit. They also wanted to repeal the restrictions upon the inheritance of noble estates. The new empress knew how to take advantage of the officers' discontent, and promised them civil and economic privileges. The "conditions" were torn up, the Supreme Privy Council was dissolved, and autocratic power triumphed again.

6. Ann and Elizabeth

The reign of Empress Ann was marked by the ascendancy of the German party at the Russian court. Its leaders were Ernest Johann Biron, duke of Courland; Osterman, and Field Marshal Burkhard

Christoph von Münnich. After the death of Empress Ann, during the short reign of Ivan VI (grandson of her sister Catherine, duchess of Mecklenburg) the members of the ruling German group began to intrigue against each other. This made a coup d'état possible. The officers of one of the Guards regiments called Peter's daughter Elizabeth to the throne, and the youthful Ivan VI was arrested on January 5, 1742.

The leading members of the group supporting Elizabeth—the Vorontsovs, Shuvalovs, Chernyshevs, and others—belonged to the Russian gentry. The triumph of the "Russian" party over the "German" did not bring with it a return to the national ideals that prevailed before Peter's time. German cultural influence at court was exchanged for French culture. Henceforth French, English, and German influences persisted at court until the mid-19th century.

Russia during the reign of Ann and Elizabeth did not succeed in achieving any permanent results in foreign policy. Austrian and, later, French policies exercised their pressure and in part determined Russian activity. During Ann's reign Russia interfered in Polish affairs and opposed the French candidate to the Polish throne, though this struggle did not affect Russia's interests. War with Turkey also brought no result, despite the victories of Field Marshal Münnich.

During Elizabeth's reign Russia participated with Austria and France in the Seven Years' War against Prussia. The war went in Russia's favor. East Prussia was occupied by the Russian army under Gen. Count Peter Saltykov who, together with the Austrians, inflicted a decisive defeat upon Frederick II at Kunersdorf in 1759. Russian troops occupied Berlin, but the death of Elizabeth in 1762 put a stop to Russia's gains. Elizabeth's successor, Peter III, a nephew from Holstein, was an ardent admirer of Frederick and immediately concluded a separate peace. He wanted to go even further and to send an army to help Prussia against Russia's recent allies; but this gave rise to an officers' revolt, and the Russian throne was given to Peter's wife, Catherine, by birth the German princess of Anhalt-Zerbst, in 1762.*

The period of almost forty years from 1725 to 1762 between the

* According to Baron Michael de Taube's as yet unpublished study, Catherine II's actual father was Frederick II of Prussia. (Courtesy of Baron de Taube.)

death of Peter the Great and the coronation of Catherine II was thus of little significance in the foreign policy of Russia with respect to Europe. Unproductive also in internal changes, it nevertheless had great importance in Russia's eastern policy. At this time a sound basis was laid for the new period of Russian expansion in the east. The main lines of the new eastern policy were laid down by Peter the Great, who set up the guideposts for it in both the Far and Middle East. He attempted to enter into relations with China. He sent a Russian embassy to Peking in 1720–22. He also tried to enter into relations with Japan. When Russian Cossacks occupied Kamchatka in 1697, they met a Japanese survivor of a shipwreck. Peter called him to Moscow and ordered him to teach several Russian children Japanese. After Peter's death Russia concluded a permanent treaty with China. Trade relations between the Russians and the Chinese were limited to a single point —Kyakhta-Maimachin on the Siberian-Mongolian border; Russia received the right to have a religious mission in Peking, which also functioned as a diplomatic mission.

Peter also organized the Bering Expedition which was sent to discover whether Asia and America were joined. The fact that this problem had already been solved by Dezhnev in 1648 was not known in St. Petersburg. Capt. Vitus Bering's first expedition in 1724–30 had few practical results, but in 1732 the navigator Fedorov and the geodesist Gvozdev stumbled upon the "Great Land," the American continent, at Alaska. In the course of the next decade, 1733–43, the Russian Government organized the so-called "Great Northern Expedition," which was of lasting importance and one of the remarkable undertakings in the history of science. In 1741 Captain Bering reached the shore of America at latitude 58° 28′ N. Captain Chirikov, in charge of another ship, also reached America at latitude 56° N., but was not able to make a landing. From the islands near Alaska Chirikov's crew brought many valuable furs, which stimulated the initiative of Siberian merchants. The first "merchant sea voyage" was undertaken in 1743, to be followed by many others.

The Middle East attracted Peter's attention no less than the Far East. The objective of his policy in this region was to establish direct trade relations with India. This was not easy to achieve. Peter's first plan was to conquer the central Asiatic khanates,

Khiva and Bukhara. It was unsuccessful. A division of troops sent
to Khiva was betrayed and massacred in 1717. Equally unsuccessful
was the attempt to expand south of the Irtysh River into the Middle East. But the failure did not put an end to Peter's hopes, and
in 1721 a Russian envoy was sent to Khiva and Bukhara.

The policy pursued by Peter aroused the fears of Persia, which
led to a war in 1722. Persia he regarded as a step on the road to
India. As one of his contemporaries said: "The hopes of His Majesty were not concerned with Persia alone; if he had been lucky
in Persia and were still living, he would of course have attempted
to reach India or even China. This I heard from His Majesty my-
self."

The Russian army moved from Astrakhan southward along the
western shore of the Caspian Sea, occupying the cities of Derbent
and Baku. By the peace of 1723 Russia received from Persia all
the western and southern shore of that sea. After the death of Peter
the Russian Government renounced these acquisitions because of
the great expense of defending them, and they were returned to
Persia (1729–35). Following the Persian war Peter thought of
opening a sea route to India. In December 1723 two warships were
sent out from Revel. The commanding vice admiral received two
instructions, one to seize Madagascar, the other to sail to the East
Indies and Bengal. The vessels were to sail secretly in the guise of
trading ships. The plan, however, was not carried out as the ships
turned out to be unfit for such a long voyage—one sprang a leak as
soon as it entered the open sea.

At the time of Peter's death the frontier of the Russian Empire
in the Middle East formed an angle from the Altaic Range down
the Irtysh River to Omsk, and from Omsk to the upper reaches of
the Iaik River and thence along the Iaik to the Caspian Sea. The
Middle Eastern steppe was at the very frontier. The Iaik was a
feeble barrier, and the untamed steppe peoples entered and left
the territories of the Russian Empire without even being aware
of it.

Three leading ethnic groups had to be taken into consideration
at that time in Russian policy. The Bashkirs, the Kalmyks, and
the Kirghiz (now known as Kazakhs) moved over a huge area
lying approximately between the Volga River and the Altai and
T'ien-shan Mts. The Kirghiz were divided into three hordes—

eldest, middle, and youngest. Pressure from the Kalmyks forced them to seek aid from the Russians.

Ivan Kirilov, an outstanding Russian statesman of the 18th century, took advantage of this situation. Kirilov regarded the Kirghiz horde as the key to all Asiatic lands, and insisted upon building a town at the mouth of the river Or in the southern Urals. His plan was to extend Russian domination to the east of the Aral Sea, and he dreamed of "picking up the provinces of Bukhara and Samarkand"—that is to say, of occupying Turkistan.

Empress Ann approved Kirilov's policy, and he was made leader of the expedition to the Or. He first suppressed an uprising of Bashkirs, who opposed the extension of Russian domination to the southern Urals, and laid the foundation of a new town at the junction of the Or and the Iaik in 1736, which was named Orenburg.

Kirilov died in the spring of 1737, but his program was not abandoned. In 1742 the new government agent, who was also a pupil of Peter's, moved the town of Orenburg to another site near the mouth of the Samara river, and fortified lines from Orenburg to Samara and to the Caspian Sea were constructed to enforce the obedience of the Bashkirs, the Kalmyks, and the Kirghiz. The former town of Orenburg became known as Orsk. In 1754–55, in view of the oppressive measures of the Russian Government against the Mohammedans, another abortive Bashkir uprising occurred under the leadership of Batyrsha, who attempted without success to arouse the Kirghiz.

7. *Expansion in the Far East and policies in the Middle East*

The reign of Catherine II (1762–96) raised new problems in Russian foreign policy and transferred the focus of Russian diplomacy from the Far and Middle East to the Near East and the West. The Far East was left to the initiative of individual traders. In the second half of the 18th century they founded Russian settlements in Alaska and the neighboring islands. Unusual energy was shown by the merchant Gregory Shelekhov, nicknamed "the Russian Columbus." He had migrated to Siberia at the age of twenty-eight; in 1777 he had chartered his first ship to the Kuril Islands, and then made voyages to the Aleutians. In 1784 Shelekhov formed a trading company with the brothers Golikov and occupied Kodiak Island near Alaska. From this center the Shelekhov company rapidly increased its possessions on the continent. Its chief activity was purchasing the valuable furs of seals and beavers from the natives.

In the Middle East the government of Catherine II aimed primarily to maintain order among the Turkish peoples by making its peace with the Mohammedan faith, in contrast to Russian policy during the reign of Empress Elizabeth. In 1785 Catherine published a charter of toleration of Islam. The Russian Government began to take great interest in the education of the Kirghiz, and school books were published for them in both Kirghiz and Russian. Mullahs from Kazan were appointed teachers of the natives, in the absence of trained candidates among the Russians and Kirghiz. These measures led to the encouragement of Mohammedanism and medieval Mohammedan learning among the Kirghiz.

8. The Polish question

In the West Catherine's foreign policy falls into two distinct periods. The first, prior to 1780, was characterized by the existence of the so-called Northern Accord among Russia, England, Prussia, and Sweden. The second was marked by an understanding between Russia and Austria. The turning point between the two periods was the Act of Armed Neutrality of 1780. It was published in connection with the American War of Independence and favored the revolutionary colonies against England. It insisted upon the right of neutral ships to trade with belligerent states and to import all goods with the exception of arms and munitions.

Catherine's European policy was closely connected with the Polish and Turkish questions. Her first problem was to determine the fate of the West Russian lands, a large part of which were in Poland's possession at the beginning of the 18th century. The second was to extend the territories of Russia to the shores of the Black Sea.

The Polish question first arose with respect to the rights of the Orthodox population of Poland and Lithuania. During the diplomatic rapprochement between Russia and Poland in the late 17th and early 18th centuries the rights of the Orthodox population in Poland were curbed in favor of the Uniate Church. The Prussian king, Frederick II, was protecting the rights of the Protestants in Poland. Russian diplomacy consequently sought an agreement with

Prussia. Meanwhile, the Polish seim or parliament rejected the petition of rights of the "dissenters" or non-Catholic portion of the population. This led to quarrels between the various parties of the Polish nobility, which in turn brought about an intervention of the powers and a partition of Poland. Prussia received western Poland, which was populated chiefly by Poles; Austria received Galicia, populated by Poles and Ukrainians; Russia took Polotsk, Vitebsk, and Mogilev, populated by Belorussians. Nineteen years later, under the influence of revolutionary ideas coming from France, great changes took place in Poland. On May 3, 1791, the seim adopted a new constitution. The right of liberum veto was rescinded; the central power was strengthened. The constitution of May 3 turned the former loosely knit Polish state into a centralized state. The Grand Duchy of Lithuania was formally incorporated in Poland. In the development of Poland, this constitution was a great forward step, but for Lithuania and west Russia it marked the culmination of the policy of Polonization. The publication of the constitution provoked civil war in Poland. Displeased with the document, the conservative sections of the Polish nobility requested Catherine to intervene. Russia sent troops into Poland and occupied Warsaw. The second partition of Poland took place in 1793. Russia took a considerable portion of Belorussia and Ukraine—Minsk, part of Volynia, and Podolia. The boundary between Poland and the Soviet Union from 1921 to 1939 corresponded approximately to the Russo-Polish boundary after the second partition. Prussia occupied Poznan. What remained of the Polish Kingdom was forced to rescind the constitution of May 3. In 1794 uprisings took place in Warsaw, organized by Polish patriots in protest against the plight of their country. The Russian garrison was forced to retreat from the city. A Polish revolutionary government was formed, headed by Thaddeus Kosciuszko. This government declared war upon Prussia and Russia. Catherine sent the best Russian troops, headed by Gen. Alexander Suvorov, against Poland. In 1794 Suvorov occupied Praga, a suburb of Warsaw, while Kosciuszko was taken prisoner by another detachment of the Russian army. After this Poland ceased to exist as a separate state. By the third partition, in 1795, Prussia received Mazowia, with the city of Warsaw; Austria took Little Poland, with the city of Cracow; Russia took Courland, Lithuania, and the western part of Volynia—that is, territories populated by Ukrainians, Lithuanians, and Letts. As a result of the partitions of Poland, Russia retook possession of all the southwestern Russian lands, with the exception of Kholm, Galicia, Carpatho-Ukraine, and Bukovina.

9. *The Black Sea question*

A solution of the Black Sea question was essential to Russia, for both economic and political reasons. Only by reaching the Black Sea and destroying the Crimean Khanate could southern Russia be freed from constant dangers which hindered economic development. As late as 1750 Crimean Tatars still made destructive incursions into the Ukraine. The expansion of the Russian state to its natural frontier at the Black Sea required strenuous effort, and took the greater part of the 18th century. Under Empress Ann the government, following the old muscovite method, constructed a fortified line between the Dnieper and the northern Don. Twenty regiments of territorial militia were settled along this line. The fortress of St. Ann was constructed on the lower Don. This was later renamed for St. Dmitri of Rostov and is now known as Rostov-on-the-Don.

In 1736 a war with Turkey broke out. It was burdensome to Russia in view of the difficulty of conducting campaigns at great distances in the Crimea and Moldavia, but Russian troops under Field Marshal Münnich achieved a series of important victories— the capture of Perekop, Ochakov, Azov, and the battles of Stavuchany and Khotin. The settlement in the peace of Belgrade of 1739, however, was felt not to be commensurate with Russia's enormous effort and successes in the war. All Russia received was a portion of the steppe from the Bug River to Taganrog. It was agreed that the fort of Azov should be torn down and a neutral strip of territory left between Russia and Turkey. Russia, moreover, did not receive the right to have a fleet in the Black Sea. Elizabeth's government however strengthened Russia's southern boundary by extensive military colonization. In 1752, 16,000 Serbs settled on the right bank of the Dnieper, and were organized into two regiments. In 1759 new Serbian settlements were established at Lugansk and Bakhmut, the settlers receiving liberal allowances of land.

Empress Catherine's first Turkish war was connected with the

Polish complications of the 1760's. When the Polish disorders drew away Russia's forces, Turkey decided to seize the moment for attack. In 1768 she declared war upon Russia. Though completely surprised, Catherine succeeded in arousing great enthusiasm among her subjects for the war. A daring plan of campaign both on land and sea was drawn up. The army under Count Peter Rumiantsov moved to the Danube, while a fleet was sent from the Baltic Sea around the whole of Europe to the Mediterranean. In 1770 considerable success was achieved on both fronts. Rumiantsov twice defeated the Turkish army, while the fleet occupied the Aegean archipelago and destroyed the Turkish fleet in the Bay of Chesme. The Russian fleet did not succeed, however, in passing the Dardanelles. An effort to provoke a Greek uprising against the Turks in Morea did not meet with success. The Turks suppressed the rebels with great severity, and the Russian forces landed in Morea were too feeble to oppose them.

In spite of the success of the Russian army and navy, Turkey was far from destroyed. She did not plead for peace, and it was necessary to continue the war. It was concluded only in 1774 by the peace of Kuchuk Kainarji, a village beyond the Danube.

The terms of this treaty were of great importance in Russo-Turkish relations. Russia gave back Moldavia and Wallachia, occupied by the troops of Count Rumiantsov, and also abandoned the Aegean archipelago. She received, however, the mouths of the Bug and the Dnieper on the northwestern shore of the Black Sea, as well as the mouth of the Don and the Strait of Kerch on the northeastern shore of the Black Sea. The Crimean and Azov Tatars were recognized as independent of Turkey. Russian traders in Turkey were accorded special privileges. As a matter of principle it was of great importance that the Sublime Porte in one article of the treaty promised "protection to Christians and to their churches," while Russian envoys were given power to confer with the Sultan upon affairs concerning the Orthodox Church. Following the Kuchuk Kainarji treaty, Russia established herself firmly on the Black Sea, both from a military and a diplomatic point of view. That outstanding Russian statesman, Gregory Potemkin (whom Catherine secretly married in 1774), was made head of the "New Russia" and showed great energy in organizing the territories and developing their economic resources.

Simultaneously the remnants of Ukrainian autonomy were abrogated and the Ukrainian gentry were received into the Russian nobility. The stronghold of the Zaporozhie Cossacks was destroyed. Security for southern Russia was further advanced by the seizure of the Crimea in 1783. Russia sent armies to the Crimea at the request of the khan, following internal dissension in the Crimean Khanate. In 1787 Turkey declared a new war upon Russia. Thinking that Russian forces would be diverted to the south, Sweden also declared war on Russia in 1788. Prussia too prepared to attack. Finding herself surrounded by enemies, Empress Catherine II demonstrated remarkable presence of mind and strength of character. All attacks by the Swedish fleet on St. Petersburg were repulsed in 1788–89. After a preliminary struggle on the coast of the Black Sea the Russian armies, under general Suvorov, advanced beyond the Pruth River. Suvorov was victorious at Fokshany and Rymnik in 1789 and stormed the main Turkish fortress on the Danube, Izmail, in 1790. Catherine took advantage of the international situation by directing Prussia's attention to a struggle against France where the revolution had just broken out in 1789. Meanwhile, a peace was signed with Turkey in 1792. Russia expanded her possessions along the shores of the Black Sea and the Sea of Azov, including the Taman Peninsula. The Crimea remained Russian, and new territories in the Kuban were settled by the former Zaporozhie Cossacks brought from the Dnieper.

10. *Internal policy of Catherine II*

As we have seen, Empress Catherine II was put on the throne by an uprising of Guards officers. The Guards seemed to have become a Praetorian group, possessing power to dispose of the Russian throne as they saw fit. But having attained the throne Catherine made it her object to strengthen her autocratic power and free herself from all outside influences. She approached this objective first by making every effort to strengthen the state's initiative in both internal and foreign policy. In her political views, the state was called upon to be the chief moving force in Russian education and progress. In the second place, Catherine attempted to make the imperial power the arbiter in conflicts of interest between the various classes in Russia.

From the very beginning of her reign Catherine faced powerful political opposition from the nobility. Before her accession to the throne, under Peter III, a manifesto had been promulgated giving the nobility the right to serve in the army or not, as they chose. This manifesto of 1762 also contained promises of political rights. When Catherine overthrew Peter III she had to take this promise into consideration. The nobility meanwhile was preparing plans for a council of nobles similar to that of 1730. Catherine, however, did not agree to adopt these plans, and so aroused widespread discontent among the nobles. A series of conspiracies took place, and Catherine decided to counterbalance the political ambitions of the nobility by those of other classes. In 1767 a commission which was in the nature of a national congress was called to draw up a new code. This commission contained representatives from the nobility, the towns, and the state peasants. It was divided by a struggle between the nobles and the representatives of the towns. On Catherine's initiative one of the more liberal nobles raised the question of revising the laws concerning serfdom. The commission was dissolved in 1768 without having come to any agreement.

For a time public opinion was diverted by the Turkish war. Later, Russia entered a critical period. The whole southeast of Russia and the middle and lower Volga and Ural districts were stirred by a Cossack and peasant uprising under Emelian Pugachov. An uneducated, illiterate Don Cossack, he declared himself to be the Emperor Peter III, miraculously saved from death. In Peter's name Pugachov announced the abolition of serfdom and the freeing of all the peasants belonging to the estate owners. He found much support among the Iaik Cossacks, the Bashkirs, and the Russian peasants and factory workers of the Ural area. While his movement had deep roots in the social unrest of the time, it was doomed to failure because of Pugachov's weaknesses as a leader. The troops he had collected were defeated. They were almost without officers, for the officer class on the whole remained loyal to the existing regime. Isolated peasant uprisings were suppressed. Pugachov himself was seized in flight, brought to Moscow, and executed in 1775. To obliterate the memories of the rebellion in that area Catherine ordered that the Iaik River be renamed Ural and the Iaik Cossacks the Ural Cossacks.

The Pugachov rebellion had unexpected political consequences. Under the influence of the social danger, a reconciliation took place between the empress and the nobility. Catherine declared herself the "first landowner" of Russia. The nobility abandoned their political opposition and received compensation in the form of a number of elective posts in local government and the courts established by the Statute of Provincial Administration of 1775. Their personal and class privileges were confirmed by a special charter in 1785. Simultaneously a charter of privileges was issued to the cities.

The Pugachov rebellion made evident to many Russian statesmen the necessity of solving the peasant question. A new group was formed in opposition to Catherine's policy, which may be called the conservative opposition. Its leaders believed it necessary to limit serfdom and the privileges of the nobility while strengthening the imperial power. They grouped themselves around Tsesarevich Paul, who regarded himself and was officially regarded as Peter III's son by Catherine. Catherine, both in her "Confession" to Potemkin written before their wedding and in her "Memoirs," hints that her first lover, Serge Saltykov, was actually Paul's father. In any case, a political situation was created similar to that in the time of Peter the Great and the Tsarevich Alexis. Paul feared for himself the fate of Alexis. As a matter of fact Catherine was preparing a manifesto depriving him of the succession and naming as heir to the throne her grandson, Paul's eldest son Alexander. But her death in 1796 came before she had time to put this plan into execution.

CHAPTER 7

SOCIAL AND ECONOMIC DEVELOPMENT
1700–1850

1. Growth of population

THE outstanding fact of Russia's social history in recent times is the rapid growth of her population. In this respect Russia has been second only to the United States, but has greatly exceeded most European states. In the 16th and 17th centuries the Russian population numbered approximately 15,000,000. This figure varied from time to time with wars and revolutions, but the general total remained approximately the same. There was no accurate census of population in Russia before the 18th century. During the first quarter of that century the population did not increase; in fact, it probably decreased in view of the hardships of Peter's reign and the unceasing wars. At the time of Peter's death in 1725, Russia had a population of about 14,000,000. In the beginning of the 19th century the total rose to 40,000,000, while by 1850 it had reached 68,000,000.

This rapid growth is partly explained by the annexation of new lands to the Russian Empire, but paralleling this there was a steady natural increase. The great majority of the people of Russia in the 18th and 19th centuries lived in the country and engaged in agriculture; only a small part lived in cities. The urban population increased gradually, however, both in absolute figures and in proportion to the whole population. In 1700 the total population of the cities was only 500,000, of which Moscow had 200,000—that is, 3.6 per cent of the whole population. By the middle of the 19th century the town population had risen to 3,400,000, or 5 per cent of the total population.

2. *Agriculture and industry*

During the century and a half following 1700, the area of cultivated land had greatly increased. Not only had the agricultural
population increased in size but new areas were invaded by the
agriculturalists. The most important area to be so occupied was
the black earth belt in the southern Russian steppes, which was
open to cultivation following the conquest of the north shore of
the Black Sea.

But at the same time the importance of industry also rapidly
increased. In 1725 there were less than 200 factories in Russia;
at the beginning of the 19th century there were about 2,500 factories employing 100,000 workmen; and in the mid-19th century
10,000 factories employed 500,000 workmen. Metallurgy and mining increased in importance from the time of Peter the Great on.
The chief metals worked were iron, copper, lead, and later on
gold. The study of natural science fostered by Peter's Academy of
Sciences had considerable influence upon the development of mining in Russia.

An important branch of industry was manufacturing woolen
cloth, as well as linen and in the 19th century cotton goods. Simultaneously with the expansion of large-scale industry peasant handicrafts developed, brought into being partly by climatic causes. The
long winter, especially in north Russia, gave the peasants an opportunity to employ their spare time in home industry. They did not
need any complicated machinery in view of the primitive nature of
their work. There were other reasons for the growth of this kind
of small industry. The craftsmen were well acquainted with the
needs of the peasant market and were quick to supply them. They
manufactured a great variety of goods—wooden utensils, wheels,
sleds, textiles, harness, knives, and small metal objects. Peasant
handicrafts continued to develop through the 19th century.

With the progress of agriculture and industry, trade also increased. The trade turnover of the port of Archangel in the beginning of the 18th century reached 3,000,000 rubles. Following the
transfer of trade to St. Petersburg, Archangel's trade diminished,
toward the end of the reign of Peter I, to 300,000 rubles, but that
of St. Petersburg at the same time rose to 4,000,000 and that of
Riga to 2,000,000 rubles. The annual turnover of Russian foreign

trade around 1750 reached about 15,000,000 rubles, and by 1800 about 120,000,000 rubles. It must be noted that the value of the ruble in 1750 was almost double what it was in 1800.

In addition to the goods which Russia supplied to the world in the 17th century, she added all kinds of forest products and pig iron during the 18th century. In the 19th century, following the acquisition of the black earth belt of the south, Russia began to export wheat. In 1760 this export reached over 8,000 tons, valued at 822,000 rubles, and by 1800 it had risen to around 260,000 tons, valued at 12,000,000 rubles.

During the 18th and early 19th centuries inland water routes were improved. The main rivers were joined by canals, but the construction of ballasted roads was begun only in 1817. In 1813 the first Russian steamer was constructed in St. Petersburg, but steam navigation along the Volga River started only thirty years later. The construction of railroads was first contemplated in 1835. The earliest railroad to be opened ran between St. Petersburg and Tsarskoe Selo. It was built by a private company and opened in 1838. In 1842 the construction of a railroad joining St. Petersburg and Moscow was commenced by the state. In 1851 telegraphic communication was established between St. Petersburg and Moscow.

3. State economy

In its economic policy the imperial government had to take into consideration the peculiar social structure of the Russian state of the time. The social and economic tendencies noted in the Moscow state of the 16th and 17th centuries had now finally crystallized. Russia's economic system was regulated, even more than before, primarily by the needs of the state. The first of these at the time was a permanent regular army, whose maintenance called for considerably larger funds than had the army of the Moscow state. The number of men in the permanent army under Peter reached 200,000, or 1.5 per cent of the population. By 1825 the army had reached 800,000, or 1.75 per cent of the population. The soldiers had to have weapons, clothes, and food. The state treasury was consequently one of the largest purchasers in the Russian internal market, and the largest patron of Russian industry. The state needed iron, pig iron, and steel for army munitions, which led to patronage of the metal industry. The state needed cloth for soldiers' uniforms, which led to patronage of the cloth factories. The state required enormous amounts of grain, meat, and other foods for the army, and these were supplied mostly by the large estates of the nobility. Following the army-supply laws of 1758, the landowners received the exclusive right to supply the agricultural demands of the state. The needs of the army, moreover, were the chief reason for Peter's financial reforms. In the year of his death, 1725, 65 per cent of the Russian budget was being expended upon the army and navy. To cover these costs, Peter introduced a head tax. The financial needs of the army were calculated at 4,000,000 rubles, and this sum was distributed over a male population of about 5,000,000, each of whom had to pay 80 kopeks a year. The head tax in 1725 made up 54 per cent of the state revenues. Socially, the head tax became the main mark of the lower classes.

Collecting the head tax from the individual subjects of the state was impossible in view of the inadequate development of the administrative organization. So the government encouraged the formation of peasant communities, and transacted its financial affairs directly with them. On the estates of private landholders the tax was collected by assessing them for the number of "souls" they owned. Thus they became both the economic and financial agents of the government. But in spite of all efforts, the government was not able to purchase all of the necessary supplies at the market price. Hence the state was forced to supply the factories and landowners with cheap labor in the form of serfs. In the course of the 18th century about 1,300,000 peasants were apportioned to factories and estates. Almost half of Russia's economy between 1700 and 1850 was based on serf labor.

4. Serfdom

In the 17th century the holders of the pomestie estates were chiefly military agents of the government. In the 18th century, on the other hand, the landowning nobles considered themselves primarily the economic and financial agents of the government. They also bore administrative responsibilities. In the words of a government official of the beginning of the 19th century, each landowner was a "free policeman." In particular the landowners were responsible for supplying recruits to the army from their estates. These functions explain to a considerable degree the government's encouragement of the growth of the landowners' authority over the peasants in the 1700's. The institution of serfdom in the 18th century was completely different from what it had been in the 17th century, when it merely consisted in fixing the peasant to the soil but not to the person of the landowner. As we have seen, this policy toward the peasants was motivated by the needs of the state. Peter the Great, even more than his predecessors, stressed the importance to the state of the institution of serfdom. But beginning with his reign, serfdom was rapidly transformed into slavery. The peasants became bound not to the land but to the landowner. One of the reasons for this was the merging of the serfs and the slaves into one social category. We have seen above that in the Moscow state there were both serfs and slaves; the latter had no juridical identity and were regarded not as individuals but as chattels. For considerations of fiscal policy, Peter ordered that in drawing up the head tax, slaves were to be listed with serfs. From the legal point of view, slavery was now abolished. Actually, however, the position of the serfs deteriorated since they now were treated as slaves in many respects. The proprietors paid the tax for both, and thus, first in practice and later by legislation, received complete authority over both groups. In the mid-18th century the noblemen received the right to punish their serfs and to exile them to Siberia, and they also acquired the right to sell serfs. Not until 1827 was a law passed making it necessary to ensure a sufficient quantity of land for the serfs; and in 1833 another forbade the partition of families by sale. Although the laws provided that the noblemen should not misuse the power of punishment, the serfs were completely defenseless. They were divided into two groups—the house serfs, who lived in the household of the owner, and the peasants. The position of the house serfs was particularly burdensome, and they were completely unprotected. The peasants were usually better off because their owner valued them at least for economic reasons. The arable land of an estate was usually divided into two parts, the owner's personal fields and the peasants' fields. In large estates the peasants of each village usually formed a separate community (*obshchina* or *mir*), with an elected elder at its head. The elections were to be confirmed by the proprietor. All the duties of the individual serfs were allocated by the mir. The peasant duties consisted either in payment of a rent (*obrok*)—this being the custom in northern provinces of Russia—or in working on the owner's land a fixed number of days a week, usually three, which was customary in the black earth belt.

Serfdom reached its fullest development in 1775–1800, after which the government began to take measures to modify the institution.

5. *Growth of individual rights*

While the serfs were losing the remnants of their personal rights, the nobility and merchants successfully struggled throughout the 17th century to extend their privileges. As we have seen, Catherine II satisfied them by issuing the charters of 1785. By these documents both the noblemen and upper class townspeople were finally and fully freed from their former obligations toward the state. This amounted to the abrogation of the basic pattern of state-society interrelations of the Muscovite and the Petrine periods. A new type of free society was in process of emerging starting from the top of the social pyramid. So far only the upper classes were emancipated but, once started, the process could not stop at that. Slowly and gradually the rights of the lower middle class and other intermediary groups were enlarged. The bulk of the nation—the peasants—had to wait for their emancipation several more decades although nobody could explain to them the reason for the delay. From the point of view of pure logic, there was no reason.

Among the trends which led to the emancipation of the upper classes from state tutelage and to the growth of middle class individualism in Russia, the extension of owners' rights on land is of great importance. We have seen that in the early Muscovite state there were two types of property in land: the patrimonial estates of the boyars and the military fiefs or pomestie, which were held on condition of government service. In the 17th century these two types practically merged into one, for the government then demanded service both from the patrimonial estate and from the fief, while on the other hand temporary and conditional possession of the pomestie was gradually being transformed into hereditary ownership. In the beginning of the 18th century the two types of possession were finally merged by legislation. By the law of 1714 a single concept of real property was introduced.

Neither under Peter the Great nor under his immediate successors did the owners of real property have full possession of it. The legislation of Peter and Ann introduced material limitations upon property rights. Thus title to subsoil rights was vested in the state, and permission to exploit them was granted to all who desired on the payment of a small sum to the owner of the land. Timber suitable for the construction of ships was also declared government property. The owner of the land had no right to fell oak on his own land, under threat of death. These examples demonstrate how circumscribed was the right of private property in land in the first half of the 18th century and to what an extent the state interfered in private matters. Only in the second half of that century were protests heard against this interference, and in 1782 Catherine II rescinded the limitations. It was at this time that the modern Russian word for "property" (*sobstvennost*) first appeared in Russian legislation.

The struggle which this legislation involved affected only the nobility, for in the mid-18th century the right to private property in land became a privilege of the nobility. The lands of the Cossacks and of the state peasants were not owned by individuals. The next phase was the extension of property rights to other classes of society. In 1801 Alexander I issued a manifesto granting the right to own land to individuals of all classes, except serfs. From this time on the only remaining exclusive privilege of the nobility was the right to private property in "populated" lands—that is to say, to own land with serfs.

The law of 1801 was an important step forward in the development of modern juridical concepts and in the creation of a new type of middle-class society. The recognition of the right of all classes, except the serfs, to private property in land was evidence of the fact that new groups in Russian society were acquiring full civil status.

6. *Social changes as reflected in the state budget*

The social changes of the 18th and 19th centuries intimately affected the Russian state budget. The constant growth of population and of the national economy permitted a steady increase in the whole budget, while the relative weight of budgetary items underwent modification. The expenses of the army grew, but its proportion to total expenditure steadily decreased. Military expenses in 1725 swallowed up 65 per cent of the budget, which that year was 9,100,000 rubles. In 1801 the proportion had decreased to 50 per cent and in 1850 to 42 per cent of a total expenditure of 284,-500,000 rubles. Thus it may be said that the Russian budget gradually became demilitarized. This relieved the government of anxiety about means to support the army.

The sum derived from the head tax decreased in importance as a source of revenue. In 1725 the head tax brought in 54 per cent of all state revenue. In 1801 it accounted for only 30 per cent, and in 1850 for 24 per cent. In place of direct taxation the revenue was made up by indirect taxation, and in particular by the tax on spirits. The changes in the budget made the former system of state economy less necessary and permitted the government to undertake the fundamental reconstruction of the whole social system begun by the reforms of Alexander II.

CHAPTER 8

CULTURAL DEVELOPMENT, 1700–1850

1. The eclipse of the Orthodox Church and the growth of dissenters

THE Europeanization of Russia, begun under Peter, consisted primarily in the secularization of Russian culture. The church, which had played such a leading part in Russian life before his time, gradually lost its importance. The upper circle of society, which came under European influence, no longer felt the need of a church, or, at any rate, the church definitely lost its position as the chief source of cultural life. In the 18th century the aristocratic and official classes of Russian society were educated in the spirit of the French Enlightenment. They were devoted to Voltaire and had no real respect for the church.

For a large section of the lower classes the church also lost its original meaning. Following the schism of the Old Ritualists in the 17th century, half the population of some districts in north Russia turned away from it. Thus, the Orthodox Church in the 18th century lost the support of a large part of the noble classes and a considerable portion of the trading and peasant classes.

It has been pointed out above that the church administration was made subservient to the state by Peter's reforms. The management of the church became one of the functions of a special government department. Important positions in the new ecclesiastical hierarchy were given to supporters of Peter's reforms, such as Archbishop Theophan Prokopovich, who drew up the "Spiritual Regulation" which determined the activity of the Holy Synod. A government appointee, the overprocurator of the Holy Synod, had almost complete authority in church administration. In the 18th century the government all but ceased to value the church as a moral authority either with regard to its own activities or as a force in society at large. The church was considered essential only for the moral education of the lower classes.

A change in the government's attitude took place at the end of the century during the reign of Emperor Paul. But Paul, while recognizing the moral value of the church, regarded it as subject to his authority. It was he who said in 1797, "The tsar is the head of the church." This formula under Nicholas I found its way into the laws of the Russian Empire in the form of a note to one of the articles of the basic law, commenting that it was intended to define the role of the tsar as protector of the interests of the church and not in any wider sense.

Throughout the whole 18th century the government did not hesitate to limit the material rights of the church. Its land was confiscated by Empress Catherine II in 1764. The archbishop of Rostov, Arseni Matseevich, who protested against this measure, was deprived of his office and imprisoned in a fortress where he subsequently died. At the same time a large number of monasteries were closed. But while the government itself felt no compunctions in its dealings with the church, it demanded obedience from the masses of the people to the institution whose authority it was itself undermining. Old Ritualists and the sectarians who desired to leave the church were subjected to government oppression during the greater part of the century. Naturally these forcible measures did not check the widening of the schism and the growth of sectarianism.

The movement of the Old Ritualists by 1800 ceased to be a unit and broke into several separate sects. It was essentially a protest against the innovations of Nikon by defenders of the old ritual; but the break-up of the old organization of the church forced the Old Ritualists to enter upon paths of even greater innovation. Thus, it became necessary to choose a new way to select priests. The Greek Orthodox Church held that only the bishop could ordain new priests and that the priest could not transfer his office to another person. The Old Ritualists had no bishops. The priests named before the schism were gradually growing old and dying and there was no way in which to secure new ones. The Old Ritualists were faced with the possibility of remaining without priests. This question served as a basic ground of difference between the two chief divisions of Old Ritualists. One decided to be consistent in its beliefs and to remain without priests. This eventually made its organization somewhat similar to that of the Protestant churches. The other sought a bishop outside of Russia. In the 19th century the latter finally succeeded in having a bishop ordained beyond the limits of the Russian Empire, in Bukovina, which then formed part of Austria.

The break-up of the Old Ritualists into smaller groups was only one of the sources of weakness of the opposition to the Russian church. Another was the rapid growth of various sects. One of the oldest, the *Khlysty* (flagellants), took definite shape at the end of the 17th century. The Khlysty were mystics who believed in the possibility of the continuous and recurrent incarnation of God in man. They repudiated the official church and its organization and also denied marriage. They organized secret meetings at which they attempted to call forth the presence of the Holy Spirit by means of ecstatic dances. These meetings at times terminated in orgies. Gregory Rasputin, who played such a tragic role in the fall of the imperial regime in Russia, was associated with the Khlysty in his youth.

At the other extreme, seeking liberation from the darker aspects of the Khlysty, was the Spiritual Christianity of the Dukhobors, who arose in the mid-18th century in central and southern Russia. In the last quarter of the century, among the Spiritual Christians of Tambov province, appeared a sect of Evangelical Christians who received the name of Molokane, that is, people who drank milk during Lent, which was forbidden by the rules of the Orthodox Church.

Prior to the 19th century, the Old Ritualists and the sectarians converted many of the trading and peasant classes. In the early 1800's, under Alexander I, sectarianism, especially the Khlysty, began to penetrate into the higher circles of society. Branches of Khlysty were organized in the time of Alexander I by the upper groups of society in St. Petersburg.

All the dissenters, as we have said, were subjected during the 18th century to constant repression on the part of the government. The leaders of the Dukhobors in southern Russia were sentenced to be burned as late as 1792, but Catherine II commuted the sentence from death to exile to Siberia. The government began to be more tolerant toward the Old Ritualists in the latter half of the century; but the repression of sectarians was terminated only at the beginning of the 19th century under Alexander I, on the advice of Senator Ivan Lopukhin, who conducted an investigation in one of the southern governments in 1801. Under Nicholas I, in the mid-19th century, a reaction set in and the government again pursued the policy of repressing religious dissenters. The total number of Old Ritualists and sectarians in 1850 was estimated as close to 9,000,000.

2. Education

The secularization of Russian culture in the 18th century was noticeable first in education. In the Muscovite state, education had a narrowly religious character. Practical needs during the reign of Peter the Great brought about a new system of education intended to prepare officers for the army and navy. Peter in 1700 founded in Moscow a School of Mathematics and Navigation and invited a Scot, Henry Fargwarson, to direct it. In 1715 the school was moved to St. Petersburg and named the Naval Academy. The pupils of the academy became teachers in the mathematical schools instituted in the principal cities of Russia, where children were taught chiefly arithmetic and geometry. In the last years of the reign of Peter there were about 40 such schools, with 2,000 pupils; part of these came of their own free will, others were recruited from soldiers' and civil servants' families.

It cannot be said, however, that Peter did not understand the value of abstract sciences as well. On the advice of the famous German philosopher Leibnitz he created the Russian Academy of Sciences which began functioning in St. Petersburg in 1725, soon after his death. The first academicians were called from Germany and Switzerland, among them the well known mathematicians Daniel Bernoulli and Leonhard Euler. The academy also opened a gymnasium or upper school where a number of boys, chiefly sons of government servants and merchants, were educated. The nobility preferred to send their sons to the Cadet Corps, which had been instituted in 1730 to prepare officers for the army. Further steps in public education were made in the second half of the 18th century. In 1755 the first Russian university was founded in Moscow, the first professors being chiefly Germans. Moscow University had as adjuncts two gymnasiums—one for the children of nobles and one for those of all other classes. In 1782 a Commission for the Creation of Public Schools was set up. This commission, under the direction of Jankovich de Mirievo, a Serbian educator brought over from Austria, drew up a plan for the development of public teaching in Russia. High schools were to be opened in the chief cities and primary schools in the small cities; because of inadequate funds only part of the program was realized. By 1800 there were 315 schools in Russia with 20,000 pupils, for the most part children of merchants and craftsmen. When the Ministry of Public Education was founded in 1802, Russia was broken up into six educational districts, each under a curator. The first appointments to these posts were very well judged and the reform greatly advanced education. According to this plan a university was to be founded in each educational district, a gymnasium in each provincial capital, and a school in each county. This program was practically completed by the end of the reign of Alexander I. Russia then had 6 universities (Moscow, Derpt, Vilno, Kazan, Kharkov, and St. Petersburg), 48 gymnasiums, and 337 schools. There were 5,500 students in the gymnasiums and about 30,000 in the schools. The University of Derpt was German until the end of the 19th century. The University of Vilno, until it closed after the Polish rebellion in 1831, was Polish. Instead of it, a Russian university was opened in Kiev in 1833. The chief progress, compared with education in the 18th century, was in the development not of primary but of secondary and higher education. Private initiative aided the government in the educational movement, for instance in opening Kharkov University. Two higher schools, Demidov Law School in Iaroslavl (1805) and the Historico-Philological Institute of Prince Bezborodko in Niezhin (1820), were established by private means. The Imperial Lyceum was opened in Tsarskoe Selo in 1811 for children of the nobility; among its early graduates were the poet Alexander Pushkin and the future chancellor, Prince Alexander Gorchakov. During the reign of Nicholas I several technical schools were opened, among them the Institute of Technology of St. Petersburg (1828) and the Institute in Moscow (1844). In 1835 the Imperial School of Jurisprudence was founded in St. Petersburg. Many of those responsible for the judicial reform of 1864 were graduates of this excellent institution.

3. *Science*

Organizing the Academy of Sciences before either universities or high schools seems at first sight an impractical idea; but it had a great influence upon the development of Russian learning, and particularly in mathematics and natural science. Russian scientists had a center at a time when a particularly intensive study of the natural sciences was beginning in the West. The academy immediately took an important place in the broader world of learning of the 18th century. While the first members of the academy were imported from abroad, learned men of Russian origin soon joined them, among them that universal genius, Michael Lomonosov (1711–65), son of a peasant shipbuilder from the north of Russia, who made himself equally proficient in chemistry, physics, mineralogy, history, philology, and poetry.

The academy did significant work in making a geographical survey of Siberia and supporting the great Siberian expedition of 1733–43. It also contributed to the growth of technical education in Russia, thus preparing the ground for important inventions. A Russian technician, Ivan Polzunov (1730–66), experimenting simultaneously with James Watt but independently, constructed a steam engine which was used in the Barnaul metallurgical plant in the Altai region in 1766.

The greatest Russian scientist of the first half of the 19th century was not an academician but a university professor from Kazan, Nicholas Lobachevsky (1793–1856), who began teaching in 1811. It was some time before his originality was appreciated and his ideas understood by his contemporaries in Russia and abroad. Lobachevsky's mind was one of the most productive in the history of mathematics. He created a new geometry which uses a hypothesis of space differing from that of Euclid.

The study of social sciences and history was less emphasized in the 18th and early 19th centuries than the natural sciences. The Academy of Sciences produced an energetic collector of historical documents, Gerhard Friedrich Müller, a naturalized German. But the outstanding Russian historians of the period were not professional men of learning. One was an administrative official, another a politician, and a third a military man. The leading Russian historian of the first half of the 19th century, Nicholas

Karamzin (1766–1826), was not associated with any institution of learning. The publication of his exhaustive *History of the Russian State* (1816) was a great event in the spiritual life of Russia. His breadth of learning and deep knowledge of sources were combined with a masterly literary presentation. It was commonly said that Karamzin had discovered ancient Russia as Columbus had discovered America.

The growth of interest in science in Russian society around 1800 was evidenced by the foundation of several learned societies such as the Free Economic Society, St. Petersburg, 1765; the Friendly Society of Learning, Moscow, 1782; the Society of Russian History and Antiquity and the Society of Experimental Science, both opened in 1805. There was significant activity too by private individuals in organizing scientific investigations. At the initiative and expense of Chancellor Count Nicholas Rumiantsov, a man of unusually wide interests in both geography and history, a valuable collection of ancient Russian documents was brought together and published. Rumiantsov supported geographical expeditions and historical research. He conducted an extensive correspondence with many Russian scholars, took an interest in the details of their work, and stimulated them to further activity. His collections were housed in the Rumiantsov Museum in Moscow, now known as the Lenin Library.

4. *Literature and the theater*

Before the reforms of Peter the Great, the literature (written and oral) and art of Russia had had an equal appeal to all classes of society, as both groups had religious training. Conditions now, however, had completely changed. The upper circles of society had broken away from the church, whose creative powers had at the same time been materially weakened. They began to create for themselves a new art and literature, while the lower classes remained without the cultural leadership they had formerly had. By 1850 the new literature was widely popular; the rift between the "intellectuals" and the people, in literary matters, was gradually being closed. But in the 18th century, this literature was available only to the upper classes. A typical 18th-century "poet of the nobility" was Gabriel Derzhavin, some of whose verses demonstrated genuine artistry. The first half of the 19th-century saw the rise of a number of writers and poets who attracted wide circles of readers, among them Pushkin, Lermontov, and Gogol.

Alexander Pushkin (1799–1837), the "Sun of Russian Poetry" as he was justly called, remains to this day the greatest genius of Russian literature. Because he wrote chiefly in verse he is more difficult to appreciate in translation than Russian prose writers. This partly explains the fact that his works are little known outside Russia. Pushkin had an unusually harmonious personality, and a keen and brilliant mind. He could both feel and express the most intimate experiences of the human soul, as well as manifestations of mass psychology. Pushkin was deeply interested in history and in contemporary political questions. His political ideas passed through two phases. During his youth, up to the second half of the reign of Alexander I, he was sympathetic with liberalism, being close to many of the so-called "Decembrists." Later, in the reign of Nicholas I, he held moderately conservative views. But all his life Pushkin was a sincere humanitarian, unhappy, at times, in the midst of the political and personal intrigue which characterized Russian higher society of the day. He was ultimately ruined by intrigue, being killed in a duel at the age of thirty-seven while defending the honor of his wife.

Michael Lermontov (1814–41), a guards officer, was a brilliant poet but a more one-sided personality than Pushkin. An ancestor of his was George Learmont, a Scottish adventurer who in the early 1600's entered the Russian service. Lermontov's youthful poetical work was strongly influenced by Byron. The source of his inspiration was the Caucasus, with its natural beauty, the primitive customs of its mountaineers, and its state of constant war. He was transferred to the Caucasus in punishment for his verses "On the Death of Pushkin," which blamed court society for the death of the poet; and he took part as an officer in the Caucasian war. His best known poem, "The Demon," is set in the Caucasus. The Demon was the Spirit of Negation and Doubt, which had fascinated Lermontov from his early youth. Like Pushkin, Lermontov died in a duel at the age of twenty-seven.

Nicholas Gogol (1809–52) was of Ukrainian origin and introduced many Ukrainian words and idioms into the Russian language. The subjects of his first stories were incidents in the life of the people of southern Russia. Later he described the world of landowners and civil servants in his comedy, *The Government Inspector,* and in his novel, *Dead Souls.* The chief characteristics of Gogol's work are realistic satire and humor. But behind the humor lies profound grief for the imperfection of human society. Through his realistic descriptions of the external world, one senses his search for spiritual values as the real basis of life.

Pushkin, Lermontov, and Gogol laid the cornerstones of the foundation upon which subsequent Russian literature was to rise.

The drama was an important branch of Russian literature of this period. Peter the Great built the first theater in Russia that was open to the public—and tried to use it to influence his subjects in favor of his reforms. He was handicapped, however, by lack of good plays and good actors. It was only in the reign of Elizabeth that serious interest in the theater appeared in Russia. A leading producer and actor of the period was Theodore Volkov, son of a merchant, whose productions in Iaroslavl became highly popular in 1750. Empress Elizabeth invited him and his company to St. Petersburg and was so pleased with their art that she decided to create with their help a permanent theater in St. Petersburg. Thus the first Imperial Theater was founded in 1756, to be followed by others, both in St. Petersburg and Moscow. From the late 18th century on there were also several private theaters in Russia. The art of acting in the first half of the 19th century followed chiefly French patterns. There were a number of talented Russian actors and actresses, both in tragedy and comedy. The most popular was Michael Shchepkin (1788–1863), son of a serf, whom his contemporaries considered the greatest comic actor of the age. The repertory consisted of both translations of western dramatists, including Shakespeare, Racine, Corneille, and Molière, and Russian plays, which at first had been pale imitations of western patterns but later developed qualities of their own. Toward the end of this period there appeared a playwright of great talent and originality, Alexander Ostrovsky (1823–86). Most of Ostrovsky's plays are genre comedies, but in some of them tragic situations arise, and one of his plays, *The Storm,* is a masterpiece of Russian dramatic literature. Most of his works deal with the lower middle class, and merchants of old patriarchal traditions. That his creative genius also had other, only partly developed, aspects is evidenced by his charming fantasy play, *The Snow Maiden,* which is based on Russian folklore.

5. *Fine arts*

The art of ancient Russia was tied even more closely than the literature to the church. Architecture, painting, and music served first of all the needs of the church. For this reason, as we have seen, instrumental music and sculpture were very little developed in ancient Russia. Art did not cease to serve the church in the 18th century, but religious art became only one of the branches of a general development.

The fact that imperial palaces and the houses of nobles in town and country became the chief objects of artists' endeavors in part explains the character of Russian art during the 18th and early 19th centuries. Catering to the tastes of society, art was entirely western in spirit. The Academy of Arts, founded in 1757, which sponsored the technique and ideals of western art, played an important role in the development of the fine arts.

Western architects and painters, among them many Italians and Frenchmen, were called by the court to construct and decorate the imperial palaces and, to a certain extent, the churches as well. Among the western architects working in Russia were the well known Italian, Bartolomeo Rastrelli, and the Scot, Charles Cameron. Many of these foreigners became naturalized, like Carlo Rossi. Gradually native Russian artists and architects appeared too, possibly the most gifted one of this period being Basil Bazhenov. The new architecture was exemplified first in the new capital, St. Petersburg, as well as in the nearby imperial palaces. The favorite style was the classical. Columns of different types were a feature of both lay and church architecture. The style set by the imperial palaces was followed by the nobles. During this period many nobles' estates were adorned with architectural masterpieces. The style of the manor houses was similar to the colonial style employed in the United States, but they were often built of stone. The classical style of architecture soon became adapted to the Russian environment and ceased to appear foreign. Early in the 19th century a variant of this style, known as Russian "Empire," was developed.

The most famous sculptural work of the time was the monument to Peter the Great in St. Petersburg, cast by two French sculptors, Etienne-Maurice Falconet and Marie-Anne Collot. Several good pieces by Russian sculptors are less renowned. The portrait busts of Fedot Shubin were fine pieces of work, as were the monuments of Ivan Martos. Russian sculpture, like the architecture of the period, was inspired by classicism. Michael Kozlovsky represented General Suvorov as a youthful Mars, while Martos showed Minin and Pozharsky, the heroes of 1612, as citizens of ancient Rome.

Several remarkable portrait painters appeared, among them Dmitri Levitsky, Vladimir Borovikovsky, and Orest Kiprensky; and a landscape painter of great talent, Simeon Shchedrin, who died at an early age. The most famous painter of the early 19th century was Karl Brullov, who in 1830 painted the "Last Day of Pompeii," a cold and theatrical picture, which nevertheless produced a great impression. More profound was Alexander Ivanov, who was moved by deep religious sentiment. His picture "Christ Appearing before the People" combines depth of feeling with technical mastery. Ivanov was more than twenty years (1833–55) in completing this work.

6. Music

Church singing in the 18th century fell under Italian influence. An Italian operatic troupe performed in St. Petersburg and the court singers took part in the choruses. Italian influence may be noted in religious compositions of the period. The most famous and competent composer was Dmitri Bortniansky (1751–1825), who was trained in St. Petersburg by an Italian master and studied in Italy. In 1796 he was appointed director of the Imperial Choir. This choir even before his appointment had reached a high degree of excellence, so Bortniansky directed his attention to selecting voices and perfecting the ensemble. He sought singers in southern Russia and the Ukraine, where the people were famed for their voices. As a result he achieved enormous success. His successor as director of the choir was Alexis Lvov, composer of the Russian national anthem (1833). The French composer Berlioz thought the choir under Lvov superior to the papal choir.

During the 18th century secular music, both instrumental and vocal, flooded Russia from the West. Music was used as entertainment, accompanying banquets, dinners, balls, and performances of all kinds. Landowners, imitating the court, organized orchestras and choirs among their serfs. In 1735, in the reign of Empress Ann, the Italian Opera was invited to visit St. Petersburg. Later, several Russian operas were written, in the Italian manner, in which attempts were made to use Russian tunes. They were only moderately successful. In the 19th century the musical life of Russia became more serious and significant. The Russian Philharmonic Society was founded in 1802. After the War of 1812 many operas of a patriotic character were written. Textbooks on music became available; the number of serious professional musicians increased; and musical education improved.

This atmosphere of interest and creativity made possible the appearance of the real founder of modern Russian music, Michael Glinka (1803–57). He occupies in the history of Russian music the same central position that Pushkin holds in the history of Russian literature. They were contemporaries; and Glinka, who had great respect for Pushkin, set a number of his poems to music. The composer belonged to a noble family from Smolensk province. His first musical impressions came from hearing his uncle's orchestra of serf musicians. The Russian folk songs Glinka had heard sung in the country from childhood had a great influence upon the character of his later work. He studied in Berlin and, having acquired great skill in musical technique, developed a symphonic and operatic style entirely his own in conception. He composed two operas, *A Life for the Tsar* (now called *Ivan Susanin;* 1836) and *Ruslan and Ludmila* (1842); the libretto of the latter is based on a poem by Pushkin with a brilliant eastern theme.

A decade after Glinka the second great Russian composer, Alexander Dargomyzhsky (1813–69), was born. He is representative of realism and of the declamatory style in music. He sought a perfect union between speech and music. As he expressed it: "I want the sound to express the word directly. I want the truth." His highest achievement in this direction was his opera based on Pushkin's play, *The Stone Guest.*

CHAPTER 9

THE RUSSIAN EMPIRE IN THE FIRST HALF OF THE 19TH CENTURY

1. *The reign of Emperor Paul*

EMPEROR PAUL, who reigned five years, from 1796 to 1801, came to the throne with many interesting ideas about Russian policies, domestic as well as foreign, but his despotic caprices marred all efforts to realize these plans. At the time of his accession Paul was mentally unbalanced. The program of the conservative circle which had formed around Paul before his coronation was primarily intended to procure fundamental laws which would define the imperial power; it was partly carried out by the acts of April 5, 1797. A law of succession to the throne was promulgated, laws concerning the imperial family (the internal organization of the imperial house), and, finally, a decree which limited serf labor for the landowner to three days a week. This last was the first serious attempt at imperial legislation to restrict serfdom. The decree was of small practical importance, since the government did not have enough agents to secure enforcement, but it had great significance as a matter of principle. Simultaneously, the privileges granted by Empress Catherine to the nobility were suspended. The government of Emperor Paul also began reforms in the administrative departments, with the aim of replacing collective responsibility by personal leadership.

Foreign policy under Emperor Paul was significant, particularly with respect to the Black Sea and the Mediterranean. The anti-Turkish policy of Empress Catherine had secured for Russia the northern coast of the Black Sea. This had very great value for the development of Russian trade and the prosperity of agriculture in the south. Meanwhile there arose the possibility of developing relations with Turkey on entirely new lines. The government of

THE ROMANOV DYNASTY

Part II

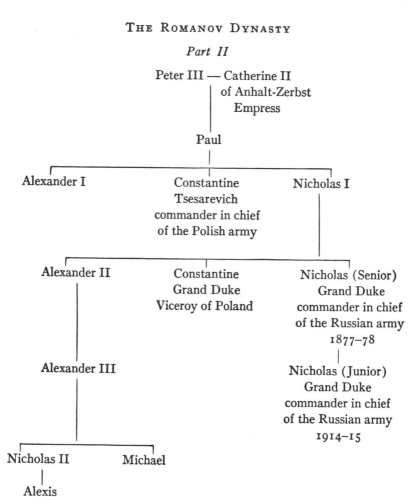

Peter III — Catherine II
of Anhalt-Zerbst
Empress

Paul

Alexander I

Constantine
Tsesarevich
commander in chief
of the Polish army

Nicholas I

Alexander II

Constantine
Grand Duke
Viceroy of Poland

Nicholas (Senior)
Grand Duke
commander in chief
of the Russian army
1877–78

Alexander III

Nicholas (Junior)
Grand Duke
commander in chief
of the Russian army
1914–15

Nicholas II

Michael

Alexis
Tsesarevich

Emperor Paul succeeded in taking advantage of this opportunity in a manner which gave its foreign policy special importance in the history of Russian diplomacy. The guiding principle was the extension of Russian influence in the eastern part of the Mediterranean Sea, by means not of war but of cordial relations with Turkey. In 1798 Russia and Turkey joined England, Austria, and the Kingdom of Naples in a coalition against France, motivated by the common purpose of resisting the expansionist policy which had brought Switzerland, northern Italy, and the Ionian Islands under her sway.

In 1798 France sent General Napoleon Bonaparte to Egypt to seize the route to India. Russia concluded a special convention with Turkey for joint action. The Turks agreed to allow the Russian fleet to pass through the Straits of the Bosporus and the Dardanelles, while undertaking to hold them closed to the warships of other nations. The Russian Black Sea squadron, under Adm. Theodore Ushakov, together with Turkish vessels, was sent into the Adriatic Sea. Ushakov drove the French from the Ionian Islands, where he organized a republic formally under the suzerainty of Turkey but actually under the control of Russia.

Ushakov succeeded in securing great influence in the Adriatic. In 1799 Montenegro offered its allegiance to Russia. Thus policy under Emperor Paul led to the establishment of a Russian base in the Adriatic Sea, from which assistance could be given the Orthodox and Slavonic peoples of the Balkans. Desirous of extending Russia's power still further in the Mediterranean, Paul became patron of the order of Knights of St. John, known as the Maltese Knights, who owned the island of Malta.

The naval campaign in the Mediterranean was supplemented by an overland campaign. In 1799 Paul sent to Austria's aid choice Russian troops under general Suvorov, who soon succeeded in defeating the French armies in Italy and forcing them to retreat. He was ready to invade France when Paul, yielding to the advice of Austria, ordered him to eject the French troops from Switzerland. Consequently Suvorov made the extremely difficult march across the Alps over the St. Gothard Pass and entered Switzerland. At that juncture Paul became convinced of the selfishness of both Austria and England, and not wishing to be a toy in their hands broke relations with them and called Suvorov back to Russia. Russia then began to negotiate with her recent enemy, France.

Russia's change of policy with regard to France did not lead to altered relations with Turkey. That alliance continued, and the Adriatic base was retained to further Russian policy in the Balkans. But the agreement with Napoleon automatically led to a complete break with England. Paul imposed an embargo upon all English goods in Russia, and ordered the Don Cossacks forthwith to conquer India. This only proved the unbalanced condition of Paul's mind. The Cossacks were ordered to march without any preparation. They lacked even maps, and before reaching the Russian frontier had lost half their horses in the desert. They were summoned back immediately after Paul's assassination.

England's reply to Paul's new policy was to dispatch the British fleet to the Baltic Sea. At the same time the British representative in St. Petersburg attempted to utilize the discontent which Paul's regime had aroused in court circles and among the officers to sponsor a coup d'état. This plan did not prove difficult of execution. Paul's insanity expressed itself in recurring attacks of wild fury during which none about him could feel secure. For a mistake at a military parade, he would send officers into exile; the highest government officials went in continual fear of his displeasure and of being dismissed. Paul used to say, "In Russia he is great with whom I speak, and that only while I speak to him." The result was an unceasing change of personnel in high military and civil posts.

It is not surprising, under the circumstances, that the courtiers and officers who plotted against Paul were led by the military governor of St. Petersburg, Count Peter Pahlen. On the night of March 24, 1801, Paul was assassinated by conspirators who succeeded in entering his bedroom.

The new emperor was Paul's son Alexander, who was then twenty-four years old. He had consented to his father's overthrow but had not supposed that assassination would be the means. There is evidence that he suffered a nervous collapse when he received the news. He was brought back to his senses by Count Pahlen's angry remark, "C'est assez faire l'enfant, allez regner."

2. Alexander I's policies to 1807

Alexander I had a brilliant political mind, and few equals among contemporary diplomats. He has often been regarded as a weak man who frequently changed his policies. Actually he usually held stubbornly to his objectives, but he reached them not by direct means, as did Peter the Great and Alexander's chief opponent, Napoleon, but by devious methods—first instilling his ideas into the minds of those around him and then pretending that he was following their views. Alexander had unusual ability to charm his auditors. He was particularly attractive to women and succeeded in attaining many of his goals with their aid. Only a few contemporaries saw through his diplomatic methods. It was said of him, "Alexander is as sharp as a pin, as fine as a razor, and as false as sea foam." Napoleon referred to him as a "Grec de Bas Empire" (Byzantine).

A remarkable trait in Alexander's mentality was his broad world outlook. He was internationally minded and felt that his main responsibilities were to the European community of nations rather than to the particular national state whose head he happened to be. Because of this, throughout his reign stanch Russian nationalists accused him of betraying or neglecting Russia's national interests and objected to the prominent role played by foreigners in the Russian army and diplomatic service. An autocrat by birth, Alexander favored the constitutional form of government, which he actually introduced in Finland and Poland and intended eventually, but failed, to introduce in Russia. Still another facet of Alexander's complex personality was his mysticism, which became apparent after the struggles of the Napoleonic wars and found expression in the declaration of the Holy Alliance in 1815.

Alexander's accession to the throne was greeted enthusiastically by the whole nation. He opened his reign with a series of liberal measures, such as abolishing the "Secret Chancery" (department of political police) which had flourished under Paul; granting amnesty to political prisoners and exiles; abrogating torture, which until then had been a regular part of procedure in the investigation and trial of criminals; and restoring the charters of the gentry and the towns. Further reforms were discussed and partly prepared by the so-called "Intimate Committee" which formed around Alexander, consisting of four "young friends" of the new tsar; Count Victor Kochubey, Nicholas Novosiltsov, Count Paul Stroganov, and Prince Adam Czartoryski. All of these were enlightened men who sympathized with the liberal ideas of the period. Czartoryski, a Pole, was chiefly interested in the possibility of restoring Poland as a nation under the patronage of Alexander. Among the decrees issued upon the recommendation of this committee was that granting the right to individual ownership of land to all the tsar's subjects except the serfs (see p. 177). A measure of considerable im-

portance replaced the antiquated system of "colleges," introduced
by Peter the Great to handle the central administration, with
ministries modeled on the French pattern. Eight ministers were
appointed to direct the following branches of administration: War,
Navy, Foreign Affairs, Judiciary, Interior, Finance, Commerce,
and Education. A Committee of Ministers was created, each minister, however, being personally responsible to the tsar.

Alexander stopped the practice of turning state peasants into
noblemen's serfs, the policy in his father's and grandmother's
reigns. All rewards to high officials were now made in money and
not in men. Moreover, the peasant question became a weapon in
Alexander's hands against the aristocracy. The political opposition
of the nobles expressed itself in 1802 in demands that the Senate
be made a council of nobles, and even in advocacy of a limitation
of imperial power in favor of the nobility. In the decree concerning
the reorganization of the Senate in 1802, Alexander did not follow
the plans advocated by the nobles, but he did leave the Senate
a shadow of political authority. This was the right to protest against
imperial decrees which were at variance with the established laws
—something in the nature of the *droit de remontrance* of the French
courts of the 18th century.

The Senate soon desired to take advantage of its right when it
felt that the government was violating the privileges of the nobility. In December 1802 the Committee of Ministers approved,
and the tsar confirmed, a proposal of the minister of war that nobles
who had served in the army without securing promotion to the
grade of officer could not retire until they had served at least
twelve years as noncommissioned officers. The ordinance was sent
to the Senate for publication. A senator expressed the opinion that
the new regulation was at variance with the fundamental privileges
of the nobility, and the Senate supported this opinion. A deputation of senators was received by the tsar, who told them dryly that
special legislation would be promulgated. At the beginning of April
1803 a decree was published announcing that the right of the Senate
to protest was limited to laws and decrees published before
1802.

To counterbalance the opposition of the Senate and to warn the
nobles, Alexander raised the peasant question. On March 4, 1803,
a decree was published regarding "free landowners." This con-

cerned the rules for emancipating the serfs and providing them with land; the granting of liberty, however, was left to the decision of the estate owners.

The practical result of the decree was not great. The total number of serfs freed following its publication was about 50,000. But it had great significance in principle. The nobles recognized the possibility that Alexander might grant freedom to the peasants to counterbalance their own privileges. They retired, and Alexander remained victor in the political duel. After that time nobles desiring to advance a practical political program were forced to include in it a solution for the peasant problem. This was done by the "Decembrists" at the end of Alexander I's reign.

The law on free landowners was only a first step. In 1804 and 1805 new regulations were issued concerning the status of the peasants in Livonia and Estonia. They received limited rights of self-government and were to be tried in courts of their own. Their work for the proprietor was limited to two days a week.

The progress of reform in Russia was seriously hampered by international complications. At first Alexander tried to avoid intervening in European affairs, but in 1803 there was a new rupture between Great Britain and France, and Russia was involved in the international crisis which followed. While preparing for a war against France on the side of Great Britain, Alexander made a significant attempt to introduce new principles into international diplomacy and to create an ideological basis for European solidarity. In 1804 he sent one of the members of his Intimate Committee, Nicholas Novosiltsov, as his envoy extraordinary to England. In the "Instruction" given to Novosiltsov, Alexander suggested that the principle of European federation be opposed to Napoleon's imperialistic policies. Part of the plan called for a regional federation of the Slavs, both of central Europe and of the Balkans. The British dismissed the plan as utopian but welcomed alliance with Russia. In 1805 Austria joined the coalition, but the combined Austro-Russian army was defeated by Napoleon in the battle of Austerlitz—which is vividly described by Leo Tolstoy in *War and Peace*. Austria concluded a separate peace with Napoleon, but Prussia now joined the alliance against him, only to be defeated in her turn (1806). While the Russians continued the war for some time in cooperation with the remnants of the Prussian army, they too were defeated at Friedland in 1807. Alexander then sued for peace.

Since Russia could have continued resistance if necessary, Napoleon proposed conditions of peace more favorable than might have been expected. Alexander and Napoleon negotiated personally, without intermediaries, meeting on a raft in the middle of Nieman River at Tilsit. The result was a treaty of both peace and alliance. It was Prussia that was to pay the price of defeat. Besides losing some of her western possessions she had to give up a good part of her Polish lands. An autonomous state, the Duchy of Warsaw, was created from them, and its throne given to the king of Saxony, one of Napoleon's vassals. Actually, Napoleon became master of the restored fragment of Poland. (Two years later Austria, too, had to cede some of her Polish lands to the Duchy of Warsaw.) The Belostok district was given to Russia. Napoleon also agreed to give Russia a free hand with both Sweden and the Balkans. On the other hand, the Treaty of Tilsit put an end to Russian naval expansion in the Adriatic, which had started under Paul and continued in the first years of Alexander's reign. The Ionian Islands were now handed over to France. Furthermore, Russia had to join the "Continental Blockade" sponsored by Napoleon and aimed at disrupting British commerce.

During the first half of Alexander's reign the Russians were active in the North Pacific area. Under Paul in 1798 Shelekhov's trading company was reorganized into the Russo-American Company and received a trading monopoly, as well as power to administer justice in the Russian colonies on the Pacific Ocean. Under the charter granted by Paul, the chief director of the company had to be a member or relative of the Shelekhov family. Nicholas Rezanov was appointed director, but the leading role in the company was played by the manager, Alexander Baranov, a merchant from north Russia.

In 1805 the fortress of Novoarchangel was built and became the center of Russia's possessions in Alaska. Baranov was not content with Alaska alone, but formed extensive plans. In 1812 he established a Russian colony in California and dreamed of making the Pacific Ocean a Russian sea. In 1815 he sent an expedition to the Hawaiian Islands, but this failed. In 1818, when about to retire, Baranov died in the Sunda Straits while returning to Russia and was buried at sea according to custom. His far-reaching Pacific policy was not continued after his death.

3. *Alexander and Napoleon: peace and war* (*1807–15*)

The sudden turn in Alexander's foreign policy baffled the Russians and almost cost Alexander his popularity. Even his former closest advisers—the members of the "Intimate Committee"—considered the Treaty of Tilsit a surrender and betrayal of the basic principles of his earlier policy. The committee ceased to exist and new men took their place, among them the chancellor, Count Nicholas Rumiantsov (1754–1826), and an official of the Ministry of the Interior, Michael Speransky (1772–1839). Both of these were immediately dubbed "pro-French." Irritation among the nobility because of the French alliance was widespread, and Napoleon's envoys to Russia were at first snubbed by St. Petersburg society. Economic reasons accentuated the opposition of the nobility. The breaking of commercial relations with England deprived Russian landowners of their main export market. At the same time importation into Russia of so-called "colonial goods," such as coffee, sugar, cotton, and so on, all but ceased, and their prices became prohibitive. The fact that the state treasury, drained by previous war expenses, now lost a considerable portion of the revenue from customs duties, contributed to the depreciation of the ruble and made the issuance of more paper money unavoidable.

Undaunted by the opposition of the nobility and the general dissatisfaction, Alexander decided to continue his reforms and even to tackle the basic constitutional problem. He had discussed some aspects of this question earlier with the Intimate Committee, but no decision had been taken. In 1806 Alexander entered into correspondence with President Jefferson of the United States to obtain firsthand information about American principles of government. Now he entrusted the task of preparing a comprehensive plan of constitutional reform to his new adviser, Michael Speransky. The son of a village priest, Speransky had entered government service after graduating from a divinity school. A man of outstanding ability, he rose rapidly in the ranks of service and soon achieved nobility. Many aristocrats continued however to consider him an upstart. Alexander was much impressed by his logical mind and his personality, and before long Speransky became the tsar's "right hand," as Alexander himself put it.

Speransky intended both to improve the administrative machine of the empire and to revise the fundamental laws of Russia, by which he meant introducing constitutional government. In order to raise the intellectual standard of the civil service personnel he recommended that court ranks be considered honorary only and not a step to a higher position; and that the higher ranks in civil service be open only to university graduates or to those who passed a special examination (1809). Two decrees were issued accordingly, which greatly irritated both the nobility and the bureaucracy. The same year Speransky submitted to Alexander a well balanced plan of general reform. The separate branches of government were to be differentiated. The Committee of Ministers was to assume control of administration, while the Senate's competence was to be limited to judicial matters. A house of representatives (State Duma) was to be created to handle legislation. The system of representation proposed called for landowners and state peasants to elect a duma in each township, the township dumas to send deputies to the district duma, the latter to the provincial duma, and the provincial dumas to the State Duma. (The hierarchy of elective bodies proposed by Speransky was actually introduced in 1917 by the Soviet under entirely different circumstances.) A State Council was to be appointed by the tsar to coordinate the activities of the three branches of government.

Alexander approved Speransky's plan in principle but decided to keep it secret for the time being while introducing it gradually from the top. As the first move toward its realization, the State Council was created and formally opened in 1810. The next year a new statute was issued on the ministries, which defined more clearly the authority of each minister and of the Committee of Ministers.

About the same time, Speransky was put in charge of the reorganization of the state finances, with the main object of restoring the value of the ruble. Among the measures he proposed was the introduction of an income tax, which contributed little to his popularity. Having made few friends and many enemies, he could keep power only so long as the tsar was firmly behind him. While Alexander trusted Speransky, there was a limit to his holding firm against the pressure of public opinion. When Russia's relations with France deteriorated and war seemed imminent, Speransky's enemies pointed out to Alexander that the only way to pacify public opinion was to get rid of his "pro-French" adviser. In March 1812 Alexander dismissed Speransky and ordered him deported first to Nizhni Novgorod and then to Perm. Speransky's plan of constitutional reform fell through when he fell.

Cordial relations with France inaugurated by the Treaty of Tilsit lasted only about two years. Then misunderstandings arose between the two powers which led to a new crisis. An early by-product of the Russo-French alliance was the war of 1808-09 between Russia and Sweden, which had remained in the British fold. As a result of this war Finland was annexed to Russia and organized as an autonomous grand duchy. Alexander granted her a constitution based on her old privileges under Sweden.

According to the Tilsit agreements, the Balkan area was considered within Russia's sphere of influence. Russia's plan was to support the uprising of the Serbs against Turkey (started in 1804) and eventually to create a federation of the Balkan Slavs under Russian protection. A protracted war between Russia and Turkey followed (1806-12). The Treaty of Bucharest which ended it required Turkey to cede Bessarabia to Russia.

The equivocal—and later openly unfriendly—position of France, which in 1811 offered Turkey her support, could not but offend the Russians. Napoleon in his turn was vexed by the leniency of Russian customs officers toward the illicit import of British goods. Petty incidents, such as Alexander's unwillingness to give one of his sisters in marriage to Napoleon, added fuel to the fire. Early in 1812 relations between France and Russia became tense, and in June Napoleon's armies invaded Russia.

The war was carefully prepared by Napoleon from the point of view of military technique. His march to Moscow was strategically outstanding, but the great battle of Borodino was a draw, and because of the strategic skill and sound judgment of the Russian commander in chief, Field Marshal Michael Kutuzov, Napoleon did not succeed in destroying the Russian army.

With the core of that army still undefeated and all classes of Russian society aroused, Napoleon could conquer Russia only by bringing about a social revolution. The elements for such a revolution were present then to an even greater extent than in 1917, par-

ticularly in view of the existence of serfdom. Eyewitnesses of
the Pugachov rebellion were still alive. It is now known that several
Russian statesmen of the time feared war with Napoleon because
they expected him to bring about another such rising. If he had
succeeded in this, he might have had Russia under his thumb, for
a time at least.

There were evidences of unstable conditions among the Russian
peasants at the beginning of the War of 1812. Several revolts occurred among the recruits. Later the attitude of the peasants
changed, especially because of the looting and violence of Napoleon's multinational army. Napoleon either did not wish, or did
not know how, to take advantage of the situation. Moreover, he
did not have a "fifth column" in Russia. Suspicions of Speransky's
enemies that Speransky was ready to collaborate with Napoleon or
to organize a revolution in Russia were, of course, completely un-
founded. And without organizing a revolution Napoleon could
not hold Moscow, hundreds of miles away from his base. Retreat
was inevitable. It became a rout, with the French soldiers exposed
to hunger and cold and to the attacks of the Russian army and
of guerrilla bands.

Many Russians including Kutuzov regarded Napoleon's expulsion as the end of Russia's part in the war. The further struggle
must be attributed to the personal initiative of Alexander. He was
the soul of the European coalition against Napoleon and the chief
manager of all military activities. After Kutuzov died, in 1813,
Alexander's adviser was the Russian general Michael Barclay de
Tolly, a descendant of a Scottish family. Napoleon's resistance was
broken only after a stubborn struggle. The Russians and the allied
troops entered Paris in the summer of 1814. Napoleon's forces,
following his return from Elba, were defeated by the British and
the Prussians at Waterloo in 1815 before the Russian troops had
arrived.

4. Policies in the second half of Alexander I's reign

In 1815 Alexander I was at the height of his glory. His dream of
creating international peace and stability seemed almost achieved
in the mystical form of the so-called Holy Alliance. Alexander
at that time supported liberal trends in Europe. It was chiefly
upon his insistence that France was granted a constitutional

government although of a limited nature. In 1815 he granted a constitutional charter to Poland. He still contemplated constitutional reform for Russia as well.

Alexander's hopes and expectations were high—but destiny had bitter disappointments in store for him. By the end of his reign the international organization he valued so much was shattered. At home, his reforms had not been completed and some of his measures were decried as reactionary; opposition to him grew rapidly both in Russia and in Poland.

On the international stage, Alexander encountered setbacks as early as 1815 at the Congress of Vienna. At one time Austria and Great Britain threatened him with war, and only Napoleon's return from Elba restored the unity of the allies. Nevertheless, Alexander finally obtained from the congress what he wanted: the core of Poland known since 1807 as the Duchy of Warsaw. He intended to preserve that nucleus of the Polish state intact under himself as king of Poland. The alternative was to divide it again between Prussia and Austria. When the congress agreed to cede it to Russia Alexander granted the Kingdom of Poland (within the boundaries of the Duchy of Warsaw) a liberal constitution.

On September 26, 1815, on Alexander's initiative, the tsar of Russia, the emperor of Austria, and the king of Prussia signed the Act of the Holy Alliance. In November the king of France adhered to it, and gradually all the other Christian monarchs except the pope and the prince regent of Great Britain followed suit. In its form and spirit the act was an unusual diplomatic document, religious rather than political. The undersigned solemnly declared their determination "to take as their sole guide . . . the precepts of religion, namely the rules of justice, Christian charity and peace . . . . Considering each other as fellow countrymen, they will on all occasions and in all places lend each other aid and assistance . . . They will consider themselves as members of one and the same Christian nation." To their subjects they promised to "extend a fatherly care and protection . . . in the same spirit of fraternity."

While this declaration was meant as evidence of the best of intentions on the part of Alexander and his fellow monarchs, many diplomats of the old school viewed it cynically as either idealistic nonsense or a cover for Russia's imperialistic designs (which it certainly was not). Some liberals saw in it a potential conspiracy of the monarchs against their peoples aiming at preventing and crushing any incipient revolutionary movement. Actually the Holy Alliance proved to be of little importance in practical politics. International affairs were at this time controlled by the so-called Quadruple Alliance (Austria, Great Britain, Prussia, and Russia) to which later on France was also admitted (the Quintuple Alliance). During the first years of its existence the alliance met in several pan-European congresses: Aachen in 1818, Tropau (Opava) in 1820, Laibach (Ljubljana) in 1821, and Verona in 1822. By 1821 Alexander's dominant influence on international policies in that organization had been superseded by that of the Austrian prime minister, Prince Klemens Wenzel von Metternich, who opposed Alexander from fear both of Russia and of liberalism. When the Greek uprising against the sultan started in 1821 and Russian public opinion demanded intervention in Greek affairs, Metternich argued that it was against the spirit of the Quintuple Alliance to support a revolutionary movement. Metternich's opinion prevailed and Alexander, unwilling to destroy the unity of the European nations, was not able to give the Greeks any assistance. Simultaneously the Congress of Verona decided to intervene in Spanish affairs to restore the authority of the king. The French assumed this task in the name of the congress.

At that juncture, however, there occurred a sharp turn in British policies under the new foreign secretary, George Canning. Canning was worried by the intention of the "Holy Alliance" to continue intervention across the ocean in order to suppress the uprising of former Spanish colonies in Central and South America against Spain. On Canning's recommendation, Britain broke with the Quintuple Alliance and thus destroyed it. It was in connection with these events that President Monroe sent his famous message to the Congress of the United States announcing the doctrine which has ever since been associated with his name. Canning meanwhile approached Near Eastern affairs in the same spirit in which he had dealt with Spanish-American matters. In 1823 Britain recognized the Greeks as belligerents. Canning's new policy in the Near East threatened to eliminate Russian influence in Balkan affairs and replace it by British. From a desire to help their coreligionists, the Orthodox Greeks, and because of traditional Russian interest in the Near East, many Russians urged Alexander to intervene in favor of the Greeks too. While he started concentrating a strong army in south Russia, he made several more attempts to coordinate his policy with that of Austria. Having failed in this, Alexander considered himself entitled to freedom of action and in 1825 secretly got in touch with Canning through Princess Dorothy Lieven, wife of the Russian ambassador in London, to propose joint action with Britain in the Near East. This was a complete reversal of his former policies.

In internal policy in the second half of his reign, Alexander continued experimenting with plans for far-reaching political reform. His chief adviser in these matters at the time was Nicholas Novosiltsov, who in 1820 submitted a well balanced plan for reorganizing the central and regional governments along constitutional lines. In contrast to Speransky, who favored centralization, Novosiltsov suggested dividing Russia into a number of large provinces, each with its own seim (diet) and administrative council. The provincial diets were to send representatives to the national diet. It is obvious that Novosiltsov was influenced by the constitutional pattern of the United States. Alexander indicated his satisfaction with the plan but hesitated to approve it at once. He finally decided to introduce it piecemeal, starting with the local councils. The councils were formed, as an experiment, in the province of Riazan in 1823.

Meanwhile Alexander continued to seek a solution of the peasant problem. Within the span of three years, 1816–19, serfdom was abolished in Estonia, Courland, and Livonia. The peasants were given their personal freedom but no land allotments. For Russia, Alexander asked a number of people he trusted to submit projects for peasant reform. One was prepared by the commissary general of the army, George Kankrin; another by Gen. Alexis Arakcheev who was then Alexander's chief assistant in internal administration. Arakcheev was poorly educated, a martinet but an honest and efficient administrator. Among his other services, he is credited with modernizing the Russian artillery before the War of 1812. Alexander trusted him unreservedly, as one of the few men who had remained loyal to his father to the end. Both Arakcheev and Kankrin recommended gradual emancipation of the peasants. Arakcheev suggested that the treasury assign 5,000,000 rubles annually for buying nobles' estates. Alexander was well aware that any attempt to abolish serfdom would provoke the wrath of the landowning nobility. He remembered the role of the nobles in the overthrow of Peter III as well as of his own father. So he believed it necessary, before attacking the peasant problem, to strengthen his authority until he could feel secure against any opposition. After careful consideration he decided to make the army his main support. But the army itself depended on the nobility to a considerable extent, since half the recruits were drafted from among the serfs and most of the food supplies came from the large landed estates. Thus the first step must be to make the army self-sufficient. From this came the idea of "military settlements," which Alexander asked General Arakcheev to realize.

A military settlement was established either by settling a military unit on a plot of land or by turning a community of state peasants into a military camp. Military drill was to be combined with productive work. The whole plan might be called an experiment in military communism. The advantages expected from the new system were that 1) the army would become self-sufficient, both economically and financially; 2) the soldiers would be provided with land and means of subsistence for their old age; 3) the majority of the population would not be liable either to pay taxes or to supply recruits for the army. Whatever might be the value of the military settlements in theory, in practice the system met with opposition from both soldiers and peasants. Each party regarded it at first as a new burden loaded on them by the administration. There were many cases of open revolt, which were ruthlessly quelled by Arakcheev and his assistants. The system was continued, however, and at Alexander's death some 250,000 soldiers had been settled, or about one-third of the standing army. The military settlements existed throughout the reign of Nicholas I. Some of them became quite prosperous. In each settlement area hospitals and schools were established, at a time when no such facilities existed for the average peasant and his family.

Preoccupied with the grave problems of foreign policy, Alexander toward the end of his life delegated to Arakcheev most of his authority in internal administration. Meanwhile, both Arakcheev personally, as well as the military settlements he headed, had become very unpopular in Russia. Another unpopular appointment was that of Prince Alexander Golitsyn, in 1816, to the post of minister of religion and public education. Golitsyn was a pietist and a mystic, and his activities were resented by both the conservative part of the Orthodox clergy and the liberals. The conservatives were aroused by his patronage of the Russian branch of the British and Foreign Bible Society (established in Russia in 1812; closed in 1826). The liberals objected to the emphasis he required on religion in schools and universities. As a matter of fact, some of the curators of educational districts that Golitsyn appointed issued absurd orders in their pietist fervor which stifled the teaching of both humanities and sciences in the name of religion. A number of professors of the universities of St. Petersburg, Kazan, and Kharkov were either dismissed or resigned in disgust. In 1822, under the pressure of the conservative section of the Orthodox clergy, Alexander dismissed Golitsyn, replacing him by a conservative Orthodox, Adm. Alexander Shishkov. While the latter had the reputation of a reactionary, even some of the liberals welcomed the change.

Alexander kept his constitutional plans secret from the public. And nobody knew beforehand of the impending turn in his foreign policy in 1825. He was accused of subservience to Metternich, of betraying Russia's national interests, of being ready to cede Belorussia and western Ukraine to Poland, and of reactionary policies at home. For a group of liberal Guards officers, the contrast of present gloomy conditions with the glory of 1812–15 was too much to bear. They decided to take matters into their own hands and to bring about reforms by pressure of public opinion if possible, by a coup d'état if peaceful methods failed.

Soon after 1815 secret societies began to be formed with the aim of completely reorganizing internal affairs in Russia. These were set up partly under the influence of the Masonic lodges and had some connection with them. The lessons of history were not missed by the liberal nobles who formed the opposition. The program of all the secret societies included the abolition of serfdom. Among the revolutionary groups, two had especial importance: the Southern Society, which was composed of officers of the southern army and was headed by Col. Paul Pestel, and the Northern Society of St. Petersburg. The plan for a constitution drawn up by Pestel was known as the *Russkaia Pravda* (Russian Law). Pestel visu-

alized the future Russian state as a centralized republic with democratic policies. He also recognized the necessity of a powerful dictatorship in the revolutionary government. In these matters Pestel
was a pupil of the French Jacobins and a forerunner of Lenin. For
the Northern Society Col. Nikita Muraviev drew up a plan for
a constitution which retained a liberal monarchy and gave primary
importance to the rights of the individual. According to this plan,
which was written under the direct influence of the constitution
of the United States, Russia was to be organized along federal
lines.

Alexander received a report on the activities of the secret societies in 1821. The next year he ordered the Masonic lodges closed,
together with all other semisecret or secret societies affiliated with
them. After that the conspirators became more cautious and increased their secrecy. No arrests were made, however, and no attempt to prevent the further growth of revolutionary activities.
Presumably Alexander did not consider the threat serious enough.

The matter of succession to the throne in case of his death called
for Alexander's attention. As he had no sons, his brother Constantine, commander in chief of the Polish army, had been recognized as heir to the throne. But Constantine, who was happily married to a Polish lady, was not inclined to accept the responsibilities
and risks of the imperial office, and so informed Alexander as early
as 1819. After waiting four more years, Alexander signed a manifesto confirming Constantine's refusal to accept the throne and, in
accordance with the law, appointed his next younger brother,
Nicholas, his successor. For unknown reasons, Alexander did not
publish this manifesto but deposited three copies in sealed en-
velopes in various places. One reason for secrecy may have been
fear of exasperating the officers and bringing about an uprising.
Nicholas, who was married to a Prussian princess, was very unpopular among the officers for his Prussian contacts and sympathies as well as for his conservative point of view.

As years went by the strain of his various duties became heavier.
He still believed in the possibility of satisfactorily solving the
urgent problems of both foreign and internal policy, but he was
weary and mentioned to several intimate friends his desire to abdicate and retire to private life as soon as circumstances permitted.
To Prince William of Prussia (the future emperor William I), in

1823, he intimated that he would retire at fifty in any case. He was not destined to reign that long. At the age of forty-eight Alexander fell ill of a fever contracted in the Crimea and died in Taganrog on December 1, 1825. The suddenness of his death gave rise to a legend that he had taken the disguise of a pilgrim who many years later appeared in Siberia as an old man under the name of Fedor Kuzmich.*

5. The December uprising

At the time of Alexander's death, Constantine was in Warsaw and Nicholas in St. Petersburg. Both of them knew of Alexander's manifesto, but only Constantine acted upon it. He ordered the military and civil officials of Warsaw to swear allegiance to the new emperor. Nicholas, on the other hand, having been informed by the military governor of St. Petersburg of his unpopularity among the officers of the Guard, did not dare to demand allegiance to himself in St. Petersburg and had the officials take their oath to Constantine.

With no telegraph service or railroads—connections between St. Petersburg and Warsaw were maintained by post horses—the crisis was drawn out over a long period of time. The news of Alexander's death was received in St. Petersburg December 8, 1825. It was two weeks before the correspondence between Nicholas and Constantine was concluded and Constantine renewed his categorical refusal to accept the throne. December 26 was set for taking the oath of loyalty to Emperor Nicholas I. This moment was chosen by the plotters for an uprising—and from that fact they have taken the name of Decembrists. The plotters succeeded in convincing the soldiers of several regiments that the oath required of them was illegal, that they must uphold the rights of Emperor Constantine and demand a constitution. It was said that some simple soldiers thought "Constitution" was the name of Constantine's wife.

* Two books have recently appeared supporting the opinion that Fedor Kuzmich actually was the former tsar Alexander I, one in English, by L. I. Strakhovsky, *Alexander I of Russia* (New York, W. W. Norton, 1947), the other in Russian, by M. V. Zyzykin, *The Mystery of Emperor Alexander I* (Buenos Aires, 1952). Professor Strakhovsky surmises "that the proof of his thesis can be found in the private papers of the Cathcart family in England, access to which has been refused to every investigator including the late Grand Duke Nicholas Mikhailovich."

The rebels occupied the Senate Square and efforts to send negotiators to them failed. The military governor of St. Petersburg, one
of the heroes of the War of 1812, who approached them to negotiate, was killed. The rebels, however, evidenced no plan of action
and limited themselves to forming a square in the middle of the
city. Nicholas succeeded in bringing up the remaining loyal troops
and in planting cannon at strategic points in the capital. The rebels
had no artillery. When toward evening they were asked to surrender and refused, they were fired upon with case shot. The square
broke, and the rebels fled. The uprising was immediately suppressed. The attempt at a military revolt in southern Russia also
failed.

Arrests and investigations were immediately started. A hundred and twenty men were tried, among them many members of
leading noble families in Russia. Although the sentences were light-
ened by Nicholas, five ringleaders were hanged, among them
Colonel Pestel; thirty-one were condemned to hard labor in Siberia;
the remainder were exiled to Siberia or committed to prison for
various periods of time.

6. *Nicholas I and his internal policy*

Nicholas I was quite unlike his elder brother Alexander. He had
a very much more primitive nature, more limited interests, and not
a shade of liberalism in his political views. He was not entirely lacking in knowledge of how to handle people but even here his capaci-
ties were very limited. He loved to play the plain, honest officer
and servant of the state.

His political wisdom consisted primarily in imposing strict discipline in military and civil matters. Nicholas was guided by the
same idea of a "regulated" or "policed" state as Peter the Great,
but of course he was far less capable than Peter. A contemporary
of Nicholas, the great Russian poet Pushkin, said of him: "Il y a
beaucoup d'enseigne en lui et un peu de Pierre le Grand." Nicholas
undoubtedly felt responsible before the bar of history and desired
to be of service to Russia, but as he had received no education except in military matters he was unprepared for the task of ruling.
Still he attempted to supervise all the departments of government.
As he distrusted liberalism in general, he put a stop to all preparations for constitutional reform, and in connection with this re-

voked the new experiments in local administration. Nonetheless, it is impossible to deny that he made efforts to introduce improvements in the governmental and social organization of Russia. He ordered that a summary of the views of the Decembrists regarding the need for change in governmental affairs be drawn up, and studied it carefully.

One of the principal deficiencies of the Russian political system in the eyes of the Decembrists was the absence of any system of laws and the consequent confusion of procedure in the courts. To correct this deficiency, Nicholas called a committee to codify the law and to compile the *Svod Zakonov* (Code of Laws). The great statesman and jurist Speransky was placed in charge of this work. As we have seen, Speransky had been exiled in 1812. In the second half of Alexander's reign he was admitted into the civil service in the provinces; he became governor general of Siberia in 1821–22, and later was allowed to return to St. Petersburg but without the importance he had had before. Nicholas tested his loyalty by appointing him one of the judges in the trial of the Decembrists. After several years of concentrated work Speransky published in forty-two volumes a *Complete Collection of Russian Laws* in their chronological order from the Code of Tsar Alexis of 1649 to the coronation of Emperor Nicholas. On the basis of this work, a systematic Code of Laws of the Russian Empire was compiled in 1832. A second edition of this code was published in 1842 and a third in 1857. Thus the codification of laws which neither Catherine II nor Alexander I had been able to achieve was accomplished under Nicholas I.

Another serious defect in Russian life noted by the Decembrists was of course serfdom. We have seen how, under Alexander I, the government thought seriously of abolishing or at least limiting serfdom. Nicholas I continued to work in the same direction. For him as for Alexander the peasant question was of political importance in the struggle with the nobles. Following the Decembrist uprising, which was primarily a movement of the nobility, Nicholas never ceased to be distrustful of the political intrigues of the nobility.

Under Nicholas I several measures were taken to limit serfdom. The laws of 1827 and 1833—both of only slight importance—have been mentioned in another connection. The government was motivated by the idea of regulating the exploitation of peasant labor by the landowners. The law concerning peasants bound to the land, proclaimed in 1842, had this purpose. It called for a definition by the landowners of the duties of the peasants, but left the matter to their good will. The attempt to impose fixed responsibilities in respect to serf labor was made only in certain districts of Russia. In the Kingdom of Poland the so-called "tables" were introduced in 1846, in view of peasant uprisings in Austrian Galicia; in the southwestern provinces "inventories" were introduced in 1853. Both tables and inventories were lists of peasant liabilities. Everything pointed to a general peasant reform, but it did not take place until the next reign.

Another evil in the governmental system of Russia pointed out by the Decembrists was the confusion in finances, and the depreciation of the ruble caused by the paper money inflation as a result of the prolonged wars under Alexander I. The financial reforms of Nicholas were carried out by Kankrin, whom he appointed minister of finance. The first measure Kankrin introduced stabilized paper money in 1839 at 3.5 to one. Following this, new paper currency was introduced backed by a gold reserve and maintained at parity; the old bills were purchased by the State Treasury.

After carrying out many reforms of the Decembrists in the judicial and administrative machinery of the state and accepting some of their suggestions about social and economic matters, Nicholas reasserted the principle of autocracy. All manifestations of liberalism were mercilessly suppressed. The press was limited; the universities were placed under strict supervision; a special "third" division of the Imperial Chancellery was organized for the secret police. This was reinforced by the newly created Corps of Gendarmes. The slightest suspicion of political untrustworthiness terminated the career of any civil or military official, however talented. As a result, the proportion of capable officers and civil servants in higher posts decreased considerably. Arrest and exile threatened anyone having independent political views. The outstanding conservative political thinker of the "Slavophile" group, George Samarin, was imprisoned, if only for a short time, in 1851 for opposing the German party in the Baltic provinces. The young author Dostoevsky, a genius of the first rank, was exiled to Siberia in 1849 for being a member of a group interested in French socialism.

The system of Nicholas I was enforced harshly and without

right of appeal. When the military collapse of Russia in the Crimean war showed it to be poor, its creator was incapable of surviving it. Nicholas I died in the midst of the war, on March 2, 1855, from a cold and nervous fatigue. There was a rumor that he poisoned himself.

7. The foreign policy of Nicholas I

Emperor Nicholas' foreign policy had followed the same firm principles as in his internal policy. Its basic concept was legitimism; hence his opposition to all liberal and revolutionary movements. But his first move—the Russo-Turkish war of 1828–29—was not in complete consistency with this principle. In supporting the Greek revolution he was guided not by his general principles of foreign policy but rather by the traditional objectives of Russian diplomacy in the Balkans. Moreover, the war had been prepared in the preceding reign. Nicholas really followed his brother by inertia, and probably out of a desire to divert the attention of Russian society from the effects of the Decembrist uprising by a foreign war. In 1827 an agreement was conducted by Russia, England, and France to aid Greece. In the autumn of 1827 the combined Russo-Anglo-French squadron destroyed the Turko-Egyptian fleet at Navarino. The immediate consequence of this was a war between Russia and Turkey in 1828–29.

According to Nicholas' plan, the Polish army was to take part in the war in the Balkans, the object of which was to free the southern Slavs. But Grand Duke Constantine refused to consent to the dispatch of the Polish army to the Balkans. Its participation in the war, however, was symbolized by the presence of a special mission of Polish officers. The war progressed slowly in 1828; in the course of the next year the Russian commander in chief, Gen. Ivan Diebitsch, finally delivered a telling blow to the Turks at Kulevche and crossed the Balkans. At the same time Gen. Ivan Paskevich succeeded in capturing Erzerum on the Caucasian front. Turkey was forced to conclude peace at Adrianople. By the treaty of peace, Russia took possession of the mouth of the Danube and improved her position along the Caucasian coast of the Black Sea. The independence of Greece was secured as well as the autonomy of Serbia, Moldavia, and Wallachia, the Danubian principalities.

The conditions of the Peace of Adrianople astonished the diplomats of Europe by their moderation. This was not the result of weakness or of error but of farsightedness and strength. It was a continuation of the Turkophile policy of Emperor Paul. The moderation of the Peace of Adrianople bore fruit four years later in the Treaty of Ungiar-Iskelessi between Turkey and Russia. Three years after the Peace of Adrianople, Turkey found herself on the verge of disruption from civil war. The Egyptian pasha, Mehmet-Ali, rose against the sultan, and his son Ibrahim succeeded in defeating the sultan's army. The country was saved by the intervention of Russia. A small corps was sent under the direction of Gen. Nicholas Muraviev to the Bosporus to defend Constantinople against the Egyptian army.

General Muraviev was one of the outstanding military personages of the reign of Nicholas. He had prepared himself for action in the east by learning several oriental languages, so that he could converse without interpreters. He prepared the ground for the conclusion of the Treaty of Ungiar-Iskelessi which placed Russia in the position of protector of Turkey. By its provision the Straits of the Bosporus and the Dardanelles were to remain closed to all military vessels except those of Turkey and Russia. The treaty was a great victory for Russian diplomacy, but Russia did not succeed in utilizing its benefits. Emperor Nicholas tied his own hands with an agreement concluded the same year with Austria at Münchengrätz. Later on, Russia adhered to the London conventions of 1840 and 1841, according to which the straits were closed to military vessels of all nations, under international guarantee.

Even before the conclusion of the Treaty of Ungiar-Iskelessi, Nicholas had a chance to demonstrate the true nature of his foreign policy. The revolution of July 1830 in France overthrew the Bourbons and replaced them by the liberal monarchy of Louis-Philippe of Orleans. Nicholas decided at first to intervene in favor of the Bourbons. A revolution in Poland prevented this. The uprising cannot be explained by Nicholas' Polish policy, for while he never sympathized with constitutional principles, he was careful to maintain the Polish constitutional charter. But his nationalistic policy made it evident to the Poles that there was no chance of their being ceded the Lithuanian and west Russian provinces for which they still hoped during the reign of Alexander I. The Polish uprising was suppressed in 1831, after a year of heavy fighting. The Polish constitution was then repealed. The Organic Statute of 1832 left Poland with only administrative autonomy. This further confused the Polish question for both Russians and Poles.

The reactionary foreign policy of Nicholas found expression a second time in 1848–49, when the whole of the European continent was swept by a new wave of revolution. At the personal entreaty of the young Austrian emperor, Francis Joseph, Nicholas moved an army of 100,000 Russians under General Paskevich to suppress the Hungarian uprising against Austria in 1849. The Hungarian army was soon forced to surrender, and Austria was saved. The Austrian minister Schwartzenberg immediately took steps to forestall excessive Russian influence upon Austria's subsequent policy. His remark is famous: "Austria will surprise the world with her ingratitude." An opportunity for this soon arose with a new turn in international affairs.

It was already easy in the 1840's to foresee a complete breach between Russia on the one hand and England and France on the other, over the eastern question. The French revolution of 1848 completely disrupted the relations between Russia and France. The situation was not improved when the French Republic became the empire of Napoleon III. Napoleon attempted to strengthen his internal power by an effective foreign policy. In the hope of attracting the French Catholics to his side, he demanded that Turkey grant privileges to Catholics in the Holy Land. The keys of the Church of Bethlehem were taken away from the Orthodox Greeks and given to the Catholic Church. Emperor Nicholas, in his capacity of patron of the Orthodox population of Turkey, under the provisions of the Treaty of Kuchuk-Kainardji of 1774, demanded the re-establishment of the rights of the Orthodox Church. Having been refused by the sultan, he sent Russian troops to the autonomous principalities of Moldavia and Wallachia, which were under sultan's suzerainty.

In the autumn of 1853 Turkey declared war against Russia. The Russian Black Sea squadron destroyed the Turkish fleet at Sinope in November. Following this the British and French squadrons entered the Black Sea and a war started between Russia and the west European states. England and France were later joined by Sardinia. The position of Russia became difficult when Austria demanded the evacuation of the principalities of Moldavia and

Wallachia. Schwartzenberg's prediction began to come true. Nicholas submitted to the demands, considering that Russia was not prepared to fight Austria as well, especially with Prussia acting in an unpredictable manner.

War on the Danube, which formed the basis of the Russian military plan, became impossible. The chief forces of the Russian army were brought back to defend the Russian frontiers against possible attack by Austria. Meanwhile, the Russian fleet of sailing vessels could not oppose the united and incomparably stronger Anglo-French fleet, which contained a number of steam vessels. During the autumn of 1854 the allies landed their troops in the Crimea near Eupatoria and moved against Sevastopol. The city was hurriedly fortified by Gen. Edward Todtleben, and the Russian fleet was sunk at the entrance of the harbor to prevent the entrance of the Anglo-French fleet. The siege of Sevastopol began. The city could have been saved, perhaps, if Paskevich had agreed to send reinforcements from the main Russian army which was defending the Russian frontier against Austria, but he did not want to take this risk.

On March 2, 1855, Emperor Nicholas I died, but the accession of his son Alexander was accompanied by no change in military plans. Sevastopol was in fact left to take care of itself. On September 8, 1855, the French succeeded in taking Fort Malakoff, the key to the fortress of Sevastopol. After this the Russian army abandoned the fortress.

Meanwhile the Rusian troops were victorious on the Caucasian front, where General Muraviev took the fortress of Kars, regarded as impregnable by the Turks. Russia had taken Kars in 1829, but it had been returned to Turkey by the Treaty of Adrianople.

At the beginning of 1856, by the mediation of Austria and Prussia, peace negotiations were opened between Russia and her enemies. The Treaty of Paris was concluded on conditions highly unfavorable to Russia. She received back Sevastopol in return for Kars, but lost the right to maintain a fleet in the Black Sea. The Straits of the Bosporus and the Dardanelles were closed to military vessels of all nations. The southern part of Bessarabia was annexed to Moldavia, depriving Russia of any access to the Danube River. Finally, Russia had to abandon the right of exclusive protection over Orthodox peoples in Turkey. All the Christians in

Turkey were placed under the joint protection of the great powers.

Thus the foreign policy of Nicholas I ended in failure. Russia's military prestige was seriously undermined and her influence in European affairs was at an end. These were severe blows to national self-esteem. Russia's defeat in the Crimean war was one of the causes of the series of important internal reforms which were carried out by Alexander II.

CHAPTER 10

THE RUSSIAN EMPIRE IN THE SECOND HALF OF THE 19TH CENTURY

1. *The reforms of Alexander II*

IT cannot be said that Alexander II's political views differed greatly from those of his father. He had, in fact, the same ideals of enlightened absolutism as Nicholas I; but he was of a much gentler and more tolerant disposition and had been educated in a more humane spirit. His tutor was the poet Basil Zhukovsky, who was one of the finest characters of his time.

Alexander's patriotic sentiments, like those of many of his contemporaries, were deeply hurt by the outcome of the Crimean war. Reforms in Russia seemed inevitable, as the old regime had proved itself incapable of organizing the defense of Russia. Nicholas I admitted this before his death, telling Alexander: "I am handing you command of the country in a poor state." The basic defect of the old regime was the institution of serfdom. So it was natural for Alexander II's reforms to start with this, especially since the ground had been prepared during Nicholas' reign.

In January 1857 a secret Committee on Peasant Reform was set up. It was composed of several top government officials, but fear of taking decisive action retarded its work. A decisive step was taken on Alexander's initiative in the late autumn of 1857, when the governor general of Vilno was authorized to organize provincial committees of the nobility in the Lithuanian provinces to discuss the terms of the proposed reforms on December 2, 1857. This move left no possibility of retreat; the reforms became inevitable. The nobles of other provinces were forced to request the government's authorization to form similar committees. Their motives were clearly expressed in a famous speech Alexander made to the nobility of Moscow: "Better that the reform should come from above than wait until serfdom is abolished from below."

Working out a general plan of reform and detailed provisions for its execution occupied more than three years. The work of the provincial committees was revised by special commissions in St. Petersburg. These "editing commissions" consisted primarily of partisans of reform. They were composed of government officials, from ministries directly concerned in the proposed reform, and experts from among the progressive estate owners. James Rostovtsev headed the commission until his death in 1860. One of its leading members was the vice minister of internal affairs, Nicholas Miliutin. Several leaders of the Slavophile movement exercised great influence, notably Prince Vladimir Cherkassky and George Samarin. The editing commissions showed great initiative, making proposals which went much farther than those of the majority of the provincial committees. The plan of the commissions was revised by the main committee, and by the State Council. After this the plan was confirmed by the emperor in a manifesto abolishing serfdom which was signed on March 3, 1861.

The basic principles of the reform were as follows: Household serfs were to be freed within a period of two years without redemption, but were to receive nothing on gaining their freedom. Peasant serfs were to receive not only their personal freedom but also allotments of land. The serfs had formerly worked both their own lands and those of their owner. The allotments granted them now were approximately equal to the area retained by the landowner. Thus, the land they received had previously absorbed only half their labor.

By the terms of the emancipation, it did not become their private property. It continued to be regarded as the landowner's property, held for the benefit of the peasant. The peasants, though now freedmen, were called upon to pay for the use of this land or to perform certain services for the landowner. The government, however, was willing to help, if both landowners and peasants desired to terminate this relationship. Help was provided in the form of long-term credit to purchase the land. Where estate owners agreed to sell to their former serfs, the government paid for the land with an interest-bearing bond, and this sum the peasant paid back over a period of forty-nine years. Within twenty years following 1861 about 85 per cent of the landowners actually sold to the peasants their portion of land in each estate, with the government assistance described. Even so, the peasant did not have full personal ownership; each peasant commune or village received the land in communal ownership, with collective responsibility for the redemption payments of all the members of the commune. Special government agents called mediators, named for the purpose of putting the reform into operation, drew up charter deeds for the land in the name of a whole commune. The commune itself allotted the land to its members according to the size of families. These reallotments took place periodically every few years.

Thus, even after the reform, the peasant did not become an individual property owner or possess full civil rights, but remained subject to the authority of the commune. Actually the peasants became dependent upon those bureaucratic government agencies which concerned themselves with peasant affairs. It should be added that outside of the commune each peasant could purchase land on the basis of full ownership. This whole situation is important for understanding future events. It explains the continued juridical isolation of the peasants even after the reform. It also preserved in their consciousness the memory of serfdom. The firm bonds of the commune did not permit changes in the manner of owning land. The peasants never forgot that the commune had only half of the former estate. The reform of 1861 seemed incomplete and they dreamed of completing it. And from the conception that the land was not the property of individuals but was granted in the form of an allotment to serve the uses of the individual the peasants came to regard the land within the whole state as a fund which could be drawn upon for further allotments until it was used up. These were the embryonic ideas of the subsequent revolution.

In spite of its incompleteness, the reform of 1861 greatly altered the old order. After the peasant reform it seemed easier to undertake other reforms which, taken together, completely transformed the nature of the Russian state. Alexander II's other outstanding "great reforms" were of the zemstvo, the towns, the courts, and military service.

The reform of the zemstvo in 1864 created the first real local self-government for all classes that had existed since that of Moscow in the days before Peter. The basis of the reform consisted in granting to elected representatives of each county (*uyezd*) control over schools, public health, and roads. The elective law provided for the division of electors into three *curias:* the private landowners (nobles and merchants), peasant communes, and townspeople. The representatives elected a board known as the *uprava* for a term of three years. The representatives of the uyezd formed a provincial assembly which elected a provincial zemstvo board. Measures similar in spirit to the zemstvo reforms were introduced for town government in 1870. The electors again were divided into three curias, according to a property census; the amount of taxes paid was totaled and divided into three equal parts, each having an equal number of representatives. Both the zemstvo and the town authorities succeeded in carrying out work of great cultural importance in Russia prior to the revolution of 1917.

Of no less significance was the judicial reform of 1864, of which Serge Zarudny was the chief promoter. Its basic points were the improvement of court procedure, introduction of the jury system and justices of the peace, and the organization of lawyers into a formal bar. The new courts proved equitable and efficient, and in this respect Russia could be compared favorably with the most progressive European countries. However, the peasants in the vast majority of small civil litigations had to be content with their separate township (*volost*) courts, especially organized for them. The last of the major reforms was the introduction of universal military service in 1874. This law was profoundly democratic in spirit. The recruits were granted privileges according to their family position. The only son, the only grandson, or only supporter of a family received full privileges and was registered in the reserve of the second category; that is, in practice, prior to World War I, he was never called into service. With respect to the term of service and promotion, special privileges were given persons having secondary education. Class differences were not in any way reflected in military service, with the exception of the traditional selection of the Guards officers from the aristocratic circles of society.

Most of the characteristics of the society created by the reforms of Alexander II lasted until 1905, and some until 1917.

2. *Alexander II's foreign policy*

The foreign policy of Emperor Alexander II may be divided into two main periods. During the first, Russian policy was inspired primarily by the idea of revising the Treaty of Paris of 1856 and

particularly of abrogating the humiliating clause prohibiting maintenance of a Russian fleet in the Black Sea. Taking advantage of
the Franco-Prussian war of 1870, Russia succeeded in overthrowing the limitations of the Treaty of Paris. Then began the second
period of Alexander's foreign policy, in which Russia sought the
emancipation of the Balkan Slavs. But the union of Europe against
Russia at the Berlin conference in 1878 deprived both Russia and
the Balkan Slavs of the fruits of these efforts. This marked a further turn in policy.

Finding herself thrust out of the Near East as a result of the
Crimean war, Russia attempted to carry on an active policy in
the Caucasus, the Middle East, and the Far East. In all these
directions the opening moves had been made during the reign of
Nicholas I. The government of Alexander II succeeded in achieving its most important successes in the Caucasus and Middle East.
Gen. Alexis Ermolov, appointed viceroy in the Caucasus in 1816,
had gone far toward conquering Caucasia and Transcaucasia in
the second half of Alexander I's reign. Ermolov was a prominent
Russian statesman of the 19th century with a recognized talent for
both military and administrative matters. Personally of a modest
and simple nature, he could be harsh when he considered it necessary in Russia's interests. However, neither Ermolov nor his immediate successors succeeded in finally subjugating the Caucasus.
Throughout the reign of Nicholas I Russia was forced to maintain
troops there to protect her possessions from incursions of the
mountaineers. An exhausting mountain war continued for many
years.

The conquest of the Caucasus was concluded only in the reign of
Alexander II. In 1857 the new viceroy in the Caucasus, Prince
Alexander Bariatinsky, began a methodical advance into the hills
of Daghestan against the leader of the mountaineers, Shamil.
Shamil conducted a heroic defense but was overcome by the Russian armies and taken prisoner in 1859. After conquering the eastern Caucasus from the Georgian military road to the Caspian Sea,
the Russians turned to the western part of the Caucasus. The
Circassians were given the choice either of moving to the valleys
where they could be controlled or of emigrating. About 200,000
went to Turkey.

The renewal of Russian activity in the Middle East commenced,

as has been said above, during the reign of Nicholas I. The energetic governor general of Orenburg, Count Basil Perovsky, in the
winter of 1839–40 opened a campaign to punish the Khivans for
their raids. It ended in failure, owing to the severity of the winter.
But in 1847 a Russian detachment reached the Syr Darya, not far
from its mouth in the Aral Sea. Here the fortress of Aralsk was
constructed. This event marked the turning point in Russia's policy
in the Middle East.

The fortress of Aralsk became the basis of Russian domination
of the Aral Sea. Two vessels were brought in sections from Orenburg, and a Russian flotilla was organized on the sea. Kirilov's
dream of seeing the Russian flag float over the Aral Sea had become a reality in less than a hundred years.

In view of the incursions of the Khokands, it was decided to
move up the Syr Darya to the fortress of Ak-Mechet. This was
seized and renamed Fort Perovsk in 1853. With the conquest of
the lower Syr Darya and the bringing of a flotilla into the Aral
Sea, the Russian frontier moved from Orenburg to the boundary
of Turkistan. The fortified line of Orenburg became obsolete. At
the same time the eastern Kirghiz line was advanced by the occupation of the basin of Lake Balkash, the frontier was carried
from Irtysh to Semirechie. Thus, less than 120 years after Kirilov,
the provinces of Bukhara and Samarkand were within the Russians' reach. But these provinces no longer lacked in unity as they
had in the time of Kirilov. At the beginning of the 19th century
a new dynasty of khans in Bukhara had succeeded in strengthening their power by means of a cruel despotism. The new center of
government was in the valley of the Fergan, where one of the local
Uzbek princes, having founded his capital in Khokand, took the title
of khan. The Khanate of Khokand was a troublesome neighbor.
The Khokands attempted to conquer the Kirghiz, who had long
ago become Russian subjects. The ensuing struggle made it necessary for Russia to intervene and connect the Syr Darya and the
Semirechensk lines. In 1865 the occupied territories were united
to form the province of Turkistan and were made part of the region
under the control of the governor general of Orenburg. Gen.
Michael Cherniaev was made head of the new territories. On June
27, 1865, he captured Tashkent, the largest Khokand city. This
capture by a small force had a tremendous effect upon all Turk-

istan and decided the further course of the struggle. The amir of Bukhara attempted to assist the Khokands and demanded that the Russian troops immediately leave the territories they occupied. A struggle began with Bukhara which was conducted by Gen. Constantine Kauffmann, who had been appointed governor general of Turkistan in 1867. In 1868 Kauffmann occupied Samarkand, and the amir of Bukhara recognized the suzerainty of the Russian tsar.

The attention of the Russian Government and public opinion was attracted to the Far East in the 1840's. At this time the basin of the Amur River, ceded to China at the end of the 17th century, was thinly populated by native tribes. In the early 1840's the zoologist Alexander Middendorf headed a scientific expedition into Siberia. On his way home he passed through the region of the Amur and saw no Chinese officials there. Middendorf's report made a deep impression in St. Petersburg. In 1847, in appointing Nicholas Muraviev governor general of eastern Siberia, Emperor Nicholas I mentioned the "Russian" river Amur. In naval and diplomatic circles in Russia, the Amur was not regarded as having great importance, since it flowed only into the Sea of Okhotsk. While Sakhalin was believed to be connected with the mainland, the mouth of the Amur seemed to have no direct outlet to the ocean. Capt. Gennadi Nevelskoy, sent to the Sea of Okhotsk on the brig *Baikal,* decided to investigate the mouth of the Amur and the shores of Sakhalin on his own responsibility. He left Petropavlovsk (Kamchatka) June 11, 1849, and sailed to the eastern shore of Sakhalin. On September 15 he passed through the Tatar Strait to the Bay of Aian. Sakhalin was proved to be an island and the importance of the Amur as a line of connection became evident. On August 19, 1851, Nevelskoy raised the Russian flag at the mouth of the river. For these acts "of the greatest impertinence" he was sentenced to be demoted to a sailor. Only the personal intervention of Nicholas I saved him from the punishment. Nicholas said at that time: "Where once the Russian flag has flown it must not be lowered." The region of the Amur was occupied by Russia in 1858 by the Treaty of Aygun, while in 1860 the Usuri region was ceded by China to Russia, and the town of Vladivostok was founded. For the conclusion of the Treaty of Aygun Muraviev was created count and became known as Muraviev-Amursky. Sakhalin was for a long time under the joint dominion of Russia and Japan, but in 1875 Japan recognized Russia's rights over the whole island in exchange for the Kuril Islands.

Her success in the Middle and the Far East increased Russia's international importance and aroused concern among the great powers, particularly Great Britain, which by 1869 was so anxious over Russia's moves in Turkistan as to enter into negotiations with the Russian Government. Great Britain proposed to form a neutral zone between Russian and British possessions in the Middle East, with the provision that Afghanistan would be included in the sphere of British influence. The Russian Government long refused to answer this proposal, perhaps awaiting an offer of compensation in the Black Sea.

Meanwhile, the desire to secure allies against the European powers induced Russian diplomats to reach an understanding with the United States. The tradition of Russo-American rapprochement goes back to the 18th century. During the Crimean war the United States Government gave moral support to Russia, which on its part supported the Union forces during the Civil War. Fearing a war with Great Britain and as a measure of precaution, the Russian naval authorities decided to send the Russian Pacific squadron to San Francisco and part of the Baltic squadron to New York. This move was also meant as an expression of sympathy with the Federal Government. When Alexander II barely escaped assassination in 1866, the United States assistant secretary of the navy, G. V. Fox, was sent to Russia to bear congratulations. The fact that serfdom had just been abolished in Russia and slavery in the United States led to mutual understanding and sympathy. Desire to meet the wishes of the United States was one of the reasons for Russia's selling her American possessions. She sold Alaska to the United States in 1867 for $7,200,000, a nominal sum considering the region's natural wealth. The Russian colony in California—Fort Ross—had already been sold by the Russo-American Company to J. A. Sutter in 1844.

The rapprochement with the United States, however, could not serve as a firm support to Russia against Great Britain and France in her Near Eastern policy. Alexander II attempted to strengthen his position in European diplomacy by means of an understanding with Germany and Austria (the League of Three Emperors, 1872).

Russia took advantage of the helpless condition of France during the Franco-Prussian war in 1870 to announce her determination to abrogate the Black Sea clauses of the Treaty of Paris. Great Britain alone, without France, she did not fear.

Having achieved success in the Black Sea, Russia was ready to make concessions to Great Britain in the Middle East and agreed to the British demands. Prince Alexander Gorchakov announced Russia's willingness not to seize Khiva. Events, however, proved otherwise. A struggle with Khiva was unavoidable in view of the increasing raids of the Khivans. In 1873, 13,000 Russian troops under the command of Kauffmann moved against Khiva from Turkistan and the Caspian Sea, and conquered the country. Part of its territory was merged with Russia and part became a vassal state. Because uprisings of Dungan (Chinese Mohammedans) in Chinese Turkistan, which the Chinese Government proved unable to suppress, threatened the peace of the Kirghiz, Russia occupied the Kuldja region on the frontier in 1871. She did not return it to China until 1882. In the middle of the 1870's the khan of Khokand rose against Russia; the uprising was suppressed and the khanate was incorporated into Russian territory.

Russia's attention was again directed toward the Near East in the late 1870's. The Russo-Turkish war of 1877–78 was caused by serious internal complications in the Balkans. Turkish oppression of the Slavs led to uprisings in Bosnia and Herzegovina, as well as in Bulgaria. The Turks attempted to suppress the uprising with extraordinary cruelty. As the great powers did not intervene, Serbia and Montenegro declared war on Turkey in 1876. The Serbian Government invited General Cherniaev, famed for his Turkistan campaigns, to command the Serbian army. A few volunteers accompanied him from Russia. The forces of the Serbs and the Turks were so unequal that after a heroic resistance at Alexinac Cherniaev was forced to retreat. Serbia was saved from complete defeat by the timely intervention of Russia. When Turkey refused to carry out the demands of the conference of European diplomats in Constantinople in 1876 respecting the reform of government over the Slavonic lands, Alexander II declared war on Turkey, April 24, 1877. Russia was joined by Rumania, a principality formed in 1859 from the union of Moldavia and Wallachia. The war was difficult, especially as the reorganization of the Russian army on the basis of universal service was far from completed when it began. In the autumn of 1877 Russian troops achieved considerable success on both the Balkan and Caucasian fronts. At the end of November Kars was taken by the Russian troops for the third time in the 19th century. In December Plevna, where the main Turkish army of Osman Pasha was besieged, fell to Russia. During the winter Russian troops crossed the Balkans. In February 1878 they neared Constantinople. The success of the Russian armies led to the interference of Great Britain. The British fleet entered the Sea of Marmora. On March 3, 1878, at the small village of San Stefano near Constantinople, the preliminary conditions of peace between Russia and Turkey were signed. Turkey agreed to form a new princedom, Bulgaria, including the Vardar River and the whole of Macedonia, out of its Balkan possessions between the Danube and the Aegean Sea. It further agreed to recognize the independence of Serbia, Montenegro, and Rumania. Russia received Batum, Kars in Transcaucasia, and the southern part of Bessarabia, which she had ceded in 1856. (Kars was returned to Turkey by the Treaty of Brest-Litovsk in 1918.) But the Treaty of San Stefano aroused the opposition of Great Britain and Austria. The creation of a big Bulgaria was contrary to the provisions of the secret conventions between Austria and Russia, concluded in 1876 and 1877. Russia was threatened with a new war. Desiring to avoid it, Alexander II accepted the mediation of the German chancellor, Bismarck, and agreed to revise the conditions of the treaty at a European congress in Berlin. The Congress of Berlin was a defeat for Russian diplomacy. The territory of Bulgaria was reduced by half, Macedonia being left to Turkey. What remained was cut in two, forming the principality of Bulgaria and the autonomous province of Eastern Roumelia, both remaining vassal to Turkey. Bosnia and Herzegovina were "temporarily" occupied by Austria.

3. *The revolutionary movement and the assassination of Alexander II*

Alexander II's internal policy did not bring political peace in Russia. In spite of his far-reaching social and administrative reforms, he had to face bitter opposition and open revolutionary movements. The political opposition came primarily from the nobility. The idea was current that the nobility, having been deprived of their social and economic privileges, should receive in exchange political privileges, that is, a part of the governing power. This idea originated during the discussion of the peasant reforms, among members of the provincial committees who were discontented with the radicalism of the editing commissions. In addition to the political programs of the nobles, other plans, looking to the reorganization of Russia along constitutional and democratic lines, were advanced, as a continuation of Decembrist tradition.

The revolutionary idea was chiefly current among the *raznochintsi,* that is, individuals of no definite class: children of peasants and merchants who had received secondary or higher education, children of clergy who did not desire to enter the church, children of small civil servants who did not want to follow their fathers' vocation, and children of impoverished nobles. These raznochintsi rapidly formed a new social class of intelligentsia, which included many members of the nobility. With the reforms of Alexander II, the institution of the legal bar, the growth of newspapers and magazines, the increase in number of teachers, and so on, this class continued to expand. It consisted of intellectual people in general, but at first primarily of those connected with newspapers and magazines or with universities. The university students contributed the majority of the radical and revolutionary leaders. Many of the students had no means whatsoever. The average student lived in a state of semistarvation, earning his way through the university by giving lessons or by copying. Most were unfamiliar with sports and had no taste for them. The ill health that resulted from lack of adequate nourishment and physical exercise had a deleterious effect upon their psychology. The leaders of the intelligentsia desired not only radical political changes but also a social revolution, in spite of the fact that Russian industry was too undeveloped to supply a firm basis for socialism. They criticized the government for not being radical enough. The more moderate criticism was expressed in the legalized press, while the more bitter criticism appeared in revolutionary organs published abroad, the best known of which was *Kolokol* (The Bell), published by Alexander Herzen in London. Revolutionary propaganda against the government took a harsh tone. A proclamation of 1862 to the youth of Russia called for terrorism, murder of members of the government and supporters of its policy. Simultaneously a number of cases of incendiarism occurred in St. Petersburg. The government took decisive steps, arresting and exiling several radical leaders.

The activity of the Russian revolutionists was connected with a movement which was plotting an uprising in Poland at the same time. The Polish revolution broke out in 1863. Just before this the Russian Government had started a more liberal policy in Poland, and put the introduction of the reform in the hands of a prominent Polish statesman, Marquis Alexander Wielopolski. The radical elements in Poland decided to sabotage the reform. The uprising was suppressed by military force, after which the last remnants of Polish independence were abrogated. The official title of the former Kingdom of Poland became the By-Visla provinces. A land reform was introduced in 1864 under the supervision of Miliutin and Cherkassky, who had been the chief figures in the Russian reform movement. They succeeded in carrying it out more successfully in Poland than in Russia, and thanks to this measure the great mass of Polish peasants remained loyal to the Russian Government almost up to the World War.

The Polish uprising had an important influence on the evolution of the opposition and revolutionary movements in Russia. It aroused the patriotism of the great majority of the people and thus strengthened the position of the government. The Russian revolutionary leaders who had been connected with the Polish uprising rapidly lost prestige in Russia. The circulation of Herzen's *Kolokol* fell from 3,000 to 500. For some years the revolutionary and opposition movements in Russia did not receive the support of any important groups there. The attempt of Dmitri Karakozov to assassinate Emperor Alexander II in 1866 was an isolated fact and the work of a very small group of conspirators.

A new wave of antigovernment activity arose in the 1870's. In liberal circles the desire grew for elective representation not only in local self-government (zemstvos and towns) but also in the central agencies of government. A parliament was needed to complete the unfinished reforms. This movement became particularly strong following the Turkish war of 1877–78: when liberated Bulgaria received a constitution the desire for a constitution in Russia was given clear utterance. The activity of the revolutionary organizations increased. From 1870 to 1875 the radical intellectuals abstained from direct struggle against the government, but undertook preparatory propaganda among the masses. Many intellectuals of that time went "to the people," living among the peasants and workmen, teaching school, or becoming agricultural or industrial laborers.

The government, fearing the results of the propaganda, tried to check the movement by arresting revolutionaries who took part in it. At times the harmless members of the movement suffered arrest together with the dangerous ones. Many were imprisoned or exiled on mere suspicion by the police. The government's measures aroused bitter feeling among the radical intellectuals. Around 1875 the revolutionaries began to use terrorism and assassination. In 1879, in Lipetsk in central Russia, the leaders of the revolutionary movement met in secret conference. An executive committee was elected to overthrow the government. This committee decided to abandon all attempts against individual members of the government and to bend every effort to assassinating its head, Emperor Alexander II. From that time on, Alexander II was the object of a man hunt. Attempts were made in rapid succession but without success, until that in St. Petersburg in the spring of 1881, which resulted in the emperor's death on March 13.

The assassination of Alexander II occurred the very day he had signed a statement on the Representative Committee to advise the State Council. This was the so-called "constitution" drawn up by Michael Loris Melikov, the minister of the interior. Loris Melikov's idea was that the revolutionary activity of the intellectuals could not be stopped by police measures alone. In his opinion the revolutionaries had the moral support of the moderate classes of society who were discontented with the autocratic policy of the government. He believed that the government should placate the moderates by granting a constitution. This measure, he believed, would deprive the revolutionaries of the moral support of these classes. The assassination prevented the execution of this plan. The emperor's son and successor, Alexander III, withdrew the constitutional plan, and the statement signed by Alexander II was never published.

4. *Alexander III and Nicholas II*

The impression made upon Alexander III by the assassination of his father lasted all his life. He retained a distrust for all liberal movements, and influenced by the overprocurator of the Holy Synod, Constantine Pobedonostsev, a philosopher of extreme conservatism, he expressed a firm belief in the principle of autocracy. The political program of Alexander III was simple. It consisted in opposing all liberal and revolutionary movements in Russia and in satisfying, to a certain degree, the urgent economic demands of the Russian people. These principles of policy were handed down by Alexander to his son Nicholas, who ascended the throne on his father's death in 1894. Under pressure of the revolution of 1905 Nicholas agreed to grant a constitution; but up to the revolution of 1917, and probably until his death in 1918, Nicholas continued to believe in his father's principles.

Through the twenty-five years between 1881 and 1905 the political program of the Russian Government remained unchanged; but the actual course of events was very different during the reigns of Alexander III and of Nicholas II. Father and son had common traits: love of home and simple private living. Both Alexander and Nicholas were model husbands and fathers. Coupled with these qualities went a certain cautiousness and stubbornness. But in spite of these similarities, the son did not closely resemble the father. Alexander III had a masterful nature and knew how to secure obedience both from his ministers and from the members of the imperial household—the grand dukes. He was not particularly well educated, but he had the instinct and the tact of a statesman and could grasp without difficulty the essential points of questions presented to him. Alexander had an uncomplicated nature, but he was a born emperor.

Nicholas II, on the other hand, had a more complex personality. His education had not been very thorough, but he was fond of reading. In private life Nicholas II could easily have succeeded in applying his talents. But he totally lacked the qualities of a statesman and a leader. Soon after his coronation, intrigues sprang up among his ministers and the grand dukes, whom he never succeeded in mastering and putting in their proper place. He had a weak will, and like many weak men attempted to hide the fact by stubbornness. He was not interested in political matters; his mind slipped along their surface and seized only the superficial aspects. Nicholas never attempted to penetrate to the substance of the questions submitted to him.

Nicholas did not like to admit that anyone exercised any influence upon him. Actually, however, he was constantly under someone's influence, until he became completely dominated by his wife, Empress Alexandra. An episode illustrating Nicholas' character took place in Moscow during his coronation. Because of the incompetence of the police, a panic occurred during the distribution of gifts in honor of the occasion; over a thousand people were crushed to death. This happened at the very height of the coronation festivities. If such a thing had occurred at the coronation of Alexander III he would have immediately canceled all further celebration. Nicholas, however, had the idea of showing his firmness and made no change of plans. Even the ball at the French ambassador's the same evening was not canceled.

Nicholas II's domestic policy consisted in continuing by inertia the policy of his father. The internal policy of Alexander III had been first of all to strengthen government control in all directions where free public opinion might be expected to manifest itself. Pursuant to this policy, the laws regarding local self-government were revised. The power of the government, in the person of the provincial governors, was strengthened as against the power of the zemstvos. According to the new law of 1890, the peasants elected only candidates for the zemstvo, while the governor chose representatives from among these candidates. This law was repealed in 1906. In order to extend governmental supervision over the peasants, the office of *zemsky nachalnik* or land captain was created in 1889. The zemsky nachalniks, who were appointed by the government from the nobility, had administrative power in local affairs as well as the function of judge over the peasantry.

Many measures were also taken to repress the intellectuals. The universities were reorganized in 1884. Education became subject to government control. Censorship of the press was strengthened and the majority of newspapers and magazines became subject to the "preliminary censorship" of government agents. The political tendencies of the intellectuals became subject to redoubled watchfulness by the police. Persons who were suspected were subject to police supervision. Attempts at political conspiracies were mercilessly crushed. In 1887 the police discovered a plot to assassinate Alexander III. Among those who were executed was Alexander Ulianov, Lenin's eldest brother. In order to grant the police greater freedom, many provinces of Russia were declared in a state of "special protection." This enabled the administration to suspend the normal laws of procedure with respect to political offenses. Several of the territories of Russia inhabited by non-Russian peoples also fell under suspicion. The government began a policy of forcible "Russianization," a policy which was applied particularly to Poland. Measures were also taken against the cultural dominance of the Germans in the Baltic provinces where they formed a minority of the population. Religious life was also subject to restrictions. The Old Believers and the evangelical sects were equally affected. Particular suspicion was leveled against the Jews.

The Jewish question had arisen in Russia in the 18th century. A great many Jews had become subjects of the Russian state, after the division of Poland and the annexation of the southwestern Russian territories, which had a large Jewish population. According to the regulations of 1804, Jews were forbidden to settle in the central Russian provinces. The statutes fixed a "pale of settlement" within which Jews must live. This included the western and southern provinces. Under Alexander III the restrictions upon Jews were increased. They were forbidden to settle outside the towns and villages, even within the territories which they might inhabit. The line of demarcation was further restricted in 1887 when the city of Rostov-on-Don was excluded from the pale. In 1891, 17,000 Jews were deported from Moscow. A quota for Jews, limited to their proportion of the population, was introduced in government educational institutions. With few exceptions the Jews were not admitted to government service.

Seeking to hold the various classes under close observation, the government sought a group in society upon which it could itself depend. This seemed to have been found in the nobility. During the reigns of Alexander III and Nicholas II, the government attempted to secure the support of the nobles by granting them special privileges in respect to local self-government and local justice, as well as a number of financial privileges. This dependence was a fatal political error. The Russian nobility was politically dead after the reforms of Alexander II and the beginning of the democratization of Russian life. The attempt to bring it back into political life was an attempt to revive a corpse. Even when the nobles had been a powerful force in Russia, in the 18th and early 19th centuries, the imperial interests and theirs had seldom coincided. The short-sighted attempt to establish a union with them now only aroused further discontent with the government on the part of other classes.

However, it would be unjust to point only to the negative aspects of Russian policy in the last quarter of the 19th century, for the government also carried out reforms improving the social and economic conditions of the majority of the people. Many measures were directed toward improving the condition of the peasantry. First, in 1882, a decree was issued ordering compulsory sale to peasants of land on those estates where the sale had not been completed after the emancipation. The instalments to be paid by the peasants for the land were lowered and the head tax was abolished (1886). New regulations made it easy for peasants to rent government lands and aided them to migrate to the free lands in the eastern part of the empire. It was partly to further migration that the Siberian railroad was begun in 1892. The reign of Alexander III also marked the beginning of labor legislation in Russia. In 1882 government inspection of factories was instituted and the government undertook to regulate the conditions of the workers. At the same time the working day of minors and women was limited by law. Labor legislation was continued during the reign of Nicholas II.

The government also undertook financial reforms. We have seen that the nation's finances were greatly improved under Nicholas I, but since that time two wars and expensive internal reforms had succeeded in shaking them, and the currency had again depreciated. An outstanding statesman, Serge Witte, succeeded in reorganizing the finances and in introducing gold standard in 1897.

All these measures directed toward improving the economic condition of the country could not, however, outweigh the irritation caused by the police supervision instituted by the government. Alexander III's internal policy suppressed social discontent and political opposition only for a short time. Actually, throughout his reign and the first half of Nicholas II's, everything was quiet, but then the accumulated social discontent expressed itself in a violent explosion. The immediate cause was the failure of Nicholas' foreign policy.

5. *Foreign policy to 1899*

Foreign policy following the Congress of Berlin of 1878 was characterized by fatigue and disillusionment. The congress was a serious defeat for Russian diplomacy. Russia's sacrifices during the Turkish war of 1877–78 seemed to have been useless. The emancipation of the Balkan Slavs was only half accomplished. Misunderstandings soon arose in Bulgaria which further diminished the role of Russian diplomacy in the Near East. The cause was partly the tactlessness of Russian advisers, who took too imperious a tone toward the government of Prince Alexander Battenberg, a German nephew of Alexander II who had been placed upon the Bulgarian throne in 1879. That same year an alliance was concluded between Austria and Germany, directed against Russian influence in the Balkans. Despite this, Bismarck succeeded in 1881 in reviving the League of Three Emperors (Russia, Germany, and Austria) which had first been organized in 1872. This alliance was concluded only for a period of three years with the option of renewal. It was renewed in 1884, and terminated in 1887 when Austria broke with Russia. The alliance between Germany and Russia continued for three more years. Bismarck's success may be explained by the fact that Russia at the time was looking for an ally against Great Britain. Relations between the two countries were growing worse each year as Russia continued to advance in central Asia. In the beginning of the 1880's she sent a punitive expedition against the Tekins; and Gen. Michael Skobelev captured the fortress of Geok-Tepe in 1881. In 1884 the lower reaches of the Murgab River, with the town of Merv, were annexed to Russia. In 1885 Afghan troops were met and defeated on the Kushk River. In 1885–88 the trans-Caspian railroad from Askhabad was extended to Samarkand. Gen. Michael Annenkov, who was in charge of the construction, carried it out with great efficiency, despite the natural barriers of desert and windswept sands that had to be overcome. The Russian policy in central Asia aroused much excitement in Great Britain. The battle of the Kushk almost led to war between the two powers. Russia was enabled to retain her acquisitions, thanks to her alliance with Germany as well as to the conciliatory policy of both Alexander III and Gladstone.

The Russo-German understanding could not, however, be permanent if Germany continued to support Austria in the Balkans. The impossibility of relying on it forced Alexander III to seek for other allies. This prepared the ground for a Franco-Russian understanding. The rapprochement between Russia and France started in the realm of finance. Russia needed loans to develop her industries and to improve her armaments. Prior to 1880 Russia's foreign loans had been floated chiefly by German bankers. After 1880 Germany was herself in need of funds for the development of her fleet and colonies, and was, for this as well as other reasons of a political nature, less anxious to extend loans to Russia. In 1888 a group of French bankers offered to grant a loan. The offer was accepted, and in 1890 three loan agreements were concluded. After that France repeatedly extended loans to Russia, in 1893, 1894, 1896, 1901, 1904, and 1906. The financial rapprochement was followed by a political and military understanding. On July 25, 1891, a French squadron visited Kronstadt, and the sailors were cordially greeted. The visit made a deep impression upon Russian society. It was ironic that the autocratic tsar should order the playing of the "Marseillaise," that product of the French Revolution which is filled with revolutionary sentiment, for the Russian revolutionaries regarded it as their hymn too, and their text was a call to revolution in Russia. A month later a military agreement was concluded between Russia and France.

The agreement with France was not, in the eyes of the Russian Government, a direct threat to Great Britain or Germany. It was regarded rather as a measure preventing the possibility of an attack by one European power upon another. For this reason, several years after the conclusion of the French alliance Russia proposed a general agreement among the European powers. On her initiative a peace conference was called at The Hague in 1899. It met for two months but led to no practical results. Its only significance was one of principle. For the first time since the Holy Alliance, an attempt had been made to bring about international peace; and again, as in 1815, the initiative had come from the Russian emperor.

6. *Crisis in the Far East*

The failure of The Hague conference was due primarily to the general distrust felt by the great powers toward each other. Conflicts took place between France and Great Britain and between Great Britain and Germany. In this state of affairs there was little opportunity for creating international order. Possibly the only way to guarantee peace would have been an understanding between the chief continental powers: Russia, France, and Germany. In Russia this scheme was supported by Witte. But a working agreement between Russia and Germany was rendered difficult by the competition in the Balkans between Russia and Germany's ally, Austria, not to speak of the difficulties in the way of a Franco-German understanding. The efforts of German diplomacy were consequently directed toward transferring Russia's attention from the Near East to the Middle and Far East, while attempting to restrain Austria and to discover a modus vivendi between Russia and Austria in the Balkans.

To a certain extent German diplomacy was successful. The year 1897 opened a decade of cooperation between Russia and Austria in the Balkans. Meanwhile, even without German encouragement, Russia's economic interests attracted her to the Middle and Far East. Here, too, Witte stood as the chief exponent of Russia's new policy, which was to encourage Russia's economic penetration in the east. In the early 1890's Witte first directed attention to Russia's economic interests in Persia. A Russo-Persian bank was organized, supported by the Russian Government, to finance Russian concessions in Persia and to aid Russian trade with Persia. Somewhat later, Witte turned his attention to the Far East. In the war of 1894 between China and Japan, Japan was victorious and China was forced to cede the Liaotung Peninsula. China's finances following the war were completely disrupted. Witte urged Russia's diplomatic interference in favor of China. Both France and Germany backed Russia, thus giving an example of the possibility of a Russo-Franco-German understanding such as Witte advocated. Japan was forced to abandon the Liaotung Peninsula; and with the aid of France Russia extended China a loan of 400,000,000 francs. Germany and Great Britain also granted Chinese loans of £16,000,-000 each. The Russian loan was at the rate of 4 per cent, the British 4½, and the German at 5 per cent. Soon after this, upon the occasion of the visit of the Chinese minister, Li Hung-chang, to Russia, a treaty of friendship between China and Russia was concluded (1896). Russia undertook to aid China in case of aggression by a third power, it being understood that the treaty had special reference to Japan. At the same time China agreed that Russia should have the right to construct a railroad through northern Manchuria, connecting Chita and Vladivostok. A company was organized for this purpose, known as the Chinese Eastern Railway Company, which was controlled actually by the Russian Government.

Russian diplomacy, however, did not confine itself to economic penetration, as Witte advised. At the suggestion of Germany Russia took a more aggressive tone. Germany advanced the idea that the European powers should guarantee their financial interests in China by occupying several Chinese ports. Germany took Kiaochao, leaving the Liaotung Peninsula to Russia and Weihaiwei to Great Britain. The Liaotung Peninsula was forcibly occupied by Russian troops and taken from China under the terms of a twenty-five year lease, March 27, 1898. This move, as might well have been expected, aroused the keenest dissatisfaction in China. All the favorable effects of the Russo-Chinese Treaty of 1896 were obliterated.

The next Russian move in the Far East occurred when Russian forces in 1900 joined with those of the European powers in suppressing the Boxer Rebellion. At this time Manchuria was occupied by Russian troops. These events did not advance friendly relations between Russia and China. They resulted, moreover, in straining Russo-Japanese relations. Japan had been deeply offended by Russia's seizure of the Liaotung Peninsula. She also feared Russia's economic competition in Korea. These fears were stimulated by the activities of an irresponsible group of Russian concessionaires on the Yalu River, as well as by the aggressive policy pursued by Adm. Eugene Alexeev, the Russian viceroy in the Far East. Russia did not succeed in solving her difficulties with Japan by peaceful means. On February 9, 1904, without any declaration of war the Japanese fleet attacked the Russian squadron in the outer harbor of Port Arthur.

7. The first Russo-Japanese War

The war with Japan in 1904–05 resulted in a series of defeats for Russia. The Japanese fleet showed itself to be considerably stronger than the Russian, whose vessels were less well constructed and had weaker armament. The Japanese soon succeeded in blockading Port Arthur and then in landing troops on the mainland.

Although the Russian army was larger than the Japanese and not inferior in quality, the war on land was as unfortunate for Russia as at sea. The first failures might be explained by the difficulty of rapidly concentrating Russian troops at the distant battlefield. The whole army depended upon the one-track Siberian railway, which was not even completed. There was no line around Lake Baikal. But the subsequent defeats must be explained on psychological grounds. The Russian army went into battle without enthusiasm. The deep dissatisfaction of the Russian people with the government could not fail to be reflected in the army. The war was unpopular in Russia from the very beginning. Its objects were not understood by the Russian people. It did not seem to them to affect the vital interests of the country, while every Japanese soldier understood that vital interests of Japan were concerned.

The Russian army was led by inferior commanders. At its head was Gen. Alexis Kuropatkin, who had a high reputation, having been chief of staff for popular General Skobelev in the reign of Alexander III. But while he had been an excellent chief of staff, he did not possess the qualities of a commander in chief. He lacked initiative. A leading Russian general said to a friend who expressed his opinion that Kuropatkin was made commander in chief because he had been chief of staff for Skobelev: "Who, then, is going to take the place of Skobelev?" After several failures Kuropatkin was dismissed and his place was taken by the old general Nicholas Linevich, a much better strategist; by that time, however, the government was already thinking of peace.

Soon after the beginning of the war, the Japanese succeeded in cutting off Port Arthur and forcing the Russian army back to the north. A great battle at Liaoyang in the autumn of 1904 was lost by the Russians as a result of Kuropatkin's mismanagement. Early in 1905 Port Arthur surrendered to the Japanese, and several months afterward Russia suffered two new setbacks. The army was defeated at Mukden, and the Baltic fleet, sent under the command of Admiral Rozhdestvensky around Africa to the Far East, was destroyed by the Japanese in the battle of Tsushima.

The defeats in the war led to internal disorders in Russia. The financial condition of the country was greatly disturbed. These conditions led the Russian Government to accept the mediation of President Theodore Roosevelt and to agree to negotiate with the Japanese at Portsmouth. At the head of the Russian peace delegation was Witte, who succeeded in concluding peace on more favorable conditions than were generally expected. He was subsequently granted the title of count in recognition of his services. As to the provisions of the treaty, Japan abandoned her original demand for a money indemnity, but Russia agreed to cede to Japan the southern half of Sakhalin. She also ceded the "lease" to the Liaotung Peninsula but retained control over the railroads in northern Manchuria. The Peace of Portsmouth of September 5, 1905, was concluded just in time to save the Russian Government from complete internal catastrophe. Russia was already in a state of revolution.

INTERNAL DEVELOPMENT FROM THE MID-19TH CENTURY TO THE FIRST WORLD WAR

1. *Social changes*

A GREAT change occurred in Russia between the reigns of the two Nicholases. In half a century the nation underwent complete social reconstruction. The Russia of Nicholas I was based upon serfdom and its own sort of state socialism. As a result of the reforms of Alexander II, there arose on the ruins of the earlier regime a capitalist economy. A typical aspect of the change was the abolition of the head tax in 1886. As we have seen, the financial importance of the head tax decreased rapidly in the middle of the 19th century, when it comprised only 24 per cent of the total national income. In the early eighties its importance lessened still further; but its complete abolition was a significant move. This tax was associated with the old regime; its repeal terminated the division of the people into the two classes of those who paid it (*podatnoe sostoianie*) and those who were exempt. However, instead of this tax there were now the payments for lands given to the peasantry at the time of their emancipation. These payments were the chief financial reason for continuing the special legal condition of the peasantry. In this way, notwithstanding the reforms of Alexander II, a good part of the Russian people were isolated from the new citizenship and placed in a special category. This was the chief social anachronism of Russia prior to the revolution of 1905.

As a result of that revolution, a constitution of limited scope was established in Russia and a House of Representatives, called the Duma, created. This was followed by important social reforms. The peasants' redemption payments were discontinued and, at the initiative of Prime Minister Stolypin, the peasants were allowed to leave the commune and their ownership of individual farms was greatly encouraged. The dissolution of the commune and the termination of the redemption payments put an end to the juridical isolation of the peasant class, and its members received the same civil rights as those of the upper classes. In 1906 the peasants were given back their right to elect deputies for the zemstvo councils (which they had lost in 1890). In 1912 the justices of the peace were re-established and the land captains lost their judicial functions. Thus, the defects of the Emancipation Act of 1861, as well as some of the painful features of the counterreforms of 1889 and 1890, were now eliminated, and so on the eve of the first World War Russia became a society of citizens with full rights.

2. Economic development: agriculture

The creation of the new capitalist structure was accompanied by rapid economic development. The basic factor in this, as in the preceding period, was the swift growth of population, which doubled between 1850 and 1900. During the first 15 years of the 20th century it increased 30 per cent. In 1914 the population of the Russian Empire without Finland totaled 170,000,000.

Particularly significant was the growth of the cities. In 1851 there were less than 3,500,000 people in the towns or about 5 per cent of the total population. By 1897 the number had risen to 16,500,000 or 13 per cent of the population, and by 1914 to around 25,000,000 or 15 per cent. These figures indicate the growth of the industrial population as compared with the agricultural. However, in spite of the growth of the cities and of industry, about 85 per cent of Russia's population before the first World War lived in rural districts, and most of these were occupied in agriculture.

Agriculture remained the foundation of Russia's economic life. The area under cultivation increased steadily. In 1905 it amounted to around 100,000,000 hectares; in 1914 to about 120,000,000 hectares. The grain harvests per hectare in Russia were considerably smaller than in other countries. However, they gradually increased, thanks to the introduction of modern methods of cultivation. The average annual harvest of grain in European Russia in the decade 1861–70 was half a ton per hectare. In the decade 1901–10 it increased to five-sixths of a ton per hectare.

The total production of grain in 1913 reached over 92,000,000 tons. In view of the occasional droughts, the grain harvest in Russia was subject to wide variation. The years of poor harvest led to food shortages or even famine for part of the population, as in 1891 and 1906. The tragic extent of the famine of 1921–22, however, was due not only to natural but also to social and political conditions. Russian economic life up to very recent times was dependent directly upon "his excellency the harvest," as Minister of Finance Vladimir Kokovtsov said in the Duma in 1911.

Ownership of land in Russia, following the peasant reforms of 1861, underwent great changes. Land rapidly passed to the peasants, who not only retained the lands distributed in 1861 but also acquired new lands by purchase. Thus, simultaneous with the growth of the area under cultivation in Russia during the fifty years preceding the first World War, a radical change in the social structure of the agricultural population took place. As a result of the Stolypin reforms the peasant communes began to disintegrate, and by 1913 5,000,000 households had left the commune and applied for consolidation of their allotments. The consolidation had been completed for 1,500,000 of them. Russia was moving with great strides toward small individual landownership.

3. Industrialization

The industrialization of Russia which began in the second half of the 19th century increased rapidly until 1914, and in some branches of industry until 1917. We will trace this process briefly in three of the most important branches of Russian industry: textiles, metallurgy, and food products.

The Russian cotton industry, prior to the first World War, occupied fourth place in world production. It was surpassed only by Great Britain, the United States, and Germany. In 1905 it employed 7,350,683 spindles and 178,506 looms. By 1911 the productive forces of the industry had grown to 8,448,818 spindles and 220,000 looms. The increased production was absorbed partly by the home market and partly by foreign trade. In 1890 the per capita consumption of cotton cloth in Russia was 2.31 pounds and in 1910, 4.56 pounds. The principal foreign market was Persia, where Russia's cotton industries competed successfully with British goods. Russia's cotton exports to Persia in 1906–07 were valued at 10,189,000 rubles, as against British exports of 13,999,000 rubles. In 1912–13 Russian exports rose to 16,180,000 rubles as against British exports of 14,238,000 rubles. The growth of cotton manufacture in Russia led to a rapid increase in the area of cotton cultivation in Turkistan and Transcaucasia, where, before the war, over 600,000 hectares were planted in cotton.

The metallurgical industries showed a similar development. In 1900 around 1,500,000 tons of pig iron were produced in Russia. By 1914 production had grown to over 3,500,000 tons.

The principal products of Russian food manufacturers were sugar, alcohol, and flour. Sugar was an important commodity both of internal consumption and of export. In 1909–10 over 80,000 tons of it were exported. In 1911–12 sugar exports reached 500,000 tons.

The growth of industrial production was reflected also in mining. Eighty-five per cent of the coal used in Russia was of domestic extraction. The chief center of coal mining was the Donets basin which supplied 55 per cent of Russia's needs for coal. In 1900, 11,000,000 tons were mined in the Donets basin and in 1913 25,000,000 tons.

Forests were exploited to serve both domestic needs and foreign trade. In 1904, 13,200,000 rubles worth of lumber was exported and by 1913 exports had reached 164,900,000 rubles. Of great importance also was the production of oil, chiefly in the neighborhood of Baku. In 1860 oil production in that area hardly exceeded 160,000 tons. By 1905 it had risen to over 7,000,000 tons and by 1913 to around 9,000,000 tons. As world production of oil in the 20th century grew by gigantic strides, the proportion of Russia production to the total fell during the years preceding the war. In 1905 Russia supplied 27 per cent of world production, but in 1913 only 16.5 per cent.

No less rapid than the expansion of industry was the development of railroads in Russia. Around 1850 the total length of lines in operation in Russia did not exceed 660 miles. By 1912 the Russian railroad system comprised 40,194 miles and was second in length only to that of the United States. The greatest achievement was the completion of the Trans-Siberian Railroad, built between 1892 and 1905. Its construction was one of the outstanding railroad projects of the time. The length of the line from Moscow to Vladivostok is 5,542 miles. Great natural and technical difficulties had to be overcome—frozen subsoil and wild country—and the cost exceeded $200,000,000. It was originally a single-track line, but later a second line was laid down.

4. Labor

The rapid expansion of Russian industry was accompanied by the creation of a working class on a scale previously unknown in Russia. Gradually the social character of the laboring class changed. At the beginning of the century the majority of Russian workers were still connected with the peasantry; they were in fact peasants temporarily engaged in factory work. This partly explained the psychology of the worker, who had little interest in his occupation or his factory; he could almost always return to his village, if he wished, and secure an allotment of land. But with every year conditions changed. The Stolypin reforms, in creating a new class of small landowners, cut off the village peasants from those who had become factory workers and thus stimulated the growth of a city proletariat.

The organization of labor unions was very slow because of the government's fear of any kind of organization. Finally in 1902 it consented to legalize some unions, and after the revolution of 1905 unions were permitted on a large scale by the law of March 4, 1906.

By artificially retarding the development of unions the government unwittingly fostered the formation of illegal revolutionary organizations. But it did make efforts to satisfy the principal needs of the workers by means of legislation. Labor legislation in Russia goes back to the 1880's in the reign of Alexander III. In 1897 day work was limited to 11.5 hours and night work to 10 hours. Night work was forbidden for children under 17, and children under 12 were not allowed to engage in industrial work of any kind. The legislation of the 20th century introduced workers' accident compensation in 1903, health insurance in 1912, and accident insurance in 1912. The condition of the working class gradually improved, thanks to increasing wages, particularly in St. Petersburg and Moscow. In 1900 the average wage of the Russian worker was only 187 rubles a year. By 1913 it had risen to 300 rubles and in some branches of industry in St. Petersburg and Moscow to five times this sum. In many factories the low money wages were augmented by free lodgings, hospital services, and factory schools.

5. *State economy and private initiative*

During the reign of Alexander II the government apparently desired to refrain from interference in economic matters and to allow the fullest degree of private initiative. These principles were expressed in the policy stimulating the construction of railroads by private companies on the concession basis. A number of government-owned factories in the Urals were sold to private individuals, and the salt mines in the southeast were leased to private capital. At the same time a policy of free trade was instituted. The government's policy, however, led to confusion in many branches of Russian industry. Chaos reigned in railroad administration. In 1871 the unpaid obligations of the private railroad companies to the Treasury amounted to 174,000,000 rubles. The sum rose in a few years to 500,000,000 rubles. As a result the government changed its policy. In 1876 the tariff on imports was raised, and it continued to be raised steadily until the first World War. The government also started buying up private railroad lines and undertook the construction of new railroads. In 1889, 23 per cent of the railroads were government controlled, while in 1900 60 per cent were. It was the government that constructed the Trans-Siberian Railroad and the Orenburg-Tashkent Railroad in Turkistan.

Of great importance in the period 1892–1903 were the policies of Serge Witte, minister of finance. At Witte's suggestion, the government undertook the ambitious scheme of introducing the alcohol monopoly, and this reform, begun in 1894, gradually spread over the whole country. The consumption of alcohol in Russia in 1905 totaled 200,000,000 gallons and in 1913, 280,000,000 gallons. The income from the monopoly in those years was 443,200,000 and 675,-100,000 rubles respectively. Besides, Witte greatly expanded the operations of the State Bank, which he tried to make a "bankers' bank." Its turnover in 1909 amounted to 162,324,000,000 rubles and in 1913 to 234,000,000,000.

The steady growth of the budget was a reflection of this economic policy. Government expenditures in 1900 were 1,889,000,000 rubles and in 1913, 3,382,000,000 rubles. About one-third of the budgets in the 20th century were appropriated for government-operated railroads and other industries and less than one-quarter for the army and navy. If the budgets of the Russian Empire in the time of Peter I could be called military budgets, those under Witte may be termed industrial budgets.

It would be erroneous to think, however, that Russia's growing prosperity depended mainly on government patronage. Private initiative of both Russian and foreign businessmen played a role of paramount importance in the rapid industrialization of Russia from the 1880's on. Witte was in favor of attracting foreign capital to Russia, and by 1913 about one-fourth of the capital of industrial corporations and private plants in Russia was derived from foreign investments—British, French and Belgian, German, Swedish, and American. The percentage of foreign interests was highest in the chemical industry, and lowest in the textile, which was controlled chiefly by Russian capital. Most of the Moscow textile magnates— the Khludovs, the Konovalovs, the Morozovs, and others—were descendants of operators of small shops grown out of cottage industries. Large wholesale trade firms were also built up by Russian merchants, such as the Vtorovs who started their activities in Siberia. By the turn of the century Russian industrialists and merchants turned their attention to banking. The Guchkovs and the Riabushinskys were prominent in this group.

Of the owners of Moscow's 50 largest industrial and trade concerns as of 1900, 29 were descendants of peasants; 8 of petty merchants, and 5 of noblemen. Five were of foreign descent; the origin of 3 is uncertain. Those families that were descended from peasants and petty merchants went through a great cultural change. While their forefathers were often illiterate, and the next generation still followed the old ways of life, the younger generations received the best education available and became not only wealthy but often cultivated. Many captains of industry became noted patrons of the arts and the theater.

6. *The cultural work of the zemstvos. Education and public health*

In 1700–1850 Russian culture centered chiefly around the large cities and the nobles' estates. From 1850 on, the basic elements of modern civilization such as education and medical care spread far and wide, reaching the lowest levels of the city population and the peasant huts. A prominent part in this movement was played by the zemstvos and city organizations introduced by the reforms of Alexander II. Notwithstanding the imperfections in the electoral law, local self-government in Russia in the half century preceding the first World War fulfilled an immense cultural task. The zemstvos were first introduced in thirty-four provincial governments. The reform did not extend to Turkistan, Siberia, the Caucasus, Poland, the Baltic provinces, the western Russian provinces, or the Cossack regions. By the law of 1864 the zemstvos were given the task of supervising public education, public health, charity, roads, fire insurance, in fact all questions relating to local life and economy. Their budget was raised by self-assessment and was derived chiefly from the taxation of real property.

The zemstvos first directed their attention to public education and to matters of health. The population of the rural districts of Russia, which before the reforms of Alexander II had been almost entirely illiterate and without medical care, was gradually provided with schools, hospitals, and dispensaries. In 1895, in the regions having zemstvos, there was one hospital bed to every 6,500 inhabitants, while where there were no zemstvos there was only one hospital bed to every 41,000 persons. The expenditure of the zemstvos on public health increased each year. In 1892 the average expenditure on medical assistance was 34 rubles per 100 inhabitants; in 1904, 56 rubles.

The same trend may be observed in public education. In 1911, in provinces having zemstvos, there were 46 pupils in zemstvo schools for every 1,000 rural inhabitants. In nonzemstvo provinces of European Russia there were 34 per 1,000 receiving schooling, and only 18 per 1,000 in Siberia. By the laws of 1911–12 zemstvos were introduced in 9 additional provinces.

The total budgets of the zemstvos grew steadily. In 1875 the expenses of all the zemstvos in 34 provinces totaled 28,870,000 rubles; in 1905, 124,185,000 rubles. In 1914 the budget of the zemstvos of 43 provinces reached 347,512,000 rubles; and if the sums expended upon the commercial undertakings of the zemstvos and insurance be included, the 1914 budget approximated 400,-000,000, i.e., one-ninth of the total state budget.

Over two-thirds of zemstvo expenditures were for public health and education. In 1914, 82,000,000 rubles was spent by the zemstvos for public health. The rural population, prior to 1864, when the zemstvos were introduced, almost wholly lacked medical care. Fifty years later, at the eve of the first World War, the zemstvos had covered the rural territories with hospitals and dispensaries. The average radius of the medical districts was 10 miles. In 1914, in the 43 provinces having zemstvos, there was a total of 3,300 medical districts. Many zemstvos introduced special agencies to handle medical supplies—pharmacies and warehouses —and in some cases stations for vaccination against smallpox and rabies. Sixteen of the 29 Pasteur laboratories in Russia were under the management of the zemstvos or city organizations.

The expenditure of the zemstvos on public education in 1914 was 106,000,000 rubles. Most of this went to primary schools. In 1914 there were 50,000 zemstvo schools with 80,000 teachers and 3,000,-000 school children. The zemstvos paid particular attention to the construction of new schools in accordance with modern pedagogical ideas and hygienic requirements. They also opened their own teachers' colleges and organized special courses for the improvement of teaching methods. They established extension courses for adults and built libraries. In 1914 there were 12,627 rural public libraries in 35 of the 43 zemstvo districts.

In addition the zemstvos undertook to assist the population in agriculture, insurance, and the development of roads and telephones. In 1914 they were authorized to open 219 regional telephone systems. There were at this time 163 systems already in operation, with about 42,900 miles of lines and 100,000 miles of wire.

The work of the zemstvos was at first little appreciated by the peasant population for whose benefit it was intended. This may be explained partly by the poverty of the Russian peasant who associated the zemstvo first of all with new taxes. Moreover, as has been explained, the electoral law on the basis of which the zemstvos operated from 1890 to 1906 gave little actual responsibility to the peasants in the election of representatives. Although the zemstvos were operating for the benefit of the people, they were often regarded not as popular but as aristocratic organizations.

The cooperative societies were nearer to the popular masses than were the zemstvos. Their rapid development, however, began only in the decade preceding the first World War. On January 1, 1915, there were 32,300 cooperatives with a membership of 12,000,000, most of them peasants.

Following the revolution of 1905 the Duma paid much attention to promotion of education. In 1908 it adopted a comprehensive and integrated plan providing for training teachers, and began the construction of many new schools. Largely because of the success of this program, illiteracy in Russia was considerably reduced during the early years of the 20th century. According to data collected in the census of 1897, only 24 per cent of the population of the empire above the age of 10 could read and write, in 1914 the figure was around 45 per cent. The figures revealed certain other facts about the condition of education in Russia: the degree of literacy was higher in the cities than in the villages; higher among men than among women; and higher among those in the younger brackets, from 10 to 30 years, than among the older generations. This breakdown makes understandable the fact that, in 1914, 73 per cent of the army recruits were found to be able to read and write. Taken as a whole, this evidence indicates that the literacy rate in Russia had continued to increase rapidly from 1890 until the disruptive effects of the civil war were felt—a significant fact that is too often overlooked by students of Russian history.

7. Universities and scientific progress

Higher education in Russia during the half century preceding the revolution of 1917 also made considerable progress. First of all, the number of students increased. In the second half of the 19th century three new universities were founded (Odessa 1865, Warsaw 1869, Tomsk 1888). In the 20th century another was opened before the first World War and one during the war (Saratov 1909, Perm 1916). The University of Simferopol (Crimea) was opened during the revolution in 1918. During the war Warsaw University was transferred to Rostov and Iuriev University to Voronezh.

There were eleven universities in Russia in 1917, plus a number of separate technical schools: institutes of technology, mining academies, a land survey institute, institute of roads and communications, institute of forestry, several law schools and philological schools, several women's colleges, and four theological academies.

The character of the instruction in Russian universities in the 20th century reached a very high level and cannot be considered inferior to the universities of Europe and America. Nearly all the above institutions were under state control, although some received assistance from private funds. Shaniavsky University in Moscow, the Makushin College in Tomsk, and several others were municipal or private universities. There were 137,000 students of both sexes in Russian universities in 1912. Prior to 1905 the universities played an important part in the political development of the country. The professors mostly took part in the liberal movement, and a considerable portion of the students were socialists. In 1905 some liberal groups were organized by students, but by 1917 the political role of the universities was of little importance.

University life under Alexander III was closely regulated by the law of 1884. In 1905, however, the management of the universities was handed over to the professors. The restrictions remaining after 1905 led in 1911 to a dispute between the government and the faculty of Moscow University which resulted in the resignation of a large number of the professors.

The Academy of Sciences at the end of the 19th century also participated actively in the development of Russian culture. Its various institutes before the first World War grew into large institutions enjoying a high degree of autonomy in their scientific research. Many learned organizations came into existence. Their fields included not only the natural sciences and mathematics but history and philology. Russia came to be covered with a network of the learned societies, and Russian science held an important place internationally. Such men as the chemist Dmitri Mendeleev and the physiologist Ivan Pavlov became world famous.

Russian scientists contributed their share to the technological inventions of the modern age. In 1874 A. Ladygin, then a student at the University of St. Petersburg, applied electricity for purposes of illumination and built a lamp which was perfected by two other Russian physicists, demonstrated in Paris in 1875, and later tested in the Siemens-Halske plant in Berlin. Simultaneously Paul Iablochkov (1847–94) constructed his carbon arc "candle" which was produced commercially in 1876. It was in 1878 that the news of Thomas Edison's incandescent lamp was reported in American press. In the 1890's Alexander Popov (1859–1905) entered the then entirely new field of radiotelegraphy. Having constructed a new device for receiving electromagnetic waves—the antenna—he demonstrated his apparatus for wireless transmission at a meeting of the Russian Physical Society in St. Petersburg in 1895. He applied to the Ministry of the Navy for funds to enlarge his researches but was granted only 300 rubles ($150.00). Nevertheless he continued his experiments and in 1897 was able to operate transmission stations at a distance of five kilometers. By that time, however, Guglielmo Marconi, who knew of Popov's experiments, had produced his paper on radiotelegraphy, and it is with his name that most people usually associate the invention of the radio.

8. *Literature, drama, and fine arts*

The flowering of Russian literature in the second half of the 19th century was an event which has been fully recognized both in Europe and in America. The works of outstanding Russian writers have been translated into many languages and become part of the literary heritage of tens of thousands of foreign readers.

The three giants of the period were Count Leo Tolstoy (1828–1910), Theodore Dostoevsky (1821–81), and Ivan Turgenev (1818–83). Both Tolstoy and Turgenev belonged to wealthy noble families. While Dostoevsky too was a descendant of an old family it had become impoverished and lost contact with the nobility; for practical purposes, Dostoevsky may be said to have belonged to the classless intelligentsia.

All three of these writers received an excellent education and were well versed in western culture and literature, but only Turgenev was sympathetic to the West. Turgenev spent many years abroad and finally settled near Paris. There he became intimate with French writers; it may be noted that Henry James included his essay on Turgenev in a volume on French novelists. In contrast to Turgenev, while neither Tolstoy nor Dostoevsky was a "Slavophile," both of them, in feelings as well as in reactions to life, were close to the Russian soil—and the Russian "soul"—and this affected their whole literary production.

As to the characteristics of that production, Dostoevsky stood apart from the other two. Both Tolstoy and Turgenev may be said to have belonged to the school of literary realism (or naturalism). Dostoevsky was a mystic and a religious thinker, chiefly interested in the intricacies and aberrations of human psychology. His life was cruelly cut into two pieces by his being sentenced in 1849 to four years of penal servitude for participation in a socialist circle. He described his own and his fellow prisoners' sufferings in his *Memoirs from the House of Death*. Among his other best known works are *Crime and Punishment* and *The Brothers Karamazov*. In the latter he tried, among other things, to portray the ideal type of Russian monk. *The Possessed*, a less known and less readable, yet significant, novel, contains a remarkable analysis of the mentality of the early Russian revolutionaries.

Turgenev first became known with the publication of *A Sportsman's Sketches* (1852), a collection of short stories in which the quiet life of provincial noblemen and peasants—then still serfs— was vividly described. This book had political as well as literary importance since it was, in a sense, a plea for emancipation of the serfs. Among the readers impressed by it was the future tsar Alexander II. Of the series of novels which followed, *A Nest of Gentlefolk* and *Fathers and Sons* are perhaps best known; Turgenev created a gallery of portraits of Russian noblemen and intellectuals of the important period of change from the old regime to modern times in Russia. Most of his men are weak and irresolute and the women dynamic and fascinating.

Leo Tolstoy's masterpiece is his great historical novel *War and Peace* (completed in 1869), which describes Russia in the period of the Napoleonic wars. It is more than a novel in the usual sense —it is a vast panorama of life, love, and death. As Tolstoy had been an army officer in his youth and had taken part in the defense of Sevastopol, he was familiar with the sordid reality of the war as well as with the gamut of human feelings it engendered, from quiet courage to cruelty and vanity. His second great novel, *Anna Karenina*, is of somewhat narrower scope. Of the two romances it describes, one is tragic, and in a sense signalizes the approach of a moral and religious crisis in Tolstoy himself. That crisis came into the open when Tolstoy completed his *Confession*, in 1882. Tolstoy's new teaching was a rationalized Christianity based on the principle of nonresistance, or not repaying evil by evil. This led him to the denial not only of military service, the state, the courts, and private property, as based on violence, but also of all higher forms of science and art. Manual labor he came to consider the only decent way of life. His attempts to give up his wealth and to practice what he preached led to conflict with his family. At the age of 82 he secretly left his home to live the life of a wanderer—only to die of pneumonia at a small railroad station. While Tolstoy had been as critical of revolutionary terrorism as of governmental compulsion, his opposition to the state, the courts, and the established church contributed greatly to the rise of the revolutionary spirit in Russia.

Among the prominent writers of the younger generations Anton Chekhov (1860–1904) and Maxim Gorky (1869–1939) may be mentioned. Maxim Gorky is the pen name of Alexis Peshkov ("Gorky" means "bitter" in Russian). Both Gorky and Chekhov were commoners. Anton Chekhov's grandfather was a serf who succeeded in purchasing his freedom; Anton's father was a boy of nine at that time. Gorky's father was a shipping clerk; he died when Alexis was five. While Chekhov received a good education, Gorky was left to his own devices from his boyhood on and what knowledge he acquired came from casual but eager reading. As writers, both Chekhov and Gorky belong to the realistic school, yet they differed greatly from each other. Chekhov, to a certain extent, continued Turgenev's traditions. The milieu he described, however, was rarely that of the nobility and mostly that of intellectuals and petty government clerks. He left excellent pictures of peasant life, all of them very grim. His style is concise and direct, with careful avoidance of rhetoric. He never succeeded in writing a lengthy novel; most of his works are short stories. In addition, he also wrote several plays, of which *The Three Sisters* and *The Cherry Orchard* are best known to American theater audiences. There is little action in his plays; their charm is in the shades of feeling and mood. Their initial popularity owed much to the Moscow Art Theater, where most of them were first produced. Taken as a whole, Chekhov's works gave a sympathetic, though melancholy, picture of some aspects of Russian life and society of the 1890's. Like Turgenev's men, most of Chekhov's men are gentle and amiable but incapable of enduring effort. His women are less dynamic than Turgenev's, and while some of them are charming, on the whole one feels a strain of aversion if not of contempt in his attitude toward them. Chekhov like Turgenev had a deep admiration for western civilization and was in favor of gradual political and cultural progress as against terrorism and violent revolution.

In contrast to the gentle Chekhov, Gorky usually searched for heroes and dramatic situations. While hoboes were his first favorites, he later looked to factory workers for inspiration. There is much cheap romanticism in Gorky's early creations and much political bias in his later works. Of his novels, his first, *Foma Gordeev,* is decidedly his best; it describes the merchants who controlled the Volga shipping. Gorky's plays are, on the whole, of higher literary quality than his novels; *The Lower Depths,* first produced by the Moscow Art Theater, is the best known. In contrast to Chekhov, Gorky took active part in politics, eventually joining the Bolshevik party; Lenin and some other Bolshevik leaders were his personal friends. Under the Soviet, Gorky was recognized as the dean of Russian letters.

Of less fame abroad are the Russian poets of this time. In the period around 1900 Russian poetry like that of so many other countries was dominated by the symbolist movement. The whole world, according to the view of this school, is merely a combination of symbols. Its poets attempted to combine verse and music so that they would supplement each other. The founders of this tendency in Russian poetry were Constantine Balmont (1867–1942) and Valerius Briusov (1873–1924). At first misunderstood and laughed at by the public, they finally secured recognition. Of the younger symbolist poets the most important was Alexander Blok (1880–1921). The next generation of Russian poets moved away from symbolism: "We want to admire a rose because it is beautiful, not because it is a symbol of mystical purity." At the head of this movement were Nicholas Gumilev (1886–1921) and his wife Ann Akhmatova (b. 1889). Gumilev was shot by the Bolshevik government on suspicion of having taken part in a counterrevolutionary organization.

By 1900 the realistic theater had become the dominant type in Russia. The Imperial Alexandra Theater in St. Petersburg and the Imperial Little Theater in Moscow achieved renown which was based largely on a succession of great actors and actresses famed for their performances in both tragic and comic roles. Ostrovsky's plays occupied an important place in the repertory of both these theaters. There were many theaters in Russia besides the imperial ones, and one of the greatest of all modern Russian actresses, Vera Komissarjevsky, became known only after she left the Alexandra Theater.

The Moscow Art Theater created by Constantine Stanislavsky (1863–1938) and Vladimir Nemirovich-Danchenko (1858–1943) brought the realistic theater to its finest expression. Its success was based mainly on Stanislavsky's insistence that the total performance was of greater importance than the dazzling display of the talents of a few great actors and actresses, a principle that eventually resulted in a series of magnificent performances by a perfectly trained ensemble in which each player—and no one player —was the star. Stanislavsky's theater was bulging with extraordinarily talented people, and he was a great actor himself, but he demanded of every member of the cast the self-effacing restraint necessary for a flawless and luminous interpretation of the play. As has been mentioned, both Chekhov's and Gorky's plays were produced by the Moscow Art Theater with great success.

When the Moscow Art Theater was founded in 1898, and for several years thereafter, little attention was paid to the artistic quality of the scenery or to the place of the pictorial artist in the production. Later, however, this weakness was corrected, and after 1909 several painters—including Mstislav Dobujinsky, Nicholas Roerich, and Alexander Benois—joined Stanislavsky and Nemirovich and added new beauty to the theater's productions.

Russian sculptors in the period did not form any recognizable movement. One of the most prominent was Prince Paul Trubetskoy. Russian architecture was at the crossroads and partly engaged in imitating 16th- and 17th-century architecture. However, in the period just before the first World War new constructive tendencies appeared. A certain analogy may be found between the development of painting and of modern literature. The second half of the 19th century saw the rise of a new group of artists who in 1870 broke with the classical traditions of the Academy of Arts. The ideal of this new movement was to depict historical subjects and scenes of everyday life realistically. Some wished to reveal social evils. Among these artists was one of the best known Russian painters, Elias Repin. A special place was held by Victor Vasnetsov, who attempted to combine modern technique with the manner of the old Russian and Byzantine religious painting. His murals in the Cathedral of St. Vladimir in Kiev, painted between 1885 and 1895, are the best known of his works.

By the end of the century a new movement was to be observed in

Russian painting, devoted to "pure" art. For the members of this school art must not serve any social or political purpose; it must serve only beauty. The magazine *Mir Iskustva* (*The World of Art*) was the organ of this group, and the artists included Valentin Serov, Russia's greatest portrait painter, and Michael Vrubel, whose masterpiece is "The Demon" (based on Lermontov's theme), as well as the above-mentioned Benois, Dobujinsky, and Roerich. A remarkable leader in the promotion of Russian painting and ballet abroad was Serge Diaghilev who started his activities in Paris in 1906.

Distinct from the "intellectual" painting of the above groups was the popular art. Until 1917 peasant artists continued painting icons in the traditional manner, particularly in the province of Vladimir. A great interest in this work was shown by the archaeologist Nikodim Kondakov. A special committee was organized at his initiative, under the patronage of Nicholas II, to promote icon painting (1901). The committee succeeded in aiding the peasant iconographers and providing them with special training.

9. *Music*

For Russian music 1850–1900 was a period of great creative activity. In the early 1860's a group was formed in St. Petersburg whose object was to develop a national style in Russian music. The leading spirit was Mili Balakirev, and the group included Nicholas Rimsky-Korsakov, Modest Musorgsky, Alexander Borodin, and César Cui. The name of the "Mighty Band" given them by their admirers was seized upon by their enemies, who for many years taunted them with it. But time has justified the name. The basic idea of the "Band" was, first, the utilization of folk song themes and, second, realism in music. In their first idea the "Band" followed the views of Glinka. Their realism, on the other hand, was a continuation of the views of Dargomyzhsky. They drew their themes from folk music and folk tales. Their operas have historical or mythological subjects, and frequently eastern or Russian folk themes.

The prime mover of the group was Mili Balakirev (1836–1910). His compositions are few but of high quality. He left a small number of orchestral overtures and symphonic poems, a few collections of songs—among them the best in Russian vocal music—and some pianoforte music. He was a remarkable pianist and for many years director of the imperial choir.

Modest Musorgsky (1839–81) is perhaps the most famous of all the members of the "Band." He opened new paths in music and his work had an influence upon modern French music. The operas *Boris Godunov* and *Khovanshchina* have historical plots. The first is concerned with the Time of Trouble and the second with the streltsy and Old Ritualists of the late 17th century. Musorgsky succeeded in giving to his music, which is full of drama, the pathos of great popular movements.

The music of Borodin and Rimsky-Korsakov is more harmonious and clear than that of Musorgsky. Borodin (1833–87) was both an outstanding composer and a scientist. His opera *Prince Igor* is founded on the narrative of the old Russian heroic song, the Lay of Igor's Campaign. Borodin also left three symphonies, the last of which is unfinished, as well as a symphonic picture entitled *In Central Asia,* in which two themes, the oriental and the Russian, meet.

Rimsky-Korsakov (1844–1909) was the youngest member of the "Mighty Band." He was technically the most skilled of the group and completed as well as orchestrated the unfinished works of Borodin and Musorgsky. His own music is characterized by the brilliance of his instrumentation. Most of his fifteen operas deal with mythical and eastern subjects; *Sadko* is based on an old Novgorod trading song, and *The Golden Cock* on a story by Pushkin. Another of his operas, *The Invisible City of Kitezh,* deals with the epoch of the Mongol invasion of Russia.

Peter Tchaikovsky (1840–93) was not a member of the "Band." His music is of a totally different character, being concerned with the spiritual experiences of 19th-century man, and bears fewer national traces in the sense of describing national character and popular movements. Like Dostoevsky, Tchaikovsky looks into the human soul and expresses the struggles and sufferings there. In the blind and helpless moods of the Sixth Symphony there may be a prophetic and sorrowful utterance of approaching calamities. He also composed songs, many of which demonstrate a remarkable depth of feeling. His operas, *Eugene Onegin* and *The Queen of Spades,* acquired great popularity in Russia. His soft lyricism is universally understood and appreciated.

The scene of the activities of the "Mighty Band" was St. Petersburg. Tchaikovsky, on the other hand, lived for the most part in Moscow, with which the majority of Russia composers of the turn of the 20th century were connected. Outstanding among these were Alexander Skriabin and Sergei Rachmaninov. Skriabin (1871–1915) was a mystic and a theosophist. He never composed vocal music, considering it too materialistic. The best known of his symphonic pieces are the *Poem of Ecstasy* and *Prometheus*. Skriabin attempted to find the relationship between sounds and colors and to complete the musical symphony with color. His dream was to reform the world by sound.

Rachmaninov (1873–1942) is well known in this country, both as a composer and as a pianist. His first opera *Aleko,* with a libretto based on a poem by Pushkin, was composed in 1892. In the early 1900's he produced a number of orchestral as well as chamber compositions.

A decade younger than Skriabin and Rachmaninov, Igor Stravinsky (b. 1882) was a pupil, though not a follower, of Rimsky-Korsakov. Before the first World War he moved to Paris, where in 1911 his ballet *Petrushka* was given for the first time. He is now in the United States.

10. *Religious life*

Most characteristic of Russian religious life prior to the first World War was the wide spread of evangelical teachings denying the complex dogma and ritual of the Orthodox Church. The movement of rationalism among the intellectuals took the form of Tolstoyanism, following the religious teachings of Leo Tolstoy. Among the masses, especially in the south of Russia, this tendency found expression in the Stundo-Baptist movement. The term "stunda" was derived from the German *Stunde* (hour), and signified to certain German evangelical and reforming groups of the 18th century the hour of religious congregation. The Stundists appeared in the south of Russia in the first half of the 19th century and expanded rapidly in the second half. In the 1870's they fell under the influence of Baptist teachings coming from Bessarabia and Transcaucasia. By the end of the century, the Baptists had spread over more than thirty provinces of Russia.

The government attempted to put a stop to the movement by police measures. In 1894 the sect was recognized as "specially harmful" and forbidden the right to congregate. The natural consequence was to stimulate the growth of the movement. It was only after the revolution of 1905 that policy toward dissenters changed. In 1905 a manifesto was issued permitting religious freedom. By that time there were probably over 20,000,000 dissidents in Russia, counting Old Believers, Baptists, and others.

The manifesto of 1905 was the beginning of the liberation not only of the dissenters but of the Orthodox Church itself. In the years preceding the first World War a great internal upheaval took place in the Orthodox Church. This was a sign of life. The church, notwithstanding the decline of its moral authority in the 18th century and the beginning of the 19th, was alive and capable of assuming the religious guidance of its members. Proof of its continued vitality, even in the most lifeless period of the 18th century, was the appearance of a man of such outstanding character as Bishop Tikhon Zadonsky, one of the first Russians to raise his voice against serfdom.

In the 19th century the Russian church produced a number of outstanding elders who exercised a great influence upon members of both the upper and lower classes by the purity of their moral life. The elders were monks of strict habits to whom believers came for advice and consolation in their spiritual or practical difficulties. The elder was available to anyone, no matter what his class in society. The elders of the Optina Pustyn monastery were especially esteemed, and visited by Gogol, Dostoevsky, and Tolstoy. The elder Amvrosy served as a prototype of the monk Zosima in Dostoevsky's *The Brothers Karamazov*.

Around 1900 some members of the Orthodox Church raised the question of calling a church council (*sobor*) to secure the liberation of the church from the guardianship of the state and to carry out internal reforms in its organization. One of the chief internal reforms sought was the right of congregations to self-government, which they had had in the days before Peter the Great. As a result of Peter's church policy the congregation became merely a section of people living in the vicinity of a given church and possessing no right of self-government in church affairs. It also was suggested that the patriarchate (abolished by Peter) should be restored. No council was called prior to the revolution of 1917, and up to that time the Russian church continued to be under the official guardianship of the government through the Holy Synod.

CHAPTER 12

THE REVOLUTION OF 1905 AND THE CONSTITUTIONAL EXPERIMENT

1. Political parties at the beginning of the 20th century

THE Japanese war was the outward cause of the first Russian revolution. Its inner causes lay very deep in social conditions. The widespread dissatisfaction among the most diverse groups of the population in Russia during the period preceding 1905 has already been described. Political parties were formed, but the long period without freedom of political expression made it impossible to establish large political groups now. Consequently, political organizations in Russia were illegal or "underground" agencies. Their programs and the activities did not express the real needs of the people but were rather theoretical declarations. Political platforms originated primarily among the intellectuals, who were isolated from the life of the masses and were often forced into exile for their activities against the government. Russian Jews played an important role among political émigrés abroad, partly because so few were permitted to enter the universities in Russia that many were forced to seek education abroad. They attended universities in Germany, Switzerland, and France.

The conditions of the period of "underground" development go far to explain the activities of the Russian parties. Because of the enforced secrecy and restriction they were forced to stress theoretical discussion rather than to face practical problems. They did not seek to understand the real desires of the people but rather to utilize popular emotion in order to achieve success for their programs.

At the earlier stage of the revolutionary movement, in the 1860's and 1870's, the leading socialist group was that of the "populists" (*narodniki*). Their doctrine was a mixture of the ideas of French "utopian" socialism and those of some Russian radical thinkers such as the publicist Peter Lavrov and the literary critic Nicholas Mikhailovsky. The Narodniki preached a kind of agrarian socialism to be based on the idealized peasant commune, and at the same time many of them recommended terrorism against the government officials as the best method of shattering the tsar's administration and arousing the masses. Their monopolizing influence on the radical intelligentsia was broken around 1895 by the rise of Marxism in Russia. The first Russian Marxist group was organized in Switzerland in 1883 by an émigré publicist and former narodnik, George Plekhanov, who established close connections with the so-called Second (Socialist) International founded in Europe in 1889.* In 1895 an active Marxist group was secretly organized in St. Petersburg for propaganda among the factory workers. At the head of this "circle" was Vladimir Ulianov (b. 1870), universally known under his pseudonym of Lenin. Lenin's father was a civil servant of lower middle class origin who achieved nobility through his service. Both Vladimir Ulianov and his brother Alexander engaged in revolutionary activity at an early age. The brother was executed in 1887 for his connection with a plot against the life of Tsar Alexander III. In 1895 Lenin was arrested for his propaganda activities among the workers in St. Petersburg and exiled to Siberia for three years. Through correspondence during his exile he kept in close touch with his fellow Marxists in Russia. In 1898 representatives of several Marxist circles met in Minsk and announced the organization of the Russian Social Democratic Workers' party, on the model of the German Marxist party of similar name.

In 1900 Lenin, having returned from exile, left Russia. He remained abroad until 1905, at first cooperating closely with Plekhanov; later the two men split apart because of differences in interpreting the Marxist doctrine. Plekhanov, having spent many years abroad, was in favor of milder political methods and of achieving a democratic regime in Russia first, under which it would be easier to organize the workers. Lenin, on the other hand, emphasized the necessity of creating a strong and active revolutionary

* The First International was founded by Karl Marx and Michael Bakunin in 1864 and dissolved in 1872.

Marxist group which would lead the proletariat in their struggle for an immediate social revolution. At the second convention of the Russian Social Democratic party in 1903 a clash took place between Lenin's followers and their opponents and the party split into two groups. Lenin and his followers became known as the Bolsheviks and their opponents as the Mensheviks.

Meanwhile the Narodniki, feeling that they were losing ground in Russia, decided to strengthen their organization and in 1900 formed the so-called Socialist Revolutionary party which undertook to defend the interests of the peasants and tried to organize cells among them. A special "Fighting Organization" within this party assumed the direction of terroristic activities against the administration and its agents.

Both the Social Democrats and the Socialist Revolutionaries succeeded in obtaining a large following among university students of both sexes; they also attracted members of the professions: lawyers, doctors, and teachers.

In 1903 moderate liberal groups also organized a semisecret Union of Liberation consisting primarily of professors and liberal estate owners. The real bourgeois classes, the merchants and manufacturers, did not enter any political organizations at this time. In 1905 the liberal Union formed the Constitutional Democratic party, whose program was based upon the political teachings of constitutional democratic groups of western Europe and America. This party attempted to influence the thought of government employees and the bourgeoisie in the cities. It was the political organization of the middle classes.

All these parties were united in desiring the end of autocracy and the introduction of a representative government elected by universal, direct, and secret ballot. But between the programs of these political parties and the concrete needs of the people there was a gap. The Social Democrats regarded themselves as the representatives of the workers, but were interested only in propagandizing socialism among the workers; the Socialist Revolutionaries regarded themselves as representing the peasants, but advocated the nationalization or socialization of all land, including that of the peasants, in spite of the fact that the peasants desired only the division of the large estates among themselves. The Constitutional Democrats advocated a parliamentary government after the French or British model, without taking into consideration the peculiar historical background of Russian politics.

In view of the theoretical character of the activities of these parties the imperial government could easily have continued to dominate by rapidly and energetically introducing political reforms; but being under the influence of the reactionary wing of the nobility, it was incapable of undertaking this task. Although the government always retreated in the face of overwhelming criticism, it never undertook action on its own initiative. Its indecision was the principal factor in the success of the revolutionary groups.

2. The revolution of 1905 and the October Manifesto

The revolutionary sentiments of the Russian people in 1904–05 expressed themselves in the most diverse forms. The political activity of the intellectuals took the form of lectures on politics, the organization of societies of a semipolitical nature, and, in some cases, of riots by the students. The liberal landowners, members of the zemstvos, organized conferences to discuss reforms, and a deputation from one of these congresses was sent to the emperor on June 19, 1905. The workers took recourse to strikes, the chief aims of which were political, rather than economic, reforms. The discontent of the peasantry found expression in agrarian riots, which resulted frequently in the destruction of landowners' houses or even in the murder of the landowners. Finally, after the Japanese war, the disorders spread to the army. The soldiers were affected by socialist propaganda and in many cases revolted against their officers. Socialist agitators urged the formation of councils composed of soldiers, an idea which in 1917 proved fatal to the Russian army. Riots spread from the army to the navy, and on the battleship *Potemkin* the sailors succeeded in temporarily seizing control in June 1905. The whole period was characterized by a series of assassinations of government officials by terrorists.

The government first attempted to deal with the revolutionary sentiments of the people by suppressing disorders with armed force and by disrupting the revolutionary organizations. The Department of Police introduced secret agents into revolutionary organizations to secure evidence against their leaders. These agents sometimes became leaders of the revolutionary parties and took so active a part in the movement that it became impossible for the government to determine where provocation ended and revolution began. The plot against the minister of the interior, Viacheslav Plehve, who was assassinated in July 1904, was actually directed by the *agent provocateur* E. Azef, who later explained that by this action he attempted to divert the terrorists' attention from a plot against the tsar. The Police Department also attempted to get control over the workers' movement by satisfying their economic demands and thus drawing them away from political activity. Serge Zubatov, an agent of the secret police, succeeded in the spring of 1902 in organizing the workers along purely economic lines in Moscow and in some other towns. In the strikes which followed, the police did not interfere. The alarmed industrialists complained to the government and Zubatov was dismissed. The workers' organization, however, continued to develop of its own momentum. Its new leader, the priest George Gapon, thought of petitioning the tsar in person to effect the reforms demanded by the workers. On January 22, 1905, a huge crowd of workers made their way to the Winter Palace in St. Petersburg to appeal to Nicholas II. The day had a tragic end, for although the workers were peacefully disposed and unarmed, the crowd was fired upon by the soldiers and several hundred people were killed or wounded. "Bloody Sunday" became a turning point in the history of the opposition of the working classes. It had as its immediate result their alliance with the socialist parties. The government by this time realized that with no plan to alleviate the situation and no firm support among the people it must make concessions in the matter of political reform. But even in this it moved unwillingly. On August 19, 1905, the order was given to convoke a Duma, which was to have deliberative but not legislative functions. This was, however, a half measure which satisfied no one. That autumn the situation became critical. A general strike was called throughout Russia. In the cities even electricity and water were cut off; all railroads save the Finland Railway came to a standstill. Leadership of the revolutionary groups in St. Petersburg was taken by a special council composed of the heads of the socialist parties and representatives of the workers. This was the so-called Soviet of Workers' Deputies which was to take a prominent part in the events of 1917. At the first session of the Soviet there were only 40 workers' representatives; they were increased later to 500. The chairman of the Soviet was a lawyer, George Khrustalev-Nosar, but the actual leader was the vice president, Leo Bronstein, subsequently known as Trotsky. The pseudonyms employed by many revolutionary leaders were assumed for self-protection against the espionage of the government police. All revolutionary instructions were signed with fictitious names.

The Mensheviks, of whom Trotsky at that time was a prominent member, held the majority in the Soviet. The Bolsheviks after failing to capture control of the first Soviet regarded it with suspicion. Soviets were formed in some other cities—Moscow, Odessa, and elsewhere—but before they achieved any important results the government decided to make far-reaching political concessions. At the initiative of Count Witte a manifesto which amounted practically to capitulation by the government was issued on October 30, 1905.

By this manifesto the emperor granted the Russian nation: 1) the fundamental principles of civil liberty—inviolability of person, and freedom of thought, speech, assembly, and organization; 2) democratic franchise; 3) no law to be made henceforth without the consent of the Duma. Count Witte, as newly appointed prime minister, with power to appoint assistants from opposition circles, was named to put the manifesto into effect.

The principal demands of the liberal opposition were embodied in this manifesto in the hope that it would stop their revolutionary activity. In this respect the manifesto was an attempt to unite the government and the liberal parties against the imminent social revolution. And for this reason leaders of the social movement who desired revolution at all costs opposed the manifesto. They held that the government was not sincere in its promises, that it desired only to stop the revolutionary movement, and that as soon as conditions permitted it would rescind the manifesto. The government did indeed hope that the manifesto would stop the revolution; but it did not wish to withdraw the concessions. In fact, it did not do so after its victory over the revolutionaries. Count Witte personally believed in the necessity for reform and had naturally no intentions of retraction. Only the inexperience of the leaders of the Russian liberal movement can explain the decision of the liberal groups to decline all Count Witte's invitations to enter his ministry. The result was that the manifesto of October 30 did not stop the revolutionary movement at once.

The socialist parties sought only the triumph of their revolutionary doctrines. The leader of the Bolsheviks, Lenin, who returned to Russia from abroad following the manifesto of October 30, became the firmest opponent of the government's policy. The strikes went on; a second railroad strike lasted from the end of November to the middle of December, and an armed insurrection occurred in Moscow at the end of December 1905. The irreconcilable policy of the revolutionaries was not supported, however, by the majority of the people, who were fairly well satisfied with the program set forth in the manifesto. The government was enabled to retake control of the situation. The Soviets were disbanded and the riots were suppressed by force. In several cities *pogroms* against Jews took place, organized by a reactionary group called the Union of the Russian People, whose ideology was of the same pattern as that of German Nazism.

On December 24 the government published a decree on the procedure of elections. At the beginning of March, a manifesto appeared on the new parliament, which was to be formed of two houses: the State Duma and the State Council, the first consisting of members elected by the nation, the second of members of whom half were appointed by the emperor and half elected by the nobility, zemstvos, and university faculties. The electoral law gave the right of suffrage to the people, but it was neither equal nor direct. The peasants were given a fairly large representation. This was prompted by the government's desire to draw them away from the opposition parties. As a further means of appeasing the peasantry, Count Witte had the idea of expropriating the large estates and handing over the lands to the peasants. This project was developed by one of Witte's ministers, Nicholas Kutler, who subsequently took a prominent part in the financial reorganization of the Soviet Government. The expropriation of large landholdings, however, was bitterly opposed by the estate owners. Witte did not have enough power to insist upon the measures he proposed, and was forced to cancel Kutler's project. This failure reacted upon the operation of the electoral law, which was primarily a bid to the peasantry. Like the earlier attempts to organize the workers in a manner favorable to the government, it merely succeeded in stirring up social unrest without either satisfying or being able to control it.

3. The first two dumas

The elections to the first Duma took place in March 1906. On May 10 the State Council and Duma were opened by Nicholas II. The majority of the Duma consisted of opposition deputies; of the 490 members, 190 belonged to the Constitutional Democratic party and 94 to the moderate peasant group. The Constitutional Democrats, led by Ivan Petrunkevich, were the strongest party represented. Their other leader, Paul Miliukov, had been removed under a pretext from the list of voters. The socialist parties boycotted the elections, but a number of socialist deputies were elected nevertheless. The peasants formed a faction of their own known as the Labor Group. The nationalist and conservative parties were defeated at the polls and secured only a small number of seats. The results of the elections were disappointing to the government.

Finding a hostile group in control of the State Duma, Nicholas II dismissed Count Witte and appointed Ivan Goremykin in his place. The new prime minister was a typical civil servant of the old regime. He was chosen not because he had initiative and political convictions but because he lacked these qualities and was ready to execute the orders of the emperor. The appointment was a political error. Relations between the government and the Duma rapidly took on an unfriendly character.

Supported by other opposition groups, the Constitutional Democrats demanded that the cabinet resign and a new one be appointed upon the recommendation of the Duma. A prominent deputy expressed the feelings of the Duma members as follows: "Let the executive power be subordinated to the legislative power." The Duma thus tried abruptly to change nascent Russian constitutionalism from a constitutional government of the German type to a western form of parliamentarian government. Another point of dispute between the cabinet and the Duma was the agrarian problem. Its discussion in the Duma aroused the passions of all groups. An agrarian bill, sponsored by the Constitutional Democrats, proposed expropriation of the large estates and the transfer of land to the ownership of the peasants, granting compensation to the owners. This led to increased agitation against the Duma by the reactionaries. Nicholas II faced the dilemma of either submitting to the Duma and displeasing the nobility, or dismissing it and provoking the hostility of the liberals. On July 21 the Duma was dissolved. As a concession to the liberals, Goremykin was dismissed and Peter Stolypin was appointed prime minister. Stolypin had been minister of the interior in the cabinet of his predecessor in office. He began his service to the Crown as governor of one of the western provinces. Before that he had managed his own estates. He had a profound comprehension of the agrarian problem in Russia and possessed the qualities of an outstanding statesman. He was firm, patriotic, and a man of ideas. The opposition parties did not support Stolypin and his program, but they were obliged to reckon with him. Following the dissolution of the Duma, the opposition groups were undecided as to their course. Their psychology was not that of peaceful parliamentary opposition but that of revolution. The members of the Duma, after the dissolution, issued an appeal to the nation to resist the government by refusing to pay taxes and to refuse conscription into the army. The appeal had no effect upon the people. Its only result was that its authors lost the right of voting in the subsequent elections.

Stolypin first tried to attract some of the leading members of the moderate liberal groups into his cabinet. They refused to cooperate with him, and he was obliged to draw upon professional bureaucrats. On November 22 his decree dissolving the peasant commune was published. Each peasant was given the right to receive his share of the common land in full ownership; and simultaneously measures were taken to finance the peasants' purchase of Crown lands. Stolypin's attempt to repair the defects in the reform of 1861 and to create in Russia a new class of small landowners to form the basis for the reformed state required a score of years to produce lasting results.

When the second Duma gathered on March 5, 1907, it proved to be even more hostile to the government than had been the first. It had a stronger left wing than the first (180 socialists); Lenin had abruptly changed his tactics, and the socialists did not boycott the Duma. The conflict between the government and the Duma in 1907 was more acute than in 1906. The government now had a practical program of reform, which the Duma did not possess. When fifty-five socialist deputies were charged with organizing a plot against the emperor, the second Duma was dissolved, in June 1907. To suppress similar expressions of opposition, the electoral law was changed, in violation of the constitution. The large landowners were given preference over the peasants in selecting representatives to the electoral colleges. The third Duma, elected in November 1907, had a membership different from that of its predecessors. The majority of deputies now belonged to parties of the right, and the liberal and socialist deputies were in the minority. The result of the two years of political conflict was the victory of Stolypin and the moderate conservative parties.

4. *Foreign policy to 1907. Formation of the Triple Entente*

Simultaneously with the internal political struggle, important events were shaping Russia's foreign policy. At the turn of the century the international situation had not as yet taken the form of alliances of mutually antagonistic states. Germany was allied to Austria and Italy, Russia to France, but Great Britain had no political ties with Russia. Germany was seeking an agreement with Russia. During the Japanese war, Russia needed an ally to counterbalance Great Britain, which in 1902 had entered into an alliance with Japan. She signed a commercial treaty with Germany in July 1904, which greatly favored German trade and was unprofitable to Russia. This expression of Russia's fear of Great Britain resulted in strengthening German foreign policy. In the spring of 1905 the German Government demanded an open door in Morocco where previously France had special privileges. In July Emperor William II visited Nicholas II at Björkö and concluded a secret alliance with Russia. Nicholas regarded this as a move against Great Britain and not against France. The Björkö agreement was to take effect immediately following the Japanese war, but after the conclusion of the Portsmouth peace it became evident that the friendship of France would be lost if the agreement was maintained. Russia's interests dictated a French alliance for purely financial reasons. The expense of the war and the economic instability caused by the revolution made foreign borrowing absolutely necessary. A tentative effort made by Count Witte to secure funds in the United States did not meet with success. Russia's strained relations with Great Britain closed the London market. Only France could supply the necessary loans. As compensation for financial support, France demanded Russian support against Germany in the Morocco controversy. The result of this international tangle was Russia's decision to cast her lot with France. At the Algeciras conference Russia and Great Britain supported France, and Germany was forced to give way before the united pressure of the three powers. Nine days after the close of the Algeciras conference France agreed to extend the necessary loan to Russia.

The French loan of 1906 exceeded two billion francs. It came at a critical moment in the Russian Government's struggle with the political opposition, and served to strengthen the bonds that tied Russia to France. At the same time, Russo-British relations took a turn for the better. Russia's position in the Far East had been materially weakened by the Japanese war, so that she became more cautious in the Middle East as well. In August 1907 Great Britain and Russia signed a convention concerning Persia, Afghanistan, and Tibet. Afghanistan was recognized as being within the exclusive sphere of British influence; Persia was divided between Great Britain and Russia into two spheres of influence; and Tibet was recognized as being neutral territory. This convention in which Russia agreed to curb her pretensions in central Asia opened the way to further agreements between the two countries.

At the suggestion of President Roosevelt, a second world peace conference was called at The Hague. Pursuant to this suggestion, in 1907 Nicholas II invited the representatives of all the powers to discuss the problem of disarmament. The Hague Conference failed to achieve its purpose and gave evidence only of the new political alignments in Europe. On one side stood the Triple Alliance (Germany, Austria, and Italy); on the other, the Triple Entente (France, Russia, and Great Britain). A clash between the two groups was hard to avoid.

5. *The third and fourth dumas*

The revolutionary period, with its bitter struggle between the government and the Duma, was followed by a period of relative quiet. The third Duma sat without interruption throughout its legal existence, from 1907 to 1912, and the elections of 1912 resulted in a triumph of the conservative nationalist groups.

While the political conflict between the government and the

Duma was temporarily solved by the change in the electoral law in 1907, there remained the more troublesome question of dealing with the aftermath of the revolutionary spirit of 1905. The dissatisfaction of that period found continued expression in a number of assassinations of government officials and so-called "expropriations"—raids on the banks and robbing of the wealthy. Premier Stolypin adopted a course of merciless suppression of revolutionary terrorism. Those caught in terroristic activities were subject to trial by court-martial, and when found guilty were punished by death. This policy of Stolypin's met with severe criticism from the opposition, but was supported by the majority of the conservative members of the Duma.

Just as political equilibrium seemed to have been reached, Stolypin was assassinated in September 1911. His place was taken by the minister of finance, Vladimir Kokovtsov, who, like his predecessor, was a moderate constitutionalist. He lacked Stolypin's firmness and had increasing difficulty in dealing with the opposition as well as with the reactionary circles at the emperor's court. Even some of the members of his cabinet proved unmanageable and ready to accept direct orders from the emperor without the premier's knowledge. But notwithstanding irritating incidents of this kind, the Duma succeeded in bringing about many favorable changes in the country. Of great importance was the legislation by which the precarious legal status of the peasants was done away with and they were given the same civil rights as other citizens.

The reform of local justice was an important measure in this connection. By a law of June 28, 1912, the general judicial system was to be gradually extended over the peasant population. The land captain was replaced in judicial matters by a justice of the peace. The Duma also continued its efforts to speed up the growth of the educational system and provided for an annual increase of 20,000,000 rubles in the educational budget, so that the budget grew steadily from 44,000,000 rubles in 1906 to 214,000,000 in 1917. The number of pupils in the primary schools rose from 3,275,362 in 1894 to 8,000,000 in 1914. Thus on the eve of the war over half the children of school age in Russia were receiving instruction. The educational committee of the Duma estimated that universal education would be achieved in Russia by 1922. The war and the initial chaos of the revolution, however, upset the projected timetable.

6. *International tension*

The defeat of Russia in the Far East and her agreement with Great Britain in matters concerning central Asia had the effect of stimulating Russian diplomacy in the Near East. Great Britain now showed signs of abandoning her traditional fear of Russia's seizure of Constantinople. This may be explained in part by the fact that she now feared Germany more than she did Russia. This change in policy became evident following the Turkish revolution of 1908, which brought a pro-German group into power in Turkey. In the autumn of 1908 the Central Powers opened a diplomatic offensive in the Balkans. On October 6 Austria, supported by Germany, announced the annexation of Bosnia and Herzegovina. The leader of Austria's foreign policy, Count Aehrenthal, made very skillful use of some preliminary parleys with the Russian foreign secretary, Izvolsky, who was himself surprised by the Austrian step. France and Great Britain too were caught unawares; not one of the members of the Triple Entente desired war or was prepared for it, and it appeared that any effective protest against the Austrian move might lead to war. There was nothing for it but to accept the *fait accompli*.

The incident, however, had the important consequence of accelerating the armament race between the two groups of powers. In 1911 Germany decided to interfere again in Morocco and dispatched the gunboat *Panther* to Agadir to protect German interests. The diplomacy of the Entente on this occasion was more effective than in 1908; the united front it presented forced the German Government to recognize a French protectorate in Morocco.

Tension in Europe increased after this incident. The situation in the Balkans, the proverbial "powder keg" of Europe, was particularly serious.

The Serbs could not reconcile themselves to Austria's annexation of Bosnia and Herzegovina, which resulted in the complete domination by Austria of territories peopled by Serbs. So long as Austrian influence in Bosnia was unlegalized, the Serbs could still secretly hope that the Slavs of the western Balkans would achieve unity. The annexation of 1908 deprived them of these hopes and sharpened the national feelings of the Serbs against Austria.

In view of these circumstances the object of Russian diplomacy after 1908 became the emancipation of the Balkans for both Austrian and Turkish influence. By 1912 this aim seemed near to realization. Four Balkan states, Serbia, Montenegro, Bulgaria, and Greece, united in an alliance against Turkey. The Balkan war, which was a victory for this alliance, deprived Turkey of almost all her European possessions populated by Slavs or Greeks. Then a disagreement arose between the allies. A second war immediately followed between Bulgaria on the one hand and Serbia and Greece on the other. Rumania joined the latter. Bulgaria was defeated, and, finding herself alone, turned to look for new allies. Since Serbia had now gained the patronage of the Entente, Bulgaria joined the Central Powers.

The diplomatic situation in the Balkans in 1914 was thus radically different from that at the beginning of the century. Bulgaria was now aligned with Austria; Serbia and Rumania with Russia. The whole situation was extremely unstable. The Bulgarians hoped for revenge against Serbia and Rumania. The Serbs thought only of emancipating their brothers by race from Austrian rule, as they had been from Turkish. Nationalist feeling in Serbia threatened at any moment to provoke a revolution among the Serbs in Austria. There began a series of attempts to assassinate prominent members of the Austrian Government.

On June 28, 1914, the Archduke Ferdinand was assassinated in the Bosnian town of Sarajevo. Within a month of this, on July 23, Austria presented an ultimatum to Serbia, impelled by the idea that the murder was sanctioned by the Serbian Government.

Serbia's reply was practically complete submission to Austria's demands. Nevertheless, the Austrian minister in Belgrade declared the Serbian reply unsatisfactory and immediately left for Vienna.

It was quite clear that Russia would not leave Serbia without help at this moment and remain an indifferent spectator of Serbia's annihilation by Austria. It was also plain that if a war broke out France would side with Russia against the Central Powers. The position that Great Britain would take was not clear, and Germany might have reasonably hoped she would not enter into the struggle. British diplomacy and Sir Edward Grey, personally, worked hard to avert the war, but the only means which might have succeeded during these fatal days would have been to declare Great Britain's complete solidarity with France and Russia. This was not done.

Russian diplomacy too did what was possible to avoid war. But all attempts to settle the Austro-Serbian dispute by diplomacy failed, and on July 28 Austria declared war on Serbia. Russia had the choice either of doing nothing and seeing Serbia invaded or of ordering mobilization. She decided to support Serbia. After some hesitation Nicholas II ordered partial mobilization of the Russian army on July 29 and general mobilization on July 30. He explained in his telegram to William II that his action did not mean war. Nevertheless on August 1 Germany declared war on Russia.

CHAPTER 13

THE FIRST WORLD WAR AND THE REVOLUTION OF 1917

1. *The Russian attitude toward war*

GERMANY'S declaration of war aroused in the Russian people entirely different feelings from those caused by the beginning of the Japanese war ten years previously. The gravity of the situation was realized by many. Patriotic demonstrations were held in the big cities. A strike going on in St. Petersburg was immediately called off.

The Duma met in special session and expressed complete agreement with the government's policy. On August 12 the representatives of the zemstvos created an All-Russian Union of Zemstvos to aid the wounded. Thus the war opened under the best political auspices—all Russia seemed to be united. The rise of national feeling was further enhanced by the policy of Slavonic emancipation declared by the government. The war was commenced avowedly to free the Serbs, and at the outset the Russian commander in chief, Grand Duke Nicholas, called for the liberation of another Slavonic people—the Poles, promising to reconstitute "the living body of Poland cut into three parts." The three parts in the possession of Russia, Germany, and Austria were to be united under a Russian protectorate. A little later an appeal was made to all the oppressed peoples of Austro-Hungary. To appease Pan-Slav feelings, the German-sounding name of St. Petersburg was changed to the Slavonic form, Petrograd.

Germany had calculated that disorganization would develop in Russia, but the mobilization, according to a plan prepared by Gen. Alexander Lukomsky, was carried out with no difficulties. It was materially aided by the prohibition of all alcoholic beverages and closing of all liquor shops. In the first months of the war it became evident that Russia had profited greatly by her experiences in the Russo-Japanese war. Without that preparation the Russian armies could not have withstood the German forces.

2. *The first year of the war*

On August 3 Germany declared war against France. Within two days Austria declared war on Russia and, following the German breach of Belgian neutrality, Great Britain declared war on Germany. In October Turkey entered the war on the side of the Central Powers. The forces of the Triple Entente seemed to be greater than those of the Central Powers, but this inequality of manpower and wealth was compensated for by the unity of the Central Powers under the direction of Germany. The forces of the Allies were not united under a general military command and their military activities were not coordinated. At first the Entente forces were divided into three unequal parts: those of France and Great Britain on the western front, those of Russia on the eastern front, and Serbia's on the southeastern front. The Serbian forces were so much weaker than those of the Central Powers opposing them that that front could be effectively maintained only if the attention of the Central Powers were drawn to the struggle on the main fronts. Thus the progress of the war depended primarily upon the success or failure of the opposing sides on the main fronts.

The principal feature of Germany's military plan for a war against France and Russia simultaneously was to throw most of her forces against France first. Hence it was important to France that Russia, by attacking promptly on the east, should compel the German command to withdraw some of the forces taking part in the western offensive. By a military convention with France of 1913, Russia undertook in case of war to start an offensive against Germany on the 16th day after mobilization. She fulfilled this agreement exactly on schedule. The war started on August 1. On August 17 a Russian army under Gen. Paul Rennenkampf started an offensive in East Prussia, and in a few days a second army under Gen. Alexander Samsonov advanced into East Prussia from the south. These armies were insufficiently prepared for an offensive; the second was in a particularly precarious situation for lack of supplies. The Germans, according to plan, prepared to retreat beyond the Vistula, leaving East Prussia to Russia. However, the

Russian advance into Prussia had so strong an effect upon German public opinion that the high command was forced to change its plan and oppose the attack. A new commander, General Hindenburg, with Ludendorff as chief of staff, was appointed on the northeastern front, and part of the troops engaged against France were withdrawn to stem the Russian tide. Ludendorff succeeded in surrounding and annihilating five Russian divisions of Samsonov's army at the battle of Tannenberg on August 31, 1914, at the same spot where in 1410 the Polish, Lithuanian, and Russian troops defeated the German Knights. In the following weeks Ludendorff succeeded in driving the Russian armies out of East Prussia.

The transfer of German troops from the western front contributed to Germany's successful repulse of Russia, but it upset the whole German plan for an offensive on the western front and had a profound influence upon the general course of the war. The weakening of the German army on the eve of the Marne enabled the French to arrest the German advance.

While the first engagement between Germany and Russia resulted in a German victory, Russia succeeded in defeating the Austrian army on the southeastern front and occupying Galicia. During this operation of Gen. Michael Alexeev, the Russian army occupied important strategic posts in Austria and took over 200,-000 prisoners. Following her success in East Prussia, Germany was forced to engage in further operations on the eastern front in order to support Austria. In late September 1914 Ludendorff moved 52 divisions of German and Austrian troops in the direction of Warsaw. After nearly a month of bitter fighting the battle was won by the Russian troops, and on October 27 Ludendorff gave orders to retreat.

The Russian army, after suffering enormous losses in the course of the first three months of the war, needed rest, and in order to undertake an offensive it required preparation. But the French and British military commands insisted upon an immediate Russian advance to draw away the German reserves from the western front. The Russian troops were ordered to attack Silesia and Poznan on November 14, 1914. Germany acted first. Fourteen divisions were withdrawn from the western front and thrown against Russia. The Russian advance failed after sizable losses.

The failure of the German offensive in France led to a reversal of Germany's military plans. It was decided now to attack Russia first. In the spring of 1915 Germany brought to the eastern front 13 new divisions originally intended for use in the west. A great quantity of heavy artillery was concentrated on the Russian front, and General Mackensen took charge of operations. It soon became plain that the Russian troops, who were very short of supplies, could not withstand Mackensen's furious attack. A general retreat during the whole summer resulted in the loss not only of all enemy territory that had been occupied but also of Poland, Lithuania, Courland, and a huge stretch of the Ukrainian and Belorussian provinces.

The inadequacy of supplies was keenly felt throughout 1915. In August the number of unarmed Russian soldiers reached 30 per cent, and the troops had to take up the arms of those wounded or killed in order to continue fighting. The German advance came to an end when the distance from bases in Germany made supply difficult. In the autumn the advance stopped along the line Riga-Dvinsk-Tarnopol.

After that, the Russian supply of munitions gradually improved, with increased production and relative quiet on the line of battle. Supplies from abroad began arriving only in 1916. At no time during the retreat of the Russian army in the summer of 1915 or during the collapse of Serbia in the autumn of 1915 did the French and British undertake large-scale operations on the western front to draw away the forces of the Central Powers. They tried to help Russia and Serbia by attacking the Dardanelles, but this attack failed. The entry of Italy into the war in May 1915 brought Russia no assistance. Thus during 1915 Germany had the opportunity to deliver terrific blows at Russia's military power. At the beginning of the war the Central Powers had 63 divisions on the eastern front and 93 on the western. In September 1915 they had concentrated 161 divisions against Russia and 84 on the western front. While successful in driving back the Russian armies, Germany failed to obtain her main objective—the destruction of Russia's military power. At the same time, the fighting on the eastern front allowed the British and French to concentrate their forces to continue the struggle.

3. *Political crisis*

A crisis in the supply of munitions was experienced by all the warring countries. Not one of the powers had calculated the duration of the struggle correctly or the quantity of materials necessary to conduct it. As it became evident that the war would be prolonged, measures were devised to supply enough munitions. The result was the militarization of industry in Germany, Great Britain, and France. Russia's position was harder than that of the other powers since Russian industry, in spite of its great progress in the decades preceding the war, remained comparatively feeble. The Russian army, moreover, being larger than those of the other Allies, was in greater need of supplies. During the first year it was engaged in fighting almost without pause, while the British and French, after the battle of the Marne, dug into permanent positions. The Russian situation was further complicated by an internal political conflict. The failures of 1915 created a rift between the government and the Duma. The inadequacy of munition supplies was attributed to the shortsightedness of the government and the general staff. This was in part true. Moreover, as the army retreated it ordered great numbers of the population to evacuate the abandoned territories—a mistake which brought to the public's attention the defects in the military command.

To assist the government in dealing with the problems it faced, the Union of Zemstvos and Towns as well as other public organizations took over the relief of refugees and the furnishing of the army with necessary supplies. Industry was mobilized by a War Industry Committee, and the Duma became the center of a vast system whose object was to aid the government. The work of the various agencies soon brought relief to the army, but as their work grew in popularity the prestige of the government fell. In the most of this internal transformation, the Allies found themselves on the side of the Duma. They could not help seeing that its activities were of the greatest assistance to Russia in waging the war. The Duma, on the other hand, felt that only the Allies could satisfy Russia's need for munitions, as Russian industry alone was not capable of dealing with this problem. There grew up an important relationship between the Duma and the public organizations, on the one hand, and the representatives of the Allies on the other.

This aroused political jealousy in court circles, prompted by justifiable fears. The political rift was widened by personal animosities. The head of the government was Goremykin, whose part in dissolving the first Duma had made him unpopular in Duma circles. The government agreed to a short session of the Duma in August 1915, and dismissed the minister of war, Vladimir Sukhomlinov, who was held responsible for the military setbacks experienced by the Russian army. But Tsar Nicholas soon showed his unwillingness to accept the Duma's leadership in directing the organization of the army and the country. There followed a split between the Duma and the government, reminiscent of the situation during the first two dumas of 1906–07. At the initiative of the liberal leader, Miliukov, a progressive bloc, composed of moderate rights, and liberals, was formed, which controlled a majority in the Duma. The Duma now demanded a cabinet that would have the confidence of the country. Only two courses were open to the tsar: either to yield to the Duma or to end the war at the cost of betraying the Allies. He could not reconcile himself to betraying the Allied cause, and attempted, by taking over personally the supreme command of the Russian armies, to avoid yielding to the Duma. It was hoped that this act would raise his prestige in the country at large, in the army, and with the Allied powers. It was a risky undertaking, since further failures would bring popular condemnation upon the tsar himself. On September 5, 1915, Grand Duke Nicholas was transferred to the Caucasian front and Nicholas II became commander in chief. The political atmosphere in Russia thickened. The Duma was called for the shortest possible periods and the tsar made a supreme effort to find leaders capable of solving problems without its aid. Since he failed to find competent assistance, ministry supplanted ministry without apparent reason or improvement. The precarious internal situation in Russia aroused the suspicions of the Allies, particularly when Boris Sturmer, who was suspected of being pro-German, was appointed to succeed Sazonov as foreign minister.

Gradually the tsar became politically isolated, abandoned by the groups of the left and of the right and finally by the Allies. The Duma felt that he was incapable of conducting the war with sufficient energy. The members of the extreme right faction, on the other hand, desired a separate peace, and everyone secretly suspected that the real source of power was the Tsarina Alexandra, under whose sway the weak-willed emperor had completely fallen. The tsarina, in turn, was known to be under the influence of Gregory Rasputin, an uneducated peasant "prophet" whom the tsarian regarded as a saint. Rasputin's ascendancy was due to his magnetic personality and the neurotic condition of the tsarina. She credited him with the power to protect the health of the tsarevich, who had suffered since birth from the incurable hereditary disease of hemophilia.

Political conflict between the Duma and the tsar was especially dangerous in that it weakened both sides. The disagreement tended to destroy authority in general and opened the road for the destructive forces of the social revolution which had taken cover since 1906. The situation became favorable for the spread of "defeatist" propaganda by the extreme socialist parties. During the war the socialists of all countries had abandoned internationalism in favor of nationalism. Among the Russian socialists there were many patriots, but there was also a powerful group of Socialist Internationalists.

The most active agents of Russia's defeat in the war were the Bolsheviks. Although Lenin had been abroad since 1907 he had continued to exercise a strong influence upon Russian politics. The Bolshevik members of the Duma first expressed their adherence to the "defeatist" policy of their leader in November 1914. In the spring of 1915 they were arrested, and after trial for cedition were imprisoned or exiled. But their ideas slowly sank into the minds of the mass of Russian labor. Lenin continued his preparatory work in Switzerland and in 1915 proposed the founding of the Third International. During 1915 and 1916 he succeeded in reasserting his "defeatist" policy at two international socialist conferences. He now openly advocated civil war of the lower classes against the higher classes to end the "imperialist" war between peoples.

4. *Economic difficulties*

Not only did the political conflict between the government and the representatives of the people prepare the ground for revolutionary propaganda, but the economic condition of the country contributed to the breakdown of popular morale. The war brought about the mobilization of vast numbers of men in all countries. The Russian

Government, under the influence of Allied policy, called to the colors almost all those capable of carrying arms. By the beginning of 1917 over 15,000,000 men had been recruited. There was no immediate need for all these men, nor were there sufficient munitions to arm them effectively. Millions of soldiers who lived in the rear of the battle line in complete inactivity presented a fertile field for political propaganda. The mobilization of such large numbers led to economic difficulties: enormous expenditures to care for them, shortages in transportation, and manpower shortages in production. The cities, which depended entirely upon foodstuffs imported from the country districts, were the first to suffer. In the autumn of 1916 Petrograd had difficulty in securing sufficient supplies. The government was forced to undertake to support soldiers' families, which increased its administrative and financial burdens. Finally, there were 2,000,000 refugees from the abandoned areas of western Russia also dependent upon government aid.

To procure munitions the government subsidized industry. By the end of 1916 more than 73 per cent of industrial workers were exclusively engaged in military production. State expenses increased and income decreased. The families of those called to the front could not pay the usual taxes, while in introducing prohibition the government also lost the proceeds of the largest indirect tax.

The Treasury was compelled to issue paper money out of proportion to the gold reserve. This led to an increase in prices, which in turn necessitated repeatedly increasing the pay of officials and workers. The economic insecurity was evident all over the country.

5. The course of the war from the autumn of 1915 to the spring of 1917

Following the setbacks of 1915, the condition of the army began to improve. In March 1916 an offensive against the center of the German front was tried, but failed in its objective.

The operations undertaken in the summer of 1916 against the Austrian army were more successful. At Italy's insistent request an offensive on the southwestern Russian front was started on June 4. The Russian army under the command of Gen. Alexis Brusilov succeeded in smashing the Austrian army and capturing over 400,-000 prisoners. The Central Powers were forced to withdraw troops

from other fronts to stem the Russian advance. In the autumn of
1916 Rumania entered the war against the Central Powers, but
was soon defeated. The consequence was the further extension of
the Russian front south to the Black Sea in order to bring relief
to Rumania.

The counteroffensive against Brusilov and the Rumanian offensive called for extraordinary efforts on Germany's part. In gaining
Pyrrhic victories in the east, the Central Powers failed to secure
decisive victory on the western front. In 1917 Germany's position
became critical. Meanwhile, the forces of the Allies in the west,
now the principal opponents of the Central Powers, continued to
grow. At the same time, with the arrival of some supplies from
abroad and the reorganization of Russian industry, the Russian
army in the spring of 1917 was amply provided with munitions. In
spite of all the hardships in the past, it was possible to expect that
the new Allied campaign of 1917 would crush the Central Powers.

6. *The March revolution*

During the winter of 1916–17 the conflict between Nicholas II and
the Duma became particularly acute. Some drastic solution was inevitable. Both sides were embittered. The Duma feared the possibility of an alliance between Rasputin and the reactionary circles
for the purpose of concluding a separate peace with Germany. At
the session in November 1916 several speeches were made in the
Duma attacking the influence of the tsarina. Meanwhile, in the
highest circles of society, the decision was made to do away with
Rasputin, who was regarded as the evil genius of the empire. On
December 30 he was killed by a well-known aristocrat, with assistance of a conservative Duma deputy and of a member of the
imperial family. The policy of the tsar, however, did not change
following this act. A plot was formed in one of the court circles to
overthrow him and put another member of the royal family on the
throne. But the moment for such an act had already passed; before a court revolution could be effected a popular uprising took
place.

The disintegration of the Imperial Government and the history
of the attempts to create a new organ of power may be traced
chronologically.

The tsar was in Mogilev, headquarters of the Russian army,

when a telegram was received informing him of the murder of Rasputin in Petrograd. The same day, December 31, 1916, he left for Tsarskoe Selo to join the tsarina and from then on he took no further interest in political affairs.

It happened that the chief of staff, General Alexeev, had previously fallen seriously ill and was also absent from headquarters, recovering in the Crimea. He was temporarily replaced by Gen. Basil Gurko. Alexeev returned to headquarters on March 3, 1917, although not completely recovered. Nicholas returned on March 9. The next day a telegram came telling of disorders in Petrograd caused by food shortages. The following days brought further alarming news about the disorders. The president of the Duma, Michael Rodzianko, described events very gloomily. He requested that a new cabinet be formed to satisfy the Duma and command the full confidence of the people. On March 12 Grand Duke Michael, the tsar's brother, informed General Alexeev that he believed this alone could save the situation, which had become further aggravated.

A few hours later a telegram arrived from the prime minister, Prince Nicholas Golitsyn, requesting similar measures. The only alternatives open to the tsar seemed to be to accept this advice or to take energetic measures to crush the uprising. Some measures were taken, but they were wholly inadequate to meet the situation. The new session of the Duma, which opened on February 27, was discontinued by an imperial ukaz of March 11, and Gen. Nicholas Ivanov was dispatched with one battalion to Petrograd with orders to suppress the revolt. These acts were not sufficient to crush the revolution, but they were enough to prevent the Duma from assuming control of the forces now in motion.

The immediate cause of the rioting in Petrograd was lack of food. However, this did not affect the soldiers, who received their normal supply. On the morning of March 12, Petrograd was overrun by a revolutionary mob. Policemen were killed in the streets, the Kresty jail was forced open, and the courthouse set afire. The soldiers of reserve battalions staying in Petrograd joined the crowds. Some officers were killed. The government, the military command, and the chief of police were helpless. Anarchy began.

The members of the Duma, instead of obeying the ukaz to disband, gathered on the morning of March 12 in the Taurida Palace.

Since the Duma seemed to be the only authority which could control the situation, crowds of soldiers and civilians rushed to the
palace. About noon the members of the Duma decided to act, and
a temporary committee of 12 members was elected, with Rodzianko
as chairman. Liberals and moderate conservatives were in the
majority on this committee, which included two socialist members,
Alexander Kerensky and Nicholas Chkheidze. Chkheidze at once
refused to serve, wishing to have his hands free to advance purely
socialistic policies. The socialist leaders arrived at the Taurida
Palace at the same time as the Duma members, but instead of
joining with the Duma they tried to create their own government
on the pattern of the soviets of 1905. All that day the Duma leaders
hesitated to break with the old regime. They merely followed the
lead of the mob, which arrested the ministers and brought them
to the Duma. In the evening the Temporary Committee decided
to take the initiative. Commissars were appointed to all government
offices. It seemed for a moment as though the Duma would succeed
in mastering the revolution.

But at the same time the Petrograd Soviet of Workers' and
Soldiers' Deputies was being organized. Deputies of workmen, one
for each thousand, and of soldiers, one for each company, were
summoned to gather at the Taurida Palace at 7 P.M. The socialist
chiefs who led them did not even ask permission of the Duma committee to occupy the Duma hall. Chkheidze was chosen chairman
of the Soviet at its first meeting.

Early on the morning of March 13 the tsar left Mogilev for
Tsarskoe Selo, not wishing to be separated from the tsarina during
these troublous days. His train was stopped at Dno by the railroad
staff, already informed of the revolution by telegram. On the evening of March 14 the tsar reached Pskov, where he decided to
abdicate.

The Duma committee was already taking the next step in the
revolution. It appointed a Provisional Government, with Prince
George Lvov as chairman, Alexander Guchkov as head of the War
Office, and Paul Miliukov as head of the Foreign Office. Among
the ministers there was one socialist deputy, Kerensky, who was
minister of justice. The Labor Office was offered to Chkheidze, but
he refused again.

The first care of the new government was to eliminate the tsar.
On March 15 the new war minister, Guchkov, and Basil Shulgin,

a member of the Duma committee, left for Pskov to secure his abdication. Because the tsar did not wish to be separated from his son, he abdicated in favor of his brother, Grand Duke Michael, instead of in favor of Alexis. First he appointed Grand Duke Nicholas commander in chief of the army and named Prince Lvov premier. Grand Duke Michael did not choose to accept the supreme power and passed it on to the Provisional Government. The Romanovs had ceased to rule Russia. The tsar was soon arrested, with the tsarina and their children, and then exiled in Siberia.

7. *The Provisional Government and the Soviets*

The revolution in Petrograd was accepted not only by army headquarters but by the whole of Russia. Supporters of the old regime made no sign of resistance. But it soon became evident that the new government did not possess real authority. From the first hour of its existence the Provisional Government was hampered by the Workers' and Soldiers' Soviet. The first decree it issued, on March 14, was written under its pressure.

This decree laid down the following principles: 1) a general amnesty for all political, religious, and military prisoners; 2) freedom of speech and of the press, freedom for unions and strikes; 3) abolition of all social, religious, and national distinctions; 4) the summoning of a constituent assembly; 5) a people's militia to replace the police; 6) elections to be based on universal suffrage; 7) troops that took part in the revolution to remain in Petrograd and not be transferred to the front; 8) soldiers to have the same public rights as civilians when not in active service.

In spite of the fact that this declaration was a compromise between them, the Soviet issued another declaration independently and without the approval of the Provisional Government. This was the notorious Order No. 1 of March 14 which was the principal agency in the destruction of the Russian army. Its main features were: 1) soldiers' committees to be chosen in each military detachment; 2) each detachment to obey the Soviet's political decisions; 3) orders of the military commission of the state Duma to be obeyed only if they did not contradict the Soviet's orders; 4) all weapons to be under the control of the soldiers' committees and not to be delivered to the officers.

This order brought about confusion in the control of the army.

It was clear that its authors desired to make the continuance of the war impossible. The Provisional Government attempted to have it revoked, but failed. It was now plain that the real administration was the Soviet and not the Provisional Government. Yet the Soviet did not wish to seize power openly because it feared a reaction among the conservative elements of society at this moment. The Provisional Government was indispensable to the Soviet because it was still the recognized authority for the country and the army. The Soviet preferred to maintain it in nominal authority as bait for the antisocialist groups, controlling it and checking its measures when they conflicted with Soviet policy.

Consequently, there were two governments in Petrograd from the first day of the revolution: the Provisional Government representing the political revolution, and the Soviet of Workers' and Soldiers' Deputies representing the social revolution.

The helplessness of the Provisional Government is explained partly by the inexperience of its members and partly by the difficulty of the problems it had to face. Most of the members of its first cabinet belonged to the Constitutional Democratic party. Brought up in the principles of European constitutionalism, they tried to apply these principles to Russia, without taking into account the revolutionary temper of the time, which demanded rapid decisions rather than scrupulous constitutional procedure.

For both the local zemstvo and the national elections, the Provisional Government formulated new laws establishing universal, equal, direct suffrage, and secret balloting. First of all, reorganized local bodies or zemstvos were to take charge of the lists of those voting for the members of the Constituent Assembly. Thus the election of representatives was delayed until the autumn of 1917.

The second government of Russia during this period, the Soviet of Workers' and Soldiers' Deputies, consisted of 2,500 workmen and soldiers chosen without any technical formalities in the factories and by military detachments in Petrograd. It also comprised the leaders of the socialist parties who, ever since 1905, had regarded themselves as the real representatives of the interests of labor. All nonsocialist parties were classified as bourgeois or "capitalist" and refused admission to the Soviet. The largest group in the Soviet was the Socialist Revolutionaries, who regarded themselves as representing the peasantry. The next group in importance was the Socialist Democratic party, which thought of itself as representing the workers and, as we have seen, was split into Mensheviks and Bolsheviks. After Lenin's return from exile on April 16, 1917 the Bolsheviks finally broke relations with the Mensheviks and organized a separate party which later was called the Communist party. The partisans of Lenin formed but a small minority of the Petrograd Soviet during the first months of the revolution, but owing to the lack of organization of the Soviet and their own tireless activity, they managed to play a part far out of proportion to their numbers. While the more moderate socialists desired to see the Provisional Government continue in control, the Bolsheviks loudly demanded that all power be given to the soviets immediately.

The peculiar strength of the Soviet lay in the fact that, despite its clumsy size and heterogeneous membership, it had far closer contact with the masses than the Provisional Government. Very soon every town in Russia formed its soviet. These were supplemented by similar organizations in the army and in many villages.

Then an All-Russian Congress of Soviets was convoked.

The congress opened on June 16. The strongest party present was the Socialist Revolutionaries, with 285 deputies. The Mensheviks were represented by 248 and the Bolsheviks were in a minority with only 105 delegates. A Central Executive Committee of the Soviets was elected to sit permanently. Current matters were to be decided by the Presidium of this committee.

The leading political question of the time was, of course, the war. There were two views about this. The moderate elements wanted to continue the war to a victorious end. This view was frequently expressed by Foreign Minister Miliukov, in conversations with the Allied representatives in Petrograd and in public statements. The Bolsheviks and a number of Socialist Internationalists argued the need of immediate peace and openly admitted themselves to be "defeatists." Between these two extremes lay a group composed of a majority of the socialists in the Soviet. They realized that popular feeling did not support a war policy, but they were unwilling as yet to accept the fact of the complete collapse of Russia's military power.

The bitter opposition between the two views of Russia's war policy remained unreconciled. On March 18 Miliukov addressed the representatives of the Allies in Petrograd, assuring them that Russia "would fight by their side against the common enemy until the end." On March 27 the Petrograd Soviet issued a proclamation to the peoples of the world calling for "concerted and decisive action in favor of peace." From this day the socialist leaders began an intensive struggle against the "imperialistic policies" of Minister Miliukov. Under the pressure of the soviets, the Provisional Government accepted the resignations of the two ministers most severely criticized, Miliukov and Guchkov, and on May 17 formed a new cabinet. On May 18 it disavowed Miliukov's war aims and accepted the soviets' view that the future peace—when it came —should be on the principle of "no annexations and indemnities, on the basis of self-determination of nations."

The new government retained Prince Lvov as premier, but its real leader was Kerensky, who was minister both of war and marine.

8. *The Kerensky offensive and the Bolshevik uprising of July 1917*

Kerensky's program for the army contained two principles: the preparation of a general Russian offensive and a democratic reorganization of the command. The idea of an offensive did not seem to him to conflict with his earlier commitments to a purely defensive war or his renunciation of imperialistic aims. The chief purpose of the offensive would be to force the Central Powers to abandon the territories of Russia which they then occupied. The chief defect in this policy was its failure to take account of the soldiers' attitude since the revolution.

The proposed reorganization of the army destroyed the last vestiges of discipline. On May 22 Kerensky approved an order to the army and navy known as the Declaration of Soldiers' Rights. This confirmed nearly all the points of Order No. 1 and in some respects went even farther.

A new feature in the organization of the army laid down by Kerensky was the appointment of commissars, empowered with political leadership, to represent the government in the army. The high command found itself checked from above by these government appointees and from below by soldiers' committees organized at the outset of the revolution.

The army was well along toward dissolution. The authority of the officers collapsed. The army soviets issued orders contrary to those of the commanding officers, and the troops were subjected to a flood of defeatist literature. Soon the soldiers at the front began to fraternize with the enemy. The German command decided to suspend military operations, as the best method of furthering the disintegration.

Meanwhile, Kerensky sincerely tried to prepare an offensive. After his tour of the front, which earned him the nickname of "persuader-in-chief," an offensive was planned for July 1917. The first days of fighting were successful; a wide breach was made in the Austrian lines and the enemy was put to flight. But soon it became evident that the "reorganized" Russian army could not continue the advance. Whole regiments refused to carry out orders and even left the front when they were weary of fighting. The early success had been due to the enthusiasm of the officers and a small minority of the soldiers, most of whom perished in the first days of the fighting. Meanwhile the Germans broke the Russian line at a spot where one of the unruly regiments had abandoned the front. A complete collapse was imminent. The German troops stopped at the river Zbruch, but they could easily have occupied the whole southwest of Russia. The catastrophe compelled Gen. Laurus Kornilov to send a bitter message to the government requiring the immediate restoration of military discipline and of capital punishment for all deserters. The government commissars supported his demands.

This produced a deep impression on the whole country. It was the first time that firm language had been used since the beginning of the revolution. In one day Kornilov became the center of patriotic feeling. Kerensky on July 30 appointed him commander in chief.

The disorganization of the army and of the administration was accompanied by an economic crisis. Agricultural as well as industrial production declined, transportation broke down, and the finances of the government grew rapidly worse.

Simultaneously with the collapse of the Russian offensive, an armed uprising took place in Petrograd, the Bolsheviks on July 16–18 leading a group of sailors and some of the regiments of the Petrograd garrison in an attempt to overthrow the government.

A cavalry division summoned from the front succeeded in suppressing the movement.

The strength of the Bolsheviks lay in the forceful appeal of their slogans and the efficiency of their organization. Their program contained three points: 1) immediate peace; 2) immediate distribution of land to the peasants, and the control of factories by the workers; 3) all power to the soviets. Though they had only a minority in the Petrograd Soviet and the Soviet Congress, they played a dominant role in these bodies. Their activity became particularly effective after Lenin and Trotsky had returned from abroad. Both men were well known "defeatists." Trotsky had been living in the United States. On his way home through England he was arrested by the British as a dangerous propagandist, but was released at the insistence of the Provisional Government and allowed to proceed to Russia. Lenin, while living in Switzerland, had negotiated with the German Government through Platten, a Swiss socialist, to be allowed to return to Russia through Germany. The German Government, hoping to use Lenin as a weapon to destroy Russia's military power, agreed to allow him passage from Switzerland to Sweden in a sealed railroad car.

A few days after his arrival Lenin began to expound his ideas at meetings of workmen and soldiers. He appealed to the socialists to discard their old-fashioned methods of parliamentary opposition and espouse the class war of communism.

The failure of the first Bolshevik uprising might have been a turning point in the history of the Russian revolution. It was the right moment to enforce the authority of the government in Petrograd. But this opportunity was not seized. Some Bolshevik leaders, including Trotsky, were arrested; Lenin fled to Finland; but the Bolsheviks were not outlawed in the Soviet. The government meanwhile was reorganized. Prince Lvov resigned; Kerensky became prime minister, while remaining head of the war and marine ministries. The majority in the cabinet was now socialist.

9. *The Kornilov rebellion*

In the first months of the revolution the high command of the army had passively submitted to all the measures of the Provisional Government. But after the collapse of the July 1917 offensive, and with the appointment of General Kornilov as commander in chief, the attitude changed. Army headquarters became a political force. Kornilov accepted his new post only after laying down his conditions. These were that 1) the commander in chief should have full authority; 2) the government should not interfere with his military orders; 3) military discipline should be restored. Kerensky accepted the conditions. It was clear that he must break with the Soviet in order to carry out his promise. But even after the suppression of the Bolshevik revolt of July he was unwilling to do so. The political situation became extremely confused. Before the Bolshevik uprising there were two powers in Russia: the Provisional Government and the Soviet. The main strength of the Provisional Government consisted in the loyal support of the army command. The Soviet's active strength was in its left wing, the Communist party. Now both extreme groups broke away from the moderate forces. The Bolsheviks, while continuing to act in the name of the soviets, carried out their own policies, undeterred by the failure of their first uprising. The army command likewise prepared to act for itself.

In spite of his growing popularity, General Kornilov was not in a position to be wholly self-reliant. He had to cloak his moves with the authority of the Provisional Government, just as the Bolsheviks cloaked theirs in the authority of the soviets. Kornilov's plan to reinstate discipline in the army depended upon the cooperation of the Provisional Government. But a rift soon opened between army headquarters and the government.

On August 27 a National Political Conference was held in Moscow under the auspices of the Provisional Government. Representatives of the main political and economic groups of the nation were summoned. Kornilov was applauded with enthusiasm by the conservative members. The socialists gave Kerensky an ovation. The split was evident and the break prepared.

On September 9 a telegram from Kerensky informed General Kornilov of his dismissal and ordered him to proceed immediately to Petrograd. The blow was unexpected, and a violation of Kornilov's first condition. He decided the moment had come to act. On September 10 he issued a proclamation by telegraph to all Russian citizens in which he announced his refusal to give up the post of commander in chief and asked for support against the Provisional Government. At the same time he ordered General Krymov to move the Third Cavalry Corps against Petrograd.

Kerensky meanwhile joined forces with the left groups of the Petrograd Soviet and ordered the Petrograd garrison to prepare to fight General Krymov. All the socialist organizations in Russia hastened to Kerensky's support. A particularly important part was played by the executive committee of the railroad workers who had control over transportation and refused to obey Kornilov's orders to let reinforcements proceed to Krymov. The latter's troops were disconcerted and eager to hear the propaganda appeals of the socialists. Finally Krymov accepted Kerensky's invitation to report to Petrograd. The day after his arrival he committed suicide.

After the failure of General Krymov's mission, Kornilov and his assistants, Gens. Anton Denikin and Alexander Lukomsky, were arrested by order of the Provisional Government.

10. *The November revolution*

With the collapse of the Kornilov movement the revolution entered a new phase. On the surface Kerensky had triumphed over the two opponents who had threatened his position: Kornilov was under arrest and Lenin had sought refuge outside of Russia. The victory, however, was an illusory one. Kerensky was no longer the real power but a political ghost unable to control or direct the political and economic anarchy which was rapidly overwhelming the country. Indeed, the defeat of the military party itself immediately reacted against the Provisional Government, for thereafter the dominant force was not the alliance of the government and the army but that of the soviets and the Bolsheviks.

Kerensky's government had but one hope; to retain at least the forms of power until the Constituent Assembly met. The election had been set for November 25, and the first session of the Assembly was to open on December 12, 1917. But the Bolsheviks were equally aware of the political importance of these events and, as the dates approached, hastened to summon the Second All-Russian Congress of Soviets for November 7 in order to forestall the government. They planned to carry out a coup d'état immediately after the official opening and then secured the approval of the Congress for constituting a new government.

During the night of November 7 the principal government buildings in Petrograd were occupied by Bolshevik troops. Posters fresh off the presses announced the program: 1) immediate opening of peace negotiations; 2) partition of large estates; 3) control of all factories by the workers; 4) the creation of a soviet government.

Kerensky at last realized the danger. Leaving the government under the temporary leadership of a colleague, he fled from Petrograd to rally troops against the Bolsheviks. Since the Petrograd garrison had joined the Bolsheviks, the government was without armed defense; when the Bolsheviks attacked the Winter Palace where the cabinet was in session, only a few military cadets and a battalion of women attempted resistance. They were quickly crushed and the members of the cabinet were arrested. The government was in Lenin's hands.

When the Second Congress of Soviets opened immediately after the fall of the Provisional Government, Socialist Revolutionary and Menshevik members protested futilely. They did not succeed in blocking the meeting of the Congress, nor were they, on the night of November 8, able to prevent it from approving the program advanced by the Bolsheviks. A cabinet called the Council of People's Commissars was formed, with Lenin as president. Trotsky was appointed commissar for foreign affairs, Rykov commissar of internal affairs, and Stalin commissar of nationalities.

The first acts of the council were to adopt unanimously the Decree of Peace and the Decree of Land. The former proposed that all warring peoples and their governments begin immediate negotiations for a just and democratic peace without annexations or indemnities. The latter abolished private ownership of the soil, which henceforth was to be shared equally by all laborers. Thus in one night the Bolsheviks succeeded not only in organizing a government but also in proclaiming revolutionary new policies on the most important questions of the day.

Kerensky's attempts to regain power failed. He fled from the country and thereafter took no part in the struggle between the Bolsheviks and their opponents, whose countermoves became increasingly futile. The Bolsheviks were confident that nowhere in Russia at that moment was there an organized group capable of blasting them from their positions, and they could look forward to a relatively long period in which to secure and consolidate their control over the whole of Russia. They had arrived. In the course of a single week the Bolsheviks had come to power in the largest nation in the world.

They were now faced with the task of translating the policies they had proclaimed into concrete governmental and administrative terms. The problems before them were pressing. They must terminate the war, and quickly; they must suppress the rapidly growing counterrevolutionary movement in southern Russia before it had become a challenge too great to meet; they must solve the economic crisis which held the nation in its grip. So long as the Bolsheviks had been the opposition party, it had been easy for them to criticize the policies of the government and to make attractive promises to the people. Now they were confronted with the necessity of bending the vast government machinery inherited from Kerensky to their will.

In March 1917, after the first revolution, the functionaries of the central state offices and the local authorities throughout Russia had accepted the leadership of the new government. The Bolsheviks, however, met only with resistance. Everywhere government employees refused to cooperate with the Soviet Government, and in Petrograd state employees went out on strike. Unlike the soldiers and workers, the intellectuals and the middle classes regarded the Bolsheviks with the utmost distrust; in the eyes of many they were simply agents of the Central Powers who were intent upon betraying both Russia and the Allied cause, a cause to which the bourgeoisie in Russia was still devoted. Moreover, almost everyone considered the new government a wild swing of the political pendulum which would soon be corrected. It seemed doubtful that the Bolsheviks could hold power for more than two or three weeks, and government employees everywhere felt it was neither wise nor necessary to throw in their lot with a temporary regime.

They miscalculated. The Soviet Government continued to extend its power and the Council of People's Commissars gradually mastered the situation. New men from the Bolshevik party took over the important posts, some of the recalcitrant government employees were dismissed, and others, moving with the times, submitted and entered the service of the new government. Within a few weeks the governmental machinery of Moscow and Petrograd was firmly under Bolshevik control.

The Bolsheviks then extended their authority to the provinces, for the most part without exercising force. The fact that the Soviet Government was a dictatorship of the Communist party was evident only in the capitals. The Bolshevik revolution officially consisted merely in the transfer of power from the Provisional Government to the soviets, which in the provinces merely meant that the local soviets took the place of the commissars of the Provisional Government. At this time the authority of the Bolsheviks extended only to the towns; the village communities, which even under the Provisional Government had shown opposition, were now entirely independent of the central government and reverted to the rule of the traditional village assembly. Accordingly, the forms of local government varied from province to province, and dependence of local soviets upon the national government was purely nominal until the Bolsheviks gained control of each soviet. This was accomplished in time by dispatching agitators and armed supporters to the sections where persuasion was needed.

The chief instrument used by the government to suppress disorder was the political police. By order of Lenin on December 20, 1917, the Extraordinary Commission for the Suppression of Counterrevolution (Cheka) came into existence. The Red Terror was proclaimed, under the direction of Felix Dzerjinsky, against all enemies of the state. During the winter of 1917–18 the Cheka claimed a considerable number of victims; but it was not until the autumn of 1918—following attempts on the lives of the Bolshevik leaders, manifestations of counterrevolution in the south, and the intervention of the Allies in Russia—that the Red Terror reached its height. The atrocities committed in its name during this period were not accidental abuses of authority. The Red Terror was a recognized and integral element in the process of subjecting the nation to the Bolshevik will. Lenin himself declared, "No dictatorship of the proletariat is to be thought of without terror and violence." Officially the activities of the Cheka were directed at the bourgeoisie alone. "We are not waging war against separate individuals; we are exterminating the bourgeoisie as a class," said Martin Latsis, one of the leaders. As a matter of fact, however, the Cheka exterminated without discrimination all of those suspected of opposing the Soviet Government. The victims were not confined to the upper or middle classes but included peasants and occasionally even workers as well. The Cheka moved without compunction and ruthlessly. Taking hostages from the non-Communist groups of a community was a favorite method. In the event of an uprising against the government—and especially of an attempted assassination of Communist leaders—the hostages, commonly nonpolitical people who themselves had done nothing to oppose the authority of the state, were shot without hesitation. Nor was the Cheka unwilling to resort to torture to obtain confessions or information which it considered necessary. In addition, individual Bolshevik groups in the provinces not infrequently took the law into their own hands and dealt death where they felt it was warranted—as in the case of the collective execution of officers in Sevastopol in the spring of 1918. The active period of the Red Terror was a bloody one in which the normal processes of justice were supplanted by an all-powerful organization operating on a system of suspicion and summary judgment. Thousands suffered for the crime of opposing the dictatorship and more thousands completely innocent of any political activities suffered with them.

In addition to the political police who were used against dissident groups, the Soviet Government had the active support of the Red Army, the Workers' and Peasants' Army, which was organized on February 23, 1918. It consisted at first largely of hired troops recruited from the ranks of the old army and young workers; the soldiers received good pay and special rations and could be counted upon to carry out government orders loyally and zealously. The discipline of this body was much better than that of the demoralized remnants of the old army. Using to the utmost the Cheka, the Red Army, and whatever other instruments they could bend to their will, the Bolsheviks succeeded during the winter of 1917–18 in getting complete control of the governmental machinery.

To solve the economic crises facing the country was more difficult, and as time went on they grew increasingly critical. The value of the ruble fell; prices rose higher than ever before; the condition of the railways became desperate; industrial production slumped after the committees of workers seized control. The Bolsheviks did manage to supply certain groups of the urban population with food, particularly members of the Communist party, employees of government institutions, and workers. This was accomplished by requisitioning all the food available in the cities and all deliveries of foodstuffs from the country and distributing them by means of a system of ration cards to certain categories of inhabitants. Members of the Communist party and workers were placed in the best-fed category, government employees in the second best, and craftsmen and the unemployed in the third group. All others were declared "unproductive elements" and as such were not objects of government care. The average ration was about half a pound of bread a day. It was difficult to purchase any food in excess of the ration by legal means, and to have no card meant almost certain death by starvation. Control of the food cards which had virtually become permits to live delivered the city population into the hands of the Bolsheviks.

The distribution of food was, however, only one aspect of the difficulty. The first problem was to obtain food in the villages. Because of the Provisional Government's inability to supply manufactured goods or to pay for produce in stable currency, the peasants had already refused to cooperate with the Kerensky regime. The Soviet Government was even less capable than its predecessor of satisfying their demands. The Decree of Land of November 8 had been an attempt to appease the dissatisfied peasants, but its importance was largely documentary and it had little effect on the attitude of those who on their own initiative had already partitioned a substantial part of the landowners' estates. Finding that it could not enlist their voluntary cooperation, the government did not hesitate to take grain from the peasants by force. "Food battalions" of Red Guards and Cheka employees were organized and sent into the villages, and, though the peasants tried to hide their grain or even to destroy it, some was secured and shipped to the cities. The measures used to solve the food problem of the city population inevitably produced another problem, the natural and widespread opposition of the peasants. In time this resentment grew into armed resistance, and the Bolsheviks faced a serious threat to their authority precisely in the regions where they were weakest, in the provinces remote from the center of power.

11. *The peace of Brest-Litovsk*

The Decree of Peace approved by the Second Congress of Soviets was just a theoretical declaration. Further measures were needed to get Russia out of the war. On November 20, 1917, the Soviet Government ordered army headquarters to propose to the enemy a cessation of hostilities. The acting commander in chief, General Nicholas Dukhonin, replied that this was the task of the government, not of the army, and refused to carry out the order. The next day he was dismissed and later murdered. On November 22 Trotsky addressed a note to all the Allied ambassadors in Petrograd proposing "an immediate armistice on all fronts and the immediate opening of peace negotiations." At the same time a similar note was presented to the diplomatic representatives of the neutral nations who were then in the capital. Although the military agents of the Allied Powers in Petrograd immediately protested against the suggestion of a separate peace with Germany, it seems clear that at the time they did not fully realize the seriousness of the military and political situation in Russia.

The November 25 elections to the Constituent Assembly—elections which had been called by a decree of the Provisional Government and had not been canceled by the new government—showed that the Bolsheviks were in a decided minority. They controlled only 168 votes in a body of 703 deputies, where the majority were members of the Socialist Revolutionary party. It is probable that the results of the election convinced the Germans of the unstable position of the Bolsheviks and alarmed them sufficiently to make them willing to hasten peace. Negotiations for an armistice between the Central Powers and Soviet Russia began on December 3.

On January 18, 1918, while peace negotiations were still going on, the Constituent Assembly met in Petrograd. The Bolsheviks were determined to exclude opponents who could not be influenced, and as a first step in this direction they arrested all the nonsocialist deputies, two of whom, being ill, were brutally murdered in hospital. When the remaining non-Bolshevik deputies still refused to acknowledge the Council of People's Commissars as the legal government of Russia, the Bolshevik delegates withdrew from the conference. In the streets demonstrations broke out against the government but were quickly suppressed. At 1.30 A.M. on January 20 the Central Executive Committee of the Soviet issued a decree disbanding the Assembly. The deputies were ejected from their meeting place and a Bolshevik military force guarding the building refused to allow any further sessions.

Though the disbanding of the Constituent Assembly strengthened the Bolsheviks at home by buttressing their control of the government machinery, it weakened their position in the armistice negotiations in Brest-Litovsk. The Germans, no longer afraid of an imminent collapse of the Bolsheviks, now demanded that Russia renounce her control of Poland, Ukraine, and Lithuania. These proposals were more than the Bolsheviks were prepared to accept, and in a proclamation on January 23 they protested the German peace conditions. The time for protests had passed. With her army disbanded, Russia was now helpless before the military power of Germany.

To increase the pressure on the Soviet Government and to ensure the complete annihilation of Russia as a military power, the Germans encouraged and supported the Ukrainian separatist movement, and on January 28, 1918, Ukraine proclaimed itself an independent republic. The history of this Ukrainian state is brief, for on February 8 Kiev, the capital, was occupied by Bolshevik troops.

The peace conference at Brest-Litovsk meanwhile dragged on in deadlock. Trotsky, who was negotiating for the Soviet Government, refused to accept the German conditions, but on February 10 he announced that the war with Germany was at an end and the Russian army was demobilized. The German reply was an order to their troops to advance into Russia. The Soviet Government was forced to accept the peace terms which had been offered and on March 3 signed the Treaty of Brest-Litovsk.

The peace conditions were disastrous for Russia. Ukraine, Lithuania, Esthonia, and Latvia were taken over by Germany, and after the defeat of the Central Powers the Allies recognized the three Baltic states as independent republics. In December 1917 the Soviet Government itself had recognized Finland's status as an independent state. In the south, part of Transcaucasia was ceded to Turkey. Such were the results of a war in which Russian casualties were about 2,500,000 soldiers killed and wounded.

And yet the Bolsheviks were able to take some satisfaction from the turn of events. By signing the peace treaty they had gained a breathing spell which they badly needed. They were able to build up their own strength so that they could break formally with the moderate socialists. A small but significant step was taken by the Seventh Convention of the Bolsheviks which approved the ratification of the Brest-Litovsk Treaty, when it adopted a new name for the party. Until then known as the Russian Social Democratic Party, Bolsheviks, it was now renamed Russian Communist Party, Bolsheviks. The change was a concrete indication that the political dividing line which had formerly been drawn between the bourgeois parties and the socialist parties had now been shifted leftward to establish the boundary between the Communists and the socialists. The change meant, too, that the new regime had completed the consolidation of its position, and, to add a final touch to the break with the past, the capital was soon afterward transferred from Petrograd to Moscow.

12. Civil war and foreign intervention

Though the Soviet Government was able to establish its control over stunned and demoralized Russia with almost incredible rapidity, it could not, of course, completely eradicate all the potential sources of opposition. In order to seize and hold power the Bolsheviks had resorted to harsh and ruthless means which inevitably bred discontent and resentment in certain sections of the country and among various groups of the population. As the feeling of indignation spread in widening circles about the government, opposition groups were organized and gradually established interconnections. By merging their forces and by recruiting dissident elements antagonized by the new government, some of these opposition groups in time became strong enough to engage in open revolt. The Bolsheviks were thus confronted with yet another crisis—civil war.

The causes of the civil war were many and complex. In the political sphere, the Bolsheviks had openly violated the principle of democracy by disbanding the Constituent Assembly. It was only natural that the duly elected deputies—most of them Socialist Revolutionaries—not only protested against the action but attempted to form an opposition government of their own. On the military side, a number of the officers of the old army refused to accept the German peace, which they considered detrimental to Russian interests and a betrayal of Russia's allies—a view which was very generally shared by intellectuals, especially the university students. This group of officers eventually created the so-called

Volunteer Army in the south and set up contacts with the Don and Kuban Cossacks who traditionally had existed as a separate and privileged group within the Russian Empire. Enjoying a measure of self-government and being somewhat wealthier than the average Russian peasant, the Cossacks were in no mood to submit to communist rule without a struggle, and from the very beginning of the conflict became the mainstay of the opposition in the south. Furthermore, certain national groups such as the Ukrainians, the Georgians, the Kalmyks, and others saw in the revolution and subsequent disorganization the opportunity to separate from Russia and establish themselves as autonomous states and were consequently willing to support a movement against the central government.

Driven by the absolute necessity to supply food for the army and the city proletariat and met by the stubborn resistance of the peasants who must provide that food, the Soviet Government had to break the peasant opposition. A method was devised to neutralize the power of the whole peasant class by dividing the village population into separate categories and setting one group against the other. This division was accomplished by creating committees of the poor. The village inhabitants were classified in two groups, one composed of richer peasants (*kulaki,* rich peasants, and *seredniaki,* middle peasants) and the other of poor peasants (*bedniaki,* those who possessed no cattle or stores of grain). The Bolsheviks then delegated authority in village affairs to the poor peasants, who were to form committees to see that the richer peasants did not hide grain from the government collectors, and were empowered to seize any surplus grain or cattle discovered. By these measures the Bolsheviks succeeded effectively in planting the "class warfare" of communism in the villages.

The slogan of "loot the looters" with which rich and poor peasant alike had justified the seizure of land from the large landowners was now turned against many of those who had at first profited by it, peasants who owned no more than a few acres of land and two or three head of cattle. The committees of the poor worked with a will and within a short time had brought about a serious disorganization in agriculture and great hardships for all classes. For the Bolsheviks, however, this did accomplish one purpose. The revolutionary struggle which had thus been transported to the very heart of the village community completely absorbed the powers of the whole peasant class, and the government was free to proceed with other plans. In the villages the committees of the poor had become the chief support of the Bolsheviks.

In view of the government's difficulties and the means the Bolsheviks had chosen to handle the situation, the Whites would seem to have been provided with ample opportunity to secure for themselves the support of the rich and middle peasants. Almost without exception, however, they failed to exploit their advantages. When they expelled the Reds from an area, the White governments usually re-established the laws that had been valid in the pre-November period. This meant, of course, that the former owners of the large estates were free to return and evict the people who had occupied their land—which aroused the indignation of all the peasants, rich and poor alike. The peasants were, therefore, caught between two forces, neither of which they were willing to support. In certain agricultural areas they occasionally tried to organize a government of their own which would be neither Red nor White, a "Green" government, as it was sometimes called, intended to serve their interests and protect them from the other contenders. On the whole, however, the peasants remained unpredictable, moving from side to side as the occasion demanded, first supporting the Whites to get rid of the Reds and then turning to the Reds for help in driving out the Whites.

One rather curious political fact emerges as we study this period. Though most of the White governments were definitely conservative and though they sprang up in different parts of Russia, were organized along various political lines, and were led by representatives of many different groups, none of them ever attempted to re-establish tsarism. This may have been partially accounted for by the fact that the overthrow of tsarism in 1917 had been legalized by the last tsar himself when he abdicated in favor of his brother Michael. Michael had never accepted the throne, however, and was later kidnapped and killed by the revolutionaries. Nicholas II and his wife and children were brutally murdered by the Bolsheviks in Ekaterinburg (now called Sverdlovsk) on July 16, 1918, and other members of the imperial family were either killed or escaped to exile. Grand Duke Nicholas, the former commander in chief of the Russian armies, was the only one of the remaining grand dukes who enjoyed any real or widespread popularity, but he would not think of accepting the throne. Grand Duke Cyril, who was later to assume the imperial title among the émigrés, was too cautious to risk taking the lead in Russia in the midst of a civil war. Among the other grand dukes there were probably some who would gladly have accepted an offer of the title, but nobody cared to support their claims. So one of the chief reasons that there was no effective movement for a restoration at the time of the civil war was the lack of a suitable candidate. And, finally, the most influential leaders of the White armies themselves had no monarchistic inclinations, and those among their followers who had such sympathies were afraid to espouse them openly.

Contrary to the general opinion, which was particularly widespread in the United States, the Whites were not tsarists, certainly not officially so. The government established in Samara (now Kuibyshev) on the Volga, by a committee of the Constituent Assembly consisting mostly of Socialist Revolutionaries, was clearly republican. In the event of victory, it was the intention of the two strongest leaders of the White armies, General Denikin in the south and Admiral Kolchak in Siberia, to establish a strong military government for the transition period and then to convoke a National Assembly. Throughout the whole period the main struggle of the Whites was against communism rather than against the constitutional or republican form of government.

The underlying issues and the course of the civil war itself were greatly complicated by foreign intervention. The Allies were irritated by the cancellation of Russia's foreign debts and obligations which was announced by the Soviet Government in February 1918, and they were even more indignant, of course, about the separate peace which the soviets had concluded with Germany. Most of the Allied statesmen refused to recognize the peace even after the Soviets had signed the Treaty of Brest-Litovsk, and proceeded with plans to re-establish the eastern front with or without the consent of the Soviet Government; if necessary, against the will of the Russian people. This determination was carried so far that at one time the French even suggested a plan whereby Japan would send her troops through Siberia to fight the Germans, a plan which failed to materialize chiefly because of the opposition of the United States.

Besides these general problems about the attitude of the Soviets, there were certain specific tasks in Russia which demanded the Allies' immediate attention. By the time of the revolution, huge stores of ammunition which had been bought by Imperial Russia from the United States, Great Britain, and Japan had accumulated in Russia's two northern ports, Murmansk and Archangel, and in Vladivostok on the Pacific. The Allies had no desire to see this vast amount of precious material fall into the hands of the Bolsheviks. In addition to the danger that the revolutionaries would take over the supplies, the Germans were now in a position to threaten the capture of the stores in Murmansk. Early in 1918 a civil war had started between the Finnish Reds and Whites, and the Senate of Finland had asked for German assistance. With this aid the Reds had soon been crushed, and German troops were now well along in a drive northward toward Murmansk.

It was obviously necessary for the Allies to act quickly; in April 1918 Allied troops landed at Murmansk and, later, at Archangel.

There was no danger that the Germans would penetrate as far as Vladivostok, yet the Allies were eager to lay hands on the stores in that port as well. A suitable pretext was produced. It was suggested that, according to information available to the Allies, the Soviet Government was believed to be releasing German and Magyar prisoners from the Siberian camps in which they had been confined and arming them for attack against the Allies. Subsequent thorough investigation proved these rumors to have been fabrications: the number of prisoners actually freed was shown to have been insignificant and, in addition, only those who accepted communism and agreed to join the Red Army had been liberated. Nevertheless, Allied contingents intended to forestall this nonexistent threat began landing in Vladivostok in April 1918.

There was by no means complete agreement between the Allies about the objectives of the intervention. While originally the motive of guarding the military stores against possible German seizure was kept in the foreground, at a later date both the British and French established close connections with the anti-Bolshevik forces in Russia and talks about a crusade against communism were begun. The attitude of the United States was somewhat different. Considering the presence of American troops in Siberia primarily as a check to Japanese aspirations to establish a base of their own in that area, President Wilson instructed the American commanders to remain neutral in the Russian civil war and to give direct assistance only to the Czechoslovaks. However, since the Czechs themselves were in active opposition to the Bolsheviks until November 1918, it was difficult to preserve actual neutrality.

The Czech anabasis was one of the most spectacular episodes in the whole civil war. Among the Austrian soldiers captured by the Russians before the revolution there had been a substantial number of Czechs who, as subjects of the Austrian emperor, had been conscripted and sent to the front. Inspired by the hope of establishing an independent Czech state, many of them had agreed to form a special brigade to assist the Russian army and in the summer of 1917 had taken part in the Kerensky offensive against the Central Powers. After Russia's withdrawal from the war these Czechoslovak troops, who at that time numbered 40,000, requested transfer to the western front to continue the struggle against Germany and her allies. This required transporting them the whole width of Siberia as the first leg of their journey around the world. In May 1918 the first units of the Czech troops reached Vladivostok; the balance of the force strung out across the continent to the other side of the Volga. Apparently under the influence of the German ambassador in Moscow, Count Mirbach, Trotsky then ordered the Czechs to disarm. They agreed, but when a new order came from Moscow directing that they again be interned as prisoners of war, they rose against the Bolsheviks. During the early part of June they took possession of all the principal cities between Samara and Vladivostok, a stroke which was soon followed by political revolt against the Bolsheviks throughout all eastern Russia and Siberia.

While the Allies were intervening in both the north and the Far East—and, through the Czechs, along the whole Trans-Siberian Railroad as well—the Germans lost no time in occupying the southern regions. To be sure, it was not technically an intervention in Russian affairs, since by the Treaty of Brest-Litovsk the Soviet Government had recognized the independence of Ukraine. Actually, however, the Ukrainian Reds who were now compelled to retreat before this new German onslaught were part of the all-Russian Communist movement. Coming officially to Ukraine in response to the émigré Ukrainian Government's call for assistance,

German troops quickly overcame the scattered resistance of the poorly organized Red Army and occupied Kiev, while the Austrians captured Odessa in April 1918. In a further German advance to the Don, the city of Rostov fell on May 8. Thereupon Ataman Peter Krasnov entered into negotiations with the invaders who, anxious to secure an opportunity for the economic exploitation of south Russia, willingly agreed to support him with arms and ammunition in his struggle against the Bolsheviks. While all this was in progress in the south, it is interesting to note that in Moscow the Germans, through their first ambassador to the Soviet Government, Count Mirbach, were expressing their friendship for the new regime. On April 23 the German forces of occupation concluded an economic treaty with the Ukrainian Government which secured for Germany the rights to the rich resources she coveted. They re-established the landowners on their estates and soon accomplished the overthrow of the half-socialistic Ukrainian Government. A little later General Paul Skoropadsky was proclaimed head of a government which was in reality a puppet of Germany.

Though Germany may have had some semblance of legal justification for occupying Ukraine, in the capture of Rostov in the Don area, the seizure of the whole Crimea, and the excursion into Transcaucasia she clearly and openly violated the boundaries of the Soviet state she had officially recognized.

13. *The course of the civil war to January 1920*

Though the total amount of territory subject to the control of the Soviet Government was reduced by the outbreak of counterrevolutionary movements in the south, southeast, and east, within that circle of enemies the Bolsheviks had, by the middle of 1918, extended their power not only to the towns but to the rural districts as well. In order to regain the regions in revolt, the Communists now began to reorganize the Red Army, which was still not an efficient fighting force. Within a few months the whole structure was thoroughly overhauled. Trotsky was appointed chief of the Military Revolutionary Committee—the War Office—and in June 1918 the government determined to conscript a new army on the basis of compulsory service. The soldiers' committees which had been formed in 1917 were abolished and replaced by "Communist cells" directed by political commissars and composed of party members, which were charged with the maintenance of strict discipline.

Generals of the old army and officers of the former general staff were given the task of reorganizing the Red Army after the traditional pattern; and though some Communists were promoted from the ranks by the Bolsheviks, the majority of the commissions in the new Red Army were held by line officers of the old army. Even the high command of the Red Army during the civil war was largely in the hands of these trained soldiers—though new leaders also arose among them, such as Lt. Michael Tukhachevsky, Sergt. Simeon Budenny, and Commander Frunze. Lack of other means of support, the habit of professional military service, and fear of the Cheka were perhaps the main reasons which impelled officers of the demobilized old army to accept service in the Red Army. After they had enlisted, it was a matter of self-preservation to serve in good faith, for in the event of capture they faced reprisals by the anti-Bolshevik forces—and indeed many Red officers were shot when they fell into the hands of the Whites. In addition, these men were well aware that treason to the Soviet Government would entail swift retaliation against members of their families who were considered by the Cheka as hostages for their loyalty.

Paradoxically enough, it was the civil war which transformed the Red Army into a fighting organization and the Soviet Government into a strong centralized power. Even though the conscription of 1918 succeeded in raising only half the number of men called, by November of that year the Soviet had an army of 400,000 men under competent leadership. The efforts of the anti-Bolsheviks had produced a result diametrically opposite to that which they had intended. By constituting a threat to the stability of the Bolshevik regime they had indirectly provoked the formation of a strong military power in Russia subject to the will of the Soviet Government.

From the military point of view, the most important center of opposition to the Bolsheviks was in south Russia, where the Volunteer Army led by generals Alexeev and Kornilov (and later, by Gen. Anton Denikin) was formed in February 1918 as a small group of army officers, cadets, university students, and even high school boys, poorly armed and ill equipped, but strong in spirit. Surviving through incredible hardships, the Volunteer Army eventually received support from the Kuban and Don Cossacks, and during the summer of 1918 the three forces succeeded in clearing the Bolsheviks out of the North Caucasian and Don areas. The Samara government became another center of opposition; and in Omsk, Siberia, still another anti-Bolshevik government was formed. Both the Samara and Omsk governments were in close touch with the Czechs.

Of all the land previously held within the Russian Empire, the Bolsheviks by the autumn of 1918 exercised control over only the central part of European Russia. The balance of old Russia was split into small segments divided against each other and the mother state. In the south, Ukraine was under German and Austrian occupation; the Don valley was independent of the Bolsheviks and friendly to the Germans; the Kuban area had been cleared of Bolshevik forces and was opposed to the Germans; the southern Ural region and Siberia were under the control of the Czechs and local governments—a potential threat to Germany; the extreme north and east had been occupied by Allied forces. Russia, under the Soviet, had been reduced to the boundaries of Muscovy of the early 16th century. At that moment, when Soviet fortunes were at their lowest ebb, the World War ended with the capitulation of Germany on November 11, 1918.

The armistice produced unexpected results in Russian affairs. On the surface, this sudden turn of events seemed to favor the policy of those among the Allied leaders who had been thinking of a crusade against communism. The whole military might of the Allies seemed now to be available for a crushing blow against the Bolsheviks who, in the eyes of the victors, had betrayed the common cause by signing a separate peace with Germany in March 1918. And yet the blow was not to fall. Instead the Bolsheviks profited greatly by the collapse of the Central Powers. Like the Russian army of the year before, the Germans who had occupied Ukraine and propped up the ephemeral Ukrainian Government now withdrew from this territory in a state of complete demoralization. The anti-Bolsheviks hoped that after compelling the Germans to evacuate southern Russia the Allies themselves would occupy that area rather than let it be exposed to the Bolshevik armies, but contrary to the expectation of the Whites no Allied troops made their appearance. Since the Ukrainian Government under Skoropadsky had not been allowed by the Germans to maintain any armed troops of its own, within a few weeks after the evacuation of the German army of occupation it fell before the socialist Ukrainian leader Petlura. Detachments of French troops did occupy Odessa on December 18, 1918, but by that time the opportunity to seize the control relinquished by the Germans had already been lost. By then considerable force would have been necessary to reconquer southern Russia, and the Allies were in no position to undertake another military campaign.

A number of circumstances made any large-scale Allied intervention impossible. The soldiers of the Allied armies were tired and anxious to return to the ways of peace; they were far from eager for a new war. The British and French differed in their evaluation of the forces available to them in southern Russia, and agreed only in their lack of confidence in the anti-Bolshevik movement with which they would have to work. This division between the Allies most concerned in the situation resulted in scattered and disorganized action.

The whole of southern Russia was divided by the Allies into a British and a French zone of influence, roughly separated by the Don area. On their side the British attempted no military operations on any substantial scale but limited themselves to occupying the Transcaucasian area. At the end of November 1918 a British detachment occupied Baku, the center of the oil industry on the Caspian Sea, and a month later took Batum, terminus of the Transcaucasian pipe line. The British Government provided the Volunteer Army with assistance in the form of war supplies and arms. In the territory under their control, however, the French attempted more aggressive action. On March 13, 1919, they proclaimed themselves the supreme authority in the Odessa area and with the support of local Russian forces began operations against the Bolsheviks. This policy of direct attack on the Soviet armies resulted in complete failure. The French soldiers soon fell under the influence of Bolshevik propaganda and refused to fight the Red Army. The French command in the end was unable to trust even its own troops, and in time a comparatively feeble Bolshevik army drove the French completely out of south Russia.

The armistice on the western front also affected subsequent developments in Siberia. With the termination of the World War the Allies of course lost interest in the creation of a front along the

Volga, and the Czech troops who had been fighting in that area lost heart in their battle with the Bolsheviks, which to them had been nothing more than an episode in their struggle against the Central Powers. They were with difficulty induced to remain in Siberia to protect the Trans-Siberian Railroad while the Allies tried to settle their difficulties with the Russians by diplomatic means. During the winter of 1918–19 the Russian situation was discussed at the Peace Conference in Paris. On January 22, 1919, President Wilson issued an invitation "to every organized group that is now exercising or attempting to exercise political authority or military control in Russia" to send representatives to a conference to be held on the Island of Prinkipo in the Sea of Marmora, a truce of arms to be operative meanwhile.

Thus within a few months the desperate situation faced by the Soviet Government had entirely changed. Bolsheviks and anti-Bolsheviks were now invited to attend a conference and discuss the future of Russia. The Bolsheviks immediately accepted President Wilson's proposal, for such a conference promised them relief from the terrific pressure they were under both from the opposition within the territories they occupied and from the circle of external enemies which had been drawn around them. All of the anti-Bolshevik forces, however, considered the invitation insulting. They refused to negotiate with a group which had, they felt, usurped political power within the country, betrayed Russia to the Central Powers, and was at the moment pursuing an intolerable policy within the territory under its control. From their point of view the proposed conference would amount to indirect recognition of the Soviet Government by the Entente and would in itself give significant moral support to the Bolsheviks.

The civil war continued unabated. During the winter of 1918–19 and the first half of 1919 the anti-Bolshevik forces scored impressive successes. General Denikin's army, now numbering about 150,000 men, extended its control over all south Russia, occupying such important cities as Tsaritsyn (now Stalingrad), Kharkov, and Kiev. Moscow was now its goal. In Siberia, Adm. Alexander Kolchak was proclaimed supreme ruler and assumed dictatorial power. His army of 125,000 men succeeded in taking Perm, Orenburg, and Ufa, and it too seemed ready to march on Moscow. A political understanding was reached between two White leaders,

Denikin recognizing Kolchak's supreme authority. The achievement of the White armies, while spectacular, proved ephemeral. Denikin's position was undermined by the opposition of both the peasants and the Ukrainians; Kolchak's authority was shattered by the sabotage of the Socialist Revolutionaries, whose leader, Victor Chernov, announced the slogan "Neither Kolchak nor Lenin." Actually, Chernov's activities helped Lenin considerably. The leaders of the Red Army decided to stop Kolchak first and then to turn their attention against Denikin. In the summer of 1919 Kolchak's armies suffered several defeats and were thrown back to Siberia. The Soviet's first counterattack against Denikin failed, but in October it succeeded not only in stopping his advance column at Orel but in turning back his whole army. Peasant uprisings in the rear of Denikin's armies compelled him to order retreat, which soon became a rout. The remnants of his army made for Novorossiisk on the northeastern shore of the Black Sea, where they were finally compelled to ask the British to help evacuate the troops, their families, and the wounded. On March 27, 1920, Novorossiisk was abandoned, and the remnants of the Volunteer Army, as well as most of the Don and part of the Kuban Cossacks, were transported by sea to the Crimean Peninsula. Denikin resigned his position as commander in chief and appointed Gen. Peter Wrangel his successor.

Meanwhile the fate of Kolchak had already been sealed, for the complete disintegration of the forces under his command was obviously only a matter of time. The support of the Allies, upon which Kolchak depended and which had been promised in June 1919, never materialized. Throughout Siberia his government was harassed by peasant revolts incited by the Socialist Revolutionaries. To add to the confusion, the only means of communication over these vast distances, the Trans-Siberian Railroad, was under the control of the Czechs who had joined the opposition. Cut off from his troops, Kolchak was finally seized by the revolutionary committee in Irkutsk with the connivance of the Czechs and the consent of the French general, Janin. A few days later he was shot.

With the arrival of the Red Army troops in Irkutsk two weeks later, the Soviet Government established its control over all the territory west of Lake Baikal. The Far Eastern portion remained in effect under the control of Japanese troops. It was only after two more years of alternate fighting and diplomatic negotiation that the Soviet Government was able to complete the occupation of the whole of Siberia.

The collapse of the anti-Bolshevik forces all along the line at last compelled the Allies to alter their stand in regard to the Soviet Government. They began to realize that after two years in power the Bolsheviks had entrenched themselves and were, indeed, growing stronger. As early as November 8, 1919, Lloyd George declared that the Bolsheviks could not be conquered by arms, and on January 16, 1920, the Supreme Council of the Allies voted to withdraw the economic blockade of Russia. A little later Archangel was evacuated and soon afterward all Allied troops were withdrawn from Russian territory.

14. *Soviet internal policy during the civil war*

During the civil war the Soviet Government enjoyed certain advantages over its opponents. The most important of these, perhaps, was controlling the central regions of Russia, a circumstance which secured for the Red Army the use of shorter internal lines of communication. Within their territory, also, the Soviet armies had at their disposal enormous reserve stocks of armaments and munitions which had been accumulated by the Imperial Army for a huge offensive planned for 1917 and which had been only partly used by Kerensky in his abortive advance in July. Politically, too, the Soviet Government was a centralized power with the advantages of unity of purpose and clearness of program, while the many peripheral White governments opposed to it were muddled and divided among themselves. Although the bourgeoisie and part of the intelligentsia objected to the Communist dictatorship and the peasants remained more or less neutral, the Bolsheviks were able to base their program solidly on the factory workers who, with few exceptions, supported the government wholeheartedly.

The policy of the Soviet Government in this period is known as "war communism." Motivated partly by theoretical Marxist concepts and partly by grim necessity, it set about the task of transforming the whole country into a huge military camp. As we have seen, the land was divided among the peasants in 1917–18. This solution of the agrarian problem was regarded by Lenin and other Communist leaders as a temporary one dictated by considerations of practical expediency. Theoretically, the Bolsheviks were inclined to regard the peasant not as a proprietor but as a workman operating government-owned land. All his produce was considered government property and, as such, subject whenever necessary to government seizure by means of a levy in kind. Under the circumstances, of course, food requisitioning continued to be necessary for the duration of the war.

In industry the Soviet Government at first introduced the so-called "labor control" policy by which representatives of the workers shared the direction of plant operation with the former owners. Since there were incessant altercations between the two groups and since the working of the plan became increasingly involved in red tape, the labor control system failed to produce adequate results. In the summer of 1918 all large-scale plants were seized by the government, and from then on the nationalization of industry gradually spread downward even to small machine shops. In 1920 a decree nationalized all plants which employed more than five workers and used mechanical power and all those without mechanical power which employed more than ten workers.

National production as a whole was thus taken over by the government, which was then to arrange to supply the manufactured articles to the public. At first it was intended that the distribution should be free, not only for such things as fuel and machinery but for articles of personal use. The latter were apportioned by means of ration cards issued on the basis of a predetermined scale. Trade and commerce were, of course, eliminated under this system of Communist economy and in 1918 were officially abolished. Banking having also become an unnecessary function, the banks were nationalized and in their place a People's Bank was created in 1918. This organization, a bank in name only, was in reality a department of the Commissariat of Finance, and by the decree of January 19, 1920, it was merged with another branch of the same bureau and became the Budget Accounting Department.

Money was not abolished but the continual issuance of paper currency soon made it worthless. This can be demonstrated graphically by a few figures on money and prices during those years. On March 1, 1917, there were 11,786,000,000 rubles of paper money in circulation. By November 1 this sum had doubled. Two years later the total was 225,014,000,000 rubles, and January 1, 1921, it had reached the astronomical figure of 1,168,596,000,000 rubles. At the beginning of 1918 the dollar was worth about 9 rubles; at the beginning of 1919, about 80 rubles; at the beginning of 1920, 1,200 rubles. Naturally prices soared with this inflationary spiral, and every decline in the value of money led to a corresponding increase in the cost of goods. In 1917 the general index of prices was three times as high as in 1913. At the beginning of 1918 it was 23.5 times as high. In 1920 it rose to 2,420 and at the beginning of 1921 to 16,800 times the 1913 figure.

Having destroyed the delicate and sensitive organization of trade and money exchange, the economy of war communism was now forced to substitute clumsy and bureaucratic systems regulating both the production and distribution of goods. At the head of these organizations was the Supreme Council of the National Economy. The real difficulty of this situation lay in the necessity not only to develop a new economic organization but also to provide new psychological incentives for the whole economic machine. In overthrowing the old regime the Communist system had also destroyed the natural incentives of individual enterprise which heretofore had been basic in all social schemes. Demand now lost touch with supply. The market for goods no longer depended upon the value of work done but upon membership in one or another category of consumers. No longer able to depend upon the usual incentives which had caused people to work, the Soviet Government was forced to resort to the practice of forced labor. This policy, first proclaimed in 1918, was finally confirmed by the Decree of Compulsory Labor of January 1920, which stipulated that it was to apply not only to factory work but to agriculture as well. A further step in this direction was taken in the same year when an attempt was made to organize military workers' communes, a move which was an interesting parallel to the establishment of the military settlements of Alexander I.

The essential difficulty at this time was not necessarily that the government's plans were faulty but rather that it had no means to make them work. The situation was complicated especially by the fact that at the time of the Bolshevik revolution both industry and agriculture in Russia had already been seriously disorganized by the World War. All of these factors now brought a steady year-by-year decline in agricultural and industrial production. In order to tighten its control over the workers, the government moved to restrict the freedom of trade unions which had been legalized in Russia only in 1906. Although the Bolsheviks favored another form of labor organization—shop committees—trade unions had shown a rapid increase in membership under the Provisional Government and the movement was largely captured by the Mensheviks. Finally at the First Congress of Trade Unions in January 1918 the Bolsheviks succeeded in gaining an absolute majority, and under their influence the All-Russian Central Committee of Trade Unions was made the agency of factory and shop committees. After that the trade unions became for all practical purposes government-controlled. In 1920 the Ninth Convention of the Communist Party passed a resolution that "the trade unions . . . must gradually be transformed into auxiliary agencies of the proletarian state. The tasks of the trade unions lie chiefly in the field of economic organization and education."

The same method and policy were applied to the cooperative societies which were especially popular among the peasants. Here, too, the normal functions of the cooperatives were gradually transformed, and in 1920 the agencies of the consumer cooperative societies became mere subdivisions of the People's Commissariat of Food Supply.

It was the attitude of the peasants which remained the thorniest problem for the government throughout the whole period of the civil war. In spite of the establishment of the committees of the poor—or rather, precisely because of them—the peasant masses continued to look upon the Soviet Government with suspicion and distrust. Because of the constant opposition in the villages the Bolsheviks decided that some concessions should be made to the middle peasants at least. As early as August 8, 1918, Lenin consented to a threefold rise in the fixed price of grain, but by that time depreciation in value made the increase little more than a gesture. The peasants would, of course, have been glad to accept manufactured goods in exchange for their grain, but the government had no surplus of such articles at its disposal. The whole problem was like squaring a circle. "We have no blessings to bestow upon the middle peasant" was Lenin's frank avowal before the Eighth Convention of the Communist Party in March 1919. However, he did suggest certain palliative measures such as improving the apparatus of village administration, correcting the corrosive abuses, and, in general, attempting to establish a working agreement with the middle peasants. As a sort of moral consolation for this group, a middle peasant, Michael Kalinin, was elected chairman of the All-Russian Central Executive Committee—a post corresponding to the position of president in a republic.

Life in Soviet Russia was desperately hard during those troubled years, and even some of the government leaders were at times overcome by despair. That the government was somehow able to pull through seems to have been due principally to two forces—Lenin's iron will and the support of the factory workers.

15. *The Whites' last stand in the Crimea and the Polish-Soviet war*

After the defeat and evacuation of the anti-Bolshevik forces in the north and east of Russia, there remained but one center of opposition to the Soviet Government—the remnants of Denikin's army under General Wrangel's command on the Crimean Peninsula. Attempting to reorganize that army and to continue armed resistance to Moscow, Wrangel ordered that the troops be given a rest, discipline reinstated, and severe measures taken against the forced requisitioning of food from the peaceful population. This last order was particularly important to his plans for he relied upon the support of the peasantry of south Russia and had declared that his basic policy would be the satisfaction of their demands. Another move in this direction was his new agrarian law of June 7, 1920, vesting ownership of land in the peasants, a reform which was to be carried out by Alexander Krivoshein, former imperial minister of agriculture, who had taken a prominent part in the Stolypin reforms. Widening his search for allies against the Bolsheviks, Wrangel made overtures both to Poland and to leaders of the peasant movements in Russia. He even dispatched a representative to Nestor Makhno, leader of a group of anarchical peasant bands, in the hope of making an alliance with him. Makhno killed the messenger who had brought the offer.

Wrangel was convinced that his army, which consisted of only 70,000 men, could not hope to defeat the Soviet Government alone. He did believe, however, that his agrarian policy would draw the support of the peasantry when they understood its purpose, and that it would at the same time undermine the discipline of the Soviet armies. But his hopes were not realized. The peasants, weary of civil war, were not to be won over by new agrarian laws. Indeed, in many localities in south Russia the news of Wrangel's agricultural reforms never even reached them. An attempted uprising of the Don and Kuban Cossacks against the Soviet Government failed, and the Red Army, at that moment at the high point of moral exaltation, remained completely unaffected by Wrangel's program.

The war against Soviet Russia which Poland began at that time, instead of strengthening the anti-Bolshevik movement, actually had the opposite result. By taking advantage of the national patriotism which had been aroused in Russia by the Polish intervention, the Soviet Government was able to secure the cooperation and assistance of many of its staunchest enemies. At the invitation of the government the World War veteran, General Brusilov, issued an important and effective proclamation urging all Russian officers to support the Red Army in its struggle against Poland.

Poland's first moves were successful. After a brief campaign, Kiev, the capital of Ukraine, was occupied on May 6, 1920. An immediate counteroffensive by the Red Army, however, drove the Poles out of Kiev and back to the very gates of Warsaw. Finding herself hard pressed, on July 10 Poland appealed to the Allies for assistance, and a French military mission under General Weygand was sent to Warsaw while the Allies simultaneously attempted to reconcile the two warring governments.

Aware of the ever-increasing military power of the Soviet, France however decided to support General Wrangel, and on August 12, 1920, recognized his administration as the de facto government of south Russia. Meanwhile, with the arrival of additional French supplies in Warsaw, the Poles launched another attack against the Soviet armies and drove them back in disorder almost to Minsk. There the advance halted and, with both sides seeking peace, a truce was concluded on October 12, 1920. The peace was finally signed in Riga on March 18, 1921, on terms that were patently unfavorable to Russia. The eastern frontier of Poland was drawn along the line of the German front at the outbreak of the Bolshevik revolution, which meant that several million Ukrainians and Belorussians became subject to Polish rule.

The cessation of military activities on the Polish front in October enabled the Soviet Government to throw the Red Army over to the attack against General Wrangel in the south. In November a fierce battle was fought on the Perekop Isthmus connecting south Russia with the Crimea. Realizing that he could no longer withstand the assault, Wrangel ordered the evacuation of all the anti-Bolshevik elements from the Crimean Peninsula. In all, about 130,-000 soldiers and civilians, with their families, took ship and sailed for the Bosporus. The civil war was over.

CHAPTER 14

THE NEW ECONOMIC POLICY AND THE FIVE-YEAR PLAN

1. The legacy of the civil war and the New Economic Policy

RUSSIA survived the civil war, but it had taken all her strength to achieve that bare survival. She emerged from the cataclysm in a state of collapse unique in modern history. She had been devastated from end to end by the combined destruction of three contending forces—Reds, Whites, and foreign interventionists—who had fought along battle lines that writhed over a vast part of the nation. The blockade had throttled the already crumbling economic system. Peasant opposition to the government's enforced policy of food seizure had reduced agriculture to a level far below national requirements. The whole industrial system, burdened by a cumbersome and unworkable management scheme, was grinding to a halt. As a nation Russia had endured, but at a fearful cost in human suffering.

The continuing decline of industry and the disorganization of transport now led step by step to the total impoverishment of the country. Each year industrial production sank further until in 1920 it came to no more than 13.2 per cent of the volume in 1913. Transportation reflected the disappearance of manufactured goods and produce of all sorts. Daily carloadings in 1916 were 31,164; in 1920, 10,738. All this could only mean increasing hardship and want for the population. The scarcity affected nearly all articles of daily use. Before the war, for example, the consumption of sugar and molasses per person was 4.87 gold rubles worth. By 1920 it had fallen to .24 gold rubles. Prewar consumption of textiles per person was 6.77 gold rubles worth; in 1920 it was only .91.

The catastrophic decline in agricultural production was a far more serious condition. All arable land had passed into the hands of the peasants at the time of the revolution through their appropriation of the large estates, a shift which had increased their land holdings by about 31 per cent. But though the revolution had given the peasants the land which they wanted, the civil war, with its train of military difficulties driving the government more and more to the literal application of communist theory, brought them the economic policy of war communism which they abhorred. To them the new system was a compound of regulation and robbery which took away all of the old incentives for cultivating the land. Since the peasant no longer had any desire to raise more crops than he needed for his own purpose, the total area under cultivation began to shrink. In 1916 there were about 90,000,000 hectares of land under cultivation in the territory later under Soviet control; by 1921 that area had been reduced to 60,000,000. In addition, the yield per hectare had declined with the destruction of the large estates where production had generally been more efficient, and the collection of grain had consequently fallen off even more than the area of cultivation. In 1916 the harvest had totaled 74,000,000 tons of grain; in 1919 it was estimated at only 30,000,000 tons. Livestock raising inevitably would have been curtailed by the fodder shortage alone, but the economic policies pursued by the Soviet Government hastened and intensified the reduction. The 1916 total of 31,000,000 horses had been cut by 1920 to 24,000,000, and the number of cattle from 50,000,000 to less than 37,000,000.

In Russia's already terribly impoverished condition the drought of 1920 and 1921 led to a famine which had appalling consequences. The collection of grain in 1920 barely reached 18,000,000 tons; in 1921 the harvest failed in the whole of southeast Russia. The loss of life during the famine years of 1921–22 has been estimated at 5,000,000, a figure twice as great as the total Russian casualties in the World War. The death toll would have been even higher had not assistance come from outside the country, mainly from the United States. The chief organization engaged in the work was the American Relief Administration under Herbert Hoover. The ARA administered $61,566,231.53 and furnished 718,770 tons of commodities. During August 1922, it fed daily a high of 4,173,339 children and 6,316,958 adults—or more than 10,000,000 individuals. It also shipped and distributed $8,072,256.03 worth of medical supplies furnished by the American Red Cross and the United States Army.

Devastation, disorganization, chaos, and starvation were the legacy which the civil war left to a nation already bled white by the enormous losses of the World War.

The widespread dissatisfaction which the Russian people felt under the regime of war communism was expressed during 1920–21 in a series of peasant uprisings. Finally, at the beginning of March 1921, a serious outbreak occurred in Kronstadt among the sailors of the Red Navy, a group which had previously been the chief support of the Bolshevik revolution. The principal demands put forward by the rebels were for the calling of a constituent assembly and the reintroduction of freedom of trade. Though the uprising was soon quelled by armed force, the Soviet authorities considered it an ominous symptom. Grasping the seriousness of the situation, Lenin determined to supplement repressive police measures with a change in policy which was calculated to eliminate the causes of discontent.

Here again, as in the question of the Duma elections in 1906, Lenin showed that he was willing to make a sharp turn in his policy. He was prepared to make any compromise, to adjust his plans to the realities of the time, if by so doing he retained command of the situation. "We are in a condition of such poverty, ruin, and exhaustion of the productive powers of the workers and peasants," said Lenin in a speech at the Tenth Convention of the Communist Party in March 1921, "that everything must be set aside to increase production." With that announcement, Lenin began the creation of the New Economic Policy which in time came to be known simply as the NEP.

In its beginning the NEP involved a fundamental revision of the policy which had previously been enforced with the agricultural population. In place of the levy in kind which had created violent resentment that found outlet either in armed opposition or in a passive resistance which was even more crippling, the new economic setup substituted a definite quota of taxation. At first the tax was an assessment in kind and was collected principally in grain; later it became a money tax. The peasants were now granted the right to dispose of the surplus as they wished—that is, to sell it in the open market. The decree replacing the levy with a tax opened the way for a thorough alteration of the economic system, for by restoring the peasant's right to sell his grain the government had started a process which led inevitably to the introduction of freedom of trade. Indeed, in July 1921, before the collection of the harvest, a decree was promulgated sanctioning free trade in internal commerce, though foreign trade, of course, still remained a government monopoly.

Simultaneously with the liberation of agriculture, a similar reform was put under way in industry. The purely socialist form of production was replaced by a new system of "state capitalism." The central, unified management of industry gave way to a system of "trusts" in which the state retained control over large-scale production but allowed smaller productive units to revert partly to private individuals. In a limited sphere the investment of foreign capital was permitted by the introduction of a system of concessions. The plan for supplying raw materials and tools to factories gratis was dropped; every manufacturing plant, whether owned by government or privately, now had to pay for everything it used. These changes logically led to the reintroduction of currency, in its proper economic function, as well as to the re-establishment of a credit and banking mechanism. At the end of 1921 a State Bank, operating on an orthodox business basis, was set up.

The general retreat from the socialist system in the whole realm of production was necessarily accompanied by the abandonment of socialist principles in the distribution of goods. The state no longer undertook to supply the needs of great sections of the population. The right to receive goods free of charge was restricted to groups roughly similar to those so provided for in nonsocialist countries—members of the Red Army and Navy, and the police forces, as well as prisoners held in confinement. A final and important reform accompanying the extensive economic revisions of the NEP was the abolition of forced labor which had been resorted to in the violent period of war communism.

2. *The Genoa conference and the Communist International*

The introduction of the New Economic Policy was received favorably and with pleased anticipation by statesmen and business interests throughout Europe. Both groups very generally misunderstood the essential meaning of the revision in Soviet economic policy. To them the NEP meant only the capitulation of the Bolsheviks to the capitalistic world, and almost without exception it was interpreted as a sign of weakness rather than the mark of strength and political flexibility which it actually was. On the continent hopes ran high that the supposed feebleness of the Bolsheviks would provide opportunities for the exploitation of Russia's natural resources by foreign interests. A Soviet Government amenable to "capitulations" and extraterritorial rights similar to those already established by European powers in Turkey and in China was anticipated. The governments of most of the European states nervously edged toward favorable positions from which they hoped to capture the lead in the expected rush for concessions. But here again failure to reach any common agreement hampered the Allies. Lloyd George, in the British tradition of free trade, advocated independent action by each individual country, while the French continued to insist that the Allies act only in concert. The Germans, fearful of being left entirely behind, offered their services as middlemen between Russia and the West. It was also proposed that a *Europa Consortium* be organized to facilitate the reconstruction and exploitation of Russia. Though no plan was adopted officially and no agreement reached between Great Britain and France, the main contenders, these tentative moves made it abundantly clear that a thoroughgoing discussion of Russian affairs on an international scale could no longer be postponed.

At the session of the Supreme Council of the Entente at Cannes on January 6, 1922, the general terms under which the economic reconstruction of the countries prostrated by the war might be undertaken were discussed. Though not specifically recognized as such, Russia was, of course, the chief subject of the deliberations. The two principal conditions laid down for the work of rehabilitation were 1) recognition of all previous debts and obligations and 2) development of a normal financial and trade organization. At the same time the Supreme Council affirmed its belief in the principle of noninterference in the economic life of each country.

The succeeding conference which opened in Genoa on April 10, 1922, was the first international diplomatic gathering to include representatives of the Soviet Government. The first declarations of the Soviet delegates were businesslike in tone and led European statesmen to hope that an agreement of some kind might be possible. In tentative and preliminary terms, George Chicherin declared Russia ready to recognize both her prewar and war debts and either to return confiscated property to foreign owners or to give them compensation. In return he demanded immediate de jure recognition of the Soviet Government and large credits. In addition, he advanced a number of counterclaims for damages caused by the Allied intervention in Russia during the civil war. Once more the Allies showed by their reaction to Chicherin's proposals that they were hopelessly divided among themselves. Great Britain and Italy were willing to examine the Russian proposals. France and Belgium, concerned about the disposition of the concessions they had formerly held in southern Russia, flatly refused even to discuss them. At the same time Lloyd George was attempting to secure economic privileges for Great Britain through a direct agreement with the Soviet Government by which the entire production and export of Russian oil was to become a monopoly of the Royal Dutch-Shell Company. To put the finishing touches to the snarl, when word of the English negotiations leaked out, the American "observer" warned the conference that the United States would insist that an "open door" policy be applied in exploiting Russian oil.

Although it was basically the conflict of interests among the Allies which caused the failure of the Genoa conference, the situation was aggravated by the Soviet Government's conclusion of a separate agreement with Germany in Rapallo on April 16, 1922. This treaty disposed of all mutual claims of the two countries for war damages. Germany abandoned the support of her citizens' claims for compensation for property confiscated by the Soviet Government "provided the Government of the Russian Socialist Federative Soviet Republic does not satisfy similar claims of other states." Full diplomatic and consular relations beween Germany and Russia were to be resumed. Article V of the treaty further provided: "The two governments shall mutually assist each other in supplying the economic requirements of the two countries . . . The German Government declares itself ready to facilitate as far as possible the conclusion and execution of economic contracts between private enterprises in the two countries."

At the conclusion of the Genoa conference those questions remaining unsettled had been left to "commissions of experts" which were summoned to meet at The Hague in June and July 1922. However by the time this assembly met, Moscow, wearied by the previous failure to come to terms with the "capitalistic" governments, had assumed a much firmer attitude. Hence The Hague conference also proved a failure, even though the Entente negotiators appeared prepared to work more willingly for an understanding with Russia.

In negotiations with the western powers the Soviet Government represented Russia's national interests as it understood them; and simultaneously plans were made for spreading communism abroad. The call for the First Congress of the Third, or Communist, International was issued by Lenin and Trotsky on January 22, 1919—a date which almost coincided with President Wilson's invitation to the Prinkipo conference—and the delegates assembled in Moscow in March 1919. Chiefs of the various departments of the new body were elected, and a long manifesto was issued to the working people of the world.

The first period of activity by the International was characterized by immediate attempts to incite Communist revolutions in all countries. Uprisings did actually occur in a few nations, but their achievements were short-lived: the Communist government of Bela Kun in Hungary lasted from March 21 until August 1, 1919, and a Bavarian Soviet government, founded on April 7, 1919, held power for an even shorter period. Revolutions were also planned for England and the United States, though in these countries the "plans" could hardly have been more than vague hopes.

After these failures the Second Congress of the International in July 1920 adopted a new plan. Instead of relying so heavily upon spontaneous insurrection in the capitalist states, the Bolsheviks, through the headquarters of the International in Moscow, launched a systematic program of propaganda all over the world. The globe was divided into special propaganda areas, of which no less than six were in Europe. Presumably the sums expended on this scheme of preparation for "world revolution" were considerable. It is clear, nevertheless, that the Executive Committee of the Communist International was originally intended as the nucleus of a potential Soviet world government, though actually it remained merely a supplement to the Russian Communist party. The existence of the

International did, however, definitely establish Moscow as the center of the Communist world.

The Communist party was particularly active at that time in efforts to inculcate revolutionary theories among the Asiatic peoples; the leaders of the party and of the Soviet Government feverishly set about training propagandists to carry on that part of the work. Largely because of their growing resentment against Europeans who possessed special economic and political privileges in the East, the Asiatics were ready to listen to the call. The Bolshevik agitators at first met with considerable success in the Near and Middle East, but they were greatly handicapped in the consolidation of their gains by an excessively literal interpretation of Communist doctrine, especially by their insistence on its violent opposition to all religion. At the Congress of Eastern Peoples in Baku in September 1920, Mohammedanism showed itself to be stronger than communism and adherents to that faith were aroused to indignation by an exceptionally bitter antireligious speech by Zinoviev. In general, nowhere in the Middle or the Near East, in Persia or in Turkey, was the existing social organization suited to the adoption of communism. The Russian revolution had demonstrated that the doctrine of revolution was attractive chiefly to factory workers and a part of the intellectuals. In Persia and Turkey there were few industrial workers, and the small intellectual class had little if any political importance.

Farther east, communism met varying degrees of resistance. In India, where the British had greatly feared the penetration of insurrectionary beliefs, the strong religious feeling of the people served as an effective deterrent to the growth of the Communist idea. In China, however, Russian communism achieved greater success than it had in Asia Minor, and a substantial number of Chinese intellectuals, as well as a portion of the laboring class, accepted the belief. The left wing of the Kuomintang was sympathetic to the movement, and a little later a Chinese Communist party was formed and formally enrolled in the International.

3. Far Eastern affairs, 1920–27

In its relation with the Far East the Soviet Government faced a complicated situation, and the whole area was swept by political cross-currents which made a direct or speedy solution impossible.

For a time during the civil war Moscow had been entirely cut off from the whole of Siberia, and the region during that time had fallen under the control of the Whites and foreign interventionists. With Siberia lost and the road eastward blocked, the Soviet Government for some time was not in a position to establish direct contact with China. Japan, foremost champion of intervention in the Russian Far East, was, of course, actually a hostile power. Handicapped as she thus was, the Soviet Union was at first limited almost exclusively to issuing reassuring declarations in which she expressed her willingness to cancel all remnants of Russian imperialism such as the various concessions and extraterritorial rights which the former Russian Government had enjoyed. This attitude was in line with the policy pursued in the Near East, but it by no means represented the total Soviet effort in the Far East, which in time proved to be much more vigorous and realistic than it had been in Persia and Turkey.

Even after the defeat of Kolchak in western Siberia, the eastern end remained outside the Soviet Union. The government was unable to undertake its conquest by arms since it was entirely occupied with the Polish War and with the struggle with Wrangel in south Russia. Toward the spring of 1920 the Allied troops and the Czechoslovaks left Vladivostok, the last American withdrawing on April 1. The Japanese, however, continued their occupation of Vladivostok and the coastal area, and Ataman Semenov, their agent, maintained control of the Transbaikal region. When the Whites' retreat to the Manchurian border released a large territory which they had previously ruled, the Soviet Government decided to incorporate it in a buffer state east of Lake Baikal. Accordingly, on May 14, 1920, the Soviet recognized the Far Eastern Republic, whose capital was at Chita. Its prime minister was Krasnoshchekov (Tobelson) who, interestingly enough, had formerly been a Chicago lawyer. Immediately after its formation, the Far Eastern Republic protested against the continued presence of Japanese troops in the Maritime Province farther east and against the support the Japanese were giving to the remnants of the White forces. At the same time it called upon the Soviet Union for armed assistance, and in the autumn of 1920 Red Army troops entered Chita.

Japanese policy in Siberia, meanwhile, was vacillating and undecided. In the spring of 1921 Japan lent support to the organization of an anti-Bolshevik government in Vladivostok but insisted upon disarming the remnants of the White armies, which were to be the military forces of that government, before they were admitted to the coastal area. By the fall of 1921 there were signs that Japan was considering relinquishing her hold on Siberia. In September she opened negotiations with the Far Eastern Republic at Dairen. When these conversations broke down, they were followed by further conferences at Washington in February 1922 and at Changchun in September. Japan finally announced that she would voluntarily withdraw her troops from the mainland of Siberia by the end of October 1922. With the exception of the Japanese claim to the northern part of the Island of Sakhalin, this step effectively removed Japan from interference in Russian affairs.

Without active Japanese support the government set up at Vladivostok was incapable of resisting the Bolsheviks. The remnants of the White forces were soon evacuated to Shanghai, and Vladivostok was occupied by Soviet troops. The conquest of Siberia having been completed, the Far Eastern Republic was now of no further use to Moscow, and when, on November 13, 1922, the "National Assembly" of the Republic voted the transfer of all its powers to a revolutionary committee appointed by the Soviet Government, the Far Eastern Republic ceased to exist.

The Soviet Government formally readjusted its relations with Japan in a treaty signed on January 20, 1925. By this agreement both parties reaffirmed the terms of the Peace of Portsmouth. Japan abandoned North Sakhalin in return for a number of concessions which the Union of Socialist Soviet Republics agreed to grant her in the northern half of the island.

In its relations with China, the Soviet Government had to consider two involved and interrelated problems which it had inherited from Imperial Russia: the Chinese Eastern Railway and Mongolia. In 1915 a tripartite agreement had been concluded among China, Outer Mongolia, and Imperial Russia which had established a joint protectorate of the two powers over Mongolia. During the Russian upheaval in 1919 the Chinese Republic had decided to revise the situation by annexing Mongolia, but even this move failed to prevent the civil war in Siberia from rolling across the border. In the beginning of 1920 when a part of the Russian White armies was driven into Mongolia by the Bolsheviks, Mongolian and Chinese authorities were equally incapable of preventing the invasion. Soon afterward Soviet troops entered Mongolia to crush the last vestiges of the White forces, and a little later a Moscow-instigated uprising set up a revolutionary Mongolian Government. Shortly thereafter, on November 5, 1921, the Soviet Union concluded with the Mongolian Government a treaty of friendship in which no mention of China was made, a circumstance which provoked considerable indignation among Chinese ruling groups.

The problem of the management of the Chinese Eastern Railway was intimately bound up with the question of Sino-Russian relations. In the declaration of 1919 the Soviet Government had, of course, renounced its rights in the railway. This declaration, however, had been made at a time when Siberia was under the control of the White armies and when the Chinese Eastern was being managed by an Allied commission. The Soviet Government had then given up something which it did not actually possess. With the improvement of the Bolshevik position in Siberia in the next year, the attitude of Moscow toward the problem of the railroad altered. When Soviet troops occupied Vladivostok, the Chinese Eastern again assumed the importance it had formerly held—that of the shortest route between two portions of Russian territory. In 1922 Adolph Joffe, the Soviet representative, frankly informed the Chinese of the new Soviet view of the question. In response, the Chinese Ministry of Foreign Affairs demanded the withdrawal of Russian troops from Mongolia and the recognition of Chinese sovereignty in that region. The two countries remained adamant in their positions, and Joffe's negotiations eventually broke down in this deadlock. No agreement was concluded until 1924, when Leo Karakhan, the new Soviet representative, finally yielded on the Mongolian issue. According to Article V of this treaty the Soviet Government "recognizes that Outer Mongolia is an integral part of the Republic of China and respects China's sovereignty therein." The Soviet Union further agreed to withdraw its troops from Mongolian territory. But while the principle of Chinese sovereignty over Outer Mongolia was recognized, actually Chinese control was not re-established, and for practical purposes Mongolia remained a people's republic under Soviet protection. As for the Chinese Eastern Railway, the Soviet and China agreed to regard it as a purely commercial enterprise; the USSR recognized China's jurisdiction and police control over the territories owned by the railroad and affirmed China's right to purchase the railroad. The management of the Chinese Eastern was to be in the hands of a board of directors, half of them appointed by the Chinese Government and half by the Soviet Government, the chairman to be chosen by the Chinese. In addition to this arrangement with China, the demands of Marshal Chang Tso-lin, who was at that time dictator of Manchuria, had to be considered, and on September 30, 1924, the Soviet was able to conclude an agreement with him on substantially the same terms as that with China. Though these arrangements did much to resolve the most vexing problems of the Chinese Eastern, they did not completely clear up the situation, since the claims of the creditors of the railroad, including Japan, the United States, and the Russo-Asiatic Bank, were still outstanding.

Just when the older problems which had separated the Soviet Union on the one hand and China and Japan on the other were approaching settlement, the whole Far Eastern situation was plunged into a new crisis by the outbreak of the Chinese revolutionary movement, which was directed to a large extent against the special privileges the British and other foreigners held in China. Russians were comparatively little involved in this resentment which flared up in China. Though the Soviet had preserved its interest in the Chinese Eastern Railroad, its administration had assumed a much more moderate form, and since all the rest of Russia's exclusive rights in China had been given up, the Soviet Union was in a position to enjoy neutrality in the Chinese-British conflict. Nowhere was there any ill-feeling against Russia on the part of the Chinese.

Instead of remaining aloof from the Chinese troubles, however, the Russians eventually became involved in them. To the leaders of the International the Chinese revolution seemed to provide an opportunity to undermine the forces of the European capitalist powers, since according to Lenin's theory the main strength of international capitalism and imperialism lay in their ability to exploit the "colonial and semicolonial countries." Because China's political and economic conditions fitted this theory so perfectly, it fell to her lot to become the principal battleground of the struggle of the Communist International against European imperialism.

The great Chinese leader Sun Yat-sen, who had been in touch with Lenin and who, although he was not a Communist himself, was sympathetic to Russian communism, died in 1925. His work, however, was continued by the party which he had organized under the name of the Kuomintang. In it a labor and peasant movement was united with a nationalist movement which was led by intellectuals and students who opposed the imperialist policies of certain of the European powers. The Kuomintang also included a strong Communist wing, and while Sun Yat-sen was still alive his party had entered into close relations with the Communist International in Moscow. The Soviet Government was quite willing to support the Chinese movement and during 1925 supplied about a thousand military and political instructors as well as some $3,000,000 which was cleared through the banks of Shanghai and Canton. A prominent Communist, Borodin, was appointed adviser to the Canton Nationalist Government, which during 1925 and 1926 continued to expand its sphere of control along the coast toward Shanghai and inland toward the middle section of the Yangtze River. A dictatorship patterned after the Moscow model was introduced in the areas occupied by its armies. When the Nationalists swept into Hankow in September 1926, Soviet influence in China was rising to a high point.

This movement seemed to have been so successful that the Communist International now confidently tried to extend its activities from China to the Dutch East Indies, where an abortive Communist uprising was organized in November. During a general strike in Hankow early in January 1927 a boycott of foreign goods was proclaimed and violent anti-British demonstrations took place, a mob invading the area of the British concession on January 4. On March 22 the Nationalist forces occupied Shanghai, with the exception of the foreign concessions, and the next day Nanking was taken. The Communists were at the peak of their influence in China.

At this point internal dissension put a halt to military operations by the Nationalists. Differences between the conservative and moderate members of the Kuomintang and the Communist wing had in fact arisen as early as the autumn of 1926. By the following spring these differences had grown greater, and antagonism flared up between Chiang Kai-shek, who was then a general in the Chinese Nationalist forces, and the Soviet adviser, Borodin. On April 6 the police raided the Soviet Embassy in Peking. Documents seized there revealed the close connection between Russian diplomacy and the Communist wing of the Kuomintang and plainly established Borodin's dominating position in that party. The publication of these documents led to a full break between Chiang Kai-shek and Borodin, who then tried unsuccessfully to organize a purely Communist government in Hankow but was forced to leave on July 27, 1927.

In December Canton was seized in a Communist-aided uprising, but after three days the insurrection was put down by the Nationalist forces. It was suppressed with severity; many revolutionary leaders, among them some Russians, were executed. All over China the influence of the Communist International, which only two years before had promised so much was being relentlessly crushed.

4. *Recognition of the Soviet Union by the western powers*

While the western powers agreed to negotiate with the Soviet as early as 1922, they were for some time hesitant to grant the Soviet Government formal recognition. The Soviet leaders, on the other hand, were eager to normalize relations with the West in order to gain time for the internal reconstruction of the country. Their efforts were crowned with at least partial success after the victory of the Labor and the radical parties in the British and French elections. As early as the end of 1923 recognition of the Soviet had been included in the platform of the Labor party in England, and after that party's victory at the polls Ramsey MacDonald's cabinet voted at its first meeting on February 1, 1924, to fulfill its pledge. Within two months Italy, Norway, Austria, Greece, and Sweden had followed suit. However, the recognition granted by Great Britain was by no means unconditional and was followed by a series of prolonged negotiations. First of all, the British note accorded recognition only to those parts of the former Russian Empire which were then willing to accept Soviet authority. Second, the Soviet must recognize Russia's pre-Soviet debts. And third, it must abstain from anti-British propaganda, especially in the Orient. In April 1924 a Soviet delegation came to London to discuss the terms of the note, but after several months the negotiations broke down without having produced any results. The British continued to demand Soviet recognition of Russian debts, and the Soviet delegates countered by asking for a loan with which to begin to pay them. On August 8 an agreement was finally signed; but it was a strange document, which left unsettled almost all the important questions and agreed only that the two parties would try to reach a real agreement later.

MacDonald's unsuccessful attempts to enter into friendly relations with the Soviet resulted only in making him unpopular. On October 8 he was defeated in Parliament and was obliged to dissolve the House of Commons, setting new elections for October 29. A few days before the election English newspapers published what purported to be a secret letter written by Zinoviev and containing instructions for the preparation of a Communist uprising in England. The letter was a forgery, but its publication accomplished its purpose by arousing the indignation of the voters and thus contributing to the defeat of the Labor party. The new Conservative government canceled the agreement of August 8 but it did not withdraw the original recognition which had been accorded to the Soviet Union on February 1. This compromise in Soviet-British affairs, by which the formality of diplomatic recognition was retained, was a highly unsatisfactory arrangement which led only to the further estrangement of the two countries.

In spite of the failure of British negotiations, France followed the example of England and the course of diplomatic events in that country fell into roughly the same pattern. In May 1924 the left bloc headed by Herriot won the elections, and on October 28 the French Government extended de jure recognition to the Soviet. The question of Russian indebtedness to France remained unsolved, however, and subsequent negotiations between the two nations proved futile.

Great Britain and France were at this time particularly anxious to achieve some stability in European affairs. Since their recognition of the Soviet Union had not promoted real friendship between Russia and the West and since they still continued to distrust Communist activities, they now turned to Germany and Italy in an effort to organize European relations. An important step in this direction was taken at the Locarno conference on October 16, 1925. Through it a system of agreements was set up providing for the settlement of disputes by arbitration. Moscow, however, regarded the conference as an international attempt to "isolate" Soviet Russia and form "a united anti-Soviet front." Soviet tacticians, searching for a method of piercing this front, readily agreed upon Germany as its most vulnerable point. Although Germany had been invited to attend this conference, she had not yet attained equal membership in European diplomatic society since she had not yet been admitted into the League of Nations. It was natural for the Soviet to attempt to enter into closer relations with Germany, which, in turn, was quite willing to threaten the western powers with the possibility of a Russo-German alliance in order to hasten her admission into the League. On October 12, 1925, just before the departure of the German delegates for Locarno, Foreign Commissar Chicherin succeeded in concluding a trade agreement with Germany which, among other points, provided that Soviet Russia was to receive a loan amounting to 100,000,000 marks. On April 24, 1926, a Soviet-German political treaty was concluded in Berlin; both sides were bound to maintain friendly contact and to remain neutral if one of them should face armed attack by a third power. This was Germany's reply to the western powers for the affront she had received at the March session of the League of Nations, when she was not accepted as a member although her representatives had been summoned to Geneva. In addition to the broad terms of the treaty, a German note attached to the text specifically stated that one of the aims of the pact was to oppose anti-Soviet tendencies within the League. The treaty proved to be a skillful move for both countries; it strengthened the Soviet Union's hand in Europe and led to the admission of Germany into the League of Nations on September 7, 1926.

Following the Locarno conference, Soviet diplomacy intensified its attack on Great Britain. "Chamberlain believes he encircled us at Locarno," wrote *Pravda*, the official organ of the Communist party in Moscow. "On the contrary, we will encircle him with the masses of labor in his very home."

The labor situation in England at that time was indeed unstable. In September 1925 the Congress of English Trade Unions at Scarborough, by a vote of 2,456,000 to 1,218,000, passed a radical resolution which was opposed in principle to the development of peaceful methods of settling differences between capital and labor. In December of that year Zinoviev stated at the Fourteenth Convention of the Russian Communist Party: "A huge movement of miners is to be expected in England before May 1926. A real revolutionary labor movement is beginning in England." In a further elaboration of the Communist position, he prophesied in March 1926 that Britain was on the eve of a social catastrophe. "If the strike really begins, it will be our first task to help it, along the European and international front of industrial war." The rupture of negotiations between the English mine owners and the miners did eventually lead to a general strike which, contrary to Communist expectations, soon ended in complete failure. The miners themselves, however, remained out of the pits until the autumn of 1926 and during the whole period of the strike received support from the Soviet workers both in money and propaganda. By July this aid to the striking miners amounted to $2,225,000.

About this time the Anglo-Russian Committee of Trade Unions attempted by mediation to bring about an understanding between the Moscow leaders and the Council of English Trade Unions. These efforts were fruitless, however, for the council was not willing to accept the firmly dogmatic point of view adopted by the Moscow representatives. The Communist position was not entirely without support, however. The London Conference of the Minority of English Trade Unions on August 30, 1926, did accept the Moscow viewpoint, but the Congress of English Trade Unions meeting in Bournemouth the following September rejected it by the decisive majority of 2,416,000 votes.

The English public was, not unnaturally, considerably irritated by Communist interference in British labor affairs. And the participation of Russian Communists in a Chinese revolution which also had anti-British implications was an added source of worry for British statesmen. Finally, as a result of growing suspicions in both these groups, a break with the Soviet was decided upon. Disregarding Russian claims of diplomatic immunity, representatives of Scotland Yard on May 12, 1927, raided Soviet House, the London headquarters of both the Soviet Trade Delegation and Arcos, Ltd., the trading company for the Soviet cooperative societies. The secretary for home affairs justified the raid with the explanation that a document containing military secrets, which had been stolen from the government, had been traced to these premises. Although this particular document was not found, the police seized other papers which, in the opinion of the cabinet, amply justified the action. The Soviet Government protested in a note that the British authorities had violated the immunity granted to the Soviet Trade Delegation by the agreement of 1921. Toward the end of May the whole question was discussed in the House of Commons. Some of the documents seized were laid before the House by Prime Minister Baldwin who declared that they proved "the existence, under the direct control of the Soviet authorities, of a regular system whereby documents of a subversive character from various organizations in Russia were conveyed secretly to various persons engaged in Communist activities in this country and elsewhere."

Rupture of diplomatic relations with Soviet Russia was recommended by the ministry and approved by Parliament, and on May 27, 1927, the decision of the British Government was communicated to the Soviet chargé d'affaires in London. Baldwin made the following announcement: "I wish to state emphatically that our rupture of diplomatic relations does not in any way mean, or imply, war against Russia." The break was not followed by a serious disruption of normal commercial contact between the two nations. The usual facilities for trade were not disturbed, and after the deportation of certain employees of Arcos, Ltd., the balance of the personnel was allowed to remain and continue its work.

While the British attitude toward the Soviet Government varied thus from time to time, the policy of the United States throughout this period rested firmly on the one principle of nonrecognition. The break which had developed between Great Britain and Soviet Russia seemed a substantial argument in favor of the continuance of that position. But some financial circles in the United States, approaching the question from a different point of view, advanced reasons for resuming relations with Moscow. Trade between the United States and Russia in 1927 reached $100,000,000, twice the prewar total, and the prospects of its continued growth constituted a strong inducement to establish diplomatic contacts.

The division among American business interests on the question of Soviet recognition came to a head in the fall of 1927 when a sharp conflict arose between a group of English and a group of American interests over Soviet oil. In July the Standard Oil Company of New York and the Vacuum Oil Company, another member of the Standard group, concluded agreements covering the purchase of oil from the Soviet Naphtha Syndicate. The Standard Oil Company of New Jersey protested against these arrangements, insisting that, before any deals with the Soviet Government, former owners who had been deprived of their property rights should receive compensation. An even stronger protest was made by Sir Henry Deterding, head of Royal Dutch-Shell. At this point representatives of the Soviet Government revealed that both Standard Oil of New Jersey and Royal Dutch-Shell had been trying for some time to obtain a monopoly of the oil exported from Russia, and expressed their conviction that the resentment of these two companies arose from the refusal of the Soviet Government to grant them exclusive privileges. Deterding admitted that he had negotiated with the Soviet but asserted that he had always demanded compensation for former owners. The confusion resulting from this three-cornered dispute was finally resolved in February 1929 by an agreement drawn up between the Soviet Petroleum Trust and the Anglo-American interests. By this arrangement prices for Soviet oil were fixed low enough to enable the purchasers to build up a fund for settling the claims of former owners.

In 1927, at the end of this period, Soviet relations with the western countries were still in an unsettled state. A number of countries had formally granted full recognition to the Soviet, but their actions were frequently hardly more than gestures. In general, though the Soviet Union had made some progress toward re-entry into the world community of nations, especially in the field of trade, she was still refused the status of an equal member.

5. *Political structure of Soviet Russia*

It was largely during the period 1921–27 that the political forms and governmental mechanisms which were to prevail in the Soviet Union until 1936 took shape. In 1917 the Bolsheviks seized power under a slogan calling for the concentration of all power in the soviets, and this principle determined the general character of the new political structure of Russia. The Second All-Russian Congress of Soviets, meeting at the time of the revolution, sanctioned this new political form and itself assumed the functions of the Constituent Assembly which had actually been elected two weeks after the upheaval but was dismissed by the Bolsheviks after its first session. Acting in the capacity of a legislative assembly, the Third Congress then officially confirmed the government of the Council of People's Commissars which was headed by Lenin.

Lenin's government did not, however, hasten to define the precise political structure of the state. It had neither the time nor the inclination to present a detailed governmental system. At the time it was nearly overwhelmed with practical problems affecting the very existence of the new state which demanded immediate solution, problems involving the consolidation of Bolshevik power within the country and the conclusion of the promised peace with Russia's enemies without. It was not until the meeting of the Fifth Congress of Soviets on July 10, 1918, that a new constitution for the Russian Socialist Federative Soviet Republic (RSFSR) was adopted.

The soviet or council system written into the constitution of this first Soviet republic was the model upon which the governments of the subsequent members of the Union and of the Union itself were based. According to the provisions of this constitution, the highest agency of power was the All-Russian Congress of Soviets, a large and somewhat cumbersome elected body, which met whenever necessary but never less than once a year. The Congress of Soviets elected a Central Executive Committee in whose hands the supreme power reposed between sessions of the congress. The Executive Committee, a body of more than 300 members which met regularly, took the place of a parliament. Its members were accorded the equivalent of parliamentary immunity; they were not subject to arrest without the consent of the Presidium or the chairman of the Committee and could be tried only upon the authorization of the Committee itself or its chairman.

When the Central Executive Committee was not in session, its power in turn resided theoretically in its Presidium, which was, in effect, a collective president of the Soviet state.

In contrast to the precise limitations set upon the power of each branch of government in European and American states, no distinction was made in the constitutional power of the several higher branches of the Soviet Government. The principle of replacement applied throughout, and rights and duties passed automatically from one body to another. The Central Executive Committee had the same legislative and administrative power as the

Soviet Congress when the latter was not in session. Its Presidium was the supreme legislative and administrative branch between the meetings of the Committee. The Council of People's Commissars had the right to assume supreme authority whenever it was necessary to do so.

As the power of the Soviets extended beyond the border of Russia proper—the RSFSR—other socialist soviet republics were founded—such as the Belorussian, the Ukrainian, the Esthonian, Latvian, and Lithuanian; the latter three existed for only a short time in 1918–19 and were restored in 1940. Each of these republics was organized on the pattern of the RSFSR, and each in turn concluded an alliance with the larger state. Gradually, however, the need for a closer link between the sister republics was felt, and in December 1922 all of them issued a joint declaration of union. On July 6, 1923, the new constitution of the Union of Socialist Soviet Republics (USSR) was passed. At that time the Union consisted of the following four republics: 1) the RSFSR; 2) the Ukrainian SSR; 3) the Belorussian SSR; and 4) the Transcaucasian SFSR, which included Georgia, Armenia, and Azerbaijan. In 1924 two central Asian Soviet republics, the Uzbek and the Turkmen, were formed and accepted into the Union. Later on, three new republics were formed in central Asia, the Tadjik, Kazakh, and Kirghiz, and the Transcaucasian Federation was dissolved, each of its three parts receiving the status of a full-fledged constituent republic. As a result of these admissions, by 1929 the number of constituent republics in the Union had risen to 11.

The constitution of the USSR was basically that of the RSFSR elaborated to fit it to the needs of a wider federation. An All-Union Congress of Soviets was elected, and it in turn elected an All-Union Executive Committee composed of two chambers, the Union Soviet and the Soviet of Nationalities. The Soviet of Nationalities consisted of five representatives from each of the allied and autonomous Soviet republics and one from each of the autonomous regions of the RSFSR.

The electoral system adopted by the Soviet Union was a frank expression of the principle of the dictatorship of the proletariat. The factory workers, who constituted only about 15 per cent of the population in the early 1920's, were represented in the Congress by one deputy to 25,000 voters; the peasants, the bulk of the population, had only one deputy for every 125,000 inhabitants.* Several million people, including remnants of the bourgeois class, the gentry, the clergy, and members of the former police force, were disfranchised altogether. Members of this disfranchised group were not only denied the right to vote; they were also ineligible for civil service, were prohibited from working in factories, and their children were refused admission to college.

There were several stages of elections—for township, district, province; the members of each assembly elected a certain number of that body to represent them in the next higher body. This system worked to eliminate all opposition, for in each stage voting was by a show of hands and was thus easily controlled by the political police. The task of restraining the voters and of supervising the elections generally was at first entrusted to a force headed by the so-called Cheka (Extraordinary Commission to Combat Counter-revolution and Sabotage). In 1922, following the NEP reforms, the Cheka was replaced by the OGPU (United Department of Political Police) which was supposed to work within certain legal restrictions. The change, however, was in name only, not in policy or method.

Whatever might have been the advantages or disadvantages of the Soviet system as it was organized in 1918–23, the real power at that time lay not with the soviets but with the Communist party. Although no mention of the party was made in the constitutions either of 1918 or 1923, control of the country from top to bottom was firmly in Communist hands. The party had its branches in each of the republics of the Union; its "cells" operated wherever decisions were made—in every factory, every local soviet, every army unit. Its rule prevented the rise of opposition or conflict between either the republics of the Union or the highest bodies of the Soviet Government itself. It was the only political party allowed to exist in Soviet Russia. In those years the Soviet system was not so much a dictatorship of the proletariat as of the Communist party.

The activities of the party itself were directed by a Central Committee of about one hundred members and a smaller group of nine members called the Political Bureau (Politburo). Both of

* Since the voters constituted at that time about 50 per cent of the population in Soviet Russia, 25,000 voters corresponds to around 50,000 inhabitants.

these bodies were elected at party conventions and both had authority over party institutions throughout the Soviet Union. The membership of the party was severely restricted, and each applicant had first to pass through a rigorous trial period as a candidate before he gained admission. Training and indoctrination had as their aims both doctrinal and political preparation of the candidate for his task. He must give complete adherence to Communist philosophy and unswerving loyalty to the party. While a candidate—or a party member—might criticize minor defects in Soviet administration, he was denied any freedom of thought in a broader sense. Besides the party itself, a Communist Youth Movement, the Komsomol, was inaugurated. By 1927 there were about 2,000,-000 party members and candidates and something over a million young people enrolled in the Komsomol. These were considered the elite of the nation to whom was entrusted the creation of the new society. They had—and still have—many privileges in everyday life, but such honors and prerogatives as they enjoy are paid for in obedient and strenuous labor for the party. They are members of an organization which prides itself upon the discipline it enforces and they cannot refuse the heavy tasks of administration, propaganda, or military service which are allotted to them. The rewards for success are sometimes considerable, but the punishments for failure are equally great.

6. *Economic reconstruction and intraparty struggle*

The introduction of the NEP in 1921 was an emergency measure forced upon the party by Lenin to save the sick and sinking economy of the Soviet state. It was successful beyond the hopes of most Bolshevik leaders. Reluctant as many of the more zealous Communists must have been to admit the achievements of a program which seemed to contradict the principle upon which the new world was to be built, the beneficial results of the retreat on the economic front were almost immediately evident. In both agriculture and industry production began to recover. The area under cultivation, which by 1921 had fallen to 60,000,000 hectares, by 1923 had risen to 65,000,000 and by 1927 almost reached the 1916 level of 90,000,000. Grain collections, at the famine level of 18,000,000 tons in 1920, had increased to 37,000,000 tons in 1924 and by 1926 doubled again to produce a harvest of over 74,000,000 tons. There was a gradual increase in livestock to more than 27,000,000 horses and 55,000,000 cattle by 1926. Productivity in the various branches of industry showed similar gains. Coal production, which in 1922–23 had declined to 11,500,000 tons, rose in 1925–26 to 24,500,000 tons. During the same period the manufacture of cotton fabric shot up from 560,000,000 meters to two billion meters. Released from the suffocating restrictions of war communism, the Russian economy had started on the road to recovery.

The new stability introduced by the economic reconstruction of Russia made possible the reorganization of the currency and establishment of a stable monetary unit. The State Bank, which had been re-established in 1921, was authorized in 1922 to issue chervonets bank notes. The chervonets—equal to ten gold rubles, or about $5.00 *—was to be backed by a quarter of its value in gold, platinum, or stable foreign currency. The rest of its value was to be guaranteed by readily negotiable short-term obligations. The old paper currency was not withdrawn, however, with the issuance of the chervonets; the state treasury in fact continued to produce still more of it. Thus, for a time there were two kinds of paper money in circulation—one stable and the other continuing to fall in value. The chervonets was quoted on the exchange like pounds sterling and dollars: one chervonets was worth 117 rubles of the 1923 paper currency, and each of these rubles was in turn worth 1,000,000 rubles of any previous issue. The value of the old paper currency sank rapidly; in December 1923 the chervonets was quoted at 13,700 "1923 rubles" and in April 1924, at 500,000 "1923 rubles."

In the spring of 1924 the treasury was authorized to issue small currency notes of one, three, and five rubles. Simultaneously the State Bank announced that it would accept an unlimited amount of new currency notes in payment of all liabilities at the official rate of ten rubles to the chervonets which had been established in 1922. At the same time the printing of the old paper currency was suspended, and silver and copper coins were put in circulation. On March 17, 1924, the redemption of "1923 rubles" at the rate of 50,000 to the gold ruble was announced. The end of the circula-

* The ruble contains 17.424 dolyas of pure gold. One dolya is equal to 0.68576 grains.

tion of the old currency was set for May 10, 1924, and the final date for its redemption fixed as May 31. The withdrawal of the depreciated paper money left only chervonets, stable currency notes, and metal coins in circulation, and the consequent strengthening of the monetary system greatly increased public confidence in the government.

The introduction of the NEP was generally regarded outside the Soviet Union as the first step toward return to a capitalist economy. Indeed, had the tendencies implicit in the new policy not been carefully controlled, the reforms might well have led to that conclusion. But the Soviet Government was fully aware of the dangers (from its point of view) and made extraordinary efforts to prevent the situation from getting out of hand. In March 1922 the Eleventh Conference of the Communist Party announced that the "retreat on the economic front" must end. Nevertheless, several further concessions were later made to the NEP in connection with the reintroduction of produce exchanges and the important annual fair at Nizhni Novgorod. Toward the end of 1922, however, "the retreat" was actually brought to an end, with the exception of the currency reform which was then in progress and a few temporary measures favorable to the peasants, which were canceled by 1927. The economic system which prevailed in Russia from this time until 1927 was a hybrid plan, neither socialist nor capitalist but something between the two. It differed from a true socialist system to the extent of all the reforms instituted with the NEP; it varied from the capitalist form in that it involved government control of economic matters, especially foreign trade.

Both government-owned and private industry shared in the increased production of the period, but the relative strength of the state industries increased steadily. The tendencies are clearly shown in the figures that follow. In 1923–24 the production of government industries amounted to 2,400,000,000 gold rubles in prewar prices, while production by private industry, including foreign concessions, was about a third of that. Two years later state industries produced 5,333,000,000 rubles' worth of goods and private industry less than a quarter as much. Although production had been released from the more stringent restrictions of war communism, the Soviet Government still retained the essential direction. It continued to exercise a monopoly of foreign trade and through the Gosplan, or State Planning Commission, to shape the course of the economy for several years in advance.

The agricultural policy of the Soviet Union had two objectives: to increase the production of food material and to prevent the development of private property in landholdings. The provisions of the NEP carefully avoided reintroducing the right of ownership in small individual farms. According to the Land Code of 1922 all land belonged to the state and the peasant was merely accorded the free use of it. It was to be cultivated either by the community or by an individual, but Section 27 of the code categorically forbade the sale, purchase, mortgage, bequest, or gift of the land. The Soviet Government was in no wise committed to the support of the old commune but in general it gave less encouragement to the peasant to leave the commune and become an individual tenant than had the Stolypin legislation.

The reforms of the NEP so successfully revitalized the Soviet economy that by 1927 production in many fields had already reached the levels of 1913 and in some instances had slightly exceeded them. For example, in 1913 the value of agricultural goods produced within the territories later held by the Soviet totaled 12,790,000,000 rubles; by 1927 it had reached 12,775,000,000. Industrial production, which in 1913 was valued at 6,391,000,000 rubles, had risen by 1927 to 6,608,000,000 rubles; coal production moved from 29,000,000 metric tons to 30,000,000; oil from 9,000,- 000 to 10,000,000 metric tons; and the manufacture of cotton cloth from 2,238,000,000 meters to 2,342,000,000. The theoretical "retreat" on the economic front carried the Soviet Union well on its way to a stable economy.

Because of the inner contradictions in the NEP, a difference of opinion developed among the Soviet leaders on the best course to follow, especially after Lenin's death on January 21, 1924. For a time Lenin's spirit continued to rule over Russia. His tomb was made a Communist shrine, and Petrograd, City of Peter (the Great), was renamed Leningrad in his honor. No party orator could fail to quote from his work, and his words became the bible of communism to which his followers returned again and again for political guidance.

The task of directing the destinies of the country and the problems of guiding a world-wide organization made it necessary, however, to find a successor to Lenin—both as leader of the Communist party and as head of the Soviet Government. These duties were at first assumed by a triumvirate consisting of Kamenev, Zinoviev, and Stalin—all three Bolsheviks of long standing. Leo Kamenev, whose real name was Rosenfeld, was the least revolutionary in temper and at the same time the best educated. Gregory Zinoviev, whose name was Radomyslsky, was an insolent man without either moral principles or great ability, who had attained a leading position in the party chiefly because of his servile attitude toward Lenin. Joseph Stalin, a Georgian whose real name was Djugashvili, had already exhibited the firmness of will and undeniable organizing ability which were eventually to bring him to a dictatorial position in the Soviet Government.

Trotsky, the most prominent leader next to Lenin and most brilliant orator of the Russian revolution, was prevented by the "Triumvirate" from sharing power, and soon started an opposition movement. His policy was an amalgam in which personal motives and political principles were intricately combined. He had never been an orthodox Communist. In the revolution of 1905 and the years following it he had wavered between the Bolsheviks and the Mensheviks, in many cases making common cause with the latter. Only after the revolution of March 1917 did he finally throw in his lot with the Bolsheviks and in the months following he rose rapidly to a position of leadership. Even after the revolution, however, Trotsky often expressed views which were not approved either by Lenin or by the majority of the Communist party. That he should, after Lenin's death, become an exponent of "pure" communism was an unexpected reversal of his previous position.

Pointing out that Zinoviev and Kamenev had voted against the majority of the Central Committee of the Communist party as late as two weeks before the Bolshevik uprising, Trotsky now charged them with lacking the true revolutionary spirit. Trotsky was an able antagonist. His oratorical ability, combined with his prestige in the party, were such that the leadership was soon involved in intense debates which led to a bitter struggle for control of the party mechanism. Soon factions had arisen, and Trotsky assumed the leadership of a group, dubbed the "Trotskyites," who accused the party of bourgeois tendencies and proclaimed themselves the true followers of Lenin and the guardians of communism pure and undefiled.

As early as 1922, while Lenin was still alive, the party convention had declared that the "retreat from the economic front" was complete. By the spring of 1925, however, relations between the Soviet Government and the peasants had become so strained that a new series of compromises was necessary. Nicholas Bukharin, the chief theorist of the party and editor of *Pravda,* admitted that in spite of the NEP the effects of war communism were still evident in the village economy. The peasantry still had no confidence that their farms would be secure under the Soviet regime. Because of these difficulties the Soviet Government decided to adopt a more lenient agricultural policy which the Fourteenth Party Conference approved in the spring of 1925. Defining the party aims at that conference, Stalin said: "The chief problem now is how to rally the middle groups of peasants around labor; we have to conquer the sympathies of the middle groups of the peasants." At the same meeting the policy of providing relief for the peasantry was also strongly supported by Michael Kalinin, chairman of the Soviet Federation, and by Alexis Rykov, chairman of the council of people's commissars.

It was against this new peasant policy of the Soviet Government, conceived as a further development of the NEP, that the opposition within the Communist party centered its attack. The situation became especially dangerous for the unity of the party when two leading members of the Politburo, Zinoviev and Kamenev, made peace with Trotsky and joined the opposition. The critics excoriated the new policy as an example of the abandonment by the Soviet leaders of the principles of pure communism, and accused the Central Committee of giving relief to the richer peasants. They also charged the majority leaders with despotism in the party management and asked that the Politburo be deprived of its autocratic power. Yet in spite of this vitriolic criticism the majority of the delegates to the Fourteenth Conference of the Party in December 1925 approved the policy presented by the Central Committee.

Stalin's program had been sustained. Consequently he did not yet consider it necessary to take punitive measures against the opposition leadership but confined himself to the following warning: "The party desires unity, and will achieve it with Kamenev and Zinoviev if they wish it, without them if they do not wish it."

The victory of the Central Committee was not final. The defeated leaders, masters of the techniques of political maneuvering, tried all sorts of measures to increase their influence within the party. By 1926 they had built up their own organization which was guided by its own committee and operated its own secret printing office. In September and early October 1926 this group tried to win labor over to its side by attacking the Central Committee in meetings of the workers of various large factories in Leningrad and Moscow. However, when the workmen remained loyal to the Central Committee, the leaders admitted their failure and on October 16 drafted a petition to the Central Committee promising to cease the struggle and to work with the party majority. Stalin, however, was not ready this time to accept their statement as a bona fide recantation, and in an address before the Fifteenth Conference of the Party, held in October and November of 1926, subjected the opposition to merciless criticism. While its leaders were trying to mask their intentions with a pretense of pure Communist principles, he charged, their policy was in reality permeated with opportunism and favored the restoration of a middle-class regime. This point of view was accepted by the party conference and approved by the Central Committee.

The truce within the Communist party was not lasting. In the summer of 1927, when relations between the party majority and the opposition again became critical, Stalin decided to inflict penalties on the opposition leaders. Declaring that they were causing a split in the party and endangering the future of the Soviet system, he demanded that Trotsky and Zinoviev, as the two most active leaders, be formally excluded from its rolls. This expulsion was carried out in November 1927 by the decision of the Central Committee of the party. The purge which Stalin thus achieved secured the dominance of the majority within the party, and although it did not terminate the conflict it did assure the party an opportunity to carry out its program with a minimum of internal dissension.

7. The five-year plan: industrial revolution

The Fifteenth Convention of the All-Union Communist Party which was called in December 1927 marked the beginning of a new era in Soviet Russia. It was an event of the first magnitude not only in the development of internal party policy but also in the re-molding of the political and economic system under which the Soviet Union itself was henceforth to operate. As subsequent events were to prove, it was the decisions of the Fifteenth Convention which turned the energies of Soviet Russia away from the drive toward international revolution and concentrated them in a move-ment for internal revolution.

The immediate business of the Fifteenth Convention was the conflict which had split the Russian Communist party. From the first session it was clear that the Central Committee would triumph over the opposition. On December 18 all opposition leaders were excluded from the party and passed into a political oblivion that at the time seemed final. In January 1928 Trotsky was exiled to the city of Alma-Ata in Turkistan and early in 1929 he was de-ported from Russia to Turkey. Expressing their willingness to abandon their opposition, Kamenev and Zinoviev sought pardon from the Central Committee and thus escaped formal exile. They were assigned for a time to obscure positions in provincial towns of central Russia, and in the summer of 1928 were received back into the party.

A substantial part of the Fifteenth Convention was devoted to the problems of economic reconstruction.

The decisions eventually resulted in that total reshaping of the Soviet economy to be known as the five-year plan. The Russian people were plunged into a twin revolution—industrial and ag-rarian—which, in a sense, affected their destinies even more than the cataclysm of 1917. In some ways the new upheaval was a reversal of the usual revolutionary pattern. In contrast to the rev-olution of 1917, when the masses took active part in the move-ment, this new revolution was deliberately instigated by the gov-ernment itself. It was a violent readjustment originating above and exerting pressure downward. The earlier uprising had been chiefly destructive in nature, a clearing away of old forms to make way for new; the upheaval which began in 1927 was con-structive both in its spirit and in its purpose. But revolution it was—in scope, intent, and consequences. Remembering that with-out this period of readjustment Russia might have fallen before the German onslaught of 1941, the future historian may well consider these events the decisive turning point in modern Russian history.

The idea of a planned economy was not a new one. Indeed, all the belligerent countries had turned to such planning on a greater or lesser scale during the first World War. In Russia the conditions which had caused all countries to adopt planning continued long after the war was over and after the capitalist states were well advanced in reconstruction. The Gosplan itself had been organized in 1921 to facilitate the recovery of Russian industry both from the damage resulting from the war itself and from the destruction and disorganization of the civil war. Even before that, at Lenin's suggestion, a Commission of Electrification had been set up in 1920, but because of economic circumstances it was unable to make any substantial progress. The Marxist theoreticians were not alone in their interest in the problem of building a more efficient economy; engineers and technicians were, by their training, attracted to the possibilities of such an organization. Many plans had been suggested, but the most important and clearest blueprint for the reconstruction of Russian industry had been presented in a remarkable book written by Basil Grinevetsky, a prominent engineer of prerevolutionary training.

Grinevetsky's book, *Postwar Prospects of Russian Industry,* which was published in 1919, proposed that Russian factories and plants should be geographically adjusted to the natural resources of the country and located near the principal supplies of raw materials, in order to avoid unnecessary transportation. Basing his thesis on the practical possibilities for such a shift, Grinevetsky suggested the rapid development of two areas of great potential wealth—the Ural region and the vast territory of western Siberia which had not hitherto been sufficiently exploited. Besides its economic aspects this mammoth relocation of Russian industry involved at least one change of great military importance—the shift of productive centers far to the east out of reach of any foreign invader.

On the basis of Grinevetsky's ideas and others, the members of the Gosplan prepared the outline for the first five-year plan, which was announced early in 1928 and went into operation that autumn. The following year the quotas originally set were revised upward, and it was decided "to complete the first five-year plan in four years"—that is, between October 1, 1928, and December 31, 1932. While the plan was not fulfilled in all details, its actual achievements during this shortened period were tremendous. In four years Russia's yearly national income rose from 27 billion rubles (1926–27 price level) to 45 billion rubles in 1932. Capital invested in industry rose from 2 billion to over 9 billion rubles. On the basis of this enormous capital investment the Soviet Union was able to proceed with a vast industrial expansion.

But the over-all figures and quantitative increases did not tell the whole story. The quality of the industrial products was usually poor and the cost of production almost invariably high. Everywhere there were waste and mismanagement, due chiefly to the shortage of skilled labor, technicians, and engineers. The reserve pool of skilled workers in Russia had always been low, and after the revolution many trained engineers and technicians emigrated, reducing the supply still further. Foreign engineers were invited to supervise the building of the more important industrial plants, but they were too few to take care of all details of the work personally, and in addition they could not always be trusted by the government. Gradually, however, the labor situation improved. Every year greater numbers of engineers and technicians were graduated from Russian schools and more and more raw peasant recruits were trained in mechanical skills. Indeed, from one standpoint the very deficencies in the execution of the first five-year plan had their positive uses. While a great deal of valuable and desperately needed machinery was ruined by newly drafted peasant boys and girls who were totally unfamiliar with mechanical processes, and while much time had to be spent teaching them even the simplest tasks, the whole process amounted to a practical course of experimental education. In time millions of untrained youths had been poured into the creation of a reserve of machine-minded workers. More important, perhaps, was the fact that the traditional inertia of the Russian peasant had finally been broken, even though at a tremendous cost in lives, machinery, and money.

In spite of the almost unbelievable hardships the Russian people were called upon to bear, the government carried through its plans. It is sometimes difficult to understand how any people who had passed through the cataclysms which had descended upon Russia in 1914, 1917, and 1920–21 could have endured the privations to which they were now subjected. That the government was able to carry the reorganization to a successful conclusion was, in the main, the result of its ability to combine the efforts of several groups. The Soviet leaders were aided, of course, by the cooperation of those engineers and technicians who saw in the new system an opportunity to exploit and develop the potential wealth of the nation. They had the unflagging assistance of party members and Komsomols, who were inspired by the prospect of "building socialism in a single country," of achieving the economic independence for Russia of which they had long dreamed. Recalcitrant elements were held under a discipline that was often harsh and sometimes cruel. As a nation, the Soviet Union felt the threat of "capitalist encirclement" and was intent upon using this brief span of years to prepare for the attack which seemed imminent. The mentality of the Russian people in the early years of the first five-year plan was that of a nation going through a revolution and a war simultaneously. The Russians believed that they were battling for survival, and under those circumstances they could and did bear extremes of privation.

Sociologically, the most important result of the successive five-year plans was the transformation of Russia from a predominantly agrarian country into one 50 per cent industrialized. At the same time, this change resulted in a new relationship among the economic groups within the Soviet Union. The collectivization of agriculture did away with the class of peasants as small farmers, and the members of the collective farms (kolkhozes) and state-owned farms (sovkhozes) no longer stood apart as a separate segment of the population but became as much a part of the new society as the factory workers. The end result of this "deepening of the revolution" was a new combination of social classes which had an over-all cohesion in spite of the fact that here and there new group distinctions arose as time went on.

In retrospect, it is clear that this significant period of the first five-year plan established the basis for later successes, and in spite of all the shortcomings the essential work accomplished then laid the foundation for the further development of Russian heavy industry. But what is so plain today was then obscure both to contemporary students and to those actively engaged in the day-to-day work. Doubts and worries were continually arising, and at times during the first five-year plan even the Soviet press was gloomy or alarmed. The most disturbing feature of the new system was the uncertainty of production. Industry appeared to function in spurts and spells, and months of feverish progress were frequently succeeded by equally long periods in which production slumped and bottlenecks developed in many crucial sectors.

The first quarter of the second year of the first plan—from October through December 1929—was typical of the recurring periods in which production figures showed disquieting regressions. Indeed, in January 1930 the Soviet press was talking of serious "breaks" at various points on the economic front. For that first quarter the Donets coal basin fulfilled only 94 per cent of the program set for it, which meant that industry received 500,000 less tons of coal than had been anticipated. The smelting of pig iron in the Ural region reached only 90 per cent of the planned output, and factories of the Yugostal or southern steel trust were only slightly higher, with 92 per cent. In October 1929 Leningrad factories turned out goods valued at 172,000,000 rubles, about $86,-000,000; but the following month the output fell to 160,000,000 rubles. In general, heavy industry fell short of the quota set for it by 4 per cent, though in some factories the gap between plan and performance amounted to 10 per cent or more. Lumbering enterprises in the north of Russia fell behind by more than 25 per cent, a failure which adversely affected the balance of foreign trade, since lumber and petroleum were at that time the chief items of Soviet export.

The Soviet Government stubbornly refused to admit failure. Characteristically enough, each time a new crisis developed the government increased quotas for production rather than adjusting them to a lower level. Wherever the situation became critical, extraordinary steps were taken, such as forming "shock brigades" of best workers or sending in battalions of Komsomol members to prevent a breakdown in production. Because of the government's single-minded insistence upon its objective and its complete disregard of the hardships and privations which the population was called upon to endure, the general rise in production at the end of the first five-year plan was impressive enough. In the period 1928–32 the yearly output of coal had increased from 35,000,000 to 64,000,000 tons; of oil from 11,000,000 tons to 22,000,000; of pig iron from 3,000,000 to 6,000,000. In 1928 less than 1,000 automobiles and only slightly more than 1,000 tractors had been produced, but in 1932, 24,000 automobiles and 50,000 tractors rolled from Soviet plants.

It is worth calling special attention to the most ambitious undertaking of the first five-year plan, the construction of the Dnieper River Power Station. An American engineer, Hugh L. Cooper, was engaged to design and supervise the construction of this enormous project, which was completed in October 1932. Its annual output soon reached 2.7 billion kilowatt-hours, and its ultimate capacity was estimated as 558,000 kilowatts. This industrial unit, the pride of Soviet industry and a memorial to Russian-American cooperation, was to stand hardly ten years: during the retreat of the Red Army in the first summer of the German war it was blown up by the Russians themselves.

Of even more importance to Russian industrial development was the huge steel mill erected at Magnitogorsk in the Ural area, which was completed in the course of the second plan. Several automobile, tractor, and agricultural machinery plants at Gorky (Nizhni Novgorod), Kharkov, Rostov, Stalingrad, and Cheliabinsk were completed during this period. To the list of important milestones in industrial development reached at this time must be added the construction of the oil pipe line from Grozny in the northern Caucasus to the Black Sea port of Tuapse, and the building of the vital Turkistan-Siberian railroad.

The first five-year plan was not, however, entirely a story of successes. There were many disturbing factors, especially the continued problem of the poor quality of goods, the low rate of production, and, as a result, the high unit cost. The government, of course, recognized these deficiencies, but there was little that could be done about them at first. Only gradually, during the second and the beginning of the third five-year plan, was the situation to improve, and even in 1940–41 the legacy of the haste with which the first five-year plan had been started and fulfilled was still being felt.

A serious problem was the "fluidity" of labor, which resulted in a continual and hampering turnover among workers in the plants. Because of poor housing conditions and, at times, because of food shortages at the sites of new construction projects, workers were always on the move in search of better accommodations and better conditions elsewhere. As a result, almost no factory except those situated in long-established industrial regions like Leningrad and Moscow had a permanent staff of skilled workers on whom it could rely.

The normal length of the work day was seven hours until 1940, when it was increased to eight because of the pressure of external danger. The comparatively low real wages which prevailed during the first five-year plan were compensated for, in part at least, by a comprehensive system of unemployment and health insurance. Nevertheless, though the average annual wage expressed in monetary terms rose from 703 rubles in 1928 to 1,427 rubles in 1932, because of a corresponding increase in prices the average worker was able to obtain less food and manufactured goods for his wages. Both real and monetary wages, however, improved during the sceond five-year plan. Largely as a result of the spread of a system of piecework and bonuses, certain groups of workers reached a comparatively high standard of living by 1940. This new piecework system, begun in 1935 by a coal miner named Alexis Stakhanov, soon came to be called Stakhanovism. By the institution of "brigades" of workers who were trained in a method of teamwork based on strict division of labor, the Stakhanovites were able to produce much more rapidly than was possible when individuals worked alone, and in time their methods were applied in various forms to many branches of industry. Economists outside the Soviet Union were apt to observe that the Stakhanovite spirit of competition and "speed-up" was essentially more suited to the capitalist system of industrial management than to the socialist scheme. Whatever its faults or virtues may have been, it is clear now that in spite of certain technical deficiencies Stakhanovism contributed to the general upward trend in Russia's production standards and enabled her to engage the capitalist countries on a more equal basis.

8. *The five-year plan: collectivization of agriculture*

The agrarian revolution which accompanied the industrial one involved total readjustment of both the social and economic foundations of the NEP agricultural system. The central fact of the new policy was the shift from the millions of small farms—the traditional basic division of the Russian peasant economy—to the enormous socialized agricultural units called kolkhozes. A social movement of such vast proportions is inevitably attended with great hardships even when scores of years are allowed for the readjustment. In Russia, compressed as it was within the space of a few years, it resulted in a social convulsion.

To rebuild agriculture according to the new plan, it was first necessary to raze the existing farm structure. The work of demolition was carried out ruthlessly and with a total disregard of the rights, needs, or desires of the recalcitrant peasants. The richer peasants, the kulaks, suffered especially. As their farms were liquidated and their possessions confiscated, they must have remembered the days of the revolution when they themselves were looting and dividing the estates of the landed gentry; the wheel had turned and they were suffering the same fate hardly twelve years after their own hour of triumph. Entirely aside from the violence with which it was accomplished, from the economic point of view the "dekulakization" ordered by the government seemed at the time an act of cruel madness. The kulaks were the most efficient group among the whole peasant class, and to knock out this mainstay of Russian agriculture seemed the certain way to bring the whole structure down in ruins. To be sure, the intent was to move the structure to a new foundation and to replace these uncertain props with new and massive pillars. But the kulaks were eliminated before the collectives were either numerous or strong enough to support the whole national weight. As a result agriculture was plunged once more into chaos, and as production slumped to new lows the threat of starvation again hung over the whole country.

The new Soviet agricultural program was not a scheme completely prepared beforehand and applied at once all along the line. It was the result of a number of experiments which were carried out over a considerable time. Several plans of collectivization ranging from a free cooperative association of farmers to a strict kolkhoz economy were offered. It was proposed at first to introduce collectivization gradually, using either persuasion or comparatively mild coercive methods such as a gradual increase of taxes levied against the wealthier group of peasants.

The final decision to prepare for a rigorous and thoroughgoing collectivization of rural life in Russia came on January 6, 1930. The whole process was to be completed in the region of the lower and middle Volga and in the northern Caucasus by the autumn of

1930 or at the latest by the spring of 1931. In other regions it was to be put into effect by the autumn of 1931 or the spring of 1932. The huge collective farms were to be operated by the use of an enormous amount of mechanical equipment—tractors, harvesting combines, and other labor-saving machinery. Hence their productivity was expected to be markedly higher than that of individual peasant enterprises. Here again, however, the element of timing defeated the theoretical schedule, for the supply of tractors and combines did not match the growth of the collectives. Until 1930 there were not more than 25,000 tractors in the whole RSFSR, and because of the lack of repair shops and the scarcity of experienced operators nearly half of these were chronically in poor condition. The shortage of harvesting combines was even more acute. Although two immense factories capable of turning out 25,000 combines a year had been planned, in 1930 there were almost no such machines actually in operation anywhere in Russia. Few of the new farms could be furnished with the equipment which alone could justify their organization from the economic point of view. For most of them "columns of tractors" remained only a slogan, and the great majority had to be content to try to operate vast tracts of land with "horse and ox columns," the traditional equipment of the peasant farmer.

But still the policy of collectivization continued unabated, spurred on by the slogan, "Attack the rich peasants." Actually, of course, the burden fell upon all classes among the peasantry, and in 1928 and particularly in 1929 all except the very poorest peasants were crushed by excessive taxation and numerous direct levies. Life in the villages reverted to the conditions which had existed in 1918 under the committees of the poor. In the course of 1929 all the more or less well-to-do farm enterprises were disrupted. Because of the penalties attached to ownership of property, thousands of peasants who owned only two or three cows, for instance, chose to butcher and eat one of them rather than be listed among the richer classes. Many others were unable to endure the hardships, and numbers of these, particularly those whose ancestors had settled in Russia in the 18th or early 19th centuries, emigrated to escape liquidation. A considerable number of Swedes and a good part of the German Mennonites were among the groups who escaped in this way. But escape was out of the question for the majority of peasants, and as they fought against the new government policy to preserve their way of life, civil strife again flared up in nearly every village. Agents of the government were frequently attacked and sometimes killed by groups of the rich and middle peasants, and the buildings of the kolkhozes and sovkhozes were never safe from the torches of vengeful farmers. The government's response was a relentless reign of terror in which all known or suspected instigators of discontent were shot. The fall of 1929 was a bloody one in the villages, and before it was over hundreds of the richer peasants had been executed.

In January 1930 the government decided to exterminate the whole class of richer peasants. To end their participation in running village affairs, the old village soviets were dismissed and replaced by new ones consisting solely of poor peasants. The homes of the well-to-do peasants were given to hired workers or homeless peasants, and all their herds and property were turned over to the collective farms. The expropriated peasants were forbidden to join the collectives and, stripped of their possessions and without means of support, they were soon reduced to poverty. While the dekulakization was in full swing, hundreds of thousands of these men with their families were deported to the north and the east where they were placed in concentration camps and set to work, under the supervision of the OGPU, at lumbering, canal digging, railroad building, and other heavy labor.

Since no peasant who possessed even a comparatively small amount of property could be sure that he would not eventually be classed as a kulak and treated accordingly, dissatisfaction and then despair swept through the villages. Some of the well to do peasants had sons serving in the Red Army and it was possibly these soldiers who by their protests were first able to secure some abatement in the violence against the peasants. The government made a few concessions; and deported kulaks who had children in the army, in civil service, or in the factories were returned to their villages—if they were still alive. In March 1930 *Pravda* published Stalin's famous letter on "Dizziness from Success," in which he expressed disapproval of the more violent methods of achieving collectivization and put the blame for their use on the excessive zeal of local party members. The peasants were now allowed to join the kolkhozes or not, as they wished, and those who had been forced into the collectives were permitted to leave. At first there was a concerted rush to return to the old system of individual farming, and for a brief period kolkhoz membership decreased rapidly. In time, however, most of the peasants who had left the collective returned, bringing with them many others who had not previously been members. The acceptance of the collectivized system was in part the result of the repeal of the more extreme regulations which had applied to the kolkhoz members—such as the one providing that all property, including even a peasant's few chickens, must be held in common ownership. In addition, the individual farmers who still remained outside of the new system were subjected to increasingly prohibitive taxes. Lastly, the general conditions of life in the collectives were greatly improved by the provision of more and more machinery for their operation. By 1933 the number of tractors actually in use reached the impressive total of 200,000, and 25,000 combines were in operation in the grain districts. For the first time service stations for the repair and maintenance of agricultural machinery became generally available, and in the south, in particular, great numbers of "machine-tractor stations" were set up to serve the neighboring kolkhozes.

By 1932 the government had won the battle of the kolkhozes—in the sense that the peasants had at last reluctantly accepted the new regime. In its broader aspects, however, the struggle was far from ended, for the advantages which had been claimed for collectivization had still to be proved. Indeed, for a considerable time the government's success appeared to be a Pyrrhic victory, since in winning it the backbone of the Russian agricultural system seemed to have been destroyed. The first reports showed a catastrophic decrease in production, particularly in the raising of livestock. The famine of 1930–31 followed close on the heels of the chaos which existed everywhere in agriculture, and in Ukraine in particular the suffering and starvation reached a scale which almost passes human comprehension.

Even this disaster did not permanently cripple the Soviet economy. Within a comparatively few years the tremendous innate vitality of the Russian people once more asserted itself in the reestablishment of a working agricultural and industrial system. Then, after a respite of less than a decade and at the moment when they seemed on the verge of achieving at least a taste of comfort, the Russian people—kolkhozes, factories, and all—were engulfed in a new and even more terrible catastrophe, another World War.

9. The Communist International and Soviet foreign policy

The industrial revolution which had been inaugurated by the decisions of the Fifteenth Convention of the Communist Party, and especially the agricultural revolution which accompanied it, were watched by foreign observers with anxiety and distrust. The revival of militant communism which had been revealed in the new domestic policy of the Soviet Government was expected to be reflected in Soviet foreign affairs as well, and a new outburst of the activities of the Communist International seemed at the time almost inevitable. Actually, however, the internal revolution in the Soviet Union had a reverse effect on Soviet diplomacy. Instead of intensifying the revolutionary trends which had existed in Russia's foreign policy, the shift of emphasis in internal affairs was accompanied by a turn away from rabid internationalism and the growth of a kind of nationalism. For some time, however, the new orientation was cloaked in the traditionally turgid Communist phraseology which has so frequently misled foreign observers. Basically, the slogan of "building socialism in a single country" signaled the abandonment—for a time at least—of any far-reaching plans for promoting revolution abroad. The tremendous task of national reconstruction absorbed all the energies of the new revolutionary state and served to concentrate interest almost completely on domestic problems. If Leninism was the adaptation of Marxism to the era of international conflicts, Stalinism amounted to the nationalization of the revolution.

Since the Communist party in reality controlled the government of Russia, the party decisions actually determined the subsequent course of Soviet foreign policy. In one of its aspects, as we know, the Communist party of the Soviet Union was a member of the Communist International and the leading group within that body. Its decisions, therefore, could not but substantially affect the policies of the International. The Sixth Congress of the Communist International was held in Moscow from July 17 to August 28, 1928. While it had been originally intended that congresses should be called yearly, four years had elapsed since the fifth congress had met—a delay which was partly explained by the struggle that had been raging within the Communist party of the Soviet Union after the death of Lenin. The rise of the Trotskyite opposition in 1926 and the subsequent exclusion from the ranks of the party of both Trotsky and Zinoviev had also had serious repercussions in revolutionary circles the world over. The struggle between Stalinists and Trotskyites was repeated in most of the national Communist parties. The calling of the sixth congress, therefore, had been possible only after a great deal of maneuvering and countermaneuvering within the various parties. The Moscow leaders had been faced with the extremely delicate task of securing for themselves a majority of the delegates without applying drastic measures that might result in the total breaking up of at least some of the foreign Communist groups. By 1928 it was clear that they had been successful in achieving their ends, but it was also plain that, as a result, the Communist International as a whole had lost its independence, and its non-Russian groups—which theoretically at least had enjoyed complete equality with the Russian branch—had now become satellites of the Communist party of the Soviet Union.

While the domestic problems of the Soviet Union had been monopolizing the attention of the Russian Communist party, it had lost much of its original enthusiasm for internationalism. Consequently, from this time forward the Moscow leaders looked upon the Communist International as an instrument for advancing the national interests of the Soviet Union. The International became actually a subsidiary organization of the Moscow government, charged with assisting the latter in the development of its foreign policy.

The resolutions passed by the sixth congress, emphasized the growing danger of another world war which, in the opinion of many of the delegates, was likely to assume the form of an attack on the Soviet Union either by one of the capitalist powers or by a coalition. Working on this assumption, the congress was concerned with what tactics the laboring masses should employ to avert the supposedly imminent war. After long debate it passed a resolution outlining labor's threefold task. First, the proletariat of each capitalist country must continue the struggle against its own government. Second, the proletariat of the whole world must unite to defend the Soviet Union against the imperialism of its enemies. Lastly, it must promote the revolutionary movement in the colonies subject to the great powers.

In order to carry out the first of these tasks the proletariat of each country must immediately establish a secret organization of workers' "cells," especially in heavy industry and in industry concerned with the manufacture of war materials. At the outbreak of war these groups were to adopt a "defeatist program" and by vigorous propaganda to attempt to turn the imperialist war between states into a class war between the proletariat and the middle class within each capitalist country. A special resolution carrying instructions for the development of the "revolutionary movement in colonial and semicolonial countries" was passed by the congress. The essential core of the program proposed by the International was the development of Communist parties throughout the world and especially in the colonial and semicolonial countries of Asia, as well as in Latin America.

The program thus outlined by the sixth congress was not calculated to allay the fears of nonsocialist governments throughout the world. Indeed, from the capitalist standpoint it appeared to be alarmingly revolutionary. From the point of view of the Muscovite leaders, however, it was not intended as an aggressive policy but was meant chiefly as a measure of self-defense. Whatever the intentions may have been and however they may have been misunderstood in other countries, it is clear now that in all probability they did more harm than good to the Soviet Union.

While the Soviet cultivated the radical parties abroad for whatever help they might someday be, the main efforts of Russian officials were directed toward the prevention of war by diplomatic means. The Soviet Foreign Office characteristically approached the problem from several angles. At first Soviet spokesmen—particularly Maxim Litvinov, as vice commissar and then as commissar for foreign affairs—stressed the necessity for total disarmament and offered a number of formulas designed to expedite such a movement. When all such suggestions failed, they attempted to secure peace by collective security to be based upon a series of multilateral nonaggression treaties.

The logical instrument for the development of interlocking pacts was, of course, the League of Nations, but this organization did not at once commend itself to the Soviet Union. For a number of years Russian diplomats had pretended to ignore the League which, in the eyes of the Communists, had been designed merely to promote the political and economic objectives of the capitalist powers. As late as February 1926 the Soviet Union refused to participate in the Geneva conference on disarmament on the ground that she had had no relations with the Swiss Government since the assassination of the Soviet envoy, Vorovsky, on Swiss territory on May 10, 1923. A little later, however, in spite of the fact that she was not yet a member of the League, the Soviet Union decided to attempt to use the League machinery in the international situation. On November 1, 1927, Moscow let it be known that the Soviet Union was prepared to participate in the disarmament discussions and that, in the words of Soviet Prime Minister Rykov, "the Soviet Union was ready to propose, support, and carry out the most complete program of disarmament for the whole world simultaneously." The draft presented to the Geneva conference by the Soviet delegates provided for the immediate demobilization of half of all existing armed forces, the corresponding destruction of arms and munitions, and the cessation of all military and naval construction. Demobilization and destruction were to continue progressively for four years until only such forces as were necessary for police and frontier guards remained. National navies were to be supplanted by an international maritime police force, and control and enforcement of the entire disarmament agreement were to be entrusted to a permanent international commission to be formed on the basis of national equality and with the participation of all working classes.

A long speech explaining and elaborating upon the various aspects of the proposal was delivered on March 19, 1928, by the Soviet delegate, Litvinov. German and Turkish representatives voiced general approval of the Soviet program, but Lord Cushendun strongly opposed the suggestion in the following remarks: "There are two kinds of war, and where there are two kinds of war, there are two kinds of peace. There are international and civil wars, and of these the civil is more horrible. It is a fair question to ask whether the Soviet Government sets its face against civil war as resolutely as against international war. . . . For years past the whole basis for the Soviet world policy has been to produce armed insurrection amounting to civil war in every country where they can exercise influence. If that is so, before we proceed much further some assurance should be given to us by the Soviet that in that respect there is to be a complete change in policy. We ought to be told whether the Soviets now have decided no longer to interfere in the affairs of other nations." The chairman of the American delegation, Hugh S. Gibson, joined in disapproving the Soviet proposal, explaining that the government of the United States supported instead a system based upon a multilateral compact renouncing war as an instrument of national policy.

On August 27, 1928, the Kellogg Pact for the Renunciation of War was signed at Paris by representatives of fifteen states, including the British Dominions. Soviet Russia, however, was not invited to participate as an original signatory power, nor was she included in the list of states which later received the note of the United States on the subject of adherence to the general pact. Since there were no diplomatic relations between the United States and the Soviet Union, France, acting as an intermediary, formally approached the Soviet, which signified, on August 31, 1928, acceptance of the pact.

In addition to general concern with the problem of the preservation of peace, the Soviet Union at this time was working toward an immediate and more specific goal—the restoration of diplomatic relations with Great Britain which had been severed by the latter in 1927. The prospects were brightened in 1929 by the return of a Labor government to power. However, since Prime Minister MacDonald did not command an absolute majority in the House of Commons, he had to proceed cautiously in the matter of Soviet relations and indeed in many difficult political problems. Negotiations got under way slowly. In July 1929 correspondence between the two governments was begun. Again the British suggested that Russian debts and guarantees that the Soviet would refrain from anti-British propaganda be discussed as part of the whole question of recognition; again the Soviet Government insisted that the question of the resumption of relations should be discussed separately, without preliminary discussions relating to special problems.

When the House of Commons debated the proposed agreement in November 1929 Arthur Henderson, secretary for foreign affairs,

declared his belief that the Soviet assurances it contained about re-
fraining from propaganda applied to the activities of the Communist International. Although the Conservatives in Commons
voted against the measure—and the House of Lords later repudiated it—the agreement nevertheless received the support of the
majority in Commons which was necessary to ratify it. As its envoy
to London the Soviet Government appointed Sokolnikov, chairman
of the Soviet Petroleum Trust. Sokolnikov, whose real name was
Brilliant, had been a member of the party since before the revolution; although he had at one time belonged to the opposition headed
by Trotsky, he later renounced these views, achieved a responsible
place in Soviet councils, and as head of the Petroleum Trust was
responsible for the conclusion of the agreement with English oil
interests which had been signed in February 1929. On December
20, 1929, he presented his credentials, and also exchanged formal
assurances with Henderson that both governments would in the
future abstain from agitation against each other.

Relations between the Soviet Union and the United States failed
to improve in this period in spite of the fact that Moscow obviously hoped to establish closer contacts. If anything, Secretary of
State Stimson's attempted mediation of the dispute which had
arisen at this time between Russia and China, and Litvinov's blunt
rebuff, had widened the breach between the two countries. The
Soviet Government endeavored energetically to extend commercial
relations with the United States. In connection with the launching
of the first five-year plan and the program for industrializing
Russia, a number of contracts had been assigned to American firms
for constructing or equipping factories in the Soviet Union, and a
sizable group of American engineers had been hired to work in
Russia as experts and consultants. The volume of trade continued
to rise during this period and in 1929 reached the round sum of
$155,000,000. But although trade relations proceeded on a mutually
satisfactory basis, diplomatic relations with the United States remained in a state of suspension.

10. *Far Eastern affairs, 1929–32*

Meanwhile there came a period of crises in the Far East. Once
again the troubles had their origin in the circumstances surrounding
the ownership and operation of the Chinese Eastern Railway. The

agreement providing for joint operation of the railroad which had been negotiated in 1924 between the Soviet Government and the military governor of Manchuria, Marshal Chang Tso-Lin, had from the first functioned under difficulties. Relations between the Soviet and Marshal Chang were complicated by his undisguised animosity toward the Russian system, and his son, Chang Hsueh-liang, who succeeded him, was scarcely better disposed toward the Bolsheviks than his father had been. The Chinese authorities— both the Nanking government and Marshal Chang Hsueh-liang —suspected the Soviet of a desire to interfere in the internal affairs of China at the first favorable opportunity.

At length, information that the Soviet Government was providing funds for General Feng Yu-hsiang, who was suspected of conspiring against Nanking, led the Chinese authorities to raid the Soviet consulate in Harbin on May 27, 1929. The results were similar to those obtained in the various other raids on Soviet property. No documents implicating Feng were discovered, but others were found which contained evidence of Communist propaganda by Soviet agents in Manchuria. Since such propaganda was in violation of the agreement of 1924, the Chinese felt justified in abrogating the treaty altogether. On July 10, 1929, they arrested more than a hundred Soviet civil servants in Harbin, among them the general manager of the Chinese Eastern, and deported them to Russia; this left the administration of the railway entirely in Chinese hands. In addition, all institutions of the Soviet trade unions in Manchuria were closed, since they were suspected of being the principal instruments of Bolshevik propaganda.

Within a few days diplomatic relations were broken between Moscow and Nanking. When it became apparent that war was imminent, international diplomatic bodies began hastily to consider how to prevent hostilities. Under Article XI of its covenant, the League of Nations had a formal right to take the dispute under advisement since China was a member. Practically, however, it was clear that intervention by the League would be ineffective, and so another approach was attempted. Both Soviet Russia and China had signed the Kellogg Pact of Paris, and Secretary Stimson considered that he would be justified under the circumstances in calling the attention of both governments to the moral obligations they had assumed as signatories of that agreement. Since no diplomatic relations existed between the United States and the Soviet Union, however, the note—which had the support of both Great Britain and France—had to be delivered to the Soviet Government by an intermediary, Briand, the French minister of foreign affairs. The Soviet and China both responded curtly that they were aware of their obligations and that they had no desire for war. The Soviet Government, however, also announced that it would conduct negotiations only after China had agreed to the return of the expelled Soviet employees to their positions; and since the Chinese adhered to their stand the Manchurian crisis remained dangerously explosive. Both parties, in fact, began preparations for war. This uncertain situation continued for several months, punctuated from time to time by border skirmishes in which, it is worth noting, companies of White Russians recruited from the refugees who had settled in Manchuria during the Russian civil war took part on the Chinese side.

The Soviet Government assembled in Siberia a military force organized as the so-called special Far Eastern Army, but it may be presumed that from the very beginning of the dispute the Russians had depended upon a recurrence of internal strife in China and so had not wished to carry affairs at once to the stage of war. These expectations of Chinese internal difficulties were soon justified: in October a series of clashes began between troops loyal to Nanking and the armies of the generals who had refused allegiance to the central government. The leading role among the opposition was played by General Feng, who had established contact with the radical wing of the Kuomintang. But in spite of the military and political embarrassments which resulted from this internal dissension, neither Nanking nor the military governor of Manchuria was willing to accept the demands of the Soviet Union.

On November 17 Soviet troops began to advance into Manchuria from both the east and west ends of the Chinese Eastern Railway, and the Chinese fell back in disorder on both fronts. Red Army soldiers occupied the town of Hailar and pressed on in the direction of Harbin. In several localities in their advance they wreaked vengeance on Russian émigrés who had settled in Manchuria. Defeated decisively, Chang Hsueh-liang was compelled to satisfy the Russian demands, and on December 3 a protocol was signed on behalf of the Soviet Government and China.

While the invasion of Manchuria was actually in progress another attempt was being made to deal with the conflict through international diplomatic channels. On November 28 Secretary Stimson addressed to the governments of Great Britain, France, Germany, Italy, and Japan a note proposing joint diplomatic intervention to maintain the Kellogg Pact and to prevent war. The note he eventually dispatched to China and Russia bore the signatures of fourteen of the fifty-three signatories of the Kellogg Pact.

Litvinov, acting Soviet commissar for foreign affairs, responded on December 3 with a biting protest against Secretary Stimson's interference. He contended that Soviet Russia had taken military action only for purposes of self-defense, and further that the Stimson note, which had been sent at a moment when peace negotiations were already under way, conveyed the impression that Stimson wished to influence the negotiations, a desire which could not be regarded as a friendly act. As Stimson took no further steps, the incident was closed. In the meantime conferences between the Soviet Government and the Mukden authorities were continued, and on December 22, 1929, an agreement was signed providing for the return of the Chinese Eastern to the status which had prevailed before the conflict.

Soon after the Far Eastern situation appeared to have reached at least temporary stability, a new series of important events occurred in Manchuria which completely overshadowed the skirmishes of 1929. Japan, having completed the preparation of her grandiose plans for establishing the "Greater Asia Co-prosperity Sphere," now began the conquest of Manchuria as the first step toward attaining her ambitions. Paradoxically, it appears to have been the Russian venture of 1929 which demonstrated to Japan her precarious position in this area and encouraged her to move at this time. Working cautiously toward her objective by seizing the coveted territory piece by piece, she first occupied only southern Manchuria—an area, incidentally, which in 1907 had been recognized by Imperial Russia as within the Japanese sphere of influence. The principal protest came not from Russia but from China, which considered that her rights of sovereignty had been violated. In the League of Nations, of which both China and Japan were members at the time, there was a flurry of excitement which culminated in futility with the holding of a few meetings, the delivery of several speeches, and the appointment of committees of investigation.

When no effective action was initiated either by the League or by any of the individual powers, Japan took her second step by occupying in the spring of 1932 the northern part of Manchuria. This area included the city of Harbin, a great part of whose population was Russian—both Red and White. Some of the anti-Bolsheviks welcomed the arrival of the Japanese and offered their services in the event of a war against the Soviet Union. However, Japan contented herself for the time being with installing a puppet government in Manchuria—or Manchukuo, as the country was now renamed.

Viewed from almost any standpoint, the occupation of northern Manchuria was a threat to Russia's Asiatic interests. In 1907 Japan had specifically recognized this area as lying within the Russian sphere of influence. Entirely aside from the question of historical precedent and diplomatic commitment, however, it was clear that the presence of Japanese troops so near to the vital Chinese Eastern Railway threatened the military position of the Soviet Union in the Far East and endangered Russian commercial relations throughout the whole area. The Japanese action was a challenge which demanded an immediate decision from Moscow. If the Soviet Union were to preserve even the remnants of her control over the Chinese Eastern, she must protest strenuously and, if diplomatic means failed, fight to protect her rights. But Russia neither desired a full-scale war nor was prepared for one. She declined to risk her position in a struggle for Asian hegemony; she took no action to forestall Japanese advances, and a few years later agreed to sell her share in the Chinese Eastern Railway to Manchukuo.

Although the Soviet Government was forced to adopt a position of outward acquiescence in the occupation of Manchuria, the lesson of Japan's venture in northern Asia was neither overlooked nor forgotten in Moscow. The whole episode inaugurated an era of instability in international affairs.

CHAPTER 15

THE SOVIET UNION IN THE 1930's

1. *The rise of Hitler and its impact on Soviet foreign policy*

WHILE the results of the first five-year plan were in the main satisfactory, and in not a few fields even better than had been anticipated, the economic reconstruction of the Soviet Union as a whole was, in 1933, far from complete. In the industrial sphere, many of the most essential factory units had already been built but many more were either only under construction or still in the blueprint stage. While these gaps existed, the whole industrial structure lacked stability and cohesion. The railroad network, vitally important to any industrial nation and particularly to a vast country such as Russia, was still entirely inadequate to the requirements of an expanding economy. The reorganized agricultural system was in such a chaotic state that even in 1933 the government could not be certain collectivization was a workable principle or would yield adequate returns within a reasonable length of time. The people as a whole were depressed by the severe and continuous privations by which they had to pay for the fulfillment of the plan, and in spite of the wholesale deportation of kulaks—or perhaps precisely because of it—the loyalty of the peasant masses was especially doubtful.

Keeping the nation out of war had been the central objective of Soviet foreign policy ever since the beginning of the NEP, and the Russians now redoubled their efforts to avoid and prevent war. Most Soviet leaders realized that Russia dared not become involved in a war, and that any attack against her by a major power was likely to result in an economic breakdown and perhaps even in serious peasant revolts. Because they were aware of the essential weakness of Russia's position, Soviet leaders had cautiously

avoided conflict with Japan in 1932, and for several years thereafter their main energies were to be devoted to avoiding every
danger of war from any quarter. The resumption of relations with
Great Britain had to some extent allayed the fears of an attack
from that direction, but the diplomatic coolness which continued on
both sides was not conducive to the growth of understanding or
confidence. Under the circumstances, the Soviet sought security
through her new European alliances. Friendship with Germany,
with whom they had first been able to come to terms, continued
to be regarded by the Russians as their best insurance of peace in
a threatening and unsettled world.

Hitler's rise to power in 1933 and the subsequent nazification of
Germany destroyed the cornerstone of the security framework
which the Soviet Union had labored long to build. Nor was Russia
the only nation caught unawares by the destruction of democratic
Germany. The ominous implications of Hitler's victory and the
passing of the Weimar Republic were nowhere recognized at first
—not in Great Britain or in the United States, or even in those
European states most intimately acquainted with the turns of continental politics. Few people outside of Germany had read *Mein
Kampf* and most of those who had were unable to accept it seriously. Finally, in some conservative circles in both Great Britain
and France there was a lingering belief and hope that Hitler's ag-
gressiveness might someday be diverted toward the east against
the Soviet Union.

The Soviet leaders themselves were watchful of events in Germany but at first were not greatly alarmed. In the first place, until
Hitler had consolidated his position in the purge of 1934 they did
not consider that the Nazi government was firmly in the saddle.
For some time Russian leaders continued to cherish hope that the
new German Government would prove to be realistic enough to
continue Russo-German relations which had proved mutually
beneficial. The conclusion of the nonaggression pact between Germany and Poland in 1934 finally made them realize the menace
of Nazi Germany. It was clear to them that nothing good could be
expected from a rapprochement between Hitler, who did not conceal his intention of eventually trying to seize Ukraine, and Pilsud-
ski, who had already tried and might at any time be expected to
repeat the attempt.

The rise of the Nazis to power in Europe and the danger revealed in the Far Eastern crisis of 1932 were responsible, directly and indirectly, for the very considerable improvement of relations between the Soviet Union and the western world during this time. On November 17, 1933, the long-delayed de jure recognition was granted by the United States to the Soviet Government. This was but the first of a series of events which greatly improved Russia's position. The general betterment of her relations in Europe was, to a large extent, due to the efforts of Dr. Eduard Beneš, then minister of foreign affairs in Czechoslovakia, who contributed much to Russia's reappearance as a full-fledged member of the community of nations. In June 1934 two of the three members of the Little Entente—Czechoslovakia and Rumania—recognized the Soviet Government, and in September of the same year the Soviet joined the League of Nations, being granted a permanent seat on the council.

This appeared to have prepared the ground for a further rapprochement between the Soviet Union on one hand and France and Czechoslovakia on the other. On May 2, 1935, a treaty of mutual assistance was signed between France and the Soviet Union. Its provisions were worded so as to place the agreement within the framework of the League of Nations. Referring to the League covenant, each country pledged the other aid and assistance in the event of "an unprovoked attack on the part of a European state," a reference which obviously applied to Germany. Two weeks later a similar treaty was signed by the Soviet Union and Czechoslovakia. In this case, it was understood that Russia was obligated to come to the assistance of the smaller state only in the event that France had acted first to fulfill the terms of her treaty with Czechoslovakia. It may be assumed that by such an arrangement France hoped to obtain some insurance against rash action on the part of the Soviet Union. The attitude of mistrust exhibited by France in itself did not augur well for the solidity of the Franco-Russian pact. It later became even more apparent that the French Government was not solidly behind the treaty, principally because influential French conservatives were reluctant to see any effective association with Moscow which might strengthen the radicals.

The Soviet Union, on the other hand, took pains to solidify the treaty. Evidence of the Soviet attitude was provided in the adoption of an enabling amendment to the draft of the new constitution which was then being prepared. According to this amendment, which was incorporated as part of the constitution of 1936, the Presidium of the Supreme Soviet was authorized, in the intervals between sessions of the Supreme Soviet, to proclaim a state of war not only "in the event of armed attack on the USSR" but "whenever necessary to fulfill international treaty obligations concerning mutual defense against aggression." At the same time the policy of the Communist International was adjusted to the new world situation. The Seventh Congress of the Comintern which met at Moscow in July and August of 1935—the last ever held—recommended the establishment of a "united fighting front of the working class" which was to be open to all, irrespective of the political organization to which they might belong—Communist, socialist, or Labor party. The "united front" which was thus launched was to become an important part of Russia's drive to prevent the victory of the growing "fascist" * menace.

2. The assassination of Kirov and the first Trotskyite trial

The second five-year plan, which was officially inaugurated on January 1, 1933, was even more ambitious than the first. The annual gross output of Soviet industry, which by 1932 had reached 43 billion rubles (calculated on the 1926–27 price index), was to be expanded to 93 billion rubles by 1937, the last year of the second plan. Under the new program it was proposed to unify and consolidate the production of newly constructed industrial units and to continue the upward drive by building a series of mammoth new factories in the various industrial centers being developed throughout the nation. The railroad system was, at the same time, to be expanded to keep pace with the increasing burden it was required to bear. Recognizing that hardships arising from the shortage of consumer goods had greatly hampered the progress of the first five-year plan, Soviet planners now decided to lay particular emphasis on light industry. Plans which would largely have alleviated the distress of the preceding years were incorporated in the new direc-

* In Soviet terminology the term "fascist" is applied not only to Italy but to Germany as well—in fact to any brand of totalitarianism similar to either fascism or nazism.

tives; but before the revisions of policy could have any substantial effect the balance between heavy and light industry was once more upset by the ominous trend of events in the international sphere. The Soviet Union was forced again to concentrate on heavy industry in order to build up her military potential. But even though she had to abandon some of the program looking toward satisfaction of the people's wants, the production of consumer goods nevertheless continued to increase during this period.

A number of vitally important industrial projects were completed and put into operation during the first two years of the second five-year plan. Outstanding among these were the Magnitogorsk plant, the Kramatorsk heavy machinery plant, and the Cheliabinsk tractor factory. As railway transportation rose, showing a 10 per cent increase in carloadings for 1934 over 1933, several new lines such as that between Moscow and the Donets basin were laid down. A step of great importance to the economy of the whole country was the completion of the Baltic-White Sea Canal in 1933. The whole period was characterized by the enormous amount of building everywhere under way. Perhaps the best known of these projects was the Moscow subway, the first to be built in Russia.

The critical condition in agriculture was eased somewhat at the beginning of the second plan. A vast amount of capital was poured into the collectives which were constantly being expanded and equipped for more efficient production. In 1933–34 alone agricultural investments totaled 5 billion rubles, most of which was spent on machinery and equipment. The extraordinary efforts previously put forth by the government to bolster the agrarian structure began to show results. The annual yield of grain crops in both 1933 and 1934 totaled more than 89,000,000 metric tons as compared to slightly more than 80,000,000 tons in 1913. The livestock situation continued to be troublesome. The number of horses continued to decline—though not at the previous catastrophic rate—but the general food situation was improved somewhat by an increase in hog production. With the mechanization and collectivization of farming, thousands of peasants were released for work in factories and the pool of skilled labor available to industry was rapidly augmented. On the whole, the morale of the Russian people was improving. Better fed, stirred by sweeping industrial achievements of great national significance, the people caught the spirit of growth and expansion which was being cultivated by the government.

While Soviet leaders were wary of relinquishing control over the social organizations and the productive machinery of the country, some moderation in the harshness of the dictatorship now seemed possible. Since the passing of Zinoviev and Trotsky from the political scene, a group of men had risen to positions of prominence in both the party and the government who were more interested in the practical administration of the new system than in the abstract theories from which it had arisen. Typical of the new type of leadership was Serge Kirov, a member of the Politburo and the chairman of the Leningrad Soviet, who took the lead in urging the democratization of Soviet governmental machinery and the abolition of class distinctions. In order to achieve these reforms a number of revisions in the constitution were necessary. A significant step in this direction was taken on July 10, 1934, when the OGPU was abolished as an independent institution, its juridical functions partly transferred to regular courts and its administrative functions to the People's Commissariat of Internal Affairs (NKVD). In the light of subsequent events it is easy to argue that the reform was in the name rather than in the essence of the institution of political police, but it might have been originally meant as a real improvement. At the same time, several other reforms were contemplated, and the work of drafting them was begun.

The new tendencies, however, were secretly opposed by certain groups in Russia. The results of underground agitation became increasingly apparent in the numerous acts of sabotage which occurred in industrial plants in various parts of the country, and though these acts were usually attributed officially to foreign spies, it was known that in part, at least, they were committed by members of the opposition groups. On December 1 Kirov was assassinated by a former member of the Komsomol. Numerous arrests were made and the circle gradually widened to include such prominent figures as Kamenev and Zinoviev. Aided by the confessions extorted from some of the accused, the prosecution drew a picture of a far-reaching conspiracy of the Trotskyite, Zinovievite, and rightist groups, which were found to have established working alliances between themselves. Also, some of the confessions revealed that a number of opposition leaders had been in touch with "certain foreign powers," by which the world understood Germany, Poland, and Japan.

The preliminary examination of the accused lasted for almost two years, and it was not until August 1936 that Kamenev, Zinoviev, and eleven other leaders of the alleged conspiracy were at last put on public trial by the Military Collegium of the Supreme Court. The prosecution claimed that in addition to Kirov several other Soviet leaders, including Stalin, had been slated for assassination. The campaign of political murders, according to the government, was only part of a larger scheme worked out in detail by the plotters. The central objective behind the "direct action" campaign was alleged to have been the overthrow of Stalin's government and the destruction of both the five-year plan and the kolkhoz system. Private property was to be re-established among the peasantry and a semicapitalist regime introduced in industry and commerce. Furthermore, the prosecution claimed that the conspirators had entered into an agreement with Germany, promising the latter control of Ukraine in return for her support of the new government which was to be established in Russia after the fall of Stalin. After a spectacular trial which was fully reported in the world press, the court found most of the accused guilty, and several, including Kamenev and Zinoviev, were sentenced to death.

The trial and the executions evoked strong reactions in public feeling abroad, especially in the United States. Trotsky vehemently denied any connection between himself and his avowed followers in Russia, and American Socialists and Trotskyites conducted a violent campaign of protest against the trial. The attitude expressed by the dissident Leftists at this time raises a number of interesting questions. Throughout the early years of the revolution, when only bourgeois conspirators were being executed by the Soviet Government, no charges of cruelty had ever been made by either the Socialists or the Trotskyites. Both Trotsky and Zinoviev had supported the Red Terror during the period in which they were in power and, indeed, had approved extreme measures including even the taking of hostages. Only when they themselves were the objects of these violent repressive tactics did they find it necessary to protest against them.

In the grim atmosphere of fear, abjection, and utter confusion created by the trial thousands of people were arrested on the flimsiest of evidence and many of them hastily executed. When a prominent member of the opposition had been arrested, his friends, associates, and even his secretaries frequently fell under suspicion and in some cases were imprisoned or deported to Siberia.

3. The constitution of 1936

In spite of the political conflict which raged within the party during the period from 1934 to 1936, Kirov's reforms were not altogether abandoned; they were, in fact, largely embodied in the draft of the new constitution which was completed at the beginning of 1936. After the revisions had been codified, they were submitted to the party membership and to meetings of factory workers for criticism and discussion. Modified somewhat as a result of these discussions, they were officially approved in December 1936. Several fundamental changes in the basic constitutional law of the Soviet Union were introduced in the new code. Both the constitution of the RSFSR, which had been adopted in 1918 and revised in 1925, and the 1923 constitution of the Soviet Union had been frankly instruments of the "dictatorship of the proletariat": as has been mentioned, by their provisions factory workers were given much stronger representation in Soviet assemblies than were the peasants, and the bourgeoisie as a class were disfranchised altogether. Now the structure of the state was considerably altered. The All-Union Congress of Soviets had originally been designated as the supreme authority. The congress proved to be an unwieldy body whose chief function was to elect the Central Executive Committee, which roughly paralleled the parliament of democratic countries. By the provisions of the new constitution the All-Union Congress was abolished, and the "parliament," now called the Supreme Soviet, was elected directly by all citizens of the nation. The new Supreme Soviet, like the former Central Executive Committee, consisted of two chambers: the Union Soviet and the Soviet of Nationalities. The former body was elected by the nation according to electoral areas and on the basis of one deputy for every 300,000 of the population; the latter was elected by republics and national areas on the basis of twenty-five deputies from each union republic, eleven from each autonomous republic, five from each autonomous region, and one from each national area. The secret ballot was substituted for the show of hands which had previously been the normal procedure in all elections. The right of nominating a candidate was reserved to "public organizations and associations of the working people: Communist party organizations, and cultural societies."

There was no fundamental change in the organization of the Union itself. Each of the union republics retained, theoretically, its right to secede from the Union. Prior to 1940 there had been eleven union republics: the Russian, Ukrainian, Belorussian, Azerbaijan, Georgian, Armenian, Turkmen, Uzbek, Tajik, Kazakh, and Kirghiz. To these in 1940 were added five more: the three Baltic republics (Estonia, Latvia, and Lithuania), the Karelo-Finnish, and the Moldavian.

Neither in the first constitution of the Soviet Union nor in the earlier constitutions of any of the single Soviet republics had there been any mention of the Communist party. For the first time in Soviet constitutional history the party was, so to speak, legalized in 1936. In one of the provisions which has just been mentioned it was frankly given the right, together with other "public organizations," to nominate candidates for election. In addition, in the section on "Fundamental Rights and Duties of Citizens" there appeared the following statement: "The most active and politically most conscious citizens in the ranks of the working class and other sections of the toilers unite in the Communist party of the Soviet Union, which is the vanguard of the working people in their struggle to strengthen and develop the socialist system, and is the leading core of all organizations of the working people, both public and state."

In a sense the legalization of the Communist party was an indication of the fact that it had become a permanent national institution. A tendency to emphasize the close cooperation between party and nonparty men now became evident, and it was a bloc of these groups which won—or rather was allowed to win—in the first elections held under the new constitution. The new orientation of the party may be explained as another result of the struggle which had been going on between the Stalinist and the Trotskyite groups within the party, and which had culminated in the elimination of such influential Old Bolsheviks as Kamenev and Zinoviev. The clash had been bitter and prolonged, and had eventually resolved itself into a split between the new nationalist generation of Communists and the older proponents of internationalism. This struggle within what had formerly been a solid and united party weakened both partisan groups, and the nationalist wing now bid for nonparty support in an effort to strengthen its position.

The new constitution was hailed both by the Russians themselves and by Stalinist sympathizers in other countries as "the most democratic constitution in the world." Foreign critics pointed out that it was in reality a legal fiction of no importance whatsoever, since the dictatorial regime of the Communist party had not been abolished. Merely introducing the secret ballot did not make the elections comparable to those customarily held in democratic countries; there was only one ticket and that was made up exclusively of candidates nominated and sponsored by "public organizations." Although the nominees were widely discussed both in the press and in public meetings, the deputies were invariably elected by almost unanimous vote. While the guarantees which the constitution provided for the rights of individual citizens may seem to an outsider to be of little value, under the circumstances they were actually of considerable importance to the remnants of the old disfranchised classes such as the deported kulaks and clergy, whose children were now admitted to schools and for the first time became eligible for positions of any kind both in civil service and in industry.

Simultaneously with the constitutional reform, the Soviet judiciary was reorganized. According to such evidence as is available, the Soviet courts function efficiently in both civil litigation and trials of ordinary criminals. Most political offenses and crimes are subject to the authority not—or not alone—of the regular courts, but of the NKVD (whose former authority is now divided between two institutions, the Ministry of Internal Affairs and the Ministry of State Security). The punishment, in most cases, is confinement to the labor camps, for terms varying from three to twenty-five years. While forced labor as a general principle of state organization was abrogated in 1921, it was continued as a measure of punishment of both political offenders and plain criminals. After the trials of the late 1930's the population of the labor camps grew steadily. The number of the inmates is not known since no comprehensive statistics on the subject have ever been published by the government. Private estimates vary greatly. On the basis of an analysis of general population statistics of the Soviet Union Professor Timasheff arrived at the figure of 2,000,000, and Kulischer at 5,000,000.* While the primary purpose of confinement to the camps was to suppress any actual or potential political opposition to the regime, the reservoir of forced labor thus formed was also used for various economic enterprises, such as building canals and railroads in north Russia and Siberia, as well as mining gold in the Far East. According to the reports of former camp inmates published abroad, conditions of life and work in some of the camps were immeasurably hard, especially for political prisoners.

4. Troubles: international and domestic, 1935–38

After the Japanese occupation of Manchuria in 1932 and Hitler's rise to power in 1933, the international political situation became each year more tense, more explosive, and more delicately balanced. At a time when armed clashes—trials of strength for the coming death grapple—were becoming more frequent throughout the world, the Soviet Union continued trying to improve its position in Europe and Asia. It cannot be said that Russian policy was merely appeasement or that it was entirely passive and evasive. It was, indeed, a combination of several methods applied in various ways in different situations.

As always the problem was complicated for the Russians, for they were exposed to danger in both of the principle storm centers, Asia and Europe. To begin with the Far East: In 1935 the Soviet Government had agreed to sell to the Japanese-sponsored Manchukuo Government the Soviet half interest in the Chinese Eastern Railway for the rather modest price of 170,000,000 yen, the yen at that time being quoted at 28 12 cents. Upon the outbreak of the "China Incident" two years later, on July 7, 1937, and during the subsequent invasion of China by the Japanese, the Soviet officially abstained from intervention in the Sino-Japanese struggle. Unofficially, however, the Soviet Union aided China both with material and with military instructors and advisers who were sent to work with the defending armies. The situation was made additionally difficult by the fact that since 1927 the Chiang Kai-shek government had been at bitter odds with the Communists and had

* N. S. Timasheff, "The Postwar Population of the Soviet Union," *The American Journal of Sociology,* 54 (September 1948), 150. E. M. Kulischer, "Russian Manpower," *Foreign Affairs* (October, 1952), p. 77.

harried what remained of the movement from province to province in an attempt to crush it. Nevertheless, a nucleus of the Chinese Communist army was still in existence at the time of the Japanese invasion, and the amount of Russian aid which the beleaguered Chinese could expect depended to a large extent on the degree of cooperation which could be instituted between the Communists and other political groups in China. When a temporary understanding had been worked out on this question, unofficial Soviet aid was extended to some degree to both Chiang's army and the Communist army, although the bulk of the aid quite naturally went to the left groups.

Even before she embarked upon the Chinese venture, Japan had signed the Anti-Comintern Pact with Germany and Italy in November 1936. It is safe to accept this action as presumptive evidence that at that time the Japanese intended to turn their forces against Russia as soon as China was conquered. However, in spite of a series of resounding Japanese victories, months passed and China's resistance remained unbroken. Unable to conclude the China Incident, Japan was faced with the necessity of preparing for an attack against Russia even though her armies were still heavily committed along a winding and elastic front in Asia. By 1938 considerable Japanese forces had been concentrated in Manchuria, and Nipponese secret agents were busy in Mongolia, in Sinkiang, and in the Soviet Union itself. Still not in a sufficiently favorable position to attempt an all-out war against Russia, the Japanese on several occasions chose to test the strength of Russian defenses by various border incidents. Several clashes of this kind occurred during 1938, and the next year a full-scale battle was fought between Russian and Japanese troops on the border between Manchuria and Mongolia. In reality an undeclared war at that time existed between the two satellite states, with Russia and Japan each assisting her respective ally. The results of the test proved disappointing to the Japanese, for their forces were thrown back with heavy losses. The Russians, however, were not encouraged by the success of this one encounter to allow the incident to develop into a war. They were determined not to become involved in any conflict which they could avoid, particularly in the Far East, since it had already become plain to them that the immediate danger now lay upon their western frontiers.

In the west the delicate political equilibrium which had existed for a number of years was at last destroyed by Italy's Ethiopian venture in 1935. Encouraged by the success of fascism in Africa, Spanish rightists under the leadership of General Francisco Franco revolted against the Republican government of Spain on July 17, 1936. Public opinion in the democratic countries had not been greatly aroused by the fate of a remote and little known African country, but war on the European continent was a matter of direct concern to all. France, already confronted by powerful totalitarian nations on two borders, was especially affected by the turn of events beyond the Pyrenees.

Although the USSR was geographically remote from Spain, politically she was considerably closer than the democracies. Litvinov, the spokesman for Moscow in foreign affairs, had always insisted that peace was indivisible and that war anywhere in the world threatened the security of all peoples. Moreover, the Spanish Communist party threw its support to the Republican government and immediately appealed to the Executive Committee of the Comintern—that is, to Moscow—for help.

It was decided to engage in direct action of a limited nature; and Soviet "volunteers," military equipment, and other supplies were dispatched to Spain. Although the Soviet Union did more to assist the Loyalist cause in Spain than any other European government, its intervention in Spanish affairs was limited to half measures, and under the pressure of inimical public opinion in France and Great Britain the help that was originally offered was gradually withdrawn. Thus, because of the failure of the democratic countries to reach any basic understanding on the issue, Franco was eventually allowed to win (the Spanish Civil War dragged on well into 1939), and his victory considerably increased the prestige of both Germany and Italy.

The failure of Russian intervention in Spain, the deterioration of Russian relations with France and Great Britain, and the ominous ascendancy of fascism and nazism in Europe and Africa made the Soviet Government apprehensive about the repercussions these events might have at home. The Soviet leaders' fear and concern were evidenced by the great purge of 1937–38. In January 1937 several members of the so-called "Trotskyite Center," including Piatakov, Radek, and Sokolnikov, were tried for participation in a

plot to overthrow the Soviet Government and for alleged contacts
with Germany, Poland, and Japan. Of the important political figures tried, Radek alone escaped with a sentence of ten years in
prison; most of the others were executed. In March 1938 still another mammoth public trial took place, that of the "bloc of rightists and Trotskyites," in which Bukharin, Rykov, and Iagoda, the
former chief of the OGPU, stood among the accused. Here again
most of the defendants were eventually condemned to death.

It was Radek who during his testimony first hinted at the existence of a conspiracy in the Red Army under the leadership of Marshal Tukhachevsky. Soon afterward Tukhachevsky and a number
of other prominent army leaders, most of them civil war veterans,
were arrested, tried by court martial, and promptly executed.

Abroad the purge was almost universally interpreted as a sign
of inner weakness in the Soviet Government and even as an indication that the Communist regime was beginning to disintegrate.
There was also a new outburst of public indignation against Russia both in Europe and in America; Stalin was accused of taking
revenge on his personal enemies under pretext of guarding the integrity of the state. The confessions of the condemned men were
credited by comparatively few, and it was believed that they had
been made under threat of torture or as a result of a breakdown
after months of duress.

5. *Economic progress, 1935–38*

In spite of political turmoil and party intrigues and in spite of the
purges and executions which struck down many of the guiding figures of the revolution during those five fateful and significant years
from 1934 to 1939, Soviet efforts to industrialize the nation were
pressed forward with unabated vigor. Many industrial projects
begun earlier were put into operation with the completion of the
second five-year plan, and still others were launched during the
third plan, which was inaugurated toward the close of this period.
At the very beginning of the period the Seventeenth Convention
of the Communist Party, meeting in January and February 1934,
recommended a number of revisions designed to speed up the
second plan, which had just entered its second year. This revised
plan, which was approved by the Central Executive Committee and
the Council of People's Commissars of the Soviet Union in 1934,

called for increased productivity of labor, reduction in unit costs, improvement in the quality of goods produced, and greater mechanization, particularly in heavy industry. In order to increase the output of consumer goods it was also decided to decentralize the administration of light industry by reorganizing a part of it on a regional instead of a national basis, and placing the major responsibility upon local administrators. The geographical redistribution of heavy industry was also speeded up. More effort than ever before was made to develop the Ural and Siberian industrial bases, both in order to exploit the natural resources of these vastly wealthy industrial regions and in order to shift at least part of Russia's military industries to the east out of reach of potential invaders.

A number of huge industrial combinations were built or further developed during the second plan, of which the so-called Ural-Kuznetsk *combinat* was perhaps the most important. The development of mining and the erection of metallurgical plants in the Ural area had already made substantial progress under the first plan, when the huge Magnitogorsk project was begun and brought into partial operation in 1934. As early as at the Sixteenth Convention of the Communist Party in 1932 it had been decided to pool the iron resources of the Ural area and the coal resources of the Kuznetsk basin in western Siberia. Since the distance between these two points is more than 1,200 miles, it was decided to transport coal from the latter region to the former by rail and, in order to use the freight cars to fullest capacity, to load them with iron ore for the return trip. In spite of the magnitude of the task thus laid down, the plan was in time put into operation and worked well for several years. A little later, however, huge new coal deposits were discovered in northern Kazakhstan, which was much nearer to the Ural area, and when the exploitation of this new field had got under way the Ural projects became independent of the Kuznetsk basin. In the meantime, metallurgical plants had already been begun in the Kuznetsk region, and a number of important single plants producing tractors, automobiles, locomotives, turbogenerators, and other machinery were completed in various cities on both sides of the Volga—in Moscow, Kharkov, Stalingrad, Gorky, Ufa, and Sverdlovsk.

As the international situation grew more and more threatening, the importance of the Ural and Siberian industrial bases for defense became increasingly clear, and by the time the third five-year plan was launched in 1938 the government had decided to accelerate still more the development of industry in the east.

Until this time most of the Soviet oil industry had been concentrated in the Caucasus—an area which was vulnerable to attack from either the northwest, through Ukraine, or the south through Iran and Turkey. The Soviet Government therefore considered it most fortunate when new oil deposits were discovered between the Volga and the Urals. Feverish work was immediately begun to develop this new area, soon nicknamed "the Second Baku," and as early as 1939 a number of oil wells were already in operation.

The amount of increase in the output of Soviet heavy industry may be seen in Table 1.

TABLE 1

Industry	Unit	1932	1938
Coal	million tons	64	132
Oil	million tons	22	32
Pig Iron	million tons	6	14
Steel	million tons	6	18
Automobiles	thousands	23	211
Tractors	thousands	50	176
Machinery	billion rubles (1926–27 price level)	18	33
Chemicals	billion rubles (1926–27 price level)	2	6

In light industry (Table 2) the progress was less spectacular. The troubled international situation had compelled Soviet leaders to concentrate the national effort on producing arms and munitions and on developing those industries which either were essential for defense or might readily be converted to war uses.

A parallel expansion was also taking place in communications. The construction of the Moscow-Volga Canal in a sense made Moscow a seaport, and ranks as one of the most important engineering undertakings of the period. Considerable railroad building was under way, the most ambitious project being the construction of a second trunk line to the Far East, skirting the northern shore of

Lake Baikal in the direction of the Sea of Okhotsk. This important addition to the transportation system, however, was still incomplete at the time of the beginning of the German war. Generally speaking, the railroad network expanded rather slowly. Railway trackage, which had totaled slightly more than 58,000 kilometers in 1913, reached 83,000 in 1932, and by 1940 had climbed to 100,-000. The carrying capacity of the railways, however, expanded much more rapidly than the mileage. While in 1931 only 132,000,-000 tons had been transported by rail, the figure had risen by 1932 to 260,000,000, and by 1940 to 553,000,000.

TABLE 2

Industry	Unit	1932	1938
Cotton textiles	million meters	2,694	3,491
Woolen textiles	million meters	88	114
Footwear	million pairs	94	213
Paper	thousand tons	479	834
Sugar (granulated)	thousand tons	828	2,530

The progress of agriculture was directly affected by the steady increase in the production of tractors and agricultural machinery at home and in imports from abroad, chiefly from the United States. By the end of the second five-year plan more than 6,000 machine-tractor stations serving collectivized agriculture had been organized in the main farming districts of the Soviet Union—in Ukraine, the north Caucasus, and western Siberia. At the same time, the number of tractors operated by the stations increased from 7,000 in 1930 to 454,000 in 1941, and harvesting combines from 3,000 in 1932 to 125,000 in 1939. In addition to the technical service which the machine-tractor stations provided to agriculture, they performed an almost equally important economic and sociological function as links between industry and agriculture, and as training centers in which young men and women were made familiar with new mechanical processes.

Originally, two types of socialized agriculture had been tested by the government—sovkhozes (state farms) and kolkhozes (collective farms). The second of these two became by all odds the more important. By 1939 there were about 4,000 sovkhozes in the Soviet Union controlling something more than 12,000,000 hectares of arable land; 242,000 kolkhozes included more than 117,000,000 hectares. As a leftover from the period of the NEP there remained 1,300,000 individual farmers who still continued to cultivate privately used land, although its area had shrunk to less than a million hectares. At first there had been considerable confusion about the internal organization of the kolkhozes; two different plans had been put into operation simultaneously, the one providing for strict collectivization and the other for a looser association. By the end of 1934 an intermediate form which included some elements from both of the original plans had become the prevailing type, and in 1935 a revised code for the kolkhozes, called the Stalin Code, was promulgated. Presumably this new system of organization was in part the result of the advice given by Kirov. Each kolkhoz received a charter or deed for the land in its possession, and although the land still legally belonged to the state it was expressly provided that the farms should remain permanently in the control of each kolkhoz. Thus the members of the more prosperous collectives were assured that the fruits of their common labor would be theirs alone, and would not be used for the benefit of other less efficient groups.

In addition, the members were granted certain new rights within the collective. Each member was now permitted a small plot of land, varying from one quarter to one hectare in size, for his personal use, and the products of such plots could be disposed of by the holder for his own profit. Each member was also to share in the collective profit of the kolkhoz according to the amount of work he had contributed. All collectives were bound to sell a certain quota of grain and other products to the government at fixed prices, and to pay the machine-tractor stations, usually in grain, for their services. They were free to dispose of the balance on the open market.

Though the economic reconstruction of Russia was not completed by 1939, some stability had undoubtedly been achieved by the new regime. The demand for clothing and other consumer goods still greatly exceeded production, but the situation was decidedly on the upgrade. The abolition of ration books for bread and other food products in 1935 and for manufactured articles in 1936 was a characteristic sign of the basic improvement in the standard of living.

6. *The Munich Pact*

The purges of 1937–38 seriously under-mined the international prestige of the Soviet. It became possible to urge the diplomatic isolation of Moscow on two grounds: it was first argued that any contact with the terroristic Soviet Government was an offense against political morality, and, since realistic politicians were frequently not to be swayed by moral considerations alone, it was simultaneously suggested that, as the Soviet was obviously weak and racked by dissension, any agreement with it was likely to be useless. Though Litvinov continued to present the Soviet position at Geneva, Russia's political and military reputation had been so thoroughly blackened in the world press that the Soviet Union entered the fateful year 1938 with hardly one firm friend in the community of nations.

On March 10, 1938, Hitler's troops marched into Austria. From more than one point of view this week-end enterprise was a master stroke. At the time there seemed to be little evidence to indicate that the Austrian people themselves did not want to join the Third Reich, and although the union of two Germanic peoples had previously been opposed by the major European powers, it now began to seem a natural and almost inevitable event.

The reshuffling of power in central Europe rapidly brought on the hour when the validity of the Franco-Czechoslovak alliance was to be tested. Torn by inner political dissension, disheartened by her failure to meet the threat which had arisen in Spain, and still distrustful of the aims of the Soviet Union, France now turned to Great Britain for advice. In England the policy of appeasement was at its height, although from time to time Chamberlain was forced by the pressure of liberal groups to make some slight demonstration of anti-Nazi feeling. Certain of the British conservatives hated the Soviet more intensely than they feared Hitler, and to them the ideal policy was one which diverted Hitler's attention toward the east and thus allowed them to hope for relative quiet in Europe. Unfortunately, later events were to prove that although Hitler was indeed planning war against Russia, he meant first to round out his possessions in central Europe. Nevertheless, he had enough cunning to move cautiously, preferring to take what he wanted piece by piece and applying wherever possible the policy of "infiltration," which he had laid down in *Mein Kampf*, before risking outright invasion. Had he attacked Czechoslovakia as a whole immediately after the annexation of Austria, it is probable that even Chamberlain would have been forced to let France honor her Czech alliance. Since this must have been perfectly clear to Hitler, he chose to achieve his purpose by manufacturing the Sudeten problem. It was then possible for him to obtain in due time the Czech "Maginot Line" along Bohemia's northern boundary and reduce Czechoslovakia to a defenseless "rump" state without firing a single shot.

When the Czechs protested Hitler's threat to their sovereignty, the British sent to Prague a special mission headed by Lord Runciman who spent considerable time exploring conditions and preparing recommendations on the possibilities of a compromise. That they agreed to this method proved unfortunate for the Czechs for, psychologically at least, it made the subsequent Munich Pact almost inevitable. It now became possible to put the blame for the explosive situation on the uncompromising attitude of the Czechs toward minority groups, and both the British and French quickly agreed that under the circumstances it would be foolish to fight to "keep the Sudeten Germans within Czechoslovakia against their will," as the situation was summed up in appeasement circles. Even so, the Czechs continued to object and in September 1938 war began to appear unavoidable. Fearful that the desired compromise might not materialize, both the British and French approached the Russians to inquire what they meant to do in the event of an open conflict. The Soviet Union gave the impression it intended to fight. Litvinov stated the case plainly in the League of Nations, and in addition Russia took the opportunity to warn Poland to keep her hands off Czechoslovakia should Hitler decide to attack. Although French opinion was divided on the question and confusion prevailed in diplomatic circles, until mid-September the French press continued to insist that France would honor her word. At this point Chamberlain decided to go to Godesberg to confer with Hitler. The weak and insecure anti-Nazi front which had been built in Europe seemed about to collapse completely. Since Russia was obligated to intervene only in the event that France honored her agreement, President Beneš of Czechoslovakia approached the Soviet Government through its ambassador in Prague, Aleksandrovsky, asking whether Russia would support Czechoslovakia even if France refused. Once more the answer was affirmative, but by the time it was received the Czech cabinet had already agreed to entrust the fate of Czechoslovakia to Great Britain and France. At the suggestion of Mussolini, four statesmen representing Great Britain, France, Germany, and Italy (Chamberlain, Daladier, Hitler, and Mussolini) met in Munich to settle the problem. Not only was Russia not invited to participate but she was not even informed beforehand of the impending conference. Quietly and almost casually, the fate of Czechoslovakia was sealed by four men who late on the night of October 1 decided to hand over to Hitler the Sudeten province and the Little Maginot Line which was the Czechs' only defense barrier.

7. The Soviet-German Nonaggression Pact

The Munich Pact alarmed and dismayed the Russian leadership. It appeared to them an open rapprochement between the western democracies and Germany and her satellites—an agreement which could only mean that the Nazis were to be given a free hand in the east. Soviet relations with France and Great Britain at their best had never been cordial, but with the signing of the Munich agreement Soviet leaders lost what little confidence they had had in the sincerity and ultimate purposes of the democracies. It was evident that had Hitler at that time struck directly at Russia he would have encountered little if any opposition from France or Britain.

Hitler's new ambitions, however, proved to be too extreme even for Chamberlain. While it is true that when Hitler invaded Prague on March 14, 1939, he was allowed to overrun the Czech state without opposition from any of the western powers, it is also true that from that day onward Great Britain began to prepare for war. The preparations, however, proceeded in leisurely fashion, and even at that late date the British Government appeared to have no realistic estimate of the danger, no accurate notion of the forces involved, and, above all, no conception of the absolute necessity for an immediate and binding agreement with the Soviet Union.

On April 8, 1939, Litvinov resigned as commissar of foreign affairs, and his portfolio was taken over by the premier (chairman of the Council of People's Commissars), Viacheslav Molotov. The meaning of the change should have been obvious to anyone who troubled to think about the matter, for Litvinov for years had been closely associated with the policy of collective security. His resignation was open notice to the world that the Soviet Government no longer expected the common action which Litvinov had so long advocated, and was now determined to free itself of previous commitments in order to follow the course it deemed best. Strangely enough, however, the implications of the event were not at the time fully grasped by either the British or the French. The German appraisal of the situation was much more correct. There it was understood that since Chamberlain had chosen to play the role of appeaser in the west at the expense of Russia, Stalin was now prepared to play the same game in reverse. Nevertheless, Stalin did not immediately close the door to negotiations with the democracies; on April 17 Molotov proposed to the British and French ambassadors in Moscow the formation of a triple alliance against German aggression. The French representatives were willing to accept the Russian proposal, but London demonstrated no interest. On May 31 in a speech before the Supreme Soviet Molotov repeated the offer, and this time—again under pressure from left and Labor groups—Chamberlain agreed to send a special envoy to discuss the situation in Moscow. Instead of assuming the duty himself or assigning it to an important representative of the British Government, he sent William Strang, a man who then held no high official position and moreover was not given sufficient latitude or authority. The negotiations instituted by Strang in Moscow dragged along for weeks without achieving appreciable results. The Russians insisted that both Poland and the Baltic countries be guaranteed against indirect as well as direct aggression. The British were prepared to speak only of direct attack. Though this may well seem a minor technicality, it proved to be the point on which the negotiations broke down. The Russians were concerned about the possibility of German "infiltration" into one or more of the Baltic countries, and wished to be protected by Allied guarantees to the border states against the piecemeal dismemberment suffered by Czechoslovakia. The British position on the matter was fixed: they were reluctant to give such a guarantee for fear Russia would then be in a position to determine by herself under what circumstances Britain would be obligated to go to war.

Unable to make any headway in the conversations with Great Britain and convinced that the British were merely delaying a decision, the Russians made a friendly gesture in the direction of Berlin by undertaking new negotiations concerning a trade treaty with Germany. Meanwhile, however, the conversations with Great Britain and France were not broken off and, as a matter of fact, entered a new stage—staff talks. The Anglo-French military missions chose to journey to Moscow by boat through the North Sea to Leningrad, the slowest possible way in an age of air travel. Conversations were begun immediately upon their arrival, but once again a snag was soon encountered. The Russians insisted on the adoption of a plan which would authorize them to send troops into Poland and the Baltic countries in the event of a German attack. The British were afraid this would open Europe to Russian armies; and both Poland and the Baltic states resisted any suggestion that the Red Army be allowed to enter their territory. The Russians immediately pointed out that under such circumstances no realistic or effective plan of cooperation could be devised. Soviet leaders were becoming convinced that the only way to keep Russia out of war was to choose the other alternative—to come to terms with Germany.

On August 21 a new Soviet-German trade agreement was signed in Berlin by which the Germans agreed to advance a credit of 200,-000,000 marks to the Soviet Union. Two days later German Foreign Minister Ribbentrop arrived in Moscow by plane, and a nonaggression pact between Germany and the Soviet Union (dated August 23) was signed at 1 A.M. on August 24. According to the provisions of this pact, the two contracting parties pledged to "refrain from any violence, from any aggressive action, and from any attack against each other, either individually or jointly with other powers." Any disputes or conflicts which should in the future arise between the two contracting powers were to be solved "exclusively in a peaceful way through an amicable exchange of views." The pact was to be effective for ten years.

On August 25 Great Britain countered by signing a mutual assistance pact with Poland. The British act was a demonstration of gallantry but it was hardly evidence of a realistic appraisal of the situation. Nothing was done to prevent the final step being taken on the agreement between Russia and Germany, and on August 31 the Supreme Soviet unanimously ratified the German-Soviet pact.

CHAPTER 16

RUSSIAN CULTURE UNDER THE SOVIETS

1. *Education and public health*

LET us now turn to the cultural aspects of life in Russia in the 1920's and 1930's. The steady progress of education from 1890 to 1914 was accomplished on the basis of the program which has already been discussed in Chapters 11 and 12. The destruction resulting from the first World War, and especially the complete disruption which attended the initial years of the revolution, played havoc with the Russian educational system. During the civil war the collapse of educational services was intensified not only by the physical destruction of thousands of school buildings but also by general deficiencies, such as fuel shortages, which made it impossible to continue classes even in those buildings that remained standing. Since the loss of life during the first World War and the civil war was heaviest among the youth of military age, and since that generation was also the best educated in the country, a serious setback resulted to educational progress. Only with the gradual return of comparatively normal conditions and the healing of the wounds of the civil war in the years following the introduction of the NEP were further advances possible. Almost immediately after the restoration of order, however, the upward trend which had been interrupted by the war was resumed. By 1926 the country had achieved 51 per cent literacy, surpassing the 1914 level of 45 per cent, and from that time forward education in Soviet Russia made steady gains. By 1934 the goal of universal primary education for children of school age was at last achieved, and special efforts were simultaneously taken to "liquidate" illiteracy among adults. While the progress in education was essentially the continuation of the cultural process started long before the revolution, indoctrination of the people in Marxist principles now became an additional motive for the Soviet educational drive.

Though it is true that during the early period of the revolution education suffered severe limitations because of the destruction of physical facilities, it is only fair to add that during those same years the Russians had been engaged in bold experimentation with progressive educational methods. Those charged with the organization of the new system were familiar with modern pedagogical techniques; for example, many of the methods adopted indicated the influence of the theories of John Dewey. During this experimental period a number of extreme types of "revolutionary" educational systems were adopted—such as student self-government—but after a brief trial they were, for the most part, either abandoned or modified. In spite of the fact that a few unworkable schemes were for a time seriously attempted, the whole experiment, in so far as it provided the opportunity to test a variety of new ideas, was undoubtedly beneficial.

Soviet authorities were as concerned about the progress of secondary and technical education and university training as about elementary instruction, and with the introduction of the first five-year plan the expansion of facilities for advanced learning began to be noteworthy. Scores of new colleges were opened throughout Russia, and hundreds of training schools specializing in technical subjects were set up in conjunction with many of the large industrial projects. In addition the Soviet Union has developed a number of new types of training centers adapted to her unique problems. The special courses for tractor drivers are typical of the arrangements which have been made to provide both general and vocational training—these particular ones being especially designed to supply essential information relating to the collectivization of agriculture. Within a few years the Soviet Union had produced thousands of young scientists, medical and social workers, and technicians upon whom the growth of the new mechanized, socialized, and industrialized nation must and did depend.

Typical figures covering education during these years will give an idea of the results. In 1914 there were 104,610 primary schools with an enrollment of 7,236,000 students in Russia within the boundaries as of 1921. In 1936 there were in the Soviet Union 164,-081 elementary schools with an enrollment of around 20,000,000 students. Between 1936 and 1940 10,000 more schools were established, and the number of children attending elementary schools in 1940 was over 25,000,000. The number of secondary schools and universities and of students enrolled increased at an even greater rate. Between 1913 and 1939 universities and technical schools of university rank rose from 71 to 448 and their students increased from 85,000 to 371,000.

The educational system of the Soviet Union, with the exception of that part directed by the Committee on College Education, is under the control of the People's Commissariat of Education of each of the constituent republics of the Union. It has, for the most part, evolved from the basic organization developed by the zemstvos in prerevolutionary Russia. Under the new regime the duties previously carried out by the zemstvo councils have been assumed by the local soviets and adapted to the changing needs of the various communities.

The zemstvos had, of course, a number of other functions in Imperial Russia, among which one of the most important was the supervision of public health, the building of hospitals, and the organization of free medical care for the population. The system of medical service administered by the zemstvos was admirably adapted to the needs of the Russian village, the ingenious program developed by the zemstvo workers being in many ways the best in Europe at the time. But the program needed considerable expansion, especially since a number of provinces of the Russian Empire were not included in the zemstvo system. Like the educational program, public health and medical service suffered greatly during the civil war. However, after the re-establishment of order, the Soviet Government succeeded not only in restoring the wrecked facilities for medical service but also in enlarging them. Under the general supervision of a Commissariat of Public Health, the local soviets took over the whole zemstvo hospital system. Utilizing the best elements of the mechanism which it had inherited, the Soviet was in time able to build up a far-reaching and well-balanced system of socialized medicine which continued to yield increasing benefits until the day of the German attack.

The present system of health service in the Soviet Union is based upon the organization of "health centers" in all factories and other large industrial enterprises as well as in city and rural districts. Over 7,000 factory "health stations" had been established by 1940. The 90,000 hospital beds in Russian urban districts in 1913 had increased almost fivefold by 1937. Hospital facilities in rural areas trebled between 1913 and 1938, the number of beds increasing roughly from 50,000 to 150,000. Considerable attention has been paid to maternity institutions as well as to child care. New types of medical institutions have been developed, such as the traveling serological laboratory to combat infectious diseases in rural areas. The increase in medical facilities has a solid foundation in the rapid expansion of medical education during the Soviet period. The number of trained physicians increased from 30,000 at the time of the first World War to 120,000 in 1940. It goes without saying that, for all the achievements of socialized medicine in the Soviet Union, there is much room left for improvement. The shortage of doctors became especially evident during the second World War, and, as in Great Britain, there is endless paperwork for both doctors and patients. But the system works, even if not always smoothly.

2. Marxist ideology

In medieval Russia and indeed throughout all Europe, Christianity was the basic moral and intellectual foundation upon which the structure of the state and society rested, and the Christian church for several centuries exercised complete and unchallenged control over the thought and action of the people. After the Renaissance in Europe, and after the reforms instigated by Peter the Great in Russia, the church began to lose its unique position, and free thought, in one form or another, increasingly challenged church dogma. On the eve of the Russian revolution, however, Christianity was still considered the fundamental moral basis of civilization, both in Europe and in Russia, though its authority was considerably more restricted than it had been during the Middle Ages. Even after carefully weighing the events of the French revolution and the anticlerical trends that developed in France toward the end of the 19th and the early 20th centuries, one is still forced to the conclusion that Russia was the first and only country with a Christian background to break with the church deliberately and openly. What is perhaps more important historically is the fact that communism's conflict with religion did not arise, like other antireligious movements, as a crusade to establish intellectual tolerance or to secure freedom of thought for all mankind. On the contrary, communism sought the destruction of the authority of the church only in order to seize for itself the control of social thought; the ideology of the church was to be replaced by the equally inclusive ideology of Marxism. In this sense, indeed, the regime established by the Communists may well be considered a new ideocracy. Not only were the principles of Marxism made obligatory for members of the select ruling group of the Communist party but a strenuous effort was made to instill Marxist doctrine into the minds of the masses.

Since Marxism in Russia became the official doctrine to which all who were engaged in any field of intellectual endeavor necessarily subscribed, it is important to consider briefly the essential features of the philosophy with some special attention to its interpretation and application in the Soviet state. In this connection the philosophical core of Marxism must be differentiated from its political aspects, and the original teachings of the Marxian fathers, Karl Marx (1818–83) and Frederick Engels (1820–95), must be distinguished from the later modifications of their theories. The evolution of the concepts they first enunciated has been a continuing process which has been reflected even in the variations in the name under which the movement has operated. The qualifying term "Leninism" was the first to be added, and then "Stalinism" came to be used in a descriptive sense, so that a three-word, hyphenated term, Marxism-Leninism-Stalinism, became necessary to designate adequately the theoretical foundation of the official Russian system of thought.

The original Marxian doctrine is a direct outgrowth of that branch of philosophy usually described as Hegelian. Deriving its theories, as it does, essentially from the dialectical logic formulated by Hegel (1770–1831), it has in time come to be known as dialectical materialism. In its political aspect, Marxism is based primarily upon the theory of class struggle and upon the belief that because of the relationship of economic forces a unique and revolutionary role has been assigned to the working class. Because of its emphasis upon the decisive importance of economics and social change, Marxism has also been known as economic materialism, a term that has frequently been used by Michael Pokrovsky, the Soviet historian. In still another of its aspects, that of "scientific socialism," Marxism claims to provide a formula for social progress which is equally applicable to all modern forms of society.

According to Marx, capitalism by its very nature is driven constantly and inexorably toward its destruction. Communism, the social instrument of the working class, simultaneously is rising irresistibly to seize the control which capitalism can no longer exercise. The era of industrialism contains within it both the seeds of the destruction of the capitalist system and the elements of the working class revolution. Lenin carried these original Marxist concepts still further. In his study of imperialism as the final stage of capitalism, he elaborated on the international aspects of capitalism which Marx had described, and analyzed the role of colonial and semicolonial countries in the development of capitalism in highly industrialized nations. Another—and perhaps more important—contribution made by Lenin was his specific definition of the active part to be taken by the revolutionary party in leading the masses of the working class in the overthrow of the capitalist state and system. According to the common interpretation of classical Marxism, the revolution, which was to be expected first in the most highly industrialized nations, was to come as an inevitable result of the dialectics of the historical process. It followed that revolutionaries need only await the day and prepare themselves to greet revolutionary events as they unfolded in history's own good time. This, essentially, was the attitude adopted both by the German Social Democratic party and by the Russian Mensheviks. Lenin, however, insisted upon the necessity of building a compact and disciplined revolutionary party which would be prepared to force the issue at the critical moment, to seize control of the situation before the dying economic system of exploitation could despoil the world in its violent death agonies.

When in 1917 Lenin was confronted in his own country with the revolutionary situation he had long hoped for, he was not deterred from putting his plans into operation by the incontrovertible fact that at that time Russia was the least industrialized of all the major European countries. Somewhere, somehow, he reasoned, it was necessary to break the capitalist front, and since the opportunity had arisen in Russia, it must be exploited there. Once the ring had been broken, he thought, other nations better suited for the further development of the new system would be prepared to assume the leadership as the workers rose to power.

Thus there arose the paradox of the first Communist revolution occurring in a country the socialists had always considered "semifeudal." Both Lenin and Trotsky placed all their hopes in the immediate spread of the revolution over the European continent. Their expectations, of course, were not fulfilled, but by the time it had become clear that support was not forthcoming from outside the Communists already controlled the Russian Government. They had no alternative but to consolidate their position in Soviet Russia in order to preserve and secure this newly won bastion for the world revolution which was to follow. In the meantime, in order to prevent the complete decay and collapse of the Russian economic system, it became necessary to compromise with capitalism. This adjustment was made in the NEP. After Lenin's death and after the Soviet Union's recovery from the devastation of the civil war, Trotsky, representing one branch of the Communist party, continued to concentrate his interest on fomenting revolution throughout the world. By that time, however, the great majority of the Russian people were concerned mainly with the reconstruction of their own country rather than with a political program which offered only the prospect of engaging them in interminable international adventures. Stalin's strength rested chiefly in his ability to evaluate these new tendencies, and he took advantage of public sentiment by organizing his government under a slogan which promised the people the ultimate success of socialism in their own country.

The distance between Stalinism and Leninism is no less than that between Leninism and Marxism. Lenin had boldly determined to drive through a revolution in a country which was insufficiently developed industrially to function properly under the new system. He was able to achieve his immediate objective, but for a time the industrial weakness of Russia threatened to prevent the broader success of socialism in that country. To overcome this weakness, Stalin was compelled to strengthen the industrial foundation so that it might safely support socialism. Thus, from the standpoint of classical Marxism, the Russian revolution was actually a chain of paradoxes. In a sense, the historical process had been inverted: superindustrialism, which by all the logic of Marxist thought was to precede the revolution, in reality came last. In Russia not only did economics not determine the course of political development but the political system was used as a lever to revise and reform the economic system. Apparently then, that part of the Marxist theory which emphasizes economic materialism proved to be inaccurate or meaningless in the Russian situation. Although in the Soviet Union lip service is still paid to the whole Marxist philosophical concept, the underlying principle of "dialectics" is the only part of the doctrine which actually functions. Stripped of moral and philosophical components, dialectics may serve almost any purpose. In the Soviet Union today it is used to promote a national system of political realism as well as the expansion of Soviet power through the international Communist movement.

3. *Religion and atheism*

Marx's hostility toward religion was made abundantly clear in his much quoted phrase describing it as the "opium of the people." Though the German Social Democrats recognized Marx's formula in principle, in actual practice they adopted a much milder program which recognized religion as the private affair of each individual. Among the Russian socialists, the Mensheviks chose to follow the policy of the German Social Democrats. The Socialist Revolutionaries—who were in any case not adherents of the Marxist philosophy—in general demonstrated no hostility toward religion; indeed, some of their leaders were quite ready to grant it an important place in the reconstruction of society. The Kerensky government not only adopted a policy of complete religious tolerance but also was cautious in curtailing any of the historic privileges which had previously been enjoyed by the Orthodox Church. The Bolsheviks' attitude, on the other hand, had from the very first been militantly antagonistic. Not only was Lenin suspicious of the Orthodox Church as an institution; he disliked and distrusted all religious sentiment. Since Lenin himself was prepared to apply Marx's definition of religion to the letter, atheism was made obligatory for members of the Communist party. Although it was apparent to the leaders of the revolution that it was impossible to destroy religious belief in Russia entirely and to replace it by atheism overnight, nevertheless, by sponsoring a program of atheistic propaganda, they made every effort in the early years to weaken the position of the church and to undermine the authority of all religion.

It is quite evident that the personal philosophical convictions which Lenin and other Communist leaders held on religious questions were largely responsible for the antireligious policies of the Soviet Government. Other reasons which from time to time have been put forward as the basis of the party's attitude—such as the Soviet leaders' fear of the alleged reactionary role of the church—were in the last analysis of only secondary importance. The course pursued by the Soviet Government was aimed at all religious beliefs, and though the Orthodox Church was the first to suffer from the Communist attack, other denominations were later placed under identical government restrictions.

Even under the imperial government the activities of the Orthodox Church had been somewhat curtailed, although it still retained a number of special privileges which were granted to no other denomination. The re-establishment of the patriarchate, which had been abolished by Peter the Great, had for years been urged by some religious leaders as a step toward regaining the independence of the church from the state, and shortly after the revolution of 1917 a council or *sobor* of the church was called for this purpose. A few days later Archbishop Tikhon was elected patriarch, and set about his new duties under the most trying conditions of political anarchy and governmental disapproval. Although the government had not actually forbidden religious activities, persecution of representatives of the clergy by many of the local soviets had already been begun, and in the years between 1917 and 1920 several hundred bishops, priests, and monks were either shot or starved to death in prisons. However, in spite of his issuing a severe denunciation of Communist measures in January 1918, Patriarch Tikhon was not at that time molested by the Soviet Government.

By the decree of January 23, 1918, the Soviet Government officially severed the connection between church and state. All property owned by the churches, including the buildings themselves, was nationalized. In order to continue to use the churches for divine services, the congregations were now compelled to sign contracts with the local soviets, providing always that local leaders had not previously decided either to use the buildings for other purposes or to demolish them. It was even necessary to obtain permission from the soviets to use articles of the ritual such as the chalices and vestments, although for the time being these articles remained in the possession of the parishes. The churches were also forbidden by law to acquire any new property in place of that which had been confiscated. In spite of all these restrictions, however, when the first constitution of the RSFSR was adopted on July 10, 1918, the church was still granted at least a vestige of liberty by an article which guaranteed freedom of both religious and antireligious propaganda. This clause was later included in the constitution of the Soviet Union of 1923 in substantially the same form.

In the spring of 1922 the Soviet Government issued a decree authorizing requisition of the ritual implements of the church, with the explanation that the proceeds were to be used for famine work. This seizure of the church treasures was accompanied by a new wave of persecutions in which many priests were arrested and a number executed, among them the bishop of Petrograd, Benjamin. At the same time Patriarch Tikhon was incarcerated in one of the Moscow monasteries.

During this period the Soviet Government had attempted to instigate internal disorganization in the Orthodox Church by supporting a group of priests, the so-called Living Church, who were engaged in a campaign urging radical revision of the church organization. In the spring of 1923 this group called representatives of part of the clergy and laity to a meeting which was then declared to be a legal sobor of the Orthodox Church. Although this sobor accused the imprisoned Patriarch Tikhon of counterrevolutionary opinions and deprived him of his position, he was released soon afterward by the Soviet Government. Until his death on April 7, 1925, Tikhon continued to be regarded as patriarch by the majority of the church membership. After his death his *locum tenens,* Metropolitan Peter, became the head of the church. When he too was imprisoned by the Soviet Government, Metropolitan Sergius became the keeper of the patriarchal throne, and in the summer of 1927 announced his loyalty to the Soviet state.

In 1925 the Militant Atheists' League was organized, and immediately launched a nation-wide campaign against the church. Although atheism had achieved considerable popularity by that time, especially among the younger generation, and although membership in the churches had shown a correspondingly rapid decrease during the preceding years, the vulgar and blasphemous tone of the official atheistic propaganda seemed to repel more than it converted. By 1928 the league had recruited only 123,000 members, a figure representing less than 10 per cent of those active in the

Communist party. Later on the membership increased rapidly, but the members showed, on the whole, little enthusiasm for their cause. When the five-year plan and the collectivization of agriculture were undertaken, the government made an attempt to administer a death blow to religion. Since its plan called for complete collectivization, and since it was supposed there would be no room for church activities in the kolkhozes, Soviet authorities confidently expected the total elimination of religion in the villages. To make doubly certain of the destruction of the church, however, the government on April 8, 1929, issued a new decree forbidding religious societies to participate in any kind of cultural or social activity except religious services. On May 22, 1929, the constitution was amended to include this regulation. The new statement of the government's position contained a significant modification. Instead of guaranteeing both *religious and antireligious propaganda,* it now proclaimed "freedom of religious *worship* and freedom of antireligious *propaganda"*—a turn in phraseology which allowed the atheists to carry on a militant campaign and at the same time prevented the faithful from engaging in any proselytizing activities. The wording of the 1929 decree was repeated in the clause on religious worship which was inserted in the new Soviet constitution of 1936.

In spite of all the restrictions raised against it, religion demonstrated a remarkable tenacity and resiliency. The chairman of the Militant Atheists' League, Emelian Iaroslavsky, in 1937 estimated that although more than half the workers in the cities considered themselves atheists, more than half the population in the villages still expressed their belief in God. If this statement is correct, it would mean that after twenty years of Soviet rule around 50 per cent of the population of the Soviet Union was still religious. However, 30 per cent would be perhaps a safer estimate. In any case it is known that in 1940 there were over 30,000 religious communities of every kind in the Soviet Union. Significantly enough, whereas during the initial years of the revolution the youth, especially the boys, had deserted the church in droves, in the 1930's it was possible to organize a Christian Youth Movement, the Christomol, as a parallel to the Komsomol, or Communist Youth Movement. Since no official statistics on religion are issued by the Soviet Government, it is impossible to say how important the new movement is numerically today. In recent years Protestant denominations, notably the Baptists, have secured a sizable number of converts among the Russians.

In 1937 there was a sudden and comparatively brief flare-up of antireligious propaganda in the Soviet Union, and a number of bishops and priests were arrested and tried. The clergymen were not charged with unlawful religious activities but rather with having had connections with the espionage and sabotage groups which were then on trial or under investigation. Whatever purposes may have been behind this action, no further outburst of anticlericalism has since occurred in the Soviet Union.

In later years there was a change in the attitude of the Soviet Government toward religion. One of the first signs of the return to a more tolerant position was the admission of the failure of the Militant Atheists' League and the gradual reduction in government support. A little later there came a series of events which indicated that the government's estimate of the church's place in history was being revised. At a joint session of the Historical Institute of the Acadamy of Sciences and the Central Committee of the Militant Atheists' League in December 1938 the essentially progressive role of the church in the historical process was admitted in general terms, and the close connection of Christianity with the development of Russian art and literature during the early periods of Russian history was specifically acknowledged. The same trends were visible in many of the official and semi-official activities of the government. Alexander Nevsky—a prince of medieval Russia who had been canonized by the church—was glorified in the Soviet Union as a great national hero who had valiantly defended Russia against German invasion In the 13th century. Before long the Soviet Government discovered that support of its policy by various religious groups could be useful on many occasions.

In 1939 the Soviet adopted a new religious policy in fact if not in legislation. After that the government demonstrated an increasingly mild attitude toward the church and religion in general. The church has showed itself willing to cooperate with the authorities, and especially with the beginning of the German war made every effort to assist the government in rallying the people to meet the emergency. The new relations which developed between government and church during the early months of the war culminated in the re-establishment of the patriarchate in Moscow, a move which undoubtedly strengthened both church and nation. The locum tenens, Metropolitan Sergius, was elected patriarch, on September 12, 1943.

4. *The sciences and humanities*

From the very beginning the attitude of the Soviet Union was as warmly favorable toward the sciences as it was hostile toward the teachings of the church. The reasons for the government's interest in the advancement of scientific learning are, for the most part, self-evident. In the first place, Marxism itself is considered a science by its adherents—indeed, *the* scientific form of socialism which asserts that the natural and social sciences have played an important role in human progress. In the second place, Marxian socialists believe that as science explores the vast unknown in which man exists, and reveals more of the structure and function of the universe, it will displace religion which has, in their opinion, existed primarily as an integrated system of belief attempting to explain the mysteries lying beyond the horizon of man's understanding. A third—and eminently practical—reason was simple necessity. The physical and mathematical sciences are the foundation upon which the social and technical progress of the Soviet Union must be constructed. Technology is obviously the most necessary tool in the construction of the new society, in the creation of socialism which, in Lenin's words, was to be "Soviet power plus electrification."

Even though the Bolsheviks have in general been generous in aiding the development of scientific learning, their dictatorial political methods have sometimes frustrated scholarship. At the time Marx was writing, scientists were already abandoning the extreme mechanistic conception of the world typical of the 17th and 18th centuries, and consequently Marxian materialism was a step forward compared with the doctrine of materialistic philosophers of the period of the French Enlightenment. However, the progress of science in the span of the century which has elapsed since the original formulation of Marx's doctrine has been so rapid that an entirely new approach to nature and reality is now possible. No rigid philosophical schemes, whether idealistic or materialistic, can monopolize the development of modern science. It is characteristic of the rigidity of Marxian tenets as applied in Soviet Russia that certain scientific doctrines such as the Mendelian theory and the quantum theory of modern physics were regarded with disfavor by the government.

A controversy over the Mendelian theory in the 1940's upset the whole science of genetics in the Soviet Union. A number of Soviet scientists, led by Trofim Lysenko, attacked neo-Mendelism (the generally accepted theory of heredity based on the genes) as a "mystical," "bourgeois," and "reactionary" doctrine. Lysenko attempted to prove that characteristics which are acquired through environmental influences are inherited—a concept known as Michurinism after the Russian horticulturist Ivan Michurin (1855–1935). In 1940 the leading Russian geneticist, Nicholas Vavilov, who was the main target of Lysenko's attacks, was accused of being a British spy and deported to Siberia where he died in 1942. In 1948 the issue was settled by the Central Committee of the Communist party approving Lysenko's views. The Presidium of the Academy of Sciences of the USSR thereupon resolved that its Division of Biological Sciences "shall be guided by Michurin's teachings." The partisans of neo-Mendelism were removed from the scientists' councils of the biological institutes and replaced by supporters of "progressive Michurinite biology." As the British scientist Julian Huxley commented, "The major issue at stake was not the truth of falsity of Lysenko's claims, but the overriding of science by ideological and political authority."

The obstacles which Soviet scholars encountered in the field of the humanities were equally serious; from the beginning of the revolution the teaching of both philosophy and sociology was seriously hampered by official Marxian dogmatism. In the initial years of the revolution the teaching of history was entirely suspended in most Russian universities and was replaced by courses in sociology tailored to fit the Communist interpretation of social relationships. Professors who happened to teach Russian history were in an unenviable position since as a group they were suspect as believers in nationalism and as carriers of a reactionary attitude. Among the leading Russian historians of the older generation there were only two Marxists—Nicholas Rozhkov and Michael Pokrovsky—and they were at once put in control of the new academic set-up. Under the Soviet regime Pokrovsky became the more important of the two, and for a number of years served as the official exponent of Marx's theories as they applied to Russian history. An able scholar, he contributed much to the reorganization of historical archives, and was instrumental in the publication of important historical documents—among them the well-known series of Russian diplomatic papers covering the period of the first World War. His general approach to history was that of an "economic materialist," and he was an especially rabid foe of the spirit of Russian nationalism which he fought wherever he found it or suspected it. During the period in which he enjoyed the position of a virtual dictator of historical studies in the Soviet Union, Pokrovsky subjected all teachers and students in that field to a strict supervision which forced them to keep within the rigid limits he had established. Those who proved to be recalcitrant or insufficiently cooperative were frequently punished by imprisonment or exile, a disciplinary technique which resulted in the premature death of many of the most gifted Russian scholars—among them Serge Platonov who, after Basil Kliuchevsky's death in 1911, was considered the dean of Russian historians. Another noted historian, Eugene Tarle, having survived several years of exile in central Asia, returned after Pokrovsky's death, to become a member of the Academy of Sciences. The regime of academic terrorism which Pokrovsky instituted in the field of history temporarily broke down with his death in 1932. It later became apparent that his passing had come none too soon, since his activities too were becoming increasingly "suspect" each year.

It was characteristic of the position of learning in the Soviet Union that a decision of the Central Committee of the Communist party and another by the Council of People's Commissars were necessary to establish more normal conditions in history research and teaching after Pokrovsky's death. According to the "theses" proposed by Stalin, Kirov, and Zhdanov, history was now to be taught as a separate subject and not as a subdivision within the framework of sociology. Russia's past was not to be deliberately distorted and maligned as it had been while Pokrovsky held the dominant position in the field; instead the constructive elements in Russia's background were to be emphasized in order to explain the historical position of the Soviet Union in the proper light.

Under the Soviet a number of important changes have been instituted both in the type and in the organization and administration of centers of learning. At the beginning of the revolution the emphasis was placed almost exclusively on the creation of institutions of a strictly Marxist type, such as the Communist Academy which was founded in 1918 and the Marx and Engels Institute organized in 1920. Later, however, the government devoted more attention to sustaining and developing older institutions like the Academy of Sciences and the prerevolutionary universities. The All-Union Academy of Sciences, which included an ever-increasing number of special research institutes in various fields, now became the leading center of scientific research in the Soviet Union. Branches were established in various parts of the country and separate academies were founded in a number of the constituent republics of the Union, such as Ukraine,* Belorussia, and Georgia. Since one of the functions of the All-Union Academy of Sciences was to sponsor the exploration and supervise the exploitation of natural resources in the Soviet Union, the tendency has always been to connect the activities of the academy with the specific needs of industry in the country. Nevertheless, it should be emphasized that a number of the research institutes are still dedicated to "pure science" and that there appears to be no intention on the part of the government to abandon this type of study.

The Soviet Government has gone to unusual lengths to provide adequately trained technicians for the rapidly expanding industries of Russia. In order to insure a steady and continuous flow of scientific personnel, a school of "aspirants" was founded at the Academy of Sciences and at each university and research institute. A considerable network of research institutes—which are more closely connected with industry than are the academies—has recently been developed. In 1935 the People's Commissariat of Heavy Industry alone sponsored more than 100 such scientific institutes in which nearly 12,000 men and women were engaged in research work with the aid of some 10,000 technicians, engineers, and laboratory assistants.

Some of the older generation of Russian scientists who had achieved prominence before 1917 played a leading role under the Soviet as well. Among these were the mathematician Alexis Krylov; Vladimir Ipatiev (in the United States after 1929; died in 1952), Alexis Favorsky, and Nicholas Zelinsky in chemistry; Constantine

* The Ukrainian Academy of Sciences was founded in Kiev in 1918 and later taken over by the Soviet.

Tsiolkovsky in rocket research; Vladimir Vernadsky and Alexander Fersman in mineralogy and biogeochemistry; and Leo Berg in geography. Most of these have died in recent years; each created a school of students and followers to take over and continue his research. Among the outstanding scientists of the younger generation the physicist Peter Kapitsa may be mentioned here.

5. *Trends in literature, arts, and music*

In literature and the arts the initial period of the revolution was full of contradictions. On the one hand, the Soviet Government attempted to sponsor "proletarian culture" by opening schools for training young writers and artists of working class origin. On the other hand, among the intellectuals, symbolism and futurism became the strong influences.

In the winter of 1917–18 Alexander Blok wrote *The Twelve,* a famous poem which is perhaps the most penetrating interpretation that has been made of the tumultuous spirit of the first months of the revolution. The poem, which is available in an English translation by Babette Deutsch and Avrahm Yarmolinsky, is symbolic in meaning, but it nevertheless provides dramatic and realistic insight into life in Petrograd during those intense and turbulent days. It is a grim picture of chaos and destruction, of debauchery and drunkenness, of blood and misery, but it shows beneath the outer violence the firm and simple faith with which the workers and soldiers then looked to the future of international brotherhood.

Perhaps the most colorful figure of that transitional epoch was the futurist, Vladimir Maiakovsky (1894–1930), a poet of great talent who, realizing the government's need for propaganda in the arts, boldly attempted to monopolize the field for futurism. Although Maiakovsky and his followers succeeded in creating a distinctive style in propagandistic literature and art, the average citizen's attitude toward futurism remained cool if not negative. Most of the Old Bolshevik leaders, including Lenin, who had been brought up on realistic art and literature, were soon weary of the new style.

The subjects most frequently treated in the novels and plays published during the NEP were the civil war and the national effort to reconstruct industry and agriculture. There were also a number of books written on the familiar pattern of the historical and psychological novel. On the whole, realism was the prevailing literary style, although some authors, especially those writing of the civil war period, leaned somewhat toward romanticism. At the same time there was a healthy amount of experimentation with new literary techniques, such as the inverted chronology used with skill by Constantine Fedin in his *Cities and Years.*

During this period quite a number of new writers came to the public's attention, and a few of them should at least be mentioned here. One of the most prominent was Isaac Babel, whose short stories showed the influence of Guy de Maupassant. Babel's best known work, *Red Cavalry,* was published in 1926, and his *Jewish Tales* in 1927. Leonov (b. 1899) is the author of "Tuatamur," a story of the period of the Mongol invasion, which was in the romantic rather than the historical tradition. In *Badgers* (1925) Leonov returned to a modern theme in a story of peasant life. The reputation of Alexander Fadeev was built on his colorful stories of the civil war period, of which *The Nineteen,* published in 1927, is the best known. George Olesha (b. 1899) is known chiefly as the author of *Envy,* a remarkable psychological novel based on the clash between the old and new ways of life in Russia. Michael Zoshchenko (b. 1895) enjoyed a unique and universal popularity for his humorous tales and short stories, which were virtually literary candid camera shots of everyday life. A novel by Michael Bulgakov (b. 1891), whose setting was the Ukraine in 1918, at the time of the civil war and German occupation, was dramatized as *The Days of the Turbins* and produced first by the Moscow Art Theater, later in America.

We can best conclude this selective catalogue by recalling the best known of the Russian novels of the period—the monumental *And Quiet Flows the Don,* by Michael Sholokhov, which has been compared by many enthusiastic readers to Leo Tolstoy's *War and Peace.* Although it is not as wide in scope and is definitely weaker in those sections in which the author turns from the Don Cossack life with which he is most familiar and attempts to sketch individuals from other classes, Sholokhov's novel has something of Tolstoy's breadth of style in historical literature.

The inauguration of the first five-year plan in 1928 had a direct effect on the government's attitude toward literature. In the opinion of Soviet leaders, the tremendous effort of the industrial revolution and of the collectivization of agriculture demanded the full and unstinting cooperation of all Soviet citizens, the concentration of every effort on the gigantic task of securing Russia's place in the world. Because the mood of the period was much like that of a nation at war, the desire to use every ounce of the people's physical and mental energy toward achievement of the common goal is understandable. Nevertheless, the attempt to convert literature to the tasks of the day was fraught with danger to the personal freedom of the writer and the artist. The authorities now contrived the principle of "social command" to serve the government's purpose. Writers were expected to illustrate the developments of the five-year plan and to contribute to its fulfillment by clarifying and glorifying its aims and by firing the imagination of the people with the immense importance of the new policies. Constructive criticism of mistakes which occurred in the details of the operation of the plan was allowed at this time. But even this policy proved to be too rigid and mechanical to operate for any length of time, and regulations were gradually relaxed. At the same time the government abandoned its sponsorship of "proletarian literature." As the remnants of NEP capitalism were done away with and the individual kulak farmers were liquidated, Russia began to enter the stage of a "classless society"—or so the government announced. Under these circumstances, it became possible to abolish the distinctions between proletarian and nonproletarian writers, and in 1932 all writers were accepted into a single Union of Soviet Writers.

In 1934 the first All-Union Literary Congress met to discuss the role of the writer in the Soviet Union and to establish the general principles under which creative literary work was to be done. The tendency of the time was to harness literature as closely as possible to contemporary social and political needs. It was argued that the chief function of the true Soviet writer was to be "an engineer of human souls," and the principle of "socialist realism" was agreed upon as best describing the road that literature should follow. Soviet literary critics made it clear that while a critical attitude toward the realities of life was characteristic of bourgeois realism, socialist realism must be constructive rather than destructive, optimistic rather than pessimistic. It was the Soviet writer's duty to accept life as fundamentally sound and beautiful. Although this limitation was not to prevent criticism of the remnants of the "ugly past" or discussion of the mistakes of socialist construction, the reader was always to be left with a feeling of faith and hope in the future of the new collectivized system.

Even though the principle of socialist realism somewhat widened the limits which had previously been set by the social command policy for literary work, it soon became evident that not all writers could adjust themselves to the new requirements. As a result, a good part of the writing done during the period of the first two five-year plans was dull and lifeless. On the other hand, writers whose interest and style coincided with the official interpretation of socialist realism were able to create works of force and distinction. A number of novels were written around the theme of the collectivization of agriculture, and of these Sholokhov's *Seeds of Tomorrow* (1935) is perhaps the most remarkable. It is a grimly realistic picture of civil strife growing out of the dekulakization of a Don Cossack village. In spite of the circumstances under which it was written, it is not a political pamphlet but a work of art describing a world in which kulaks have virtues as well as vices and Communists sometimes have their foibles as well as their fortes.

An outstanding novel of the period—and one characteristic of the spirit of the day, although it tells a story laid in the early days of the revolution—is *The Making of a Hero* by Nicholas Ostrovsky (1904–36). In addition to being a first-rate literary work, it is interesting from a historical and psychological point of view, for it reveals with exceptional clarity the qualities of the new Soviet youth—their ardor, strength of will, realistic attitude toward life, and constructive abilities. No less interesting from the same standpoint is *The Pedagogic Poem* by Makarenko, a semifictional diary of a teacher in a reform school.

Considerable attention was devoted to the historical novel. In his *Peter the First* (1934) Alexis Tolstoy drew a striking portrait of Peter the Great. Though he dwelt at length on the "barbaric" aspects of Russian life in early days and on the brutal features of the mighty tsar's personality, he also emphasized Peter's thirst for knowledge, his appreciation of technological skills, and the progressive aims of his reforms. Taken as a whole, the picture is not an unfavorable one, and, indeed, the tsar appears to be represented as an early forerunner of Bolshevism. Just before the German invasion an author of an older generation, Sergeev-Tsensky, who had

won a modest following before the first World War but had never
been especially prominent, wrote a monumental novel on the siege
of Sevastopol during the Crimean War of 1854–55, *The Martyr-
dom of Sevastopol,* in the grand historical style of *War and Peace,*
although not on Tolstoy's level.

Turning now to the graphic arts, during the early years of the
Soviet regime, we find that they too, like literature, were first
plunged into a state of confusion and then passed through similar
stages of futurist and *proletkult* experimentation. Soon after the
November revolution a number of prominent painters belonging
to the original *World of Art* group * emigrated—among them
Benois, Dobujinsky, and Somov. They were joined in exile by a
group of younger Russian painters, some of whom later won fame
abroad—men like Boris Grigoriev, Iakovlev, and Shukhaev. A
number of those who had originally fled, however, fearing that
separation from their native country would eventually result in
the fading of their creative abilities, returned to Russia after a few
years.

The adoption of the NEP established in the realm of art the
same modicum of freedom it had brought to literature. A number
of artists of the *World of Art* school were now given the opportunity
to resume their work. The inauguration of the five-year plans in
1928 resulted in the application to art of the social command policy
and later that of socialist realism—with much the same results as
in literature.

Prominent among Russian painters of modern times is Igor
Grabar (b. 1871), who was originally a Moscow associate of the
World of Art group. A talented artist who in the course of his creative life has developed several different styles, Grabar has been
called the Russian Cézanne because of the still lifes done in his
earlier years. He has furthered many art activities in the Soviet
Union, including the rearranging of museums and organizing of
exhibitions, and has also made a reputation as a historian of Russian art. Grabar and his associates have done important work in
restoring old Russian paintings, in particular icons and frescoes.
The elaborate process of cleaning and eliminating later coatings,
which has restored the colors of the old icons in all their brilliance,

* See above, p. 257.

has for the first time made adequate knowledge of the old Russian schools of painting possible.

The theater has been defined as the bridge between literature and the pictorial arts. Because of its peculiar position it can be approached either as pure art or as a practical medium and for propaganda and the education of large groups of people. Small wonder, therefore, that from the very beginning of the revolution the Soviet Government was interested in using it as a tool in building the new society. Directors and producers, actors and scenic designers, on the other hand, considered the theater an art, and for the most part were interested primarily in the expression of their own artistic beliefs—which in some cases coincided with the government's program and in other cases did not. These divergent conceptions resulted, as in other fields of art and literature, in a long-drawn-out and bitter conflict between official Soviet critics and advisers and the theater people, who in some cases continued to insist upon their right to artistic freedom. From the very beginning of the revolution the directors of the Moscow Art Theater affirmed their loyalty to the government and as a result the activities of that theater continued without interruption.* Season after season new plays were added to the repertory, among them *Days of the Turbins* by Bulgakov, and, in 1937, a dramatization of Tolstoy's *Anna Karenina* which was also shown in Paris the same year.

At the time of the revolution there were several other prominent directors and producers in Russia. One of them, Theodore Komissarjevsky, emigrated, and after twenty years in England, during which he produced plays in London, Paris, and other European cities, came to the United States and opened a studio in New York. Of those who remained in Russia, V. Meyerhold and A. Tairov are perhaps the best known. Meyerhold, although a product of the Stanislavsky school, eventually became one of Stanislavsky's bitterest opponents. He rebelled against realism and turned to "constructivist" theories in which he advocated a "biomechanical" style of acting. His attitude resembled that of Maiakovsky, and like the poet he attained a certain popularity with the government during the early years of the revolution; but eventually he found himself out of sympathy with governmental policies and unwilling to accept the principle of socialist realism. He finally fell into disgrace and

* On Stanislavsky and the Moscow Art Theater see above, p. 256.

was prevented from continuing his work in any important group. He was arrested in June 1939 and has not been mentioned since in the Soviet press.

Alexander Tairov (b. 1885) began to organize his Chamber Theater in Moscow in 1914. The revolution helped him to realize his plans for a radical revision of the relations between actor and audience, which he hoped to achieve by doing away with the traditional three-dimensional stage. "The actor must no longer be merely a component part of the décor" was one of Tairov's favorite sayings. In the course of his experimentation he used many novel arrangements, such as vertical sets, "dynamic decorations," and movable surfaces in various combinations. His basic objective, in his own words, was to create a "synthetic theater." Tairov's "organic realism," compared to the conventional and naturalistic theater, was difficult to harmonize with the principle of socialist realism, and in 1935 he was subjected by the Soviet press to a series of blistering attacks pointing out his "errors" and "lack of ideas." In 1937 he was dismissed from his post as director of the theater.

Music, that most abstract of the arts, bears something to the same relation to the other arts that the physical sciences do to the humanities. Less controversial in content, music might have been expected to escape some of the effects of the revolutionary upheaval, but even though it was spared some of the political restrictions of the time, it was not to avoid the confusion in which all the arts were caught. The disruption of the normal intellectual and psychological life of the country and the physical privations and suffering during the years of the civil war and war communism resulted in at least the temporary disorganization of musical activities. Many musicians joined the exodus of intellectuals after the revolution, and among the émigrés and exiles there were, of course, a number of gifted Russian composers. Paris had become Stravinsky's home even before the revolution, and later he chose to move on to the United States. Rachmaninov, Grechaninov, Medtner, and later on Glazunov, all emigrated. Prokofiev, on the other hand, after several years in Europe elected to return to Russia.

In the initial years of the revolution there was a short-lived outburst of futurist and ultramodernist tendencies in music, but extreme musical forms had even less appeal to the masses than futuristic painting and literature. Since only a relatively small circle of sophisticated music lovers could appreciate the subtleties of the new style, the little popularity that it did attain was confined to a very circumscribed group. No more successful was the attempt to "democratize" orchestras by eliminating the "dictatorial" power of the conductor. In 1922 a conductorless orchestra known as the First Symphony Ensemble was organized, and though audiences at first received it enthusiastically, it soon became apparent even to the plan's supporters that this route led nowhere.

The re-establishment of social order which followed the adoption of the NEP had its effect in bringing to an end the more extreme types of experimentation, and thereafter musical education and training were once more based on firm foundations. A great deal of attention was paid to the thorough mastery of details of mechanical technique. The number of music schools increased steadily from 1920 to 1939; in 1936 there were in the Soviet Union 12 conservatories and 95 "musical technicums," many of them with excellent standards.

Under the five-year plans the principles of social command and later of socialist realism were applied to music. Symphonies were commissioned on such civic themes as the kolkhozes and the anniversaries of the revolution. Composers who showed "formalistic tendencies" in their work were sharply rebuked, among them one of the most popular of Soviet composers, Dmitri Shostakovich, creator of several symphonies. While his music to *Lady Macbeth of Mtsensk* (on the theme of a story by N. Leskov) was well received in New York, performances of this opera were suspended in Moscow. Yet the creativity of Russian composers has not been altogether stifled. Forced to recant, they have started anew, and continued work in spite of everything. Among the younger generation of Soviet composers Dmitri Kabalevsky, like Shostakovich, is outstanding. To American concert audiences and radio listeners he is perhaps best known for the overture to *Cola Brunyon*. Prokofiev, who was several times harassed by the censors, died in 1953. Among his last works were an opera on the theme of Leo Tolstoy's *War and Peace* and the ballet *Romeo and Juliet*.

CHAPTER 17

RUSSIA IN THE SECOND
WORLD WAR

1. *The Soviet Union as a neutral*

THE second World War began under circumstances differing sharply from those which prevailed at the start of the first. Russia's neutrality in 1939 was, of course, the most striking difference. In the system of alliances organized by Britain and France during the two decades between wars, Poland—a country that did not yet exist in 1914—was depended upon by the Allies to assume the role of Imperial Russia. There were other differences. Austria, now a shadow of the powerful empire of 1914, had been merged with Germany and absorbed into the Nazi economy. Hungary had been reduced to the status of a satellite nation and was firmly under German control. Fascist Italy, in 1939 as in 1914, was bound to Germany by an alliance, but this time the actions and the repeated declarations of both dictators had made it abundantly clear that the totalitarian nations would adhere to the provisions of the pact. In the second World War the conflict which led to hostilities first crystallized in the Baltic area rather than in the Balkans, although the issues were such that the Balkans could hardly hope to avoid involvement and were sucked into the vortex in their turn.

Yet, in spite of these and other obvious differences, the underlying causes of the two wars remained fundamentally similar. The aggressive spirit that had characterized Germany under the Kaiser was proclaimed in much more violent form in the tenets of Nazi ideology. Between Germany and Great Britain there had arisen the same rivalry that had culminated twenty-five years earlier in the first World War. The Russian uneasiness about the German *Drang nach Osten*—the centuries-old conflict of eastern Europe—

was daily aggravated by the differences in the official ideologies and governmental systems of the two countries, though throughout the initial period of the war efforts were made by both parties to conceal them, somewhat clumsily, under the cloak of the nonaggression pact. In an insecure and uncertain situation the Soviet Government chose the road of hard-boiled realism: Its leaders had the interests of the Soviet Union in mind, and at the time those interests seemed best served by neutrality.

Under the circumstances, however, while it was comparatively easy to proclaim Russia's neutrality, it was obviously difficult to define its limits and still more difficult to keep within them. Moreover, the assumption of neutrality and the actions that flowed logically from such a position brought down upon the Soviet Union the almost universal condemnation of the democracies. The conclusion of the nonaggression pact with Germany and the Soviet occupation of western Belorussia and western Ukraine aroused violent indignation not only in Britain and France but in the United States as well—an indignation which arose (in part, at least) from the failure of the Anglo-Saxon countries to realize the peculiarities and intricacies of the involved political background of eastern Europe. This initial strain opened a breach which was widened by subsequent events. At the time of the Soviet-Finnish war there arose actual and immediate danger of Franco-British intervention against Russia—in Transcaucasia as well as in Finland—and the collapse of Soviet neutrality seemed then to be almost a matter of hours. Moreover, the Soviet on principle consistently objected to the British blockade of Germany which threatened maritime commerce. During the whole period of neutrality, relations between the Soviet Union and the western democracies were so precariously poised that it was only with the utmost effort—the result, in part, of the foresight of a few British statesmen and scholars such as Sir Stafford Cripps and Sir Bernard Pares—that the outward appearance of normality was preserved.

No less precarious were the relations between the Soviet Union and Germany. Expressions of friendship toward Germany were frequently and conspicuously displayed both in the press and in the official statements of Soviet leaders, and the government demonstrated great caution in eliminating anything that might serve the Germans as a pretext for irritation. This caution extended to almost all official activities, from the withdrawal of the anti-German historical movie, *Alexander Nevsky,* to the meticulous observance of every clause of the commercial treaties governing delivery of goods to Germany.

While bending every effort to avoid conflict with Germany, the Soviet Government continued to be acutely aware of the danger of a Nazi attack, and, particularly after the fall of France, took diplomatic and military steps of a precautionary nature. It was chiefly the necessity to provide for national safety which dictated the occupation of the strategic regions along Russia's western frontier. These movements along the border areas were paralleled and reinforced by internal readjustments. Considerable attention was directed to retraining the Red Army and to modernizing its tactics and supply services. Industries were put on a war footing, and drastic steps were taken to increase production. The seven-hour workday was lengthened to eight. To stop labor turnover and increase the productivity of war plants, workers were frozen in the industries in which they were employed and forbidden to move from plant to plant without special permission. During 1940 and 1941 armament plants were transferred from the exposed Belorussian and Leningrad areas to the Urals; and along the Volga and beyond it new plants, such as the high-octane gasoline refineries at Ufa and Saratov, were rushed to completion. The Russians hoped for peace—and prepared for war.

2. *The rectification of the western frontier*

The German invasion of Poland on September 1, 1939, and the British and French declarations of war which immediately followed came while the Soviet Union was in this geographically somewhat disadvantageous position of neutrality. Her immediate object, therefore, was to improve her strategic position all along her western borders; and neutrality was not allowed to interfere with attempts to achieve this end.

The attitude of the Soviet leaders at this time can be better understood, perhaps, if we reconsider the effect of the territorial changes along the western fringes of Russia which had occurred at the end of the first World War and as a result of foreign intervention at the time of the civil war. These revisions fell into several different categories. On Lenin's initiative the Soviet Government itself had granted independence to Finland in December 1917. The Baltic area, western Belorussia, and the western Ukraine had been taken from Russia by Germany as one of the conditions of the Brest-Litovsk peace in 1918. These regions had not been returned to Russia by the Allies after their victory over Germany. Instead, the Baltic provinces were organized as independent states, and in 1920 Poland was allowed to attack Russia and then to annex western Belorussia and the western Ukraine. In the south the Allies had consented to and eventually approved the seizure of Bessarabia by the Rumanians. The Soviet Government steadfastly refused to recognize Rumanian sovereignty in Bessarabia but in time had accepted all the other changes, for a variety of reasons: first, in the Soviet's weakened state at the time there was no alternative; second, that was the period of the Russians' belief in world revolution and Soviet leaders still pinned their hopes on the spread of communism across national borders; third, acceptance made it possible to establish a European peace—however unstable—and since relations with Germany were friendly, there seemed to be no immediate danger of an attack on Russia by any major power.

Hitler's rise to power in Germany, however, had changed the whole international picture. Russia could no longer exclude from her calculations the possibility of the nazification of the Baltic states. Moreover the tension which now existed between the Soviet Union and Nazi Germany made it necessary for Russian leaders to provide for any eventuality. Ever since the early years of the five-year plan and the inauguration of the program of building socialism in a single country, the Soviets had wished to control the Baltic area for both economic and strategic purposes. Leningrad, the only Baltic port left to Russia at the conclusion of the first World War, could obviously not handle all her Baltic trade in view of the rapid expansion of the Russian economy at the moment and that foreseen for the future. The situation became urgent with the outbreak of the second World War, and when Great Britain and France refused to give Russia a free hand in the Baltic there remained no alternative but to attempt to snatch concessions from Germany in this area as payment for Russian neutrality. The paradox of this situation was that Russia needed these borderlands in order to strengthen her position against a future German attack. Although the Anglo-Saxon countries appear consistently to have misunderstood this need, Germany was perfectly aware of the use to which the new territory was to be put. However, she was not then in a position to bargain further, and was forced reluctantly to accept the revisions which were later to prove so crucial.

According to the secret additional protocol attached to the Soviet-German Nonaggression Pact of August 23, 1939, western Belorussia, western Ukraine, Latvia, Estonia, and Finland were considered within the sphere of influence of the Soviet Union. Moreover, Germany recognized the Soviet's interest in Bessarabia. Following the German attack on Poland and the collapse of Polish resistance, Red Army troops on September 17 crossed the Polish frontier and raced westward to the Vistula River which was recognized the boundary line between the German and the Soviet spheres of influence. On September 28 a new agreement on the German-Soviet boundary was concluded: Lithuania was conceded to be in the Russian sphere of influence; the Russians, in turn, agreed to making the western Bug River, instead of the Vistula, the new line of demarcation. By this the Soviet Union was left in control of an area whose population was predominantly non-Polish. With minor exceptions, the peasants in the occupied area were of Belorussian and Ukrainian stock, and in the cities throughout the territory a considerable percentage of the population was Jews.

In the elections for the people's assemblies of western Belorussia and western Ukraine which were organized by the Soviet Union and were held on October 22, 1939, more than 90 per cent of the eligible voters participated, and of these over 90 per cent cast their ballots for the single ticket of "candidates of social organizations"—trade unions, cooperative societies, etc. Within a few days the two people's assemblies passed resolutions expressing their desire to join Soviet Belorussia and Soviet Ukraine respectively, and on November 1 the Supreme Soviet of the USSR approved their incorporation.

Even before these annexations had been legalized, the Soviet Government began a series of diplomatic moves in the Baltic states. Singly and individually representatives of Estonia, Latvia, and Lithuania were invited to Moscow to negotiate pacts with the Soviet Union, which in each case included a provision granting the Soviet the right to establish and garrison with Red Army and Navy men certain naval and air bases within the territory of the smaller country. In the case of Lithuania the Russians were able to provide a token of goodwill which was enthusiastically received by the Lithuanians—the offer to return to them their ancient capital, the city of Vilno, which the Poles had seized in 1920 and which the Russians had taken over when they occupied eastern Poland.

The situation in the Baltic now seemed to have been stabilized, at least for the time being; but in June 1940 the political status of the three Baltic states was suddenly and drastically changed again. Latvia, Estonia, and Lithuania were incorporated in the Soviet Union, each receiving the status of a constituent republic in the Union. This new move seems to have been prompted by the unexpected and alarming collapse of France before the Nazi juggernaut in May and June. The immediate reaction on the part of Soviet leaders was to hasten all diplomatic efforts to complete and consolidate the strategic occupation of the Baltic area at the earliest possible moment. Following the procedure adopted by both western Belorussia and western Ukraine, a "people's government" was established in each of the Baltic countries on the basis of hurriedly conducted elections which resulted in more than 90 per cent of the votes being cast for the single party and its platform. These new governments almost immediately pleaded for and received admission into the Soviet Union.

Simultaneously an ultimatum was delivered to the Rumanian Government, and upon its expiration Soviet troops occupied Bessarabia and northern Bukovina. The parts of these two districts in which Ukrainians predominated were incorporated in the Soviet Ukraine, and the balance of the territory, populated chiefly by Rumanians, was organized as a constituent republic of the Soviet Union, the Moldavian SSR.

Executed in the face of the constantly increasing irritation of the Germans, who still were in no position to offer effective opposition, this series of swift and bold diplomatic maneuvers restored within the space of a few months the western boundaries of the Russian Empire, except for the Polish salient to which the Soviet laid no claim. Indeed, the new gains included in eastern Galicia and northern Bukovina a Ukrainian population which had never been part of the Russian Empire, although during the Middle Ages the area had been part of the Kievan federation. In general, from the Soviet standpoint, the revisions had resulted in a favorable realignment of the central and southern border regions and only the northern frontier remained an immediate danger.

The rectification of that last segment, the Finnish frontier, proved to be the most difficult and dangerous issue of all. The border with Finland ran only twenty miles from Leningrad, Russia's second largest city, and only a few miles beyond the border lay the Finnish line of fortifications, known as the Mannerheim Line. Therefore the Soviet Government demanded that Finland cede the Karelian Isthmus to the Soviet Union in exchange for a large piece of territory north of Lake Ladoga. The Finns rejected the Soviet offer, expecting support from the western countries. In starting war the Soviet Government apparently did not take into account all the dangerous implications. For one thing, the Russians seem not to have expected any resolute defense by the Finns, and appear to have counted on a revival of the Finnish Communist movement which had been suppressed by the White Finns and Germans in 1918. At the very beginning of the Soviet-Finnish war O. Kuusinen, leader of the Red Finns in 1918 and a prominent leader of the Communist International, hastened to organize a People's Government of Finland, but his efforts evoked no enthusiasm among the Finns. In spite of this, the Soviet Government signed a treaty of friendship with the Kuusinen government, and continued the war under the guise of protecting this new government against the White Finns. But this fiction of legality did not prevent the League of Nations from convicting the Soviet Union as an aggressor and depriving her of her League membership. The League, however, had awakened from its lethargy too late. Since for years it had done nothing to prevent acts of aggression on the part of Italy, Japan, and Germany, its sudden action against the Soviet Union could hardly be expected to produce the moral effect that had been hoped for. The political effects were, of course, infinitesimal.

Immediately after the beginning of the war on November 29 it became plain that the Soviet Union, overestimating the strength of Communist tendencies in some sections of the Finnish population and depending upon them to arouse a crippling civil strife in Finland, had failed to amass enough military power. The Finns, united and sustained by a glowing patriotism, knew and took advantage of every feature of the terrain to throw up a stout defense.

They were bolstered by expressions of sympathy and promises of equipment and volunteers which poured in from almost every country of the world, and from day to day they held on in the hope that concrete aid would soon reach them. Only Germany, still caught in the dilemma, stood aloof. In spite of the fact that the traditions of 1918 had not been forgotten, Berlin was forced to suppress all expression of pro-Finnish sympathy.

During the first two months of the war the Finns were able to beat off and parry most of the Russian attacks, but in February 1940 the Red Army was reorganized to meet the realities of the situation and began waging war in all seriousness. In a short time, driving against the center of the Mannerheim Line in the depths of an arctic winter, Soviet troops succeeded in piercing the Finnish fortifications which had been considered impregnable by many a military analyst. The Finns, having found the outside world more free with promises than with actual help, had no alternative but to sue for peace, which was concluded on March 12 on conditions less favorable to Finland than those in the original Russian demands. In addition to the Karelian Isthmus itself, the city and the district of Vyborg were annexed by the Soviet Union. Furthermore, the Finns were forced to lease the Hankoe Peninsula to Russia for a term of thirty years, a condition to which they had specifically objected during the negotiations preceding the war. A new constituent republic of the Soviet Union, the Karelo-Finnish Republic, was formed from the territory annexed from Finland and from a part of Soviet Karelia, and Kuusinen was elected chairman of the Presidium of its Supreme Soviet.

One result of the Finnish war was the disclosure to the Soviet leaders of many serious deficiencies in the organization of the Red Army. The weaknesses and mistakes were frankly recognized and discussed among army men, and under War Commissar Timoshenko feverish work was immediately begun to increase efficiency throughout the army. Particular attention was paid to matters of organization as well as to training and tactics and the service of supplies. One of the most serious difficulties encountered had been the confusion and delay that had resulted from the conflicts arising between political commissars and army officers, since the latter were not allowed to make any important decisions without the approval of these official political advisers. The institution of political

commissars has been a matter of contention almost since the founding of the Red Army. Created at the time of the civil war for the
dual purpose of directing the political advancement of the soldiers
and controlling the army leadership, they were later abolished, then
restored in the period immediately following Tukhachevsky's execution, and were now eliminated once more.

For the Soviet Union the first months of the second World War
were tense and difficult. However, the Russians were able during
this troubled period to strengthen their strategic position and, to
some extent, to secure their most exposed frontiers. Their action
was often hasty and sometimes aggressive and ill considered; but
they felt that there was no time to debate method; they must reach
their first and single objective in the shortest possible time: adequate defense of the Soviet Union.

3. *The German attack and the first stage of the war*

During the summer of 1940 the outward air of friendship which
had characterized relations between Germany and Russia began
to evaporate and the underlying tensions gradually became apparent. Though not abrupt, the changes were profound in their
implications—just how profound we can understand now when
we remember that Hitler himself later admitted in a proclamation
at the beginning of the Russian war that his decision to invade the
Soviet Union was made as early as August of 1940. But for the
time being the moves were veiled. In the 1939 agreement Germany had recognized the Soviet Union's interests not only in the
Baltic area but also, to some extent, in the Balkans. Hitler, it appears, had felt that circumstances would force the Russians to
move slowly and warily and that consequently the agreement was
being bought at the cost of comparatively small German sacrifices
in the Baltic area. However, the speed with which the Russians
moved to absorb the Baltic states into their defense system and to
consolidate their control of the whole region must certainly have
alarmed German military leaders. Having disposed of France, the
Germans now felt sufficiently secure to take steps to prevent the
further westward expansion of the Russians, and they determined,
as the first move, to exclude Russia from the Balkans. The Germans
conceded Russia had some right to Bessarabia, but the annexation
of northern Bukovina had seemed to them nothing less than po-

litical impertinence which required immediate and strong counter-measures. Accordingly, German troops were sent into Rumania and it was discreetly made clear that they would be used to "protect" that country against any further Russian aggression. They served an additional purpose as well, for a little later these protectors compelled the protected to cede considerable slices of territory to Hungary and Bulgaria—an exchange which cost the Germans nothing and secured them the support of two countries. As for Rumania, she was quietly promised ample compensation in the form of territory which was to be seized in the future dismemberment of Russia.

The Soviet Union was well aware of the ominous implications behind the German penetration of the Balkan Peninsula, but Russian leaders were forced to move cautiously in countering the threat. Russian foreign policy was geared to one aim—to avoid conflict with Germany altogether, or, failing that, to postpone it until the Soviets were better prepared. Obviously any direct provocation must be avoided. On the other hand, the very imminence of German attack made it all the more necessary for the Soviets to take immediate steps to insure themselves against simultaneous blows in the east and west which would make necessary the division of forces between two enormous fronts some 6,000 miles apart. The Kremlin had been deeply concerned about this possibility ever since the signing of the Three Power Pact. Preliminary negotiations with Japan had been under way for some time, and on April 13, 1941, the Soviet was able to conclude an important neutrality pact with that country which to some extent reduced the hazard. Article Two provided that "should one of the contracting parties become the object of hostilities on the part of one or several third powers, the other contracting party will observe neutrality throughout the duration of the conflict." This agreement, while it strengthened the position of the Kremlin by weakening the ties between Japan and Germany, itself contributed further to the deterioration of relations between Russia and Berlin, which were going from bad to worse. As early as in November 1940 Molotov, the Soviet foreign commissar, had gone to Berlin in an attempt to iron out the diplomatic conflicts by direct and frank discussions of the situation. His mission, though distinguished by a show of official courtesy, had been fruitless, and the German push southward had continued unabated throughout the winter. With the attack on Yugoslavia and Greece in April 1941 all possibilities of a Russo-German understanding appeared to have vanished.

The disastrous defeat of the democratic powers in Greece and the spectacular German invasion of Crete seemed to observers to open the way for an immediate attack on Egypt. Speculation on the probable date and method ran through the world press, and the Germans assiduously encouraged such beliefs as a new weapon in the war of nerves. As we now know, however, German plans had by this time undergone a radical revision, and under cover of the threat to drive into the Near East feverish preparations for the invasion of Russia were already in full swing. With Great Britain driven from the continent and the British Isles themselves menaced with invasion, Germany could look forward confidently to a period of comparative quiet in Europe which would make it possible to throw the whole weight of the Nazi army against the Russians. Indeed, Hitler seems to have believed it entirely possible that in England's extremity a German promise not to dismember the British Empire would be sufficient to enlist the English in a crusade against Bolshevism.

It was in line with this belief that deputy Nazi leader Rudolph Hess undertook his astounding flight to Scotland on May 10, 1941. According to a statement issued by Anthony Eden on September 22, 1943, Hess suggested that England should be allowed a free hand in the British Empire, Germany a free hand in Europe, and that Russia should be "included in Asia." However, Germany was ready to negotiate only with a "reasonable" British Government and not with Churchill's. If his terms were refused, Hitler was prepared "to destroy Great Britain utterly." The conditions which Hess stated merely amazed the British, and Hess himself was dealt with as a prisoner of war. However, even after the abrupt and ignominious failure of Hess's mission Hitler apparently hoped that his own armies would achieve a swift and resounding victory over the Russians which would demonstrate German invincibility once and for all and bring England to terms.

That the Germans confidently expected to destroy the Russian army within the space of a very few months—if not, indeed, within weeks—is clearly demonstrated in their official statements. In time it became clear that they had vastly underestimated the strength of the Red Army, a miscalculation which Hitler later complained bitterly was the result of Russian tricks in concealing their real military might. It seems probable that the Germans not only depended upon military successes to accomplish the destruction of Soviet power but also reckoned on the political disintegration of the state, and in particular they hoped to take advantage of peasant uprisings, especially in the Ukraine. They believed, apparently, that resentment against collectivization could be tied in with the separatist movement which had been to a certain extent nurtured in Berlin, to produce a crippling civil war.

On June 22, 1941, Hitler ripped to shreds the nonaggression pact which he had signed and at dawn sent German troops pouring over the Russian border for the supreme test of the Soviet system and the ultimate trial of the Red Army. The German blow was perhaps unequaled in military history; it was calculated to stun the Russians and to bring about their defeat before they could properly organize their defenses. The immediate danger which faced the Russian army at that moment was enormously greater than that of 1914; in the first World War German forces were engaged on two fronts, while the onslaught of 1941 was directed at Russia alone and backed by the whole force of the formidable German military and industrial machine. In addition the attack had been meticulously prepared and the Germans were now able to enlist and extort support from conquered and satellite countries throughout Europe—among them France, Finland, Slovakia, Hungary, Rumania, and Croatia—as well as from Italy.

Even before the German attack, in order to strengthen the Russian administration and to coordinate party and governmental institutions, Joseph Stalin had assumed the post of chairman of the Council of People's Commissars, i.e. premier (May 7, 1941). Immediately following the news of the invasion a Supreme Defense Council headed by Stalin was organized to direct the total national resistance. Made up of Communist officials representing every phase of Soviet life, the council included only one military figure, Marshal Boris Shaposhnikov, who served as an associate member and as Stalin's adviser. (In 1943 he was replaced by Marshal Alexander Vasilevsky.) Subsequently Stalin himself assumed the office of commander in chief of the Soviet Armed Forces, and still later the title of marshal of the Soviet Union was granted to him by the Red Army. As retreat followed retreat and the number of prisoners taken by the Germans grew (620,000 by July 7), the strain on Russian morale mounted. In order to prevent any deterioration of the fighting spirit in either the army or the civilian population and to facilitate the coordination of the army and civilian fighters harassing the enemy in the rear, the system of political commissars—or military commissars, as they were now called—was restored in an order of July 16.

Lack of training in combat conditions of modern war proved costly to the Russians on other parts of the vast front. While the Nazi machine was stalled in the Smolensk area for more than two months, the Germans scored dangerously both to the north and to the south. Moving through the Baltic states with little resistance, the vanguard of their armies finally reached the outskirts of Leningrad; in the south Kiev was occupied by September 20 and the Perekop Isthmus was forced on October 30. By November German pincers extending through both the northern and southern sectors threatened to nullify the stand at Smolensk, and for a time it seemed that Moscow itself might fall in an enormous enveloping move.

Hitler's confidence reached its height when he declared on October 3, "The enemy is already broken and will never rise again." His speech served as signal for the start of a German offensive to smash the Smolensk armies and drive on to take Moscow by direct frontal assault. At this juncture there came a shift in the Russian command, Marshal Zhukov being assigned the heavy task of holding the lines around Moscow. Throughout November the Germans launched a series of battering attacks on both the central and southern fronts. At the high point of their advance in the south on November 22, they made their way into Rostov, but a week later the Russians recaptured the city in a counterdrive that stopped the Germans at the gateway to the Caucasus. Meanwhile, the German army piled up at the approaches of Moscow and sent troops swinging around the capital to cut communications with the rear. In the bitter Russian winter hundreds of thousands of soldiers stormed backward and forward over the ringing ground as the great armies struggled for a mortal grip. And there, almost within artillery rang of the spires of the Kremlin, with victory at its fingertips, the German army was stopped.

On December 6 a carefully prepared and successfully executed counteroffensive was hurled at the numbed, ill-clad Germans. Armed with special winter equipment designed to function efficiently at temperatures far below zero, and clothed in uniforms adapted to the Russian climate, Red Army men were able to take advantage of every weakness in the German army and to exploit every crack they could open in the Nazi lines. The noose that had been drawing around Moscow was cut and Soviet troops, pressing on the heels of a frozen and dejected German army, forced them to fight a bitter retreat which lasted until the spring thaws ended the campaign in March 1942. Having suffered tremendous losses and endured one of the cruelest ordeals in modern military history the Germans were at last able to establish the center of their forces on the line running from Rzhev to Viazma. The first stage of the war had ended.

4. The effect of the war on Russia and Soviet-Allied relations in 1941 and 1942

The war affected the Russian national consciousness much more deeply and in many more ways than the first World War ever had. A nationwide drive for volunteers for the civilian and army services was immediately organized among the youth. Factory working hours were increased and machines speeded up in order to enlarge the production of military equipment and munitions. The reaction of the peasants appears to have been somewhat slower than that of the urban workers. The village population, however, soon learned the meaning of war from the German occupational authorities who instituted a regime replete with seizure of hostages, deportation of Russian laborers to Poland and Germany, and the requisitioning of all available food supplies.

In spite of careful governmental planning and in spite of the help, especially from America, which the Soviet Union received through Lend-Lease channels, the civilian population had to endure severe deprivation and hardship. Because of the loss of enormously rich agricultural regions such as the Ukraine and, in 1942, the northern Caucasus—which was held by the Germans for only a brief period, but, unfortunately for the Russians, a period coinciding with the harvest—the supply of basic foods was dangerously reduced. Especially in north Russia shortages became alarming, and to insure the distribution of food even on a subsistence level it became necessary to institute strict rationing. Since all industrial facilities were turned over to the production of military supplies immediately after the invasion, the scarcity of clothing and other consumer goods soon created additional hardships. Even though the controls set up by the Soviet Government have functioned much more efficiently than those instituted in 1914–17, it seems certain that the actual suffering of the civilian population was far greater in this war than at any time during the first World War.

Before Hitler's attack on Russia, relations between the Soviet Union and the Anglo-Saxon countries had been characterized, as we have seen, by mutual distrust and suspicion. The first result of the German invasion was the immediate installation of the Soviet Union in the camp of the Allies; whether it was formally recognized or not, the logic of the situation at once made Russia an ally of Great Britain. Circumstances forced the two countries to coordinate their efforts against a common enemy, and, as events transpired, for the next two years it was the Soviet Union that had to bear the full brunt of the German assault. It is possible that even after the internment of Rudolph Hess the Germans hoped that Great Britain might tacitly, if not openly, accept his message and refrain from interference with the German offensive in Russia. If they did entertain such hopes, they were soon disillusioned. Within the space of hours after Germany's invasion Winston Churchill had declared his country's complete solidarity with Russia. Sir Stafford Cripps was immediately sent to Moscow to establish a working contact with the Soviet Government, and on July 12, 1941, a solemn agreement for joint action between the two governments was signed.

A secondary result of the German war in Russia was the beginning of a measure of relief for the bomb-shocked, weary English people. As the Germans thrust deeper into Russia, they threw all their available forces to the east, and London and other shattered British cities were spared, for the time being at least, the devastating bombing raids of the preceding months. The average Briton could not but feel gratitude to the Russians who, by their determined stand, had provided some respite for Great Britain. It is true there remained conservative circles in which an attitude of fear and coldness toward the Soviet was much in evidence; early in September, for example, a member of the British cabinet, J. T. C. Moore-Barbazon, rose to express the hope that the Red Army and the German army would exterminate each other. However, such statements were not representative of the opinion of the general British public.

In the United States—at that time, of course, not officially in the war—public opinion changed more slowly. President Roosevelt, however, at a press conference two days after the German attack made it clear that the United States would help Russia. The Treasury Department immediately released part of the Soviet funds which had been frozen in the United States at the time of the Russo-Finnish war, and on October 30 a billion dollar loan was granted to the Soviet Union for the purchase of armaments and supplies. There remained, nevertheless, a very tangible difference between the British and American attitudes toward Russia. The United States was still at peace, officially; she was remote from the war, psychologically and geographically; bombs had never fallen on an American city. Consequently, the turn in public opinion toward Russia did not come as quickly as in Britain, nor was it as far reaching. For a long time Russia was considered in a special category—not so much an ally as an enemy of our enemy. Later, after Pearl Harbor and the German declaration of war against the United States, and after a feeling of admiration for Russia's continued resistance had had time to develop in wide sections of the American public, the rapprochement with the Soviets found broader support.

Just as it was not easy for the United States and, to a lesser extent, for Great Britain wholeheartedly to accept Russia as an ally, Russia found it difficult to adjust her attitudes to the new situation. Soviet leaders continued to fear that the Anglo-Saxon countries intended trying to use Russia as a pawn; statements such as that of Moore-Barbazon and occasional articles in the press were fuel for their suspicions. In a speech on July 3, 1941, Stalin expressed the hope that in her war of liberation Russia would have "loyal allies in the peoples of Europe and America," but he was careful to avoid any definite commitments in regard to the Anglo-Saxon countries. Russia needed Britain's help, and when the trickle of supplies which she received in the beginning gradually began to assume important proportions, she was grateful. But as time went on she hoped for more direct support; she began to demand a more active military effort on the part of Great Britain. However, she expressed willingness to come to terms with both Great Britain and the United States by adhering to the Atlantic Charter of August 14, 1941, as well as by signing the Declaration of the United Nations of January 1, 1942.

As Russian defenses stiffened toward the end of the first year of the Soviet-German war, British and American confidence in the seriousness of the Russian effort grew. The warming of relations encouraged the visit of Foreign Commissar Molotov to both London and Washington in June 1942. In London a twenty-year treaty of alliance was signed by Great Britain and the Soviet Union, providing not only for common action between the two countries during the war but for their collaboration afterward for "the organization of security and the economic prosperity of Europe." In Washington Molotov met with less success than he had in London; the United States avoided a formal alliance with the Soviet Union, in all probability because of her reluctance to recognize Soviet control over the Baltic states. That did not mean that the United States Government would not continue to support the Russian military effort; the Soviets were included in the Lend-Lease plan, and an agreement to that effect was signed by both countries. Indeed, from then on supplies were shipped both through Murmansk and Iran in constantly increasing amounts, and by July 1943 the United States had achieved the goal of moving a million tons of equipment a month over the Iran route alone.

It appears, however, that the main purpose of Molotov's visit was to secure the opening of the so-called second front in Europe. Although neither Prime Minister Churchill nor President Roosevelt could do more than express his desire to establish such a front before the year was out, both Stalin and Molotov seem to have considered that statement a definite commitment. The misunderstanding which appears to have arisen here resulted in considerable disappointment in Moscow when the summer came and went without the Allies having taken any action. In his letter of October 4, 1942, to Henry Cassidy, an American correspondent in Moscow, Stalin said bluntly that "the aid of the Allies to the Soviet Union has so far been little effective," and recommended that "the Allies fulfill their obligations fully and on time." The landing of Allied troops in North Africa in November 1942 somewhat improved the situation, since it was recognized in Moscow that thenceforward German attention would necessarily be divided and that the African campaign was certain to result in psychological if not material help to Russia. The North African landing was not, however, accepted by the Russians as a full-fledged second front and they continued to remind the democracies that the promise of an invasion of Europe had so far not been realized.

The United States Government, on the other hand, did not find conditions in Russia always to its liking. Admiral Standley, American ambassador in Moscow, in a public statement on March 8, 1943, expressed his dissatisfaction with the Soviet Government's reluctance to exchange information on the conduct of the war. He complained, too, that American aid to Russia—through Lend-Lease, Russian War Relief, and other channels—could not be sufficiently appreciated by the Russian people because the Russian Government told them little about it. After this the Soviet Government went to considerable lengths to publicize American aid through the press and the radio.

As the war progressed and the democracies began to move toward invasion of the continent of Europe, there was a noticeable improvement in relations between the Soviets and the Anglo-Saxon countries. In his order of the day on May 1, 1943, Stalin took cognizance of the Allied successes in Africa. The capture of Tunisia, which constituted a German rout similar in some ways to that at Stalingrad, and especially the landing in Sicily in July, seem to have convinced the Russians that the Allies were waging war in earnest and intended to open a second front. Only the question of when continued to be a sore point.

5. The campaign of 1942

On April 26, 1942, Hitler unequivocally declared that the decision of the war must fall on the eastern front, and Russia was thus warned that a renewed German drive was imminent. In spite of the substantial successes which they had achieved during the campaigns of the preceding winter, the Russians did not minimize the dangers that now threatened them. The concentration of almost the whole of Europe's manpower and industrial facilities in Hitler's hands made the German army the most formidable military machine in the world. RAF raids over Germany and France which were later to take a heavy toll of German production were still in an experimental stage, and the German industrial system had nowhere shown any signs of disorganization. In 1942 it is probable that German and German-controlled production of armament and munitions was rising to its peak, and, in spite of substantial German losses in men and material in the campaigns of 1941, the Russians could reasonably expect the German army to be stronger in 1942 than it had been a year before.

The Red Army, however, had also been gathering strength during the preceding year. It had acquired valuable experience both in defensive and offensive warfare; a substantial percentage of the troops was battle-trained, and the military leadership was in competent hands. Russian industries in the safe areas of the Urals were now pouring out equipment, and British and American aid in material was beginning to be felt on a larger scale. More important, perhaps, was the strengthening of national morale which had resulted from the successes of the preceding winter. The elimination of the military commissars on October 9, 1942, was a concrete demonstration of the Soviet leaders' belief in a new spirit of mutual confidence between the army and the nation as a whole.

The main German blow was delivered against the Don area between Voronezh and Rostov. The German plan was an ambitious one, and had they succeeded in the opening drive all along the line, they would have provided themselves with a number of possibilities, the most likely of which would probably have been a deep and dangerous flanking movement against Moscow itself. However Voronezh, at the very northern end of the front, held against their heaviest assaults, and the German offensive consequently could develop only in a southern and southeastern direction— against the Caucasus and lower Volga. That, in turn, posed other problems: in order to protect their western flank while they drove into the Caucasus, the Germans needed to establish complete control over Crimea. This done, they penetrated into the northern Caucasus and seized the important Maikop oil fields. Next they turned against another Russian bastion, a city on the Volga— Stalingrad.

The story of the defense of Stalingrad is one of unbelievable endurance in the face of overwhelming odds, of bloodshed and sacrifice on a scale unequaled in modern military history. So tenacious was the Russian resistance and so determined was Hitler to break it that the conquest of that one city lying in a bend of the Volga at last became a cardinal point of German military honor. As if hypnotized by the magnitude of the task they had set themselves, all through the fall of 1942 the Germans sent division after division, wave after wave crashing against the citadel. Meanwhile, north and south of the city Russian troops began hacking at the flanks of the attackers. The German command dismissed these attacks as desperate sallies designed to relieve the pressure on the center, and flung still more men against the tight little knot of resistance still clinging to the icy bank of the Volga. The jaws of massive Russian pincers moved around the German army, and, apparently before the Nazi command was aware of the danger, closed around 350,000 exhausted German troops. The Red Army, under the command of Marshal Zhukov and General Rokosovsky, proceeded with the annihilation of this tremendous force, destroying it piece by piece. In January 1943 some 90,000 Germans surrendered—all that was left of the mighty German army that had stood before Stalingrad.

While the battle of Stalingrad was in progress, the Russians had been able to mount attacks in several other sectors. In time the drives which they developed near Voronezh and Vladikavkaz threatened all of the German armies on the southern front and finally forced them to retreat in order to avoid a catastrophe like Stalingrad. In the extreme north, too, the Russians took advantage of the changed situation to improve their position around Leningrad. In January 1943 they succeeded in retaking Schluesselburg on the shore of Lake Ladoga and in driving the Germans back from the Leningrad-Vologda railway. While these operations did not relieve Leningrad from siege, they did establish at least one rail link with the rear and thus improved somewhat the desperate condition of the people within the city. Meanwhile the Red Army continued offensive action all along the southern front. As the Russian armies swept on from newly captured strong points, it seemed for a time that the Germans would be forced to continue their retreat to the Dnieper. The Russians, however, overreached themselves. The recaptured railways upon which they depended for the movement of much of their supplies all had to be laboriously reconverted from the narrow European gauge to which the Germans had adapted

them, and in their rapid sweep across the Donets the Russians out-
ran the work of reconversion and dangerously weakened their extended lines of communications.

A resurgence of German power now compelled the Russians to
attempt to drain some of the Nazi armies from the southern front
by creating a "second front" of their own in the Lake Ilmen and
Velikie Luki sector. In this new Red Army drive the Russians
scored an important success by eliminating the powerful triangle
of German fortresses in Rzhev, Gzhatsk, and Viazma which
throughout the winter had remained a potential threat to Moscow.
The Germans were able to muster enough strength to retake Kharkov and Belgorod by the end of March, but all their attempts to
force a crossing of the Donets River collapsed after three weeks
of severe fighting. By the beginning of April the eastern front was
once more stabilized and both armies took advantage of the period
of the spring thaws to rest and prepare for renewed summer offen-
sives.

6. *The dissolution of the Comintern and Soviet-Slavic relations*

The circumstances surrounding the outbreak of the second World
War and the developments of the first two years of the conflict
revealed clearly enough that, contrary to the expectations of
many, the division of forces had been drawn on the basis of nationalities rather than classes, that national boundaries rather than
international class lines separated the opposing groups. The emphasis on Russian patriotism reflected Soviet recognition of the
national character of the war and foreshadowed other adjustments
which the Soviet Union could be expected to make to meet the
situation.

We have already seen (p. 374) that the Seventh Congress of the
Communist International in 1935 revealed a curtailment of activities and a marked diminution of fighting spirit. For various reasons,
principally fear of Trotskyite opposition, no more congresses were
allowed to convene, and in the years after 1935 the executive committee of the International more and more assumed the character
of a subsidiary organ of the All-Union Communist party. It was
brought forward when and if the foreign policy of the Soviet Union
required its support, and even on these relatively infrequent occasions—notably in the case of the Soviet-Finnish war—its activities

often resulted in more harm than help. As a result of this progressive disuse of the body, the presidium of the executive committee of the Communist International on May 22, 1943, moved the dissolution of the whole organization. After emphasizing the important role of the International in accomplishing historically necessary functions, the presidium concluded that, since in the present war the division definitely did not correspond to class lines but was rather a conflict between the Hitlerite military machine and an anti-Hitlerite coalition, the International no longer served an essential political purpose. The national Communist parties which had previously been affiliated with the International were advised to shape their policies in accordance with their own judgment of the national situation; and the International at least officially ceased to exist.

Coincident with the weakening and dissolution of the Communist International and paralleling the growth of Soviet nationalism came the revival of Pan-Slavism. Russia now reverted to her old technique of seeking friends among her kin beyond her borders. Whereas religious affiliations between Imperial Russia and the Orthodox Slav peoples of the Balkan Peninsula were once the firmest ties, now ethnic and cultural affinities were the primary links. However, the Soviet leaders did not entirely neglect the religious aspects; the re-establishment of the patriarchate in Moscow (September 12, 1943) could not fail to produce a favorable impression among the Orthodox peoples of the Balkan Peninsula.

A powerful sponsor of Soviet Pan-Slavism was, of course, none other than Hitler himself. By his propagation of the doctrine of German racial superiority over the Slav, by his brutal attempts to reduce the Slavic peoples to an amorphous mass of German serfs through the systematic extermination of all cultural leaders in Bohemia, Poland, and Serbia, Hitler gave Russia the opportunity to lead at least for a time a kind of Pan-Slav crusade. Spokesmen for all Slavic peoples participated in the first All-Slav Congress which met in Moscow as early as August 1941, and among the organizers and speakers were many prominent Slavic writers, historians, and artists. The emphasis at this meeting was on the cultural ties which bound all the peoples represented in an ethnic unity.

As always, Russo-Polish relations presented a delicate problem and at once became a stumbling block in the way of Slavic unity. There is a long history of Polish antagonism toward the Russians, and it was only natural that the older resentments should have been increased by the Soviet occupation of eastern Poland in September 1939. On the other hand, Russia remembered the Polish attack of 1920 which had resulted in the Polish annexation of a considerable part of western Belorussia and western Ukraine. The reoccupation of that territory in 1939, from the Soviet point of view, represented nothing more than the recapture of land which had been forcibly taken from Russia during the turmoil of the civil war. In addition to these specific points of contention, the general tone of relations between the two countries during the interval between 1921 and 1939 had been anything but friendly, and at times had been especially complicated by Soviet antireligious moves and by the opposition of Polish Catholicism to every aspect of communism.

When the German attack placed Russia on the side of the Allies, to whose camp Poland had, of course, belonged from the beginning of the war, some sort of working agreement between the Soviet and the Polish Government-in-Exile became imperative. A preliminary arrangement, in which such thorny problems as that of the frontiers were avoided, was signed on July 30, 1941. Two weeks later representatives of the two countries concluded a military agreement which provided for the formation in Russia of a Polish army to participate in the common struggle against the German invader. Relations seemed to be progressing on a mutually satisfactory basis and in Moscow on December 3, at the end of a friendly conference with General Sikorski, head of the Polish Government-in-Exile, Stalin took the opportunity to declare his belief that a strong Poland was essential for a lasting European peace.

Relations between the two nations were not, however, to continue on the same smooth course. The Polish army provided for in the agreement was to be recruited among the Polish officers and men who had been taken prisoner by the Red Army at the time of the occupation of Eastern Poland in 1939. These men who had been interned at various places—mostly in Kazakhstan—were released upon the conclusion of the military agreement, and immediately set about organizing the army, which was to be equipped with supplies from Great Britain. But it was difficult for either side to forget the injuries of the past, and within a short time friction had once more developed between the Soviet Government and the Polish leaders. At last, toward the end of January 1942, it was decided to transfer the newly formed Polish army to Iran where it would operate under British jurisdiction. The whole incident left an unfortunate impression with both nations, and the Russians were particularly disappointed since they had hoped for the immediate participation of the Poles in the war on the eastern front.

Though the Soviet Government tended to become increasingly suspicious of the Polish Government-in-Exile, efforts were made to build and preserve close relations with the Polish people. In 1942 a group primarily of Polish Communist refugees in Russia formed the Union of Polish Patriots and began publishing a Polish language newspaper in Moscow called *Free Poland*. This group, one of whose leading members was the writer Wanda Wasilewska, as an essential part of its program urged the closest possible cooperation of the Poles with the Soviet Union. (It subsequently served as the nucleus of a "Polish Army" which was used by the Soviets in setting up a Soviet-dominated regime in Poland.) In London, meanwhile, the feeling of some groups of Polish émigrés was mounting against the Soviet Union, and early in 1943 a number of them started a campaign in both the British and American press urging the Allies to guarantee that the 1921–39 eastern frontier of Poland would be restored after the war. This campaign evoked bitter resentment in the Soviet Union, and in February *Pravda* published an article by the prominent Ukrainian playwright, A. Korneichuk, warning that the Ukrainians and White Russians would never agree to return to Polish domination. In April 1943 relations were further strained by the Germans' announcement that they had unearthed thousands of bodies of Polish officers in the Katyn forest and that the mass murder had been committed by the Russians before their retreat from this area. The Polish Government-in-Exile demanded an international investigation, to which the Russians did not agree. Later, when the Russians entered the region, they conducted an investigation of their own and laid the massacre at the Germans' door. In 1952 a committee of United States House of Representatives investigated the Katyn case and in its final report concluded that the Russians were "unquestionably guilty." (See *The New York Times*, December 23,

1952.) This episode led on April 26 to the official breaking off of relations between the Soviet Government and the Polish Government-
in-Exile.

In addition to the difficulties with Poland, further Pan-Slavic
complications arose in Yugoslavia. The anti-Axis guerrilla movement which developed in that country immediately after its conquest by the Germans was not united in the struggle against the
invaders but had divided into two rival groups whose leaders vied
for control of the patriot forces. One group, headed by General D.
Mihailović, operated under the auspices of the Yugoslav
Government-in-Exile. The other, known as the Partisans, led by
Josef Broz, now known as Marshal Tito, established connections
with the Soviet Government, and, while not officially Communist,
was more radical than the first. Within its ranks, too, both Serbs
and Croats were active, while Mihailović's movement represented
a narrower aspect of Serbian nationalism. Of the two, the Partisan
movement developed a wider range of action and tried to establish
better relations with the people of Bulgaria. In two other Slavic
countries, Slovakia and Croatia, puppet governments were established and propped up by Axis armies; and Slovenia was, until the
Italian capitulation, divided between Germany and Italy.

7. The Campaign of 1943

By the spring of 1943 the war in all its international phases had
turned greatly in favor of the Allies. On May 9 the Tunisian campaign was brought to a successful conclusion, and along the whole
northern coast of Africa the Allies stood ready to launch the Mediterranean assault against Hitler's European fortress. Once again
Winston Churchill went to Washington to discuss the larger aspects
of the war with Franklin Roosevelt in a meeting in which particular
attention could now be given to Japan and Pacific operations—a
subject which automatically excluded Russia from the discussions.
In regard to the situation in western Europe, the conferees agreed
not to hurry the landing of troops in France or Holland, but to concentrate first on an attempt to shatter German industry and weaken
German resistance by air attack. There followed almost immediately a series of powerful air raids by RAF bombers and American
Flying Fortresses aimed principally at the industrial centers of the
Ruhr. In July 1943 British experts estimated that in the Ruhr

alone nearly 1,000,000 homes had been destroyed by bombs and that German authorities had been forced to evacuate no less than 3,000,000 people from the area. This interference with the labor supply in the most concentrated factory area in Europe, coupled with the certain destruction and damage to the plants themselves, had a paralyzing effect on the delivery of essential military supplies from the whole region.

No actual invasion of western Europe, however, had yet begun, nor were there signs that one was imminent; and Hitler must have believed that he still had time for another attempt to deal the Russians a crushing blow before the second front could materialize. The Germans were now attempting to utilize the anti-Communist elements among the Russian émigrés and especially among the Russian prisoners of war in order to create an anti-Stalinist Russian army to re-enforce the German drive. General Andrew Vlasov agreed to head the movement. His Russian Army of Liberation consisted mostly of prisoners of war. A number of them were guided by the idea of overthrowing Stalin's government. Others joined to escape from the harsh regime of the German prison camps. The "Eastern Troops" organized by the Germans (including Vlasov's army) comprised 78 battalions, 1 regiment, and 122 companies, around 100,000 men in all. There were about 220,000 "Voluntary Helpers" or labor battalions besides. After having started this movement the Germans became suspicious of Vlasov's intentions and hesitated to use his troops on any large scale. Just before the end of the war Vlasov dramatically went over to the Czech side. He was later executed by the Soviet.

On July 5 the main German offensive rolled ahead on the full front from Orel to Kharkov. Since Orel lay well forward on a German salient driven into the Russian lines, the Nazis once again could attempt to break through in an effort to flank Moscow, and, should that fail once more, they would still, perhaps, have an opportunity to swing south in an encircling movement against the Russians in the exposed Kursk salient. But this time, instead of adopting their usual tactic of retreating while they wore down the enemy, the Russians were determined to stand firm on their lines and meet the attackers head on. This was a momentous decision, for failure would have entailed tremendous losses for the Red Army and possibly critical disorganization. By July 15 the German attacks had dwindled with the apparent exhaustion of the Nazi troops. Then the Red Army seized the initiative on the Orel front and surged forward in the Soviet's first summer offensive. By August 6 both Orel and Belgorod were in their hands, and two weeks later Kharkov fell to the Russian troops. These successes were tempered, however, by the fact that the Germans had systematically destroyed every town and city they had been forced to abandon. In Kharkov, for example, fully 65 per cent of the buildings had been burned and blasted to rubble before the Russians reoccupied the city, and many of the structures which still stood were too seriously damaged to be habitable. Orel was reduced to a shambles as unrecognizable as Kharkov.

By October 1 the Russians had reached the Dnieper line on a wide front from Kiev to Zaporozhie. By taking Smolensk they had not only assumed control of the upper part of the river but had spread westward beyond it. Between Smolensk and Kiev their troops had everywhere surged to a line just short of the Dnieper, and the Gomel fortress was almost the only Nazi strong point remaining in the area. To the south the Russians had reoccupied the Donets basin and by seizing the Taman Peninsula had also closed the door to the Caucasus. On October 7 the Red Army crashed through the Dnieper line above Kiev, at Pereiaslav, and in Kremenchug, and established three firm bridgeheads on the western bank of the river. Concerted German efforts failed to throw the Russians back, and the Red Army gradually succeeded in expanding the base westward at each of these points. As the snow fell along the northern part of the Russian front in the third winter of the war, the Red Army was poised for a series of drives from Leningrad to the Black Sea.

8. *Soviet-Allied relations in 1943*

The Allies, who were still somewhat skeptical of the offensive strength of the Red Army, were favorably impressed by the Russian campaigns carried through in the summer and fall of 1943. The Russians, on the other hand, could not but be pleased by the Anglo-American conquest of Sicily and subsequent amputation of the foot of the Italian "boot." The eastern and western theaters of war were thus slowly being drawn together, and the possibility of their being merged somewhere in the Balkans in the not too distant future began to occupy the minds of the Allied statesmen. Obviously coordination of the military efforts and political actions of all the Allies was now an urgent necessity. Although there already existed a fundamental unity of purpose between the nations allied against Nazi Germany, and although it was well understood in all capitals that the logic of the situation had made synchronizing the grand strategy absolutely imperative, the actual conclusion of such a working agreement was repeatedly thwarted.

At the Anglo-American parley in Quebec in August 1943 no Russian delegate participated in the conversations. Although certain sections of the American press found sinister implications in the alleged Russian unwillingness to attend the conference, Stalin, in a characteristically blunt statement, announced that because of the special nature of the meeting the Soviet Government had not been invited to participate. This was taken to mean that problems relating to the war in the Pacific constituted an important part of the agenda, and that Russia was exercising caution in an effort to avoid impairing the delicate balance of neutrality existing between the USSR and Japan. Apparently, however, this explanation was incomplete, for at about the same time Ambassador Ivan Maisky was replaced in London by Fedor Gusev, former Russian minister in Ottawa, and Andrei Gromyko was assigned the post previously held by Litvinov in Washington. In both cases veteran diplomats who were closely associated with the policy of international cooperation were replaced by able young men whose training identified them with the realistic and nationalistic Russian spirit of more recent years.

In September Ambassador Admiral Standley was called from Moscow to Washington to report on the Russian situation. He subsequently resigned his post for what he said were personal reasons. He was replaced on October 1 by W. Averell Harriman, who, because of his previous connection with the Lend-Lease program, was then persona grata with the Russian Government. The appointment on September 25 of Edward R. Stettinius, formerly Lend-Lease administrator, as undersecretary of state also created a favorable impression in Moscow.

As early as the Casablanca conference (January 1943) both President Roosevelt and Prime Minister Churchill had expressed their desire to arrange a personal meeting with Marshal Stalin in order to eliminate any misunderstandings which might still remain among the Allies. After the Quebec conference they reiterated the suggestion. The Russians, although they appeared eager to come to an agreement with the Allies, proposed that before the meeting of the heads of the governments a conference of the foreign secretaries take place to prepare the ground. Assuming that London would be the logical place for the meeting, both Great Britain and the United States readily agreed to such a conference. The Russians, however, insisted that it be held in Moscow. Their demand was motivated partly, perhaps, by considerations of prestige, and partly by Foreign Commissar Molotov's desire to be in a position to avail himself of Stalin's advice should unexpected problems arise at the parleys. After some hesitation, London and Washington accepted the Russian proposal and preparations were immediately begun for a conference in Moscow in October.

In the next weeks the Russians became noticeably more cooperative, especially in the diplomatic problems connected with the Mediterranean theater of war. When Italy declared war on her former ally, Germany, on October 13, the Russians joined with the United States and Great Britain in accepting Italy as a cobelligerent. The Russians also agreed to participate in the Mediterranean Commission, sending a vice commissar of foreign affairs, Andrew Vyshinsky, as delegate. They insisted, unexpectedly, that the commission be given full authority instead of being only a fact-finding body as had originally been planned by both Great Britain and the United States.

On October 19 the third Lend-Lease agreement between Great Britain, the United States, and the Soviet Union was signed in London, with Canada participating for the first time. The same day the Moscow conference opened and proceeded for two weeks. The results were set forth in a joint declaration which asserted that the united action of the four great participating powers—the United States, Great Britain, the USSR, and China—"pledged for the prosecution of the war against their common enemies, will be continued for the organization and maintenance of peace and security." To this end the four governments "recognized the necessity of establishing at the earliest practicable date a central international organization, based on the principle of the sovereign equality of all peace-loving states, and open to membership by all such states, large and small." The four governments would "consult with one another and, as occasion requires, with other members of the United Nations, with a view to joint action on behalf of the community of nations." In an especially significant section the governments agreed "that after the termination of hostilities they will not employ their forces within the territories of other states, except for the purpose envisaged in this declaration and after joint consultation."

Preparations started immediately for the meeting of the heads of the governments—Roosevelt, Churchill, and Stalin. The Big Three met in Teheran, Iran, on November 28, 1943, in the building of the Russian Embassy. On December 1 they signed a joint declaration expressing their determination "that our nations shall work together in the war and in the peace to follow. . . . And as to the peace, we are sure that our concord will make it an enduring peace." As for the war: "We have reached complete agreement as to the scope and timing of operations which will be undertaken from the east, west, and south. . . . We shall seek the cooperation and active participation of all nations, large and small, whose peoples in heart and mind are dedicated, as are our own peoples, to the elimination of tyranny and slavery, oppression and intolerance." Apparently the Allies considered themselves more firmly united and more ready to tackle the common tasks before them than at any time since the beginning of the second World War.

9. *The end of the war*

The successes of the Allied armies in 1943, especially the advance of the Russians along the Ukrainian front, could not but affect the calculations and plans of the German command. The idea was now put forward by Hitler's advisers that for the coming year the main task of the German armies must be to defend the "fortress of Europe" (*Festung Europa*). This was the so-called "Frederician theory" which likened Hitler's plight to that of Frederick the Great in the Seven Years' War. Owing to disunity among his enemies Frederick was able then to save himself and Prussia by a series of victorious counterblows. In contrast to Frederick, however, the German leaders of 1944 were reluctant voluntarily to abandon their overextended positions—especially in the Baltic and the Black Sea areas—and to shrink their lines of defense. By the time they realized the urgent necessity of it the opportunity for a well-planned retreat was already lost. In the period between December 1943 and early May 1944 the Russians undertook a series of vigorous campaigns which resulted, at the two ends of the front, in the liberation of the Leningrad area west to the Estonian border and south almost to Vitebsk and in the reconquest of the Crimea. In both cases the Germans lost a considerable part of their equipment and manpower. The main Russian blow in this period was directed southwest toward Bukovina, and the ground was now well prepared for Russian attack on Hungary and Rumania.

To forestall this danger the German command had to concentrate most of its attention and most of its forces in the east. The moment was favorable for an Allied attack from the west, and on June 6 the British-American troops invaded Normandy; the long-awaited second front now became a reality, and Germany was finally caught between two fires. Strategic cooperation between the western Allies and Russia now became even more imperative than before, and in full realization of this the Russians resumed their offensive on June 23. It started in Belorussia where limited though important objectives were achieved; late in August the Russians invaded Rumania; following the collapse of Rumania, Bulgaria surrendered on September 8; in October and November of 1944, crossing the Carpathian Mountains at several points, the Russians penetrated deep into Hungary. In January 1945 they attacked the very stronghold of Germanism, East Prussia. As the troops of the western Allies were advancing both in France and Italy, the situation of Germany became desperate. The question was now not whether the Germans would be able to defend central Europe but who would get there first, the Anglo-Americans or the Russians.

As events took a turn favorable to the Allies, their leaders were in a position to think not only of the immediate war tasks but of future international stabilization as well. In August and September 1944 a conference of the representatives of the main Allied nations met at Dumbarton Oaks to discuss the obligations of the nations of the world to ensure a future of durable peace. The recommendations of the conference were made public on October 9. It was suggested that henceforth all disputes, controversies, and frictions among the nations should be settled by general agreement and arbitration without resort to armed force. To achieve this aim the creation of an international organization was recommended, with a general assembly representing all the Allied and associated nations, and a smaller security council. Simultaneously an effort was made by the United States, Britain, and the Soviet Union to lay concerted plans for Hitler's final defeat. With this aim, as well as to coordinate and demarcate the lines of advance on Germany from west and east, the Big Three met again, this time in Yalta in the Crimea. The Crimea conference proved one of the most significant and debated inter-Allied meetings of the war. The report of the conference, signed on February 11, 1945, appeared in the American press two days later. Unconditional surrender of Nazi Germany was set as a goal of the Allies and, after victory and the occupation of Germany, "a central control commission consisting of the supreme commanders of the three powers" was to be established with headquarters in Berlin. A commission for compensation for damage caused by Germans to the Allied nations was to be formed in Moscow. All European states conquered by the Germans were to be liberated and restored with the assistance of the three major Allied powers. Specifically it was agreed that the Provisional Government then functioning in Poland should be recognized on a broader democratic basis. On the higher international level, the Big Three pledged themselves to follow the recommendations of the Dumbarton Oaks meeting and to call a conference of the United Nations at San Francisco on April 25, 1945. Within the framework of their major decisions announced to the world, the Big Three also made a number of agreements on specific points, such as the demarcation lines of the respective Allied armies; according to this agreement the Balkan countries (except Greece), as well as Hungary, Czechoslovakia, and the eastern part of Germany, were to be occupied by Soviet troops. While the major part of the conference was devoted to the European theater of war, the situation in the Far East was given considerable attention. Stalin promised that Russia would declare war on Japan ninety days after the fall of Germany. In return it was agreed that "the former rights of Russia violated by the treacherous attack of Japan in 1904 shall be restored" and in addition the Kuril Islands would be "handed over" to the Soviet Union.

At the very time of the Yalta conference the struggle for Budapest ended in complete victory for the Russians. Following the conference, offensive operations were continued relentlessly by both the western Allies and the Russians. In the course of March and April the Russians occupied East Prussia; simultaneously other Russian armies marched on Vienna, which was cleared of the enemy by April 13. Now the last and most difficult task was left to the Russians—to subdue the center of the Nazi state, the city of Berlin, where Hitler and his associates were preparing a desperate stand. The Battle of Berlin, ably directed by Marshal Zhukov, lasted from April 17 to May 2. Hitler was reported dead on May 1. As the western Allies pressed their offensive from the other side, the German state rapidly disintegrated. On May 7 the Provisional Government of Germany surrendered unconditionally. The formal ratification of the surrender was signed in Berlin on May 8.

The collapse of German resistance brought the European war to an end but did not result in any immediate and stable peace settlement. For the victors, to achieve durable peace proved a much more difficult task than to crush the German armies. The disruption of economic life, the destruction of cities and industrial establishments both in eastern and central Europe, presented a series of highly complex economic and social problems; psychologically it was not easy to shift from destructive operations to creative reconstruction; last but not least, it soon became obvious that there was no agreement among the Allies on the methods and objectives of the peace settlement. During the war the Allies had to cooperate of sheer necessity. Now, as the pressure of war in Europe was lifted and victory in Asia seemed near, old prejudices and mutual suspicions revived. To a certain extent this affected—for a time—even relations between the United States and Great Britain, and—for a longer period—relations between France and the Anglo-Saxon countries. But the main difficulty proved to be between the United States and the Soviet Union; subsequently, to be more exact, between the Anglo-Saxon countries, supported by France, and the Soviet Union—or between East and West.

To be sure, as the Dumbarton Oaks and Yalta conferences demonstrated, most leaders of the Allied nations foresaw well in advance the danger of victors' dissensions after victory. Since President Roosevelt was the most active supporter of the idea of international organization among the heads of the Allied governments, his death, on April 12, 1945, was a sign that the policy of concessions to Russia's demands was over. The first meeting of the Organization of the United Nations (subsequently to be known simply as the United Nations) took place in San Francisco, from April 25 to June 26, as scheduled. In spite of differences of opinion on many points the conference succeeded in laying the foundations of the new organization.

Meanwhile, more immediate problems of practical policy in regard to both defeated Germany and a weakening Japan required special consideration and brought about another meeting of the Big Three. The Potsdam conference, from July 17 to August 2, revealed the drastic change in international atmosphere which had occurred since the Yalta conference. In the opinion of both Americans and British the Soviet Government had violated the Yalta agreements on Poland and Rumania on several points. In their turn the Soviet leaders objected to British policy in Greece and were suspicious of the Anglo-American attitude toward the problem of German reparations. The change in general atmosphere was accentuated by changes in the drama's cast. Franklin Roosevelt's place was now occupied by Harry S. Truman; and on July 26, in the midst of the conference, the counting of ballots in the British elections was completed and Clement R. Attlee succeeded Winston Churchill.

One of the first decisions of the Potsdam conference was to establish a council of the foreign ministers of Great Britain, the United States, the Soviet Union, France, and China, to perform the preparatory work for the peace settlement. It was decided to carry out the Yalta declaration in regard to the occupation of Germany. A control council at Berlin and an Allied commission at Vienna were to be formed at once. Political and economic principles were set forth for their activities, with the primary objective of destroying the National Socialist party and dissolving all Nazi institutions. Methods of exacting reparations from Germany were agreed upon in a general way. Furthermore, the conference agreed "in principle" to the ultimate transfer to the Soviet Union of the city of Königsberg. "Pending the final determination of Poland's western frontier," part of the former German territory along the Oder River to the confluence with the western Neisse, and along the western Neisse to the Czechoslovak frontier, as well as the area of the former free city of Danzig, was put under the administration of the Polish state. However, transfer of German population from this region to Germany was to be undertaken without waiting for the final peace settlement. Similar arrangements for the transfer of populations were approved for Hungary and Czechoslovakia.

Besides the German problem the members of the Potsdam conference discussed the Japanese situation. The Soviet Union was still officially at peace with Japan but the date of the promised Russian intervention was rapidly approaching. Within a few days a new factor was to appear in the Asiatic theater of war: on August 5 the first atomic bomb to be used in actual warfare was dropped on Hiroshima and on August 9 a second was dropped on Nagasaki. On August 8 the Soviet Union issued its long-awaited declaration of war against Japan. This declaration was greeted with mixed feelings by American military and diplomatic leaders. Many of them felt that even before the new atomic weapon victory for the United States had been secured without Russian participation in the war. Meanwhile, the Russians had been promised important concessions in the Far East which now seemed to some Americans not only unnecessary but dangerous. On August 14 Japan accepted the terms of surrender, and on September 2 the formal terms were signed by the Japanese envoys on board the U.S.S. *Missouri* in Tokyo Bay.

While the Russians were not allowed an active part in the administration of American-occupied Japan, the Soviet Union derived substantial benefits from its participation in the Japanese war. On the basis of the Yalta conference, the Russians reoccupied South Sakhalin, which they had lost to Japan in 1905, and the Kuril Islands, which they had ceded to Japan in 1875. Moreover, by agreement with China, they got back the half interest in the Chinese Eastern Railway which they had sold to Manchukuo in 1935, including the extension to Port Arthur which they had lost in 1905. Port Arthur itself, as well as Dairen, was to be under joint Chinese-Russian administration until the conclusion of formal peace with Japan.

CHAPTER 18

RUSSIA AND THE WORLD IN THE
NUCLEAR AGE

RUSSIA survived the German onslaught but the price of victory was staggering. The destruction by the Germans was systematic and extensive in the entire Ukraine and in the Don basin, which before the war had constituted the Soviet Union's greatest single industrial region and embraced the best agricultural land in the nation and 50 per cent of the total livestock.* According to official reports 98,000 collective farms, 1,876 state farms, and 2,890 machine-tractor stations were ruined and ransacked. The resulting losses in agricultural machinery included 137,000 tractors and 49,000 harvester combines. Losses of livestock totaled 7,000,000 horses, 17,000,000 head of cattle, 20,000,000 hogs, and 27,000,000 sheep and goats—above 30 per cent of the prewar herds. In mining and metallurgical industries, capacity losses amounted to 60 per cent (of 1940 output) for coal, 48 per cent for electric power, 74 per cent for pig iron, and 55 per cent for steel. Besides the destruction of factories and industrial plants, 25,000,000 people were made homeless. As to losses in terms of human life, it was officially stated that "seven million people were killed in action, perished during the occupation, or were forcibly driven off to Germany." In this estimate neither the increased death rate due to malnutrition and wartime hardships nor the loss of population due to the decline of the birth rate during the war is taken into account. According to Professor Frank Lorimer the gross population loss on all counts could be estimated as between 20 and 25 million persons.

* For a computation of war devastation in the Soviet Union see "World Economic Conditions: A Summary of Reports by the United Nations," *International Conciliation*, No. 440 (April, 1948), chap. 9.

In his report to Congress on June 14, 1946, President Truman disclosed that to December 1, 1945 Russia received Lend-Lease goods to the amount of $11,141,470,000 (as against $30,753,304,-000 worth received by Great Britain). While the Lend-Lease shipments to the Soviet Union were eventually discontinued, the people of Belorussia and the Ukraine received substantial help in food and medical supplies through the United Nations Relief and Rehabilitation Administration. This was, however, but a palliative, and Russia lost no time in requesting further assistance to her war-shattered economy in the form of trade credits and loans. Her request was at first received sympathetically. On July 17, 1945, Foreign Economic Administrator Leo T. Crowley said that Russia was likely to receive foreign trade credits of $700,000,000 to $1,000,000,000 during the next year. Negotiations for a $1,000,-000,000 loan were reported in progress in the spring of 1946; however, nothing came of them, owing to differences of opinion of the two governments over the form of Soviet repayment and to the State Department's insistence that Russia abandon or modify her special economic agreements with eastern European countries. Under these circumstances, obtaining full reparations from Germany became a matter of paramount importance to Russia. Here again, the validity of the Russian definition of "German assets" in central and east European countries was questioned by the representatives of the western powers in many cases, which led to more misunderstandings between Russia and her former allies.

The failure of the United States and the Soviet Union to come to agree about loans was but a symptom of the rapid deterioration of relations between the two countries. In spite of the fact that both were cofounders of the United Nations, the differences between them in political philosophy, foreign policy, and methods of administration resulted before long in the formation of two blocs within the United Nations, the Soviet side being in the minority. The paradox of the situation was that, while a Communist state —the Soviet Union—was accepted as a charter member of the international organization, containing communism on an international scale became the next goal of the leading western nations.

Of the areas of tension between the West and the Soviet, Europe was in the limelight during the first four years following the surrender of Germany, and then events in the Far East drew their share of attention.

In Europe, as a result of the Soviet and Polish interpretation of the Yalta and Potsdam agreements, the easternmost provinces of former Germany were actually incorporated into Poland, while the eastern part of postwar Germany was occupied by the Soviet Union. The city of Berlin remained an island of joint Allied occupation—and of increasing Allied strife. A section of East Prussia with the city of Königsberg, now renamed Kaliningrad, was virtually annexed to Soviet Russia.

The new government of Poland, in direct negotiations with Russia, abandoned former claims on Ukrainian and Belorussian lands; Czechoslovakia agreed to cede Carpatho-Ukraine (Carpatho-Russia or Ruthenia) to the Soviet Ukraine; Rumania had to confirm the cession to the Soviet Union of Bessarabia and northern Bukovina to which she had agreed in 1940.

In all the countries of eastern Europe except Greece and Yugoslavia Russian influence now became paramount, and in all of them except Greece and Finland the Communists gradually stiffened their rule. All of the "people's democracies" concluded economic and military agreements with the Soviet Union, thus binding themselves closely to the Soviet economy and policies.

The ascendancy of communism in central and eastern Europe after the second World War cannot be explained solely by Russian pressure. The local background in most cases was conducive to the growth of bitter native opposition to the existing regimes. In the period between the two world wars Czechoslovakia was the only country in that part of Europe which succeeded in establishing a democratic government. In all other countries the trend was toward authoritarian regimes controlled by privileged groups. During the second World War all of these countries were occupied or controlled by the Germans in one way or another. While German rule was resented by large sections of the subjected populations, opposition to it varied in intensity. It was less noticeable in the nations which the Germans treated as their allies, that is in Hungary, Rumania, and Bulgaria. In Czechoslovakia the opposition ran high but the German pressure was so heavy that no general uprising was possible. In Poland the underground forces were

more active. In Yugoslavia and Greece large-scale popular uprisings took place. Irrespective of the degree and intensity of the
resistance, by countries, to the Germans, the Communists almost
everywhere represented the most dynamic element. It was only
in Poland that the non-Communist forces played a more important
role in the anti-German drive than the Communists. In both
Yugoslavia and Greece the Communists eventually assumed the
leadership in the national resistance movement.

German rule in the Balkans collapsed in the fall of 1944. As has
been mentioned, late in August of that year Russian troops entered Rumania, whose King Michael formally declared war on
Germany. This was soon followed by the defection of Bulgaria.
In October British troops landed in Greece. By an understanding
between Great Britain and the Soviet Union the former assumed
the task of maintaining order in Greece and the latter in Rumania.
Actually, this amounted to division of the spheres of political influence in the Balkan area between the Soviet and the western
powers (the guiding role in Greece was later passed on by the
British to the United States). The result was that communism
was crushed in Greece by the British and sponsored in other
Balkan countries by the Russians. The pattern of Soviet policies
was the same in the three former enemy countries—Rumania,
Hungary, and Bulgaria. At the first stage, a coalition government
of agrarian, socialist, and Communist parties was established in
each country, with the Communists in actual control of the
security police, the army general staff, and publicity. At the
second stage, the non-Communist parties were gradually curbed;
at the third stage, the Communists assumed full power. The fate
of the agrarian and socialist leaders was tragic indeed. In Rumania, Iuliu Maniu was sentenced in 1947 to solitary confinement
for life; in Bulgaria, in the same year, Nikola Petkov was condemned to death.

A similar process of communization took place in the three
Allied countries—Yugoslavia, Poland, and Czechoslovakia. In
Yugoslavia the Communist regime was established by native Com-
munists, under Marshal Tito's guidance, as early as 1945. In Po-
land that stage was reached two years later when the leader of the
Peasant party, Stanislav Mikolajczyk, left the country in despair.
In Czechoslovakia, with her democratic traditions, the Commu-

nist ascendancy at first took milder forms. The first parliamentary elections in May 1946 were freely conducted by secret ballot. The Communists won 38 per cent of the votes, which, with the support of a section of the socialists, made them the leading group in the new parliament as well as in the cabinet. In February 1948 they seized power outright through the so-called action committees. It should be mentioned that in both Poland and Czechoslovakia fear of Germany has been an important psychological factor working in favor of Russia. While the Russian-guided Communist government of East Germany recognized the new Polish-German boundary, the western powers were noncommittal in this respect.

As regards economics, in all the east European countries within the Soviet zone of influence a far-reaching agrarian reform was carried out, and the large landed estates were divided among the peasants. Up to the second World War Czechoslovakia was the only highly industrialized country in that part of Europe; Poland and Hungary lagged behind. Now a comprehensive program of industrialization, after the Soviet pattern, was put into effect for all the east European "people's democracies." Having seized the German assets in eastern Europe, the Soviet Government used them to pay Russia's share in the formation of industrial and trade concerns in Hungary, Rumania, and Bulgaria. With Poland and Czechoslovakia Moscow concluded trade agreements, securing for Russia quantities of much needed consumers' goods.

In both Britain and the United States the sovietization of eastern Europe was watched with anxiety. The first publicly to voice the concern of the western nations was Winston Churchill. In his address at Westminster College, Fulton, Missouri, on March 5, 1946, he denounced Russia's "expansive and proselytizing tendencies." Noting that an "iron curtain" had "descended across the continent," he urged a United States–British "fraternal association" to prevent further Russian advance. On that basis, the American policy of "containing" Russia was formulated and the Truman Doctrine of combatting Communist expansion was announced on March 12, 1947; military aid was also granted to Greece and Turkey. Then came the Marshall Plan, and finally the North Atlantic Treaty Organization. Soviet leaders denounced all of these measures as "war mongering." On the other side of the line, the formation of the so-called Cominform—a posthumous child of the late Comintern—made the news on October 5, 1947. Its objective was officially the exchange of information (hence its name) among the Communists of various European countries. Actually, its main purpose proved to be to direct and coordinate the policies of the Communist parties in Europe. Eventually this resulted in a series of conflicts between communism and nationalism and in Marshal Tito's revolt against Stalin. In the Soviet Union itself the international tension was reflected in the revival of intransigent Communist ideology and strengthening of the Marxist control over art, literature, and the sciences. The spirit of "bourgeois cosmopolitism" now became the main target of official propaganda.

Meanwhile, troubles were brewing in the Far East. The Communist movement in China sponsored by the Comintern since 1925 gained much prestige during the second World War by its determined resistance to the Japanese invaders. After Japan's collapse and the withdrawal of her troops from China, the breach reopened between Chiang Kai-shek's government and the Communists. In the civil war which followed, the latter, armed in large part with material taken from the Japanese, overran all of China's mainland. With the remnants of his troops Chiang had to seek refuge in the Island of Formosa. This posed a series of difficult problems for the United Nations and the United States. Not only the Soviet but some of the western nations as well favored recognition of Red China and its acceptance into the United Nations. The United States, however, stood firmly against such action.

The question was further complicated by events in Korea. Following the victory over Japan Russian troops occupied the northern part of Korea and American the southern part, with the 38th parallel as the dividing line. As in the Balkans, the military division resulted in a political one. While in North Korea a Communist regime was established under Russian guidance, the United States supported an anti-Communist Korean government in the south. Russia withdrew her troops from North Korea in 1948 and the United States withdrew hers the next year. Each Korean regime built up an army of its own, the South Korean with the help of American instructors, and the North Korean with Russian assistance and Russian mechanized equipment. When in 1950 the North Korean army invaded South Korea, President Truman immediately decided to intervene in order to stop the Communist aggression. The United Nations sanctioned the American action.

The initial goal of the United Nations intervention was to eject the invaders from South Korea beyond the 38th parallel. However, when this task had been fulfilled the United Nations, for reasons both political and military, crossed the line northward. At that juncture Communist China intervened in the conflict, sending her troops, officially known as "volunteers," to Korea. The conflict then entered the stage of protracted trench warfare. The Soviet Union, which concluded an alliance with Communist China in 1950 (supplemented by trade agreements), furnished supplies to the Communist side in Korea. Attempts to conclude an armistice led nowhere until 1953, when significant events took place in both America and Russia. In January Dwight Eisenhower succeeded Harry Truman in Washington; and on March 5 Joseph Stalin died in Moscow. Late in March the Communists agreed to the exchange, with the United Nations, of the sick and wounded prisoners of the Korean war, which had been suggested by the Red Cross in February. Following this exchange, a truce was signed by the representatives of the two opposing forces in Korea on July 27.

Stalin's death marked the end of an era in more senses than one. Son of a Georgian cobbler, once a divinity school student, and then a professional revolutionary, Stalin from the time of his victory over Trotsky in 1927 to the end of his life was the recognized ruler of the Soviet Union, who exercised absolute power over almost 200,000,000 people. More than that, he was the object of official veneration and glorified ad nauseam for his genius and wisdom. He became a myth—while yet only too real. Endowed with a practical mind, strong will, and oriental cunning, he adhered to Marxist ideology, yet turned that ideology to his own uses on many occasions. In his youth Stalin had dedicated himself to the Marxist cause, and he later identified his rule with this cause to such an extent that every opponent to his authority became an enemy of the state, to be ruthlessly eliminated. Stalin became in time the last of the old Bolsheviks by surviving them all.

In contrast to the ideologists of the party, such as Lenin and Trotsky, Stalin was a technician of the revolution and a party

boss. When he became omnipotent, he tried to direct the spiritual
and intellectual life of the nation by the same crude methods he
had used to manage its industry and agriculture. Again in contrast to Lenin and Trotsky, Stalin was not familiar with the West
and western ways of life. While, with the help of his assistants, he
accumulated considerable, if one-sided, knowledge of world economics, he never was able to grasp the spiritual imponderables
affecting public opinion in the western world.

Stalin rose to power through his control of the party machinery.
As a result the dictatorship of the party over the nation was
gradually replaced by the dictatorship of the Politburo, picked by
Stalin, over both party and nation. Through this device, Stalin
found himself in a position to canalize the revolution and to direct
it into a new stage—forced industrialization and the collectivization of agriculture. From the very beginning of the 1917 revolution the Bolsheviks showed utter disregard for human life and
indifference to human suffering. Of Stalin the dying Lenin himself
wrote that he was "too crude," and on that ground recommended
his removal from the post of general secretary of the party. Once
he came to power, Stalin proved ready to deal as ruthlessly with
his long-time party associates as he—and they—had dealt with
others. While that dread arm of the Communist regime—the
secret police—had been created by Lenin, it was under Stalin
that it became omnipotent, virtually a state within the state. With
its help Stalin was able to control information and the press and
to attempt to mold the very minds of the Soviet people.

To what extent can the success of his program (achieved at
frightful cost to the nation) be laid at Stalin's door? It is obvious
that industrialization was strongly supported by what may be
called the new elite of the nation—the managers of state industry,
engineers, scientists, and the Red Army command. Skilled labor,
granted better salaries and bonuses, represented an even wider—
and rapidly growing—group on which the government could depend. While opposition to the collectivization of agriculture was
widespread, and ruthless methods of coercion were used to suppress it, the bulk of the people went on with their everyday work
and gradually, if grudgingly, adjusted to the new conditions. Besides, in the troubled international atmosphere of the period, and
with the lessons of the first World War and the foreign interven-

tion in their minds, many Russians—Communist and otherwise—felt that only by making the national economy self-sufficient could Russia survive as a nation. Undoubtedly Stalin spoke for the groups supporting him as well as for himself when he said in 1931: "We are fifty or a hundred years behind the advanced countries. We must make good this lag in ten years. Either we do it or they crush us."

In exactly ten years Russia was attacked by Hitler's armies. She passed the test, even if at a terrible cost. Never was Stalin's prestige so high as at the end of the second World War, in the hour of victory. Russia seemed about to enter a new path, both nationally and internationally. Psychologically, this was the moment for easing the dictatorial regime. The people of the Soviet Union—and those of the outside world—expected the rigid system of Communist control over the nation to be relaxed now. But Stalin's very nature, the habit of power, the old mentality of fear and suspicion, and the dead weight of Marxian ideology prevented the initiation of a change in Soviet policies.

With the dropping of the first atomic bomb on Hiroshima, the world had entered the nuclear age. The new era required, ideally, a united mankind; consequently, it called for abandonment of the traditional forms of national, political, and military rivalry. In fact, however, the new scientific and technological discoveries, harnessed by the divided nations to their discordant policies, at first only accentuated existing dissensions and conflicts.

After Hiroshima the United States was, for a time, the only country in possession of nuclear weapons and of the knowledge required for manufacturing them. For further development of the new device, the United States Government initiated a series of atomic tests, and eventually the hydrogen bomb was invented and tested. The nuclear monopoly of the United States was broken in 1949 when the Soviet Union tested its first atomic bomb. After awhile, Great Britain entered the field. Subsequently, new types of nuclear weapons were introduced which could be used in field warfare or launched by rockets into enemy territory.

The nuclear race, bringing with it the danger of contaminating the whole earth through radiation, constitutes the major problem underlying international relations. In fact, mankind's survival depends on mutual accommodation among the great powers in their use of nuclear energy. The United States, the Soviet Union, and Great Britain eventually recognized the necessity of stopping their atomic tests, at least temporarily. In contrast, France exploded three of her own atomic bombs in 1959 and 1960 in order to be able to claim partnership in the community of nuclear powers. Under the auspices of the United Nations, a series of international conferences on a nuclear test ban began in Geneva. Standing in the way of general agreement were a number of thorny problems, such as how to organize the machinery of international inspection to assure the effectiveness of the ban in all countries and the controversy over the extent to which atomic disarmament should be linked with the proposed general disarmament.

In experimentation with atomic weapons, the rocket assumed great importance because of its usefulness both for missiles and for satellites and spaceships. On October 4, 1957, Russia launched her first Sputnik, and on February 1, 1958, the United States sent into orbit her first satellite, Explorer I. On the basis of their experiences with satellites, the United States and Russia began preparing to launch spaceships. Space exploration is of immense significance for the development of science, but under the existing conditions it also added fuel to competition among great powers and consequently led to more international complications.

Stalin's death on March 5, 1953, left a vacuum in the Communist world and could not help affecting Russia's relations with both the West and the East. During the period of his dictatorship, Stalin was not only the absolute ruler of Russia but also the recognized head of the whole Communist movement. The Communist parties of the entire world, except Yugoslavia, bowed to Stalin as the Pope of the Communist "Church." The years of Stalin's regime of terror resulted in decimating and cowing a generation of men of initiative and independent spirit. The dictator ruled with the help of aides subservient to him and distrustful of each other.

After Stalin's passing, the principle of collective leadership was announced. George Malenkov was placed at the head of the Soviet Government, and Nikita Khrushchev was appointed first secretary of the Communist party. On December 23, the chief of Stalin's secret police, Laurenti Beria, was executed by the new regime. The methods of government control over the people were somewhat relaxed. Many persons sent to concentration camps by Stalin on political grounds were released.* Some of those who had been executed under Stalin or had died in concentration camps were now posthumously exonerated (which meant removing police surveillance of their relatives). Malenkov promised that from then on more attention would be given to the production of consumer goods. In literature, censorship became more liberal. A period of "thaw" seemed to have started. '

It did not last long. On the contrary, a "freeze" was on the way. The new government was faced with tremendous difficulties and at first lacked means to solve them. The wounds inflicted by the war could not be easily healed. The casualties suffered greatly weakened the labor force. Restoring the Russian economy from the havoc caused by the war's destruction required time and great effort. Heavy industry and the manufacture of armaments continued to play the most important role in Russia's economy. Light industries, needed for the increase of consumer goods, still lagged far behind. Agricultural production had declined alarmingly. There was no unanimity among the new Soviet leaders concerning the necessary reforms. Some, like Malenkov and Molotov, continued to believe in the necessity of centralized management of Russia's economies. Others, like Khrushchev, insisted on the principle of decentralization and the creation of regional boards of economic administration.

Gradually, Khrushchev outmaneuvered his colleagues by the same method Stalin used in his time namely, obtaining control of the party machinery by appointing men loyal to him to the key posts in the party cells from the lowest level to the top. In 1955 Malenkov was replaced by Nicholas Bulganin as prime minister. In 1958 Khrushchev, while remaining the first secretary of the Communist party, took over the premiership from Bulganin and became the head of both the Communist party and the Soviet Government. By that time Molotov had been dismissed from his post of minister of foreign affairs and after an interim replaced by Andrei Gromyko. In effect, Khrushchev himself assumed the direction of Soviet foreign relations. He thus inherited

* Neither the number of convicts in the concentration camps at the time of Stalin's death, nor the number released, was officially stated.

from Stalin the cold war tension with the West. Moreover, within the Communist world, Yugoslavia developed a kind of national Communism of her own—the "Titoism" which defied Moscow's leadership. Before long, opposition to Moscow's dictatorship arose in some of the Communist satellites in central and eastern Europe. This movement was encouraged by the example of Yugoslavia and even more by the hopes of receiving active assistance from the West. An uprising occurred in East Germany, which was quickly suppressed by Soviet troops. Next, a near-revolution against Moscow's interference took place in Poland. The Polish Communist Government succeeded in controlling the national movement and in reaching a compromise with Moscow according to which a measure of national independence was achieved. In the fall of 1956, Hungary revolted. In this case the goal of the uprising was not only to secure independence from the Soviet Union, but to overthrow the Hungarian Communist regime itself. Soviet troops brutally crushed the rebellion and restored the Communist Government to power.

Relations between the Soviet Union and Communist China, extremely friendly at first, gradually cooled in spite of the fact that some potential causes for friction had been eliminated both during Stalin's rule and afterward. One of these was the control of Sinkiang (Chinese Turkestan), which was subject to Soviet political interference and economic penetration before and during the second World War. It should be noted that three quarters of Sinkiang's inhabitants are Turki-speaking Uigurs, ethnically and culturally related to the Turkic peoples of Soviet Central Asia. The Soviet Government recognized Communist China's sovereignty over the area in 1950 but at first attempted to secure for itself a number of economic concessions. By the Sino-Soviet agreement of March 27, 1950, two mixed Chinese-Soviet joint-stock companies were organized for the exploitation of, respectively, oil and nonferrous metals in Sinkiang. However, five years later the Soviet Union relinquished its claims, and its shares in both companies were transferred to China. Soon after that the Chinese Government converted Sinkiang into the Sinkiang-Uigur Autonomous Region within the People's Republic of China.

With regard to another potential area of discord—Manchuria—by her agreement with the Soviet Union of February 14, 1950,

China granted the Russians partnership in joint Sino-Soviet management of the Changchun Railway and agreed to temporary Soviet control of the naval base at Port Arthur and of the Dairen dockyard. In 1952 the Soviet Union turned over full ownership of the railway to China and in 1955 withdrew from both Port Arthur and Dairen.

One thing China continued to resent was the Soviet preponderance in Outer Mongolia. The Mongolian People's Republic, nominally an independent state, was bound to the Soviet Union by a military alliance, as well as by economic, political, and cultural ties. In 1952 China showed her interest in the area by concluding an economic and cultural agreement with the Mongolian Government. China's interest became even more apparent when she signed a treaty of friendship and mutual assistance with Mongolia on May 31, 1960. On that occasion China granted Mongolia a long-term loan of 200 million rubles.

Under Stalin and for some time after his death the Soviet Union vigorously contributed to China's industrialization by offering credits and giving China all kinds of technical assistance. As time went on and the industrialization of their country was well launched, the Chinese became less dependent on Soviet help. Differences in interpretation of Communist doctrine gradually arose between the head of the Chinese Communist party, Mao Tse-tung, and Khrushchev. The former had unreservedly recognized Stalin's leadership in the Communist world and remained Stalinist after the latter's death. For example, Communist China in the 1950's followed the same policies of forced industrialization and collectivization of agriculture that the Soviet Union had adopted in the 1930's. Mao went farther than Stalin, however, and attempted to organize fully integrated agricultural communes in place of Stalin's kolkhozes.

The Soviet Government needed China's support in its relations with the West, as well as in overcoming the actual or potential opposition of the recalcitrant members of the Communist world. The Moscow leaders—Khrushchev probably more clearly than his colleagues—felt that it was necessary to demonstrate their friendly feelings toward Mao to show that close cooperation between Russia and China would not be discontinued after Stalin's death. Consequently, it was decided to send Khrushchev and

Bulganin to Peking to greet Mao on the occasion of the fifth anniversary of his victory over Chiang Kai-shek's regime (September 1954). Khrushchev assured the "brotherly Chinese Communist Party" of Soviet Russia's support in China's struggle for the conquest of Taiwan (Formosa) and promised intensified technological assistance to China. This was more than Khrushchev's colleagues expected him to do, and Molotov (at that time still minister of foreign affairs) found it proper to explain to some foreign diplomats that Khrushchev's statements in Peking did not represent the Soviet Government's views. Be this as it may, Khrushchev succeeded in establishing personal contacts with Mao and other Chinese leaders which were to help him during the next two years. In 1956 Mao wisely advised him to come to a compromise with the Polish Communists. As to Hungary, Mao recommended ruthless suppression of the anti-Communist revolution there. In December of that year, Mao's right-hand man, Chou En-lai, visited Moscow and after talks with Soviet leaders toured the satellite countries, apparently to help Moscow diplomatically.

On Russia's internal front, the Soviet leaders, after lengthy preparations, convoked a new Congress of the Communist Party —the Twentieth (February 1956). The Congress had to approve the Central Committee's propositions of future policies. For Khrushchev and his supporters in the Central Committee, the Congress meant much more than a routine gathering. They thought that psychologically a decisive break with the past was needed. While Stalin's one-man rule was officially replaced by collective leadership, not only the people at large, but many of the Communists, could not be sure that the dictatorial policies of terror were over. Stalin's shadow still hung over Russia. Besides, a number of politicians were afraid that a relaxation of the regime would result in administrative chaos. It was important, therefore, for the post-Stalin government to kill the image of Stalin as the wise Emperor-Pope of the Communist regime and to take him—figuratively—off a pedestal. Presumably, only the top Soviet leaders took part in the discussion of the plan prior to the convocation of the Congress. Only a few of the delegates must have known what was coming. Khrushchev was given the task of delivering the main report to be read at a closed session. In this

secret report Khrushchev attempted to destroy the myth of
Stalin's infallibility by denouncing the "personality cult" of the
late dictator and condemning his cruelty and blunders. The Congress approved Khrushchev's stand. In both the theory of communism and the organization of the Communist party, a return
to Lenin was proclaimed. Khrushchev's report was not immediately published in order to give the leaders time to prepare public
opinion to grasp its full meaning. Later, Stalin's body was removed from the Lenin mausoleum and buried at the Kremlin
wall. Innumerable statues of Stalin all over Russia were taken
down from pedestals, broken, and dumped. With the abrogation
of the "cult of personality," Lenin's kind of democracy within the
Communist party was restored. However, the party's hold over
the government and administration was not removed. In the
sphere of international relations, the Congress made an attempt
to reduce the tension created by the cold war. Stalin and Lenin's
doctrine of the inevitability of war between the Communist and
the capitalist worlds was shelved, and the possibility of achieving
Communist victory without violence through peaceful competition was admitted.

On November 7, 1957, the fortieth anniversary of the Bolshevik Revolution was celebrated in Moscow, with Mao among the
guests of honor. With studied humility Khrushchev proposed to
abolish the principle of priority of the Soviet Communist party
in the Communist world. Mao declined the proposition. For the
time being, he was satisfied with Khrushchev's pledges to China
made three years before. In a sense, the day turned into a confirmation of Khrushchev as the president of international communism, the head of the Soviet Communist party and of the
Soviet Government.

Nikita Sergeyevich Khrushchev, born in Kursk Province in
1894, was the son of a miner and himself worked as a miner in
his youth in Iuzovka (later renamed Stalino) in the Donets coal
region. In 1918 he became a Bolshevik and joined the Red Army.
In 1921–22 he studied at the Iuzovka Mining Technical School
and soon was named the party political adviser of that school.
In 1925 he was appointed party secretary of a district in the
Iuzovka region, after which his steady ascendancy in the party
hierarchy began. Four years later he was transferred to Moscow

to be enrolled as a student in the Stalin Industrial Academy. He did not stay there long and completed his education by reading (he was an avid reader from his youth).

Khrushchev was a versatile man of buoyant energy, innate common sense, and an inquisitive mind. In contrast to Stalin, Khrushchev traveled extensively abroad in search of personal contacts with leaders and people in both West and East. Besides China, he visited England, Yugoslavia, India, Burma, Indonesia, and, in 1959, set foot for the first time in the United States. His travel impressions were rather superficial, however, and he was not able to grasp sufficiently the mentality of either western or Oriental leaders and people. This resulted in many blunders in his policies. But he did not take his errors seriously. When a scheme of his failed, he was always ready with another. Invested with full authority, Khrushchev undertook a series of internal reforms which seemed to him far-reaching, but the most important miscarried or proved not radical enough. They included decentralization of the national economy, reorganization of the kolkhoz system, liberalization of justice, and a partial curb on the authority of the security police.

In his policy toward the kolkhozes, Khrushchev had a twofold objective. The first was to consolidate them by combining several collective farms into one large one. Government machine-tractor stations were liquidated and the machinery and equipment transferred to the kolkhozes. The second objective was to transform some of the kolkhozes into sovkhozes. In the period between 1953 and 1959 the number of kolkhozes was reduced from 93,000 to 54,000 and the number of sovkhozes raised from about 5,000 to 6,500. While the area under cultivation in the kolkhozes remained almost the same, that in the sovkhozes rose from 15 million hectares to about 54 million hectares. But these measures did not result in any substantial increase in the volume of agricultural production, as was expected. The basic reason for the failure was the lack of incentives for the members of either the kolkhozes or the sovkhozes; their share in the profits was insufficient. In the kolkhozes, each of them really cared only for his "backyard farm"—a small private plot assigned to him. On these they worked hard, since they were allowed to sell the produce on the markets for their own benefit.

For raising the production of wheat—the basic task that faced

Russian agriculture at that time—Khrushchev initiated a vast program of intensive plowing of virgin lands in the lower Volga, the southern Ural region, western Siberia, and especially in Kazakhstan (Kazakh SSR), which had been partly used for grazing cattle. Between 1954 and 1959 the total acreage of cultivated land rose from 10 to 28 million hectares in Kazakhstan and from 38 to 52 million hectares in the other areas. The first successes soon proved illusive. The Komsomol "volunteers" sent to the virgin lands found that little or nothing was prepared on the spot for housing them and providing them with food and proper tools. What enthusiasm there was among some of them soon gave way to frustration. A great many deserted. In Kazakhstan the results were especially bad. After the plowing, the rich upper layer of land was eroded. There was not enough fertilizer at hand for the sandy subsoil, and for a time the area became unfit for agricultural cultivation and even for grazing cattle. The failure of the scheme undermined Russia's agricultural production. The harvest of 1963 was low, and the Soviet Government had to buy great quantities of wheat abroad, chiefly from Canada.

The new policy of peaceful competition with the capitalist camp did not end the Kremlin's support of subversive movements in the colonial and semicolonial countries of Asia, Africa, and Latin America. The United States countered by establishing air bases in Turkey and by pledging support to the governments of the non-Communist and neutral countries threatened by Communist propaganda. NATO and the Warsaw Pact of the Soviet Union and its East European satellites continued to confront each other. Both sides vied in offering financial, economic, and military assistance to the underdeveloped nations. Some of the neutral and nonaligned countries, like Yugoslavia and India, managed to receive aid from both the Soviet Union and the West. At the same time, neither side wanted to preclude the possibility of peaceful coexistence. Commercial relations between Soviet Russia and the West were not interrupted. Intercourse in the fields of science, literature, and art was growing. Eventually, a regular exchange of professors and students was organized on a limited scope. American tourists were welcomed in the Soviet Union, though occasionally annoyed and even arrested by the security police.

Germany proved, at that time, the main area of friction be-

tween the Soviets and the West. West Germany remained under
the occupation of the western Allies, but their attitude toward
her, stern at first, was soon softened. The United States extended
to the West German Government substantial financial aid for the
reconstruction of the country. After awhile, the western Allies
allowed West Germany to start building up her armed forces.
It is natural that the Germans of both the western and eastern
sectors, resented the artificial division of their nation. Public
opinion among the western powers likewise was sympathetic to
the idea of reuniting the two Germanys. On the other hand, to
the Poles and Czechs, as well as to the Russians, the division of
Germany into two parts, one Communist, lessened the danger of
German revanche. The Russians wanted certain international
guarantees preventing the danger. At one time they seemed interested in plans for the neutralization and demilitarization of
Germany. The unification of the two Germanys would require a
plebiscite, which the Russians would agree to on condition that
the Communist party be allowed to take part in voting in West
Germany (it was suppressed there). Nothing came of these plans.

The status of Berlin, or rather West Berlin, constituted an
especially thorny problem. At the end of the war, according to
the decisions of the Potsdam Conference, an Allied control council of the four major Allies (the United States, the Soviet Union,
Great Britain, and France) was established in Berlin as the
former capital of Germany. Berlin was put under the occupation
of the four powers, each of which was assigned a zone of its own,
with the Soviets receiving the eastern part of the city. Berlin is
located 110 miles inside Communist East Germany. With the
continued tension between the Soviet Union and the western
powers, West Berlin with its two million inhabitants became an
enclave of the western world inside Communist territory. Although according to the 1949 Constitution of the German Federal
Republic West Berlin was proclaimed an integral part of West
Germany as its eleventh state, both the Soviet and the East German governments refused to recognize the juridical value of
West Germany's action.

Khrushchev's strategic plan in foreign policy was to supplement the revolutionary agitation in the underdeveloped countries
and the counteraction in Berlin by direct negotiations with the

western powers at the summit level. Skillfully, he played on the universal fear of atomic war and on the longing for peace of the peoples of both the Soviet Union and the western nations. Every new international crisis revived demands for conciliation. In 1958 Khrushchev created such a crisis in Berlin and thereby pushed the western powers into negotiations. In his speech of November 10, 1958, Khrushchev declared that the presence of the Allied contingents in West Berlin could no longer be justified and that a treaty of peace with Germany should be concluded and signed by the four major Allied powers, members of the Potsdam Conference of 1945. Two days later Khrushchev announced that if the three western powers—the United States, Great Britain, and France—were not ready for the negotiations by May 25, 1959, the Soviet Union would withdraw from any control functions in Berlin, leaving the western powers to deal directly with the East German Government (which neither the western Allies nor West Germany recognized). Khrushchev's declaration augured serious troubles. To avert them, British Prime Minister Harold Macmillan came to Moscow in March 1959 to explore the possibilities of an understanding between the Soviet Union and the West. Vice-President Richard Nixon also visited Moscow and invited Khrushchev to come to the United States for a meeting with President Eisenhower. He eagerly accepted. His talks with Eisenhower at Camp David in November were friendly, and he received the impression that the President was responsive to the idea of an international conference in Paris at the highest level. In January 1960, the United States announced that Eisenhower would visit Russia in June. To prepare a suitable psychological atmosphere for further discussions, that same month Khrushchev ordered a substantial reduction of Soviet armed forces.

But on May 1 an incident occurred which complicated the situation. An American U-2 airplane, flying at a high altitude over Soviet territory on an intelligence mission, was brought down by Soviet antiaircraft artillery. The pilot parachuted and was arrested. A Soviet military tribunal convicted him of espionage and sentenced him to ten years' imprisonment. In February 1962, he was exchanged for a Soviet spy sentenced to thirty years' imprisonment by the United States in 1957. Khrushchev decided to

take advantage of the U-2 incident and proclaimed it an unfriendly act on the part of the United States. His aim was to
embarrass Eisenhower in order to put more pressure on him.
Khrushchev miscalculated, however, and the proposed summit
conference ended in a fiasco. The cold war was to continue.
Soviet-American relations further deteriorated as a result of
Khrushchev's economic and diplomatic support of Fidel Castro's
Cuba. African affairs, and especially the chaotic situation in the
former Belgian Congo, brought more misunderstandings. The
stormy session of the United Nations General Assembly in New
York in the fall of 1960 was marked by a series of sharp con-
flicts between the West and the Soviets.

At that juncture, the election of John Fitzgerald Kennedy as
35th President of the United States raised the hopes of the whole
world for a new approach toward the urgent problems confront-
ing humanity. Khrushchev watched President Kennedy's first
moves attentively in order to appraise his stature. The ill-fated
attempt by a force of anti-Castro Cuban refugees to invade
Cuba at the Bay of Pigs, unofficially supported by the United
States (April 1961), was interpreted in the Kremlin as evidence
of Kennedy's inexperience and amateurishness. Khrushchev
thought that it would not be difficult for him to convince the
President to hold a summit conference without demanding definite safeguards. In his turn, Kennedy believed that Eisenhower
had failed to find a right approach to parleys with the Russians
and was eager to meet Khrushchev. To Khrushchev's disappointment, Kennedy proved much firmer than he anticipated. The
two leaders met in Vienna in June 1961, but no agreement was
reached.

In August, Khrushchev authorized the East German Communist leader, Walter Ulbricht, to erect a wall between East and
West Berlin. There was an outcry of indignation in the West,
but no concerted action against the East German move was
undertaken.

The Kremlin's aim within the Communist sphere at this time
was to secure both the unity of world communism and the Soviet
Communist party's supremacy in it. However, neither task proved
attainable. The Twenty-Second Congress of the Communist Party
of the Soviet Union, meeting in October 1961, reaffirmed the

view that communism could achieve its world aims without recourse to major wars. But Khrushchev's policy of coexistence with the West brought strong opposition from China and proved to be the main factor which broke the unity of the world Communist movement. From this time on China and the Soviet Union vied for the ideological leadership of international communism, and a wordy warfare raged between Moscow and Peking over the radio and in the press. Mutual recriminations and vituperations were heaped by each side upon the other, with Mao preaching his intransigent doctrine against Khrushchev's policy of coexistence.

The result was a split of Communist parties all over the world. The Twenty-Second Congress, attempting to cope with the problem, criticized Albania for seconding China's position; but the censure proved ineffective, and in December 1961 the Soviet Union severed diplomatic relations with Albania. Meanwhile, North Korea also supported Mao, and while the Italian and French parties remained at that time loyal to Moscow, in many other countries two warring factions were formed.

Behind the widening rivalry among Communist factions, feelings of nationalism had been on the rise. Here again, China was the chief troublemaker. She began by pressing her claims on the Far Eastern areas annexed to Russia in the middle of the 19th century, especially on the Ussuri region, which includes Vladivostok. She also took steps to eliminate Russian influence in Chinese Turkestan. Poland achieved a degree of freedom of action as early as 1956. So did Hungary after awhile under the new Soviet-sponsored premier Janos Kadar. Rumania eventually assumed an even more independent attitude in her policy. All three of these nations, as well as Czechoslovakia, emphasized that culturally they belonged to the western world.

On the other hand, ties between Russia and Cuba were growing stronger. In addition to economic and diplomatic aid, Moscow promised military support to Premier Fidel Castro. Before long military advisers and technicians, as well as weapons of diverse kinds, were sent to Cuba. Among other armaments, missiles capable of striking a large part of the United States were set in position in complete secrecy. By September 1962, American intelligence agents had learned of the Soviet maneuvers, and this time President Kennedy decided to take a firm stand. On October 22 he ordered a naval and air quarantine on shipment of offensive weapons to Cuba and demanded that Soviet missile bases in Cuba be dismantled. Confronted with this ultimatum, Khrushchev had enough sense to yield, and on October 28 he agreed to take the missiles back to Russia. A world catastrophe was thus averted, but Russia's prestige was seriously damaged. Castro was indignant that Khrushchev had not consulted him before bowing to Kennedy's demands, and the Chinese could not conceal their malicious joy at the failure of another of Khrushchev's international moves.

The Sino-Soviet split was further deepened when a high-level ideological conference between the two countries, held in Moscow July 5–21, 1963, ended in failure. Later that month, Peking denounced the nuclear test ban treaty concluded on July 25 by the United States, the Soviet Union, and Great Britain. The agreement banned tests in the atmosphere, in outer space, and under water, although they were still permitted underground.

On November 22, 1963, the assassination of President Kennedy shocked the entire world, including Russia. The outcome of the Cuban missile crisis of the preceding year had produced a detente in Russian-American relations. Khrushchev was willing to continue conciliatory tactics in his dealings with the new President of the United States, Lyndon B. Johnson. He did not realize that his own position at home was becoming shaky.

Khrushchev's colleagues followed him without opposition for a number of years. Gradually, however, they became dissatisfied with many aspects of his policies, both domestic and international. On the domestic scene, the agricultural crisis could be counted as Khrushchev's major failure. With regard to foreign relations, some members of the Presidium accused him of unduly exacerbating the conflict with China. Many disliked his dictatorial ways. The opposition came into the open at a stormy meeting of the Presidium in March 1963, when Khrushchev threatened to resign but did not. The next year the Presidium decided to act. On October 14, 1964, Khrushchev was summoned to a meeting of the Central Committee, where his policies were sharply criticized. He had no alternative but to resign. Leonid Brezhnev was elected first secretary of the Communist party, and

Aleksei Kosygin, premier. The new leaders were confronted both with a chaotic economic situation inside the Soviet Union and with growing international tension.

Two days after the downfall of Khrushchev, Communist China conducted its first atomic test explosion. Since China was not a member of the United Nations and since Peking had protested against the American-British-Soviet Treaty of July 1963, her success in the nuclear competition was a portentous event. Peking interpreted Khrushchev's dismissal as a sign of impending change in the Soviet attitude toward China and congratulated Brezhnev and Kosygin. In the first half of November, Premier Chou En-lai visited Moscow for talks with the new Soviet leaders. He was disappointed to find out that, while they had criticized Khrushchev, they were not ready for complete reconciliation with the Chinese leadership. Peking answered by labeling Moscow's position as "Khrushchevism without Khrushchev."

Meanwhile a grave conflict developed in Vietnam in Southeast Asia, part of the former French Indo-China. This was the sequel to the struggle of the Vietnamese nationalists and communists against French domination. In 1954 the French stronghold of Dien Bien Phu in northern Vietnam fell to the communist forces. Following that, an international conference was convoked in Geneva, in which Vietnam, the United States, France, the Soviet Union, and Communist China were represented. Partition of Vietnam along the 17th parallel into communist North Vietnam and noncommunist South Vietnam was agreed upon.

President Eisenhower decided to support South Vietnam and in October 1954 offered economic aid. In February 1955, the United States agreed to train the South Vietnamese army. In December 1960, North Vietnam announced the formation of the National Liberation Front of South Vietnam (Viet Cong). A year later, in December 1961, President Kennedy declared that the United States was prepared to help South Vietnam. By the time of his assassination there were 15,000 American troops in South Vietnam. Their number kept increasing rapidly under President Johnson, reaching half a million in June 1968.

While the United States supported South Vietnam, Communist China and the Soviet Union helped North Vietnam. Branding American action as an aggression, the Soviet Government was careful not to interfere openly in the war, but kept shipping to North Vietnam armaments and supplies of various sorts. In turn China, in spite of her bellicose threats, limited her support to North Vietnam to sending weapons. At the same time she could only welcome help to North Vietnam on the part of the Soviet Union. Because of this she had to agree to a rapprochement between the Soviet Communist party and those of North Vietnam and North Korea (both previously under exclusive Chinese guidance).

On January 31, 1965, it was announced in Moscow that a Soviet delegation headed by Premier Kosygin would be sent to Hanoi. On the way there, the delegation made a brief stop in Peking. The next day the Russians left for Hanoi, where they were warmly received by Ho Chi Minh. On his way back Kosygin stopped in Peking once more and was received by Mao. From China, with Mao's blessings, he visited North Korea, returning to Moscow on February 14. The net result of his trip was the establishment of friendly relations between the Soviet Communist party and the North Vietnamese and North Korean Communists. However, Soviet relations with China were only temporarily patched up.

In another area of tension in southern Asia, an armed conflict developed between India and Pakistan. On July 1, 1965, a ceasefire agreement was signed by the two belligerents, but in September a new outburst of war seemed imminent. At that juncture Kosygin offered his services as mediator and invited the representatives of the two powers to Tashkent for parleys. The mediation was successful, and a declaration of peace was signed in January 1966.

Meanwhile, Soviet relations with Communist China went from bad to worse. In Moscow, China was vehemently denounced at the celebration of the 49th anniversary of the Bolshevik Revolution on November 7, 1966. In 1967, the chaos created in China by Mao's "cultural revolution" worsened China's relations with the outside world and made her further policies utterly unpredictable. It was natural in view of this for both the Soviet Union and the United States to keep in touch with each other in spite of the divergency of their policies in regard to Vietnam.

Another crisis—this time in the Middle East—was caused by the Arab-Israeli war in the beginning of June 1967. The Soviet

Union supported Nasser's Egypt and the other Arab states and called a session of the United Nations General Assembly to liquidate the legacy of the war. On June 17 Kosygin came to the United States to attend the session, which brought no agreement. More important, as a personal contact between the two countries' leaders, was an informal meeting between President Johnson and Kosygin which took place in Glassboro, New Jersey, on June 23 and 25.

In regard to the international Communist movement, Brezhnev and Kosygin continued Khrushchev's futile efforts to restore the unity of the Communist world, with as little success. The absence of Mao Tse-tung at the solemn festivities on the 50th anniversary of the Bolshevik Revolution in November 1967 could be expected. But a host of the other leaders of Communist parties in Asia— Japanese, Burmese, Pakistani, Thai, Laotian, and Indonesian— also preferred to stay home, as did Fidel Castro. Of the Communist parties of the Soviet group, Rumania openly defied the leadership of the Soviet Union, and in the summer of 1968 Czechoslovakia embarked on the road to democratization of her communism, a move that was countered by a Soviet military invasion and occupation in August.

In economic policies Khrushchev's successors concentrated their efforts on increasing industrial efficiency. In accordance with the recommendations of the economist Evsei G. Liberman, the plenum of the Central Committee of the Soviet Communist party decided to introduce a new system of profit-oriented industrial management. During 1966 the new methods were introduced in about 70 per cent of factories and plants. The first results seemed promising, though indecisive. In 1967 the Soviet industrial output increased by 10 per cent. Steel production surpassed 100 million metric tons. Output of consumer goods also went up. In agriculture, the rights of the kolkhoz member on his homestead plot were confirmed and somewhat expanded. It has been calculated that private agriculture (on the backyard farms) produced roughly a third of the Soviet Union's gross agricultural output and 13 per cent of marketed farm output, although the private plots constitute only some 3 per cent of cultivated land in the Soviet Union.*

In September 1967, by a decree of the Council of Ministers,

* H. E. Salisbury, ed., *The Soviet Union: The Fifty Years*, p. 61.

the kolkhozes were authorized to operate small factories on their own initiative. The principle of profit-oriented management applied in industry was also tested in the state-operated farms (sovkhozes). Most of these required large governmental subsidies. In March 1967 it was decided, as an experiment, to transfer 400 sovkhozes (out of the total of some 12,000) to a self-supporting profit plan.

Despite recent advances, agriculture still remains the weakest branch of the Soviet national economy. According to the official statistics for 1966, the total output of grain (wheat and rye) was slightly above 113 million metric tons. The corresponding figure for 1913 was around 50 million. The total more than doubled in half a century, but this was a much slower rate of increase than in industry. Indeed, industrial production in this period showed spectacular progress. For example, in 1966 the output of pig iron amounted to 70.3 million metric tons (4.2 in 1913), and of steel, 96.9 (4.3 in 1913).

While the material conditions of everyday life in the Soviet Union have improved recently, Russian society has entered a period of deep psychological and intellectual crisis. In general terms it may be characterized as a conflict between the rigid tutelage of the Communist party over the people's minds and the rising aspirations of the intelligentsia and youth for freedom of thought and self-expression. The basis of Communist philosophy—Marxism—has become an ossified dogma, an obligatory official ideology, which does not satisfy even many of the Communists themselves. No wonder that its validity is questioned by the people at large. Resistance to it—open or hidden—began gradually increasing when the era of Stalin's terror was over. This was felt in different aspects of Russian cultural activities— religion, literature, the arts, and sciences.

Marx preached, and his Soviet followers continue to preach, atheism. They deny any kind of philosophical idealism. Members of the Soviet Communist party are forbidden to belong to any kind of church or religious sect—Christian, Jewish, Moslem, or Buddhist. Under Stalin most synagogues were closed. As Stalin needed the moral support of the Orthodox Church during the second World War, his attitude toward Russia's traditional religion was rather benevolent; but under Khrushchev's rule a great number of the Orthodox churches were closed by the government.

Lately the tactics of the atheists in their drive against religion have become milder. In some cases they prove ready to enter into a dialogue with the defenders of religion and to try persuasion instead of violence. On August 31, 1967, *Komsomolskaya Pravda*, the newspaper of the Young Communists League, published a letter to the editors advocating faith in God. The writer, identified as A. Aiazeva, defended traditional Christian beliefs. "We got rid of Christ in our families and schools and morality disappeared with Him . . . Atheists' words are empty. There is no sense in human life without God." In his reply, a newspaper staff writer contended that "not a single one of the faithful has any proof of the existence of God" and that a belief in God was not necessary for morality.* There are no sufficient data to determine the proportion of Soviet citizens still practicing religion, openly or secretly, but it must be not inconsiderable. At the end of August 1967, the magazine on atheism, *Nauka i Religiya* ("Science and Religion") published a survey showing that 21 per cent of 4,710 persons questioned in Kazan, a city of around 700,000, were religious.

In the field of literature and the arts, the pattern of "Socialist realism" introduced under Stalin and Zhdanov continued to be applied after their deaths. An author who wanted to write in any other style, or whose attitude toward the Soviet Government was critical, was unable to publish his works and had to content himself with writing "for his desk drawer" in the hope of better times in the future.

Such hopes appeared after Khrushchev's de-Stalinization speech of 1956, but the first test case of the expected softening of censorship had unfavorable results. The publication in Russia of the now famous novel *Doctor Zhivago* by Boris Pasternak was not allowed by the government. Although the novel was published abroad, both in its original Russian and in many other languages, Pasternak was forbidden by the Soviet Government to accept the Nobel Prize for Literature awarded to him in 1958. He was ousted from the Union of Soviet Writers and spent the last two years of his life in semi-seclusion in his house in the

* *The New York Times,* September 1, 1967.

village of Peredelkino, fifteen miles from Moscow. His spirit was not broken, and his message of freedom and truth encouraged his contemporaries and the younger generation.

The search for truth motivated the development of another kind of literature—stories and recollections of former inmates of Stalin's concentration camps who had survived the ordeal. Khrushchev himself in his concluding speech at the Twenty-Second Congress of the Communist Party (1961) said that "our duty is to carefully examine the abuses of the authorities . . . in order that such things be not repeated." The first penetrating study of the grim conditions of life in the forced labor camps, *One Day in the Life of Ivan Denisovich*, by Alexander Solzhenitsyn, was published in 1963 on Khrushchev's insistence. It was the first literary work of this talented author.

Poets were in the limelight of the awakening of the intelligentsia. In Harrison E. Salisbury's words, "The poets have become a symbol to Russian youth of their own generation. Poetry readings, always popular in Russia, have become a mass phenomenon; scores of thousands turn out in the streets for recitations on the annual Days of Poetry, and recitals sometimes attract audiences of 30,000 or 40,000 to sports stadiums." * The two most popular Russian poets of the 1960's are Evgeny Evtushenko and Andrei Voznesensky.

Of a different nature are the memoirs of Stalin's daughter, Svetlana Alliluyeva, a unique human document. In 1966 she was allowed to go to India for a short visit and intended to stay there permanently with the relatives of her late husband. Under the pressure of the Soviet Government, the Indian Government refused to grant her asylum. She then managed to come to the United States, arriving in April 1967. In October her book, *Twenty Letters to a Friend*, which she wrote while still in Russia, was published in English and several other languages, as well as in the original Russian. In her book, Svetlana speaks of life with her father during her childhood and youth and the subsequent estrangement between them. It was only gradually that she became aware of his ruthlessness. Although she does not deny her father's cruel acts, she adds that many of his aides were also guilty; for her, Beria was the villain of the tragedy. She then

* *The Soviet Union: The Fifty Years*, p. 127.

proceeds to describe her disillusionment with the official ideology and the suppression of individuality under the Soviet regime. She is not interested in politics but is longing for freedom of thought, of artistic creativeness, and of religion.

The Soviet Government was not able to prevent the publication of Svetlana Alliluyeva's book, or to silence her. However, two other authors who resided in Moscow, Andrei D. Siniavsky and Iuli M. Daniel, had to pay dearly for publishing their works abroad under assumed names. Their "Fantastic Stories" (the title of one of Siniavsky's books) are biting satires on the Communist regime and the dull life of the apathetic and browbeaten Soviet citizens. Before long the identity of the authors became known to the Soviet authorities, and in February 1966 both Siniavsky and Daniel were tried in Moscow and sentenced to seven and five years' imprisonment, respectively. This, however, did not stop the ferment among the intelligentsia.

In the swing of the pendulum between the conservative and liberal tendencies in the government's policies, censorship became tighter. Among the writers whose literary activities were curbed was Alexander Solzhenitsyn. In May 1967, he wrote a letter to the Union of Soviet Writers calling for a discussion of the censorship issue at a meeting of the union and for the abolition of censorship. No action was taken by the union, and Solzhenitsyn was told to stop his protests. It was expected by many that censorship would be softened, if not abolished, on the 50th anniversary of the Bolshevik Revolution, November 7, 1967. It was not. On November 25, Solzhenitsyn received a letter from the writers' union warning him not to continue the discussion. He replied reiterating his demand that the union should protect the rights of authors from governmental interference, but the union ignored his plea.

Sympathizers of Siniavsky and Daniel among young intellectuals championed their cause. Since they were not allowed to express their views openly in the press, they started a clandestine mimeographed journal which they called "Phoenix" (as an emblem of rebirth). In December 1966, one of them, Alexander Ginzburg, circulated documents on the Siniavsky-Daniel trial to expose the violations of elementary rules of justice. On January 22, 1967, Vladimir Bukovsky organized in Pushkin Square a public demonstration of protest. This was immediately dispersed by the police. Bukovsky was arrested, put on trial, and on August 30 sentenced to three years in prison.

In December Paul Litvinov, a noted physicist and a grandson of the foreign minister of the 1930's, Maxim Litvinov, defied a warning from the Soviet security police and sent to the West excerpts from a transcript of Bukovsky's closed-door trial, including his final plea. In this Bukovsky cited passages in the Soviet constitution guaranteeing freedom of speech and the right to participate in street processions and demonstrations.

Among other persons arrested in January 1967 were Alexander Ginzburg and Iuri Galanskov. Their trial was held in the Moscow City Court, where the courtroom was closed to all but a handful of selected persons with special passes. Ginzburg was sentenced to seven years in prison and Galanskov to five years.

The friends and sympathizers of the defendants were not cowed. Paul Litvinov and Mrs. Larisa Daniel, wife of Iuli Daniel, issued an appeal "to world public opinion" denouncing many violations of the principles of law which turned the trial into a mockery. The authorities retaliated by dismissing Litvinov from his job. Other protests followed. Discontent spread among the intelligentsia at large. In mid-February 22 authoritative Russian writers, including Constantine Paustovsky and several others of the older generation, condemned the trial procedures and asserted that they evoked "gloomy recollections of Stalinist trials in the 1930's." The writers joined demands for a new trial of the accused. The security authorities became worried and attempted to stop further agitation by warning the relatives and friends of the accused that they themselves would be punished if they continued their "antisocial activity." When protests continued, some of the signers and co-signers of the petitions were ousted from their positions, but were not prevented from taking other jobs. Those who were members of the Communist party were deprived of membership. In many cases the protesters appealed to the attorney general of the Soviet Union, pointing out that according to the Soviet constitution there was nothing illegal in their actions.

Throughout the 1960's, against the background of national and international tensions, the Soviet Union and the United

States energetically promoted a vast program of exploration of outer space. The saga of their achievements symbolizes the tremendous upsurge of modern science and technology. The use of space promises vast economic benefits: it is essential for studying and eventually controlling weather and rainfall; it appears reasonable that space photography can enable geologists to speed up the rate at which mineral resources can be found. As more weather, communication, navigation, and other practical satellites come into use, greater international cooperation will be needed.*

The era of manned space navigation began with the flight of the Russian cosmonaut Iuri Gagarin, who orbited and successfully returned to earth on April 12, 1961. The United States orbited its first astronaut, John H. Glenn, Jr., on February 20, 1962. In June 1963, the Soviet Union sent the first woman into space. Among the next Russian and American achievements in space navigation were flights with two or more persons in the same craft, a "walk" in space, and the "docking" of two spacecrafts, manned and unmanned.

Simultaneously with the launching of orbital space flights, the Soviet Union and the United States experimented with sending unmanned spacecraft to and around the moon and Venus. Both nations succeeded in achieving a soft landing of a capsule on the moon's surface; a manned landing on the moon seems now to be the next task.

In 1967 preparations for new manned space flights were slowed by two tragic mishaps. On January 27 three American astronauts were killed during a sudden fire in the capsule of their spacecraft while it was on the ground at Cape Kennedy, Florida. On April 24 a Russian cosmonaut perished on the return trip to earth when his spacecraft became entangled in its reentry parachute.

On January 27, 1967, the Soviet Union, the United States, and sixty other countries (not including China) signed a treaty intended to curb the use of outer space for military purposes. The treaty prohibited the orbiting of nuclear weapons and denied claims of national sovereignty over celestial bodies. There remained the grave problem of curbing the spread of nuclear weapons and their use on the surface of the earth and in the

* *The New York Times,* February 9, 1968.

atmosphere. After protracted negotiations between the Soviet Union and the United States, as well as between the United States and its European allies, in mid-January 1968, agreement was reached between the United States and the Soviet Union on the terms of a treaty to prevent the spread of atomic weapons. President Johnson called it "a landmark in the effort of mankind to avoid nuclear disaster."

The crucial task facing humanity is to reach the stage of world cooperation and co-adjustment. The present shaky coexistence is constantly threatened by forces of destruction of every possible kind—conflicting ideologies, economic rivalries, tense nationalism, psychological instability, and ethical confusion in the changing world. The Damocles' sword of atomic catastrophe hangs over mankind, and there are threats of local wars all over the world, each potentially able to kindle a world conflagration. To prevent it, all nations and their leaders must wholeheartedly strive for the victory of the forces of cohesion and stability over those of disruption. Since the United States and the Soviet Union play such prominent roles in today's world affairs, on their shoulders lies the main burden of responsibility for the survival of mankind.

APPENDIX

Data on the Soviet Union from the Official Statistics for 1966 *

Area: 22.4 million square kilometers
Population: 234,401,000
Percentage of urban population: 54
Percentage of rural population: 46

Population of ten largest cities:

Moscow	6,507,000
Leningrad	3,706,000
Kiev	1,417,000
Tashkent	1,241,000
Baku	1,196,000
Kharkov	1,125,000
Gorky	1,120,000
Novosibirsk	1,064,000
Kuibyshev	992,000
Sverdlovsk	961,000

Population of the union republics:

Russian Soviet Federative Socialist Republic (RSFSR)	127,312,000
Ukrainian Soviet Socialist Republic (Ukrainian SSR)	45,906,000
Belorussian SSR	8,744,000
Uzbek SSR	10,896,000
Kazakh SSR	12,413,000
Georgian SSR	4,611,000
Azerbaijan SSR	4,802,000
Lithuanian SSR	3,026,000
Moldavian SSR	3,425,000
Latvian SSR	2,285,000

* SSSR *v tsifrakh v 1966 godu,* Moscow, 1967.

485

Kirghiz SSR	2,749,000
Tadjik SSR	2,654,000
Armenian SSR	2,253,000
Turkmen SSR	1,971,000
Estonian SSR	1,294,000

Note: There are now fifteen union republics instead of the sixteen mentioned on page 379. In 1959 the Karelo–Finnish SSR was liquidated and replaced by the Karelian autonomous SSR within the RSFSR.

Industrial production:

Pig iron	70.3	million	metric	tons
Steel	96.9	"	"	"
Coal	585	"	"	"
Oil	265	"	"	"
Cement	80	"	"	"
Sugar (granulated)	9.7	"	"	"
Cotton textiles	5.7	million square meters		
Woolen "	509	"	"	"
Linen "	591	"	"	"
Silk fabrics	869	"	"	"
Footwear (leather)	522	million	pairs	

Agriculture:

Grain harvest	170.8	million	metric	tons
Wheat (within the above total)	100	"	"	"

Livestock:

Large horned cattle (bulls, oxen, cows)	93.4	million	heads
Pigs	59.6	"	"
Sheep	129.8	"	"
Goats	5.5	"	"

RUSSIAN WEIGHTS AND MEASURES

The metric system has been introduced by the Soviet Government.

1 kilometer = 0.9 *versta* = 3,280.8 feet
1 hectare = 0.9 *desiatina* = 2.5 acres
1 metric ton = 61 *pud* = 2,204.6 lbs.

BIBLIOGRAPHY

1. HISTORIOGRAPHY AND HANDBOOKS

BLACK, C. E., ed. *Rewriting Russian History: Soviet Interpretation of Russia's Past.* New York, Praeger, 1956.

GAPANOVICH, J. J. *Historiographie russe (hors de la Russie).* Ed. and trans. B. P. Nikitine. Paris, 1946.

GREGORY, W., ed. *List of Serial Publications of Foreign Governments, 1815–1931.* New York, Wilson, 1932. V. Gsovski, compiler. "Russia." Pp. 517–716.

KERNER, R. J. *Slavic Europe: A Bibliography.* Cambridge, Harvard University Press, 1918.

MAZOUR, A. G. *Modern Russian Historiography.* Princeton, Van Nostrand, 1958.

STRAKHOVSKY, L., ed. *A Handbook of Slavic Studies.* Cambridge, Harvard University Press, 1949.

2. GEOGRAPHY AND ETHNOGRAPHY

BALZAK, S. S., and others. *Economic Geography of the U.S.S.R.* New York, Macmillan, 1949.

BERG, L. S. *Natural Regions of the U.S.S.R.* New York, Macmillan, 1950.

CAMENA D'ALMEIDA, P. J. "Russie," *Géographie universelle.* Ed. P. Vidal de la Blache et L. Gallois. Vol. 5. Paris, 1932.

CRESSEY, G. B. *The Basis of Soviet Strength.* New York, McGraw-Hill, 1945.

KERNER, R. J. *The Urge to the Sea.* Berkeley, University of California Press, 1942.

ZELENIN, D. *Russische (ostslavische) Volkskunde.* Berlin and Leipzig, 1927.

3. GENERAL

BILL, V. T. *The Russian People: A Reader on their History and Culture.* Chicago, Chicago University Press, 1959.

BILLINGTON, J. H. *The Icon and the Axe. An Interpretive History of Russian Culture.* New York, Knopf, 1966.

BLACK, C. E., ed. *The Transformation of Russian Society: Aspects of*

Social Change since 1861. Cambridge, Harvard University Press, 1960.

FLORINSKY, M. T. *Russia: A History and an Interpretation*. New York, Macmillan, 1953. 2 vols.

KLIUCHEVSKY, V. O. *A History of Russia*. Trans. C. J. Hogarth. New York, Dutton, 1911–26. 5 vols.

KOVALEVSKY, P. *Manuel d'histoire russe*. Paris, 1948.

LONG, JOHN. *Modern Russia*. New York, Philosophical Library, 1958.

MAZOUR, A. *Russia: Past and Present*. New York, Van Nostrand, 1951.

MILIUKOV, P. *Outlines of Russian Culture*. Ed. M. Karpovich. Philadelphia, University of Pennsylvania Press, 1942. 3 vols.

MILIUKOV, P., SEIGNOBOS, C., and EISENMANN, L. *Histoire de Russie*. Paris, 1932–33. 3 vols.

NOLDE, B. *La Formation de l'Empire Russe*. Paris, 1952–53. 2 vols.

PARES, B. *A History of Russia*. Definitive ed. New York, Knopf, 1953.

PLATONOV, S. F. *Histoire de la Russie des origines à 1918*. Paris, 1929.

Primary Sources of Russian History. 4 vols. New Haven, Yale University Press, forthcoming.

RIASANOVSKY, N. V. *A History of Russia*. New York, Oxford University Press, 1963.

SARKISYANZ, E. *Russland und der Messianismum des Orients*. Tubingen, 1955.

SIMMONS, E. J., ed. *Continuity and Change in Russian and Soviet Thought*. Cambridge, Harvard University Press, 1955.

STAHLIN, K. *Geschichte Russlands*. Stuttgart, 1923–29. 5 vols.

STÖKL, G. *Russische Geschichte*. Stuttgart, 1962.

SUMNER, B. H. *A Short History of Russia*. New revised ed. New York, Harcourt, Brace, 1949.

TREADGOLD, D. W. *Twentieth Century Russia*. Chicago, Rand McNally, 1959.

TSCHIŽEWSKIJ, D. *Russische Geistesgeschichte*. 2 vols. Hamburg, Rowohlt, 1959–61.

VERNADSKY, G. *Political and Diplomatic History of Russia*. Boston, Little, Brown, 1936. Out of print. Duopage reproduction copies available at Micro Photo Division, Bell & Howell Co., Wooster, Ohio, Catalogue No. DP 11730.

WALSH, W. B., ed. *Readings in Russian History*. Syracuse, University of Syracuse Press, 1948.

——— *Russia and the Soviet Union*. Ann Arbor, University of Michigan Press, 1958.

4. Economic History

A. Pre-Soviet

ANTSIFEROV, A. N., and A. D. BILIMOVICH. *Russian Agriculture during the War.* New Haven, Yale University Press, 1930.

BILL, V. T. *The Forgotten Class: The Russian Bourgeoisie from the Earliest Beginnings to 1900.* New York, Praeger, 1959.

BLUM, J. *Lord and Peasant in Russia.* Princeton, Princeton University Press, 1961.

FISHER, R. H. *The Russian Fur Trade, 1550–1700.* Berkeley, University of California Press, 1943.

GOETZ, L. K. *Deutsch-russische Handelsgeschichte.* Lübeck, 1922.

KOVALEVSKY, V. *La Russie à la fin du XIXᵐᵉ siècle.* Paris, 1900.

KULISCHER, J. *Russische Wirtschaftsgeschichte.* Jena, 1925.

LYASHCHENKO, P. I. *History of the National Economy of Russia to the 1917 Revolution.* New York, Macmillan, 1949.

MAVOR, J. *An Economic History of Russia.* New York, Dutton, 1925. 2 vols.

MILLER, M. S. *The Economic Development of Russia, 1905–1914.* London, 1926.

PAVLOVSKY, G. *Agricultural Russia on the Eve of the Revolution.* London, Routledge, 1930.

PORTAL, R. *L'Oural au XVIIIᵐᵉ siècle.* Paris, 1950.

READING, D. K. *The Anglo-Russian Commercial Treaty of 1734.* New Haven, Yale University Press, 1938.

ROBINSON, G. T. *Rural Russia under the Old Regime.* New York, Longmans, Green, 1932; reprinting, 1949.

TREADGOLD, D. W. *The Great Siberian Migration: Government and Peasant in Resettlement from Emancipation to the First World War.* Princeton, Princeton University Press, 1959.

B. Soviet

BALINKY, A., A. BERGSON, J. N. HAZARD, and P. WILES. *Planning and the Market in the U.S.S.R. The 1960's.* New Brunswick, Rutgers University Press, 1967.

BAYKOV, A. *The Development of the Soviet Economic System.* New York, Macmillan, 1947.

―――― *Soviet Foreign Trade.* Princeton, Princeton University Press, 1946.

BERGSON, A., ed. *Soviet Economic Growth.* Evanston, Row, Peterson, 1953.

DOBB, M. *Soviet Economic Development since 1917.* London, Routledge & Kegan Paul, 1948.

SCHWARTZ, H. *Russia's Soviet Economy.* New York, Prentice Hall, 1950.

YUGOW, A. *Russia's Economic Front for Peace and War.* New York, Harper, 1942.

5. LITERATURE, ARTS, AND MUSIC

ABRAHAM, G. *On Russian Music.* New York, Scribner's, 1939.

ALPATOV, M. *Russian Impact on Art.* New York, Philosophical Library, 1950.

CHADWICK, N. K. *Russian Heroic Poetry.* Cambridge, Cambridge University Press, 1932.

ČIŽEVSKIJ, D. *History of Russian Literature from the Eleventh Century to the End of the Baroque.* The Hague, Mouton, 1960.

GRÉGOIRE, H., R. JAKOBSON, et al. "La Geste du Prince Igor," *Annuaire de l'Institut de Philologie et d'Histoire Orientales et Slaves.* Vol. *8.* 1948.

GUDZY, N. K. *History of Early Russian Literature.* New York, Macmillan, 1948.

HAMILTON, G. H. *The Art and Architecture of Russia.* Baltimore, Penguin Books, 1954.

KONDAKOV, N. P. *The Russian Icon.* Trans. E. H. Minns. Oxford, Clarendon Press, 1927.

LONDON, K. *The Seven Soviet Arts.* New Haven, Yale University Press, 1938.

MIRSKY, D. S. *A History of Russian Literature.* New York, Knopf, 1927.

——— *Contemporary Russian Literature.* New York, Knopf, 1926.

MONTAGU-NATHAN, M. *A History of Russian Music.* London, Reaves, 1918.

NEWMARCH, R. *The Russian Arts.* London, Jenkins, 1916.

——— *The Russian Opera.* London, Jenkins, 1914.

OUSPENSKY, L., and LOSSKY, W. *Der Sinn der Ikonen.* Bern, 1952.

REAU, L. *L'art russe.* Paris, 1921–22. 2 vols.

REAVEY, G. *Soviet Literature Today.* New Haven, Yale University Press, 1947.

RICE, D. T. *Russian Icons.* London and New York, King Penguin Books, 1947.

RICE, T. T. *Russian Art.* London, Penguin Books, 1949.

SIMMONS, E. J. *An Outline of Modern Russian Literature.* Ithaca, N.Y., Cornell University Press, 1943.

SLONIM, H. *The Epic of Russian Literature*. New York, Oxford University Press, 1949.
―――― *Modern Russian Literature*. New York, Oxford University Press, 1953.
SOKOLOV, YU. M. *Russian Folklore*. New York, Macmillan, 1950.
STRUVE, G. *Soviet Russian Literature*. London, Routledge, 1935.
TROYAT, H. *Tolstoy*. Trans. from the French by N. Amphoux. Garden City, N.Y., Doubleday, 1967.
Varneke, B. V. *History of the Russian Theater*. New York, Macmillan, 1951.
VOYCE, A. *Russian Architecture*. New York, Philosophical Library, 1948.
―――― *The Art and Architecture of Medieval Russia*. Norman, University of Oklahoma Press, 1967.
WIENER, L. *Anthology of Russian Literature*. 2 vols. New York, Putnam's, 1902–03.
ZENKOVSKY, S. A. *Medieval Russia's Epics, Chronicles, and Tales*. New York, Dutton, 1963.

6. EDUCATION AND SCIENCE

BABKIN, B. P. *Pavlov*. Chicago, University of Chicago Press, 1949.
DARLINGTON, T. *Education in Russia*. London, Board of Education, 1909.
GRAHAM, L. R. *The Soviet Academy of Sciences and the Communist Party, 1927–1932*. Princeton, Princeton University Press, 1967.
HANS, N. *History of Russian Educational Policy, 1701–1917*. London, King, 1931.
―――― and HESSEN, S. *Educational Policy in Soviet Russia*, London, King, 1930.
HUXLEY, J. *Soviet Genetics and World Science*. London, Chatto and Windus, 1949.
IPATIEFF, V. N. *The Life of a Chemist*. Stanford, Stanford University Press, 1946.
―――― "Modern Science in Russia," *Russian Review, 2* (1943), 68–80.
LUR-SALUCE, DE. *Lomonosov, le prodigieux moujik*. Paris, 1933.
MENSHUTKIN, B. N. *Russia's Lomonosov*. Princeton, Princeton University Press, 1952.
ODINETZ, D. M., and NOVGOROTSEV, P. *Russian Schools and Universities in the World War*. New Haven, Yale University Press, 1929.
PINKEVICH, A. P. *The New Education in the Soviet Republic*. Ed. G. S. Counts. New York, J. Day, 1929.
POSIN, D. Q. *Mendeleyev*. New York, Whittlesey House, 1948.
SIGERIST, H. E. *Socialized Medicine in the Soviet Union*. New York, Norton, 1937.

TIMOSHENKO, S. P. *Engineering Education in Russia.* New York, Mc-
    Graw-Hill, 1959.
VUCINICH, A. *Science in Russian Culture.* Stanford, Stanford Univer-
    sity Press, 1963.

7. CHURCH, RELIGION, AND PHILOSOPHY

ANDERSON, P. B. *People, Church and State in Modern Russia.* New
    York, Macmillan, 1944.
ARSENIEV, N. *Holy Moscow.* New York, Macmillan, 1940.
BENZ, E., ed. *Die Ostkirche und die russische Christenheit.* Tübingen,
    1949.
———— *Russische Heiligenlegenden.* Zurich, 1953.
CONYBEARE, F. C. *Russian Dissenters.* Cambridge, Harvard University
    Press, 1921.
CURTISS, J. S. *Church and State in Russia, 1900–1917.* New York, Co-
    lumbia University Press, 1940.
———— *The Russian Church and the Soviet State.* Boston, Little,
    Brown, 1953.
FEDOTOV, G. *The Russian Religious Mind.* 2 vols. Cambridge, Harvard
    University Press, 1946–66.
———— ed. *A Treasury of Russian Spirituality.* New York, Sheed &
    Ward, 1948.
GRUNWALD, C. DE. *Quand la Russie avait des Saints.* Paris, 1958.
HARE, R. *Pioneers of Russian Social Thought.* New York, Oxford Uni-
    versity Press, 1951.
KOYRÉ, A. *Études sur l'histoire de la pensée philosophique en Russie.*
    Paris, 1950.
LOSSKY, N. O. *History of Russian Philosophy.* New York, Interna-
    tional Universities Press, 1952.
MEDLIN, W. K. *Moscow and East Rome,* Geneva, 1952.
PALMER, W. *The Patriarch and the Tsar.* London, 1871–76. 6 vols.
SCHMEMANN, A. *Ultimate Questions. An Anthology of Modern Russian
    Religious Thought.* New York, Holt, Rinehart & Winston, 1965.
STRUVE, N. *Les Chrétiens en U.R.S.S.* Paris, 1963.
TIMASHEFF, N. S. *Religion in Soviet Russia.* New York, Sheed & Ward,
    1942.
ZENKOVSKY, V. V. *History of Russian Philosophy.* New York, Colum-
    bia University Press, 1953.

8. HISTORY BY PERIODS

A. Medieval Russia

CHADWICK, N. K. *The Beginnings of Russian History.* Cambridge,
    Cambridge University Press, 1946.

CROSS, S. H., and SHERBOVITZ-WETZOR, O. P., trans. and eds. *The Russian Primary Chronicle*. Cambridge, The Mediaeval Academy of America, 1953.

ECK, A. *Le Moyen Age russe*. Paris, 1933.

GREKOV, B. D. *The Culture of Kiev Rus'*. Moscow, 1947.

VERNADSKY, G. *Ancient Russia*. New Haven, Yale University Press, 1943.

—— *Kievan Russia*. New Haven, Yale University Press, 1948.

—— *The Mongols and Russia*. New Haven, Yale University Press, 1953.

—— *The Origins of Russia*. Oxford, The Clarendon Press, 1959.

—— trans. *Medieval Russian Laws*. New York, Columbia University Press, 1947.

B. Tsardom of Moscow

AVVAKUM. *The Life of Archpriest Avvakum*. Trans. J. Harrison and H. Mirrlees. London, Wolf, 1924.

BACKUS, O. P. *Motives of West Russian Nobles in Deserting Lithuania for Moscow, 1377–1514*. Lawrence, University of Kansas Press, 1957.

BAIN, R. N. *The First Romanovs*. New York, Dutton, 1905.

BARBOUR, P. L. *Dimitry Called the Pretender*. Boston, Houghton Mifflin, 1966.

ECKHARDT, H. *Ivan the Terrible*. New York, Knopf, 1949.

FENNELL, J. L. I., ed. *The Correspondence between Prince A. M. Kurbsky and Tsar Ivan IV of Russia, 1564–1579*. Cambridge, Cambridge University Press, 1955.

—— *Prince A. M. Kurbsky's History of Ivan IV*. Cambridge, Cambridge University Press, 1965.

FLETCHER, G. *On the Russ Commonwealth*. London, Hakluyt Society, 1856.

FLEISCHHACKER, H. *Russland zwischen zwei Dynastien, 1598–1613*. Vienna, 1933.

GRUNWALD, C. DE. *La vraie histoire de Boris Godounov*. Paris, 1961.

HERBERSTEIN, S. VON. *Commentaries on Muscovite Affairs*. Ed. and trans. O. P. Backus. Lawrence, University of Kansas, 1956.

KIRCHNER, W. *The Rise of the Baltic Question*. Newark, Delaware, University of Delaware Press, 1954.

MAJOR, A. H., ed. *Herberstein's Notes upon Russia*. London, Hakluyt Society, 1851. 2 vols.

O'BRIEN, C. B. *Russia under Two Tsars, 1682–1689*. Berkeley and Los Angeles, University of California Press, 1952.

OLEARIUS, A. *Voyages and Travels*. London, 1662.

PASCAL, P. *Avvakum et les débuts du Raskol*. Ligugé (Vienne), 1938.

PLATONOV, S. Boris Godounov. Paris, 1929.

STOEKL, G. Die Enstehung des Kosakentums. Munich, 1953.

VERNADSKY, G. Russia at the Dawn of the Modern Age. New Haven, Yale University Press, 1959.

C. The Empire in the Eighteenth Century

BAIN, R. N. The Daughter of Peter the Great. Westminster, Constable, 1899.

———— Peter III, Emperor of Russia. Westminster, Constable, 1902.

———— The Pupils of Peter the Great. Westminster, Constable, 1897.

BENZ, E. Leibniz und Peter der Grosse. Berlin, 1947.

BLEASE, W. L. Suvorov. London, Constable, 1920.

CATHERINE II. Memoirs. Trans. K. Anthony. New York, Knopf, 1927.

DASHKOVA, PRINCESS C. Memoirs. London, 1840.

GREY, IAN. Peter the Great. Philadelphia and New York, Lippincott, 1960.

OLDENBOURG, Z. Catherine the Great. New York, Pantheon Books, 1965.

PUTNAM, P., ed. Seven Britons in Imperial Russia, 1689–1812. Princeton, Princeton University Press, 1952.

RADISHCHEV, A. A Journey from St. Petersburg to Moscow. Trans. L. Wiener; ed. R. P. Thaler. Cambridge, Harvard University Press, 1958.

RAEFF, M. Origins of the Russian Intelligentsia: The Eighteenth-Century Nobility. New York, Harcourt, Brace & World, 1966.

REDDAWAY, W. F. Documents of Catherine the Great. Cambridge, Cambridge University Press, 1931.

SACKE, G. Die Gesetzgebende Kommission Katharinas II. Breslau, 1940.

SCHUYLER, E. Peter the Great. New York, Scribner's, 1884. 2 vols.

SOLOVEYTCHIK, G. Potemkin. London, Butterworth, 1938.

SUMNER, B. H. Peter the Great and the Emergence of Russia. New York, Macmillan, 1951.

THOMPSON, G. S. Catherine II and the Expansion of Russia. New York, Macmillan, 1950.

WALISZEWSKI, K. Autour d'un trône: Catherine II de Russie. Paris, 1894.

D. The Empire in the Nineteenth Century

BILLINGTON, J. H. Mikhailovsky and Russian Populism. Oxford, The Clarendon Press, 1958.

CARR, E. H. Michael Bakunin. London, Macmillan, 1937.

CHRISTOFF, P. K. An Introduction to Nineteenth-Century Russian

Slavophilism. Vol. 1: *A. S. Xomjakov*. The Hague, Mouton, 1961.

CUSTINE, MARQUIS DE. *La Russie en 1839*. Paris, 1843. 4 vols.

CZARTORYSKI, A. *Memoirs*. London, Remington, 1888.

FISCHER, G. *Russian Liberalism from Gentry to Intelligentsia*. Cambridge, Harvard University Press, 1958.

GRAHAM, S. *Tsar of Freedom*. New Haven, Yale University Press, 1935.

GRUNWALD, C. DE. *La Vie de Nicolas Ier*. Paris, 1946.

—— *Le Tsar Alexandre II et son temps*. Paris, 1963.

GURKO, V. I. *Features and Figures of the Past*. Stanford, Stanford University Press, 1939.

HECHT, D. *Russian Radicals Look to America, 1825–1894*. Cambridge, Harvard University Press, 1947.

HERZEN, A. *My Past and Thoughts*. London, Chatto & Windus, 1924–27. 6 vols.

KARPOVICH, M. *Imperial Russia*. New York, Holt, 1932.

KORNILOV, A. *Modern Russian History*. New York, Knopf, 1924.

LEROY-BEAULIEU, A. *The Empire of the Tsars*. New York, Putnam, 1893–96. 3 vols.

MALIA, M. E. *Alexander Herzen and the Birth of Russian Socialism, 1812–1855*. Cambridge, Harvard University Press, 1961.

MAZOUR, A. G. *The First Russian Revolution, 1825*. Berkeley, University of California Press, 1937.

NICHOLAS, GRAND DUKE (Nikolai Mikhailovich). *L'Empereur Alexandre Ier*. St. Petersburg, 1912. 2 vols.

PIPES, R. *Karamzin's Memoir on Ancient and Modern Russia*. Translation and analysis. Cambridge, Harvard University Press, 1959.

POBEDONOSTSEV, K. P. *L'Autocratie russe; correspondence et documents inédits (1881–1894)*. Paris, 1927

—— *Reflections of a Russian Statesman*. London, Richards, 1898.

PUSHKAREV, S. *The Emergence of Modern Russia 1801–1917*. New York, Holt, Rinehart & Winston, 1963.

QUÉNET, C. *Tchaadaev et ses lettres philosophiques*. Paris, 1931.

RAEFF, M. *The Decembrist Movement*. Englewood Cliffs, N.J., Prentice-Hall, 1966.

—— *Plans for Political Reform in Imperial Russia, 1730–1905*. Englewood Cliffs, N.J., Prentice-Hall, 1966.

—— *Michael Speransky: Statesman of Imperial Russia*. The Hague, Nijhoff, 1957.

RIASANOVSKY, N. V. *Nicholas I and Official Nationality in Russia, 1825–1855*. Berkeley, University of California Press, 1959.

—— *Russia and the West in the Teachings of the Slavophiles*. Cambridge, Harvard University Press, 1952.

SCHIEMANN, T. *Geschichte Russlands unter Kaiser Nikolaus I*. Berlin, 1904–19. 4 vols.

SETON-WATSON, H. *The Russian Empire, 1801–1917*. New York, Oxford University Press, 1967.

TARLE, E. *Napoleon's Invasion of Russia, 1812*. New York, Oxford University Press, 1942.

WALKIN, J. *The Rise of Democracy in Pre-Revolutionary Russia*. New York, F. A. Praeger, 1962.

WALLACE, D. M. *Russia*. New York, Holt, 1905.

WITTE, S. *Memoirs*. Garden City, N.Y., Doubleday, Page, 1921.

E. The Duma Period, 1905–1917

CHASLES, P. *Le Parlement russe*. Paris, 1910.

DODD, W. F. *Modern Constitutions*. Chicago, University of Chicago Press, 1909. 2, 181–195.

GRONSKY, P. and ASTROV, N. *The War and the Russian Government*. New Haven, Yale University Press, 1929.

GRUNWALD, C. de. *Le Tsar Nicolas II*. Paris, 1965.

KOKOVTSOV, V. N. *Out of My Past*. Stanford, Stanford University Press, 1935.

LEVIN, A. *The Second Duma*. New Haven, Yale University Press, 1940.

MASSIE, R. K. *Nicholas and Alexandra*. New York, Atheneum, 1967.

PALME, A. *Die russische Verfassung*. Berlin, 1910.

PARES, B. *Russia and Reform*. London, Constable, 1907.

POLNER, T. J. *The Zemstvos and the All-Russian Union of Zemstvos*. New Haven, Yale University Press, 1930.

TREADGOLD, D. W. *Lenin and his Rivals: The Struggle for Russia's Future, 1898–1906*. New York, Praeger, 1955.

WILLIAMS, H. W. *Russia of the Russians*. New York, Scribner's, 1914.

ZILLI, V. *La Rivoluzione Russa del 1905*, Vol. 1. Naples, 1953.

F. The First World War

BRUSILOV, A. A. *Mémoires du général Broussilov: Guerre 1914–1918*. Paris, 1929.

CHURCHILL, W. *The Unknown War*. New York, Scribner's, 1931.

DANILOV, Y. *La Russie dans la guerre mondiale*. Paris, 1927.

FLORINSKY, M. T. *The End of the Russian Empire*. New Haven, Yale University Press, 1931.

GOLDER, F. A. *Documents of Russian History, 1914–17*. New York, Century, 1927.

GOLOVIN, N. N. *The Russian Army in the World War*. New Haven, Yale University Press, 1931.

———— *The Russian Campaign of 1914*. Fort Leavenworth, The Command and General Staff School Press, 1933.

KOHN, S., and MEYENDORFF, BARON A. F. *The Cost of the War to Russia*. New Haven, Yale University Press, 1932.

PARES, B *The Fall of the Russian Monarchy*. London, Cape, 1939.

WHEELER-BENNETT, J. W. *The Forgotten Peace*. New York, Morrow, 1939.

G. Revolution and Civil War

BUNYAN, J. *Intervention, Civil War, and Communism in Russia*. Baltimore, Johns Hopkins Press, 1936.

———— and FISHER, H. H. *The Bolshevik Revolution*. Stanford, Stanford University Press, 1934.

CARR, E. H. *The Bolshevik Revolution, 1917–1923*. New York, Macmillan, 1951–52. 2 vols.

CHAMBERLIN, W. H. *The Russian Revolution*. New York, Macmillan, 1935. 2 vols.

DANIELS, R. V. *Red October. The Bolshevik Revolution of 1917*. New York, Scribner's, 1967.

DENIKIN, A. I. *The Russian Turmoil*. London, Hutchinson, 1922.

———— *The White Army*. London, Cape, 1930.

KATKOV, G. *Russia 1917. The February Revolution*. New York, Harper & Row, 1967.

KERENSKY, A. *Russia and History's Turning Point*. New York, Duell, Sloan & Pearce, 1965.

LOCKHART, R. H. B. *British Agent*. New York, Putnam's, 1933.

LUKOMSKY, A. S. *Memoirs of the Russian Revolution*. London, Fisher & Unwin, 1922.

RADKEY, O. H. *The Agrarian Foes of Bolshevism: Promise and Default of the Russian Socialist Revolutionaries, March to October, 1917*. New York, Columbia University Press, 1958.

SHUB, D. *Lenin*. Garden City, N.Y., Doubleday, 1948.

STEWART, G. *The White Armies of Russia*. New York, Macmillan, 1933.

TROTSKY, L. *My Life*. New York, Scribner's, 1930.

VARNECK, E., and FISHER, H. H. *The Testimony of Kolchak and Other Siberian Materials*. Stanford, Stanford University Press, 1935.

VERNADSKY, G. *Lenin*. New Haven, Yale University Press, 1931.

WRANGEL, P. N. *Memoirs of General Wrangel*. New York, Duffield, 1930.

WOLFE, B. D. *Three Who Made a Revolution*. New York, Dial Press, 1948.

H. Soviet Russia

CHAMBERLIN, W. H. *Soviet Russia,* Boston, Little, Brown, 1930.

DALLIN, D. J. *The Real Soviet Russia.* New Haven, Yale University Press, 1944; revised ed. 1947.

DEUTSCHER, I. *Stalin.* New York, Oxford University Press, 1949.

HARPER, S. N. *The Government of the Soviet Union.* New York, Van Nostrand, 1937.

HAZARD, J. *Soviet Housing Law.* New Haven, Yale University Press, 1939.

GSOVSKI, V. *Soviet Civil Law.* Ann Arbor, University of Michigan Law School, 1948–49. 2 vols.

LITTLEPAGE, J. D. and BESS, D. *In Search of Soviet Gold.* New York, Harcourt, Brace, 1937.

PIPES, R. *The Formation of the Soviet Union: Communism and Nationalism, 1917–1923.* Cambridge, Harvard University Press, 1954.

SCHUMAN, F. L. *Soviet Politics.* New York, Knopf, 1946.

SCOTT, J. *Behind the Urals.* Boston, Houghton, Mifflin, 1942.

TIMASHEFF, N. S. *The Great Retreat.* New York, Dutton, 1946.

TOWSTER, J. *Political Power in the USSR.* New York, Oxford University Press, 1948.

VYSHINSKY, A. *The Law of the Soviet State.* New York, Macmillan, 1948.

WEBB, S., and WEBB, B. *Soviet Communism.* New York, Scribner's, 1936. 2 vols.

WHITE, D. F. *The Growth of the Red Army.* Princeton, Princeton University Press, 1944.

I. Communism

BORKENAU, F. *The Communist International.* London, Faber & Faber, 1938.

EBON, M. *World Communism Today.* New York, McGraw-Hill, 1948.

FISHER, R. T. *Pattern for Soviet Youth: A Study of the Congresses of the Komsomol.* New York, Columbia University Press, 1959.

GANKIN, O. H., and FISHER, H. H. *The Bolsheviks and the World War.* Stanford, Stanford University Press, 1940.

LENIN, V. I. *New Data for Lenin's "Imperialism."* Ed. E. Varga and L. Mendelsohn. New York, International Publishers, 1940.

SETON-WATSON, H. *From Lenin to Malenkov.* New York, F. A. Praeger, 1953.

STALIN, J. *Foundations of Leninism.* New York, International Publishers, 1932.

———— *Marxism and the National Question.* New York, International Publishers, 1942.

J. The Second World War

CHAMBERLIN, W. H. *The Russian Enigma.* New York, Scribner's, 1943.

DALLIN, A. *German Rule in Russia, 1944–1945.* New York, St. Martin's Press, 1957.

DEANE, J. R. *The Strange Alliance.* New York, Viking Press, 1947.

FAINSOD, M. *Smolensk under Soviet Rule.* Cambridge, Harvard University Press, 1958.

FISHER, H. H. *America and Russia.* Claremont, Calif., Claremont College Press, 1946.

HINDUS, M. *Mother Russia.* Garden City, N.Y., Doubleday, Doran, 1943.

SHERWOOD, R. E. *Roosevelt and Hopkins.* New York, Harper, 1948.

SMITH, W. B. *My Three Years in Moscow.* Philadelphia, Lippincott, 1950.

WERTH, A. *Russia at War 1941–1945.* New York, Dutton, 1964.

K. The 1950's and 1960's

BARGHOORN, F. C. *The Soviet Cultural Offensive.* Princeton, Princeton University Press, 1960.

CRANKSHAW, E. *Khrushchev: a Career.* New York, Viking Press, 1966.

GARDER, M. *L'Agonie du Régime en Russie Soviétique.* Paris, 1965.

———— *A History of the Soviet Army.* New York, Praeger, 1966.

GARTHOFF, R. L. *Soviet Strategy in the Nuclear Age.* New York, Praeger, 1958.

KENNAN, G. F. *Russia, the Atom, and the West.* New York, Harper, 1958.

MOSELY, P. E. *The Kremlin and World Politics: Studies in Soviet Policy and Action.* New York, Vintage Press, 1960.

SALISBURY, H. E. *Orbit of China.* New York, Harper & Row, 1967.

————, ed. *The Soviet Union: The Fifty Years.* New York, Harcourt, Brace & World, 1967.

9. DIPLOMACY AND FOREIGN RELATIONS

A. Pre-Soviet

ADAMOV, E. *Constantinople et les Détroits.* Paris, 1930–32. 2 vols.

ANDERSON, M. S. *Britain's Discovery of Russia, 1553–1815.* New York, St. Martin's Press, 1958.

BAILEY, T. A. *America Faces Russia; Russian-American Relations from*

Early Times to Our Day. Ithaca, Cornell University Press, 1950.

CRESSON, W. P. *The Holy Alliance.* New York, Oxford University Press, 1922.

GORIAINOV, S. *Le Bosphore et les Dardanelles.* Paris, 1910.

JELAVICH, C. *Tsarist Russia and Balkan Nationalism.* Berkeley, University of California Press, 1959.

[JOMINI, A.] *Diplomatic Study of the Crimean War.* London, Allen, 1882. 2 vols.

KAZEMZADEH, F. *Russia and Britain in Persia, 1864–1914.* New Haven, Yale University Press, 1968.

LANGER, W. L. *The Franco-Russian Alliance.* Cambridge, Harvard University Press, 1929.

LEDERER, I. J., ed. *Russian Foreign Policy. Essays in Historical Perspective.* New Haven, Yale University Press, 1962.

LENSEN, G. A. *The Russian Push toward Japan: Russo-Japanese Relations, 1697–1875.* Princeton, Princeton University Press, 1959.

LOBANOV-ROSTOVSKY, A. *Russia and Europe, 1789–1825.* Durham, N.C., Duke University Press, 1947.

MALOZEMOFF, A. *Russian Far Eastern Policy, 1881–1904.* Berkeley, University of California Press, 1958.

MARTENS, F. *Recueil des traités et conventions conclus par la Russie avec les puissances étrangères.* St. Petersburg, 1874–1909. 15 vols.

MOSELY, P. E. *Russian Diplomacy and the Opening of the Eastern Question.* Cambridge, Harvard University Press, 1934.

NOLDE, B. *L'Alliance franco-russe.* Paris, 1936.

—— *Die Petersburger Mission Bismarcks, 1859–1862.* Leipzig, 1936.

PAVLOVSKY, M. N. *Chinese-Russian Relations.* New York, Philosophical Library, 1949.

PETROVICH, M. B. *The Emergence of Russian Panslavism, 1856–1870.* New York, Columbia University Press, 1956.

PHILLIPSON, C., and BUXTON, N. *The Question of the Bosporus and Dardanelles.* London, Stevens & Haynes, 1917.

PIRENNE, J. H. *La Sainte Alliance.* Paris, 1946. 2 vols.

POTEMKIN, V. *Histoire de la diplomatie.* Vols. 1–2. Paris, 1946–47.

PRIBRAM, A. F., and COOLIDGE, A. C. *The Secret Treaties of Austria-Hungary.* Cambridge, Harvard University Press, 1920–21. 2 vols.

PRICE, E. B. *The Russo-Japanese Treaties of 1907–1916.* Baltimore, Johns Hopkins Press, 1933.

PURYEAR, V. *England, Russia and the Straits, 1844–1856.* Berkeley, University of California Press, 1931.

Bibliography 501

Rosen, Baron R. *Forty Years of Diplomacy.* New York, Knopf, 1922. 2 vols.

Sazonov, S. *Fateful Years.* London, Cape, 1928.

Seton-Watson, R. W. *Disraeli, Gladstone and the Eastern Question.* London, Macmillan, 1935.

Sumner, B. H. *Peter the Great and the Ottoman Empire.* Oxford, Basil Blackwell, 1949.

—— *Russia and the Balkans.* Oxford, Clarendon Press, 1937.

—— "Tsardom and Imperialism in the Far East and Middle East, 1880–1914," *Proceedings of the British Academy.* Vol. 27. 1940.

Zabriskie, E. H. *American-Russian Rivalry in the Far East, 1895–1914.* Philadelphia, University of Pennsylvania Press, 1946.

B. Soviet

Beloff, M. *The Foreign Policy of Soviet Russia.* New York, Oxford University Press, 1947–49. 2 vols.

Dallin, D. *Soviet Foreign Policy after Stalin.* Philadelphia and New York, Lippincott, 1961.

—— *Soviet Russia and the Far East.* New Haven, Yale University Press, 1948.

—— *Soviet Russia's Foreign Policy, 1939–1942.* New Haven, Yale University Press, 1942.

Fischer, L. *The Soviets in World Affairs.* New York, Cape & Smith, 1930. 2 vols.

Kennan, G. F. *Soviet-American Relations, 1917–1920.* 2 vols. Princeton, Princeton University Press, 1956–1958.

—— *Soviet Foreign Policy, 1917–1941.* Princeton, Von Nostrand, 1960.

Moore, H. L. *Soviet Far Eastern Policy, 1931–1945.* Princeton, Princeton University Press, 1945.

Pope, A. U. *Maxim Litvinov.* New York, Fischer, 1943.

Potemkin, V. *Histoire de la diplomatie.* Vol. 3. Paris, 1947.

Strakhovsky, L. *Intervention at Archangel.* Princeton, Princeton University Press, 1944.

Taracouzio, T. A. *The Soviet Union and International Law.* New York, Macmillan, 1935.

—— *War and Peace in Soviet Diplomacy.* New York, Macmillan, 1940.

United States, Department of State, *Nazi-Soviet Relations, 1939–1941.* Ed. R. J. Sontag and J. S. Beddie. Washington, 1948.

U.S.S.R. Ministry of Foreign Affairs. *Documents and Materials relating to the Eve of the Second World War.* New York, International Publishers, 1948.

WHEELER-BENNETT, J. W. *Munich: Prologue to Tragedy.* New York, Duell, Sloan & Pearce, 1948.

YAKHONTOV, V. *Russia and the Soviet Union in the Far East.* New York, Coward-McCann, 1931.

10. NATIONALITIES, PERIPHERAL AND REGIONAL HISTORY

A. West

ALLEN, W. E. D. *Ukraine.* Cambridge, Cambridge University Press, 1940.

BAIN, R. N. *Slavonic Europe.* Cambridge, Cambridge University Press, 1908.

BUCHAN, J. ed. *The Baltic and Caucasian Countries.* London, Hodder & Stoughton, 1923.

Cambridge History of Poland, 1697–1935. Cambridge, Cambridge University Press, 1941–50, 2 vols.

DUBNOW, S. M. *History of the Jews in Russia and Poland.* Philadelphia, The Jewish Publication Society, 1916–20. 3 vols.

GREENBERG, L. *The Jews in Russia.* New Haven, Yale University Press, 1944–51. 2 vols.

HALECKI, O. *History of Poland.* New York, Roy, 1943.

HRUSHEVSKY, M. *A History of Ukraine.* New Haven, Yale University Press, 1941.

KONOVALOV, S. A. *Russo-Polish Relations.* London, Crescent Press, 1945.

LORD, R. H. *The Second Partition of Poland.* Cambridge, Harvard University Press, 1915.

O'BRIEN, C. B. *Muscovy and the Ukraine, 1654–1667.* Berkeley and Los Angeles, University of California Press, 1963.

RESHETAR, J. S. *The Ukrainian Revolution, 1917–20.* Princeton, Princeton University Press, 1952.

SCHWARZ, S. M. *The Jews in the Soviet Union.* Syracuse, Syracuse University Press, 1951.

SHOTWELL, J. T., and LASERSON, M. M. *Poland and Russia, 1919–1945.* New York, King's Crown Press, 1945.

SLOCOMBE, G. *A History of Poland.* London, Nelson, 1939.

VAKAR, N. P. *Belorussia: The Making of a Nation.* Cambridge, Harvard University Press, 1956.

VERNADSKY, G. *Bohdan, Hetman of Ukraine.* New Haven, Yale University Press, 1941.

WINTER, E. *Byzanz und Rom im Kampf um die Ukraine, 955–1939.* Leipzig, 1942.

B. East

ALLEN, W. E. D. *Problems of Turkish Power in the Sixteenth Century.* London, Central Asian Research Centre, 1963.

—— and P. MOURATOFF. *Caucasian Battlefields: A History of the Wars on the Turco-Caucasian Border, 1828–1921.* Cambridge, Cambridge University Press, 1953.

BADDELEY, J. F. *Russia, Mongolia, and China.* London, Macmillan, 1919. 2 vols.

—— *The Russian Conquest of the Caucasus.* London, Longmans, Green, 1908.

DALLIN, D. *The Rise of Russia in Asia.* New Haven, Yale University Press, 1949.

HOWORTH, H. H. *History of the Mongols.* Pt. 2, Division 2. London, Longmans, Green, 1880.

KENNAN, G. *Siberia and the Exile System.* New York, Century, 1891.

KRAUSSE, A. *Russia in Asia.* New York, Henry Holt, 1899.

LAMB, H. *Genghis Khan.* New York, McBride, 1927.

LANTZEFF, G. *Siberia in the Seventeenth Century.* Berkeley, University of California Press, 1943.

LOBANOV-ROSTOVSKY, A. *Russia and Asia.* New York, Macmillan, 1933.

SARKISYANZ, E. *Geschichte der orientalischer Völker Russlands bis 1917.* München, 1961.

SCHUYLER, E. *Turkistan.* New York, Scribner's, Armstrong, 1876.

SPULER, B. *Die Goldene Horde.* Leipzig, 1943.

VLADIMIRTSOV, B. *The Life of Chingis Khan.* London, Routledge, 1930.

—— *Le Régime social des Mongols.* Paris, 1948.

ZENKOVSKY, S. *Pan-Turkism and Islam in Russia.* Cambridge, Harvard University Press, 1960.

INDEX

Aachen, 204
Aaland Islands, 156
Academy of Arts, 188, 256
Academy of Sciences, 152, 172, 182, 184, 251, 408–409; Historical Institute of, 405; Presidium of, 407; Ukrainian, 409 n.
Act of Armed Neutrality (*1780*), 164
Adashev, Alexis, 99, 101
Adrian, patriarch, 158
Adrianople, treaty of, 213–214, 216
Adriatic Sea, 27, 62, 193, 198
Aegean: archipelago, 167; Sea, 27, 227
Aehrenthal, Count A., diplomat, 273
Afghanistan, 90, 225, 271
Afghans, 235
Africa, 240, 383, 434–435, 442, 467, 469, 472
Agadir, 273
Agrarian bill proposing expropriation, 268–269
Agriculture, 10–11, 18–19, 70, 78, 105–106, 139, 171–172, 174, 191, 242–243, 249, 264, 268–269, 316, 318, 321, 324, 343, 346, 356–357, 360–361, 371, 375, 387, 410, 412–413, 429, 453, 462, 463; collectivization of, 353, 356–359, 371, 375, 387–388, 395, 404, 460, 463, 465, 468–469, 474, 477
Ahmad, khan, 90–91
Aian, Bay of, 224
Aiazeva, A., 479
Akhmatova, Ann, 255
Ak-Mechet, 223
Alans, 21–22, 27–28
Alaska, 86, 161, 163–164, 198, 225
Albania, 473
Albert, Bishop, 43
Alcohol Monopoly, 246
Aleko (Rachmaninov), 259
Aleksandrovsky, 390–391
Aleutian Islands, 163
Alexander I, emperor, 170, 177, 181–183, 186, 192, 194–212, 222, 316

Alexander II, emperor, 178, 192, 216–218, 220–222, 225–230, 234–235, 241, 246, 248, 253
Alexander III, emperor, 192, 230–234, 236, 239, 245, 251, 262
Alexander, grand duke of Lithuania, 91
Alexander Nevsky, prince, 61–62, 65–66, 83, 87, 405
Alexander Nevsky (movie), 420
Alexandra Feodorovna, empress, 232, 282, 284–287, 304
Alexandria, 133
Alexandrov, 103–104
Alexeev, Eugene, admiral, 238
Alexeev, Michael, general, 278, 285, 309
Alexinac, 226
Alexis, son of Nicholas II, 287
Alexis Michaelovich, tsar, 123, 128–129, 132, 136, 140, 147, 211
Alexis, tsarevich, 147, 158–159, 170, 192
Algeciras conference, 271
Allied Commission, 451
Allies, 277, 280–281, 284, 289–290, 297, 300–301, 305–307, 310–314, 319, 325–326, 329, 331, 392, 418, 421, 432, 434–435, 440–442, 444–450, 455, 456, 470, 484
All-Russian Congress of Soviets; First, 289, 292; Second, 294–295, 299, 339; Third, 340; Fifth, 340–341
All-Russian Union of Zemstvos, 276
All-Slav Congress, 439
All-Union Communist Party, 438
All-Union Congress of Soviets, 341, 378
All-Union Literary Congress, 412
Alliluyeva, Svetlana, 480, 481
Alma-Ata, Turkistan, 350
Alps, 193
Altai Mts., 7, 20, 26, 162, 184
Amastris, 31
America, 125–126, 167, 185, 251–252, 306, 365, 384, 411, 431, 433, 441, 459, 475; Central, 204; Latin, 363, 469; South, 204